VAR

Understanding and Applying Value-at-Risk

VAR

Understanding and Applying Value-at-Risk

Published by Risk Books,
a specialist division of Risk Publications
Haymarket House
28–29 Haymarket
London SW1Y 4RX
Tel +44 (0)171 484 9700; fax +44 (0)171 930 2238

ISBN – 1 899332 21 9 - Hardback
ISBN – 1 899332 26 X - Softback

Editor: Sue Grayling
Production Editor: Miles Smith-Morris
Expert Readers: Frank Iacono, Capital Market Risk Advisors, Inc.; Peter Zangari, JP Morgan

The introductions to each section and Chapters 25, 29–33, 39 and 46 are published here for the first time. Chapter 27 is an edited version of an article due to appear in the December 1997 edition of the ***Journal of Financial Services Research***. The remaining chapters are slightly revised versions of articles previously published in the following journals:
Chapter 1 ***Risk VAR Supplement***, June 1996; Chapter 2 ***Risk***, January 1996 (originally entitled "Value at Risk"); Chapter 3 ***Risk***, February 1996 (originally entitled "Value at Risk 2"); Chapter 4 ***Risk VAR Supplement***, June 1996; Chapter 5 ***Risk VAR Supplement***, June 1996; Chapter 6 ***Risk***, September 1996; Chapter 7 ***Risk***, October 1996; Chapter 8 ***Risk***, January 1995; Chapter 9 ***Risk***, January 1995; Chapter 10 ***Risk VAR Supplement***, June 1996; Chapter 11 ***Risk*** September 1995; Chapter 12 ***Risk***, May 1996; Chapter 13 ***Risk***, May 1996; Chapter 14 ***Risk***, September 1996; Chapter 15 ***Balance Sheet***, Autumn 1996; Chapter 16 ***Risk VAR for End-Users Supplement***, March 1997; Chapter 17 ***Financial Analysts' Journal***, September–October 1995; Chapter 18 ***Bank Accounting and Finance***, Fall 1996; Chapter 19 ***New England Economic Review***, September–October 1996; Chapter 20 ***Federal Reserve Bank of Philadelphia Business Review***, September–October 1996; Chapter 21 ***Federal Reserve Bank of New York Economic Review***, April 1996; Chapter 22 ***Journal of Derivatives***, Spring 1997; Chapter 23 ***Financial Analysts Journal***, November–December 1996; Chapter 24 ***Journal of Derivatives***, Winter 1995; Chapter 26 ***Journal of Portfolio Management***, Fall 1996; Chapter 28 ***Journal of Derivatives***, Spring 1997; Chapter 34 ***Risk***, December 1995; Chapter 35 ***Risk***, September 1995; Chapter 36 ***Risk***, March 1996; Chapter 37 ***Risk***, June 1996; Chapter 38 ***Risk***, July 1996; Chapter 40 ***Risk***, July 1996; Chapter 41, ***Energy and Power Risk Management***, October 1996; Chapter 42 ***Risk VAR for End-Users Supplement***, March 1997; Chapter 43, ***Risk Firmwide Risk Management Supplement***, July 1996; Chapter 44 ***Risk Firmwide Risk Management Supplement***, July 1996; Chapter 45 ***Risk Firmwide Risk Management Supplement***, July 1996.

FOREWORD

The advent of VAR as a generally-accepted methodology for quantifying market risk and its subsequent embrace by bank regulators are milestones in the evolution of risk management. KPMG is pleased to join with the publishers of *Risk* in presenting this collection of significant papers that trace the development of VAR, its applications and its future role.

This book includes a number of articles that have appeared before in *Risk,* as well as important selections from academic and practitioner journals and new papers which are published here for the first time. The material is organised into four sections in a way that shows the history of the process: how VAR was developed, assessed and improved and, finally, how it is deployed in the marketplace. The papers are intended not simply to outline the mechanics of VAR, but to prepare readers for an active role in its ongoing assessment, the discovery of new applications, and the development of broader risk management frameworks to make the most of this powerful tool.

Leaders from KPMG's Risk Strategy Practices in London and New York have written introductions to each section of this book. The introductions provide the necessary practical and theoretical background, and include brief summaries of the papers, highlighting their particular strengths and emphasising any recurring themes. They are designed to help readers focus on topics, authors or articles of particular interest.

I am particularly pleased with the selection, for Section IV, of a strong series of articles describing real-world VAR applications. For while the introduction of VAR was surely a milestone in the development of risk management, it would have remained merely an interesting toy unless its value had been proven in corporate life. Moreover, VAR is just *one* model, one of many tools that risk managers must master as their focus moves up the organisation from the line to the boardroom. Unless practioners learn to meld risk measurement methodologies with traditional financial models of the business firm, helping management to unlock shareholder value, the science of risk management may consist of a long list of passing fads.

The key is the link to equity. That is what drives current efforts to develop an enterprise-wide risk management framework. And that is what makes this the most exciting time in the history of risk management.

Joseph Erickson

Chairman, KPMG GlobeRisk

September 1997

CONTENTS

III. SELECTING AND IMPROVING VAR METHODOLOGIES: NEW RESEARCH

IV. CORPORATE APPLICATIONS AND FIRMWIDE RISK MANAGEMENT

AUTHORS

Robert Allen is presently head of global investments at Westpac in Sydney. Previously he was responsible for the development of credit and market risk measurement policy. Robert's banking career has spanned 27 years, with 12 years at Westpac preceded by 15 years at Bankers Trust. He has had wide ranging exposure to both credit and market risk management in senior line and staff management roles in North America, Asia and Australia. He holds a Bachelor of Economics degree from the University of Sydney and an MBA in finance from the Wharton School of the University of Pennsylvania.

Mike Baliman read natural sciences and computer sciences at Queens' College, Cambridge. He worked for Praxis Systems as a software designer and implementer for two years before joining the investment management division of Dresdner Kleinwort Benson. He was global head of fixed interest for four years before transferring to group management where he established a group risk department.

Tanya Styblo Beder is a principal of Capital Market Risk Advisors, Inc. in New York. Prior to founding a consultancy firm specialising in financial institutions, capital markets and derivatives, she was a vice-president of the First Boston Corporation and was a consultant in the financial institutions practice at McKinsey and Company. Tanya holds an MBA in Finance from Harvard University and a BA in Mathematics from Yale University. She is currently a Management Fellow of the Yale University School of Organization and Management. Her academic work focuses on global capital markets, off-balance sheet instruments and the future of the financial system. Tanya has written several articles in the financial area, which have been published in *The Financial Analysts Journal*, *Harvard Business Review* and *The Journal of Financial Engineering*.

Jacob Boudoukh graduated from Stanford University's School of Business in 1991, and is now an associate professor of finance and international business at the Stern School of Business, New York University. He teaches a new course on financial risk measurement and management for financial institutions, focusing on market and credit risk, the value-at-risk approach, scenario analysis and stress testing. Jacob also consults on risk management, fixed income derivatives and equity trading strategies to financial institutions and corporations. His research is primarily in empirical asset pricing and the pricing of derivative securities, with particular focus on fixed income markets and financial risk management. His work has been published in a range of academic and practitioner journals, including *American Economic Review*, *The Journal of Finance* and *Risk*.

Gabriel Bousbib is currently vice-president and head of risk management at Reuters America, where he is responsible for Reuters risk management activities in the Americas, including sales and marketing, and technical and application support as well as development and financial engineering. Prior to joining Reuters, Gabriel was a managing director and principal of the CBM Group, Inc., a management consulting firm specialising in financial services and risk management. He was formerly the founder of MYCA Inc., a software company developing risk management systems for derivative dealers. Gabriel previously worked for Merrill Lynch Capital Markets as a risk manager in the derivatives area. He holds an MBA from Columbia University Graduate School of Business and is a graduate of the Ecole Polytechnique in Paris.

Michael Chen is a senior research associate in GAT's research group in the area of derivative analytics and risk management. He received his PhD in topology and dynamic systems from Columbia University.

Doug Costa was educated at Stuyvesant High School, Oberlin College, and the University of Kansas, where he earned a PhD in mathematics in 1974. From 1974 to 1997, he was on the faculty of the department of mathematics at the University of Virginia. During his tenure he published 35 articles on commutative algebra and the structure of linear groups over rings, most recently collaborating with G Keller on the theory of radices.

In 1994 he began teaching and consulting for the Susquehanna Investment Group. He is now full-time at Susquehanna in quantitative research.

Cedomir Crnkovic is a founding partner of NetRisk, a company dedicated to enterprise-wide risk management, where he is responsible for research and development in risk management methodology. Prior to that he worked at JP Morgan, first within the risk management group and then within the proprietary trading group. His research focused on time series analysis, and he pioneered work on disciplined quantitative trading strategies at JP Morgan. He received his PhD in theoretical physics from Princeton University in 1987, after which he spent six years pursuing physics research. His current interests include liquidity risk, multivariate time series models, and credit risk models.

Emanuel Derman is head of the quantitative strategies group at Goldman Sachs, where he directs the valuation modelling and the production risk management systems for equity derivative products. He has a PhD in theoretical physics from Columbia University and is a co-author of the Black-Derman-Toy interest rate model and the Derman-Kani implied tree model. Prior to joining Goldman in 1985, he worked for Bell Laboratories and held a number of academic positions where he did research in particle physics. His recent work has focused on the volatility smile using implied trees, valuing and hedging exotic options, and the static hedging of options portfolios. He is on the editorial board of *Applied Mathematical Finance* and is an associate editor of the *Journal of Derivatives*. He is also on the editorial board of the *Journal of Financial Engineering*.

Jordan Drachman is an associate in the primary management research group at JP Morgan, where he develops trading models. Prior to 1997, he was in the risk management research group, where he worked on time series analysis with applications to value-at-risk. He is a graduate of MIT and earned a PhD in theoretical mathematics from Stanford University in 1994.

Fred Eng is a financial analyst in GAT's research and consulting group. He has extensive experience in value-at-risk analysis projects for major insurance companies and international banks. He is a member of GAT's value-at-risk management system development team, and has also been actively involved in the valuation and hedging of derivatives and structured product portfolios for global asset managers and investment banks. He received his dual BS degrees in finance and mathematics from the State University of New York at Albany, and is pursuing his MS in computer science from Pace University.

Joseph Erickson is the partner in charge of KPMG's US Risk Strategy Consulting Practice and chairman of KPMG GlobeRisk, an international consulting network addressing market, credit and operational risk management and control, risk measurement methodologies and risk-adjusted performance measures. He also directs KPMG's executive education program and is a frequent seminar speaker on risk management and capital markets issues. He has previously served as a Practice Fellow for the Accounting Standards Board.

Jon Frye is a vice president within the quantitative finance group at NationsBanc and is responsible for research within the risk control group. He earned an MS in statistics from the University of Toledo and a PhD in economics from Northwestern University. Jon currently serves on the advisory board of the International Association of Financial Engineers.

Mark B Garman is Emeritus Professor of Finance at the Haas School of Business Administration, University of California. He has been professionally involved with continent pricing theory since 1975, and has published works on arbitrage, options, volatility measures, duration-related risk measures, and other computational methods of financial engineering. He is president and chief scientist of Financial Engineering Associates, Inc., a provider of spreadsheet add-ins for exotic derivatives, interest rate and equity options, Monte Carlo applications and value-at-risk software and consultancy services related to derivatives theory.

Christopher Hamilton is a consulting partner with KPMG GlobeRisk, headquartered in New York. He provides advice to international financial and corporate clients regarding enterprise risk management, risk strategy (including capital allocation), asset/liability management, financial instruments, derivative products, foreign currency issues and securitisation. He has 16 years of international financial and consulting experience at Bankers Trust, covering the Asia Pacific region, and at KPMG London. He has presented for organisations including BAI, LOMA, Wharton Executive Education Program, Risk, ICM, IRR, JCIF (Japan) and CBOT. He is a chartered accountant and a member of the Securities Industry Association. He also participated in the Group of Thirty Systematic Risk Working Team.

Gregory Hayt is a director at CIBC Wood Gundy Securities, where he specialises in risk management education for the CIBC Wood Gundy

School of Financial Products. Prior to joining CIBC, he was a vice president in the global markets sector of Chase Manhattan Bank, where he advised clients on firmwide risk management. His prior experience includes investment and futures and options trading. He holds a BS from the Wharton School and an MS from the University of Rochester.

Darryl Hendricks works in the research and market analysis group at the Federal Reserve Bank of New York, which he joined in 1992 after graduating with a PhD in public policy from Harvard University. He is currently an assistant vice-president at the bank and has been head of the Payments Studies Function since March 1997. His work at the New York Fed has focused on international risk-based capital standards for credit risk associated with OTC derivatives. He participated actively with the banking industry and international banking supervisors in the development of an internal model-based capital standard for market risk of trading activities. During 1996, he participated in the development of a report by the G-10 Committee on Payments and Settlements Systems (CPSS) on real-time gross settlement systems. He has also contributed to CPSS studies on the development of electronic money and remains involved in the work of the CPSS.

Dan Heron is a staff writer at *Risk* magazine. He graduated from Loughborough University of Technology in 1992 and joined derivatives specialist Chicago Research and Trade in London. At CRT, he worked on a variety of exchange-traded options products before specialising in oil and gasoil options. He joined *Risk* in 1995.

Martin Hiemstra joined Algorithmics as a writer and financial engineer in April 1997. Prior to that he was self-employed as a writer and consultant for a number of Canadian, US and international derivatives, finance and risk management journals. From 1991–92 he was employed by the Ontario Ministry of Agriculture and Food as an economist. From 1983–90, he was a derivatives trader with Merrill Lynch, Canada, Prudential Bache Securities, and Nesbitt Thomson in Toronto. He holds a BA in economics from the University of Western Ontario.

Thomas Ho was a professor of finance at Stern School of Finance, New York University from 1978 to 1990 and is a pioneer in the field of fixed income research. He received his PhD in 1978 from the University of Pennsylvania. He founded the Global Advanced Technology Corporation in 1987, which provides software, research and consultancy services to the fixed income market. He was research analyst at the US government bond trading desk, Yamaichi Securities, in 1988. He has published articles in the *Journal of Finance* and the *Journal of Fixed Income* and is editor of the publications *Fixed Income Management: Issues and Solutions*, *Fixed Income Investment: Research and Frontiers in Fixed Income*. Currently, he heads a research group which is incorporating his research in n-factor models into analytical software.

Douglas Hoffman is a managing director at Bankers Trust Company. He heads the firm's corporate risk and insurance services within the corporate risk management department, with responsibilities including operational and event risk management, operational Raroc methodologies, risk finance, business vulnerability analysis and continuity planning, as well as insurance strategy and business development activities. Prior to joining Bankers Trust, he was a principal and manager at a major risk management and actuarial consulting firm. He holds BBA and MBA degrees with concentrations in risk management from the University of Georgia, and is an Associate in Risk Management (ARM) and a Chartered Property Casualty Underwriter. He is a frequent speaker and author of articles on operational and event risk management.

Gregory Hopper is an economist in the credit analytics group at Morgan Stanley in New York, where he focuses on measuring the credit risk of derivative portfolios. Formerly, he was a senior economist at the Federal Reserve Bank of Philadelphia. While at the Fed, he was also on the adjunct faculty of the Wharton School of the University of Pennsylvania. He has a BA in mathematics, an MA in applied mathematics, and an MA and PhD in economics.

Richard Irving is executive editor of *Risk* magazine. A bond dealer at Lehman Brothers for most of the 1980s, he has written for the *Financial Times*, *The Times* and many other financial publications. He joined *Risk* in 1994.

Patricia Jackson is special advisor in charge of regulatory policy at the Bank of England. She has extensive experience as a financial regulator and has published on a range of issues in the banking policy field.

Marta Johnson is a vice president at Bankers Trust Company, and heads the firm's operational Raroc team, responsible for identifying and quantifying the firm's total exposure to operational risk. Prior to joining the risk management group, Marta was a product manager for new strategic initiatives. She has a BA degree from the University of California, Los Angeles with a major in quantitative economics, and an MBA from the University of California, Berkeley.

Philippe Jorion is professor of finance at the Graduate School of Management at the University of California, Irvine. He holds an MBA and PhD from the University of Chicago, and a degree in engineering from the University of Brussels. He has written more than 50 publications on risk management and international finance, as well as a number of books, including *Financial Risk Management: Domestic and International Dimensions*, a graduate level textbook on the global dimensions of risk management, and *Big Bets Gone Bad: Derivatives and Bankruptcy in Orange County*, the first account of the largest municipal failure in US history. He recently completed *Value at Risk: The New Benchmark for Controlling Market Risk*.

Paul Kupiec is a senior economist in the trading risk analysis section of the Division of Research and Statistics at the Federal Reserve Board. He received a PhD in economics from the University of Pennsylvania in 1985. He has been a member of the finance faculty at North Carolina State University, a visiting financial economist at the Bank for International Settlements, a consulting economist for the OECD, and has advised the Commodity Futures Trading Commission Staff on issues concerning futures clearing house margins policy. Paul has written many articles addressing technical issues relating to government regulatory policy and financial market volatility, the integrity of bank and clearing house risk management models, and issues related to bank capital requirements for market risk. He is a co-developer of the Federal Reserve Board's pre-commitment approach for market risk capital regulation.

Colin Lawrence is currently managing director and global head of market risk management at BZW. He was previously managing director and head of fixed income derivative trading at UBS. He has been a consultant to major financial institutions, US Congress, the Board of Governors of the Federal Reserve and a member of the Brookings Panel. He was formerly associate professor of international finance at Columbia University and holds a PhD in economics from the University of Chicago.

Kenneth Leong is risk manager at Cinergy Corp, and is responsible for the development of risk management policies, procedures, infrastructures and analytics for the firm. One of his current projects is to implement a firmwide, integrated risk management system to enable Cinergy's senior management to monitor the firm's overall market risk exposure and efficiently allocate risk capital. Prior to joining Cinergy, Kenneth was a senior manager at Deloitte & Touche, where he advised corporate clients on risk management and systems issues. Ken is a regular speaker at risk management and derivative conferences and a frequent contributor to *Risk* magazine.

Donald Lewis is a manager for KPMG GlobeRisk in San Francisco. Prior to joining KPMG, he was a marketing manger at C*ATS Software, where he was responsible for the design and implementation of the company's first VAR-based risk management engine. Prior to joining KPMG, he held positions in bank treasury management and trading, with the Resolution Trust and the US Treasury Department. He holds a BA and MIA in international banking and finance from Columbia University. He consults on a broad range of risk management issues, with emphasis on risk management systems design and implementation.

Jacques Longerstaey is a vice president in JP Morgan's risk management advisory department, focusing primarily on risks within the investment management business. Previously, he was head of market risk research, where he helped to spearhead the development of RiskMetrics. Before that, he was head of research for the Benelux markets. He has written a number of publications on risk management topics and is a regular speaker at conferences. He holds a Certificate in Portfolio Management from the Centre Inter-Universitaire d'Analyse Financière, and a Licence en Sciences Economiques from the Université Catholique de Louvain.

Hans-Jakob Lüthi studied mathematics at the Swiss Federal Institute of Technology (ETHZ) and obtained his doctorate in 1973. He has been a lecturer at ETHZ in operations research, and visiting professor at the Pontificia Universidade Catolica, Rio de Janeiro, Rensselaer Polytechnic Institute, Troy, New York and the Center of Operations Research at MIT. He was head of a consulting firm in the area of information and organisational engineering before joining the department of mathematics at ETHZ in 1993 as professor of operations research. His main research interests include the design of intelligent decision support systems in operations management.

Chris Marshall earned his PhD from Harvard Business School in 1996. He has an MA in mathematics and theoretical physics from Cambridge University and a Master's degree in artificial intelligence from Indiana University. From 1987 to 1992, he worked as a systems developer/mathematical modeller for O'Connor & Associates in Chicago, during which time he also completed his MBA in Finance from Chicago University. He has published in both academic and practitioner journals, and is also an associate with Ernst & Young's Center for Business Innovation. He will shortly be starting as an assistant professor at the University of Singapore.

David Maude is an analyst in the monetary stability wing of the Bank of England. His publications include a substantial study of private banking in the UK market and research on bank deposit insurance. He is currently on secondment to the UK Treasury.

Lyle Minton is a director of CIBC Wood Gundy Financial Products, where he is a product manager on the credit derivatives trading desk. Prior to joining CIBC, Lyle was a manager at Arthur Andersen in the global derivatives and treasury risk management group, where he provided derivatives risk management advisory services to both financial and non-financial institutions. He was a member of the Group of Thirty working group that conducted the 1994 Follow-Up Surveys of risk management practices of derivatives dealers and end-users. Lyle was also a senior policy analyst for the International Swaps and Derivatives Association (ISDA), where he participated on the working group that developed ISDA's submission to the Bank for International Settlements (BIS) regarding the amendment of capital requirements for derivatives dealers. He holds a Masters degree in Finance from the Lubin School of Business at Pace University and a Bachelors degree in economics from Auburn University.

Dori Nagar is a partner with KPMG GlobeRisk in New York. He is a member of the American Association of CPAs and offers risk management consulting services including the validation of analytical models, risk management system selection and implementation, and also advises on related control and accounting issues. He is a frequent speaker and panellist at international banking and risk management conferences.

Art Owen has been on the statistics faculty at Stanford University since 1985. He holds a PhD in statistics from Stanford and a Bachelor of Mathematics from the University of Waterloo. He was elected a Fellow of the Institute of Mathematical Statistics in 1996. His recent research interests have centred on the way that fundamental numerical problems such as approximation and integration become effectively statistical as the dimension increases, with applications in technology and finance. Randomised versions of numerical methods allow for error estimates based on replication. He has invented a randomised quasi-Monte Carlo integration, known as scrambled nets. Other interests include natural networks, image processing, value-at-risk and non-parametric inference. His teaching is focused on doctoral applied statistics, and he also consults on problems arising in pharmaceuticals, technology and finance.

Matthew Page earned a BS in mathematics from Dickinson College in 1984 and an MS from the University of Virginia in 1987. He joined Princeton Newport Partners in 1988, then moved to Morgan Stanley in 1989. He joined Susquehanna Investment Group in 1990, where he worked as the director of quantitative research from 1993–97. He is currently responsible for statistical arbitrage at SIG. His research interests include derivatives valuation, risk measurement, market microstructure, machine learning and automated trading.

Sumit Paul-Choudhury is technical editor for *Risk* magazine. As well as overseeing the refereeing and editing procedure for technical articles, he also writes and edits more general features and news stories. Prior to joining *Risk*, he was a freelance journalist specialising in media, science and technology. He holds a BSc in physics from Imperial College, London and an MSc in mathematics from Queen Mary & Westfield College, London.

Randy Payant joined the Sendero Institute in 1993. His duties include conducting research in emerging financial risk management concepts, teaching asset/liability management and performance measurement classes and developing customised educational programmes and consulting on bank financial management issues. Prior to joining Sendero, he was associated with a Minnesota-based regional bank; eight years in lending and credit management and six years in investment and fund management. He has written *Maximising Bank Value – Asset/Liability Management in the 1990s* as well as numerous articles for various industry publications. He completed his undergraduate and graduate work in finance and accounting at the University of Wisconsin. He was a guest lecturer on interest rate risk management and bank strategies at the BAI Graduate School of Banking, the University of Minnesota and for the Bank Administration Institute.

William Perraudin is professor of finance at Birkbeck College,

London and director of the Institute for Financial Research. He is also a special advisor to the Bank of England. His publications include studies of default risk and continous time pricing models.

Bjorn Pettersen is a senior manager for KPMG GlobeRisk in Chicago. He is a graduate of the Norwegian School of Management and the American Graduate School of International Management, and he serves as an adjunct professor in the Stuart School of Business at the Illinois Institute of Technology. He consults on a wide range of corporate treasury risk and technology issues, and is a leader with GlobeRisk enterprise-wide risk management product development, with particular emphasis on capital allocation and on risk-adjusted performance measures.

Andrew Priest is a staff writer at *Risk* magazine. He graduated in law from Oxford University in 1992, and was called to the Bar of England & Wales in 1994. After training as an investment analyst at Stewart Ivory, he joined *Risk* in 1995.

Matt Pritsker is an economist in the trading risk and analysis section of the Board of Governors of the Federal System. He holds a Bachelors degree from the University of Michigan and a PhD from Princeton University, both in economics. He has carried out research in the areas of risk measurement and management, market liquidity, and the behaviour of institutional investors.

Nick Reed is director and founder of RVC Associates Limited, a technology company which provides Internet-based solutions for clients in the financial and media industry and explores new ways of generating commerce on the Internet. Prior to establishing RVC Associates, he spent four years at Risk Publications, most recently as editor of *AsiaRISK* magazine, a bimonthly magazine covering the risk management and derivatives industry in Asia. Before moving to Hong Kong in 1995, he was technical editor for *Risk* magazine in London. He has had articles published in a wide variety of newspapers and magazines including the *Financial Times*, the *Journal of the Stock Exchange of Singapore* and the *Bridge Guide to Corporate Treasury in Asia*.

Matthew Richardson is an associate professor in finance at the Stern School of Business, New York University and a research fellow of the National Bureau of Economic Research. Previously, he taught at the Wharton School of the University of Pennsylvania. He teaches advanced fixed income and financial econometrics at graduate, PhD and executive levels. He has published numerous articles on asset pricing and derivative securities in leading academic and practitioner journals. His recent work on pricing and hedging fixed income securities and international derivatives has won awards form the Chicago Quantitative Alliance and the American Association of Individual Investors. He received his PhD in finance from the Graduate School of Business at Stanford University.

Gary Robinson is head of research and development at the global market risk management division of BZW. Formerly, he was a manager with the gilt edged and money markets division at the Bank of England, responsible for developing funding policy and gilt market monitoring. Before that, he was manager of the bank's quantitative financial economics group, responsible for providing analysis to the Bank's operational functions. He holds a degree in economics and econometrics, has written for many academic and trade journals and is an editor of *Net Exposure*, the electronic journal of finance and risk management.

Michael Schröder has been head of the international finance and financial management department at the Centre of European Economic Research (ZEW) in Mannheim since 1995. Prior to joining ZEW, he was a senior economist in the investment research department at Liechtenstein Global Trust. He holds a diploma and PhD in economics from the University of Mannheim.

Julian Shaw, until recently the director for derivatives risk at BZW, is head of risk policy at NatWest Markets in London. Prior to that, he was vice president for new products in the capital markets division of CIBC Wood Gundy in New York and Toronto and before that the quantitative analyst for Gordon Capital in Toronto.

David C Shimko became vice president in the risk management advisory group at Bankers Trust in April 1997. Previously, he was vice president and head of risk management at JP Morgan Securities. Prior to joining the risk management research group in May 1996, he was responsible for commodity derivatives research on Morgan's trading desk. Before joining Morgan in 1993, David was assistant professor of finance at the University of Southern California and a private consultant to financial institutions. He has published many academic and trade articles on strategic issues and the practice of risk management, has produced financial software packages and has written a technical textbook at PhD level entitled *Finance in Continuous Time: A Primer*. He writes a monthly end-user column in *Risk* magazine. David earned a BS in economics and a PhD in managerial economics and finance from Northwestern University.

Michael Siegel is a principal research scientist at the MIT Sloan School of Management. He is currently the co-director for the Finance Research Center (FRC) and associate director for the productivity from Information Technology (PROFIT) project. His research interests include the use of information technology in financial risk management and global financial systems, heterogeneous database systems, managing data semantics, query optimisation, intelligent database systems and learning in database systems. He has been leader of the risk management working group at Sloan since 1993, managing an interdisciplinary team of faculty and members of financial and corporate institutions. Michael's research has appeared in computer science, information technology, and financial journals and trade publications.

Katerina Simons is an economist at the Federal Reserve Bank of Boston. Before joining the Federal Reserve in 1989, Katerina was an economist at the Office of the Comptroller of the Currency in Washington and taught economics at Northeastern University in Boston. Her recent work includes studies of quantitative risk management models, the use of derivatives by commercial banks and agency problems in loan syndications. Katerina holds a BA from Barnard College and a PhD in economics from Yale University.

Richard Singer is a senior risk management and capital markets consultant with KPMG GlobeRisk in New York. Prior to joining KPMG, he managed New York-based interest rate, equity and commodity trading operations, including proprietary trading, for a primary US dealer for over 20 years. He consults on a broad range of market-related risk issues for capital markets and asset management clients, and is a frequent speaker on derivative and hedging issues. He has published papers on liquidity risk and risks unique to the securities environment.

Andrew Smith is the lead partner for financial sector risk management consultancy services for KPMG GlobeRisk in London. He joined KPMG in 1993 following ten years as a trader, quant risk manager and front office information technology specialist for Phillips and Drew and Union Bank of Switzerland. He has a DPhil on relativistic astrophysics from Oxford University, and has been an associate research fellow of the Financial Options Research Centre at Warwick University, where he also earned an MBA. He consults in many areas of investment banking and corporate treasury services as well as in all areas of risk management.

Charles W Smithson is a managing director of CIBC Wood Gundy Financial Products, where he is charged with developing the CIBC Wood Gundy School of Financial Products. He has held positions in academe and in government, as well as the private sector. He taught for nine years at Texas A&M University, and served with both the Federal Trade Commission and the Consumer Products Safety Division. Prior to joining CIBC Wood Gundy, he was a managing director at Continental Bank and a senior vice president at Chase Manhattan Bank. The author of scores of articles in professional and academic journals, he is best known as the originator of the building block approach to financial products. He is the author of five books, including *Managing Financial Risk*. He served as a member of the Working Group for the Global Derivatives Project sponsored by the Group of Thirty. He received his PhD in economics from Tulane University.

Shang Song is a director at CIBC Wood Gundy Securities based in Hong Kong, where she covers Chinese financial institutions. Prior to this, she was a director in CIBC Wood Gundy's School of Financial Products. From 1994–95, she was second vice president in the global markets sector of Chase Manhattan Bank, where she was responsible for mathematical analysis, model building and other technical analysis. She holds a BS degree from Peking University and a PhD from the University of Southern California, both in physics.

Gerold Studer studied mathematical engineering at the Swiss Federal Institute of Technology (Lausanne). In 1994, he joined the Institute of Operations Research at the Swiss Federal Institute of Technology in Zurich (ETHZ). His primary focus is on risk management-related issues. He is a member of the Risklab programme, a research collaboration between Credit Suisse, Swiss Bank Corporation, Union Bank of Switzerland and ETHZ. His PhD thesis is about measuring market risks of non-linear portfolios.

Domingo Tavella is president of Align Risk Analysis in San Francisco, a boutique specialising in corporate risk management. Previously, he was a director of financial engineering at Integral Development Corporation, after a spell with Bankers Trust in New York, where he pioneered analytical techniques applied to mergers and acquisitions. He holds a PhD in aeronautical engineering from Stanford University and an MBA in finance from the University of California at Berkeley. He is chief editor and founder of the *Journal of Computational Finance*.

Martin E Titus Jr is a partner for KPMG GlobeRisk in New York. Before joining KPMG, he spent over 20 years as a proprietary trader in the fixed income markets and as manager of the capital markets operations for several large regional financial institutions. At KPMG, he has engagement management responsibility for a wide variety of market and operational risk management projects, focusing primarily on process and analytical issues involving capital markets and investment management activities. He is a frequent speaker on capital markets, investment management and fiduciary risk issues.

Chris Turner is a principal of CRM Partners in New York, where he focuses on the use of risk management tools, including value-at-risk, by institutions other than derivative dealers. He is responsible for research and development of quantitative methods, tools and strategies for managing market and credit risk for the firm. In addition, he also assists clients in all aspects of the risk management process. His work has been published in a wide variety of trade and academic journals. Prior to joining CRM Partners, he was a vice president at Chase Manhattan Bank, where he was the financial economist for the bank's risk advisory function. Before that, he was an economist at the Federal Reserve Bank in Washington DC. He has a Bachelors degree in economics from Loyola College in Baltimore and a PhD in economics from the University of Washington in Seattle.

Robert F Whitelaw is an associate professor of finance at the Stern School of Business, New York University. He has also held the position of visiting associate professor of finance at the Anderson Graduate School of Management, UCLA. He teaches corporate and managerial finance and his research interests include the relation between risk and return in the stock market, the pricing and hedging of fixed income derivative securities, and risk management. His work has been published in a wide range of academic and practitioner journals, and he is an associate editor at the *Review of Financial Studies*. Robert's work experience includes two years spent in the public finance department at Shearson Lehman, where he was involved in structuring tax-exempt bond financings. He has a PhD in finance from Stanford University and a BS in mathematics from MIT.

Peter Zangari is a vice president in JP Morgan's risk management group in New York. His primary responsibility is the development of the methodology for the RiskMetrics product. He also advises clients on various issues related to market risk measurement. He has lectured and written extensively on value-at-risk. He is the principal author of the JP Morgan/ Reuters *RiskMetrics Technical Document* and edits the *RiskMetrics Monitor*. In addition, he has published articles in journals such as *Risk*, *Derivatives Strategy*, and *Financial Derivatives and Risk Management*. He holds a PhD from Rutgers University, New Brunswick and a Bachelors degree from Fordham University.

INTRODUCING VAR

Introduction

Martin E. Titus Jr and Donald Lewis
KPMG

Throughout the centuries since man became a commercial animal, investors and speculators have shared a common intuition that there is a balance between fear and greed - between the risks of investments and their potential rewards. The silk merchants of ancient China, the crowd that gathered to trade shares under a buttonwood tree near what would later become the New York Stock Exchange, and the denizens of modern high-tech trading rooms have all shared a common concern: how to quantify the risk of loss.

For a long time, risk takers just guessed. After all, to know with certainty the magnitude of potential losses was to know the future! And while methodologies for quantifying the risk of loss in various circumstances - such as "duration" for fixed income securities - were developed in recent decades, foreknowledge of market conditions was required to answer with certainty.

The problem confronting investors and speculators was not unlike that facing modern scientists: predicting future events with certainty is simply not possible. And it was only when financial market participants adopted methodologies pioneered in the sciences that a satisfactory gauge for market risk was developed.

In adopting the methods of the empirical sciences, which predict future events according to the laws of probability and statistics, risk managers were obliged to accept the highly probable, but nonetheless, conditional answers they produce. Since the question "How much can I lose?" cannot be answered with absolute certainty, market practitioners learned to be satisfied with answers to questions of a significantly different form: "With a degree of confidence chosen by me, what is the largest loss I am likely to suffer?" And it is questions of this form that we attempt to answer when we compute the value-at-risk of a position, or its VAR.

So what is VAR, and how can it help us? First, VAR is an amount of money - that is what we mean when we ask how much we can lose. Second, VAR is an estimate. It is based upon probabilities, so we cannot rely upon it with certainty, but rather with a degree of confidence we select.

In order to appreciate its complexities and challenges, we first need to understand how VAR is estimated. It is a four-step process:

- *Determine the time horizon over which we want to estimate a potential loss.* Traders are most frequently interested in calculating the dollars or pounds or yen they might lose in a one-day period - tomorrow, the next trading day. Regulators and participants in very illiquid markets, however, may want to estimate likely multiple-day exposures to market risk. But in each case, a time horizon must be specified by the decision-maker.
- *Select the degree of certainty required, the confidence interval for the estimate.* Knowing the largest likely loss we will suffer 95 times out of 100 (95% confidence interval) may suffice. But when a regulator demands to know how much is at risk, a 99% confidence interval (what happens 99 times out of 100) might be more appropriate. In each case, a confidence interval must be selected by the decision-maker.
- *Create a probability distribution of likely returns for the instrument or portfolio under consideration.* Several methods may be used, and the VAR literature debates at length how to select the right one for particular circumstances. The easiest to understand is a simple distribution of recent historical returns for the asset or portfolio, which may look like the "bell-shaped curve" often used in grading exams. After determining a

time horizon and a confidence interval for the estimate, and then organising the history of market price changes in a probability distribution, we can apply the laws of statistics to estimate VAR.

❑ *Finally, read the solution, the VAR estimate,* by observing the loss amount that appears beneath the bell-shaped curve at the critical value (the distance from the middle of the curve) that is statistically associated with the probability, the level of confidence, chosen for the VAR estimate in step 2.

In reality, of course, we do no such thing, since computers estimate distributions and read critical values for us. But it is important to understand that these are the procedures the computer performs, and that we could estimate VAR "longhand" by following these steps.

We already knew VAR was an estimated amount of money that may be lost due to market risk. Now we understand that this estimate is contingent upon both the time horizon over which we want to estimate our possible losses and the degree of certainty we require for the accuracy of the estimate. A practical working definition of VAR is as follows:

Value-at-risk is the largest likely loss from market risk (expressed in currency units) that an asset or portfolio will suffer over a time interval and with a degree of certainty selected by the decision-maker.

If that is all there is to it, why has such a simple concept generated so much debate? There are several answers. First, since VAR has been adopted as a primary market risk measure by trading firms and as a capital adequacy gauge by bank regulators, VAR estimates and VAR trading limits effectively constrain financial markets exposures in much of the industrialised world. Marginal differences in VAR estimates may have a significant impact not only on financial firms' profits but also on the supply of capital available to non-financial companies.

Second, there are a number of apparently sound methods for calculating VAR, and estimates prepared using the different methodologies can vary dramatically.

Finally, debates revolve not only around technical issues such as how to adjust portfolio VAR downward to capture diversification effects, but also around fundamental issues such as how to back test and prove the adequacy of a firm's VAR estimates. It is not just risk managers who care about VAR, but financial officers and chief executives who are seeking a better understanding of the issue. They are motivated by far more than an interest in sound risk management principles: large amounts of money as well as shareholder value are at stake.

Section I: Introducing VAR is intended to familiarise readers new to the subject with the basic VAR methodologies and the important issues that surround them. The articles selected are a useful introduction to major themes that are developed in detail later in the book, including:

❑ trade-offs between the speed, accuracy and cost of competing VAR methodologies

❑ current and planned use of VAR by regulators to measure capital adequacy

❑ relative merits of off-the-shelf VAR estimation systems developed by banks, securities dealers and other vendors

❑ appropriate methods for evaluating the accuracy of VAR estimates

❑ applications of fundamental VAR methodology to non-market risks within the firm

❑ applications of VAR-type methodologies in enterprise-wide risk management.

Treat Section I as a VAR primer. Use it to identify topics of interest in other sections. And do not be daunted by the occasional appearance of complex mathematical expressions! With the exception of Section III, which contains a series of very challenging articles on new VAR research, most papers with complex mathematical formulae in this volume also contain commentary that is of value to readers with only fundamental quantitative skills.

In "Variations on a Theme," Nick Reed of *Risk* provides a brief history of VAR, how it was driven forward by recommendations in the Group of Thirty publication *Derivatives: Practices and Principles* and by the Bank for International Settlements' capital adequacy proposals, as well as the role of the now legendary JP Morgan 4:15 report. Reed also provides useful descriptions of the three primary VAR distribution estimation methodologies – the correlation (analytic) method, historical simulation, and Monte Carlo simulation – and he highlights the strengths and weaknesses of each.

Reed's introductory article prepares the reader for two "lessons", "How to Calculate VAR" and "The Right VAR", conducted by Charles Smithson and Lyle Minton of the CIBC Wood Gundy School of Financial Products. These articles outline how to estimate VAR using each of the three basic approaches described by Reed. The special challenges of accurately estimating

VARs for options and instruments with optionality are described with particular clarity, and they support the authors' general conclusion that the composition of a portfolio should be the determining factor in selecting a particular methodology.

In "Banks Grasp the VAR nettle," Dan Heron and Richard Irving of *Risk* describe how banks and investment banks have responded to the growing importance of VAR by developing and publishing proprietary VAR methodologies as well as the data and software to support VAR implementations. Quite apart from bolstering the banks' risk management credentials, these activities are clearly intended to help the development of end-user markets for derivatives and other financial products. This article reviews the models and risk databases developed by JP Morgan, CS First Boston, Chase Manhattan, Bankers Trust and Deutsche Bank, and reports on the ongoing debate between them over their various approaches.

For a general discussion of the trade-offs that must be made in choosing a VAR estimation methodology, see "The Right Approach," by Kenneth Leong. Leong identifies the assumptions and the implementation requirements of the different VAR methodologies, and he provides a useful table comparing them. Readers seeking a clear explanation of a specific VAR estimate will find an excellent example in Leong's description of the historical simulation method. Although it is of limited use in practice because it is unsuitable to dynamic portfolios, the historical approach is perhaps the simplest method of estimating VAR, and Leong's clear exposition will benefit readers still struggling with basic VAR concepts.

Cedomir Crnkovic and Jordan Drachman provide challenging mathematics and informative prose in "Quality Control", their discussion of Kuiper's statistic, a tool that may be used to test the quality of banks' internally developed VAR models. Their findings support the conclusion that historical simulation produces superior forecasts when applied to portfolios without optionality, and that exponentially-weighted data improves the accuracy of VAR forecasts made using the analytic method. But, most importantly, the article provides both a solid frame of reference for detailed discussions of the challenges to regulatory back testing that appear in Section II, and a taste of the statistical theory required to understand the mathematically-intensive research papers of Section III.

Finally, Douglas Hoffman and Marta Johnson of Bankers Trust illustrate how techniques used to measure market risk can be applied more broadly within corporations to quantify non-market business risks, and operations risk in particular. "Operating Procedures" describes the methodology used to define and categorise operations risks, much of it drawn from analytic VAR approaches. Information about operations risks can be gathered in a similar way to market return databases, and the statistical and actuarial tools used to estimate return distributions can also identify the frequency and magnitude of potential operational risks.

Of course, the application of quantitative methodologies similar to VAR across non-market corporate risks is the basis for enterprise-wide risk management, a goal that is consuming ever more risk management resources in financial and non-financial firms, and the subject of Section IV of this book. Market risk, though critical to many companies, is only one factor affecting the future cash flows which represent the value of the firm. Recent efforts to improve risk measurement techniques will truly bear fruit when they enable not only risk managers but also chief executives and boards of directors to risk-manage all sources of volatility in the firm's future cash flows, and so directly increase shareholder value.

1

Variations on a Theme

Nick Reed
Risk

In just three years, value-at-risk has become an industry standard for measuring market risk. What does it have to offer, and what are the reasons behind its inexorable rise?

Value-at-risk (VAR) was first transformed from a pleasing concept to a working reality, it is said, when Dennis Weatherstone was chairman of JP Morgan. The story goes that Weatherstone – now Sir Dennis – demanded a one-page report be delivered to him after the close of business each day, summarising the company's exposure to moves in the markets and providing a decent estimate of potential losses over the next 24 hours.

The result was the famous "4.15 Report", so-called because it was delivered to Weatherstone at 4.15pm every day. In order to provide a brief summary of the risks and potential losses across the entire trading portfolio, the report had to aggregate diverse market positions on the basis of a single consistent measure of risk. This methodology has become known as VAR.

From there, VAR has grown to be the industry standard for measuring portfolio risks on a day-to-day basis. So much so that the Bank for International Settlements (BIS), the central banks' central bank, now sets its capital adequacy requirements for market risk in terms of banks' own VAR estimates. In the seminal July 1993 study by the Washington-based Group of Thirty (*Derivatives: Practices and Principles*), which has become a blueprint for managing risk (for all financial risks, not just those associated with derivatives), the VAR approach was strongly recommended. Software firms now provide off-the-shelf VAR packages and it is hard to open any risk management publication without finding a mention of VAR somewhere inside.

As the level of interest in VAR has grown so has the volume of research into the methodology. What has emerged is that the concept can be applied not only to market risk but also the other main financial risk facing a financial institution, credit risk. In time, banks may be able to have a single firm-wide measure of risk across all different business areas, and so measure return on risk capital consistently across the whole firm. This means institutions should be able to allocate their capital to the most profitable business areas on a risk-adjusted basis.

Different techniques have also been developed for implementing the concept. These are discussed in greater detail by Kenneth Leong in Chapter 5, but the main upshot is that choosing between methodologies for calculating VAR has forced managers to consider risk in greater detail and reconsider some of the assumptions they may have unwittingly made in the past. This, in itself, can only be good for the security of the financial system.

But what has also emerged are the limits of the concept's usefulness. VAR is now one of the essential tools of the risk manager but it is not the whole story. Its purpose is to give an estimate of losses over a short period under "normal" market conditions. It is not going to tell you what might happen during a market crash. For that, stress testing and scenario analysis are necessary. Nor do analytic approaches to VAR, such as that embodied in RiskMetrics, handle option products well. Alternative approaches are outlined in Chapter 10.

Also, as the Barings debacle showed, any risk measurement system is only as good as the numbers that go into it. A rogue trader entering false positions will undermine the usefulness of VAR reports. So the method, while extremely powerful for day-to-day risk management, is no substitute for the wider risk management process of analysing crash scenarios and keeping tabs on operational and legal risks.

VARIATIONS ON A THEME

While the concept is simple – and its power stems from this simplicity – the practical implementation of a VAR system is anything but. As financial institutions have gone about setting up VAR systems, they have often run into a number of snags. For a start, all of the firm's positions data must be gathered from around the world into one centralised database. When different offices in different time zones may be running on different – and possibly incompatible – systems, a firm may have to overhaul and maybe completely reorganise its systems in order to complete this task. Information technology vendors have not been slow to respond to their needs.

Once the position data are centralised, the overall risk has to be calculated by aggregating the risks from individual contracts across the whole portfolio. This is done by working out the effect of moves in individual "risk factors" (eg a stock index, a specific point on a given yield curve or swap curve, a foreign exchange rate or a commodity price) across the portfolio, which may involve large numbers of currencies and, within each currency, different asset classes. VAR is worked out from the relationships between the individual risk factors and the effect on the portfolio of moves in each risk factor.

This requires a huge amount of data, as the potential move in each risk factor has to be inferred from past daily price movements over a given "observation period". For regulatory purposes, this period is at least one year – ie the data on which VAR estimates are based should capture all relevant daily market moves over the previous year.

Many institutions have found that they simply do not have the data to collate and finding it can be a long and tedious process. It is perhaps fitting, then, that in 1994 the house that kick-started the concept, JP Morgan, started distributing data for VAR calculations free to anyone who wanted them.

Apart from altruism, the move was a bold step to establish JP Morgan's own system, RiskMetrics, as the industry-standard methodology. The more clients that adopt RiskMetrics, the less JP Morgan would have to tinker with its own system when discussing risk with clients in the future.

Other banks have seen the potential and developed their own risk measurement packages for clients. Bankers Trust and Deutsche Bank were first to follow Morgan's lead and have recently been joined by Chase Manhattan and CS First Boston. Dan Heron and Richard Irving describe their offerings in Chapter 4.

If the various methods of calculating VAR are to be compared and contrasted, a more precise definition is needed. This is: VAR is the maximum loss that will be incurred on the portfolio with a given level of confidence over a specified holding period, based on the distribution of price changes over a given historical observation period.

For example, the BIS rules, known as the Basle Capital Accord, specify a 99% confidence interval (ie actual losses on the portfolio should exceed the VAR estimate not more than once in every 100 days), a holding period of 10 days (ie the maximum loss is calculated assuming the portfolio remains unchanged for 10 days) and a historical observation period of at least one year (ie estimates of future losses must be based on market moves over at least the past year).

The main assumption underpinning VAR, which is also one of the concept's main drawbacks, is that the distribution of future price (or rate) changes will be similar to that of past price variations. That is, the potential portfolio loss calculations for VAR are worked out using distributions or parameters from historic price data in the observation period.

Some critics of the method say this is akin to "driving a car by looking in the rear-view mirror". However, while this assumption means risk managers may miss extreme or anomalous events in financial markets, most users say that they would use stress testing or scenario analysis to determine the risk on their portfolios in these kinds of situations. For day-to-day risk management under "normal" conditions, they say, VAR is a useful tool, provided they are aware of the assumptions built into their VAR numbers.

So far, there is no industry consensus on the best method for calculating VAR. As with any statistical model, VAR depends on certain assumptions. The choice of which method of calculation is used is normally dictated by the user's aversion to unrealistic or oversimplistic assumptions.

There are three popular methods: the correlation method (also known as the variance/covariance method), the historic simulation method and the Monte Carlo simulation method. Each has its own set of assumptions and each is a simplification of reality.

The simplest is the correlation method, which assumes the returns on risk factors are normally distributed, the correlations between risk factors are constant and the delta (or price sensitivity to changes in a risk factor) of each portfolio constituent is constant. Each of these assumptions can be criticised as not representing reality (see Chapters 5 and 10).

To calculate VAR using the correlation method, the volatility of each risk factor is extracted from the historical observation period. The potential effect of each component of the portfolio on the overall portfolio value is then worked out from the component's delta (with respect to a particular risk factor) and that risk factor's volatility.

These effects are then aggregated across the whole portfolio using the correlations between the risk factors (which are, again, extracted from the historical observation period) to give the overall volatility of the portfolio value. By scaling the volatilities of the risk factors, the desired confidence interval for VAR can be obtained. The volatility and correlation data provided free by JP Morgan can be used for this method.

Of course, there are different methods of calculating the relevant risk factor volatilities (and correlations). Simple historic volatility (correlation) is the most straightforward but the effects of a large one-off market move can significantly distort volatilities (correlations) over the required forecasting period. For example, when using a simple 30-day historic volatility, a market shock will stay in the volatility figure for 30 days, until it drops out of the sample range and correspondingly causes a sharp drop in (historic) volatility 30 days after the event This is because each past observation is equally weighted in the volatility calculation.

A more sophisticated approach is to weight past observations unequally. This is usually done to give more weight to recent observations so that large jumps in volatility (correlation) are not caused by events that happened a long time ago.

The two popular methods for unequal weighting are the GARCH (Generalised Autoregressive Conditional Heteroscedasticity) family of models and exponentially-weighted moving averages.

GARCH models need to be fine-tuned to each risk factor time series, while exponentially-weighted averages can be computed with not much more complication than simple historic volatility. GARCH volatilities capture more features of past changes in volatility. However, both methods rely on the assumption that future volatilities can be predicted from historic price movements.

The method of historical simulation for calculating VAR avoids some of the pitfalls of the correlation method. In particular, the three main assumptions behind the correlation method – namely normally distributed returns, constant correlations and constant deltas – are not needed to calculate VAR by historical simulation.

Instead, this method calculates potential portfolio losses using actual historical returns in the risk factors and so captures the non-normal distribution of risk factor returns. That means rare events and crashes can be included in the results. Yet if too many rare events are included in the historical observation period (ie the period is too long), they may obscure the day-to-day benefits of VAR as a risk management tool by unduly distorting the distributions. If the observation period is too short, the portfolio VAR will be understated because too few outlier (rare) events are included in the observation period.

The portfolio is revalued at different levels of each risk factor (which depend on the distribution extracted from the historical observation period) and so can capture the non-linear nature of options and option-like products. Also, as the risk factor returns used for revaluing the portfolio are actual past movements, the correlations inherent in the calculations are also actual past correlations. They therefore capture the dynamic nature of correlation (and its fluctuations) and also scenarios when the usual correlation relationships break down. However, the increased number of portfolio revaluations needed make this method more computationally intensive than the correlation method.

The third method, Monte Carlo simulation, is more flexible than the previous two and, correspondingly, is the most computer intensive. Like historical simulation, Monte Carlo simulation allows the risk manager to use actual historical distributions for risk factor returns, rather than having to assume normal returns.

A large number of randomly-generated simulations (say 10,000) are then run forward in time using volatility and correlation estimates chosen by the risk manager. Each simulation will be different, but in total the simulations will aggregate to the chosen statistical parameters (ie historical distributions and volatility and correlation estimates).

When all the simulations are done, the VAR can be found by listing out all of the outcomes in order of profit and loss and "cutting off" at the required confidence level. The cutting off point represents the VAR.

While this method is likely to match reality more closely than the previous two methods (and therefore estimate VAR more accurately), the price is time and computer power. The benefits of the method may be outweighed by the costs involved.

Further methods are also used, such as optimisation programs that will find the maximum portfolio loss for a given set of (user defined) scenarios, which need not be based on historical data or estimated volatilities and correlations, or fixed scenario analysis, which is more akin to stress testing, where the user inputs specific scenarios.

From the given range of methods, it is clear that calculating VAR is something that risk managers need to think long and hard about. There is no right or wrong way to do it. Each institution needs to assess which method best suits its objectives, its business, its view of the world and its pocket.

As many financial institutions found in 1995, when faced with imminent deadlines for the European Union's Capital Adequacy Directive, establishing a VAR system is not something that should be done in a hurry. As this supplement will show, the concept is still in its infancy, even though it has already had a profound effect on the risk management community and global financial regulators.

One thing is sure – it is here to stay and the scope of its potential application is still growing fast.

2

How to Calculate VAR

Charles Smithson and Lyle Minton
CIBC Wood Gundy School of Financial Products

There are several different ways in which institutions can calculate value-at-risk. This article examines the various methods, and highlights their advantages and their drawbacks.

As trading portfolios have become more complex, it has become more difficult for senior management to obtain a useful yet practical measure of market risk. Since portfolios now contain more options, simple linear measures, such as a basis point value ("the value of an 01") or duration, are inappropriate; even if convexity is included, the measures are not accurate enough to estimate the risk associated with large moves in underlying prices. Option-based measures are useful at the trading desk for determining the portfolio's sensitivity to individual risk factors but, since they cannot be aggregated across asset classes or instruments to summarise a portfolio market risk measure, they are not very useful in the boardroom.

The most widely used summary measure is commonly known as value-at-risk (VAR). VAR is obtained by translating the riskiness of any financial instrument into a common standard – potential loss.

In this chapter, we will describe the concept and review the methods of calculating VAR. In the next chapter, we will look at applications of VAR, including the debate over the "right way" to calculate it and use it as a risk measure.

The VAR concept

As illustrated in Figure 1, the concept behind VAR is extremely simple. First, value the current portfolio using today's "price list"; the components of this list will be called "market factors". For example, the market factors that affect the value of a bond denominated in a foreign currency are the term structure of the foreign interest rate (either points on the zero coupon curve or the appropriate yield-to-maturity on the par curve) and the exchange rate.

Then, revalue the current portfolio using an "alternative price list" and calculate the change in the portfolio value that would result, ie, the difference in the value of the portfolio using today's price list and the alternative price list.

If the current portfolio is valued using a number of price lists, one obtains a distribution of changes in the value. Given this, VAR is specified in terms of confidence levels. The risk manager can calculate the maximum the institution can lose over a specified "time horizon" at a specified probability level. For instance, the risk manager

The authors would like to thank Shaun Rai and Charles Henry for their contribution to this article

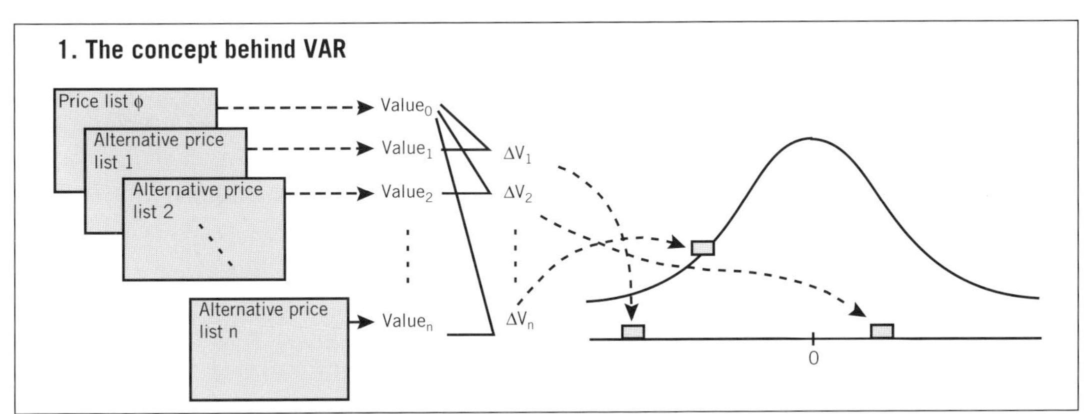

1. The concept behind VAR

can define the maximum loss for a one-day period at a 95% probability – ie, the loss that should be exceeded on only five days out of 100.

Calculating VAR

Implementation of VAR is not quite as simple as the concept. In essence, the problem is finding a way to obtain a series of vectors of "alternative market factors". Three methods are used to calculate VAR:

❑ HISTORICAL METHOD. Collect the values of the market factors for a particular historical period and calculate the observed changes in them over the time horizon to be used in the VAR calculation.

If a one-day VAR is to be obtained using the past 101 trading days, each of the market factors will have a vector of observed changes that will be made up of the 100 changes in value of the market factor. For example, look at $F(i)$, the previous values of market factor i:

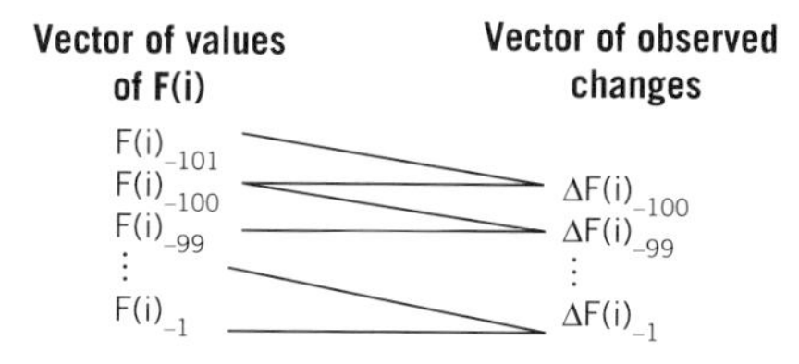

For each of the market factors, create a vector of alternative values $AF(i)_n$ by adding the current value of the market factor, $F(i)_0$, to each of the values in the vector of observed changes:

$$AF(i)_1 = F(i)_0 + \Delta F(i)_{-1}$$
$$AF(i)_2 = F(i)_0 + \Delta F(i)_{-2}$$
$$\vdots \qquad \vdots$$
$$AF(i)_{100} = F(i)_0 + \Delta F(i)_{-100}$$

Find the portfolio value VP using the current and alternative values for the market factors. Then, calculate the changes in portfolio value between the current value and the alternative values:

$$F(1)_0, F(2)_0, \ldots\ldots F(n)_0 \rightarrow VP_0$$
$$AF(1)_1, AF(2)_1, \ldots. AF(n)_1 \rightarrow VP_1 \qquad \Delta VP_1$$
$$AF(1)_2, AF(2)_2, \ldots. AF(n)_2 \rightarrow VP_2 \qquad \Delta VP_2$$
$$\vdots \qquad \vdots \qquad \vdots \qquad \vdots \qquad \vdots$$
$$AF(1)_{100}, AF(2)_{100}, \ldots AF(n)_{100} \rightarrow VP_{100} \qquad \Delta VP_{100}$$

Sort the changes in portfolio value from the lowest value to the highest value and determine VAR based on the desired confidence interval.

For a one-day, 95% confidence level VAR, using the past 101 trading days, the VAR would be the 95th most adverse change in portfolio value.

❑ SIMULATION METHOD. Define the parameters of the distributions for the changes in market factors, including correlations among market factors. Normal and lognormal distributions are commonly used to estimate changes in market factors, while historical data is most often used to define correlations among market factors. Use the distributions in a Monte Carlo simulation to obtain simulated changes in the market factors, $S\Delta F(i)$, over the time horizon to be used in the VAR calculation:

Vector of simulated changes in F(i)

$$S\Delta F(i)_1$$
$$S\Delta F(i)_2$$
$$S\Delta F(i)_3$$
$$\vdots$$
$$S\Delta F(i)_n$$

For each of the market factors, create a vector of alternative values by adding the current value of the market factor, $F(i)_0$, to each of the values in the vector of simulated changes:

$$AF(i)_1 = F(i)_0 + S\Delta F(i)_1$$
$$AF(i)_2 = F(i)_0 + S\Delta F(i)_2$$
$$\vdots$$
$$AF(i)_{100} = F(i)_0 + S\Delta F(i)_n$$

Once this vector of alternative values of the market factors is obtained, calculate the current and alternative values for the portfolio, the changes in the value of the portfolio, and the VAR, exactly as in the historical method.

❑ ANALYTIC METHOD. Similar to the historical methods, the analytic method also begins with collection of historical values of market factors, but the similarities between the two methods end there. The steps of the analytic method are: 1) decompose the instruments in the portfolio into cash equivalent positions in more elemental instruments or market factors; 2) specify the exact distributions for the market factors; and 3) calculate portfolio variance and VAR using standard statistical methods.

1) *Decompose financial instruments* The analytic method is based on the idea that the financial instruments in the portfolio can be decomposed – "mapped" – into a set of simpler instruments that are exposed to only one market factor.

For example, using the techniques one would use to "strip" a treasury, a two-year, US treasury note can be mapped into a set of zero-coupon bonds, one for each coupon and one for the principal. Each of these zero-coupon bonds is exposed to only one market factor – a specific US zero-coupon interest rate. Moving to the next level of complexity, a foreign currency-denominated bond can be mapped into a set of foreign currency zero-coupon bonds and a cash foreign exchange amount.

Suppose a US portfolio manager holds a two-year, Deutschmark Bund with a face value of DM5,000 and a 5.5% coupon, paid annually. Suppose further that the one- and two-year Deutschmark zero-coupon rates are 4.45% and 5.60%, respectively, and that the spot dollar/Deutschmark exchange rate is DM1.45. Figure 2 illustrates how this bond can be decomposed into two Deutschmark zero-coupon bonds that are subject to movement in the respective Deutschmark zero-coupon rates and a cash position subject to movement in the spot foreign exchange rate.

2) *Specify distributions* In the analytic method, one makes assumptions about the shapes of the distributions of the market factors. For example, the most widely-used of the analytic methods – JP Morgan's RiskMetrics – assumes that the underlying distributions are normal. With normal distributions, all the historical information is summarised in the means, variances and covariances of the market factors, so users do not need to keep all the historical data.

3) *Calculate portfolio variance and VAR* If all the market factors are assumed to be normally distributed, the portfolio – the sum of the individual instruments – can also be assumed to be normally distributed. This means that one can calculate the portfolio variance using standard statistical methods (similar to modern portfolio theory):

$$\sigma_p = \sqrt{\alpha_X^2\sigma_X^2 + \alpha_Y^2\sigma_Y^2 + 2\alpha_X\alpha_Y\rho_{XY}\sigma_X\sigma_Y}$$

where α_j is the home-currency present value of the position in market factor j, σ_j^2 is the variance of market factor j and ρ_{jk} is the correlation coefficient between market factors j and k.

The portfolio VAR is then simply some number of portfolio standard deviations, eg, 1.65 standard deviations will isolate 5% of the area of the distribution in the lower tail. Suppose that, using daily historical data, the variance-covariance matrix for the three Deutschmark Bund market factors has been calculated as:

	$/DM	1-yr DM zero	2-yr DM zero
$/DM	1.85E-5	–6.78E-6	–3.50E-6
One-year DM zero	–6.78E-6	2.50E-5	1.61E-5
Two-year DM zero	–3.50E-6	1.61E-5	1.85E-5

2. Mapping a German Bund

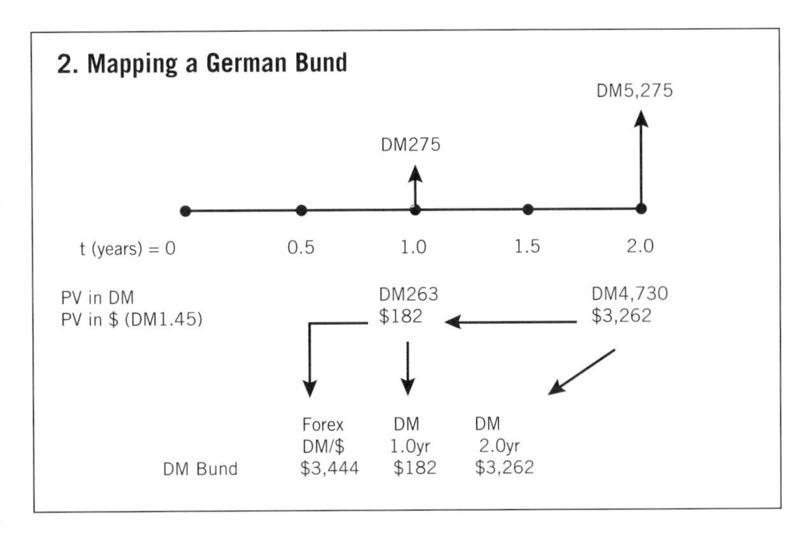

For the Deutschmark Bund, the portfolio variance is 348.57; so the standard deviation of the portfolio would be $18.67. A 95%, one-day VAR would be 1.65 × $18.67 = $30.81.

Comparison of the VAR generated by the methods

Not surprisingly, the three methods deliver different VAR measures. This is particularly true with portfolios that contain options. The analytic method usually estimates the market risk of option positions based on delta (or delta and gamma). Using only delta to measure the market risk of option positions will result in inaccurate risk estimates for large changes in the price of the underlying. It also ignores the potential effect of changes in the volatility of the underlying. The historic and simulation methods can account for potential changes in all the market factors that affect the price of an option, and the revaluation process allows the market risk of options to be more accurately measured for larger estimated changes in market factors. Therefore, analytic VAR measures can differ substantially from historic and simulation VAR measures for portfolios with substantial option positions.

Beder (1995) and Jordan & Mackay (1996) have documented these differences. Tables 1 and 2 are adapted from the Jordan & Mackay paper. Table 1 provides the Jordan & Mackay VAR calculations for a portfolio of five equities. In this case,

Table 1. Jordan & Mackay calculations of VAR for portfolio of equities (95% confidence level)

	Daily	Weekly	Monthly
Historical method	$16,142	$42,902	$76,684
Simulation method	$16,268	$30,272	$62,427
Analytic method	$15,642	$32,676	$60,500

Source: Adapted from exhibits 8, 11 and 19 of *Assessing value-at-risk for equity portfolios: implementing alternative techniques* by James Jordan and Robert Mackay.

Table 2. Jordan & Mackay calculations of VAR for portfolios of equity and equity options (95% confidence level)

	Daily	Weekly	Monthly
Historical method	$214,274	$423,322	$764,504
Simulation method	$187,605	$433,536	$865,146
Analytic method	$83,500	$178,892	$225,196

Source: adapted from exhibits 23–25 of *Assessing value-at-risk for equity portfolios: implementing alternative techniques* by James Jordan and Robert Mackay.

Table 3. The pros and cons of each VAR method

	Historical	Simulation	Analytic
Ease of implementation			
Easy to aggregate risk across markets?	Yes	Yes	Yes
Data available at no charge?	No	No	Yes
Ease of programming (spreadsheet)?	Easiest	Hardest	Intermediate
Distributions for market factors			
Must specific distributions be assumed?	No	Yes	Yes
Are actual volatilities and correlations used (so results will be sensitive to period selected)?	Yes	Possible	Yes
Will outliers affect risk measure?	Yes	Possible	Yes
Handling of individual instruments			
Are pricing models required?	Yes	Yes	No
Is it necessary to "map" instruments?	No	No	Yes
Will method accurately incorporate options?	Yes	Yes	No
Communication with senior management			
Ease of explanation?	Easiest	Intermediate	More difficult
Can sensitivity analyses be done?	No	Yes	Some

the VAR measures differ but the differences are not extreme. Table 2 provides the Jordan & Mackay VAR calculations for a portfolio made up of equity option positions (both long and short), as well as the equity positions themselves. In this case, the VAR generated by the analytic method differs dramatically from that generated by the historical and simulation methods.

Choosing among the methods

The inevitable question is: which method is best? The answer – also inevitable – is, *it depends*. Table 3 lists some of the pros and cons for each method.

The method utilised should be determined by the composition of the portfolio. For portfolios with no options (either stand-alone or embedded), the analytic method may well be the best choice because it does not require pricing models. Also, publicly available software and data, such as RiskMetrics, help to simplify implementation.

For portfolios with option positions, the historical or simulation methods are more appropriate. The historical method is conceptually simple and, since pricing models for financial products are now readily available as add-ins to a spreadsheet program, it is also easy to implement. The stumbling block to using the simulation method is the apparently complex task of doing Monte Carlo simulations; however, there is software that will take care of the simulations – again as an add-in to a spreadsheet.

Consequently, the choice between the historical and simulation methods comes down to user preference: either using actual changes in the market factors (thereby incorporating market characteristics implicit in the historical data) or specifying distributions that are based on how the user thinks the markets should behave under normal circumstances.

BIBLIOGRAPHY

Beder, T. Styblo, 1995, "VAR: Seductive but Dangerous", *Financial Analysts Journal* September–October, pp. 12–24, reprinted as Chapter 17 of this volume.

Jordan, J.V., and R.J. Mackay, 1996, "Assessing Value-at-Risk for Equity Portfolios: Implementing Alternative Techniques". Working Paper, Center for Study of Futures and Options Markets, Virginia Polytechnic Institute.

3

The Right VAR

Charles Smithson and Lyle Minton
CIBC Wood Gundy School of Financial Products

Dealers, end-users and regulators all have their own value-at-risk requirements. Which firms need VAR, and is there a "right" way of calculating it? What are the main factors to be considered in the continuing VAR debate?

The previous chapter described the value-at-risk (VAR) concept and reviewed the three calculation methods. In this chapter, we turn our attention to applications of VAR. First, we look at the extent to which VAR is used by different market participants, ie, dealers, end-users and regulators. Then we examine some of the issues from the ongoing debate about which firms should use VAR and the "right way" to calculate the risk measure.

The users

VAR is a concept whose time has come. It is being adopted by dealers and end-users and has been embraced by the regulatory community.

❑ *Dealers.* In a survey by the Group of Thirty's global derivatives project in 1993, 30% of dealers said they were using a VAR-like measure of market risk.[1] In the follow-up survey in 1994, 43% of dealers reported that they were using some form of VAR measure and an additional 37% indicated that they planned to implement VAR by the end of 1995. If we can believe this survey, 80% of dealers will now be using VAR as part of their market risk management and governance process.[2]

In November 1995, an official review of the annual reports of 67 internationally active banks and 12 securities firms from the Group of 10 countries, carried out by the Basle Committee on Banking Supervision and the technical committee of the International Organisation of Securities Commissions,[3] showed that in 1993 only four firms (all US banks) reported daily VAR exposures; by 1994, this number had risen to 18 firms (all banks).

❑ *End-users – non-financial corporations.* In the 1995 Wharton/CIBC Wood Gundy *Survey of derivatives usage among US non-financial firms*, 29% of respondents indicated that they use VAR for evaluating the risk of derivatives transactions. CIBC Wood Gundy co-sponsored a similar survey of Canadian non-financial institutions with the University of Waterloo, in which 47% of responding firms said that they use VAR. In a survey of multinational corporations in the June 1995 issue of *Institutional Investor*, 32% of firms said they used VAR to measure market risk.[4] A 1995 survey of 250 top UK non-financial companies by *Record Treasury Management* found that 25% of the respondents were using VAR to quantify their derivative exposures.

❑ *End-users – institutional investors.* A survey of pension funds' risk management practices by the New York University Stern School of Business asked funds about the techniques they used to assess risk.[5] Sixty per cent said they used VAR measures.[6]

❑ *Regulators – bank and securities firm regulators.* In April 1995, the Basle Committee on Banking Supervision proposed allowing banks to calculate their market risk capital requirement using the bank's own VAR model, with the committee specifying the parameters to load into the VAR model.

The European Union's Capital Adequacy Directive, which came into effect in January 1996, recognises VAR models as a valid method of calculating capital requirements for foreign exchange. And a recent EU decision has been made to move towards the use of VAR models to calculate other market risk capital requirements.

The "precommitment" approach proposed by

The authors would like to thank Bob Mark and Shaun Rai of CIBC-Wood Gundy, Jitendra Sharma of Arthur Andersen, Jacques Longerstaey of JP Morgan and Cathy Cole of the US Securities and Exchange Commission for their contributions to this article the US Federal Reserve in June 1995 goes one step further. The proposal would allow banks to use their internal VAR models to calculate their own market risk capital requirement (ie, the capital they should hold for market risk) for a particular period (eg, the next quarter). If, during the period, the loss experienced by the bank exceeded the capital it had reserved, the bank would be penalised. Proposed penalties include loss of the privilege of using internal VAR models, fines and public disclosure.

❑ *Regulators - Securities and Exchange Commission*. In January 1997, the SEC issued a rule designed to enhance the disclosure of market risk inherent in "derivative financial instruments, other financial instruments and derivative commodity instruments". The rule permits publicly traded firms in the US to select VAR as one of three different methods for calculating and disclosing potential loss in earnings, fair values or cashflows.[7] The VAR disclosure would include both on- and off-balance-sheet financial transactions.

The debate

VAR is still a new technique and there is much debate about the "right way" to use and calculate it. The issues include:

❑ *Appropriate uses*. Recent regulatory proposals have fuelled the debate about which types of firms should use VAR. As we noted in the preceding chapter, the VAR concept is based on valuation of the current portfolio. The value of some firms, eg, securities firms, investment funds and derivatives dealers, is closely tied to the current value of their assets. The value of other firms depends on perceived research and/or investment opportunities - growth options. The value of a firm with significant growth options is tied less closely to the market value of the current portfolio and more closely to the manner in which the firm manages these options.

A good example of a company whose value is determined primarily by growth options is a pharmaceutical firm - where research and development investments can be regarded as option premiums. The VAR concept is much less relevant to this type of firm, which is more concerned with managing the volatility of its cashflows so it can effectively manage its growth options - exercising them when optimal. (Hayt & Song, 1995, describe a cashflow analogue to VAR.)

The first two non-financial corporations to report VAR measures were British Petroleum and Mobil Oil Corporation. (Both started reporting VAR in 1994.) BP uses derivatives both to manage interest rate, foreign exchange rate and oil price risks in its core business, and to trade for profit. Consequently, it reports its derivatives positions under two headings - risk management and trading - and only reports a VAR measure for derivatives used for trading.[8] In a similar fashion, Mobil uses its VAR measure to assess the market risk of positions "that vary from management's defined benchmarks".[9]

❑ *Incorporating options into the analytic method*. We noted in Chapter 2 that the analytic method is not satisfactory for calculating VAR when the portfolio contains options. The naïve method for including options in the analytic method uses an option pricing model to obtain the delta. This hedge ratio is then used to determine the amount of a market factor that must be held to compensate for a small change (usually a 1-basis-point move) in the underlying. The present value of the delta hedge position in the underlying is then mapped into the appropriate cashflow bucket and included in the analytic formula for calculating portfolio variance.

This method for including options in the analytic VAR calculation has obvious shortcomings. Specifically, since the option's delta is a linear risk measure for small changes in the underlying price, it will result in inaccurate market risk measures for large changes in the price of the underlying - which, by definition, is precisely what VAR is attempting to measure.

The method can be enhanced by including gamma in the risk measure. Instead of measuring the slope of the option's value curve for a given underlying price, gamma adds an adjustment to compensate for the change in the value curve's slope. As an option pricing model must be used to determine the option's delta, gamma can easily be incorporated. However, since the change in slope or curvature of the option value curve is not constant for different prices of the underlying, the risk measure including gamma will again provide an inaccurate measure of market risk for larger changes in the price of the underlying. Nonetheless, including gamma in the calculation will result in a smaller estimation error for market risk than using delta alone.

Both of the above methods can be used to incorporate options into an analytic framework for calculating VAR and, depending on the size and composition of the options portfolio, can adequately measure price level risk. However, neither recognises the effect of volatility (vega) on the price of the option. To include vega in this analytic VAR model, separate buckets measuring the effect of changes in volatility (the volatility of volatility) for specified market factors would have to be included in the variance/covariance matrix. This analytic framework also fails to account for the time decay of option values (theta), which becomes a more relevant risk sensitivity measure as the VAR time horizon is increased.[10]

❑ *Length of the holding period.* Many VAR models use a one-day holding period and a 95–99% confidence interval to measure the amount of risk for the firm. Because these models measure the maximum expected losses for one day, they tend to show relatively small amounts at risk. This assumes that markets are liquid enough to unwind positions in one day. Essentially, they measure expected losses in normal markets.

Nearly all risk managers believe the one-day VAR approach is valid for trading purposes. However, they disagree on the appropriate holding period for the long-term solvency of the institution. One reason that this debate is so lively is that concerns about the appropriate holding period are, in part, due to non-linearities in value profiles. This problem becomes most evident for short option positions, where much of the attention has been given to "negative gamma" (see Figure 1).

Supporters of a one-day time horizon argue that they can capture the risk control effects of a longer holding period by multiplying the one-day risk measure by the square root of time. Opponents agree that such extrapolation works for linear products such as forwards and swaps but is not good enough to capture the behaviour of non-linear products such as options. For example, linear risk measures can underestimate potential loss for portfolios exhibiting negative gamma value profiles.

Some opponents of a one-day holding period

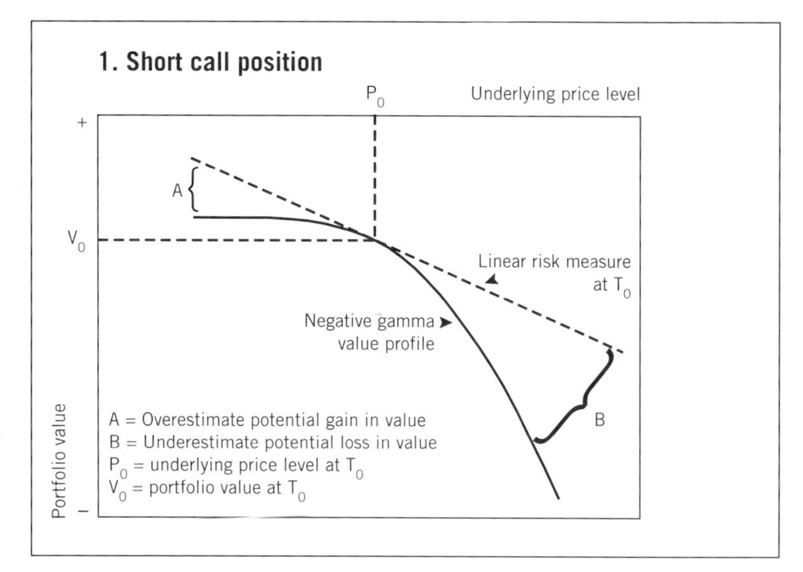

argue not only that one must use a longer holding period but also that it is necessary to perform stress tests, ie, stress simulations on extraordinary scenarios. But others doubt the merits of stress testing. They argue that, since valuation models are based on certain behavioural assumptions which may be invalid during market stress, stress testing can generate misleading results.

❑ *Degree of correlation between financial prices and aggregation.* Questions such as what is the appropriate degree of correlation to assume between financial prices and how to aggregate exposures to risk factors cannot be answered independently. Simple addition of exposures to risk factors is the most conservative way of aggregating exposures because you end up with the largest total. Simple addition implies that all factors are perfectly positively correlated, ie, that all factors can (and will) move against your positions at the same time. Most VAR models use historic correlations among risk factors to recognise market diversification. However, the debate is complicated by the fact that historic correlations are unstable. This is most evident when the markets experience stress.

1 *Specifically, 30% of the respondents indicated that the phrase that best described how they measured and determined limits for market risk was "amount at risk based on specified valuation models using confidence levels"*

2 *125 dealers from 15 countries responded to the Group of Thirty follow-up survey*

3 *Public disclosure of the trading and derivatives activities of banks and securities firms*

4 *A November 1995 survey by Emcor Risk Management Consulting got a similar percentage but gave the survey results a different interpretation: "...66 per cent of the respondents... said they do not feel that they have 'an adequate understanding or the necessary in-house expertise to effectively utilise the VAR measure'"*

5 *The survey was sent to 50 pension funds; the number of responses was not reported*

6 *However, only 33% of the funds surveyed reported that they had internal risk management systems. Eighty per cent of the funds reported that pension consultants provided risk management services*

7 *The other two options for disclosure are an analysis of sensitivity to hypothetical changes in market rates and a*

tabular presentation of expected cashflows and maturity dates. The rule does not apply to investment firms

8 *BP's measure of VAR, "assessed market risk", was defined as "a statistically based assessment of market risk, ie, of exposures to possible future changes in market values over a 24-hour period*

9 *Mobil indicated that it used a simulation method to obtain a one-day 99.7% confidence level VAR*

10 *Techniques are being developed to reflect more accurately the risks of options using the analytic method. For example, our colleague Bob Mark (1995) has developed an approach for measuring gamma over larger changes in the price of the underlying. His technique can be used to incorporate volatility and time-decay risk*

BIBLIOGRAPHY

Group of Thirty, *Derivatives: practices and principles - survey of industry practice*, July 1993.

Group of Thirty, *Derivatives: practices and principles -- follow-up surveys of industry practice*, December 1994.

Hayt, G., and S. Song, 1995, "Handle with sensitivity", *Risk* 8, 9, pp. 94-99, reprinted as Chapter 35 of the present volume.

Mark, R., 1995, "Integrated credit risk measurement", *Derivative Credit Risk: Advances in Measurement and Management*, Risk Publications.

Record Treasury Management, Derivatives survey, Summer 1995.

Slunt, J., 1995, *Survey of Risk Management Practices for Pension Funds*, New York University Stern School of Business, Spring 1995.

"The Dreaded D-word", 1995, *Institutional Investor*, June.

4

Banks Grasp the VAR Nettle

Dan Heron and Richard Irving
Risk

Where JP Morgan blazed a trail with RiskMetrics, other banks have sought to follow and other risk measurement models have hit the market. This article was first published in June 1996.

Nowhere in JP Morgan's first quarter profits for 1996 does the bank draw any correlation between its record-breaking performance in the wholesale capital markets and its state-of-the-art risk management systems. Yet the bank's high-profile attempts to promote a benchmark risk management tool to the financial marketplace is clearly doing the bottom line no harm. Although JP Morgan does not specifically break down derivatives revenues, it nevertheless confirmed that first quarter trading profits of $758 million – more than double the average for 1995 and some $200 million higher than the previous record quarter – were largely fuelled by strong demand for foreign exchange, interest rate and equity derivative products.

By its own admission, the bank's motivation for offering its proprietary RiskMetrics system free to the public was driven not by altruism but by a desire to establish an industry benchmark. It is therefore no coincidence that other banks looking to emulate JP Morgan's prowess are rushing to make their own risk management systems available to valued clients.

Shortly before JP Morgan announced its first quarter results, rival Credit Suisse First Boston (CSFB), the US investment banking subsidiary of the Credit Suisse Group, launched PrimeRisk, part of a risk management software package offering customers the flexibility to customise risk analysis systems. Chase Manhattan, Bankers Trust and Deutsche Bank have also launched products in the wake of JP Morgan's trail-blazing RiskMetrics system, first unveiled in October 1994, and other leading derivatives houses are believed to be considering following suit.

There is an on-going academic debate over the various methodologies aimed at measuring exposure to market risk, largely because regulators such as the Bank for International Settlements (BIS), the US Securities and Exchange Commission and, to a lesser extent, the European Commission are keen to incorporate some sort of market risk measurement into tighter capital adequacy rules.

Although reluctant to embrace specific methodologies, the regulators have all but accepted the validity of one particular concept – value-at-risk (VAR), which essentially defines the maximum a firm could lose given a certain level of confidence over a given time horizon, should exchange rates, interest rates and commodity prices move against it. According to the Swiss-based BIS, the simplicity of the VAR approach is the key: "VAR is an effective tool for describing and communicating risk because it assesses different risks in terms of a common loss relative to a standard unit of likelihood," it says.

Jacques Longerstaey, head of risk management services at JP Morgan, points out that effective risk management is only part science. The task is making sure that everybody has a risk management process in place, and that they are asking questions about their VAR number. The problems arise, he says, when people stop asking questions.

Fred Stambaugh, managing director of risk management advisory at Chase Manhattan in London, agrees: "As markets become more complex and interrelated, so they become more volatile. Recent well-publicised losses among both corporations and financial institutions have highlighted the need for improved risk measurement, management and control systems and the need to back up trading operations with adequate capital," he says. "One of the greatest attractions of VAR is that it can be used as a summary measure of market risk. Single position VARs can be aggregated into a portfolio of VARs or into a single VAR figure for the whole firm. Moreover, it is seen as an important input to risk-adjusted performance evaluation."

VAR models typically depend on the past being a good guide to the future. They tend to be built around statistical estimates, using probability distributions for the changes in value of a given portfolio over a specific holding period. But there is as yet no consensus among either market practitioners or their regulators as to how to generate these distributions.

Chase Manhattan's Charisma (Chase Risk Management Analyser) package, which is currently undergoing pilot testing in the US, uses perhaps the most straightforward approach. The model constructs distributions of probable future price changes using historical data. Essentially the model identifies a portfolio's exposure to specific risks - such as foreign exchange and interest rate volatility - and identifies the price changes in those markets for each of the last 100 days. The portfolio is then revalued as if each price change occurred from today's price level, thus creating 100 possible changes to the portfolio's value. From these figures, a risk manager can determine a VAR number corresponding to a given confidence level. Chase uses a confidence level of 97.5% - in other words, losses are not expected to exceed the RiskDollar (VAR) amount in more than 2.5% of cases or once every 40 days. But the system can accommodate different risk appetites (the latest BIS proposals, for example, recommend risk managers use a confidence level of at least 99%).

Stambaugh says the strength of the methodology lies in its simplicity: "We can take our model into a boardroom and explain it to any level within a firm in 15 minutes," he says. "The model does not require any subjective decisions on how to treat data, so there is no ambiguity in the results it generates. Moreover the numbers can easily be analysed in any format and to any level or type of aggregation required."

JP Morgan's RiskMetrics system uses an entirely different methodology, the so-called variance/covariance approach. It arrives at its daily VAR number (the Daily Earnings at Risk number) by using historic volatility and correlation data to predict how markets are likely to move in the future. The approach allows JP Morgan to build normal distributions for historic price changes and to aggregate the results into a diversified VAR number for a 95% confidence level. This means the volatility estimates generated by RiskMetrics will be below the actual figure on average one day in every 20.

There are a number of significant differences between the two approaches. JP Morgan exponentially weights the square of the historical returns (thus giving newer data more emphasis than the old). Chase's model, because it uses actual price changes rather than average volatility, does not adjust data. While Chase goes back 100 days, JP Morgan bases its calculations on 75 days' worth of data. This, says Peter Zangari of JP Morgan's risk management research services in New York, is due to the decay factor. RiskMetrics uses a decay factor of 0.94 which gives the best forecast when the last 75 days are used, he says. Zangari says that exponentially weighting is "not a complex computational problem", indeed "it is relatively simple over a wide variety of time series. With the well documented volatility clusters, it is important to discriminate between periods of high and low volatility".

He continues: "RiskMetrics does not unnecessarily complicate things because the volatilities and correlations that we provide allow users to isolate diversification benefits. Hence risk analysis goes beyond computing a simple value-at-risk measure." Additionally, while Chase has opted for a 97.5% confidence level, JP Morgan assumes a 95% confidence level.

Perhaps the fundamental difference between the two approaches is that the variance/covariance VAR approach of RiskMetrics assumes that portfolio return distributions are conditionally normal. As the JP Morgan RiskMetrics Monitor publication says: "Among other things, this implies that return distributions are symmetric. However, due to the pay-off structure of options many portfolios that include options have return distributions that are, at the very least, skewed." But if the bank cannot rationalise the system to include options, and subsequently ends up with a model that generates two VARs - one for options and one for the rest of the portfolio, then the model's usefulness might be compromised, suggests Chase's Stambaugh.

JP Morgan will in fact embrace another approach to market risk measurement, the so-called Monte Carlo simulation, when it adds option market risk measurement capabilities to its FourFifteen spreadsheet package, launched in March, by the end of this year. However, the full simulation, known as Structured Monte Carlo and outlined in the RiskMetrics technical document, is, as the bank admits, "computationally and time intensive". The goal, the bank says, "is to present a methodology that is relatively simple to implement and does not require a lot of computer time". Thus JP Morgan has been testing a partial Monte Carlo simulation based on an option's delta and gamma, which will be less computationally intensive.

Like the variance/covariance method, Monte Carlo simulation uses historic prices to estimate variances and correlations. The portfolio is then revalued for each new scenario and the results formatted so that a VAR number can be generated according to the required confidence level. Both the full Monte Carlo simulation and a partial simulation will be added to FourFifteen by the end of the year, says Ethan Berman of JP Morgan's risk management team. The delta and gamma questions that surround the variance/covariance matrix are being solved via this Monte Carlo add-on to the existing system in JP Morgan's so-called "delta/gamma approximation". There will be an aggregate VAR figure which can be broken down by market and which will allow users to incorporate their own portfolios, says Berman.

The Monte Carlo approach forms the backbone of Bankers Trust's Raroc (Risk-adjusted return on capital) 2020 system, unveiled to clients last June as part of a restructuring of the troubled bank's derivatives operations. The Monte Carlo simulation Bankers uses as part of Raroc 2020 is based on a correlation matrix of 400 risk factors to provide estimates of future portfolio performances.

Some 10,000 simulation trials are used to represent possible future financial market outcomes. In each trial, an independent random number for each of these market variables is selected from a normal distribution. These random moves are then adjusted to reflect historical market volatilities and correlations. The value of the portfolio is determined for each of the 10,000 scenarios by calculating a new value for each holding in the portfolio under the predicted market conditions, and these values represent the portfolio's distribution.

While Raroc 2020 calculates a portfolio's capital at risk within a 99% confidence level over one year, it also gives the user full access to the entire profit and loss distribution both on a portfolio basis and for specific portfolios. But the computing power required to do such calculations is considerable. The bank says its Dec server has to compute, in less than five seconds, the type of risk calculations that used to take PC spreadsheets more than 78 hours. This is perhaps why the bank reportedly charges $75,000 for a one-off run through the system and around $1 million for an on-site licence. Nevertheless, there appears to be no shortage of willing takers – it has already signed up three leading institutional investors, including the $12.5 billion Chrysler pension fund and a major European utility.

CSFB's recently-launched PrimeRisk is another attempt by a leading bank to set a customer-driven industry benchmark, although it differs markedly from RiskMetrics in many areas. PrimeRisk is a proprietary forecasting model for volatilities and correlations and tools to model VAR concepts. The system is part of an integrated risk management software package called PrimeClear, a central interface that allows real-time trade reconciliation and confirmation, combined with flexible account structuring. The March 18 launch is part of an ongoing product line, says CSFB, in which eight highly-integrated products should be launched this year. The system allows CSFB's clients to receive, manage, query and simulate their own transaction data as part of a customised approach to risk analysis. PrimeRisk produces risk parameters such as volatilities, correlations, prices and zero-coupon yield curves, while the PrimeClear interface produces the VAR and transaction sensitivity in its consolidation/profit centre, using its spreadsheet calculator.

CSFB has concentrated its efforts on the accuracy and depth of its volatility data. Unlike RiskMetrics, PrimeRisk does not use an identical volatility model for all markets. Research by CSFB shows that optimal volatility models for different markets are indeed different and consequently PrimeRisk uses individually tailored volatility models for each market in the search for better forecasting accuracy.

Peter Zangari of JP Morgan responds: "We maintain the same decay factor across all 454 time series because it not only keeps things simple but, if we did not, the RiskMetrics covariance matrix would be inconsistent."

Much has been written about the use of historical volatility data for predicting future market movements. The traditional method is to take a standard deviation from recent observations and determine a volatility forecast after weighting each observation equally. More modern techniques, such as GARCH (Generalised Autoregressive Conditional Heteroscedasticity) have attempted to address the shortcomings of traditional methods which imply that volatility is constant. Another method is that used by RiskMetrics, which exponentially weights historical data to guide future forecasts so that it assigns more weight to recent observations than to less recent ones. Trials of Garch have shown it to be less accurate than the exponential weighting method, says CSFB.

The advantages of this over other statistical models are that recent information can be captured relatively quickly and the nature of the weightings is computationally simple (some models are so complex that incredible amounts of computing power are required and data production can be very slow). PrimeRisk uses fractional exponential weighting of its historical data, giving lower weightings to recent and distant days and increased weight to the intermediate days. CSFB says that after extensive backtesting using daily data from 1989 over 60 different types of assets, it finds the fractional exponential method gives a lower forecasting error than the simple exponential method (as used in RiskMetrics) by up to 10% while still retaining the all-important computational simplicity.

PrimeRisk has also set out to cover as many different markets as possible, including data on futures contracts, OTC options and key equities. Data on emerging markets and other instruments will be added in the future, says CSFB. The data is also pre-formatted to make sure that data delivery is as easy as possible for the clients. Options data will also include delta and gamma statistics.

One of the crucial differences between RiskMetrics and PrimeRisk is the fact that PrimeRisk is not in the public domain but for current and prospective CSFB clients only. Varying degrees of risk management sophistication among CSFB's clients mean that some are merely taking the data provided to put into their own models and some are taking the whole package, says Philippe Buhannic, head of global listed derivatives at CSFB. He says PrimeRisk is non-profit making, the charges are to cover research costs and fund the future development of the model.

PrimeRisk data can be accessed via internet bulletin boards, proprietary web sites, electronic mail, fax and on diskettes. VAR, correlations and volatility are updated internally at CSFB every hour, and data will be downloaded to customers two or three times a day, rather than overnight.

Since Deutsche Bank's db-Analyst 2.0 was introduced in the wake of RiskMetrics in January 1995, news of the system (which was due to add a foreign exchange module capable of handling exotic options compatible with the fixed income module) has been thin on the ground. However, db-Analyst is to be relaunched in an integrated risk management system called db-treasury-network, using a Unix platform to process the increased quantity of data.

db-Analyst was never supposed to be a challenger to RiskMetrics, says Deutsche Bank, but an end-user analysis tool to help manage cashflow and understand the concepts of risk management. The system is now used by a wide spread of the bank's clients, at all points on the risk management learning curve, says Hans-Peter Preyer, vice president in charge of global marketing at Deutsche Morgan Grenfell in Frankfurt. Its interest rate module could display and calculate the risk in symmetric and assymetric interest rate sensitive positions including loans; bonds and notes; floating rate notes; deposits; forward rate agreements, and swaps and futures. In addition, db-treasury-network includes a system with which to identify foreign exchange risk, liquidity risk and credit risk. Providing gap, cashflow and sensitivity analyses and the possibility of entering various "what if" scenarios, the analysis feature implemented into db-treasury-network supports strategic decisions on the positioning or repositioning of instruments in the relevant markets.

Deutsche Bank stresses the need for an integrated solution to comprehensive risk management. The system provides data via an online link to the bank, and includes confirmation and matching capabilities for foreign exchange, bond and money market business. db-treasury-network, originally developed for Deutsche Bank's German clients, is being prepared for international demand, says the bank.

When JP Morgan launched RiskMetrics, the intention was to show the techniques it used in-house to estimate daily risk exposures, set position limits and refine asset allocation strategies. The bank's latest version still has its shortcomings, say rivals – as yet it cannot generate measurements for most derivative instruments or any securities with embedded optionality – but JP Morgan says these capabilities will be added later this year. However, RiskMetrics data currently covers some 450 instruments on 23 markets, and those numbers will be further expanded in the near future, says Longerstaey.

Indeed, the system continues to be successful in doing what it first set out to do – encourage rival banks and software companies to use its number-crunching methodology as a base from which to promote wider debate on risk management systems and ultimately the development of a new generation of risk management systems. The fact that rival systems are comparing themselves directly with RiskMetrics implies the bank has gone some way towards becoming the industry benchmark.

More work on risk management still has to be done. While arguments continue to rage over the implementation and measurement of market risk, and more specifically the relative validity of the backtesting methodologies and the data they produce, it is perhaps prescient to note that the billion dollar losses incurred at both Barings Bank and Daiwa were exacerbated, if not created, by a lack of proper internal controls, ie operational risk. The preoccupation with market risk ignores the fact that effective VAR measurements would not have prevented these losses.

The Right Approach

Kenneth Leong
Cinergy Corp

As financial institutions and corporations face greater regulation, the need for them to implement a system to manage risk is becoming paramount. This article compares and contrasts several commonly-used approaches to value-at-risk.

Academics have long evaluated investments in terms of both risk and return. They also understand there is often a trade-off between the two. But while the risk-return framework is widely accepted within the academic circle, it has yet to filter down to the practitioners' level.

Traditionally, investors and corporate managers focused primarily on earnings as a barometer of corporate health and a gauge of investment potential. Promoters of mutual funds, for example, typically provide investors with statistics of historical returns, without a corresponding warning about potential loss. While risk is a concern for many investors, the lack of an effective corporate risk measure and the absence of risk reporting requirements until now have led to an under-emphasis of this dimension of investment analysis.

A new era of risk consciousness

However, a series of mammoth losses in some of the world's largest financial institutions has begun to turn things around. The savings and loans (S&L) bail-out; Procter & Gamble's contested swaps; the well-publicised losses of Orange County; and the downfall of Barings and Daiwa Bank in the US have established beyond doubt the vital importance of a systematic approach to corporate risk management, control, reporting and disclosure. Shaken by such evidence of poor risk management and control, government regulators and oversight agencies – the Bank for International Settlements, the Federal Reserve Bank, the Office of the Comptroller of the Currency and the SEC – are drawing up new requirements for corporations and financial institutions to report and disclose their risk exposure, using the modern techniques and mathematical models developed by financial economists in the past few decades.

One of the key concepts of modern risk management, value-at-risk (VAR) is an attempt to quantify, within a specified confidence interval, the maximum potential loss for a given trading position, an investment portfolio or a firm as a whole. On December 28, 1995, the SEC released for comment a proposal for corporate risk disclosure, which discusses three alternative methods of measuring the market risk exposure of corporations. VAR is one of them.

The use of mathematical models to measure financial risk is not new. For years, modern fixed-income portfolio managers have relied on analytical concepts such as duration, convexity and basis point value to measure their exposure to interest rate risk. Option traders have relied on sensitivity measures such as delta, gamma, vega and theta to quantify option risk.

Quantitative money managers are a little more advanced in this regard. They are used to viewing investments from a risk-return perspective and have been using tools from modern portfolio theory to aid their investment decisions. But their focus has primarily been on stocks and the analytical tools they developed have never been used for risk management on a corporate level. What is new with the development of the VAR framework is the quantification of firm-wide, cross-product risk exposure and the extensive use of modern statistical techniques and concepts in the risk measurement process.

These new developments make the VAR approach more powerful than conventional ones. The well-established basis point value measure, for example, is a deterministic risk measure which quantifies precisely how much the value of a bond changes as an interest rate moves up or down by one basis point. While it provides us with some information about interest rate risk, it does not incorporate our knowledge about the historical volatilities of interest rates and gives little information about the interactions of asset risks in a portfolio context. More importantly, it offers no clues about the statistical expectation of potential loss. For example, how likely would it be for the bond to lose, say, one quarter of its market value within a day?

In contrast, as we shall see, VAR is a statistical risk measure which takes into account the historical volatilities of different assets and the correlations between them. By incorporating these relevant statistical data, it also allows us to make probabilistic statements about the likelihood of various degrees of potential gain/loss.

Risk is context-dependent

Another problem with the older risk measures is that they tend to look at risk in isolation. Risk is a holistic concept which does not lend itself easily to partial analysis. It is absurd, therefore, to say a certain financial instrument carries a big or small risk regardless of its context. The truth is that the marginal contribution that a given position makes to total portfolio risk is a function of what else there is in the portfolio. For this reason, the total risk of a portfolio is generally not the same as the direct summation of the risk of its component assets and liabilities, evaluated as if each piece stood alone. To be accurate, a risk measure system has to account for all possible interactions between all components of the relevant portfolio.

As an illustration, to perform a risk analysis of a S&L, it is not enough just to know what happens on the funding side of the institution. Let us say that the S&L funds itself with floating-rate debt. On the surface, this may suggest substantial exposure to interest rate risk. However, the net risk to the institution can turn out to be minimal if the institution's assets are also very short-term in nature. Thus, effective risk management depends on an understanding of the entire asset/liability mix. Similarly, it would be absurd to assert that trading derivative products such as futures and options is inherently dangerous. Although some market players have incurred big losses from derivatives trading, many others use derivative products successfully to hedge against market risk. Just like other instruments, the risk of derivatives is also context-dependent.

VAR: a holistic risk measure

To avoid the pitfalls of partial analysis, the modern VAR approach attempts to measure risk in a comprehensive and integrated manner, taking into account all possible interactions between all relevant assets and liabilities. While there are different ways to measure VAR, all VAR measurement systems have the following common features:

❑ *Global view* While risk measures such as basis point value and delta tend to be traders' tools which focus on the risk of individual products or instruments, VAR tends to be a general management tool which quantifies risk on a global, firm-wide level, viewing the firm as a giant portfolio of assets and liabilities with fluctuating market values.

❑ *Utilisation of statistical information* All relevant statistical information about the component assets and liabilities such as historical volatilities and correlations are used in the quantification of portfolio risk.

❑ *Recognition of interactions* This is a direct result of the previous point. To the extent that the risk measurement system correctly takes into account the correlations between different asset classes, it would accurately reflect any diversification or hedging effects in the portfolio. A fixed-income portfolio with assets spanning a wide spectrum of maturities and a variety of currencies, for example, will be subject to a diversification effect which is ignored by the portfolio duration measure but captured by the VAR measure.

RiskMetrics

In 1994, JP Morgan released to the public a new approach to risk measurement, RiskMetrics. Essentially, it is the combination of an analytical framework to measure portfolio risk and the corresponding statistical data sets necessary to do the risk computations. By providing the public with comprehensive volatility and correlation data across a wide range of asset classes, including interest rate instruments, FX and commodities, the bank delivers into the hands of corporate treasurers and risk managers a powerful tool for managing corporate risk on an integrated basis.

The introduction of RiskMetrics is historically significant because, to the extent that the methodology gains wide acceptance among market practitioners, it lays the foundation for a standardised way of measuring and disclosing risk.

The analytical approach of RiskMetrics is a direct application of modern portfolio theory and can be summarised by the following equation:

$$\sigma_p^2 = \sum_{i=1}^{n} (\alpha_i \bullet \sigma_i)^2 + 2\sum_{i=1}^{n} \sum_{j \neq i}^{n} \alpha_i \alpha_j \rho_{ij} \sigma_i \sigma_j \qquad (1)$$

where:
σ_p^2 = the variance for the entire portfolio
α_i = the portfolio weighting for asset i
σ_i^2 = variance of the logarithmic return of asset i
ρ_{ij} = the correlation between the logarithmic return of asset i and that of asset j
n = the number of assets in the portfolio.

We will not get into the details of explaining this mathematical equation. Essentially, it states that total portfolio risk is a function of two types of factors:
(a) the volatility of each distinct asset or liability in the portfolio, denoted as σ_i; and
(b) the correlations between assets and/or liabilities, denoted as ρ_{ij}.

To the extent that the price movements of the assets or liabilities in the portfolio are not perfectly correlated, there will be a diversification effect. In such a case, the total risk of the portfolio will be less than the direct summation of individual asset or liability risks.

Equation (1) quantifies the portfolio variance. But what does it mean in practice? To facilitate the translation of the portfolio variance into a meaningful number easily understood by corporate decision makers, RiskMetrics makes the simplifying assumption that the returns of all assets and liabilities are normally distributed. Since the return of a portfolio is the weighted average of the returns on the constituent assets or liabilities, this means the portfolio return is also normally distributed.

Given this simplification, we can then estimate, within a certain level of confidence, the range over which the portfolio value will fluctuate on a daily, weekly, monthly or annual basis. For a particular portfolio, we may find that there is no more than a 10% chance that its market value will increase or decrease by more than $1 million over a one-day period. Thus, the VAR in this case is $1 million.

Under the normality assumption, we can readily translate any confidence level into a specific number of standard deviations. For example, a 90% confidence level translates into 1.65 standard deviations and thus the 90% confidence interval can be constructed as

$$[\mu - 1.65\sigma, \mu + 1.65\sigma]$$

(Without the normality assumption, we can still construct confidence intervals for portfolio value fluctuation. But the translation between confidence levels and standard deviations is not necessarily easy.)

Mathematical models are, by definition, approximations of reality. To be practical and useful, they have to make certain simplifying assumptions. RiskMetrics is no exception. Although RiskMetrics is an authoritative methodology which is rapidly gaining acceptance among market practitioners, we should be aware that it is limited by its underlying assumptions. Here is a list of some of the key assumptions made:

❑ *Stability* Underlying any statistical technique or model is the implicit assumption that the future will bear some resemblance to the past. It is assumed in RiskMetrics that asset volatilities and correlations are relatively stable and can be reasonably estimated using historical data. In reality, however, volatilities and correlations do change over time, sometimes dramatically. Correlations between different currencies, for example, are known to fluctuate substantially from period to period. While the stability assumption cannot be avoided for most VAR frameworks, we have to recognise this as a potential source of error. It may help to do some sensitivity analysis, changing the estimates of volatilities and correlations, to see how much the VAR number will change.

❑ *Normality* As we have mentioned, under RiskMetrics, the translation of portfolio variance into a dollar value of potential loss is contingent on the assumption that asset returns are normally distributed. To the extent that the distribution of portfolio returns is not normal, the VAR estimate can be grossly biased. For this reason it will help to check the validity of the normality assumption on different assets and to calculate VAR using other approaches which are not so distribution-dependent.

❑ *Cashflow mapping* To facilitate the analysis, RiskMetrics specifies a methodology for simplifying the asset/liability cashflows. First, cashflows are supposed to happen only on standardised grid points on the time line. On the fixed-income side, for example, all cashflows are supposed to fall on only 18 standard dates. If a cashflow falls in between two grid points, it has to be remapped to simplify the analysis. Second, contingent cashflows (eg those resulting from option positions) have to be converted to deterministic cashflows. This is usually done through a "delta-equivalent" analysis. A detailed discussion of cashflow mapping is beyond the scope of this chapter. Suffice to say, all these simplifications lead to imprecisions in the risk measurement process. Representation of an option position by its delta equivalent, for example, means that its gamma, vega and theta risks are completely ignored (see Chapter 10).

Limitations are a fact of life. It is impossible to find a risk management methodology which does not have some kind of drawback. Effective risk management is not so much a matter of finding the perfect model or method as a matter of knowing the relative strengths and weaknesses of each alternative approach and possibly implementing a few mutually complementary ones. In what follows, we will review several commonly-used alternative approaches for measuring VAR.

The historical approach

This approach is powerful because of its simplicity and its relative lack of theoretical baggage. It differs from RiskMetrics in three key aspects:

❑ It makes no explicit assumption about the variances of portfolio assets and liabilities and the correlations between them;

❑ It makes no assumption about the shape of the distribution of asset returns. In particular, it makes no assumption of normality;

❑ It requires no simplification or mapping of cashflows.

To compute the VAR using this approach, all we need is a historical record of the daily profit and loss (P&L) of the portfolio whose risk we want to measure. Based on this historical record, we can generate an empirical distribution of the daily P&L. One major strength of this approach is that it requires minimal analytical capability. So long as the historical P&L is readily available, we do not need a valuation model to arrive at the VAR.

Besides being powerfully simple, the historical approach has the additional benefit of being "realistic". In the RiskMetrics approach, the volatilities and correlations that go into the model represent averages over a specified time period. As such, the extremes and outliers which took place historically are evened out and buried. The historical approach, on the other hand, involves no such historical averaging since it is based on the actual daily P&L fluctuations. As such, it accurately reflects the stress experienced by a portfolio during chaotic periods such as Black Monday or the breakdown of ERM. For this reason, the historical approach is particularly useful for stress testing.

An additional benefit of the historical approach has to do with the fact that there is no cashflow mapping or simplification in this method. The simplification process can create substantial risk distortion, particularly when there are sizable option positions in a portfolio. As we have mentioned, options are typically converted into their delta equivalents under RiskMetrics. This type of conversion can create serious bias in the VAR estimate, particularly in volatile periods when the market makes dramatic movements. The historical approach, by sticking with actual P&Ls, circumvents this problem.

Last but not least, the representation of risk by the empirical frequency distribution of P&L can be easily understood by most people. Many financial institutions, including JP Morgan and Merrill Lynch, have used this simple method to communicate to their shareholders the risk profile of the company in their annual reports. Although these institutions certainly have more sophisticated ways of measuring risk, the fact that this approach lends itself readily to a pictorial presentation (in the form of a histogram) has intuitive appeal.

DRAWBACKS

Because the historical approach is based strictly on what happened in the past, it is not particularly useful for scenario analysis. In the case of RiskMetrics, for example, we could alter the assumed variances and correlations to see how the VAR would be affected. We cannot do the same under the historical approach. In addition, to the extent that the portfolio mix changes over time, the historical approach may produce a VAR which does not reflect the current situation. Even if no new positions are created or old positions eliminated from the portfolio, the natural ageing process can change a portfolio's risk profile significantly over time. The ageing effect is particularly prominent in the case of options but also significant in the case of bonds over a longer time horizon.

To remedy the ageing effect, what we could do is a "historical simulation", which is more involved than the simpler historical approach discussed earlier. Instead of relying on a history of portfolio P&L, a historical simulation relies on a historical record of a basic set of market data which determines portfolio value. Using the current portfolio composition and the historical market data, we can determine what the portfolio value would have been a day, a month or a year ago. Thus, we simulate the historical portfolio P&L while keeping the portfolio character constant. The simulated history of portfolio P&L can then be used to construct an "empirical" distribution and derive the associated VAR.

This more sophisticated approach retains many of the benefits of the simpler historical approach while it eliminates the ageing bias. The price to pay for this increased precision is that we now need an analytical valuation model to derive the history of portfolio value from the history of market data. Also, more time is needed to perform the analysis since there are many more computations required. The need to resort to this simulation approach is a function of the contents of the portfolio. As long as the portfolio mix stays relatively constant and there is no substantial ageing effect, the simpler historical approach will suffice.

The stochastic simulation approach

The historical approach quantifies portfolio risk by going through one historical path ("sample path") of market evolution. However, one historical path may not be adequate to reveal all the risk associated with a portfolio, especially when there is a wide variety of random factors, all interacting with each other. In an attempt to generate a more comprehensive risk profile, some risk managers simulate the random behaviour of all the basic market variables which have an impact on portfolio value. This is commonly done using a sampling methodology called Monte Carlo simulation in which a mathematical formula is used to generate one or more series of "pseudo-random numbers" to simulate reality. The complex interplay of the risk factors is captured by generating a large sample of simulated paths. The VAR number produced by this method represents a risk measure which is averaged across a large number of potential paths sampled by this simulation process. If the sample size is large, a wide range of combinations and permutations of random events can be covered. In this sense, the VAR number is also more realistic and reliable.

Stochastic simulation only differs from the historical simulation in one respect. While the evolution of market factors is taken directly from history in the historical approach, it has to be simulated through mathematical modelling in the stochastic approach. To model the evolution of markets, we need to do the following:

- *Specify a stochastic process for each of the relevant market factors* For example, we may assume that the evolution of interest rates follows a "random walk". The specification of stochastic processes is beyond the scope of this discussion.
- *Estimate the statistical parameters for the stochastic process* For example, what are the mean and variance of a random variable? The correlations between different random variables also have to be estimated.

PROS AND CONS

Stochastic simulation has several advantages over the other approaches mentioned earlier:

- *Comprehensiveness* Because this approach generates a large collection of sample paths, it can be used to explore a wide range of possibilities and test run a myriad of scenarios.
- *Flexibility* Because this approach leaves the bulk of the analytical modelling in the hands of the risk manager, he or she has virtually boundless flexibility in specifying how the random system evolves over time. If desired, a different portfolio mix and/or a different set of statistical parameters (such as volatilities and correlations) can be specified for each future period.
- *Precision* Stochastic simulation is the most effective approach in terms of precisely capturing the risk profile of portfolios. This is because precise valuation models are used in determining the change in portfolio value as the market environment changes, in contrast with the RiskMetrics approach, where cashflows are only approximated, and with the historical approach, where the portfolio composition may already be outdated. Because of its modelling precision, stochastic simulation is the best approach to use for quantifying the effect of optionality, large market movements or deviations from normality but just like any other approach, stochastic simulation also has its drawbacks. First, the implementation of this approach requires substantial mathematical sophistication. The second major drawback is speed. Although there is no theoretical limit to the complexity of the model(s) we can build to implement this approach, there are many practical constraints. This is because in order to generate a large sample of simulated paths, the portfolio has to be revalued many times. Even in this day and age, when computing power is relatively cheap and readily available, the need to perform tens of thousands of portfolio valuations can still be daunting, especially if the portfolio contains many assets/liabilities and the simulation involves a large number of sample paths. As it turns out, stochastic simulation is the most time-consuming way to run risk analysis.

Realistically, in selecting a risk measurement approach, the risk manager has to understand the relative strengths of each alternative and the particular situation of the organisation – what is

A comparison of VAR approaches

	RiskMetrics	Historical	Historical simulation	Stochastic simulation
Assumption about asset returns	Assumes normality	No assumption	No assumption	User-defined/flexible
Valuation model(s)	Not required	Not required	Required	Required
Cashflow mapping	Yes	No	No	No
Speed	Depends on the variety of assets present and the size of the corresponding variance/covariance matrix	Quick	Medium	Slow
Data requirement	Historical price/rate data of key market variables or JP Morgan's risk datasets to the extent that they cover all relevant assets in the portfolio	Historical P&L of portfolio	Historical price/rate data of key market variables	All historical market data that are necessary to estimate the parameters of the stochastic processes used in the risk modelling
Precision of risk measure	Depends on the validity of its main assumptions – stability of asset variances and correlations, normality of return distributions, lack of option components	Good if the portfolio composition is relatively constant over time and there is little ageing effect	Good if the historical path is representative of all future market behaviour	Better precision to the extent that the stochastic simulation is more realistic and captures more market interactions and portfolio details
Best choice when...	Portfolio assets/ liabilities have no optionality eg a portfolio of stocks, FX and/or spot commodities	Portfolio mix does not change over time and ageing effect is minimal	Portfolio has optionality and historical path is representative of all possibilities	Portfolio has substantial optionality and there are many possible sample paths, each representing a different risk
Worst choice when...	Portfolio has substantial optionality	Portfolio mix has changed substantially over time	Historical path is an outlier of all potential outcomes	The portfolio is enormous and the potential sample paths are many; hardware constraints
Representative user	JP Morgan, quantitative portfolio managers	Merrill Lynch uses a combination of the historical method (actual P&L distributions) and stress testing for risk measurement. See the company's 1995 annual report for details	Some commercial risk management systems vendors such as Algorithmics, LOR/GB and Sailfish offer historicalsimulations as one of the options	Salomon, Bear Stearns, Enron

the portfolio composition, what kind of hardware, software and databases are available for the risk management effort and so on. Some of the considerations which go into this decision are presented in the table above.

Stress testing

No risk measurement model is without limitations or implied assumptions. It is therefore helpful to understand what will happen should some of the assumptions underlying the model break down. Stress testing is the catch-all term for doing a series of scenario analyses to investigate the effect of extreme market conditions and/or the effect of violating some of the basic assumptions underlying the risk model.

There is no standard way to do stress testing. It is just a way to experiment with the limits of a risk model and to "think outside the box". It is also a means to measure the residual risk which is not effectively captured by the "official" risk model, complementing the VAR framework.

VAR is the modern framework for corporate risk management. The VAR number is a statistical risk measure which quantifies, within a given confidence level, the maximum fluctuation in portfolio value within a specified time period. As distinct from the conventional risk measures, this new approach incorporates what we know about the historical volatilities of asset prices (or rates) and the historical correlations between different products.

We have introduced four different approaches to implement VAR: RiskMetrics, historical, historical simulation and stochastic simulation. Each has its own strengths and weaknesses and none is superior to the others; intelligent risk managers will seek to understand the limitations of each approach to VAR and find one – or a combination of several – which fits their organisation's constraints and needs.

6

Quality Control

Cedomir Crnkovic and Jordan Drachman
NetRisk; JP Morgan

This article presents a tool for evaluating and comparing rival risk measurement techniques. The ideas behind the tool are outlined and some potential uses illustrated.

Anyone trying to set up or evaluate a market risk measurement system is confronted with a variety of questions. Should it be based on simulation or analytics? What length of history is relevant in estimating today's risk? What parameters should be used – estimates drawn from historical data or values implied by the options market – and how frequently should they be updated?

To answer questions such as these we have developed a tool to evaluate and compare different approaches to market risk measurement. This article describes the ideas behind the tool and illustrates some of its uses.[1] We believe our work could be useful to both practitioners and regulators; the Basle Committee on Banking Supervision's proposals for the supervisory treatment of market risk envisage a role for internal risk measurement systems with a proven record of accuracy (we provide a framework for regulatory back testing in Appendix B).

At the heart of market risk measurement is the forecast of the probability density functions (PDFs) of the relevant market variables. If an institution estimates the value-at-risk (VAR) in its trading and/or investment portfolio daily, it is implicitly forecasting the entire joint PDF of the relevant market variables. Similarly, a forecast of a PDF is the central input into any decision model for asset allocation and/or hedging. In this article, therefore, the quality of risk measurement will be considered synonymous with the quality of PDF forecasts.

There are many analytical approaches to risk assessment and we need a tool capable of evaluating and comparing them all. These approaches include:

❑ Assuming all returns are normally distributed and forecasting volatilities and correlations using:
(i) a simple moving window ("simple VAR");
(ii) exponential weighting ("exponential model" – the current RiskMetrics approach);
(iii) a Garch model; or
(iv) implied volatilities.

❑ Bootstrapping from historical data. In other words, assuming that only the moves observed during the previous n days are possible and that all of those are equally likely. We will call this approach "historical simulation".

After selecting an approach, certain parameters have to be chosen – for instance, the decay factor in the exponential model. A quantitative measure of the "quality" of PDF forecasts can help one choose among the different approaches, find optimal values for the parameters and evaluate the added benefit of any potential refinements (eg increased frequency of updates).

We can define the quality of a PDF forecast as the degree of agreement between our estimate and the actual PDF of market variables. To ensure broad applicability of our proposed measure of quality, we start with as few assumptions as possible. In particular, we wish to avoid giving any parametric form to the PDF whose forecast we are evaluating and we will not assume that any of these PDFs are stationary.

Non-stationary PDFs are, by nature, ephemeral; one cannot obtain more than one sample from any given distribution. Nevertheless, given a forecast of the PDF, we can determine into which percentile that one observation fell.[2] The insight that allows us to aggregate observations across *a priori* different distributions is the fact that the percentiles are uniformly distributed for any PDF.

This is a generalisation of the simple rule of thumb used widely as a reality check of a VAR calculation. If VAR is defined as a worst-case move with 95% confidence, its accuracy can be checked by calculating the fraction of days when the adverse move exceeded VAR and comparing this with 5%. We propose to make this comparison for all fractions between zero and one instead of just for 0.95.

Let us make this more concrete and precise with an example. Say we want to evaluate the quality of some approach to daily forecasting of the PDF of dollar/Deutschmark daily returns. We will consider the simple VAR approach, taking volatility as a simple average of the squared returns over the past six months. We would proceed as follows:

❑ Each day, forecast the PDF of the next day's dollar/Deutschmark returns (in this case, a normal distribution with volatility equal to the average of the last 126 squared returns).

❑ Next day, when the actual return is known, determine in which percentile of the forecasted PDF it fell. Denote that percentile by p, where $0 \leq p \leq 1$.

❑ Over a period of N consecutive days, keep track of the values of p that have occurred.

For a forecasting method to be considered ideal, these percentiles, p, must be independent and uniformly distributed, ie, they must satisfy the following two conditions:

❑ All of them put together must look like a sample from a uniform distribution;

❑ Each individual percentile must be independent of all the others.

These conditions measure two distinct properties of the risk measurement system and therefore need to be examined separately. The first measures how well, on average, the system captures the shape of the distribution of returns, while the second measures how well the system identifies the rapidly changing structure of returns.

We take the deviation of the distribution of percentiles from the uniform distribution as the first measure of quality of the PDF forecast, and therefore of the risk measurement system that uses the forecast. The smaller the deviation, the higher the quality.

There are many ways to summarise the deviation of one PDF from another in a single number. We have chosen the following, which depends on the cumulative distribution function of the percentiles rather than the density function $f(p)$. Let $n(t)$ be the number of observed percentiles p that are less than or equal to t, where $0 \leq t \leq 1$. Then:

$$F(t) = \frac{n(t)}{N} \tag{1}$$

The quality Q of the PDF forecast is then $Q = K(F(t),t)$ where:

$$K\big(f(x),g(x)\big) = \max_{0\leq x\leq 1}\{f(x)-g(x)\} + \max_{0\leq x\leq 1}\{g(x)-f(x)\}$$

K is known as Kuiper's statistic (see Press et al, 1992, page 627). It is a measure of the distance between two cumulative distribution functions, so Q is a measure of how far away $F(t)$ is from being uniform (see Appendix A for a discussion of Kuiper's statistic as a measure of distance). The smaller the value of Q, the greater the quality. Since the distribution of Kuiper's statistic is known, the distribution of Q is also known. For example, with 1,000 data points, $Q = 0.055$ is the 95% confidence level for refuting the hypothesis $F(t) = t$. In general, this is a data-intensive procedure. In our experience, the results begin to deteriorate when fewer than 1,000 data points are used and are of little validity with fewer than 500.

An important advantage of Kuiper's statistic is that it is equally sensitive for all values of x and therefore puts all percentiles (or, equivalently, all sizes of market move) on an equal footing.[3] This is often desirable, since a significant fraction of the change in value of many portfolios today comes from non-linear instruments such as options and, therefore, the worst-case portfolio move might be due to a combination of medium-sized market moves.

On the other hand, since the majority of portfolios comprise mainly linear instruments, large market moves (ie, the tails of the distributions of market moves) may merit particular attention. Such an emphasis can easily be integrated into the definition of Q by weighting the deviations at any given point on the unit interval by the importance we attach to the precise forecast at that point.

In other words, we define a "worry function" on the unit interval with the following properties: it should be symmetric around a minimum of 0.5 and slowly divergent at 0 and 1. A function with such properties is:

$$W(t) = -0.5\ln(t(1-t))$$

(see Figure 1). Now we can define a weighted Q as:

$$Q_W = K(F(t)W(t), tW(t))$$

Note that the distribution of Q_W is different from that of Q and therefore the confidence levels are also different. The distribution can be obtained using a Monte Carlo simulation. Furthermore, as with Q, Q_W can be used to compare the relative quality of two risk measurements systems, even without knowing the precise distribution.

To complete our analysis of the quality of PDF forecasts, we need to evaluate the independence of the measured percentiles. This is necessary when dealing with time series that are not fully random. The most common example in financial markets is structure in the conditional second moments, as described by Garch-like models.

For our purposes, we consider a time series to be non-random if it fails the Brock-Dechert-Scheinkman (BDS) test for being independent and identically distributed (IID). A detailed description of the BDS test falls outside the scope of this article but, in brief, it has two steps. The first is to map all returns into the "lag space" where the co-ordinates are given by the m-tuple containing the last m returns. The second is to measure the distance between the distribution of the returns in the lag space and the expected distribution for IID returns (see Brock et al, 1991, for more details). A significant non-zero BDS score indicates some structure in the returns. This structure may be predictable, as with the volatility clusters predicted by Garch models.

If the risk measurement system we are evaluating has properly accounted for the time-evolution of the conditional PDF of returns, the percentiles, p, should pass the BDS test. In addition, since the distribution of the BDS test is known to be standard normal, we can assign confidence levels to the statement "the percentiles are identically distributed" and use these levels to rate the risk measurement system. We will define the number B to be the BDS test on the percentiles.[4]

Applications

We now illustrate a few of the many possible uses of the above formalism. We limit ourselves to only a few time series since we wish to illustrate the uses of Q and B rather than make general claims about the relative merits of methodologies.

To evaluate a risk measurement system, a risk manager should perform the appropriate analysis for each of the relevant time series, while trying to replicate how a particular methodology would be implemented. Furthermore, the quality of the forecast is only one of the relevant factors in any comparison. Others include ease of implementation and computational and data requirements.

1. Worry function for weighting Kuiper's statistic

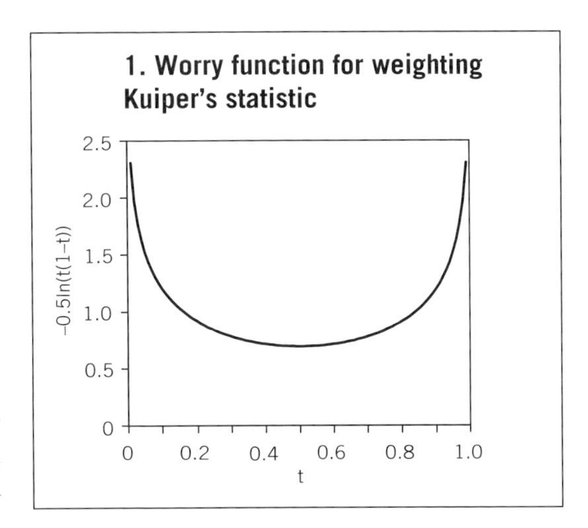

Let us assume that we wish to estimate volatilities using an exponentially weighted estimator:

$$\sigma_t^2 = \frac{1-\lambda}{1-\lambda^n}\sum_{i=0}^{n-1}\lambda^i x_{t-i}^2$$

It is useful here to view the decay factor λ as a measure of the sampling interval necessary to describe the system properly. A large value of λ (close to 1) represents a long sampling interval, while a small value (close to 0) represents a short one.

Using several years of data for the time series x, one can calculate Q for different values of λ. *A priori*, the dependence of Q on the decay factor is the result of the interplay of two conflicting forces:

- ❑ the need to capture the non-stationarity of the actual PDFs of the market variable x pushes us to use shorter sampling intervals (smaller λ),
- ❑ the need to increase the number of data points and to improve the signal-to-noise ratio pushes us to use longer sampling intervals (larger λ).

One therefore expects a graph of Q versus the decay factor to be a concave function with a minimum. This intuition is confirmed by the results summarised in Figure 2 overleaf, which are based on daily returns on the S&P 500, Nikkei 225, Dax and FTSE 100 indexes.

The optimal decay factors for each time series correspond to minima of Q. For instance, the FTSE index seems to be described best by a normal distribution with $\lambda \approx 0.92$. Forecast quality for the S&P 500, on the other hand, is best when $\lambda \approx 0.80$, but is never as good as for the FTSE.

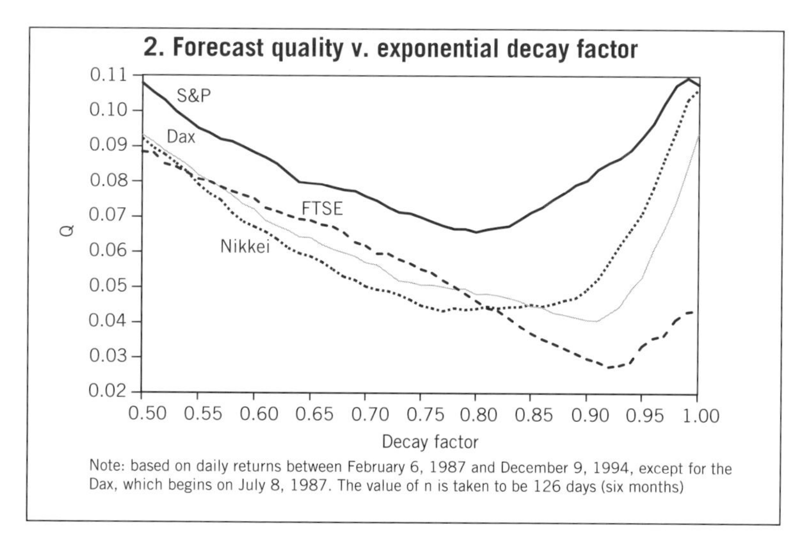

2. Forecast quality v. exponential decay factor

Note: based on daily returns between February 6, 1987 and December 9, 1994, except for the Dax, which begins on July 8, 1987. The value of n is taken to be 126 days (six months)

Note that using Q to determine the optimal decay factor avoids the use of a "benchmark" for volatilities; the latter approach begs the question of how the benchmark itself has been estimated.

An even more interesting application, given that it allows direct, quantitative comparisons of two very different methodologies, is a comparison of historical simulation with simple VAR and exponential models. Table 1 gives the values of Q and Q_W for the S&P 500 and the FTSE indexes, using simple VAR, exponential weighting with the optimal decay factor and historical simulation.

In the case of the S&P 500 index, both Q and Q_W indicate that quality improves in the order: simple VAR, exponential model, historical simulation. In the case of the FTSE index, all three methods do quite well: simple VAR performs worst but the other two are practically indistinguishable.

Having considered Q, let us turn to B. A BDS test applied to the returns on the S&P 500 and the FTSE indexes reveals that they vary only slightly from random results. As a result, measuring B does not help to evaluate how well risk measurement systems account for the time evolution of the conditional PDF of returns for these particular time series.

We therefore turn to the daily returns derived from several series of 10-year government zero-coupon rates, which show significant non-randomness, and use B to evaluate the three methodologies above. Since forecasts from simple VAR and historical simulation change slowly, we know *a priori* that both will do a relatively poor job of adapting themselves to rapidly changing circumstances. In particular, they will not capture the dynamics of volatility.

By contrast, more dynamic systems, such as exponential or Garch models, should perform better, as confirmed by the findings in Table 2. Here, the exponential model removes practically all of the time series' non-randomness, while simple VAR and historical simulation do not. Recall that B is distributed as a standard normal, so values close to 0 are consistent with the IID hypothesis.

Understanding why a given time series exhibits large values of Q can be useful in designing a risk measurement system. Simply comparing numbers, however, does not tell the whole story.

To compare Q values more intuitively, we illustrate it with a plot of $F(t) - t$ against t, where $F(t)$ is defined in equation (1). Figure 3 shows this plot for the same S&P 500 data used above. The line, which is (on average) closer to the horizontal axis, corresponds to the methodology that has (on average) produced superior forecasts; Q is equal to the difference between the maximum and the minimum values of $F(t) - t$.

Figure 3 shows what lies behind the different values of Q for the three models. The shapes of the graphs of $F(t) - t$ for simple VAR and for exponential models with two values of the decay factor are due to a persistent mis-specification of the shape of the distribution of returns. In particular, medium-sized returns, both above and below the median $t = 0.5$ (for example, the twenty-fifth and seventy-fifth percentiles), are significantly less frequent and small-sized returns significantly more frequent than predicted by a normal distribution with the same volatility, represented by the horizontal axis. The fact that historical simulation has no trouble incorporating this phenomenon indicates that the shape of the distribution changes (on average) sufficiently slowly for the last n days' returns (n = 126 here) to be a very good approximation of today's PDF of returns.

Table 1. Quality statistics for various risk measurement methodologies

	S&P 500		FTSE 100	
Method	**Q**	**Q_W**	**Q**	**Q_W**
Simple VAR	0.108	0.084	0.044	0.045
Optimal exponential models	0.066	0.076	0.028	0.035
Historical simulation	0.020	0.025	0.024	0.034

Table 2. BDS tests for 10-year government zero-coupon rates

		B		
	BDS on returns	**Exponential**	**Simple VAR**	**Historical**
Australia	3.11	0.10	3.06	3.21
Denmark	9.16	0.55	6.44	5.24
France	5.82	–1.00	2.92	1.93
UK	4.77	–0.37	2.96	2.08
Japan	7.49	0.96	5.06	3.36
Spain	6.45	–0.25	6.01	5.83

When comparing simple VAR and the exponential model with decay factor $\lambda = 0.80$, one notes that the improvement due to the exponential decay is concentrated in the bulk of the distribution, while at the tails one observes a deterioration, a fairly typical occurrence. Within these simple models, there seems to be a trade-off between adaptability and precision in the tails.

That was part of the motivation for the introduction of the weighted Q. By penalising errors in the tails, the weighting will, in general, cause the value of the optimal decay factor to increase. Although changing the decay factor from 0.80 to 0.94 (the optimal decay factor for Q_W) causes some deterioration in the bulk of the distribution, it results in a substantial improvement in the tails.

So far, we have discussed the application of Q and B to one time series at a time. There are at least two approaches to the multi-variable problem. To forecast a PDF of returns for a particular (fixed) portfolio exposed to many market variables, one can use the previous approach with minimal modification. Each day, use the methodology for forecasting a multivariate PDF that is being tested to produce the forecast of the univariate PDF of returns on the portfolio. Then calculate Q and B for the percentiles of the returns on the portfolio. Repeating the calculation with many different portfolios will result in a range of values for Q and B which will be an indication of the true, portfolio-independent quality of the PDF forecast.

Alternatively, one could use an n-dimensional analogue of percentiles, where n is the number of time series. Such n-percentiles would be uniformly distributed on the unit n-cube. We are still searching for a sensible definition of such an object.

In this paper, we have argued that the quality of any market risk measurement system is to a large degree determined by the method used to forecast the PDFs of the market variables. We have described a procedure to evaluate any such method. The procedure rests on the simple

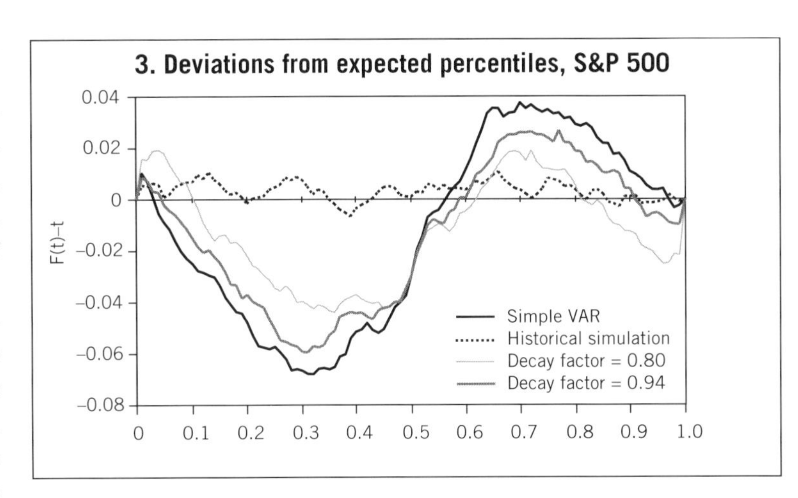

observation that a necessary and sufficient condition for an optimal forecast of a PDF is that the percentiles are independent and uniformly distributed. This allows us to aggregate observations from arbitrary, time-varying daily forecasts into two measures (Q and B) of the quality of those forecasts. We defined Q as a measure of the distance between the actual distribution of percentiles and the uniform distribution and we defined B as a measure of how non-random these percentiles are.

Some of the appealing features of the present formalism are:

- ❑ It makes very few assumptions about the processes governing market variables and therefore allows a quantitative comparison between any two approaches to forecasting PDFs.
- ❑ It allows such comparisons to be customised to the precise institutional and technological characteristics of a given user.
- ❑ It enables one not only to isolate the best possible model given the circumstances but also to perform a cost-benefit analysis of adopting one approach over another.
- ❑ It makes choosing "benchmarks" for evaluating forecasting models unnecessary.

In addition, we have presented some applications of Q and B, in the hope of illustrating how the broad range of questions that arise daily in risk measurement can be answered by this framework.

Appendix A

WHY KUIPER'S STATISTIC?

Kuiper's statistic is a sensible definition of distance because it is natural to ask the question: "What is the probability that a random variable whose cumulative distribution function (CDF) is G(x) will fall between two values a and b?" The answer is G(b)–G(a). Suppose our forecast of the CDF is H(x). Then our forecast of this probability is H(b)–H(a), and the error in our estimate is:

$$\begin{aligned}&|\{G(b)-G(a)\}-\{H(b)-H(a)\}| = \\ &|\{G(b)-H(b)\}+\{H(a)-G(a)\}| \leq \\ &\max\{G(b)-H(b)\}+\max\{H(a)-G(a)\}\end{aligned}$$

which is Kuiper's statistic. It can, therefore, be interpreted as a measure of how much error there is in a probability estimate.

We can provide further motivation for our choice of distance function as follows. If we assume that the actual $G(x)$ and the predicted $H(x)$ CDFs are not time-varying, then we can calculate that $F(t) = G(H^{-1}(t))$. Q then turns out to be:

$$Q = \max_{-\infty<x<\infty}\{G(x) - H(x)\} + \max_{-\infty<x<\infty}\{H(x) - G(x)\}$$

which is Kuiper's statistic giving the distance between $G(x)$ and $H(x)$. The Q number is thus a time-varying generalisation of this quantity.

Appendix B

BANKING ON BACK TESTING

Regulators (notably the Basle Committee on Banking Supervision) plan to "back test" risk measurement systems by comparing their outputs with the profit and loss actually realised. Such backtesting assumes that positions do not change substantially over the horizon of risk measurement. This assumption is not realistic for horizons longer than one day, so we assume a one-day horizon.

The sample distributions of Q and B are known for the case of the null hypothesis, where the profit and loss distribution is forecast perfectly. The distribution of Q_W can be obtained from Monte Carlo simulation for any worry function $W(t)$. It is, therefore, possible to associate any particular value of Q_W or B with a confidence level for the statement: "This risk measurement system accurately forecasts the probability density functions (PDFs) of profit and loss."

Those banks whose risk measurement systems are judged to produce highly reliable profit and loss forecasts by their Q_W and B statistics could be allowed to use only a small multiple when converting the output of their internal models into a market risk capital requirement. If Q_W and B correspond to lower, but still satisfactory, confidence levels, an additional factor proportional to the decrease in confidence could be applied. Finally, if Q_W and B values implied confidence levels below a certain threshold, the bank would not be allowed to use its internal models to calculate capital requirements.

Kupiec (1995) argues that a regulator will rarely have enough data to ascertain confidently whether a bank's estimate of the ninety-ninth percentile of daily trading profit and loss distribution is accurate. Back testing would therefore be impossible, and Kupiec concludes that the internal models approach is not viable. We will argue that, by using the Q-statistic, we need only 1,000 data points to narrow the margin of error in the calculation of capital to 10% or less for most cases of practical interest.

Kupiec's analysis is technically correct but it is not the whole story. We argue that the data requirements of Q and B are reasonable and that back testing is therefore possible. We will examine the case of Q_W with the worry function $W(t) = -0.5\ln(t(1-t))$. A similar analysis can be carried out for B.

The main difference between our approach and Kupiec's is the amount of available information about the quality of a risk measurement system used. Kupiec uses only a small subset: a binary indicator of whether a period's profit and loss falls below the forecast ninety-ninth percentile or not. In contrast, in using Q_W and B, we use all the available information. Therefore, we start by assuming that the quality of forecasts of all other percentiles apart from the ninety-ninth contains additional information about the quality of the overall system. It therefore also contains information about the quality of the forecasts of the ninety-ninth percentile.

On the other hand, we agree with Kupiec when he points out that the amount of data required to estimate (and subsequently verify) a given percentile of the profit and loss distribution grows exponentially as the percentile moves further out along the tail. We therefore argue that a calculation which starts from (for example) the ninety-fifth percentile and uses a higher multiple to arrive at a capital requirement will be more reliable than a calculation starting from the ninety-ninth percentile.

We now consider the greatest error in the capital requirement that can occur if Q_W is used for backtesting. We use Monte Carlo simulation to generate the sample distribution of Q_W for a "perfect" risk measurement system. The ninety-fifth percentile of that distribution, in the case of 1,000 data points, is $Q_W = 0.051$. A regulator could then choose $Q_W = 0.051$ as the "pass-mark" for back testing.

This choice means there is a 5% chance that a perfectly good risk measurement system is rejected, a so-called type I error. There is also some probability that a less than perfect system would be accepted, resulting in a type II error, although the probability of this decreases as the risk estimates deviate further from truth. Two relevant questions are:

- What is the greatest deviation from the "correct" estimate that a system could produce before its chance of being accepted would drop below 5%?
- What is the resulting error in the capital calculation?

We will answer these questions with concrete examples, starting with some of the most likely errors in the estimation of risk.

Assume that a risk measurement system has estimated the PDF of profit and loss as a standard normal distribution (SND), whereas the true distribution is normal, with mean zero, but standard deviation $x \neq 1$. If we observe $Q_W < 0.051$, we can be 95% certain that x lies between 0.91 and 1.1 and conclude that we will be forced to tolerate an error in capital calculation of no more than about 10%.

Another common error in risk estimation concerns the fatness of tails. A standard assumption is that returns are normal, whereas in practice they are much closer to a fat-tailed t-distribution. So let us assume again that a risk measurement system has estimated the PDF of profit and loss as an SND, whereas the true distribution is a t-distribution with d degrees of freedom (denoted $tD(d)$) and standard deviation 1. This time, if we observe $Q_W < 0.051$ we can be 95% certain that $d > 6$.[5] The ratio between the ninety-ninth percentiles of $tD(6)$ and the SND is 1.1, so the greatest error in capital calculation is again 10%. Note that the ratio between the ninety-fifth percentiles of $tD(6)$ and the SND is 0.96; the resulting error in capital would be approximately half as large as for the ninety-ninth percentiles.

We can combine these examples and assume that we have incorrectly estimated both the standard deviation and the fatness of the tails. For example, assume that the true distribution of profit and loss is a $tD(6)$ with standard deviation equal to 1.115, and that the risk measurement system's estimate is an SND. This combination has a 5% chance of producing a sample Q_W below 0.051 and therefore being erroneously accepted. This time, the greatest error in the capital requirement calculated using the ninety-ninth percentile is 23%; with the ninety-fifth percentile, it would be off by only 7.5%.

As we said earlier, these are the types of mistakes that we would expect from a risk measurement system. We now turn to the most extreme deviations from the true distributions. Under these (very unlikely) circumstances, some of Kupiec's estimates of the likely errors in the capital calculation can be approximated.

We are interested in the worst-case deviation from the true profit and loss distribution which would nevertheless have at least a 5% chance of sample $Q_W < 0.051$. This would be the case if we estimated all the percentiles between the ninety-ninth and 96.8th to be equal to the (correct) estimate of the 96.8th percentile. If the capital requirement were based on the ninety-fifth percentile, the equivalent percentiles are the ninety-fifth and 91.7th. The size of the corresponding error in the calculated capital requirement depends on the true profit and loss distribution. If the true profit and loss is normally distributed, the error is 26% when using the ninety-ninth percentile and 19% when using the ninety-fifth. In the case of the $tD(5)$, the equivalent errors are 42% and 25% respectively; in the extreme $tD(3)$ case, the errors are 58% and 30%.[6]

The above discussion assumes that most financial institutions' risk measurement systems perform well enough to allow perfect predictions to be used as the null hypothesis. If most of them turn in Q scores much larger than 0.051 the above discussion would have to be modified. The regulators would have to choose the level of uncertainty in the capital requirement that they are comfortable with, and then look for the critical Q score that would indicate, with 95% certainty, a violation of even that looser limit.

1 *This tool is already in use in JP Morgan's internal market risk management system, and RiskMetrics may in the future incorporate it in some form.*

2 *If our forecast for the PDF of x is $h(x)$ and the observed value is $\hat{x}$, the corresponding percentile is:*

$$p(\hat{x}) = \int_{-\infty}^{\hat{x}} h(x)\,dx$$

3 *Other statistics do not possess this property; eg the better known Kolmogorov-Smirnoff statistic: $\max\{|f(x) - g(x)|\}$ is most sensitive around the median (see Appendix A).*

4 *For those interested, B is the lag 2 BDS test using ε = 0.433, 1.5 times the standard deviation of the uniform distribution (see Brock et al, 1993, page 51).*

5 *The fewer the degrees of freedom, the fatter the tails*

6 *Kupiec also considers the $tD(1)$ case; we do not consider t-distributions with two or fewer degrees of freedom since those distributions have infinite standard deviations*

BIBLIOGRAPHY

Brock, W., W. Dechert, J. Scheinkman and B. LeBaron, 1991, "A Test for Independence Based on the Correlation Dimension", Social Systems Research Institute working paper number 8702, Department of Economics, University of Wisconsin, Madison.

Brock, W., D. Hsieh and B. LeBaron, 1993, *Non-linear Dynamics, Chaos and Instability*, The Massachusetts Institute of Technology Press, Cambridge, Massachusetts.

Kupiec, P., 1995, "Techniques for Verifying the Accuracy of Risk Measurement Models", *Journal of Derivatives*, Winter, pp. 73–84; reprinted as Chapter 24 of the present volume.

Press, W., S. Teukolsky, W. Vetterling and B. Flannery, 1992, *Numerical Recipes in C*, second edition, Cambridge University Press.

7

Operating Procedures

Douglas Hoffman and Marta Johnson
Bankers Trust Company

Operational risk is perhaps the most common and intractable risk that managers face. This article outlines how one organisation, Bankers Trust, approaches the issue.

Operational risk is everywhere. In the past few years, it has reared its head frequently. We have all seen the headlines and read the stories. Whether we are talking about failures of controls between front and back office, unauthorised trading or legal risk, the issues are large and complicated and the capital at risk is huge.

Many companies have realised that operational risk needs much risk management attention and have decided to build a risk-based capital system for business operational risk. A variety of issues need to be considered when constructing such a model, including:

- how to define the business's operational risk;
- how to quantify it – on a portfolio basis, a business-specific basis, or a product-by-product basis;
- how to attribute (allocate) capital to businesses (throughout this chapter, we use the term "attribute/attribution" to mean allocating capital/costs, etc on paper only);
- whether a portfolio number alone will be enough, or whether to aim for a broader goal, such as an incentive-based risk management tool;
- if the objective is incentive-oriented, whether the model should target behaviour in existing business operations or support invest, disinvest and/or divest decision-making?

If the system is designed correctly it can support several risk management objectives.

To begin with the first point, the attribution system must define business operational risks. These relate to all phases of the business process, from origination through to execution and delivery, spanning the front, back and middle office. Can these risks and their associated loss costs be sorted so that each risk and loss fits neatly into one category without any overlapping into another? Is it possible to identify categories that would both be logical to senior managers and imply risk management responsibility?

At Bankers Trust, we view business operational risk as encompassing all dimensions of the firm's decentralised resources – client relationships, personnel, the physical plant, property and assets for which we are responsible, and technology resources. We also capture certain external areas such as regulatory risk and fraud risk.

The first four categories are logical and convenient given our objective – proactive risk management – because they can be related back to functions and managerial responsibility, such as sales and marketing relationship managers, senior business management, human resource management, operations management, and senior technologists. Others, such as the compliance, legal and security functions, can also take on matrixed responsibilities for managing the risk (see Table 1 overleaf).

The case for a portfolio approach

The key component of Bankers Trust's operational risk attribution methodology is quantifying the firm's total capital exposure to operational risk. To do this, we apply some of the same parameters as those in the bank's own Risk Adjusted Return on Capital (Raroc) methodology that we developed internally for measuring market and credit risk over 12 years ago.

Some firms are experimenting with valuing business operational risk using an expense-based system. But there are flaws in this approach: for example, what relation does expense have to the dimensions of risk and does cutting costs reduce risk or increase it?

Table 1. Categories of business operational risk

Risk category	Functional responsibilities	Examples
People	Business line human resources Security	Human error, internal fraud, staff unavailability
Technology	Business line technologists Central infrastructure Data centre	Failure of technology, damage caused by virus/cost of eradication, loss costs due to antiquated systems
Relationship risk/liability	Sales & marketing Business management Legal, compliance	Legal and/or contractual disputes
Physical assets	Operations management	Loss of physical environment/business interruption or loss of negotiable assets
Other external/regulatory	Business line compliance, regulatory Security services	Changes in regulations, external fraud

Flowcharts and time studies can be performed to determine how many "hands" or systems are required to complete a transaction from start to finish. These approaches provide road maps for the controls that need to be reviewed or rethought. However, they do little to assist in quantifying the risks being faced by the business line.

We wanted to quantify operational risks so that severity and frequency distributions could be developed and analysed. Information on loss events was gathered from many different industries to reflect relevant parts of the financial service sector's direct and indirect exposure. An example of indirect exposure was first witnessed during 1980s litigation over lender liability, when lenders were sometimes held liable for the operational risk exposure involving their clients. Second, some operational risks cut across industries. Technology failures and "business interruption" risk events, for example, can affect any firm of a similar size and market position. Third, there are lessons for all industries in recent events involving tort litigation over tobacco, silicone and asbestos. The legal theories, outcomes and size of exposures in these cases can be analysed and used.

Some types of risks are difficult to quantify because the data is not publicly available, but to ignore them would greatly bias the overall estimate of business operational risk. One example is the cost of a technology failure. Today, a financial firm's exposure to operational risks through technology is huge, yet rarely do all the parties involved think of calculating the business impact (eg, management/staff time spent analysing the problem, the cost of developing "workarounds", and the cost of projects being delayed to solve the problem).

For these types of risks it may be worth developing estimates. Perhaps the best way to do this is to ask internal experts and outside consultants for their opinions and to develop a consensus. We found that the loss data could be supplemented by expert opinion on the potential exposure. Together, the combination can be powerful. Critics may voice their objections over the use of "soft" datapoints. However, in recent years, operational risk managers have been finding this type of Delphi technique useful in sizing exposure to loss, particularly where data points are not readily available elsewhere.

As we did not have a database that met our requirements, we had to undertake the daunting task of developing one to cover loss events. In the past two years, we have continued to increase the database daily, both in size and in depth. To date, we have 32 fields of data on each event. Each loss is sorted into its relevant risk category and analysed in the context of the transaction process in which the event occurred.

We can use sophisticated actuarial tools to develop severity and frequency distributions for the database both on a portfolio basis and for each of the five risk categories. The resulting figures show the amount of potential loss that could be expected for the firm overall and in each of the five risk categories. A range of confidence levels can be used, depending upon the uses for the data. We use the 99% confidence level to be consistent with the theoretical framework used by market and credit Raroc, and call the resulting number our "core" capital figure.

Attributing risk capital

In attributing risk capital, we need to consider several questions: what is the purpose of the allocation methodology, how will it be used, how often will it be updated and how will the target audience use the information?

One of the most common reasons why institutions become interested in attributing capital associated with operational risks is to help them make strategic business decisions. If management is making important investment decisions on existing businesses or buying a new business, it may want to incorporate operational risk exposure as part of the transaction's overall risk exposure. The magnitude of the estimated operational risks can be important in these types of decisions if used as a "pointer" to highlight the relative riskiness of one type of business or transaction compared with another.

A second reason for attributing capital associated with business operational risks is to manage efforts to finance risk more effectively. One should not fall into the trap, however, of viewing business operational risk as a subset of insurance risk. Clearly, the conditions and exclusions of insurance programmes mean that the opposite is true. However, a more detailed understanding of the operational risks involved should allow for a more efficient and more complete evaluation of existing risk finance and insurance programmes and set the framework for rigorous cost/benefit analysis of the costs and benefits of various risk finance options.

We believe that the third reason for attributing operational risk capital, which is continually overlooked, is so it can be used as a tool for actionable risk management initiatives. While defining and quantifying operational risk, much information can be harvested and trends of operational risk analysed. If designed correctly, business operational risk exposure can become an integral part of managing business risk. Capital allocation in operational risk can be used as an effective behaviour modification tool.

So, once a company has decided on the methodology for valuing the operational risk in its businesses at portfolio level, finding the "right" operational attribution methodology will make or break the process. The methodology must support the objectives established at the outset of the project. At Bankers Trust, we needed our methodology to compare different businesses, to review and refine our risk finance programmes, to act as a risk management tool and to be an effective behaviour modification tool.

False starts

We had several false starts trying to meet these objectives of the allocation methodology. The initial plan was to gather the risk profile information at the lowest level within the organisation and aggregate it up to the division level. This could be called a "granular" approach.

Working in conjunction with internal audit, we compiled elaborate questionnaires, delineating risks in each risk category. This is a common approach, as operational risks are often viewed as additive. However, there is not usually enough data on business operational risks and losses to build a statistically valid sample from which to quantify and aggregate operational risks.

Another reason why granular analyses often prove unproductive is that they require too many resources to gather information. Organisational structures tend to be fluid, so it is difficult to keep a timetable when the group components keep changing.

How could we break out of this cycle and develop a successful allocation methodology? The answer seemed to lie in finding centralised data sources and information that could be linked back to the risk categories. For example, human resources could give us information on the level of turnover within each division for the people risk category; the data centre could provide information on system failures for the technology category. The centralised data sources helped us compare the divisions with each other.

So we set the cornerstone of the attribution methodology as follows: indicators of risks within a risk category would be obtained from centralised data sources, or from the business lines; the business lines would then be compared with each other and given a risk score. The scores would be combined and used to attribute the actuarially estimated "core" capital.

Putting the methodology into practice

The loss events in the internal and external databases served as the starting point for determining the information to be used from the centralised data sources. Then two questions were asked: what types of information are predictors of control risk failures and in what risk category do the risks fall? If the centralised data sources only gave us information for one of the risk categories, say people risk, this approach was not going to work. The information in the centralised data sources was analysed against the risks that had appeared in the internal and external loss database. The risks were separated into each of the risk categories and "tested" against the loss events in the database to ensure a match between the reasons for the losses occurring and the information available from the centralised data sources.

To attribute the estimated capital number, a framework was developed within which we could categorise and rank the operational risks the business lines were taking. Our initiative resulted from a joint effort by the global risk management and internal audit teams, so that it benefited by borrowing risk analysis concepts from the audit function, such as inherent risk and control risk.

These concepts were combined with risk assessment methods and other concepts applied in risk and insurance management in the allocation of risk finance costs. The result was that the "core" capital figure was attributed using the three components - inherent risk, control risk and actual losses sustained - to rate the operational risks each division was taking.

Inherent risks are those created by the nature of the business itself. They can be thought of as the base-line risks associated with being in that particular industry. The only way to change them is to leave the business, or dramatically change it by selling or buying a major component. Examples of inherent risks would be product complexity, product life cycle, level of automation and the level of regulation, litigation and compliance. The information gleaned on each division's risk factors was compared with each of the other business lines and force-ranked on a relative scale.

Control risk factors are meant to highlight existing and potential areas of control weaknesses. These factors are controllable by management. Examples include staff turnover, level of product/compliance training, age of technology systems and the level of straight-through processing. Again, the information gleaned on each division's risk factors was compared with each of the other business lines and force-ranked on a relative scale.

The third consideration is the actual losses sustained by a division. The percentage of losses each division contributes to the internal loss event database (ie the firm's own losses) is an important part of the methodology, as it shows the importance of the contribution the losses make to the calculation of the overall, portfolio-level core capital. This component can also be controlled by management, since operational loss events can be monitored and steps put in place to minimise them.

The component scores for each division were then weighted; components that can be controlled by the business line were given a larger weighting than those that cannot (inherent risk). The core capital figure was attributed proportionally across the divisions, based upon their total, weighted score for overall operational risk.

This methodology meets the objective of risk-ranking business lines against each other, even though the businesses are different. It acts as a management tool in that the risk factors and actual losses are controllable: managers can reduce their overall capital charge by reducing their score on specific risk factors. It can also be used to look further into the business lines, and risk rank at a lower level.

Conclusion

There are six key steps in the development of an attribution methodology for operational risks. These are:

❑ Clarify the interest in operational risk by setting objectives for the initiative.
❑ Develop objectives for the attribution methodology.
❑ Define operational risk and operational loss events for your firm.
❑ Decide on a pro forma methodology for meeting the objectives.
❑ Collaborate with business lines on the methodology and how to gather information on inherent risk, risk factors, losses, etc.
❑ Attribute and follow up; gather feedback.
❑ Finalise risk management tools for business line management to use.

So how has this system worked for Bankers Trust? It has already provided valuable lessons from loss causation analysis and helped support better risk finance and insurance decision-making. But additional benefits from enhancements to risk management/controls are expected in the near future. Management information resulting from the scoring process has helped improve the management of risk across the firm. Working on the basis that everyone in an organisation plays some role in risk management, a system for attributing capital by operational risk can serve as a nerve centre for risk management action.

Most importantly, if you want to manage operational risks, there will (at least initially) be few short cuts available. You will need adequate staff resources, some difficult decision-making, a collaborative working environment between business lines, and much effort rooting out meaningful data. In the end, if done correctly, it will be well worth the effort.

ASSESSING VAR

Introduction

Dori Nagar and Richard Singer
KPMG

The objective in estimating the value-at-risk of a position, a portfolio or a firm is to provide risk takers and managers with an estimate of the largest likely loss they should expect to suffer, with a degree of confidence and over a period of time they select. Clearly, if the actual outcomes from holding such positions bear little or no relation to the VAR estimates, the entire exercise is both fruitless and perhaps dangerously misleading.

As readers of *Section I: Introducing VAR* will have noted, it seems that neither academics nor practitioners ever describe a VAR methodology without highlighting some dangers that follow from its assumptions and simplifications. So the question naturally arises, if *all* VAR methodologies are fraught with such dangers, how can we use VAR? What are the challenges that must be overcome if VAR is to be used as an effective measure of market risk? How shall we proceed?

Section II: Assessing VAR contains papers by academics, practitioners and regulators. There are articles that both criticise and defend VAR as a tool for market risk quantification; that expose the challenges of appropriately capturing the effects of asset price volatility and correlation, asset liquidity, and optionality in VAR estimates; that quantify the differences in VAR estimates generated with different methodologies; and that discuss the planned use of VAR in regulatory regimes worldwide. The criticisms far outnumber the solutions that are offered. But this section is a clear exposition of the debates surrounding VAR, and should prepare readers to assess VAR for themselves.

The RiskMetrics debate

In January 1995, *Risk* provided a unique forum in which senior risk managers from a large worldwide securities dealer voiced specific criticisms of JP Morgan's market risk measurement tool, RiskMetrics. Their counterparts at Morgan then replied to those criticisms. The exchange is particularly useful here because it identifies many of the important difficulties with VAR that are considered in greater detail in subsequent articles.

In "How Safe is RiskMetrics?" Colin Lawrence and Gary Robinson of BZW observe that RiskMetrics in particular (and, perhaps, VAR in general) does not provide any useful information about large negative rare-event returns which reside far out "in the tails" of prospective return distributions, beyond the critical values associated with RiskMetrics' 95% confidence level. RiskMetrics methodology assumes, for convenience, that the distribution of asset returns is "normal," when observed return distributions from various speculative markets generally have lower peaks and fatter tails than "normal" distributions. Since real asset return distributions have "fatter tails" than the normal distribution presumed by Morgan, RiskMetrics VAR will always underestimate actual market risk. The BZW team also asserts that RiskMetrics is critically flawed because it contains no provision for accurately estimating the VAR of options or of assets with embedded options.

In "A Transparent Tool," Morgan's response, Jacques Longerstaey and Peter Zangari argue effectively against the evidence offered by BZW. Essentially, they maintain that Lawrence and Robinson have missed the point. RiskMetrics was rolled out in 1994 with two principal goals in mind: to promote greater transparency of market risks, and to provide sophisticated risk management tools to market participants without the resources to develop such systems themselves. It was never the intent of the RiskMetrics methodology to obviate the need for stress tests or scenario analyses, which explore possible risks to a portfolio from rare market events such as the US equity crash of 1987. In fact, Morgan believes that the potential consequences of such events must be explored through stress/scenario methodologies in addition to being quantified through tools using estimated probability distributions.

As to the criticism of RiskMetrics' capacity to deal with optionality, Morgan agrees, and it clearly stated in its RiskMetrics Technical Document that early editions of RiskMetrics possessed limited capacity for accurately estimating VARs of certain instruments with optionality. Regarding the assumption that asset returns are normally distributed, Morgan notes that VAR estimations from alternative non-normal distributions do not differ significantly from those made using the assumption of normality for many asset types.

But more importantly, the assumption of normality helped Morgan to fulfil its principal goal. By simplifying its methodology and employing the more familiar normal distribution, Morgan was able to explain important risk measurement concepts to the broad population of managers possessing only fundamental quantitative skills. And it is precisely for this reason that Morgan's 1994 release of RiskMetrics and the RiskMetrics Technical Document is recognised as a defining event in the development of modern market risk management.

RiskMetrics' apparent success in revolutionising quantitative risk measurement despite its clear limitations as a model is better understood after reading Emanuel Derman's timely article, "Model Risk." A cautionary piece that states broad principles useful to all model users, it is sound advice for those wishing to avoid errors in conceptual logic and the misuse of models. It urges us to avoid mistaking a model for what it is not, for what it cannot or does not pretend to be: "...even the finest model is only a model of the phenomena, not the real thing. A model is just a toy... (and) A good toy doesn't reproduce every feature of the real object; instead, it illustrates for its intended audience the qualities of the original object most important to them." While providing important insights into the construction and use of models, "Model risk" reminds us that criticising VAR or any other model because it cannot meet all our needs in all situations is inappropriate. Like other tools, VAR models can only produce useful results in the hands of informed users.

"Optional Extras" by Sumit Paul-Choudhury of *Risk* describes some of the deficiencies in basic VAR methodology, and discusses the efforts made to overcome them. Since the value of an option is a non-linear function of the value of its underlying asset, return distributions from actual portfolios containing options will deviate, sometimes dramatically, from the frequently assumed normal distribution. Paul-Choudhury's article clearly defines the derivative measures that quantify an option's sensitivity to the price of its underlying asset, delta and gamma, and he discusses the methods that practitioners have employed to estimate VAR for portfolios with optionality.

In "Expect the Worst," finance professors Jacob Boudoukh, Matthew Richardson and Robert Whitelaw provide a very readable amplification of the requirement to supplement VAR with stress tests or scenario analyses in order to appreciate fully the risks associated with rare "market events" resident in the tails of return probability distributions. Worst-case scenario analysis (WCS), the methodology they propose, is based not upon speculation regarding possible future events, but on the historical distribution of losses during the worst real observed trading period. The particular strength of WCS is its ability to quantify the likely size, not merely the frequency, of market losses that exceed VAR estimates but appear in the tails of prospective return distributions. Their findings regarding the magnitude of outlier events are not only rather surprising, but also neatly support the application of an "hysteria factor" or multiplier, such as (VAR $\times$ 3), when VAR is used to set regulatory capital requirements as suggested by the Basle Committee.

Although risk limits for firms and product groups are now frequently set in terms of VARs, difficulties are encountered in pushing VAR limits down to trading desks or individual trading books. After all, salesmen ask traders for offerings of, say, 10,000 XYZ shares, not $200,000 of VAR! Not only is there no quick and easy method for a trader to evaluate a transaction against his VAR limit, but he is even less likely to determine the impact of a particular trade on his aggregated position VAR accurately. In "Improving on VAR," Mark Garman explains how a new methodology, DelVar, permits the rapid approximation of the per-unit impact a trade will have on trading book VAR, thus facilitating the implementation of real-time VAR trading limits at the book level.

Of course, performance efficiency is also a concern when VAR and supplementary stress test results must be computed for large complex options positions. In "More Haste, Less Precision", Gary Robinson examines practical trade-offs between speed and accuracy in measuring the risk of a derivatives portfolio, proposing a methodology aimed at generating sufficiently accurate risk estimates in the shortest time period and with the lowest degree of computational intensity. Readers will find that Robinson's article revisits a number of broad-based VAR estimation and stress-scenario selection issues, bringing both rigour and clarity to important topics discussed in preceding selections.

Randy Payant's "Why VAR is in Vogue" and Gabriel Bousbib's "Margins of Error" are interesting reviews of the VAR methodology which emphasise both the strengths and limits of VAR in addressing traditional asset and liability management risks. Both consider the difficulties encountered in using VAR to model the risks of untradeable assets, and Bousbib proposes an alternative spread-at-risk methodology that may prove more useful than VAR for measuring the balance sheet risks of retail banks.

"VAR: Seductive but Dangerous" by Tanya Styblo Beder is a classic of early VAR literature. While many early VAR assessments cite potential difficulties with various methodologies in abstract terms, Beder actually computes a series of VAR estimates based upon eight VAR techniques applied across three hypothetical portfolios. By comparing the very different VARs computed for identical portfolios using different methods, Beder provides concrete evidence of VAR estimates' extreme dependence on parameters, data, assumptions and methodology. This powerful new tool VAR is nevertheless only a tool, and just part of any firm's required risk management framework.

In a companion article, "Report Card on Value at Risk: High Potential but Slow Starter", Beder expands on her first paper, outlining seven "lessons" learned by firms struggling to implement VAR. The article is filled with important real-world examples of VAR applications and their limits and successes. Issues generally not covered elsewhere include difficulties in aggregating VARs from liquid and illiquid markets, and challenges in selecting appropriate volatilities for assets with discontinuous prices, such as instruments in short-term interest rate markets administered by central banks. It is an important and informative read, and no exceptional quantitative skills are required to reap its benefits.

Regulators assess their new tool

Section II: Assessing VAR concludes with a series of six articles that evaluate VAR not only as an estimator of market risk, but also as a regulatory tool to set market risk-based capital requirements. When authorities such as the US Federal Reserve Bank let banks use internally-developed VAR models to compute their own market risk capital requirements, they created a clear motivation for the refinement of VAR estimation methodologies, since there are significant financial incentives for banks to hold the minimum capital acceptable to meet regulatory requirements. In fact, many readers of this book may be specifically motivated by the need to understand VAR in its regulatory context. So it is noteworthy that the authors of five of the six articles assessing VAR as a regulatory tool are from the US Federal Reserve Bank or the Bank of England, and their views are a useful insight into regulators' use of VAR in capital adequacy regimes.

Since most of the papers by regulators were prepared to "stand alone" some of their general descriptions of VAR may seem redundant, but each piece also contains information and analysis not included elsewhere. For example, "Value at Risk – New Approaches to Risk Management", by Katerina Simons of Federal Reserve Bank (FRB) Boston contains not only a concise restatement of basic VAR principles but also an important description of the Basle Market Risk Standard.

On the other hand, Gregory Hopper of FRB Philadelphia (now of Morgan Stanley) breaks new ground in "Value at Risk: A New Methodology For Measuring Portfolio Risk". Hopper argues that, like bank risk managers, regulators must evaluate capital adequacy while paying particular attention to large negative return events, which may reside beyond critical values mandated for regulatory VAR, in the tails of return distributions. And he describes specific associated challenges to accurate VAR estimation such as time-varying covariances, asymmetries in market observed asset volatilities, and the directional persistence of prices and volatilities in market "events".

In "Evaluation of Value-at-Risk Models Using Historical Data," Darryll Hendricks of FRB New York compares VAR estimates using 12 different approaches to market observed outcomes for 1,000 foreign exchange portfolios in the period 1983 to 1994. He finds not only that the "best" VAR approach is highly dependent upon the confidence interval chosen, but also that "tail event" returns can be surprisingly large. His findings, which include the fact that negative tail returns sometimes approach five times VAR estimates at a 95% confidence level, further support the view that risk managers and regulators must carefully weigh risks to capital from events falling outside the critical values established for VAR estimates.

Bankers will find "Bank Capital and Value at Risk" of particular interest because it estimates VARs for the actual holdings of a large bank using several VAR methodologies, then reveals how that bank would have fared with regulators under a regime proposed by the Basle Committee. Patricia Jackson and David Maude from the Bank of England and William Perraudin of Birkbeck College find not only that simulation-based VAR more accurately estimates tail probabilities than parametric VAR, but also that estimated capital requirements based upon parametric models are generally too low.

The last two papers in this section, "Risk^2: Measuring the Risk in Value at Risk" by Philippe Jorion, and "Techniques for Verifying the Accuracy of Risk Measurement Models," by Paul Kupiec of the Federal Reserve Board, will be difficult for readers without a solid grounding in statistical theory, and, as such, they foreshadow the challenging articles which appear in Section III.

Jorion's modest conclusion, that VAR estimates should themselves be reported in terms of confidence bands, is of less importance than the elegance of its development. But Kupiec's argument may have immediate ramifications for both regulators and banks, clouding the issue of how regulators can test bank's VAR models for accuracy. He argues that because the statistical procedures typically used to verify the accuracy of model estimates such as VAR have low power in small samples, it will not be possible for supervisory authorities to verify the accuracy of bank VAR estimates without many years of performance data - data that may not be available. Even historical simulation-based tests will require long samples, with substantial error terms persisting even in samples as large as 10 years of daily data.

It should be clear to all readers of *Section II: Assessing VAR* that the evaluation of VAR, both as a measure of market risk and as a regulatory tool, is very much work in progress. In addition to firms' desires to improve their market risk measurement techniques, rating agency and regulator-mandated disclosures as well as financial incentives for optimising VAR estimation methodologies will continue to drive the assessment and the reassessment of VAR for many years to come.

8

How Safe is RiskMetrics?

Colin Lawrence and Gary Robinson
BZW

JP Morgan has offered RiskMetrics, its toolbox for managing market risk, free to other institutions. What is its potential as an industry standard? Should it be embraced whole-heartedly, or treated with caution?

The call by the Basle Committee on Banking Supervision for market risk capital requirements highlights a growing preoccupation with the measurement and management of market risk. Against this background, JP Morgan has made freely available its daily estimates of the volatilities and correlations of key interest rates, exchange rates and equity indexes, along with a comprehensive technical description of its methodology.

This move was motivated by a desire to:

❑ promote greater transparency of market risks;
❑ make available sophisticated risk management tools to other potential users, especially those players who do not have the resources to develop such a system for themselves; and
❑ establish JP Morgan risk measures and methodology as industry standards.

The release of this suite of products – RiskMetrics – was accompanied by an invitation to comment on how the JP Morgan methodology might be improved. It is in this spirit that we assess whether RiskMetrics can be safely used by other, less sophisticated players in the market and, therefore, whether it has a legitimate claim to be the industry standard.

No doubt the RiskMetrics system and risk measures will be scrutinised closely by the supervisory authorities, who will want to prevent any establishment of industry "benchmarks" without a full discussion of the measurement and management issues. Inadequate benchmarks and standards could increase systemic risk in financial markets, which is precisely what everyone wants to avoid.

We look at the scope of the system and its models of security prices before evaluating the techniques used to estimate volatilities and correlations.

The overall purpose of RiskMetrics, as of any other market risk measurement system, is to provide an estimate of the value-at-risk (VAR) of loss, due to adverse market moves, from an institution's risk-taking activities, proprietary and market-making. As it is impossible to gauge exactly how much could be lost, the potential loss is estimated with a chosen level of confidence. In the RiskMetrics system, this is chosen to be the measure of loss which we can be 95% confident will not be exceeded, ie we expect this level of loss to be exceeded, on average, on one day in 20. This level of confidence is chosen in preference to a higher level which could give a loss measure which is rarely exceeded, because rare events could not be used to check the realism of a model of market risk.

The choice of the 95% confidence level highlights a weakness of the RiskMetrics approach to risk management methodology, that is, its (acknowledged) failure to provide information on value-at-risk in unusual or extreme market circumstances. It is not enough to know what could be lost in 19 out of 20 days, since any capital set aside purely on that basis would be consumed on average once every month. Moreover, it is the more unusual market conditions – such as those which characterised the 1987 stock market crash, the more recent European currency crises and recent liquidity problems in world bond markets – that are at the centre of supervisors' concerns.

Banks, securities houses and other institutions must therefore appreciate what could be lost in extreme market conditions and know how they would cope with this. In this respect the approach outlined in RiskMetrics is incomplete and any institution which followed it would put itself at risk from the periodic market breaks and crises that have punctuated trading conditions in recent years. We hope that future versions of RiskMetrics will include this information.

RiskMetrics also does not explain how to determine the appropriate horizon for exposure measurement, simply giving one-day and one-month measures of exposure for trading/market-making activities and investment respectively. The speed with which a position's risk profile could be modified, if necessary by liquidation, depends on the instrument in question, the size of the position and the market conditions in which the position is run down or liquidated. Measuring liquidity risk is problematic but an appreciation of how quickly liquidity can dry up, and what this implies for market risk, is essential to any analysis of VAR. As a minimum, information on bid-ask spread and normal market size, where available, would usefully supplement the other market risk information given. In this respect as well RiskMetrics gives an incomplete account of the analysis of market risk and the calculation of VAR.

Its approach to measuring the market risk of a diversified portfolio of various instruments involves taking the portfolio's positions, marking them to market and using the covariance matrix of asset returns to generate the distribution of possible changes in portfolio value, on the assumption that the distribution of returns is jointly normal. As well as requiring the calculation of a large number of risk parameters, the assumption of normality is heroic and results in misleading estimates of the VAR/confidence level.

However, this method and its assumptions are not necessary to calculate a diverse portfolio's VAR. Two alternative methods may be used. The method of ex-post simulation can be used, which makes only the weak assumption that asset returns over a reasonably long period were generated in essentially the same fundamental way.

The method is simple: take today's portfolio and revalue it using past historical price and rates data, choosing the level of loss which is rarely exceeded (one day in 20 for the JP Morgan system, though a smaller chance of occurrence would be more prudent). This provides an estimate of VAR which makes only minimal assumptions about the nature of asset returns and, because of the fat tails which characterise actual asset returns, provides safer estimates of VAR. As a superior alternative, provided we can characterise both the nature of the non-normal conditional distribution (such as Student's *t*, for example – see below) and the dynamics of the volatility process (using a GARCH model, for example – see below), we can use this information to generate simulated changes in portfolio value and hence calculate VAR. Estimates calculated under the assumption of normality will mislead as to the true level of confidence, in particular giving a false sense of security about the rarity of the events against which protection is being sought.

We note that RiskMetrics supplies a highly imperfect methodology for the measurement of market risk exposure of derivatives positions. Given that concern about the risks of such positions has largely driven the concerns over market risk, the absence of derivatives analytics and risk measures must render RiskMetrics less useful than it might otherwise be to institutions with significant derivatives positions. Moreover, there is a strong sense in which the market risk of cash instruments cannot be fully evaluated independently of derivatives, since derivative prices convey important information (via implied volatilities and correlations) about volatilities and correlations.[1]

Similarly, RiskMetrics gives no account of basis risk which may, as bond markets in 1994 showed, make a significant contribution to VAR. Again, we hope future versions of RiskMetrics will cover basis risk.

In summary, we find the scope of RiskMetrics to be too limited to be safely applied to the calculation and analysis of market risk of a diverse portfolio. At BZW we have developed a methodology which overcomes these shortcomings. In particular, we distinguish VAR based on our best estimates of volatilities and correlations (though we choose a more prudent 98% confidence level) from VAR in extreme circumstances. For this, we perform stress tests which are designed to simulate the conditions experienced in recent market crashes and crises. We are also developing models of the cost of liquidation of different securities, necessary to the evaluation of market risk.[2] We always use *ex-post* simulation and non-normal *ex-ante* simulation to augment any analysis based on the assumption of normality, in order to capture the extra risks from "fat tails" in the distributions of security returns.

The model that is assumed to apply uniformly to all security prices is geometric Brownian motion (GBM) with time-varying parameters. This states that, for a security price, $p(t)$, its proportional rate of change has two components, the drift term which is non-random and the random component, the size of which is determined by the price volatility. Thus we have:

$$dp(t) = \mu(t).p(t).d(t) + \sigma(t).p(t).dZ \qquad (1)$$

where $\mu(t)$ is the drift rate of the asset price and $\sigma(t)$ is the price volatility, both assumed to vary through time. dZ is the Wiener process, which equals $\varepsilon.\sqrt{dt}$ where ε is a drawing from a standard normal distribution. The volatility of the log-difference measured over a small interval of time dt is therefore $\sigma(t).\sqrt{dt}$. The volatility term in the RiskMetrics system is allowed to vary through time, in recognition of the fact that actual volatilities vary through time.

One consequence of the GBM model of security prices is that the distribution of security returns is normally distributed.[3] However, as a vast amount of research work testifies and the examples in the RiskMetrics technical manual show, this is not the case. In the real world the distribution of asset returns has more observations in the tails of the distribution (corresponding to unusually large changes in security prices) and more observations in the centre of the distribution (corresponding to small price changes).

These "fat tails" and "high peaks" (leptokurtosis) are characteristic of most securities and speculative prices, and mean that confidence loss limits calculated on the assumption of normality will mislead (typically, underestimate) as to the true VAR. The RiskMetrics technical manual notes that, in JP Morgan's experience, it makes little difference to the measurement of VAR whether security returns are assumed to be normal.

This is surprising. A consequence of the leptokurtosis exhibited by most security returns is that in the tails of the distribution, which are the interesting parts of the distribution for the purpose of risk management, the significance points for empirical distributions and the closest fitting normal distribution can be quite different. For example, taking closing prices for the year to November 2, 1994, 1.645 standard deviations were found to correspond to confidence levels of 93.4% for the UK benchmark gilt and 91.5% for the London price of nickel, rather than the 95% which is valid under normality.

Nevertheless, in spite of these problems with the normality assumption, the normal model is used for all instruments in the RiskMetrics methodology because:

❑ there is no persuasive alternative;

❑ the sample statistics given by the RiskMetrics service are non-parametric; and

❑ the use of the stable Paretian distribution would mean risk could not be expressed in standard deviation form.

This reasoning reveals profound misunderstandings of the nature of asset returns and how to describe them. There are at least two other ways to describe security returns, both of which are more general than the assumption of normality. The first alternative for which there is strong evidence is the Student's *t* distribution, which can have much fatter tails than the normal distribution but which can take the shape of the normal distribution, provided this is consistent with the price data (see, for example, Bollerslev, 1987). Typically, empirical research has found the number of degrees of freedom of the estimated *t*-distribution to be low (below 10), which is indicative of leptokurtosis in the conditional distribution. The second is to assume that the security price follows the mixed jump-diffusion process of Merton (1976), in which the diffusion process described by equation (1) is augmented by a discrete Poisson jump process. There is strong empirical evidence for both these alternative models.

The estimates of volatility and correlation supplied by RiskMetrics are not non-parametric as claimed: they cannot be meaningfully interpreted outside the context of a particular model of security price behaviour. For example, it is of no practical use in risk measurement to know price volatilities without knowing how many standard deviations are required to calculate VAR. Similarly, it is wrong to reject the stable Paretian distribution because it would render the standard deviation a meaningless measure of risk: if the stable Paretian distribution correctly describes security returns, then the standard deviation is a meaningless measure of risk, because the stable Paretian distribution has no second moment.[4]

Just as the GBM model is retained for its simplicity, in spite of its lack of realism, it is assumed that security returns are not autocorrelated, ie related to past returns. There is plenty of evidence to refute this assumption, including JP Morgan's RiskMetrics technical paper relating to three-month Libor and 10-year US Treasury zero-coupon rates. It is true that autocorrelation may have little effect on the measurement of risk at long horizons – because the effect dies out quickly for the small autocorrelations typically observed in financial price data. But it can cause significant mismeasurement of risk over horizons of only a few days, ie precisely the horizons of most interest in the measurement and analysis of market risk.

While we would agree that the model of security price behaviour assumed in RiskMetrics offers valuable computational savings, we would argue that it is necessary to be aware that the cost of these simplifications is greater mismeasurement of market risk.

The quants at JP Morgan recognise that volatilities and correlations vary through time, and that this must be taken into account in the measurement of value-at-risk. They achieve this by estimating these parameters using a moving window of data, but one in which the most recent observations are given more weight and the weights of less recent observations decline exponentially. Thus if x_t is the return on day t, then the variance, ie, squared volatility, of return is measured as:

$$\sigma_t^2 = \frac{\lim}{N \to \infty} \sum \varpi_n \{x_{t-n} - X\}^2 \quad (2)$$

$$= \lambda.\sigma_{t-1}^{\ 2} + \lambda(1-\lambda).(x_t - X_{t-1})^2 \quad (3)$$

where ω is the weight put on the (t–n)th observation, which is set to decline exponentially so that it equals $\lambda(1-\lambda)n$, where λ is the exponential decay factor, chosen to minimise the error in forecasting future volatility;[5] and X_t is the exponentially weighted average return, where the weights applied are the same as those which are applied in the calculation of volatility.

This weighting scheme is applied to avoid the abrupt falls in volatility which would otherwise result when a large price change drops out of the data window, and presumably also because more recent data is more relevant to an assessment of today's market risk.

There are several problems with this approach. Exponential weighting is appropriate only when the process to which it is applied has unbounded variance, and is optimal when the process is Arima (0,1,1). It follows that exponential weighting in the calculation of the mean implies that the process followed by returns has infinite variance. If this is the case, why is volatility calculated at all? Further, what is the justification for applying the same weights in the calculation of the mean and the volatility of the process?

For simplicity, this method is applied to all prices, which is reasonable. However, this desire for methodological uniformity goes too far: the exponential decay factor, λ, which determines the weights given to different observations, is constrained to be numerically equal for all securities.

Why should this important parameter be needlessly constrained to be equal for all securities, when it would be no more costly of computer time to allow the data to determine the weights appropriate to each particular market? This is a potentially dangerous restriction, because in some markets an increase in volatility today will persist for many days in the future thereby causing market risk to rise, whereas in other markets a change in volatility will simply be a "blip". To constrain the parameter λ to be equal for all securities ignores such differences between markets. Similarly, the RiskMetrics technical paper gives no indication of whether the exponential parameter will be re-estimated periodically, as market conditions change.

As an alternative to the method of exponential weighting, JP Morgan considered the class of autoregressive conditional heteroscedasticity (ARCH) models (see Engle, 1982). This expression describes a stochastic process for which the volatility varies over time (ie it is heteroscedastic) in a way that depends on (ie is conditioned by) past values of a stochastic error process (ie it is autoregressive). The generalised ARCH (or GARCH) model characterises a process which, in addition, depends upon its own past values.[6] If p_t is the asset price, then the basic GARCH model has the following form:

$$d\ln(p_t) = E\{d\ln(p_t) \mid \Omega_{t-1}\} + \varepsilon_t \quad (4)$$

$$\varepsilon_t = N(0,h_t) \quad (5)$$

$$h_t = \alpha + \beta(L).h_{t-1} + \gamma(L).\varepsilon_{t-1}^2 \quad (6)$$

where $\beta(L)$ and $\gamma(L)$ are lag polynomials.

Equation (4) describes the asset return (measured as the log difference in the asset price) as the expectation of the return, given information available at time t–1, denoted Ω_{t-1}, plus the expectation error, denoted ε_t. The error is normally distributed (although this distributional assumption is not necessary) with zero mean and a variance h_t which varies through time in the manner described by equation (6): the variance in the current time period is a function of the variance in previous time periods and the squared error terms in previous time periods.

We should expect the ARCH model to be superior to the exponential method because the implicit weighting of observations and the effective length of the moving window are chosen by the data. Indeed, the study (Cho/West, 1994) reported in the RiskMetrics technical paper finds ARCH to be a better predictor of volatility than the exponential method for the short horizons of most interest in measuring market risk, ie, less than 20 days.[7] As noted above, the exponential method will be optimal only when the returns are an Arima (0,1,1) process. We would therefore prefer to use ARCH-type models to describe the tendency of volatility and correlation to vary through time, and, at BZW, the ARCH parameters on key interest and exchange rates are frequently updated.

RiskMetrics has been launched in the hope that it will become the industry standard in terms of risk measurement and methodology, to be used particularly by those banks, securities houses and other institutions unable to devote the resources required to build an adequate risk management system for themselves. In so doing, JP Morgan invited an appraisal of its measures and methodology. Though we applaud this early step in establishing a widely-accepted methodology, we have evaluated RiskMetrics and found its methods and the resulting risk measures to be incomplete. We would therefore advise extreme caution on the part of those institutions which intend to follow the methods or use the risk measures of RiskMetrics in calculating VAR.

While RiskMetrics may have served the valuable function of stimulating debate on the measurement of market risk and the development of a market standard, it does not itself represent that standard. Moreover, it is doubtful whether such standards should be set by any institution with a vested interest in promoting its own name. Rather it should be the outcome of a thorough discussion involving the whole industry, including the supervisors.

1 *Several empirical studies have established the usefulness of implied stock volatility in forecasting actual volatility.*

2 *See Lawrence, C. and Robinson, G., "Liquid Measures",* Risk, *July 1995, for a brief description of the application of this approach to equities portfolios.*

3 *Conditionally at least.*

4 *On a related point, the RiskMetrics technical manual observes that the stable Paretian distribution is unsuitable because it has a problem of instability! In fact, the compelling reason why the stable Paretian distribution is unsuitable to describe security returns is that security returns themselves exhibit instability under temporal aggregation, thereby contradicting the characteristic features of the stable Paretian distribution (see, for example, Boothe, P. and Glassman, D., 1987, "The Statistical Distribution of Exchange Rates",* Journal of International Economics *22 (May), pp. 297–319).*

5 *Note that the small number of non-overlapping monthly periods available for testing in the case of volatilities for the investment horizon leads JP Morgan to use the method of bootstrapping, by which the actual data series is randomised many times to produce many synthetic data series. This technique relies for its validity on the absence of any temporal dependence in the original series, which would be destroyed by randomisation. However, as the examples in the RiskMetrics manual demonstrate, this cannot be assumed.*

6 *Note that the ARCH model was from the start misnamed: the structure of the ARCH model is that of a moving-average process rather than an autoregressive process. Unfortunately, this error has never been rectified and it is now too late.*

7 *This is not entirely surprising judging from the graph of exponentially-weighted volatility of the sterling-DM rate shown in the RiskMetrics manual (Chart 5). Whereas the graph of daily percentage changes suggests that volatility has settled down to a new, higher level six months following the ERM crisis of August 1992, the exponential measure shows volatility declining long after.*

BIBLIOGRAPHY

Bollerslev, T., 1987, "A Conditional Heteroskedastic Time Series Model for Speculative Prices and Rates of Return", *Review of Economics and Statistics*, 69 (August), pp.542–7.

Cho, D. and K. West, 1994, "Predictive Ability of Several Models of Exchange Rate Volatility", NBER Technical Paper 152.

Engle, R., 1982, "Autoregressive Conditional Heteroskedasticity with Estimates of the Variance of United Kingdom Inflation", *Econometrics*, 50 (4), pp. 987–1008.

Merton, R. C., 1976, "Option Pricing when Underlying Stock Returns are Discontinuous", *Journal of Financial Economics*, 3 (March), pp. 125–44.

9

A Transparent Tool

Jacques Longerstaey and Peter Zangari
JP Morgan

JP Morgan argues that the value of RiskMetrics lies in its transparency and the opportunities it provides for discussion and evaluation of value-at-risk. This article outlines the advantages of the RiskMetrics methodology.

Any attempt to challenge RiskMetrics as a benchmark encompasses not only identifying potential weaknesses in the methodology but also suggesting possible alternatives. Unfortunately, potential alternatives cannot be seriously considered until details of the methodology are revealed and that methodology is in use. We would like to address BZW's principal concerns regarding the RiskMetrics product (see Chapter 8). We would also like to remind readers that one of the cornerstones of RiskMetrics is to provide potential users with a relatively simple, transparent toolkit to analyse risk.[1]

Our colleagues at BZW make three points that we will address:

- the scope of RiskMetrics is not a suitable benchmark for risk management;
- the underlying assumptions regarding the behaviour of securities prices are questionable; and
- the application of the exponential weighting scheme for estimating volatilities and correlations is too simplistic.

Scope

BZW makes the case that RiskMetrics is simply too limited for the calculation and analysis of market risk. There are two aspects to this statement, one relating to product coverage, the other to aspects of the underlying methodology.

On product coverage, we agree that the first version of RiskMetrics is limited, but its limits emanate from the target audience (participants in the global equity, foreign exchange, swap and government bond markets); we are working on expanding the instruments covered on the basis of feedback from clients.

On the methodology front, BZW first claims that the failure to provide information on value-at-risk in unusual or extreme circumstances, such as stock market crashes and Exchange Rate Mechanism crises, is a weakness of the RiskMetrics approach.

There are basically two ways to estimate market risk: using probability distributions such as RiskMetrics is one. Simulation is another. While one could argue in favour of one or the other, our position is that the two methods must be used in combination. RiskMetrics provides the building blocks for base case scenario analysis. The problem is that event risk doesn't happen often enough to provide reasonable statistics on its occurrence. Analysis of event risk therefore cannot rely exclusively on probability distributions. The consequences of event risk must be quantified through simulations, but scenarios must be constructed from a reasonable base. RiskMetrics is the part of the market risk estimation process that can be standardised and used across institutions. Simulations, on the other hand, are likely to be client-specific and therefore impractical to incorporate in a complete package.

The other issue is the choice of the confidence interval for measuring risk versus the setting of capital requirements. The argument states that since the 95% chosen by RiskMetrics is not conservative enough, it is useless from a capital perspective. Nowhere in the RiskMetrics documentation do we say that capital requirements should be equal to daily earnings at risk using a 95% interval. Capital will be a function of the risk numbers and the scalar used to calculate it will depend on the confidence interval chosen. How the function is defined is not an objective of RiskMetrics, however. That is the job of the regulators.

RiskMetrics is a risk measurement tool designed for management use. Risk managers do not want to look only at what happens in extreme events. Consequently, the preferred methodology differs from the approach of regulators aiming to protect the financial system from catastrophic and systemic risks. If internal risk measurements use only worst-case scenarios, the analysis will be useless for risk/return profiles, for example. Measuring expected return versus extreme risk makes only limited sense. This is why RiskMetrics disassociates risk management from capital adequacy.

On a related matter, BZW mentions the use of *ex-post* simulation as a potential "alternative". Without knowing the details behind this methodology, it would be both unfair and unwise to comment, especially since the technical details drive the results. The only indication on the methodology is that it relies on historical prices and yields for all instruments taken individually, an approach which has intellectual appeal but may be costly to implement in firms active in a large number of markets and instruments. If the RiskMetrics data sets seem large, the data required for long time series of individual asset prices is mind-boggling.

BZW also mentions that market risk of cash instruments cannot be fully evaluated independently of derivatives, since derivative prices convey important information via implied volatilities and correlations. This may well be true[2] but it is important to be more specific. From an implementation viewpoint, we must consider two issues.

First, as cited in the Technical Document (page 28), quality data on implied volatilities are only available for options traded on open exchanges. This limits the applicability of the method to a reduced number of time series.

Second, as will be discussed below, the estimation techniques associated with implied volatilities can be problematic. Furthermore, the properties of the estimated implied volatilities may not be as attractive as they appear. In fact, Kroner, Kneafsey and Claessens (1994) write: "Most option pricing models assume that volatility is constant, so when forecasts are extracted from these models in a world of dynamic volatility, it is not clear what is really being forecast. It is also possible that the options market is not efficient and/or the option pricing formulas are incorrect." Frankel and Wei (1994) conclude that "...the implicit volatilities extracted from options prices in the standard way are not optimal forecasts of future volatilities".

Assumed behaviour of security prices

BZW addresses some of the assumptions associated with RiskMetrics and their potential problems. The article questions our use of the normal distribution, given that recent research demonstrates that "in the real world asset returns are *not* normally distributed". In general, we cannot disagree.

However, the use of the normal assumption is more fundamental. The logic would seem to suggest that assumptions should first be validated empirically before using them to formulate a model. Consequently, the model with the most "realistic" assumptions would produce the preferred alternative. But - for numerous reasons - this does not always hold true. Assumptions simplify a model so that we can study complex phenomena while understanding the workings of the model. How well the model performs could then, for example, be based on its ability to predict.[3]

Nevertheless, in the context of RiskMetrics, it is very important that users understand what they are working with. The question of whether there are more general ways to describe returns is not as important as how well these alternatives perform in practice relative to the normal, and how easily they can be understood and applied. As a case in point, we welcome BZW's challenge of the normality assumption, claiming that there is "strong evidence" that both the Student's *t* and the Poisson jump process can be used to model asset returns.

There are a number of issues we would like to raise with respect to this claim. First, it is difficult to understand BZW's statement about the Student's *t* distribution because they cite Bollerslev (1987) as evidence of its usefulness. However, that paper estimates a GARCH model with a Student's *t* disturbance term. It would have been more enlightening to offer evidence for the Student's *t* distribution as done in Kim and Kon (1994).[4] Second, as for the "strong evidence" in favour or the Poisson jump process, not only is there a limited amount of research on this topic, but Kim and Kon find, in comparing five econometric models fitted to equity data, that its empirical results rank it second to last.[5] Finally, the nature of BZW's claim that there is strong evidence for both distributions is testimony to the lack of agreement on the best approach to modelling asset returns.[6]

As a final point, BZW questioned the statement that the volatilities and correlations are non-parametric. By describing them as "non-parametric", we do not mean that we rely on the parametric (normal) distribution as a basis for estimation. An example of imposing the normal assumption on estimation would be to perform maximum likelihood with the normal probability density function. Conversely, the normal distribution is not necessary for the current estimation of volatilities and correlations.

Measuring volatilities and correlations

BZW asks why the decay factor in the exponential weighting scheme is "needlessly" constrained? One answer is simple; if we allowed the decay factor to be unconstrained across every series then we would have to estimate a decay factor for each correlation (actually, covariance). Given 325 times series, this would require 325*326/2 or 52,975 decay factors! In addition, the calculation of the correlations would be based on three potentially different decay factors.

Similarly, BZW enquires about updating the decay factor as market conditions change. We should note that while we re-estimate the decay factor on a regular basis (every six months), simply proposing that it should be changed in line with market conditions is potentially dangerous and may lead to more instability than if the decay factor was left constant. A formal check for the retrospective detection of variance changes in a series can yield insight into the stability of volatilities.[7]

Concerning volatility estimates, BZW advocates the use of GARCH models and then relates the exponential model to GARCH. At a practical level, it does not make much sense to compare the models, for the simple reason that ARCH estimation is much more complicated and unstable.

In practice, non-linear estimation, as required by ARCH models, can be very tricky. For example, one must be concerned with issues such as convergence, starting values, and data scaling which don't arise in the context of the exponential model. In fact, note the following comment by Jacquier, Polson and Rossi (1994): "One important issue that does not receive adequate attention in the ARCH/stochastic volatility literature is the problems encountered when optimisation methods are used to construct ARCH MLE ... It is well known that many ARCH/GARCH likelihoods are difficult to maximise."

Even if the application of GARCH models was trivial, consider a simple comparison between GARCH (1,1) and the exponential model.

We generate 1,000 data points (returns) according to a GARCH (1,1) specification[8]

$$y_t = \sigma_t \varepsilon_t \qquad \varepsilon_t = \text{NID}(0,1)$$
$$\sigma_t^2 = 0.0234 + 0.0854 y_{t-1}^2 + 0.8588 \sigma_{t-1}^2$$

where NID is normally independent distribution. Then, we use this data to create variance estimates under the exponential mode:

$$\sigma_t^2 = 00.94 \sigma_{t-1}^2 + 0.94 * (1 - 0.94) * (y_t - \bar{y}_{t-1})^2.$$

Figure 1 demonstrates the variance estimates from both models for the last 500 observations. As is obvious from the graph, the dynamics of the variances of the two models are strikingly similar.

On a related point, BZW claims that in the Arch model, unlike the exponential, the "implicit weighting of observations and the effective length of the moving window" are chosen by the data. This is obviously not correct since the decay factor in the exponential method is an estimated parameter.

BZW also incorrectly infers from the charts presented in the Technical Document that there is plenty of evidence of autocorrelated returns. *None* of the correlograms on page 23 show any perceptible evidence of autocorrelated returns.

Conclusion

It appears that BZW believes RiskMetrics is too simple to be effective. Without a complete understanding of the RiskMetrics product, this is fully understandable. However, and as we repeatedly mention in the Technical Document, the

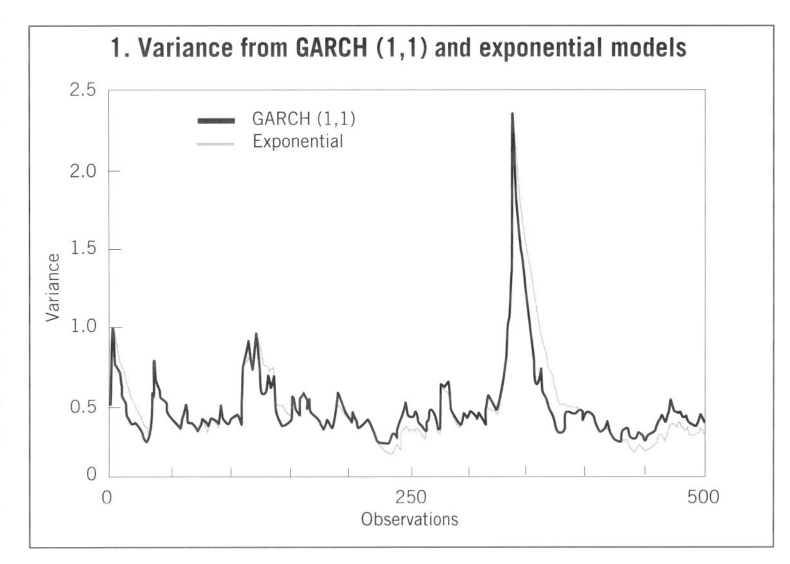

1. Variance from GARCH (1,1) and exponential models

A TRANSPARENT TOOL

RiskMetrics methodology embodies both theoretical and practical considerations.

Most importantly, we emphasise that - like any other risk management apparatus - RiskMetrics is only a tool. Computations based on RiskMetrics should be viewed in this context. BZW's critique has confirmed to us the need to reveal the detailed methodology behind calculating risk management statistics. As such, RiskMetrics is the only available tool that is fully transparent and whose shortcomings can be evaluated and understood by risk management practitioners. There are still a large number of black-box models out there which - in our opinion and regardless of their methodological merits - are significantly more dangerous to use in practice. Glossing over the practical issues of risk management statistical methodologies is potentially more misleading and heroic than recognising the shortcomings of a simple workable product.

We recognise that standards are an ever-evolving concept (particularly in the fast-moving science of risk management). The first release of RiskMetrics is aimed at providing a practical tool and will be a standard only so far as a large number of financial market participants think it is a useful one. It is clearly not the only way to measure market risk and should also not be used in isolation. It is a building block for setting up a risk management framework and a benchmark against which alternative methods can be evaluated.

Financial market participants can only benefit from open discussion on these matters. Risk measurement will benefit. The main lesson from our experience to date is that transparency is the key. As a result, we look forward to continuing these discussions. The scope of these, however, will be limited by the fact that methodologies can only be discussed seriously when they are fully transparent. To date, only RiskMetrics meets this criteria.

1 *The methodology is detailed in the* RiskMetrics Technical Document, *now in its fourth edition.*

2 *Recently, Kroner, Kneafsey and Claessens (1994) found evidence - using commodity prices - that forecasts combining both market expectations and time series outperform other methods.*

3 *On a related point, Professor P.C.B. Phillips of Yale recently noted that, "the model with the best fit to the sample data is sometimes far from being the best model of the underlying mechanism in a primitive predictive sense". See Mittnik and Rachev (1993).*

4 *This is because they are questioning the use of the normal distribution function. Alternatively, they could compare the GARCH (1,1) with normal errors with Student's* t *errors. Regardless, the model used in Bollersev (1987) is studied infrequently relative to GARCH (1,1) with normal errors.*

5 *Not surprisingly, the normal model finished last. Nevertheless, the point to question is whether there is strong evidence in favour of the Poisson model as claimed.*

6 *To understand the nature of the disagreement on modelling asset returns, the reader is referred to Mittnik and Rachev (1993).*

7 *See, for example, Inclan and Tiao (1994). This methodology is employed by the market risk research group at JP Morgan in New York.*

8 *For the GARCH (1,1) model, the parameterisation is based on the results for the Deutschmark reported in Ruiz (1993). The decay factor for the exponential model is taken from the daily decay factor in the* RiskMetrics Technical Document, *fourth edition.*

BIBLIOGRAPHY

Bollerslev, T., 1987, "A Conditional Heteroskedastic Time Series Model for Speculative Prices and Rates of Return", *The Review of Economics and Statistics*, pp. 542-6.

Frankel, J. and S.-J. Wei, 1991, "Are Option-Implied Forecasts of Exchange Rate Volatility Excessively Variable?", NBER working paper 3,910.

Inclan, C., and G.C. Tiao, 1994, "Use of Cumulative Sums of Squares for Retrospective Detection of Changes of Variance", *Journal of the American Statistical Association*, 89 (427), pp. 913-23.

Jacquier, E., G. Polson and P. Rossi, 1994, "Bayesian Analysis of Stochastic Volatility Models", *Journal of Business and Economic Statistics*, 12 (4), pp. 371-417.

Kim, D. and S. Kon, 1994, "Alternative Models for the Conditional Heteroscedasticity of Stock Returns", *Journal of Business*, 67(4), pp. 563-98.

Kroner, K., K. Kneafsey and S. Claessens, 1994, "Forecasting Volatility in Commodity Markets," *Journal of Forecasting*, 14 (2), pp. 77-98.

Mittnik, S. and S. Rachev, 1993, "Modelling Asset Returns with Alternative Stable Distributions", *Econometric Reviews*, pp. 261-375.

Ruiz, E., 1993, "Stochastic Volatility versus Autoregressive Conditional Heteroscedasticity", working paper 93-44, Universidad Carlos III de Madrid.

10

Optional Extras

Sumit Paul-Choudhury
Risk

Simple value-at-risk models do not cater well for market crashes or options positions. How can their functionality be extended to cover these areas?

Value-at-risk (VAR) may be ubiquitous but it is not a panacea. VAR, as many practitioners are keen to point out, is only a way of encapsulating a firm's market risks into a single figure which can be used to aid management understanding of its risk position. "The VAR number should be considered to have error bars around it," says Paul Dentskevich, senior manager at Tokai Bank Europe in London.

The shortcomings of VAR can be illustrated by drawing an analogy between a risk manager and an air traffic controller. The air traffic controller could encapsulate the factors critical to the safety of all the aeroplanes under her control – air speed, altitude, wind direction, and so on – into a single "passengers-at-risk" number. But a given pilot would quickly come to grief if he relied exclusively on this PAR number to fly the plane. And the carefully calculated PAR number would do little to predict the likelihood of a hurricane blowing up or the results if it did.

In the risk manager's case, the market risk of a portfolio may be quantified as a single VAR number, but management of an individual trader's book requires more careful consideration of its risk sensitivities than VAR alone can provide. This is particularly true for options, where the effect of the so-called "Greek" risk sensitivities can prove extremely significant. And a market crash is to the risk manager as the hurricane is to the air traffic controller.

Market crashes and options both pose essentially the same problem when calculating VAR. One of the standard assumptions made by conventional VAR models, such as the original form of JP Morgan's RiskMetrics, is that the returns on a portfolio are normally distributed. It is this assumption that allows VAR to be estimated, because in a normal distribution, 90% of all returns fall within ±1.65 standard deviations (the 5th and 95th percentiles) of the mean return. This allows an estimate to be made of the largest amount that is likely to be lost on a portfolio under the usual market conditions – the value-at-risk.

But returns are rarely distributed normally in practice. Outlying events (a technical euphemism for crashes) are more common in the real world than the normal distribution would suggest, which requires the use of stress testing and scenario analysis, as described in the Appendix.

Nor are the returns on an options portfolio usually normally distributed. Any instrument which includes optionality will have a non-linear payout profile. Put most simply, this means that the relationship between a change in the underlying asset price (or rate) and the resultant change in the value of the derivative is not constant. This relationship is quantified as delta, the first of the Greeks.

Consider an at-the-money call on a stock index, which is initially at a level of 1020 points. If the index value drops by 10 points to 1010, the value of the option decreases by roughly five points because it has approximately the same chance of expiring in- or out-of-the-money. If the index drops a further 10 points, to 1000, however, the value of the option might drop by just three points, even though the move in the index is the same as before. This is the non-linearity at play; the delta when the index is 1020 would be 50%, while the delta when the index is at 1010 points is 30%.

The dependence of delta on the value of the underlying is quantified as gamma. Delta and gamma are just the first two members of an infinite series of sensitivities to the underlying, the rest of which are usually ignored. The importance of non-linearity increases as the option approaches the money and also as the time to expiry increases.

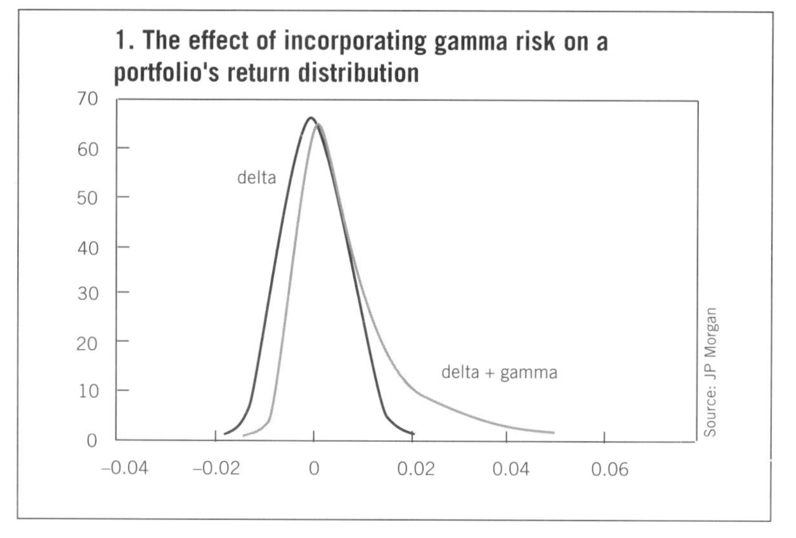

1. The effect of incorporating gamma risk on a portfolio's return distribution

Until recently, VAR models have only taken account of delta, which is the linear component of option risk. This allows the normal distribution to be used with impunity, if inaccurately. For a trading bank, whose portfolio may frequently contain large numbers of options and therefore significant exposure to gamma risk, this is not a sufficiently good approximation. Furthermore, the value of an option is also sensitive to the time remaining to expiry (the Greek tau) and the volatility of the underlying (vega). Even assuming that a bank, left to its own devices, might be happy to live with its gamma risk, the regulators are not so complacent. January's proposed amendment to the Basle Capital Accord from the Basle Committee on Banking Supervision stipulates that banks which write options will be required to measure delta, gamma and vega risk when calculating capital to be held against them.

If the effects of gamma risk are introduced when computing the potential returns on a portfolio, the distribution of returns becomes asymmetric (skewed - see Figure 1). Other variables, such as mean and variance, may also differ from a normal distribution. The statistical measures which describe the normal distribution, therefore, do not apply.

Just because the statistical measures used for normally-distributed returns do not apply does not mean similar but more refined techniques cannot be used on the skewed returns generated by the portfolio. One way to attack the options problem is to include the effects of higher-order risk sensitivities than delta, such as gamma. The portfolio's VAR can then be calculated on the basis of this skewed distribution, in one of three ways:

- ❑ the skewed distribution can be approximated to a deformed normal distribution
- ❑ the 5th and 95th percentiles can be calculated for the skewed distribution
- ❑ the skewed distribution can be fitted to a more general family of distributions whose characteristic statistical measures are known.

But an analytic approximation to VAR, by its nature, ignores some of the elements which go into making up the market risk of the portfolio, most obviously the higher-order relatives of delta and gamma, as well as the effects of crashes. These more abstruse effects can be captured by other approaches to calculating VAR, such as Monte Carlo or historical simulation.

Many banks prefer simulation for these reasons. "The analytic approach does give you a quick answer and a chance to test alternatives, but in general, simulation is the only way when there's significant optionality," says Tokai's Dentskevich. The problem with simulation is that it quickly grows extremely time-consuming and can be costly in terms of computer power. "The amount of effort required to build a good simulation is much greater than that required for an analytic approach, where simplifying assumptions can be used provided their implications are fully understood," he says.

For small users, or in situations where time is of the essence (such as checking against a position limit under trading conditions) the refinements to be made by using a simulation technique may be outweighed by the difficulty of constructing and running it. The choice, therefore, is: slow and steady, or rough and ready?

Although it has already published details of an analytical methodology for calculating option VAR, JP Morgan also suggests that users treat option market risk with a partial simulation technique for its 4.15 Excel spreadsheet add-in, incorporating delta and gamma risk only. CS First Boston's PrimeClear product also gives users the choice of a Monte Carlo or an analytic treatment.

"Many of our users may be small money managers, for whom Monte Carlo is likely to be too time-consuming and complex," says Ashok Varikooty, director of quantitative strategy at CSFB in New York. "VAR is not perfect, but you have to remember that it only captures a local risk measure. It's not a worst case analysis or a horizon analysis. What you're doing is trading off the gross imperfection [of not trying to capture option risk at all] for a slight imperfection. And any reduction in imperfection is a benefit to the client."

Appendix

SIMULATING STRESS

If a financial institution uses a confidence interval of 99% when calculating its VAR, the losses on its trading portfolio due to market price movements should not exceed the VAR number on more than one day out of every 100. For a 95% confidence interval, the corresponding frequency is one day in 20, or roughly one trading day in every month.

The question is "what are the expected losses on these days?" Furthermore, what can an institution do to protect itself against these losses? The analytics of VAR become redundant in this kind of situation. In particular, assuming that asset returns are normally distributed may provide a workable day-to-day approximation for estimating risk but when market moves are more extreme, relying on such assumptions is positively dangerous.

The 1% of market moves that are not used for VAR calculations contain events like the stock market crash of 1987, the bond market collapse of early1994 or the Mexican debt crisis at the end of that year.

In these events not only were the moves much larger than any VAR system would account for but also the correlation between markets suddenly increased well above levels normally assumed in VAR models as they all went down together.

The best that risk managers can hope to do to identify their portfolio risks in stress situations is to simulate extreme market moves over a range of differing scenarios. In the Group of Thirty's July 1993 report *Derivatives: Practices and Principles*, it recommends that "dealers should regularly perform simulations to determine how their portfolios would perform under stress conditions".

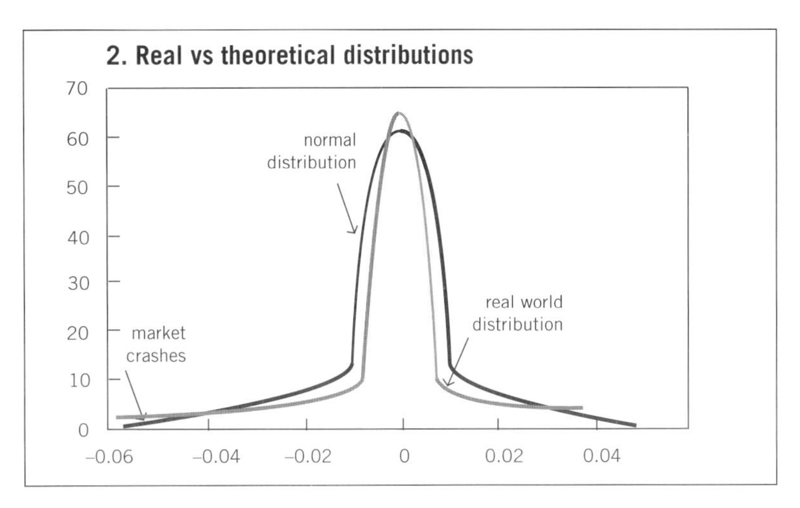

The most popular and flexible approach is to use Monte Carlo simulation. This allows dealers to push the risk factors to greater limits and is not dependent on the assumption of normality or indeed the distribution of returns over the historic observation period. For example, a 99% confidence interval captures the events up to 2.33 standard deviations away from the mean asset return. A risk manager may want to find out what will happen to the trading portfolio if a 10-standard deviation move occurs. The 1987 crash was a 30-standard deviation move.

Similarly, risk managers may want to change the correlation assumptions under which they normally work. If markets all move down together, losses are obviously going to be greater than if some markets are offset by other negatively correlated markets.

By pushing the bounds of the range of market moves that are covered in the risk management process, financial institutions have a better chance of seeing where losses might occur and therefore a better chance of managing those risks effectively.

Nick Reed

11

Expect the Worst

Jacob Boudoukh, Matthew Richardson and Robert Whitelaw
Stern School of Business, New York University

Some experts believe that value-at-risk fails to capture all aspects of market risk. This article outlines a complementary risk measure - worst case scenario analysis.

Senior management tend to prefer a single measure of the risk of their firm's assets and it is increasingly value-at-risk (VAR) that is chosen. VAR expresses the price risk of a portfolio of assets in terms of the frequency with which a specific loss will be exceeded. For example, if daily changes in the value of a portfolio are distributed normally, then the firm would expect to lose $\mu_p - 2.33\sigma_p$ one day out of every 100 (where μ_p and σ_p are the mean and volatility of the portfolio's daily change in value).

VAR is gaining support in the international supervisory community. For example, both the Group of Thirty derivatives committee (November 1994) and the Derivatives Policy Group (March 1995) have called for universal acceptance of this measure. In fact, some products, such as JP Morgan's RiskMetrics, already incorporate VAR directly.

But is VAR really what firms should care about when setting their risk management strategy? We suggest an alternative or complementary measures, related to stress testing: "worst-case scenario" risk. WCS asks the following question: what is the worst that can happen to the value of the firm's trading portfolio over a given period (eg 20 trading days)?

We build our analysis around a specific assumption. This is that the firm adjusts its portfolio positions over time to maintain the same fraction of capital invested. This is a logical assumption which corresponds to the firm increasing its bet as it makes money and reducing it as it loses.

To understand why WCS may be a more appropriate risk measure than VAR, consider the example above, where the firm's portfolio return is normally distributed with a mean μ_p and volatility σ_p. VAR tells us that losses greater than $\mu_p - 2.33\sigma_p$ will occur, on average, once over the next 100 trading periods, and that losses greater than $\mu_p - 1.65\sigma_p$ will occur, on average, once over the next 20 trading periods. From a risk management perspective, however, managers care more about the size of the losses than the number of times they will face loss.

In contrast to VAR, WCS focuses on the distribution of the loss during the worst trading period (eg two weeks), over a given horizon (eg 100 two-week periods). The key point is that a worst period will occur with probability one. The only question is, how bad will it be?

WCS analysis is similar to stress testing and scenario analysis. These concepts are most often associated with the analysis of rare or extreme events, whereas WCS is concerned with the nature of an event which, by definition, is bound to happen.

We will show that the expected loss during the worst period is far greater than the corresponding VAR. Of more importance, there is a substantial probability of a much more severe loss.

Without loss of generality, assume that the change in the value of a firm's portfolio over a trading period is normally distributed, with a mean of 0 and a volatility of 1.[1] Over N of these intervals, VAR states how many times one might expect to exceed a particular loss. In contrast, WCS states what the distribution of the maximum loss will be. That is, it focusses on $F(\min[z_1, z_2, \ldots, z_N])$, denoted $F(\underline{Z})$, where $F(\cdot)$ denotes the distribution function and z_i denotes the normalised return series, corresponding to the change in the portfolio's value over interval i.

Table 1 overleaf shows the expected number of trading periods in which VAR will be exceeded. For example, the 5% VAR corresponds

Table 1. Worst-case scenario analysis

The WCS, denoted $\underline{Z}$, is defined as the lowest observation in the vector $Z = (z_1, z_2, \ldots, z_H)$ of length H = 5,20,100,250 of independent draws which are normally distributed with mean 0 and volatility 1

	Horizon (H)			
	5	**20**	**100**	**250**
E[Number of Z_i<–2.33]	0.05	0.20	1.00	2.50
E[Number of Z_i<–1.65]	0.25	1.00	5.00	12.50
Expected WCS	–1.16	–1.86	–2.51	–2.82
Percentiles of $\underline{Z}$				
1%	–2.80	–3.26	–3.72	–3.92
5%	–2.27	–2.77	–3.28	–3.54
10%	–2.03	–2.53	–3.08	–3.35
50%	–1.13	–1.82	–2.47	–2.78

Table 2. Worst-case scenario analysis of returns on bonds and bond options

The WCS, denoted $\underline{R}$, is defined as the worst percentage return on (i) a 10-year zero-coupon bond, and (ii) an option with one year to maturity on a 10-year zero-coupon bond, in a vector R of length H = 5,20,100,250 of independent returns

Percentage return on bonds

	Horizon (H)			
	5	**20**	**100**	**250**
Expected WCS	–0.81	–1.29	–1.74	–1.95
Percentiles of $\underline{R}$				
1%	–1.94	–2.25	–2.57	–2.70
5%	–1.58	–1.92	–2.27	–2.45
10%	–1.41	–1.76	–2.13	–2.32
50%	–0.79	–1.26	–1.71	–1.92

Percentage return on bond options

	Horizon (H)			
	5	**20**	**100**	**250**
Expected WCS	-9.06	–14.28	–18.99	–21.18
Percentiles of $\underline{R}$				
1%	–21.08	–24.19	–27.24	–28.54
5%	–17.37	–20.86	–24.38	–26.11
10%	–15.61	–19.19	–22.97	–24.82
50%	–8.91	–14.05	–18.74	–20.91

to 1.65 in the normalised units of the table and is expected to be exceeded once over a horizon of length 20, and five times over a horizon of length 100.

The table also provides information regarding the WCS measures over different horizons. The distribution is obtained via a simulation of 10,000 random normal vectors (using antithetic variates) of lengths corresponding to the various horizons. For example, the WCS distribution indicates that the expected worst loss over the next 20 periods is 1.86, while over the next 100 periods it is 2.51. More importantly, over the next 20 periods there is a 5% and a 1% probability of losses exceeding 2.77 and 3.26 respectively. The corresponding losses for a 100-period horizon are 3.28 and 3.72 respectively.

Looking at the results from a different perspective, eg, for the 1%, 100-period VAR measure, the VAR is 2.33 while the expected WCS is 2.51 and the first percentile of the WCS distribution is 3.72. If the fraction of capital invested throughout the 100 periods is maintained, then WCS is the appropriate measures in forming risk management policies regarding financial distress. If the firm maintains capital at less than 160% of its VAR, there is a 1% chance that the firm will face financial distress over the next 100 periods.

Next, we discuss two specific examples involving fixed-income securities. Our main purpose is to demonstrate the effect of leverage on VAR and WCS. In Table 2 we examine the risk inherent in a position in a 10-year zero-coupon bond and a one-year, at-the-money option on a 10-year zero-coupon bond.[2] We assume that the current instantaneous interest rate is 8% a year and the daily volatility of this rate is 7 basis points (these numbers are calibrated from average past data). The bond is thus worth 46 cents per $1 of face amount.

Applying VAR, the 1% tail is represented by an increase of 16.3bp [2.33 × 7bp] in interest rates, which results in a loss of 1.62% of the value of the bond, ie, approximately, the 0.163% move in rates multiplied by the duration of the bond, which is 10. The 5% tail is represented by an increase of 11.6bp [1.65 × 7bp] in interest rates, which results in a loss of 1.15% of the value of the bond. The expected WCS loss is 1.74%, while the 1% tail of the WCS distribution is 2.57%.

Now suppose we invest in a one-year option on a 10-year zero-coupon bond. The 1% VAR of holding this option is 17.77% (12.83% for the 5% VAR) and the expected WCS is 18.99%. More importantly, the 1% tail of the WCS distribution corresponds to a loss of 27.24% during a single trading period over the next 100 periods.

Our analysis indicates the importance of the WCS facing a firm, in addition to the firm's VAR. In practice, the WCS analysis has some natural extensions and caveats, which also pertain to VAR.

First, our analysis was developed in the context of a specific model of the firm's investment behaviour, ie, we assumed that the firm, in order to remain "capital efficient", increases the level of investment when gains are realised. There are alternative models of investment behaviour, which suggest other aspects of the distribution of returns should be investigated. For example, we might be interested in the distribution of "bad runs" corresponding to partial sums of length J periods for a given horizon of H.

Second, the effect of time-varying volatility has been ignored. Assuming that risk capital measures are adjusted to reflect this, via RiskMetrics,

Garch, density estimation, implied volatility or another method, there is the issue of model risk. That is, to the extent that volatility is not captured perfectly, there may be times when we understate it. Consequently, the probability of exceeding the VAR and the size of the 1% tail of the WCS will be understated.

Third, and related to model risk, there is the issue of the tail behaviour of financial series. It is well established that volatility forecasting schemes tend to understate the likelihood and size of extreme moves. This holds true for currencies, commodities, equities and interest rates (to varying degrees). This aspect will also tend to understate the frequency and size of extreme losses. For our specific case, one could infer a distribution from historical series to obtain a better description of the relevant distribution and so capture the tails. This caveat extends naturally to the issue of correlations, where the most important question, perhaps, is whether extreme moves have the same correlation characteristics as the rest of the data. Of course, if correlations in the extremes are higher, we face the risk of understating the WCS risk.

In conclusion, our analysis of the WCS, and further investigation of the caveats discussed above, is important for the study of some of the more recent proposals on the use of internal models and the more lenient capital requirements imposed on "sophisticated" banks and major dealers. For example, the Basle Committee on Banking Supervision has suggested that banks may elect to use internal models to calculate the VAR inherent in their portfolios. This addresses the call from sophisticated participants for more flexibility in their capital requirements, which will include an allowance for the diversifying effects across various holdings in a global portfolio. They need this because they need to remain "capital efficient". More specifically, sophisticated participants believe that inflexible capital requirements make banks over-capitalised, hence reducing their return on capital.

The new degree of flexibility of the Basle Committee has been met with enthusiasm. It is also widely believed that the degree of flexibility which will be afforded to some financial institutions may result in banks flocking to use internal models, regardless of their true level of sophistication. JP Morgan, for example, introduced a "regulatory dataset" version of RiskMetrics in May 1995, entitled RiskMetrics/RD, which meets the Basle Committee requirements and only varies slightly from the original.

There is one common theme to all these proposals and initiatives. Since VAR incorporates a significant "ruin" probability, be it 5% or 1%, there is a need for an additional layer of prudence via a larger capital requirement. The approach commonly used in the context of the VAR measure is to use the VAR number as an indication, and then simply to multiply this measure by some "hysteria factor", taken out of thin air. A factor of three, for example, which is common to many of these approaches, will bring us from the VAR of a portfolio to a capital charge of $3 \times$ VAR.

For example, given a VAR measure of 2.33 standard deviations away from a given portfolio's forecast profit level, the capital charge would be 7 $[2.33 \times 3]$ standard deviations away from μ_p. This additional layer of prudence takes into account a number of factors missing in VAR, such as:

- capitalisation at the 1% VAR will be breached, on average, once every 100 periods, which is too frequent and lenient. Our WCS analysis is especially relevant as a precise measure of prudence;
- there are both estimation risk and model risk in pinpointing volatility and correlation. Our outlined treatment above provides a natural extension to WCS analysis to address this issue.

Our analysis can hence be viewed as a first step on the way to better explaining the "hysteria factor" which should be applied to VAR.

1 *This assumption corresponds to a normalised portfolio return series,* $(R_{p,t+1} - \mu_{p,t})/\sigma_{p,t}$, *where the time subscript signifies the fact that both the conditional mean and the volatility may vary over time. See our concluding remarks for a description of how the analysis there may be extended to accommodate deviations from this assumption.*

2 *As an illustration, we assume that interest rates follow a simple Vasicek process, ie,* $dr = \sigma dz$, *and that European options are priced the usual way. See Jamshidian, F., 1989, "An Exact Option Pricing Formula",* Journal of Finance *44 (1), pp. 205–09.*

12

Model Risk

Emanuel Derman
Goldman Sachs

Many firms now base their bid and offer prices for complex securities on computer models. This article analyses the various assumptions made in using models and highlights some of the risks involved.

Securities markets in the past 20 years have seen the emergence of an astonishingly theoretical approach to valuation, market-making and arbitrage in complex market sectors. Many securities firms now base their bid and offer prices for complex securities on detailed analytic or computer models built by scientists[1]. Most of this theory centres around derivatives, instruments whose value stems from their contractually defined relation to more elementary securities or market parameters. In this generalised sense derivatives encompass many products: index futures and options are derivatives on the underlying index, collateralised mortgage obligations are derivatives on interest and prepayment rates, and we can even regard bonds as derivatives on interest rates. There are many more examples, from convertible bonds to credit derivatives.

Theoretical models abound. In the fixed-income world, the theoretical approach was probably sparked by the shock to bond portfolio values as interest rates jumped in the late 1970s. Duration, convexity and other theoretical risk and sensitivity measures grew in both sophistication and popularity. You can now attend two-day courses in fitting yield curves and extracting zero-coupon rates. The increased interest rate volatility also triggered the development of caps, floors, swaps and swaptions, whose valuation and trading were all heavily model-driven. In the equity world, program trading off the mismatch between actual futures prices and their theoretical fair values was made possible by rapid electronic computation and trading. Equity and fixed-income option trading and structuring grew in part because of the confidence that developed in using the Black-Scholes model and its extensions. The growth in model building and model adoption has also depended on the rapid acceleration in computing power. Computing and modelling have played a sort of leapfrog: more power allowed for fancier models which then ran too slowly, and so in turn required even more power. Advanced users now think of hedging exotic equity index options with standard options, so that one man's derivative has become another man's underlyer[2].

This reliance on models to handle risk carries its own risks. In this article we analyse the assumptions made in using models to value securities, and list the consequent risks.

What are models?

There are at least three different meanings implied by the word *model* in finance, namely:

1. A fundamental model: a system of postulates and data, together with a means of drawing dynamical inferences from them;
2. A phenomenological model: a description or analogy to help visualise something that cannot be directly observed;
3. A statistical model: a regression or best-fit between different data sets.

Most common financial models fall predominantly into one of these categories.

Fundamental models cover models like the Black-Scholes theory, in which a set of postulates about the evolution of stock prices, data about dividend yield and volatility, and a theory of dynamical hedging together allow the derivation of a differential equation for calculating options values. These

This article was written by Emanuel Derman, head of the Quantitative Strategies Group at Goldman Sachs.

are models that attempt to build a fundamental description of some instrument or phenomenon.

Phenomenological models are less radical and more expedient, but may be equally useful. For example, some simple bond option models treat the yield of the underlying bond as being normally distributed. This is a useful picture with a plausible feel to it. But it's only a toy, good in a limited range and not as deep or insightful a description as the Black-Scholes model.

The first two classes of models embody some sort of cause and effect. The last class, statistical models, rely on correlation rather than causation. Users of these models probably hope that the correlation is a consequence of some dynamics whose detailed modelling they are avoiding or postponing. An example is a mortgage prepayment model that regresses prepayment rates against various long- and short-term interest rates and mortgage lifetimes. Modellers imagine homeowners performing certain cost-benefit analyses in deciding whether and when to prepay. Strictly, statistical models describe tendencies rather than dynamics. But knowing tendencies, if they really exist and persist, can be valuable.

Some facts about models

MODELS ASSUME CAUSE AND EFFECT

When you build a valuation model of any type, you are implicitly assuming that the objects of your concern are *causally* related to each other, and that the relationship is *stable*, at least for the time that you intend to apply the model.

FINANCIAL MODELS' VARIABLES MAY BE PEOPLE'S OPINIONS

In the physical sciences, where quantitative modelling originated, the variables in models are universal quantities like time, position and mass that (presumptively) have an existence even when human beings are absent. In contrast, in the financial world, you are dealing with variables that clearly represent human expectations. Even the simplest statement "More risk, more return" refers to *expected* risk and *expected* return, not realised quantities. These are hidden variables: they cannot be directly observed except perhaps by surveying market participants, or by implying their values insofar as they impact other measurable quantities *by way* of a theory or model. Thus, models that use concepts like return or volatility are in most cases assuming a causal and stable connection between the values of these hidden (often unarticulated) variables and security values.

You can start to see how many links there are in the chain from model to usage.

MODELS TRANSLATE OPINIONS INTO VALUES

Model users don't just switch on a model and trade according to its results. Having a valuation model doesn't absolve the model user from thinking about the value of a security. Instead, it makes the security value a dependent variable, and requires the user to think about and estimate the values of other independent variables that are easier to grasp and quantify. Mostly, a security valuation model is a way of translating one's thoughts and intuitions about these other variables into a dollar value for the security. For example, the Black-Scholes options valuation model asks a user for an estimate of future volatility, and then translates that estimate into a fair option value. Variations in volatility are much smoother and less dramatic than variations in option value. In this way, good models make it easier to extrapolate security values known under a limited range of market conditions to more distant regimes.

UNCERTAINTY IS FUNDAMENTAL

The overwhelming unknown in financial models is certainty. In the physical sciences, the mathematics of statistics and distributions and finally, the calculus of stochastic processes, made their appearance late in the drama. In the financial world, they are the first actors on stage. Everyone expects to predict the position of a man-made satellite, let alone Newton's falling apple, with high precision. No one expects to predict the value of a stock in the future with much precision at all.

MODELS NEED DOMAIN KNOWLEDGE

The financial domain is a nitty-gritty world filled with stocks that trade only at certain times and at discrete ticks. Usable models exist for some particular sector with particular trading rules, settlement conventions, and other practicalities. Models and modellers need intimate knowledge of the domain they are working in. Financial modelling is as much about content as it is about technical skills.

FINANCIAL MODELS ARE SOFTWARE

Financial models most often end up being implemented as computer programs, either because they need to do many simple things rapidly and repeatedly, or because they need to draw on large amounts of stored information, or because no simple analytic solution to the mathematics is available, and so numerical techniques are required. In addition, much of the gain from using models comes from applying them to portfolios of securities. The handling of portfolios on a computer requires the construction of databases, user interfaces and price feeds. So, both the model itself and the mechanism for employing it involve building software.

A MODEL IS ONLY A MODEL...
The real world is often an inchoate swirl of actions, occurrences, facts and figures. There are more things than we've even thought of naming or categorising. So, even the finest model is only a model of the phenomena, and not the real thing. A model is just a toy, though occasionally a very good one, in which case people call it a theory. A good scientific toy can't do everything, and shouldn't even try to be totally realistic. It should represent as naturally as possible the most essential variables of the system, and the relationships between them, and allow the investigation of cause and effect. A good toy doesn't reproduce every feature of the real object; instead, it illustrates for its intended audience the qualities of the original object most important to them. A child's toy train makes noises and flashes lights; an adult's might contain a working miniature steam engine. Similarly, good models should aim to do only a few important things well.

Constructing models

You can understand the things that go wrong with models if you understand how they are developed. Model building is as much art and apprenticeship as engineering and science. Nevertheless, it's possible to delineate some of the procedures involved in constructing a financial valuation model:

❑ Understand the securities, the markets and the way market participants think about valuation and risk.

❑ Isolate the most important variables that participants use to analyse value and risk.

❑ Decide which of these variables are susceptible to mathematical modelling.

❑ Separate the dependent variables from the independent variables. Also decide which are directly measurable and which are more in the nature of human expectations and therefore only indirectly measurable.

❑ For some variables, the uncertainty in their future value has little effect on security values[3], and they can be treated as known. For other variables, uncertainty is critical. Specify the variables that can be treated as deterministic and those that must be regarded as stochastic.

❑ Develop a qualitative picture that represents how the independent variables affect the dependent ones.

❑ Think about how to get the market values of independent observable variables, and how to deduce the implied values of indirectly measurable ones.

❑ Formulate the picture mathematically. Decide what stochastic process best describes the evolution of the independent stochastic variables.

❑ Consider the difficulties of solving the model, and then perhaps simplify it to make the solution as easy as possible. But only reluctantly give up content for the sake of an easy or elegant analytical solution.

❑ Develop a scheme for analytic or numerical solution.

❑ Program the model.

❑ Test it.

❑ Embed it in the software and organisational environment.

The types of model risk

INAPPLICABILITY OF MODELLING
The most fundamental of risks is that modelling is just not applicable. For example, it's possible that forecasting stock price movements is more like forecasting political occurrences than like projecting spacecraft trajectories, with psychology and gamesmanship more relevant than mathematics. There's always a temptation to think that complex mathematics has an applicability of its own, but you need a vision of how things work and interconnect before you use mathematics to represent it. You need the analogy or picture first; mathematics is largely the language you represent it in.

In terms of risk control, you're worse off thinking you have a model and relying on it than in simply realising there isn't one.

INCORRECT MODEL
At some level, all models are ultimately incorrect. But even without being perfectionist, here are some of the ways in which model development can go wrong:

❑ You may not have taken account of all the factors that affect valuation. For example, you may have assumed a one-factor model of interest rates. This is probably a reasonable approximation for valuing Treasury bonds, but much less reasonable for valuing options on the slope of the yield curve.

❑ You may have incorrectly assumed certain stochastic variables can be approximated as deterministic (see footnote 3).

❑ You may have assumed incorrect dynamics for a factor. For example, you might have modelled bond *prices* as lognormally distributed for the sake of analytic simplicity. In practice, bond *yields* are more likely to be lognormal. This discrepancy is worse for short-maturity bonds, but may be forgivable for long maturities.

❑ You may have made incorrect assumptions about relationships. For example, you may have ignored the correlation between corporate credit spreads and corporate stock prices in valuing convertible bonds. Is this correlation important for the particular property of convertible bonds you are interested in extracting from your model?

❑ The model you developed may be inappropriate under current market conditions, or some of its assumptions may have become invalid. For example, interest rate volatility is relatively unimportant in currency option pricing at low interest rate volatilities, but may become critical during exchange rate crises.

❑ A model may be correct in an idealised world (with no trading costs, say), but incorrect or approximate when realities (like market frictions) are taken into account.

❑ A model may be "correct in principle" but the market may disagree in the short run. This is really another way of saying the model is limited, in the sense that it didn't take account of other short-term factors (including market sentiment) which can influence price.

❑ A model may be correct, but the data driving it (rates, volatilities, correlations, spreads, and so on) may be badly estimated.

❑ A model may be reasonable, but the world itself may be unstable. What's a good model today may be inappropriate tomorrow. For example, the sentiment about interest rates may be linked to gold prices one year and to oil prices the next.

CORRECT MODEL, INCORRECT SOLUTION

You can make a technical mistake in finding the analytic solution to a model. This can happen through subtlety or carelessness. There are some well-known published errors or misunderstandings in the case of some complex derivatives, leading to so-called model arbitrage. It takes careful testing to ensure that an analytic solution behaves consistently for all reasonable market parameters.

CORRECT MODEL, INAPPROPRIATE USE

There are always implicit assumptions behind a model and its solution method. But human beings have limited foresight and great imagination, so that, inevitably, a model will be used in ways its creator never intended. This is especially true in trading environments, where not enough time can be spent on making interfaces fail-safe, but it's also a matter of principle: you just cannot foresee everything. So, even a "correct" model, "correctly" solved, can lead to problems. The more complex the model, the greater this possibility.

As an example, most Monte Carlo valuation models require the choice of a number of simulation paths and steps. Speed requires few simulations, while accuracy demands many. Different securities require different simulation parameters to get a reasonable answer. A user who values a high-variance security with the same parameters as a low-variance security can get inaccurate and even biased results.

The only practical defence is to have informed and patient users who clearly comprehend both the model and the method of solution, and, even more important, understand what can go wrong. In the above example, one should start by valuing the security with a variety of simulation parameters, and perhaps more than one solution method, to examine the accuracy and convergence of the results[4].

BADLY APPROXIMATED SOLUTION

You may have errors in the numerical solution to a correctly formulated problem, or there may simply be natural limits to the accuracy of some approximation scheme. Finite difference solution methods can be unstable, inaccurate or converge slowly. Only careful and knowledgeable testing can help here.

SOFTWARE AND HARDWARE BUGS

Many of the worst risks centre around implementation. These days, models are sophisticated programs, thousands of lines long, with rich data structures that are used to perform detailed computation. Models undergo revisions by people who were not the original authors. Equally important in making them useful, models need user interfaces, position databases, trade entry screens and electronic price feeds. Programming mistakes in any of these areas can lead to widespread and hard-to-detect errors. You can make errors in logic, rounding, counting the days between dates or the coupons to maturity, to name only a few possibilities. In addition there are occasional hardware flaws, like the widely publicised Pentium floating point error.

Similarly, as programmers strive for greater execution speed, the model is at risk from the natural tension between clarity of style and code optimisation.

UNSTABLE DATA

Many models need the future value of some volatility or correlation. This value is often based on historical data. But history may not provide a good estimate of future value, and historical values may themselves be unstable and vary strongly with the sampling period.

Avoiding model risk

There is no magical strategy for avoiding risk, but the following general guidelines based on experience in our group at Goldman Sachs may be helpful.

REGARD MODELS AS INTERDISCIPLINARY ENDEAVOURS

Models are generally not back-of-the-envelope formulas handed over to "coders" to turn into executable instructions. Modelling is multidisciplinary: it touches on the practicality of doing business, on financial theory, on mathematical modelling and computer science, on computer implementation and on the construction of user interfaces. Models end up as computational computer programs embedded in human and machine interfaces that are themselves computer programs. The risks lie in the knowledge of the business, the applicability of the financial model, the mathematics and numerical analysis used to solve it, the computer science used to implement and present it, and in the transmission of information and knowledge accurately from one part of the model, in the larger sense of the word, to the next. It helps to be knowledgeable in all of these areas in order to notice an error and then diagnose it.

But, in many firms, model users are traders, salespeople or capital markets personnel who may be physically and organisationally removed from the model creators. Furthermore, the model implementors are programmers who are often similarly separated from the model theorists. To avoid risk, it's important to have modellers, programmers and users who all work closely together, understand each other's domains well enough to know what constitutes a warning symptom, and have a good strategy for testing a model and its limits. Too much specialisation is harmful. In our group, the modellers themselves write production code for insertion into risk-management systems. Programmers and modellers work in closely-knit teams around a particular product or business area. Informed model users are particularly invaluable.

Because of the large role of computing, we also try to accentuate the importance of software engineering as a discipline.

TEST COMPLEX MODELS IN SIMPLE CASES FIRST

Test models against simple known solutions. If you can solve a model in some simple case, by constructing a tree diagram or solving some equation, compare your computer solution to the simple solution and make sure they're exactly identical.

TEST THE MODEL'S BOUNDARIES

Often, a new model overlaps on older and simpler models. In that case, test the boundaries. If it's an option model, make sure that when the option is deep in-the-money it behaves like a forward. For a convertible bond model, guarantee that it behaves like a straight bond when it's deep out-of-the-money. Too many complex models go wrong because complexity obscured the error in the simple part of the model. One of the most avoidable mistakes I saw was a convertible bond model that innovatively priced many of the options features embedded in convertible bonds, but sometimes counted the number of coupons to expiration incorrectly.

DON'T IGNORE SMALL DISCREPANCIES

If there are any small discrepancies noticed by users or programmers, don't ignore them. Track down their origin. Small disagreements often serve as warnings of potentially large disagreements and errors under other scenarios.

PROVIDE A GOOD USER INTERFACE

Thorough testing is easier with a flexible and friendly interface. We spend much time building interfaces that allow what-if analysis and graphical display of the results of a model under many different scenarios. Even after many years of use, some errors only become apparent when you notice kinks in a graphical display of the model's results.

DIFFUSE THE MODEL SLOWLY OUTWARDS

It is impossible to avoid errors during model development, especially when they are created under trading floor duress. Therefore, in addition to being careful, it's important to have an orderly procedure for disseminating the use of a model.

So, after the model is built, the developer tests it extensively. Thereafter, other developers "play" with it too. Next, traders who depend on the model for pricing and hedging use it. Finally, it's released to salespeople. After a suitably long period in which most wrinkles are ironed out, it's given to appropriate clients. This slow diffusion helps eliminate many risks, slowly but steadily.

PRIDE OF OWNERSHIP

One of the best defences against modelling error is to ensure that both models and systems are built by people who like doing it, and who take pride in their work.

1 *Or ex-scientists, depending on your opinion about what they do.*

2 *This is not as unprecedented as it sounds. Money itself is a derivative that gets its value from its convertibility into more consumable assets.*

3 *For example, in valuing stock options, the future uncertainty in interest rates is largely unimportant because option value varies smoothly with rate and so the uncertainty averages out. There is consequently no need to know the volatility of interest rates. This is not the case with bond options, whose payouts vary sharply and non-linearly with interest rates.*

4 *The following verbatim quote from someone building a model conveys a sense of the conflict involved in releasing it to users: "It's always a dilemma to release a (model)... If I do not release it, and tell people to contact me to price... options... people think I am holding back. When I tell people they should be very careful in choosing methods and parameters, they always say 'I know, I know' and get a little impatient. I guess one just has to put some trust in those people who use them."*

13

Improving on VAR

Mark Garman
Financial Engineering Associates

DelVar is a mechanism for assessing the potential impact of a trade on a firm's value-at-risk. How does it work and what are the benefits it offers?

Analytic variance-covariance value-at-risk (VAR) is an established technique for measuring exposure to market-based financial risk (Smithson, 1996i and 1996ii). Given a description of the market characteristics and the user's portfolio, the objective of VAR is to determine how much value might be lost over a given time, with a given level of probability, in a given currency. For example, JP Morgan's RiskMetrics provides a comprehensive analytical methodology for assessing VAR.[1]

This form of VAR begins by replacing a portfolio, or the trades within it, with a set of cash flows reflecting those trades' current values and their risk attributes. (This process is sometimes separately referred to as "shredding" the trades.) The resulting cashflows (which can be in any currency, commodity or other price risk source) are then aligned upon certain "vertices" representing standardised maturities and credit levels for the markets in which the cashflows are traded, again preserving their value and risk characteristics. (For example, six-month Libor Deutschmark and two-year dollar swap market flows might each represent a vertex.) The complete process of translating a trade into vertex cashflows is called "mapping". Having thus arrived at the "cashflow map" (ie the net result of mapping a portfolio of trades), one next combines this map with a covariance matrix whose index set is the set of vertices, which yields the desired result, the VAR number.

Yet after VAR is assessed, there remains an important question: "What can one do to reduce VAR?" In this article, we introduce an approximation mechanism for improving VAR, referred to here as DelVaR.

To present the issues in more concrete terms, consider what feedback the VAR calculation should provide to the trading activity of an institution. Which new trades will improve VAR and which will degrade it? And precisely how will we implement trading limits based upon VAR, when such limits evidently depend not only upon the proposed trades themselves but also on the way in which these trades interact with the existing portfolio of the institution? Unfortunately, the non-linear nature of VAR requires us to create a new portfolio incorporating the proposed trades, and then reassess the VAR of this augmented portfolio. Among other things, this means that the VAR limits imposed upon any proposed new trade necessitate the re-evaluation of all trades (perhaps tens of thousands of these) in the institution's revised portfolio, which can be a demanding process.

The DelVaR approach offers a more economical means for evaluating any new proposed trade in terms of its effect on institutional VAR, without the extensive recalculation of total VAR. This permits the realisation of rapid evaluation of candidate trades, so that real-time VAR trading limits become practical.

Also, by adding one additional feature to the DelVaR mechanism, called "trade normalisation", it becomes possible to determine not just whether certain trades will increase or decrease VAR but, indeed, what relative ranking those trades should enjoy for VAR reduction purposes.

The maths of DelVaR

In this section we discuss the mathematical basis of the DelVaR construct. As a first step, we establish appropriate notation. Suppose that:

❑ P is the existing institutional portfolio of trades;

❑ A_i is the portfolio consisting solely of the ith candidate trade, for $i=1,2,\ldots,N$;
❑ $p=m(P)$ is a (column) vector of cashflow amounts, where $m()$ is a cashflow mapping function[2], and the index set of the resulting vector is the set of vertices;
❑ $a_i=m(A_i)$ is a (column) vector of cashflow amounts for the ith candidate trade; and
❑ Q is a variance-covariance matrix scaled by the square of the VAR probability standard deviations (for example, approximately 1.64^2 for the 95% confidence level), the indexes of the matrix also being the vertex index set.

Using the definitions above, the VAR calculation of the portfolio P would be given as:

$$VAR \equiv \upsilon = \sqrt{p'Qp}$$

where the prime means transpose.[3] We now consider the standard approach, namely to perform a new evaluation of the VAR of the augmented portfolio $R_i=P+A_i$ obtained after the ith candidate trade is added to the existing portfolio. The "brute-force" method then requires a complete recalculation of VAR, namely:

$$w_i = \sqrt{r_i'Qr_i}$$

where $r_i=m(R_i)$ is the cashflow map of the augmented portfolio.[4] The test of VAR improvement occurs by examining the difference (w_i-v). When this quantity is negative, the candidate trade will improve institutional VAR; when positive, it will degrade VAR.

Compared with this standard method, the DelVaR approach offers a more economical means of evaluating (approximately) VAR improvement. The mathematical basis of DelVaR is as follows.

Consider the cashflow map vector of a candidate trade, but scaled by the small positive quantity ε, so that VAR is now given by:

$$w_i(\varepsilon) = \sqrt{r_i'(\varepsilon)Qr_i(\varepsilon)}$$

where $r_i=p+\varepsilon a_i$. If we now perform a Taylor series expansion of VAR around $\varepsilon=0$, we have:

$$\begin{aligned} w_i(\varepsilon) &= w_i(0)+\varepsilon\left[\nabla w_i(0)\cdot a_i\right]+o(\varepsilon^2) \\ &= \upsilon+\varepsilon(\mathrm{DelVaR}\cdot a_i)+o(\varepsilon^2) \end{aligned}$$

where ∇ refers to the usual "del" operator, or derivative vector (where the vector index is again vertices), giving rise to the "DelVaR" label. From the latter equation, we see that if ε is sufficiently small (and positive, since we are adding a positive amount of the new candidate trade to our portfolio), the improvement of VAR will be governed by the sign and magnitude of the second term of the last equation above; the higher order terms ($o(\varepsilon^2)$) can reasonably be ignored, provided e is sufficiently small.

But is ε "sufficiently small" in our context? In most institutions, the answer is normally "yes"; most often, the size of a candidate trade is insignificant relative to the size of the then-current portfolio holdings (as perhaps measured via aggregate cashflow volume). This is because the steady-state condition of an institution must be governed by the normal queuing principle, namely, that if K trades are performed each day, having average tenor of T days, then the size of the accumulated "book" (portfolio) will be approximately KT times as large as the average trade size. For example, if an institution is executing 10 trades a day with an average tenor of 30 days, then it will have a portfolio size roughly 10 × 30 = 300 times as large as the average individual trade size.

Nevertheless, we note that the incremental VAR as calculated via the DelVaR method is still an approximation, due to ignoring the higher order terms. Therefore, the standard approach and the DelVaR approach may yield slightly different results. Also, when an exceptionally large trade is under consideration, a standard before-and-after VAR calculation may be appropriate, as the DelVaR approximation could then break down. However, the approximation will typically be quite accurate for almost all of the small to somewhat-above-average trade sizes in most trading institutions, unless trading volume is quite low or the average trade has an exceptionally short tenor.

Direct calculation shows that:

$$\mathrm{DelVaR} = \nabla w_i(0) = \nabla\upsilon = p'Q/\upsilon$$

where $\upsilon=w_i(0)$, noting that this quantity is independent of the index i.

Correspondingly, it is important to note that the DelVaR vector depends only upon the current portfolio, and not upon the choice of any specific candidate trade. This means that, unlike the standard incremental VAR calculation, DelVaR need only be calculated once during those trading intervals over which the institutional portfolio is substantially unchanged. The incremental effect of any new trade is then approximated as:

$$\text{Incremental VAR} = \mathrm{DelVaR}\cdot a_i = \left[p'Q/\upsilon\right]\cdot a_i$$

which requires no recalculation of the new total portfolio; it is simply an inner product of the

DelVaR vector with the cashflow vector of the proposed trade. Note also that the same DelVaR vector works for all candidate trades, ie, it does not have to be calculated for more than the given portfolio P. These features make DelVaR particularly appropriate for establishing VAR-based trading limits over relatively long periods (eg, one day), without significant recomputation of VAR quantities.

The normalisation of trades

The above describes a means by which the sign of the marginal effects of individual candidate trades can be ascertained, ie, simply whether they will increase or decrease VAR, but it does not provide a means for comparing the relative amounts of VAR influence between candidate trades. This is because any single trade could be arbitrarily doubled, halved or otherwise scaled in size, so that comparison of magnitudes between candidate trades becomes meaningless. To accomplish comparability in risk contribution, it is first desirable to ensure that the candidate trades are scaled in such a way as to become comparable via some alternative criterion. In other words, we seek the VAR increment "per unit" of a trade. This may be accomplished via "normalisation".

That is, since a trade's size may be arbitrarily scaled, we must consider when one candidate trade would constitute a good substitute for another such trade. Once the candidate trades are scaled in such a way as to become otherwise "comparable" among themselves (ie, "normalised"), then it becomes sensible to assert that one candidate trade or another is to be preferred for the magnitude of its corresponding VAR contribution. The key is properly to define and implement the nature of such alternative comparability.

We suggest six methods of normalisation: cashflow, VAR, return, price, capital and notional. Each method involves dividing each candidate trade's cashflow vector ai by the positive scalar number λ_i (its "norm"), where this quantity is calculated in a manner (detailed below) depending upon the trade in question and the method selected. It is of course a matter of risk management policy as to which type of norm is chosen.[5]

❑ *Cashflow normalisation (VAR change per unit of cashflow)* In this method, some simple mathematical norm for the cashflow vector is associated with each candidate trade. If $a_i = (a_{i1}, a_{i2}, \ldots, a_{in})$ is the vector of cashflows, then the norm may be defined by:

$$\lambda_i = \|a_i\| \equiv \sqrt{\sum_j a_{ij}^2}$$

(cashflow length) or

$$\lambda_i = \|a_i\| \equiv \sum_j |a_{ij}|$$

(sum of absolute cashflow values) or

$$\lambda_i = \|a_i\| \equiv \max_j\{|a_{ij}|\}$$

(maximal cashflow). Each of these sub-cases may provide a slightly different result, but all are dictated merely by the sizes of the mapped cashflows which correspond to a candidate trade.

❑ *VAR normalisation (VAR change per unit of trade VAR)* In this method, the scaling is performed according to the VAR inherent in the candidate trade itself. (In effect, each candidate trade is evaluated on the basis of equating the risk – as measured via VAR – as if the candidate trade were held in isolation.) Accordingly, the norm is then calculated as:

$$\lambda_i \equiv \sqrt{a_i' Q a_i}$$

where Q is the scaled variance-covariance matrix described more fully in the previous section.

❑ *Return normalisation (VAR change per unit of return)* In this case, the norm λ_i is selected according to the anticipated future returns accruing to the investment in the candidate trade. For example, one might cumulate the net present value of all future revenues and payments of the candidate trade, as one such measure of future economic value.[6] Closely related is:

❑ *Price normalisation (VAR change per unit of price)* Here, λ_i is set equal to the market price of the candidate trade. This equates candidate trades according to their current mark-to-market, ie, value by present market standards.

❑ *Capital normalisation (VAR change per unit of capital)* In this approach, λ_i is set equal to the regulatory or other amount of capital which must be allocated to sustain that trade. For example, the Bank for International Settlements guidelines provide formulas involving certain amounts of capital underlying certain trade types.

❑ *Notional normalisation (VAR change per arbitrary unit of trade)* In this approach, we employ the "notional value", ie, an otherwise arbitrary market or other convention on the number of units involved in the candidate trade. For example, swap contracts are typically denominated in amounts involving $1 of principal payment, regardless of the swap interest rates involved. Because this norm is completely arbi-

1. Preferred DelVaR implementation

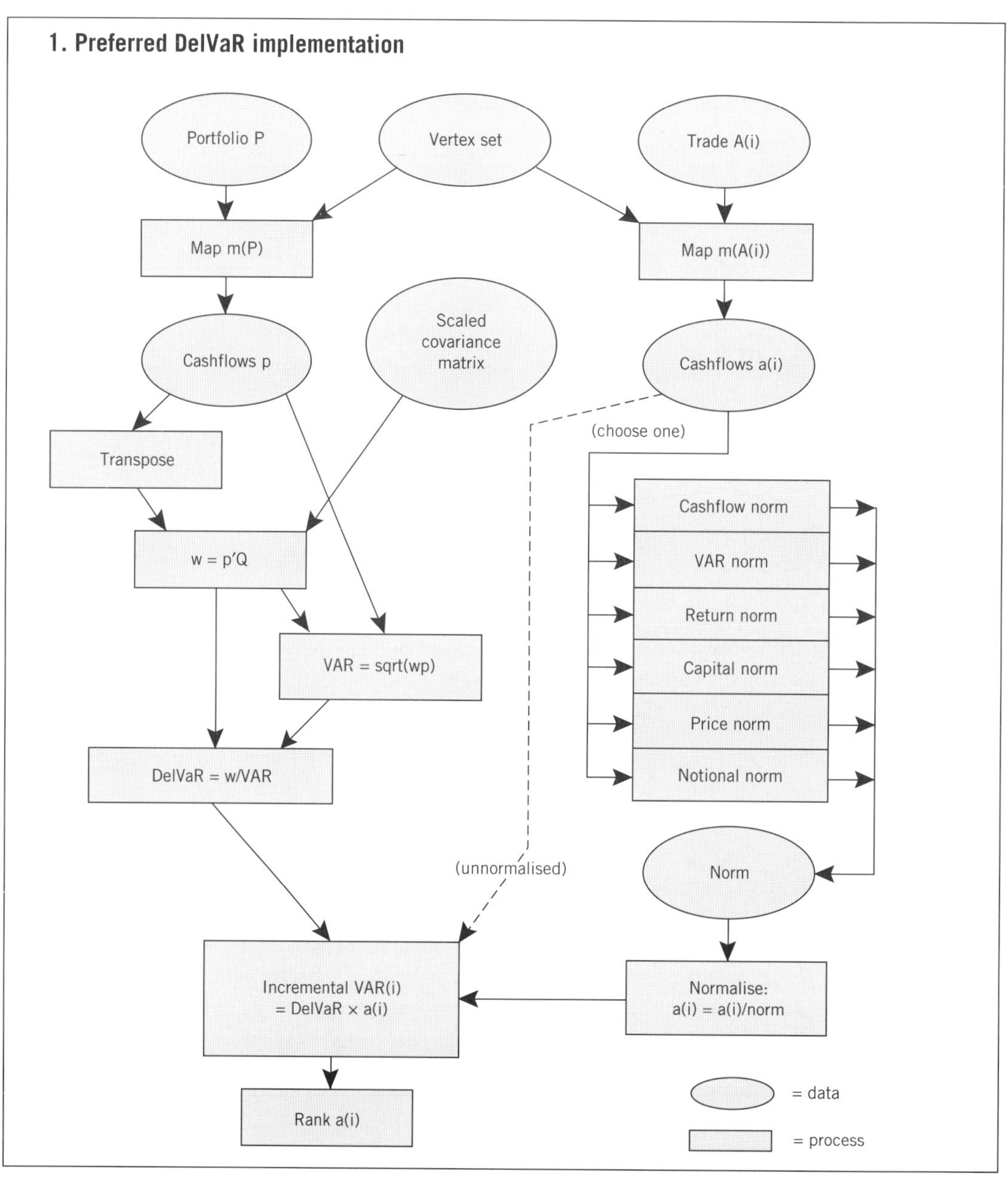

trary, it serves as a catch-all category for trade normalisation.

The importance of normalisation is that it permits a ranking of the relative risk-reducing qualities of various candidate trades. By removing the "size" issue through normalisation, trades now become subject to comparison among themselves, for risk reduction purposes. Whatever norm is selected, the ranking is then based upon the comparison of the quantities:

$$\mathrm{DelVaR} \cdot (a_i / \lambda_i) = [p'Q / \upsilon] \cdot (a_i / \lambda_i)$$

Again, we note that the same DelVaR quantity is used throughout, regardless of the (normalised) candidate trade.

Implementation

We now provide a more complete view of the preferred means of implementing the DelVaR and normalisation processes. If, say, a daily VAR cycle is selected, then the DelVaR and VAR computations may be constructed at the beginning of the day (perhaps via overnight aggregation and calculation) by analysing the complete portfolio of the financial institution. (Note that there is only a very small marginal effort required to create and store the DelVaR vector in the process of computing VAR, as shown in Figure 1.)

Subsequently, the VAR limit computation of any proposed trade during the day is done as per the right-hand side of the figure: first, the cashflow map of the proposed trade is constructed; second, ideally (but optionally), the trade is normalised using one of the methods described above; and third, the inner product of the proposed trade's cashflow map and DelVaR is computed. This latter quantity discloses whether the corresponding trade is VAR-increasing or VAR decreasing and, if properly normalised, also makes a meaningful statement about the relative magnitude of such VAR augmentation.

Conclusion

The DelVaR and normalisation processes provide a way of determining the signs and relative magnitudes, respectively, of changes to portfolio VAR resulting from proposed trades. The inner product of DelVaR and the cashflow map of any proposed normalised trade provides a good approximation of the per-unit impact that a proposed trade will have, without necessitating a full recalculation of augmented portfolio VAR. DelVaR is therefore useful for implementing real-time VAR trading limits and other related calculations which must rapidly assess the risk management impact of a proposed trade. As a result of using the DelVaR concept, the effect of VAR technology upon trading activities becomes much more direct, immediate and informative.

1 *See* RiskMetrics – Technical Document, *1995.*

2 *The cashflow mapping function* m() *embodies the mechanisms which transform cashflows arising in the trades of a portfolio into cashflows located at the vertices, for which volatility, correlation and yield data are then known; see* RiskMetrics Technical Document.

3 *Compare with equation on page 29 of* RiskMetrics Technical Document.

4 *A linear cashflow map has the property that* $m(A + B) = m(A) + m(B)$ *for all trades and portfolios* A *and* B. *Note that if linearity of the map function is present, we can speed the process of incorporating the new trade* A_i *by merging only the mapped cashflows. At present, however, even RiskMetrics contains non-linear maps, eg, for floating-rate notes.*

5 *This policy can be addressed by asking "What is the scarcest resource being employed in a trade?" If this is "lines", then perhaps cashflow normalisation might be indicated; if it is capital, certainly capital normalisation should be considered.*

6 *To be a valid norm, this must always be positive.*

BIBLIOGRAPHY

JP Morgan, 1995, *RiskMetrics Technical Document*, 3rd edition, New York.

Smithson, C. and L. Minton, 1996i, "Value-at-Risk", *Risk*, 9, 1, pp. 25–7, reprinted as Chapter 2 of this volume.

Smithson, C. and L. Minton, 1996ii, "Value-at-Risk (2)", *Risk*, 9, 2, pp. 28–9, reprinted as Chapter 3 of this volume.

14

More Haste, Less Precision

Gary Robinson
BZW

This article looks at ways in which risk managers can strike the right balance between speed and accuracy in measuring the risk of a derivatives portfolio.

A still widespread practice in the risk management of derivatives is to limit the exposure of a derivatives portfolio to each of the "Greeks" of the portfolio: delta, gamma, rho, vega etc. However, there are problems with this approach. In particular, for certain options, the Greeks are somewhat meaningless. For example, for options very close to expiry or to barriers, gamma is arbitrarily large, so that inclusion of these options would certainly result in the spurious breaking of any gamma limit. How do we aggregate the vega risks arising from changing volatility and the gamma risk associated with convexity? This problem can lead, *inter alia*, to the under-utilisation of capital. If the gamma limit were under-utilised while the vega limit was fully utilised, then it would seem sensible to be able to reallocate capital from gamma risk to vega risk. Unfortunately, under the system of Greek limits, there is no way of knowing how much a unit of gamma is worth in terms of units of vega, since these risk measures are not fungible. What is needed is a method of measuring the total risk of a derivatives portfolio which automatically assigns due importance to each of the different risks which contribute to this total.

In principle, the concept and methodology of value-at-risk provide a sound basis on which to address this problem, since they provide a probability-based measure of a portfolio's potential loss, regardless of the composition of the portfolio: the concept is as applicable to a derivatives portfolio as to a portfolio of cash instruments. However, this is not always appreciated. As the methodology has gained acceptance, it has sometimes been claimed that VAR is ill-suited to analysing the risk of derivatives portfolios and that the techniques of "stress testing" and "scenario testing" are more appropriate. This misperception may be partly accounted for by the fact that one of the main manifestations of the VAR technique, JP Morgan's RiskMetrics measurement system, has been unable to capture the risks from options.

Two essential qualities for risk measurement systems are accuracy and speed of calculation. But there is a trade-off between the two because, for any computing technology, the user must decide how much accuracy to sacrifice for increased speed. The precise trade-off will also depend on the composition and dynamics of the portfolio. The smaller and simpler the portfolio, the more favourable the trade-off. For larger and more complex portfolios, it may be impossible to achieve a minimum degree of accuracy without sacrificing speed, and vice versa. So financial institutions have chosen different points along the trade-off.

However, a minimum frequency of calculation is required for an actively traded portfolio. For example, it seems pointless to perform stress tests as infrequently as once a month, as is apparently the case in some institutions: what is the point of evaluating potential exposure once a month when the risk profile of the portfolio changes rapidly but is unobserved in the intervening periods? Again, there is a trade-off: the more frequently potential loss is calculated, the greater the chance of spotting a problem. However, at a given level of trading activity, the greater the frequency of calculation, the less likely it is that the incremental calculation will reveal anything new. It follows that the minimum frequency of calculation should depend on how actively the portfolio is traded and hence the speed with which its risk profile is expected to change.

MORE HASTE, LESS PRECISION

Two paradigms are often invoked in the measurement of derivative risk: VAR and stress-testing. These can be defined as follows:

❑ *VAR* A probability-based measure of risk in which the level of confidence is high, though not extremely high, for example 95% or 99% but not 99.99%. Probability-based means that the measure is based on the statistical distribution of the portfolio's profit and loss, as far as this can be measured.

❑ *Stress-testing* The worst possible loss from a set of scenarios to which probabilities are not assigned. This measure of potential loss is not based on the probability distribution of the profit and loss, but the scenarios are deliberately chosen to include "extreme" changes in the underlying "risk factors" that determine portfolio value.

Thus, VAR measures the potential loss which is likely to be exceeded perhaps once every month or once every quarter. The motivation for choosing such confidence levels is quite compelling: the 95th or 99th percentiles for profit and loss are quite far into the loss tail of the profit and loss distribution and are therefore good risk measures, while beyond these percentiles there may be very few observations of market prices and hence more extreme profit and loss percentiles may be difficult to estimate with any accuracy. Indeed, many decades of data are needed to estimate these probabilities with any accuracy. But this is often not available, and even if it were, it would come from different and irrelevant economic regimes. However, we are interested in looking beyond the 99th percentile, because the events beyond this percentile are the ones which could sink a financial institution. For this reason, we need to measure the potential loss in extreme circumstances, without regard to their exact probability of occurrence. Events such as the stock market crash of 1987 and the European exchange rate mechanism currency crisis in 1992 are certainly beyond the 99th percentile, occurring perhaps once a year or once every 10 years.

Any measure of a portfolio's potential loss takes a set of values for the risk factors (ie the variables that determine portfolio value), evaluates the profit and loss of the portfolio at these values of the factors, and chooses one of the resulting profit and loss figures to be the measure of potential loss. Therefore, all VAR and stress-testing measures of potential loss can be described in terms of the following framework. Let the value of the portfolio be $V(x)$, where x_i, $i = 1 \ldots n$ are the risk factors. Then the measure of potential loss of the portfolio can be expressed as:

$$L = F(dx)$$

where $dx_i = \{x_i' - x_i\}$, $i = 1 \ldots M$ are innovations in the risk factors and $F(.)$ is related to $V(.)$ in some way. The variety of different measures of potential loss arises from two sources:

❑ the particular way in which the dx, ie, the scenarios, are generated;

❑ the form of $F(.)$ – ie, the method used to revalue the portfolio.

Thus, any of the methods proposed for measuring the potential loss for a derivatives portfolio can be defined with respect to these two dimensions. We now describe in more detail the alternative ways in which dx may be generated and the form which $F(.)$ may take.

Choosing the scenarios

❑ *Monte Carlo simulation* Changes in the risk factors are generated using a multivariate statistical distribution, the parameters of which are estimated using a sample of historical changes.

❑ *Historical (key events)* In this method, actual historical changes in the risk factors are directly used to revalue the portfolio. Such data could comprise market rates and prices for only a few key market crises observed in history – particularly recent history – such as the exchange rate mechanism crisis of 1992. This method is very widely applied.

❑ *Historical (long histories)* An alternative to the above method, where the portfolio is revalued using a long history of daily market rates and prices.

❑ *Future scenarios* A set of future scenarios is devised which capture what are thought to be the most relevant/plausible risks for the portfolio in question.

❑ *Scenario matrix* A range for each risk factor is chosen which represents the maximum over which that factor could plausibly change. Thus the range should include the largest changes in prices and rates seen in recent financial history – say, the past 25 years – if not before. On the other hand, there would be no point in setting the range way beyond the biggest moves seen in recent history. For example, setting the range for movement in the S&P 500 or FTSE 100 indexes to more than twice the move seen in the 1987 crash would probably be overly cautious. This is largely a matter of risk preference and therefore subjective. Having determined a range for each of M risk factors, N points along each factor's range are selected and the portfolio is revalued at a sub-set (possibly all) of the points (of which there are M.N) in the resulting M-dimensional cuboid.

The method of revaluation

We have now looked at the choice of scenarios; how can we now revalue our portfolio at these scenarios? There are three alternatives:

❑ *Exact valuation* As the name suggests, this method uses the exact pricing formulae for the derivatives in the portfolio.

❑ *Taylor expansion (using local Greeks)* The profit and loss of the portfolio of derivative instruments is calculated as a Taylor expansion around the current values of risk factors, ie, the Greeks are evaluated at the current risk factor values. Thus, the change in value of the portfolio can be approximated by a Taylor expansion:

$$dV_t = \Sigma\Delta_i dx_i + \tfrac{1}{2}\,\Sigma\Gamma_i (dx_i)^2 + \Sigma\Lambda_i d\sigma_i + \Theta dt + \ldots \qquad (1)$$

where:

Δ_i is the portfolio's delta with respect to risk factor i;

Γ_i is the portfolio's gamma with respect to risk factor i;

Λ_i is the portfolio's vega (or lambda) with respect to factor i volatility;

Θ is the portfolio's time decay.

Each of the Greeks is a local sensitivity of V(.) with respect to a risk factor. Higher order terms and correlation effects may also be included to improve the accuracy of the approximation.

The example in Table 1 illustrates the use of this method in analysing the market risk of a long position in a single bond option and, specifically, the VAR which gives 98% confidence. The distribution of profit and loss is simulated using a local Taylor expansion (ie one which uses the current values of delta, gamma and vega – see "Data on option" in the table) by feeding into Equation (1) simulated values of the risk factors (the bond yield and yield volatility) and producing a distribution of values for profit and loss. The table also shows, under the heading "Risk calculations", the resulting estimate of the 98% daily VAR of this option position, ie the measure of potential loss over one day which we can be 98% confident will not be exceeded. This is equal to £72,500. Also given is a breakdown of the different risks which make up this total risk figure: delta risk, ie, the risk of the option, assuming that its value varies in proportion with the underlying bond price, is £75,000; gamma or convexity of the option reduces risk by £5,000, since a long position benefits from large moves in the underlying

Table 1. Example: call option on £10 million March 1997 long gilt future

Data on option[1]

Price		= 2.938
Estimated delta (for change in yield)	Δ	= –380.2
Estimated gamma (for change in yield)	Γ	= 26440
Estmated vega (for change in volatility of yield)	Λ	= 14.95

1 Rho is assumed to be zero

Risk calculations

(a) Market value of position = £293,800

(b) The 98% daily VAR is £72,500, and is arrived at as follows:

	Delta risk	£75,000
Less	Convexity risk	–£5,000
Plus	Volatility risk	£2,500
Equals	**Value-at-risk**	**£72,500**

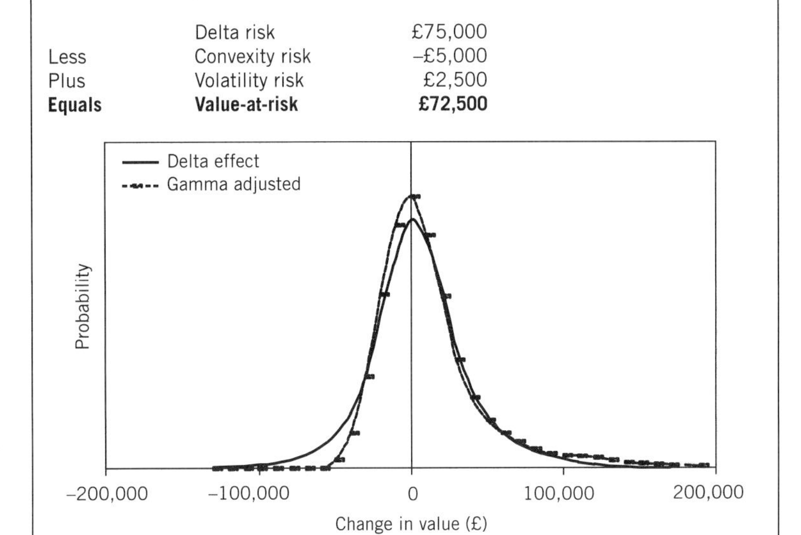

bond price; and vega risk, which measures the loss we could experience from a fall in implied volatility, adds a further £2,500.

The figure in Table 1 shows the effect on the profit and loss distribution of including gamma as well as delta. It can be seen that, because for a long position the gamma component is always positive, the distribution is shifted to the right (ie, further into profit). However, the most striking result in this example is the fact that the delta captures most of the risk at the 98th percentile. This is because, for a confidence interval of 98%, the associated move in the underlying bond price is actually quite small and the convexity of the option is not so important for this move; for higher levels of confidence, eg 99.9%, the importance of convexity would be much greater.

❑ *Taylor expansion (using global Greeks)* This technique is a hybrid of the previous two. It consists of exact revaluation of the portfolio at key values of the risk factors; between these values the profit and loss is approximated using Greeks estimated at the key points. The difference between the "local" and "global" Taylor expansion techniques is illustrated in Figure 1 (overleaf), which shows the value of a foreign exchange options portfolio plotted against the underlying exchange rate (the unbroken black

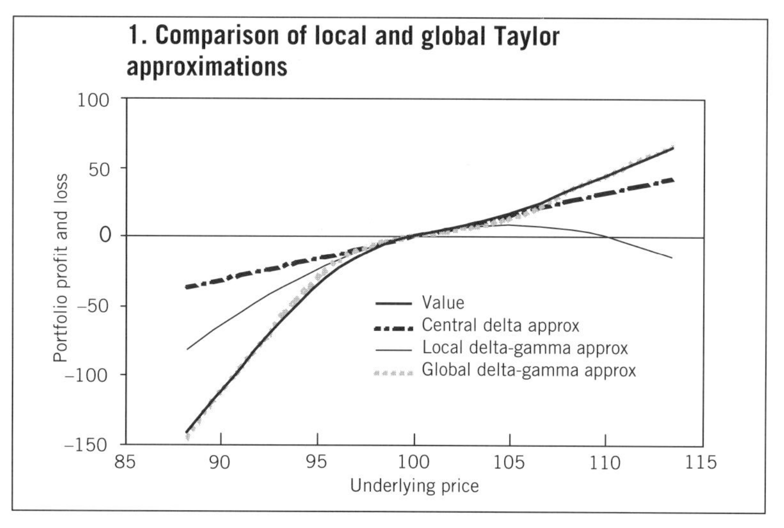

1. Comparison of local and global Taylor approximations

line). Also shown is a Taylor approximation of value, based only on the values of delta and gamma evaluated at the current exchange rate (ie, 100) - the thin solid black line. This approximation becomes very poor as we move away from the current value of the exchange rate. For this reason, we choose various other values of the exchange rate at which to recalculate the portfolio value and the delta and gamma. A Taylor approximation which uses these values of delta and gamma is then used to revalue the portfolio around these chosen levels of the exchange rate (the dotted grey line). As can be seen, the approximation is much better.

Evaluation of alternative methods

An evaluation of the alternative techniques for generating changes in the risk factors and for calculating profit and loss is summarised in Table 2.

CHOOSING THE SCENARIOS

If we first consider the attribute of accuracy in representing the risks of a portfolio, we can focus on three attributes: the presence and size of "holes" in the sample of dx; the ability of the sample to characterise the "true" distribution of the underlying risk factor; and the "meaningfulness" of the sample points.

Whichever method is used to generate the changes in the risk factors, when the sample is ordered by size there will be gaps between the sample points, ie, there will be "holes". This is true for historical changes in risk factors since, eg, history may have seen a 10% fall and a 15% fall in the S&P, but no fall of 12%. The danger is that, if the profit and loss profile of our derivatives portfolio exhibits a precipitous drop for a fall of 12% but not for a fall of 10% or 15% (perhaps because a barrier is located at a fall of 12%), then we will fail to detect the greatest risk to our portfolio.

The same is true, *a fortiori*, in relation to future scenarios. Typically, the future scenarios devised by financial institutions are few and are quite deliberately chosen to represent extreme market conditions. The portfolio for which they are devised, however, may be most exposed away from the extremes, possibly even for quite modest market moves. This can be less of a problem for a sample produced by Monte Carlo simulation, since the distribution of the sample factor changes can be made arbitrarily dense by increasing the number of simulations. This also applies to a sample which is deterministically chosen when constructing a scenario grid or matrix. The fineness of the grid can be increased in order to diminish the size of the holes. However, simple stress-testing, which revalues a portfolio only for extreme movements in the underlying risk factors, is blind to potential losses occasioned by less extreme market moves.

Table 2. Evaluation of alternative techniques

Generation of dx

Method	Advantages	Disadvantages
Monte Carlo	Holes can be made arbitrarily small	Problems capturing empirical features of the data (especially leptokurtosis); slow, inefficient
Historical (key events)	Captures empirical features of the data	History has holes in it; only big market moves are captured; can be economically irrelevant
Historical (long histories)	Captures empirical features of the data	History has holes in it; can be economically irrelevant
Future scenarios	Can be economically meaningful	There can be "big" holes
Grid points	Holes can be made arbitrarily small: can be made efficient using stratified sampling	Can be economically meaningless

Form of F(.)

Method	Advantages	Disadvantages
Exact valuation	Accurate	Slow/inefficient
Taylor expansion (local Greeks)	Fast	Inaccurate: far away from exact price; for options close to expiry or nearly at-the-money; for some exotics
Taylor expansion (global Greeks)	Fast	Inaccurate, though less so

Because there will always be "holes", regardless of how many scenarios we choose, we must develop ways of knowing where the sharp falls in profit and loss are likely to be. This requires a detailed knowledge of the portfolio's structure.

By definition, the sample of historical changes in the risk factors captures the empirical features of the data, including any leptokurtosis ("fat tails"). Future scenarios and grid points for scenario matrices can also be chosen to ensure they reflect the empirical distributions of the risk factors to which they refer: for example, by making sure the scenarios correspond to extreme market moves which would be found in the extreme tails of the risk factor distributions. Unfortunately, Monte Carlo simulations as they are usually implemented do not capture important features of real-world markets because the distributions used to generate the simulations themselves do not capture these features – in particular, the normal distribution does not allow for the leptokurtosis observed in market prices, while the Student's t distribution does not permit any skewness.

Finally, under the heading of accuracy, we might ask whether the sample of risk factor changes is economically meaningful, ie, whether the sample points represent feasible or plausible economic states of the world. This is, of course, a difficult question to answer without embracing a trading view and thereby sacrificing the independence of risk analysis. Presumably, economic meaningfulness is in-built when future scenarios are devised. This is clearly not true of scenario matrices, since typically their design is geometric rather than economically meaningful. For example, a scenario matrix for an options portfolio may have two dimensions, the price of the underlying and implied volatility. A matrix could be constructed which allows any combination of increases and decreases in these two factors, even though a simultaneous reduction in implied volatility and a large move in price may seem an implausible state of the world for most markets.

Now consider the price to be paid for increases in accuracy. The Monte Carlo and scenario matrix approaches to generating sample points may be capable of filling the holes left by history, or by our limited imagination of the future, but these methods are consequently computer-intensive.

THE METHOD OF REVALUATION

By construction, exact valuation delivers perfect accuracy of revaluation under the sample changes in risk factors, with the cost that it is slow computationally. Taylor approximations save on calculation time but at the cost of inaccuracy, as we saw above. This can be true even of the global Taylor expansion technique, when we are dealing with options close to expiry, close to at-the-money, or with certain exotic options.

2. Pitfalls of Taylor expansions: alternative techniques for measuring portfolio exposure

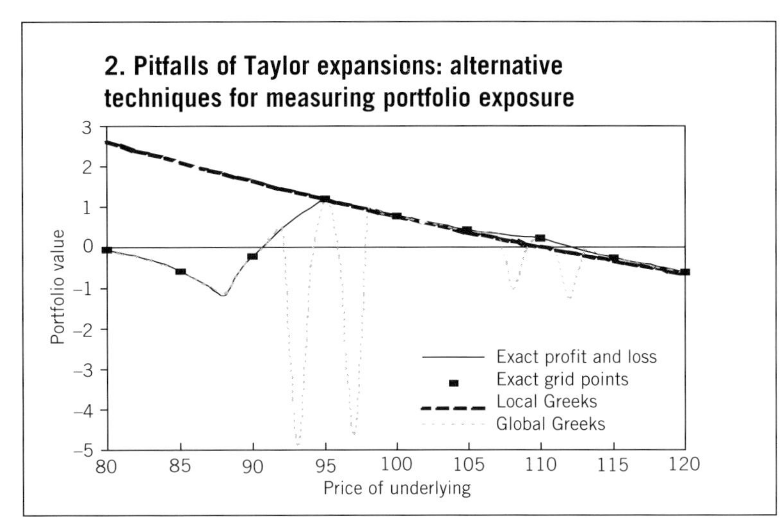

Figure 2 illustrates the potential inaccuracy of the global approximation. It shows the profit and loss of a portfolio of down-and-out/in options, plotted against the underlying price for which the current value is 100. Also shown are the local Greek and global Greek approximations (to second order in the underlying price), where the profit and loss and the Greeks are evaluated at spaces of five units in the underlying price. The portfolio was chosen to exhibit an awkwardly shaped profit and loss profile, one which would confound the Taylor expansion technique. As expected, the local Taylor expansion gives a good approximation around the current underlying price, but rapidly becomes irrelevant as we move away from this price. The global Taylor expansion gives an excellent approximation except around a few values for the underlying, for which values the approximation is extremely poor – these happen to be close to the barriers of the options which comprise the portfolio, and so the gamma at these points is very large, which has the effect of deforming the approximation.

In the following section we look briefly at a few examples of how these different techniques can be combined to deliver a measure of potential loss for a derivatives portfolio.

Some techniques

The techniques we examine are: the VAR technique using local Greeks (as proposed by JP Morgan, see Longerstaey & Zangari, 1996); the "delta-plus" method offered under the market risk supplement to the Basle Accord (Basle, 1996); and the stress test technique using global Greeks (as proposed by, eg, Wilson, 1995).

JP MORGAN'S TAYLOR EXPANSION METHOD

JP Morgan recently advocated the use of a technique which utilises the local Taylor expansion (Equation 1) in calculating VAR for option portfolios. For an option portfolio which depends upon only one risk factor, the underlying market price, p, a second-order expansion is used to approximate the profit and loss, thus:

$$P\&L = \Delta dp + \tfrac{1}{2}\Gamma(dp)^2 \qquad (2)$$

where both Δ and Γ are local partial derivatives, ie, measured at the current value of the underlying price.

As Longerstaey & Zangari note, even if the underlying risk factor is lognormal, the presence of the gamma term introduces skewness into the distribution of profit and loss, since if dp is lognormal, then $(dp)^2$ is not. To find the percentiles of the distribution of profit and loss and hence a measure of VAR, Longerstaey & Zangari use an Edgeworth expansion, which approximates the distribution of profit and loss around the lognormal distribution. Using this expansion, the approximate critical values for the distribution of profit and loss are:

$$\{\mu + z(\alpha)\sigma,\ \mu + z(1-\alpha)\sigma\} \qquad (3)$$

where $z(\alpha)$ is a multiple which is appropriate to the α-percentile and depends upon the empirical moments of the underlying price distribution and upon the Greeks evaluated at the current underlying price.

This method suffers from the drawbacks associated with using local Greeks and would also be inaccurate if global Greeks were used in the circumstances described in the previous section (ie, with options close to expiry, barrier options etc).

BASLE DELTA-PLUS METHOD

This approach consists of the following steps: the current values for delta, gamma, vega and rho are calculated for the options portfolio; the delta equivalent of the portfolio is analysed as part of the cash portfolio and capital calculated accordingly; the aggregate gamma for the portfolio is calculated as the sum of all negative gammas for the constituent options, the positive gammas being effectively set to zero, ie, portfolio gamma is calculated as $\Gamma = \sum_i \text{minimum}\ \{\Gamma_i, 0\}$, where Γ_i is the instrument-specific gamma. The gamma part of the Taylor expansion is then calculated as:

$$\tfrac{1}{2}\,\text{abs}\{\Gamma\}\{\text{risk of underlying}\} \qquad (4)$$

where the risk of the underlying is a defined large move in the underlying; and vega risk and rho risk are also calculated.

We can see several problems with this approach. First, there are the problems associated with using local Greeks. Second, the portfolio is evaluated for only a single, large shift in the underlying, whereas the biggest exposure for the portfolio may be the result of small changes in the underlying. Third, the risk will be exaggerated to the extent that only negative gammas are used in analysing portfolio risk. Lastly, it is quite possible that the calculation of delta risk and gamma risk could be inconsistent, because the delta component is analysed separately.

STRESS TESTING USING GLOBAL GREEKS

The method proposed by Wilson for calculating potential loss consists of the following steps: select a sequence of key values of the risk factor(s); at these values, calculate the value of the portfolio and Greek sensitivities[1]; and use the Greeks to revalue the portfolio at intervening values of the underlying risk factor(s). This technique suffers from the drawbacks associated with using global Greeks when the portfolio includes exotic options.

Conclusions and recommendations

There are many pitfalls in analysing the risk of an options portfolio. What is evident, particularly when considering portfolios of complex options, is that the risk management solution needs to be appropriate to the portfolio in question.

One might consider the following procedure for analysing the risk of any options portfolio:

- Partition the portfolio into those positions for which a Taylor approximation will be sufficiently accurate (sub-portfolio A), and those for which exact valuation will be required (sub-portfolio B).
- Identify the risk factors of the portfolio.
- Examine the recent history (eg the past 10 years' data) of these risk factors and identify their maximum range for this period. Do not look at risk factors as if they were unique; rather look at classes of risk factors. For example, it might be the case that some base metal prices have moved more dramatically than others in the recent past, eg, aluminium may have fallen by a maximum of 10% in a day while the maximum for nickel was 15%. But it would be silly to let the randomness of history determine the range of possible future moves, so assume that the maximum fall for base

metals is 15% to be on the safe side. Having identified the maximum range of movement, adjust this to reflect your risk preferences.

❑ For sub-portfolio A, the key values of the risk factors at which exact evaluation will be calculated must be determined. This might be done by spacing the points in a way that matches the probability distribution for each factor/group of factors, so that there are fewer points at the extremes but choosing additional points which correspond to the strikes and barriers of the portfolio.

❑ Having determined the key points for each factor, the value and Greeks for sub-portfolio A must be calculated; in between the key values, the Taylor approximation should be used. Sub-portfolio B must be exactly revalued using sufficiently fine grid points.

❑ The values of the two sub-portfolios are added for each point on the grid, the profit and loss map is drawn and the potential loss identified.

The following might also be considered:

❑ Do not rely on long histories of the risk factors or even key historical events – this is time-consuming and there is a good chance that the big risks will not be identified.

❑ Do not rely on futurology or economists to determine possible scenarios – this is fraught with danger.

Finally, remember that no risk measurement system can be perfect: it is always possible to find a derivatives portfolio with risks that will not be detected by a given risk measurement system. The art of risk measurement for derivatives portfolios lies in striking an optimal compromise between accuracy and timeliness.

1 *Shaw (1996) proposes a further refinement, which is for the algorithm to adapt to the discovery of high gamma at a certain value of the risk factor, by calculating the value and Greeks more frequently around this value.*

BIBLIOGRAPHY

Basle Committee on Banking Supervision, 1996, *Amendment to the Capital Accord to Cover Market Risks*, Basle.

Longerstaey, J. and P. Zangari, 1996, "Commoditising the VAR Framework: Incorporating Gamma Risk", *Financial Derivatives and Risk Management*, Vol. 6.

Shaw, J., 1996, "VAR Architecture", BZW internal working paper.

Wilson, T., 1995, "Practical Solutions to Address Complex VAR Problems", Mimeo, McKinsey & Company, London.

15

Why VAR is in Vogue

Randy Payant
The Sendero Institute

The volatility-corelation approach is one of the most popular methods of calculating value-at-risk. However, it does have some limitations in balance sheet management.

One of the hottest topics emerging in the risk management arena is value-at-risk (VAR). While the concept of risk to value has been around for years, its prominence has gained increasing importance due to the recent rash of financial disasters reported by industrial organisations, government bodies, and financial institutions. Traders and portfolio managers of derivatives have experienced tempestuous swings in the prices of thinly-traded and illiquid securities.

Financial instrument price swings can put strain on capital positions and cause significant damage, should the position need to be liquidated under unfavourable market conditions. The ability to ride out turbulent markets is highly dependent on a portfolio's leverage, its price volatility, and the ability to continue its financing. VAR analysis measures risk, and focuses on estimating potential negative consequences of market value reductions in a single position or portfolios of positions. While there are various interpretations of VAR, all share a common underlying focus on estimating, with a certain degree of confidence, how much a financial position or portfolio of positions could potentially decline in value over its holding period.

There are many approaches to estimating VAR. Generally the techniques fall into one of three broad classifications: volatility-correlation analysis; full scenario simulation analysis; and stochastic scenario simulation analysis. Each approach rests on a different premise and has strengths, weaknesses and appropriate applications in the measurement of risk.

The simplest, fastest and trendiest approach to estimating VAR is volatility-correlation analysis. This article will discuss the merits of this approach and its role in the asset/liability management process.

How is volatility-correlation VAR estimated?

As with all VAR estimation methodologies, volatility-correlation analysis starts with determining what factors influence the position's price and therefore its value. These may include such market variants as interest rates, foreign exchange rates, equity price indexes or commodity price indexes.

Market factors can have varying degrees of impact on the position's price sensitivity. In the simplest VAR approach, the change in the position's price is correlated to the changes in the market factor. This correlation is referred to as the position's delta and describes the degree of sensitivity the market factor has on the instrument's price. If the position's price is dependent solely on interest rates, its delta would be equivalent to the instrument's modified duration.

Correlation of risk factors

If the position's price is influenced by more than one factor, correlations of the various market factors are incorporated in multi-variant equations to estimate price sensitivity. For simplicity and speed of calculation, most volatility-correlation models use single factor analysis for estimating each instrument's price change. If the analysis is based on a single factor, it is sometimes referred to as mean-variance VAR, as only the level and volatility of a single factor influence on price is considered. With a portfolio of instruments, where each instrument's price is dependent on different factors (eg fixed income positions and forex positions) the individual market factor

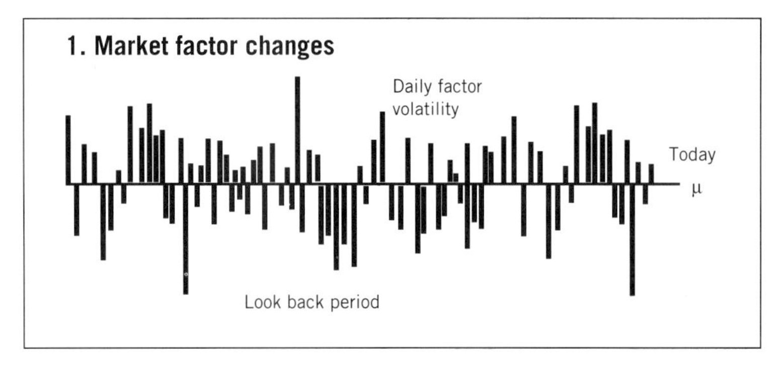

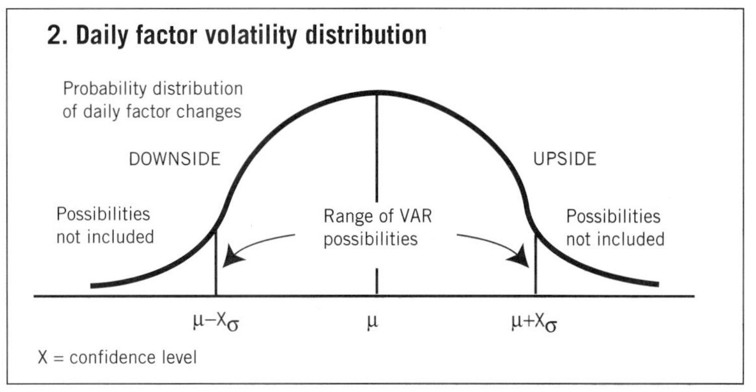

movements are correlated to one another to estimate portfolio VAR.

It is after the position's price sensitivity to market factors is determined that the volatility-correlation approach begins to differ from other methods. All VAR approaches require numerous assumptions about how to vary the underlying market factors that eventually affect price changes. Volatility-correlation VAR fits statistically-derived probability distributions of the underlying market factors to provide the assumptions used to estimate possible future price movements.

Volatility-correlation estimations require the determination of a mean and volatility for each market factor. Observed changes in interest rates, exchange rates, equity indexes and commodity prices provide raw data about the market factors. These historic factor movements are extrapolated into the future to create a basis for estimating future factor movements. Daily observations of factor movements provide the foundation used to estimate market factor volatility (see Figure 1). The data set of the market factor movements provides the distribution's mean (μ) and variance. From the probability distributions, a range of historical movements for each market factor develops, along with the measurement of the range's volatility, expressed in terms of standard deviation (σ). While this appears fairly straightforward, defining the mean and determining the length of the observation lookback period for the analysis must be done carefully.

The length of the observation period - and therefore the number of data points collected - influences the overall validity of the probability distribution. Longer lookback periods tend to provide a richer sampling of possible factor volatility changes but can hide sharp changes in the market's trend.

The mean can be a simple average, a rolling average or an exponentially-weighted average of all the observations. Simple averages completely fail to detect changes in the market's trends. A rolling average exposes a trend in the direction of the factor, such as a rising or falling trend in interest rates, but can misinterpret rapid market fluctuations that could put a position seriously underwater. An improvement - the use of exponential weighted averages - causes recent observations to be weighted heavier than earlier observations. The use of exponentially-weighted averages should provide an earlier detection of significant changes in market condition. Beyond this level of analysis, the use of GARCH-based (generalised autoregressive conditional heteroscedasticity) volatility predicting methods could be used to create a distribution of possible factor movements.

The validity of the volatility-correlation VAR estimate

The level of confidence in the VAR estimation process is selected by the number of standard deviations of variance applied to the probability distributions. A standard deviation selection of 1.65 provides a 90% confidence level that the potential estimated price movement will not be more than a given amount based on the correlation of market factors to the position's price sensitivity. This confidence level is advocated by the RiskMetrics version of volatility-correlation VAR (see Figure 2).

Higher confidence levels can be attained by selecting a larger number of standard deviations, as advocated by the international regulatory community, which recommends the use of three standard deviations, providing a 99% confidence level in the VAR estimation validity. This translates into a one in a hundred chance that the actual loss may exceed the estimated VAR.

The use of standard deviation to determine a confidence level in the estimated VAR assumes that the distribution of observations is normal, and therefore the market factors move normally. This assumption has been challenged both in terms of the non-normal movements (skewness) of actual observations of market factors and the fit (kurtosis) of the observations to the distribution. Current volatility-correlation VAR approaches usually do not address non-normal probability distributions.

The last dimension to address in any VAR measurement approach is over what time period value is at risk. At minimum this would be the time it takes to liquidate or neutralise the position from the market's influences. Volatility-correlation VAR estimates potential one-day price volatility. Multiplying the daily maximum potential price change by the number of days the position is expected to be held would overstate market risk. This is because it is unlikely the position would fall in value by the maximum amount each day of the holding period. To correct for this, daily price risk is scaled by the square root of the maximum number of anticipated holding period days.

While most volatility-correlation VAR programs measure daily volatility, observations of weekly or monthly market factor movements can be used to construct the probability distribution. This is helpful if the holding horizon is longer than several days (see Figure 3).

In reviewing the volatility-correlation VAR approach, the estimated adverse decline in value is a function of the position's size; its price sensitivity; the volatility of price-influencing market factors; a confidence level; and an anticipated maximum holding period. Daily price sensitivity is estimated using correlation, and in some cases, cross-correlation matrices of the underlying risk factors. The price sensitivity is then extrapolated to cover the time it would take to liquidate or neutralise the position from further possible price decline. For the basic volatility-correlation VAR equation see Table 1.

At its basis, volatility-correlation VAR uses statistical analysis of past market movements to estimate possible future market behaviour and the resulting impact on the position's price and value. While volatility-correlation analysis has advantages in estimating possible future price changes, it does create several areas for concern.

Much of the criticism of this approach centres on the validity of some of the underlying technical and computational aspects required and the compromise choices used to estimate VAR mathematically in the quickest, most transparent manner possible. These criticisms include: the use of normal rather than non-normal probability distributions; the prevalent use of deltas exclusively to estimate price sensitivity (particularly poor with options); the choice of appropriate confidence level used to estimate maximum value decline (1.65, 2 or 3 standard deviations); and the source of the data points used to determine the volatility of the market factors.

Most volatility-correlation VAR analyses hold the deltas constant, leaving the price change dependent only on the changes in the external market factors. The exclusive use of the instrument's delta ignores any optionality characteristics the instrument may possess. When the instrument containing options is trading around its strike price, delta estimates of price change are misleading. For volatility-correlation VAR to incorporate optionality, the non-linearity of the price/factor function must be considered. Incorporating the non-linearity of optionality complicates and slows the calculation process, thereby eliminating one of the main attractions of this VAR estimation approach.

Many practitioners agree that because the volatility-correlation approach uses statistical analysis solely to determine potential losses, its validity declines substantially as the time horizon to neutralise extends beyond 10–20 trading days.

3. Downside of value-at-risk

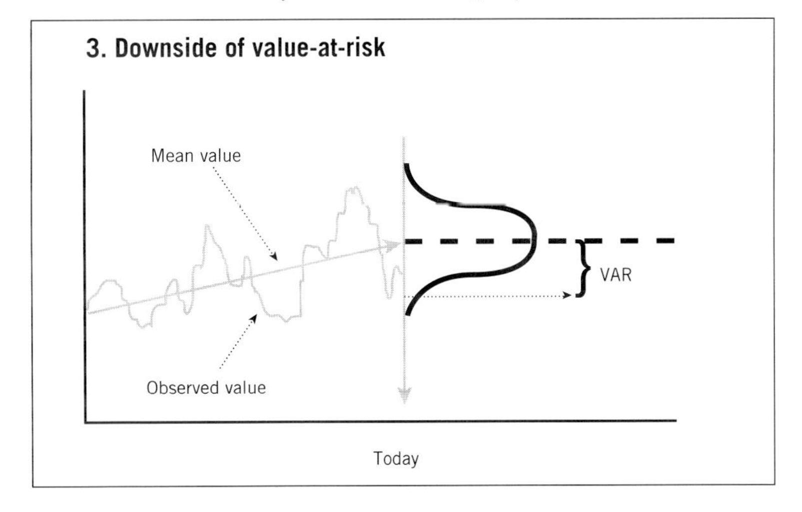

Table 1: Volatility-correlation VAR =

Position size	(Number of units)
X	
Unit price sensitivity to market factors	(Market factors deltas)
X	
Potential volatility of market factors	(Correlation of observed probability distributions of market factors)
X	
Confidence level of volatility estimation	(Standard deviations of probability distribution)
X	
Holding period horizon extrapolation	(Square root of number of days)

Beyond this, the correlations of market factors have a tendency to break down. Indeed, most uses of volatility-correlation VAR have centred in trading portfolio management where speed of computation in fast-moving markets is essential. But even here, empirical evidence suggests volatility-correlation VAR analysis becomes ineffective under abnormal and unstable market conditions.

Given these limitations of volatility-correlation VAR, are there any uses of the analysis in managing the core balance sheet businesses? The answer is a qualified yes - provided its limitations are understood and that the analysis is not pushed beyond what it is designed to address.

How volatility-correlation VAR contributes to A/LM

The greatest contribution of the volatility-correlation approach in risk measurement is its use of market-derived observations upon which hypotheses about future price movements are based. With other VAR approaches, market volatility assumptions are not directly based on market observations, and therefore non-market derived biases can be introduced in the analysis.

Under full scenario simulation analysis, suppositions about the possible movement of the value-influencing factor are left to the analyst. While he or she may opt to base the assumptions on market derived data, it is not done in a systematic, transparent fashion as prescribed in the volatility-correlation VAR approach. The analyst may look at recent levels, trends and volatility in interest rates, exchange rates and commodity and equity indexes to arrive at the assumptions used to estimate VAR. These assumptions may then be modified to reflect the analyst's assumptions about the validity of market observations. This allows the analyst to take a longer-term investment perspective rather than a shorter-term trading perspective. The biggest drawback to full scenario simulations is that a confidence level in forecasting the movement of the market factor cannot be determined statistically.

Shocking one or more of the factors by a prescribed amount - eg ±100 basis points for interest rates - estimates VAR for that magnitude of change but it could be irrelevant to actual volatility observed in the market. The improvement experienced by using observed volatility of market factors in full historical scenario simulation analysis provides the direct linkage to the market. Use of market observations to create the volatility of the market factors can lead full scenario simulations to estimate VAR with a given level of confidence.

Stochastic scenario simulations also may incorporate market-derived data but again the random nature of this method is not as structured as in the volatility-correlation VAR approach. By its very nature, stochastic analysis incorporates random and uncorrelated movements in the market factors that could potentially have an influence on price.

The second major contribution of volatility-correlation VAR is its correlated linkage of the various market factors that influence the value of a position or a portfolio of positions. Price influencing-factors such as interest rates, exchange rates, equity and commodity prices are interrelated and therefore cannot be individually summed. Volatility-correlation VAR correlates the various interrelationships among price-influencing factors so that the maximum estimated loss is not overstated.

This is particularly valuable for assessing VAR in a trading portfolio where risk estimation computation time is at a premium. In a trading setting, the decision is either to sell, buy or hold - not to understand the interrelationship of the individual risk factors.

The third contribution of volatility-correlation is its use in macro balance sheet hedging activities. The value of the balance sheet changes due to both externally derived market factors and the internal characteristics of the instruments. While the true market value of the balance sheet is not known with certainty, the relative change in value derived from changes in markets can be estimated. Based upon the volatility of the price-influencing factors, relative value can be insulated from changing market conditions. The risk factors - whether changes in interest rates, foreign currency rates, commodity or equity index changes - can be hedged, allowing for relative value to be immunised from changes in that market factor.

Shortcomings of volatility-correlation VAR in A/LM

The most troublesome aspect of using volatility-correlation analysis in strategic balance sheet management is its exclusive focus on market/price risk. Volatility-correlation VAR concentrates solely on measuring market risk, to the exclusion of other types and sources of risk that affect value. Price risk can only be measured and evaluated with precision in markets that are liquid and readily accessible. While a theoretical market price of an instrument can be estimated, the validity of that value cannot be determined outside of a market.

The market price of any instrument is the outcome of a momentary view of each financial instrument's characteristics in light of the economic outlook, where value resides, and what external factors may influence the realisation of the instrument's perceived value. Market risk therefore is an expression of the market participants' composite attitudes about underlying interest rates; default possibilities; exchange rates; optionality; legal constraints; liquidity and marketability; regulatory posture; operational complications; and so on.

Each individual source of risk contributes to the assessment of the instrument's market price. The rewards for assuming these risks can be assessed separately and then combined and cross-correlated to arrive at market/price risk. The combination of all these factors provides a single expression of risk – the potential change in price, a price that is valid only for a moment in time.

Full valuation scenario simulation VAR differs from the volatility-correlation VAR approach to risk measurement but ultimately both have the same objective. Instead of focusing on short-term price volatility, simulation takes a longer-term look at the underlying individual elements of risk and their respective influences on value. Full valuation simulation rests on the premise that the value of the balance sheet can vary for reasons outside of a change in market-derived factors.

The primary role of most financial institutions is to be an intermediary between markets, including both shorter-term liquid trading markets and longer-term investment, credit and deposit markets. While some parts of a financial institution's balance sheet are tradeable, the majority is neither liquid nor marketable. Instead of being forced to liquidate losing positions under short-term adverse market conditions, banks' financial positions are subject to the trends of longer-term market movements. The core structural assets and liabilities of financial institutions are not subject to the daily volatility of the global wholesale markets. With sufficient capital, the financial institution is able to ride out short-term market swings that may be only temporary, without being forced into liquidating positions at significant losses. This longer term doctrine provides a degree of stability to the earnings of the organisation.

Full valuation scenario simulation VAR begins with the proposition that the core balance sheet business activities of most financial institutions are not readily marketable or traded. Much of the financial institution's balance sheet is subject to administered interest rates, ambiguous maturities, significant default potential and high levels of optionality. It is due to these factors that volatility-correlation VAR begins to lose its appeal as a global risk measurement tool for the non-traded portions of the balance sheet.

Much of the financial institution's credit portfolios and most of its funding have interest rates determined and administered by management. While administered rates usually move with changes in the general level of global market rates, their correlations are far from perfect.

Default risk is the predominant risk of most financial institutions. The evolving default risk profile of a financial institution has a significantly greater impact on the changing value of the credit portfolios of the balance sheet than do changes in the external factors (such as changing interest rates, foreign currency rates, commodity or equity prices). Volatility-correlation VAR assumes that the credit risk of the position or portfolio is static over the holding period horizon. This assumption is not valid over the normal lending horizon.

A large percentage of financial institution funding is made up of accounts with either no defined maturity or at best an ambiguous maturity. Without a defined maturity for these accounts, a delta cannot be determined for them. Volatility-correlation VAR requires a delta that is based on a known or estimated maturity of the transactions. Even if a delta could be determined, there is no way to test the validity of its price movement under market conditions.

Many balance sheet items are also subject to optionality. The dynamic cashflow of these items, and therefore their value, is dependent on factors outside of those derived solely from the market. Volatility-correlation VAR ignores the influence of the internal dynamics of the instrument's cashflow on the change in value. Full and stochastic scenario simulations can provide a dynamic linkage of external factor influences with the internal characteristics of the instrument to determine the change in value.

Conclusion

Volatility-correlation VAR has provided significant contributions to the measurement of risk. It has reminded the financial community about the need to focus on value rather than simply looking only at earnings risk. But while volatility-correlation VAR clearly has a place in trading portfolio management, its usefulness in general balance sheet management is often exaggerated. As with any analysis, both the limitations and the possibilities of its application must be understood for it to be used effectively in balance sheet risk measurement. Comprehensive risk measurement is hard, dirty work that can not be boiled down to a single number, formula or analysis.

16

Margins of Error

Gabriel Bousbib
Reuters America

This article presents a value-at-risk model for financial organisations that do not trade actively in standardised instruments.

The significant market losses incurred by several financial institutions and industrial corporations in recent years have renewed pressure for regulators and senior managers to develop and implement global risk measurement techniques. These techniques assess an institution's potential loss from market movements over a given time period.

The value-at-risk concept - recommended by a growing number of regulators worldwide - measures the maximum unfavourable change in portfolio value expected to occur over a specific time period and confidence interval as a result of the movements of economic variables. The methodology, which has gained rapid acceptance in the US and Europe, can be decomposed into four steps.

First, a set of market variables (interest rates, foreign exchange rates, commodity prices, etc) is taken to represent the market. Second, behaviour is assumed for these market variables and modelled through a stochastic process (eg a normal distribution). Third, the portfolio of transactions is modelled as a function of the market variables, ie the change in the portfolio's value as a function of the market variables is calculated. Finally, VAR can be computed for the portfolio using various techniques, including historical or Monte Carlo simulations, or covariance analyses.

VAR's simplicity has led many to recommend that it become a standard risk measure, not only for financial institutions involved in large-scale trading operations, but also for retail banks, insurance companies, institutional investors and non-financial concerns. If normalised by the firm's equity capital to allow for comparisons across firms, VAR could be used by investors and analysts in the same way more traditional financial ratios are used to evaluate a company.

We believe VAR's relevance as a risk management tool depends on two key factors:

❑ The ability, or need, to mark to market the firm's assets and liabilities, whether on- or off-balance-sheet.

❑ The need to meet short-term, large, negative variations in the market value of the firm's assets through its equity capital.

As we will show, neither element can easily be applied to the kind of non-trading firms mentioned above.

Public companies' reluctance to adopt the US Financial Accounting Standards Board's directives FAS 107 and FAS 115 - which recommend adopting a mark-to-market approach for all assets and liabilities - goes beyond the issue of volatility induced by marking to market assets and liabilities. It also confirms that, in multiple cases, mark-to-market does not give an accurate economic picture of a firm.

Let us consider a typical US retail bank. Table 1 shows its simplified balance sheet. With the probable exception of its mortgage loan portfolio, it will be impossible for this retail bank to mark its assets and liabilities to market accurately. Unlike a treasury or wholesale environment, where the value of a transaction is based solely on the current level of the relevant market variables, a retail bank or an insurance company

1. Simplified retail bank balance sheet (%)

Credit cards	39	Demand deposits	15
Consumer finance	20	Time deposits	62
Mortgage loans	41	Certificates of deposit	23
Total assets	**100**	**Total liabilities**	**10**

Source: The CBM Group

2. Differing dimensions of value

Wholesale and treasury	Retail and insurance
❑ Portfolio of assets (loans, bonds) funded largely with "bought" money	❑ "Natural" combination of assets and deposits – presence of low-cost core deposits
❑ Clearly defined rigid contracts (assets, liabilities and derivatives)	❑ "Flexible contracts" open to repricing by the bank and cancellation by the client
❑ Well-informed professional counterparties	❑ Some customer segments poorly informed and/or unaware of their options
❑ A small number of large transactions with few large customers	❑ A large number of small transac tions with many small customers (actuarial model)
❑ Liquidity	❑ "Stickiness"
❑ Binary decisions based on market anticipations	❑ Price elasticity and customer behaviour influenced by factors external to market anticipations
❑ Mark-to-market accounting	❑ Multivariate models needed

Source: The CBM Group

must incorporate additional dimensions, such as customer behaviour and pricing policies (see Table 2).

For example, a retail bank could model demand deposits as a zero-coupon perpetual debt. In practice, however, the behaviour of demand deposits will depend on the alternative deposit products offered by the market, combined with the necessity of some businesses and individuals to keep demand deposits. Similarly, credit card receivables could be analysed as a series of fixed or floating cashflows, taking into account the various caps and floors embedded in the credit card (eg maximum or minimum rate on a floating-rate card and options to switch between fixed and floating rate). Again in practice, the behaviour of credit card receivables depends not only on the current level of interest rates, but also on external factors such as: customer convenience; seasonality; the bank's pricing and fee policy; and its ability to modify the terms of the transaction by changing, for example, the maximum rate charged on a credit card. Similar conclusions could be drawn for insurance products.

Furthermore, does mark-to-market give actionable information to a retail bank or insurance company's management? The need to mark transactions to market in the wholesale and treasury world is fairly clear. The organisation depends mostly on professionally managed "bought" money, which can be shifted very quickly. Its leverage is therefore significant, and the organisation must ensure it has enough equity capital to meet unexpected losses on a daily basis, or even intra-day. This leads them naturally to VAR.

In a retail bank or insurance company, funds originate from a large number of small depositors and are therefore more stable and "stickier". The organisation's objective is to maximise its net margin – ie the yield generated by its assets above the cost of its liabilities – over a fairly long time period, such as a quarter or a year. The relevant actionable information which must be provided to management is the potential variation of this net margin as a function of market variables, as well as the external factors discussed above.

Daily mark-to-market and VAR analyses do not indicate these variations. Whereas treasury market risk management aims to measure and manage instantaneous (usually meaning daily) changes in mark-to-market value, market risk management for a retail bank or an insurance company should focus on measuring and managing the volatility of the firm's net returns (asset return minus liability yield) over a given time (eg monthly or annually).

Finally, the VAR measure, as currently defined, addresses the needs of a highly leveraged institution interested in potential losses from large market movements. It gives debt and equity holders a measure of the equity capital required to sustain market losses for which the market may not be willing to provide short-term funding. Such a measure is clearly of limited value to those who hold a stake in a "non-leveraged" financial institution.

A better and easier statistic for the non-leveraged financial institution could be developed around the concept of spread-at-risk. This measures the institution's anticipated net spread (assets minus liabilities) and its expected distribution over a reporting period (say, a quarter or a year). The spread-at-risk must include the institution's projected pricing policies and incorporate the behaviour of the institution's clients. As well as providing senior management with an integrated risk profile of the institution, it could give a non-leveraged institution several other benefits, including improved pricing policies, better product design and optimised client targeting.

Let us illustrate how the notion of spread-at-risk would be implemented for a retail bank. As interest rates vary and the bank's pricing levels relative to market rates are modified, the yield or cost for each bank product (expressed as either a percentage rate or in dollars) will vary for several reasons, such as:

❑ *Market movements* Rates fall, decreasing the

cost of the certificate of deposit portfolio by a factor proportional to the change in market rates.

❑ *Product contractual features* Rates rise and a cap embedded in revolving credit lines moves into the money, capping the yield of the asset.

❑ *Retail bank pricing policies* Rates rise but prices on "super saving" accounts are not adjusted accordingly, triggering a wave of withdrawals; the balances lost must then be funded at the current market rates.

❑ *Customer behaviour* During the holiday season, retail card balances will rise, increasing the dollar amounts earned by the retail card business.

A retail bank may in practice have hundreds of products; the concept of product might represent groupings of products directly available to the bank's customer. The level of product aggregation would depend on several practical considerations, such as the availability of data and complexity of modelling, as well as the level of granularity required.

A modelling function would then determine two sets of data for each product, over a given time and for given market scenarios (generated via historical simulation, a covariance matrix or Monte Carlo simulation), ie:

❑ the expected yield or cost of the product;

❑ the expected revenue/cost of the product, taking into account the outstanding dollar balance of the product (dollar matrix).

This information would be determined in the light of:

❑ interest rate levels;

❑ pricing relative to the market;

❑ forecast balances, based on expected new business, redemptions and renewal rates.

Unlike traditional VAR analysis, spread-at-risk in the case of a retail bank must take into account pricing policies relative to the market, which can in turn affect the outstanding balances on given products.

The spread-at-risk can be evaluated by constructing a matrix that represents the expected yield or cost of the product for a combined change in market rates and pricing levels. This can be translated into a dollar matrix based on expected balances, ie the balances forecast by the business units adjusted for market movements and price changes.

Generating these matrices for each product, then aggregating them would give the retail bank a dollar matrix representing the dollar increase (or decrease) in income over the period considered. Dividing the dollar figure by the average net asset size would provide the retail bank with the spread-at-risk distribution. In other words, the spread-at-risk represents the increase or decrease in the bank's net margin as a function of market scenarios and the bank's pricing policies.

There are overlaps between strategic risk calculations for leveraged and non-leveraged financial institutions. Both need a sophisticated engine to generate a large number of market scenarios, using one of several methods which have gained market acceptance, and both must be able to model the value of a product or a transaction as a function of market variables.

Yet value, for a non-leveraged financial institution, designates the change in the product's revenue or cost over the period considered, rather than a change in mark-to-market, as it does in traditional capital markets. The concept of spread-at-risk gives non-leveraged financial institutions a more meaningful measure of market risk, as it integrates the impact of both market movements and pricing policies on an institution's net income over the horizon period.

17

VAR: Seductive but Dangerous*

Tanya Styblo Beder
Capital Market Risk Advisors, Inc

Value-at-risk (VAR) has gained rapid acceptance as a valuable approach to risk management. Not all VARs are equal, however. A study of VAR techniques used by dealers and end-users reveals that VAR calculations differ significantly for the same portfolio. VARs are extremely dependent on parameters, data, assumptions, and methodology. Calculation of eight common VARs for three hypothetical portfolios demonstrates the potentially seductive but dangerous nature of any single approach to risk management. In sum, although VAR and other quantitative techniques are necessary aspects of an effective risk-management programme, they are not sufficient to control risk.

Value-at-risk is Wall Street's latest advancement in risk measurement. Simply defined, VAR is an estimate of maximum potential loss to be expected over a given period a certain percentage of the time. Its simplicity is seductive. Used to the extreme, in a single statistic, a firm can measure its exposure to markets world-wide. VAR enables a firm to determine which businesses offer the greatest expected returns at the least expense of risk. When one considers that risk management in the early 1970s consisted almost entirely of the evaluation of credit risk, VAR's power in the context of the galaxy of risks we track, analyse, and manage today is breathtaking to consider.

VAR can be dangerous, however. A review of dozens of dealers' and end-users' VARs revealed radically different approaches to the calculation. In this study, eight common VAR methodologies were applied to three hypothetical portfolios. As illustrated in Figure 1 (overleaf), the magnitude of the discrepancy among these methods is shocking, with VAR results varying by more than 14 times for the same portfolio. These results illustrate the VAR's extreme dependence on parameters, data, assumptions, and methodology.

The implications of these discrepancies for capital adequacy standards are significant, especially given the Basle Committee on Banking Supervision's treatment of VAR in its proposed amendment to the 1988 Basle Capital Accord, *The Supervisory Treatment of Market Risks*, published on April 12, 1995. This amendment proposes that dealers use either an internal methodology or a Bank for International Settlements (BIS) standard methodology to compute VAR and that the results be multiplied by a factor of three to determine the amount of capital to be set aside for market risk. Our research indicates that this amount may be too high or too low, depending upon the method used. The need for a uniform VAR methodology or for differing multiplication factors according to the type of VAR is paramount to establish a common ground for comparative purposes.

In our analysis, historical simulations present quite different views of risk relative to Monte Carlo simulations. This difference is attributable to the extreme dependence of historical simulations on the underlying data set and the value of the relative randomness of key variables in Monte Carlo simulations compared with sample-specific values. The results also reveal the exceptional

* *This paper was first published in Financial Analysts Journal (1995). It is reprinted with permission from Financial Analysts Journal, September/October 1995.* *The author wishes to thank Frank Iacono, Maarten Nederlof, Tom Riesing, Anil Suri, and Charles Taylor for their invaluable assistance and input during the preparation of this article.*

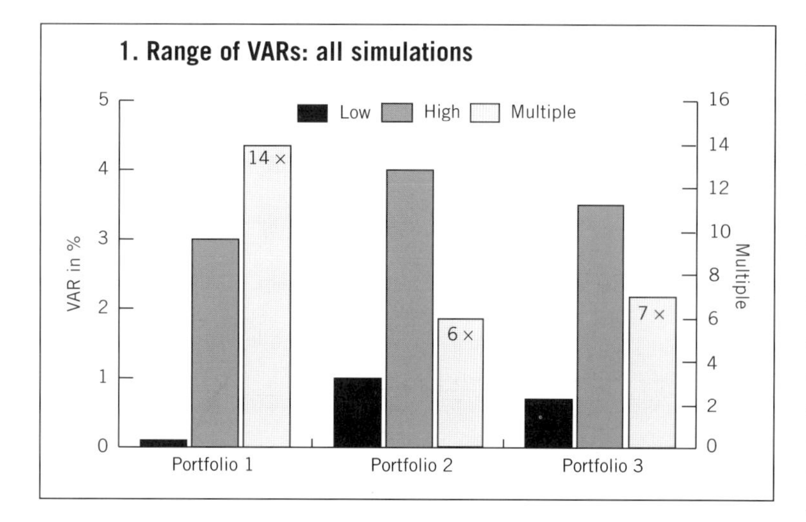

time sensitivity of certain portfolio risks and highlight the potential failure of VAR, even when bolstered by stress testing. In sum, although VAR and stress testing are necessary, they are not sufficient to contain risk.

The differences in common VARs emphasise the fact that no single set of parameters, data, assumptions, and methodology is accepted as the "correct" approach. Even if two firms use the same quantitative technique, they often apply different assumptions in implementing the technique. For example, some firms calculate the global VAR of the firm over a one-day time horizon, using historical data series on markets and a specific set of mathematical models. Others calculate regional VAR of product areas over a monthly or annual time horizon, using random or implied data series on markets and multiple mathematical models. Depending on the selection of time horizon, data base, and correlation assumptions across instrument/asset classes, the same model may produce widely divergent VAR views for the same portfolio and, therefore, different capital requirements.

The portfolios and VAR calculations

In the remainder of this article, we describe the common VAR calculations and apply them to three hypothetical portfolios. For each methodology presented, VAR is calculated for both one-day (1d) and two-week (2w) time horizons. The first methodology, historical simulation, is performed twice, changing the data base used from the past 100 trading days (Pr100d) to the past 250 trading days (Pr250d). The second methodology, Monte Carlo simulation, also is performed twice, changing the correlation estimates from the JP Morgan RiskMetrics data set to those from the BIS/Basle Committee proposal.[1] Differences in correlation estimates between RiskMetrics and BIS/Basle are significant. RiskMetrics permits correlation across all asset classes, using exponentially weighted daily historical observations. The BIS/Basle proposal permits correlation only within asset classes, not across, effectively forcing the correlation between asset classes to be plus or minus 1, whichever produces the higher estimate of VAR.

The three portfolios were constructed to have increasing complexity in terms of optionality and/or asset class composition and possess properties sought frequently by dealers and end-users. The eight VAR calculations performed for each portfolio are summarised in Table 1.

PORTFOLIO 1

Portfolio 1 consists exclusively of US Treasury strips. It was designed to satisfy three conditions at construction: the duration of the portfolio equals that of the 10-year strip[2]; the portfolio has greater convexity than the 10-year strip; and the portfolio performs at least as well as the 10-year strip under a 100 basis point parallel increase or decrease in the Treasury yield curve or under an inversion of the Treasury yield curve. Table 2 describes the composition of and constraints on Portfolio 1, which consists of a long position in two-year and 30-year US Treasury strips. The 10-year US Treasury strip, the benchmark, is included in the table for reference. The net investment in Portfolio 1 is $1 million.

The traditional risk measures show that for very small parallel shifts in the Treasury yield curve, Portfolio 1 performs similarly to the 10-year strip. Moreover, for the plus or minus 100

Table 1. Eight common VAR calculations

VAR approach	Type of simulation	Data base/correlation assumption	Holding period
1	Historical	Prior 100 trading days	One day
2	Historical	Prior 250 trading days	One day
3	Monte Carlo	Historical, RiskMetrics correlations	One day
4	Monte Carlo	Historical, BIS/Basle correlations	One day
5	Historical	Prior 100 trading days	Two weeks
6	Historical	Prior 250 trading days	Two weeks
7	Monte Carlo	Historical, RiskMetrics correlations	Two weeks
8	Monte Carlo	Historical, BIS/Basle correlations	Two weeks

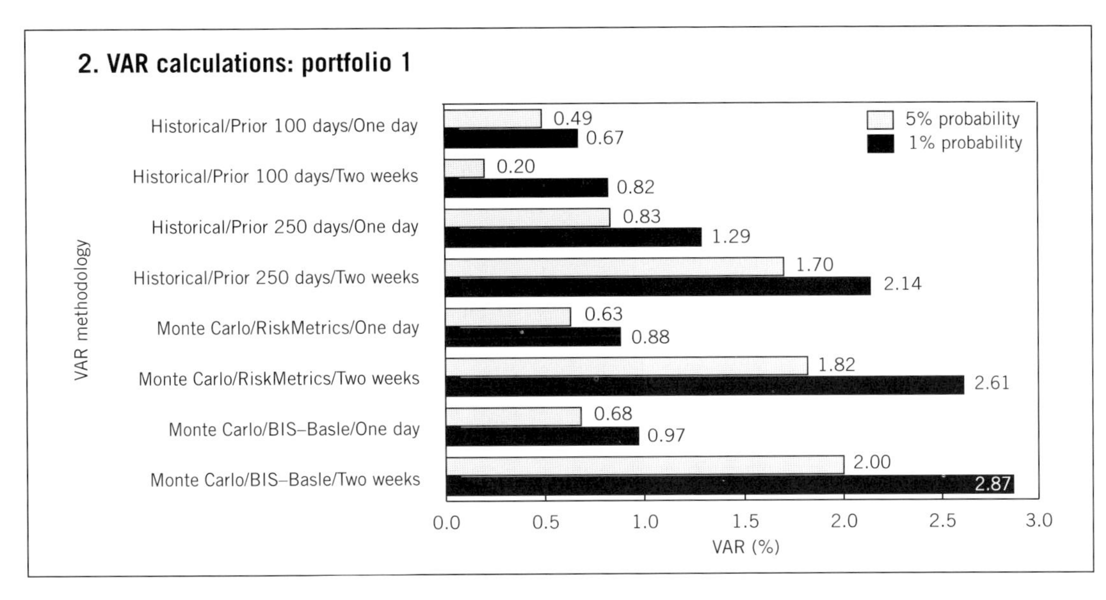

basis point parallel yield curve shifts and inversion, the portfolio's $1 million investment performs slightly better than if it had been invested in the 10-year strip.

The VAR analyses of Portfolio 1 reveal quite different risk profiles than older risk measures such as duration, convexity, and scenario analysis. Figure 2 displays the eight common VAR calculations for this portfolio. The VAR results place significantly different degrees of capital at risk both within and between methodologies. The VAR statistics to the right of each bar may be interpreted as follows: under the assumptions specific to the particular VAR calculation, the probability is 5% (1%) that the portfolio will suffer a loss greater than or equal to the statistic shown. For the third set of bars, for example, under the assumptions made to perform historical simulation over the prior 250-day period, the probability is 1% that a loss equal to or exceeding 1.29% of the $1 million portfolio investment will occur over a one-day time horizon.

Figure 3 (overleaf) compares the results of the historical simulation for Portfolio 1 with the results of the Monte Carlo simulations for one-day and two-week returns.[3] As illustrated by the graphs, the historical simulations present a different view relative to the Monte Carlo simulations. This result is attributable to their extreme dependence on the underlying data set. During the 100-day and 250-day periods included in the historical simulations, the value of Treasury strips

Table 2. Portfolio 1: composition and constraints

Characteristics	2-year strip	30-year strip	Total portfolio	10-year strip (benchmark)
Composition				
Yield[1]	5.91%	6.85%		6.58%
Price[2]	89.12	14.94		52.42
Face amount	$779,778	$2,041,424	$2,281,202	$1,907,670
Purchase amount	$694,964	$305,036	$1,000,000	$1,000,000
Duration and convexity				
Duration	1.712	4.078		5.063
Duration contribution	1.335	8.325	9.660	
Convexity	0.041	1.133		0.514
Convexity contribution	0.032	2.312	2.344	
Scenario analysis				
Yield +100bp	6.91%	7.85%		7.58%
Price/yield +100bp	87.43	11.38		47.60
Position/yield +100bp	$681,775	$232,333	$914,108	$908,051
Yield –100bp	4.91%	5.85%		5.58%
Price/yield –100bp	90.86	19.64		57.75
Position/yield –100bp	$708,743	$401,017	$1,109,490	$1,101,679
Yield curve inversion	7.20%	6.30%		6.58%
Price/inversion	86.95	17.37		52.42
Position/inversion	$678,009	$354,508	$1,032,517	$1,000,000

Note: Prices and yields as of May 25, 1995. The maturities of the two-year, 10-year, and 30-year strips are May 15, 1997, May 15, 2005, and August 15, 2023, respectively.
1 The market yield for each strip is stated on an actual/365 basis with semiannual compounding.
2 The price of each strip is stated as a percentage of face amount.

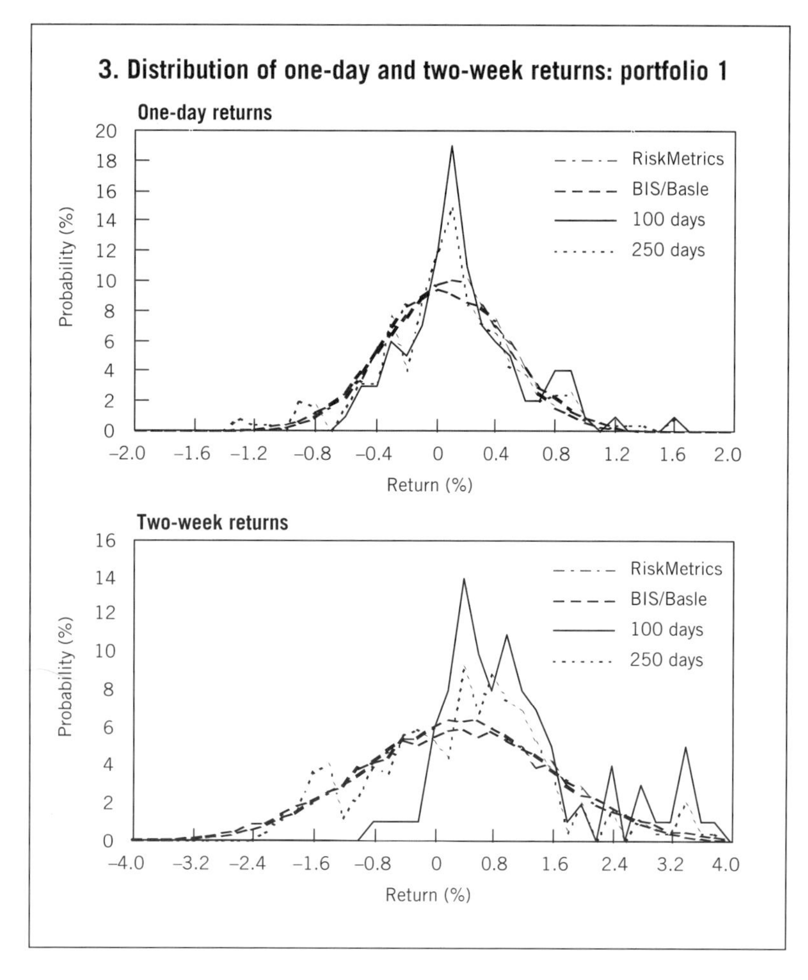

3. Distribution of one-day and two-week returns: portfolio 1

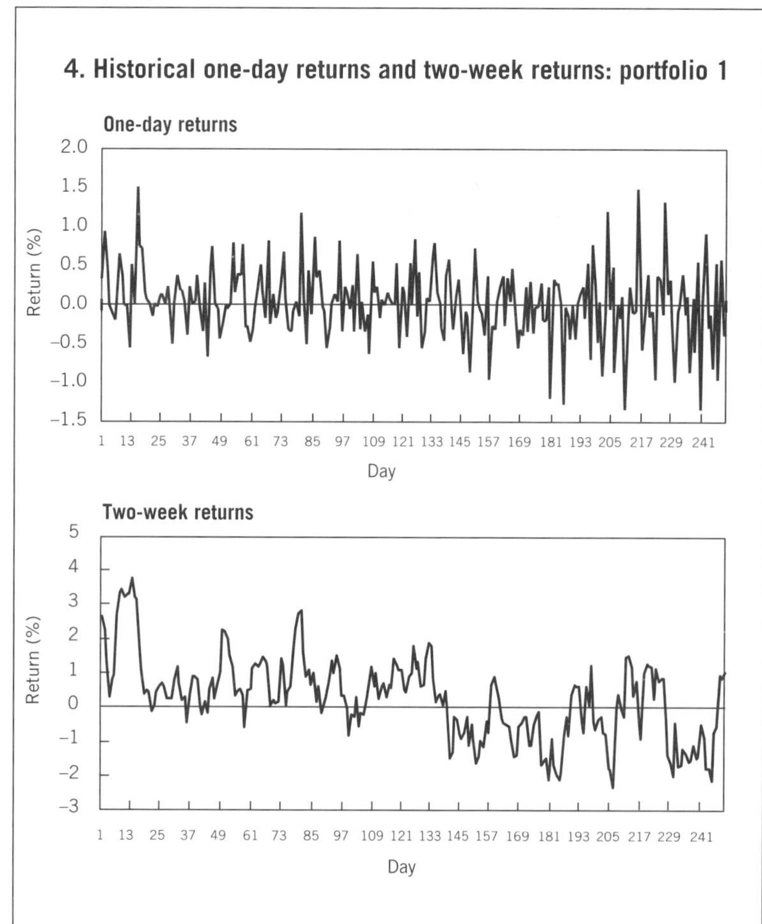

4. Historical one-day returns and two-week returns: portfolio 1

largely appreciated. Had a period of rising interest rates been selected, the result would have been the opposite. The danger in basing VAR estimates on relatively short periods or direct historical observations is apparent – history must repeat itself for the results to predict the future. Although historical estimates may be fairly accurate in a trending market, they will be less accurate when the trend changes.

As summarised in Figure 2, the result for the prior 100 trading days, 5% probability VAR equals 0.49% over a one-day horizon but then drops to 0.20% over a two-week period. For all other VAR types, the VAR result increases with the time horizon, as would be expected. This surprising result is explained by the pattern of results during the specific historical periods. Although the average return is positive during the first 100 trading days (the left side of Figure 4), negative returns are more common over the one-day time horizon than over the two-week time horizon. Thus, VAR is higher for the one-day time horizon than for the two-week time horizon.

Several other conclusions follow from this set of VAR results, as expected given interest rate trends at the time. Monte Carlo simulations indicate higher expected losses than does the 100-day historical simulation but lower expected losses than for the 250-day historical simulation. Historical simulations indicate that increasing the holding period from one day to two weeks decreases the expectation of the highest expected profits and increases the magnitude of expected losses. Note that although Monte Carlo simulations indicate a similar change in the expectation of the highest profits, they predict a larger increase in the magnitude of expected losses (three times versus two times). The difference in VAR driven by the relative randomness of key variables in Monte Carlo versus sample-specific historical simulations is clear.

Time horizon is clearly a crucial parameter in VAR. Firms select quite different time horizons to view their risk. Does the firm wish to analyse its potential capital exposure and expected profit over a short-term or a long-term horizon? In terms of risk-reward appetite, will the firm be satisfied if losses mount for two years but huge profits make up for the losses in the third year? Or, is less erratic performance desired? Often, more even performance is desired by firms that report public financial information, as well as by funds that must publish daily net asset values. Thus, two firms performing identical VAR calculations, other than selection of time horizon, may have different but not necessarily inconsistent VAR results.

Although a model may produce adequate views of capital at risk on an overnight or weekly basis, it may produce inadequate risk views over time horizons of several months, a year, or longer. For example, the calculation of short-horizon VAR may be misleading for customised or exotic products that cannot be liquidated under the assumed time horizon. To the degree that multiple horizons are required, risk systems are rarely capable of incorporating them in aggregating portfolio risks, creating a limitation in sizing true risk exposures. Note that some firms address this problem by adjusting midmarket valuations.

Yet another challenge is that although longer time horizons may be appropriate for instruments such as illiquid, path-dependent options, some mathematical functions are inaccurate beyond small market moves. For example, many mathematical models are incapable of handling discontinuities such as market gapping, or they require strict assumptions such as linearity to produce accurate information. The April 12, 1995 proposed amendment to the 1988 Basle Capital Accord suggests that firms use a single time horizon of two weeks (10 business days) for VAR calculations.

The selection of data sets is another critical component of VAR. As Portfolio 1 illustrates, alternate data sets may produce vastly different risk views. In our experience, intra-day versus end-of-day data often produce contrary views of risk during periods of high volatility. Different risk views will also be created by the use of historical as opposed to market-implied data. Although historical data are most often used to calculate VAR, the length of the historical period varies significantly from firm to firm. Several firms and software packages use a 90-day historical time horizon, but many market participants believe that, at a minimum, a one-year data set should be used. The proposed Basle amendment suggests that firms use a one-year minimum data set for VAR calculations.

Length of time is not the sole criterion to establish regarding the data set. Sampling frequency must be set high enough to ensure that the data set is statistically significant. For example, a one-year database composed of 12 end-of-month data points may be no more relevant than a data set of 12 points selected through random chance. Often, sampling frequency is also sensitive to the time the data are collected. For example, end-of-day data points are likely to produce a different VAR picture than daily high/low/close data points.

After type, sampling frequency, and length of data base are selected, the VAR user must determine whether to exclude certain data points. For example, should the data set include "outliers" caused by one-time events, market gapping, or other dislocations? Such correlations are often characterised as extreme but low probability events. Recent examples are the devaluation of the Mexican peso, the 1987 stock market crashes, and commodity volatility during the Gulf War. Two databases, distinguished by inclusion of outlier events, are likely to produce different VAR calculations.

Yet another challenge in data set selection is determining whether an outlier event is an indication of structural change in the market. For example, the prepayment patterns for mortgage-based securities in the US have changed fundamentally during the past few years, driven by mortgage broker activity. Prior to the change, a drop in interest rates had to prevail for several months before home owners refinanced their mortgages. Subsequently, the refinancing lag shortened from months to weeks during the rally that ended with the Federal Reserve's interest rate hike in February 1994. Use of historical prepayment data could thus be misleading in determining the expected life of many mortgage securities.

To reduce dependence on historical data, given that history may not repeat itself, some firms use data sets based on implied market information. Sensitivity of the VAR calculation not only to exclusion of any data points but also to use of implied versus historical data and to the specific time period covered by the data set should be tested to reveal a particular VAR's dependence on such assumptions.

PORTFOLIO 2

Portfolio 2 consists of outright and options positions on the S&P 500 equity index contract. This portfolio was designed to satisfy several conditions at construction: the delta, or price change of the portfolio, equals that of the S&P 500; the gamma, or convexity of the portfolio, is non-negative; and the portfolio significantly outperforms the S&P 500 equity index contract under downward shocks. Table 3 (overleaf) describes the composition of and constraints on Portfolio 2, which consists of a long position on the S&P 500 equity index contract plus long and short options on the same index. As with Portfolio 1, the net

Table 3. Portfolio 2: composition and constraints

Instrument	Jun 520	Jun 545	Sep 530	Dec 540	S&P 500	Portfolio
Composition						
Type	Put	Call	Call	Put	Long	
Strike versus market	+20	+45	+30	+40	0	
Price	1.95	0.60	14.90	18.45	528.59	
Number	4,157.40	–28,723.80	19,784.80	11,617.00	945.90	
Purchase amount	$8,107	($17,234)	$294,793	$214,335	$499,999	$1,000,000
Delta and gamma						
Unit delta	-0.239	0.105	0.545	-0.503	1.000	
Delta contribution	-0.001	-0.003	0.011	-0.006	0.001	0.002
Unit gamma	0.023	0.015	0.012	0.009	0.000	
Gamma contribution	0.000	0.000	0.000	0.000	0.000	0.000
Scenario analysis						
S&P +20%	634.31	634.31	634.31	634.31	634.31	
Price/S&P +20	0.00	90.02	107.91	0.25	634.31	
Position/S&P +20	$0	($2,585,725)	$2,134,983	$2,897	$600,001	$152,156
S&P –20%	422.87	422.87	422.87	422.87	422.87	
Price/S&P –20%	96.12	0.00	0.00	106.91	422.87	
Position/S&P –20%	$399,623	$0	$49	$1,241,941	$399,997	$2,041,610

investment in Portfolio 2 is $1 million.

The traditional risk measures show that the portfolio outperforms the S&P 500 equity index contract by an approximate factor of five times under a negative 20% shock to the S&P 500. This outperformance in a bearish scenario is accomplished at the price of underperformance during a comparable rise in the S&P 500. The portfolio's $1 million investment is preserved in the value of the S&P 500 equity index contract.

Figure 5 summarises the VAR results for Portfolio 2. Over a one-day horizon, VAR ranges between 0.69% to 0.91% with a 5% expectation and between 1.07% to 1.30% with a 1% expectation. Over a two-week horizon, VAR increases significantly and ranges between 2.31% to 3.93% with a 5% expectation. The two-week, 1% expectation VARs are fairly consistent across methodologies, ranging between 3.48% and 3.95% as illustrated by the bar charts.

Figure 6 compares the results of the historical simulation for Portfolio 2 with the results of the Monte Carlo simulations for one-day and two-week returns, respectively. Of note is the significant change in return patterns based on increasing the holding period from one day to two weeks. In the case of one-day returns, all simulations display low-probability high-return/large-loss expectations. In the case of two-week returns, the distribution changes to display bimodal behaviour. This behaviour is apparent in the lines that appear to be upside down "normal" distributions. A further observation is that the historical simulations produce high-probability high-return expectations and low-probability large-loss expectations relative to the Monte Carlo simulations.

The VAR calculations for Portfolio 2 expose several weaknesses of VAR, which can be managed with the addition of stress testing and limit

5. VAR calculations: portfolio 2

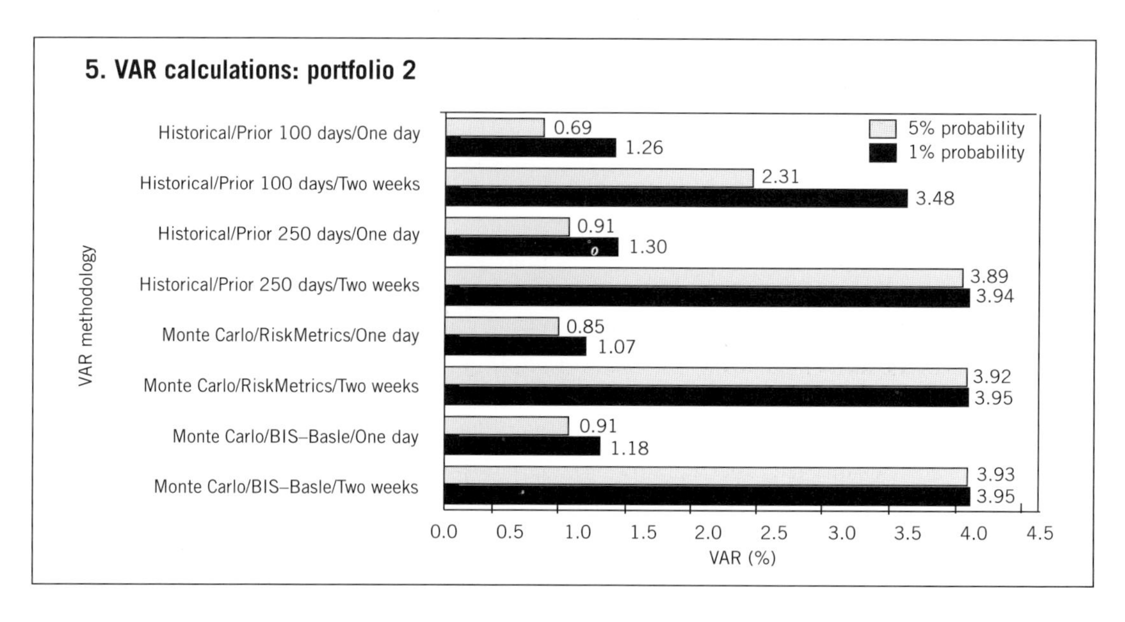

policies. These weaknesses are illustrated by viewing the differences in the portfolio's return over various time horizons. The top panel of Figure 7 shows the return on Portfolio 2 on the day of construction as a function of the underlying asset price (the S&P 500). Given the starting S&P 500 level of approximately 529, the portfolio reflects a small positive return (less than 1%) if the S&P 500 rises to 544, but its greatest returns occur if the S&P 500 drops below 510. Small downward moves of the S&P 500 (between 510 and 529), and larger upward moves (above 544) produce losses.

The centre panel of Figure 7 shows the return on Portfolio 2 at the end of the first two-week holding period, again as a function of the underlying asset price (the S&P 500). At about the S&P value of 541, the magnitude of Portfolio 2's performance changes by a factor of four from the first one-day horizon to the first two-week horizon, as illustrated by the amplitude of the graphs (1% versus 4%, respectively). The price intervals under which Portfolio 2 loses and makes money change as well.

Portfolio 2 poses significantly different risks at different points in time. For example, as shown in the bottom panel of Figure 7, prior to the expiration of the short position in the June call (strike of 545), the portfolio presents the possibility of huge loss. After expansion of the June 545 call, however, Portfolio 2 no longer presents this possibility.

From management's perspective, VAR fails as a sole measure of risk because it does not reveal the true exposure a firm faces. VAR produces a small, finite number in all eight cases (less than 4%). Another common risk control measure, a prohibition on portfolios with negative gamma, may also fail. Portfolio 2 displays slightly positive gamma at construction and as of the time horizons in all panels of Figure 7.

Most users combine VAR with stress testing to address questions such as, "How much do I expect to lose the other 1% of the time?" Note that in the case of Portfolio 2, stress tests may fail to reveal the true nature of the firm's risk, producing finite pictures of profits and losses that depend upon the level of the S&P 500 assumed. As with VAR, the quality of the answer depends on the inputs, including the financial engineer's ability to select appropriate scenarios.

As experienced during the European currency crisis, the Gulf War, and the Mexican peso crisis, not only are key factors such as maximum volatility difficult to predict but also correlation rela-

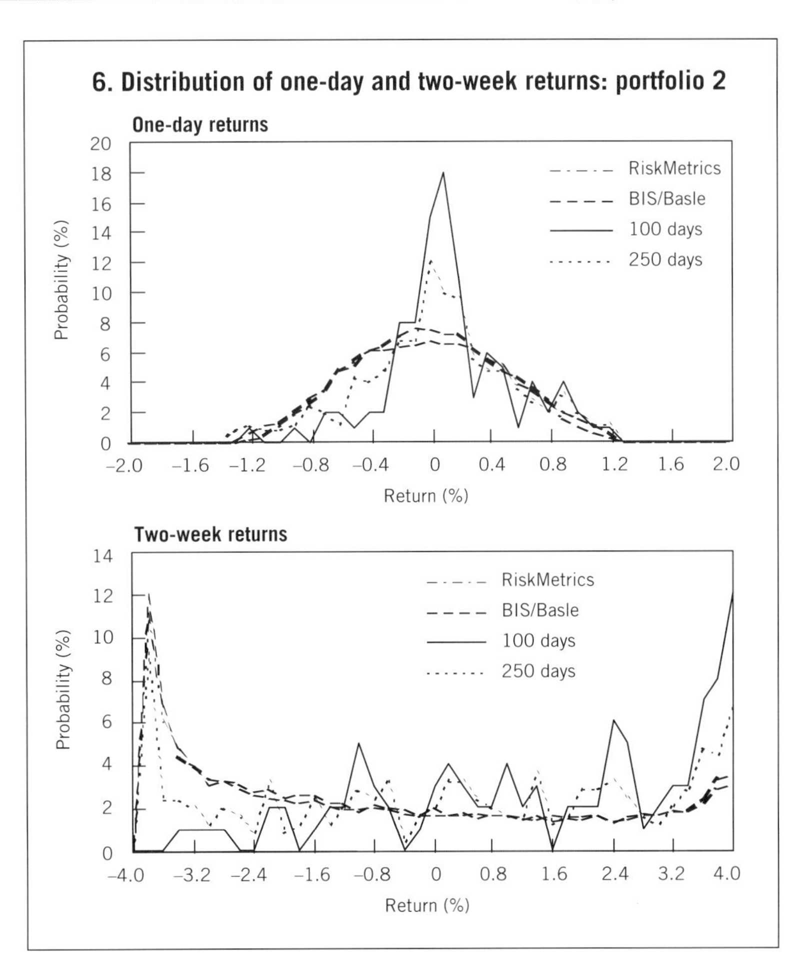

6. Distribution of one-day and two-week returns: portfolio 2

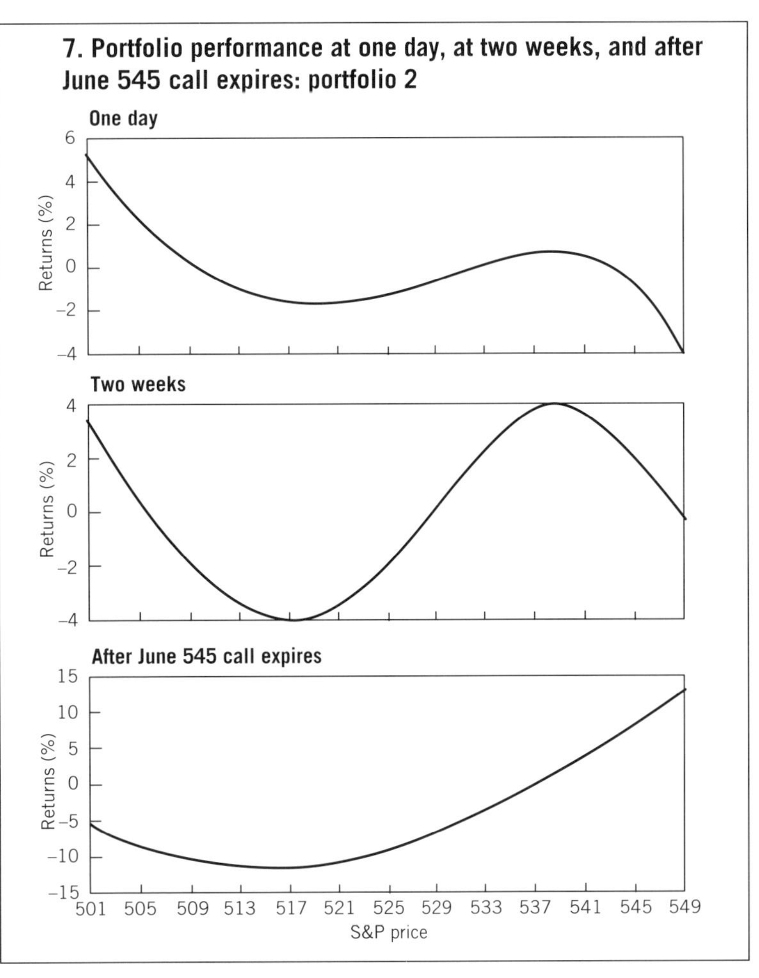

7. Portfolio performance at one day, at two weeks, and after June 545 call expires: portfolio 2

tionships often change substantially during extreme market moves. The increasing complexity and optionality of many derivatives makes relevant scenario selection even harder. Given these challenges, many firms design stress tests to analyse the impact of large historical market moves. In our experience, portfolios do not necessarily produce their greatest losses during extreme market moves. Whether asset-based or asset-plus-liability based, portfolios often possess Achilles' heels that require only small moves or changes between instruments or markets to produce significant losses. Stress testing extreme market moves will do little to reveal the greatest risk of loss for such portfolios. Furthermore, a view of a portfolio's expected behaviour over time often reveals that the same stress test that indicates a small impact today indicates embedded land mines with a large impact during future periods. This trait is particularly true of options-based portfolios that change characteristics because of time rather than because of changes in the components of the portfolio. The need for other risk measure - for example, limits that restrict writing uncovered call options - is clear.

PORTFOLIO 3

Portfolio 3 consists of the combination of Portfolio 1 and Portfolio 2. The portfolios are equally weighted, with the net investment in Portfolio 3 totalling $1 million.

Again, the VAR analyses, shown in Figure 8, reveal a wide range of risk profiles for the portfolio. As in the case of Portfolios 1 and 2, historical simulations present a different view of risk than do the Monte Carlo simulations, and Portfolio 3's VAR differences are magnified over the two-week horizon. One-day returns for this multi-asset class portfolio display more consistency under the VAR methodologies than one-day returns for the single-asset class portfolios that compose it.

The sensitivity to correlation assumptions is demonstrated by the difference in results between the Monte Carlo simulations under RiskMetrics and BIS/Basle factors. Under the RiskMetrics model, positive correlation is assumed between the Treasury strips in Portfolio 1 and the S&P 500 equity index positions in Portfolio 2. Under the BIS/Basle method, the correlation is assumed to be 1 between long positions and -1 between long and short positions. Not surprisingly, the BIS/Basle VAR factors are higher than RiskMetric factors in all cases.

Figure 9 compares the results of the historical simulation for Portfolio 3 with the results of the Monte Carlo simulations for one-day and two-week returns. As with Portfolio 2, return patterns change significantly when the holding period is increased from one day to two weeks, but high-probability extreme events no longer occur.

Correlation assumptions are an important aspect of VAR. Firms select quite different answers to which exposures are allowed to offset each other and by how much. For example, is the Japanese yen correlated with movements in the Italian lira or the Mexican peso? Is the price of Saudi Light correlated with movements in the price of natural gas? If so, by how much? VAR requires that the user determine correlations not only within markets (for example, currency underlyings or commodity underlyings) but also across markets (for example, how do changes in the bond market in the US affect the Australian equity market?). Given a portfolio with multiple instruments within and across markets, VAR varies significantly under alternate correlation

8. VAR calculations: portfolio 3

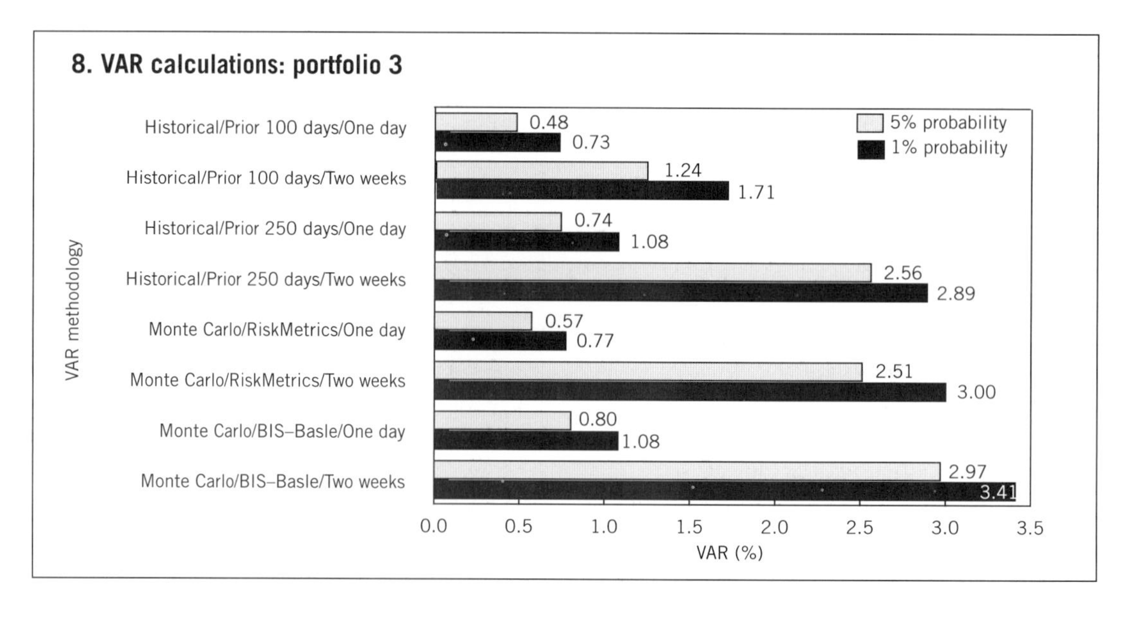

assumptions. Pension funds have addressed the issues of correlation for decades in studying strategic versus tactical allocation of assets. Correlation issues are also a crucial component of performance measurement across asset classes. A single approach to assessing correlation does not exist, and opposite views are common. For example, what happens when a market breaks through its historical or implied trading pattern and violates the correlation assumption in place?

Recently, many currencies that previously had displayed little or no correlations with the Mexican peso made sympathy moves during the devaluation of the Peso. In some cases, the increased volume of barrier options on spreads (also known as knock-out or knock-in options) has been blamed for unexpected high correlations during periods when market levels approach strike levels, with both the writers and the buyers of the barriers suspected of trading in large volume to influence the outcome.

Correlation assumptions also can mask risks that may be significant for many firms. For example, many portfolios display embedded rollover risk created through timing mismatches. An example is the common strategy that funds use to hedge long-dated foreign currency positions by rolling over short-dated forward foreign exchange contracts. Under common time horizons for VAR and its correlation assumptions, a flat currency risk position often appears. This pattern can mask the long-term rollover risk intrinsic in hedging the currency risk of 10- or 20-year securities with one- to three-month currency contracts.

In our review of different approaches to VAR, some firms assumed that all cash flows were correlated across all markets and others assumed a lower degree of correlation. Sophisticated mean-variance models - for example, the one used to compute the RiskMetrics data set - allow correlation for all instruments across all markets that are covered. At the other extreme are models that allow correlation only within asset classes (eg fixed income, foreign exchange, equity) and require perfect positive correlation across risk-factor groups. An example of this approach is the proposed amendment to the 1988 Basle Capital Accord on market risks.

VAR requires the use of mathematical models to value individual instruments, as well as to value the aggregate portfolio. Variance in the valuations produced by widely accepted models (termed "mark-to-model" risk) are well-documented and the subject of many research papers.[4] For example, the Black-Scholes versus Hull and White options models can produce differences of 5% or more in pricing, even when all input data are identical. In addition, the selection of probability distribution(s) (an assumption of anticipated or experienced market behaviour) in one VAR model versus another is a topic of great debate among theoreticians and practitioners.

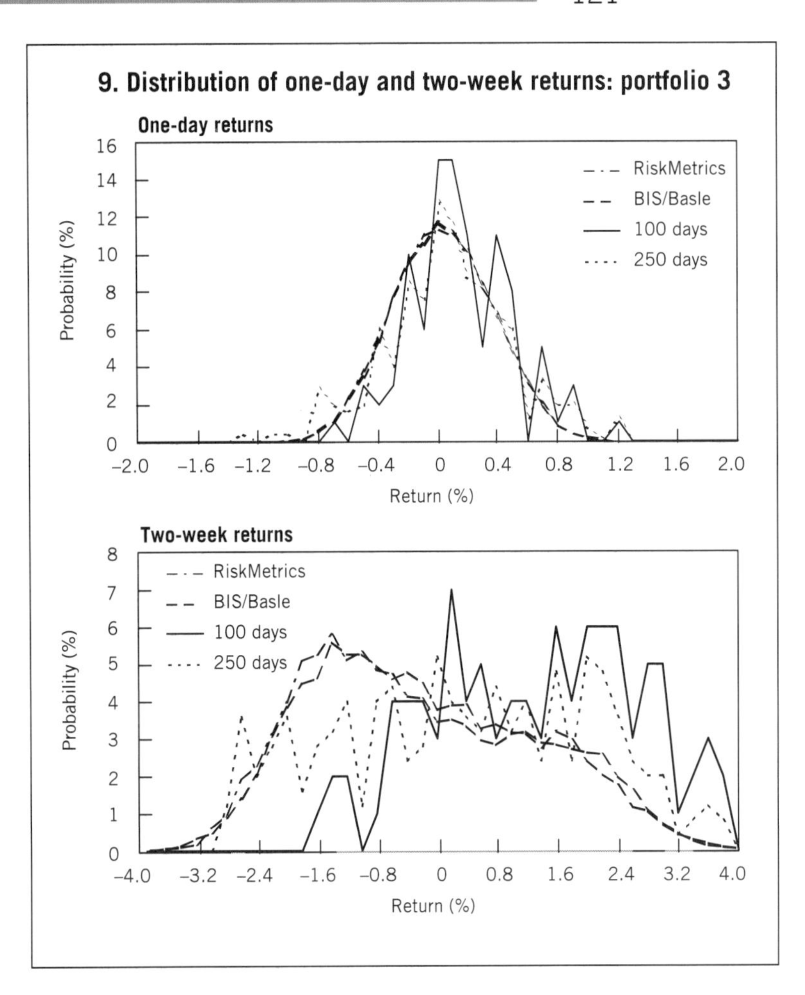

Conclusion

New studies of the differences in VAR are contemplated. Such studies will use additional computational techniques, alternate assumptions, and a broader range of portfolios in terms of number of positions, type of positions, and number of asset classes. As highlighted by the three portfolios, the picture of expected capital at risk is widely dependent upon the VAR methodology and the assumptions behind the specific calculation. Not only do the eight VAR results for the individual portfolios differ significantly, but the magnitude of the difference does not follow a clear pattern with increasing complexity of the portfolio. Thus, dealers and end-users are in a precarious position. The dependence on technology and skilled professionals is greater than ever before. Although this dependence has produced invaluable advances in financial engineering and risk management, some firms have been lulled into a false sense of security. Often, firms forget the degree to which the output of models depends upon the modeller's perspective and assumptions. A firm's senior management and directors or trustees are shocked to learn that their firm's risk reports can change dramatically under alternate assumptions. This fact is even more surprising when the alternate assumptions are those they consider to be likely or reasonable.

Some firms make the mistake of equating VAR under a 99% expectation to the certainty or confidence that the firm will not lose more than the stated amount more than 1% of the time (ie fewer than three business days a year). As demonstrated by the sample portfolios, the 99% VAR changes significantly based on the time horizon, data base, correlation assumptions, mathematical models, and quantitative techniques that are used. Accordingly, VAR does not provide certainty or confidence of outcomes, but rather an expectation of outcomes based on a specific set of assumptions. Furthermore, many risk variables such as political risk, liquidity risk, personnel risk, regulatory risk, phantom liquidity risk, and others cannot be captured through quantitative techniques. Yet, as demonstrated by recent, well-publicised losses, such variables can cause significant risk. For this reason, VAR must be supplemented not only with stress testing but also with prudent checks and balances, procedures, policies, controls, limits, random audits, and appropriate reserves.

The BIS, the Group of Thirty, the Derivatives Product Group, the International Swaps and Derivatives Association, and many national regulators have declared VAR fundamental to current best practices in risk management. But models and math, although necessary to manage risk, are not sufficient to do so. The inability to capture many qualitative factors and exogenous risk variables points to the need to combine VAR with stress tests, checks and balances, procedures, policies, controls, limits, and reserves. Perhaps the limitations of quantitative techniques explain the recent announcement by Moody's that although 25% of its volatility rating for funds will be based on VAR, the remaining 75% will be based on qualitative factors. In sum, mathematics is integral to finance, but finance does not always follow mathematics.

Some regulators propose to allow firms to use their own internal VAR models plus assumptions, but others do not. Although the Basle amendment allows banks to select their own internal models to calculate VAR (subject to the proviso that certain assumptions are required for VAR's key factors and to oversight by national regulators), the National Association of Insurance Commissioners' proposed risk-based capital standard (RBC) requires insurers to use a single, rigid approach for their VAR-type calculations.[5] The use of a single, rigid approach may have a deleterious effect. Namely, because of a rigid correlation assumption, RBC may penalise the insurer for a successful asset allocation strategy. From a regulatory standpoint, the choice of standardised versus internally-selected VAR approaches presents difficult trade-offs. The use of a single, rigid approach may stymie the development of new and improved risk measurement, creating expense for regulators, shareholders, employees, and taxpayers alike. A proper understanding of the assumptions behind VAR, as well as its limitations and pitfalls, will help all to benefit from this powerful technique.

1 *Note that selection of key statistical parameters such as the mean and variance can significantly affect distributions and, therefore, the results of simulations.*

2 *Duration is defined here as the change in price with respect to yield.*

3 *The Monte Carlo simulations are based on the assumptions that the Treasury strip yields are lognormally distributed and that the average change, or "drift," in each yield is zero.*

4 *T. Styblo Beder, "The Realities of Marking to Model",* Bank Accounting & Finance *Vol 7, no 4 (1994), pp. 4–12.*

5 *Note that a single RBC approach exists for life insurance companies, and a single alternate approach exists for property/casualty companies.*

Report Card on VAR: High Potential but Slow Starter*

Tanya Styblo Beder
Capital Market Risk Advisors Inc

For all its cachet, value-at-risk is no cookie-cutter solution to the risk management problems facing financial institutions. Implementation is hampered by the need to make simplifying assumptions. Differences in VAR methodology and the many assumptions required mean that risk managers should have a clear understanding of the components of their VAR measures and must combine VAR with other risk tools.

While value-at-risk (VAR) shows increasing promise as a risk-measurement tool, there are more questions than answers after three years of use. Despite this, the concept is widely endorsed by regulators such as the Bank for International Settlements, the Federal Reserve, the Office of the Comptroller of the Currency, and the Securities and Exchange Commission. It is mandated for many under generally-accepted accounting principles, is part of the rating process by agencies, and is encouraged by key industry groups such as the Group of Thirty, the Derivatives Policy Group, and the International Swaps and Derivatives Association. But implementation of VAR is harder than grasping the simplicity of its concept. First, not all VARs are equal. Second, vast quantities of data and significant modelling or systems efforts may be required. Third, firms must design and implement risk management add-ons to address VAR's limitations and weaknesses. While dealers typically are further along with VAR implementation than end users, few if any are finished with the process. This paper surveys the current realities of VAR and what we have learned to date.

Three main types of VAR

VAR is the great equaliser. It translates the risk of any financial instrument into its potential loss under specific assumptions.[1] There are three main types of VAR: variance/covariance VAR, historical VAR, and simulation VAR.

VARIANCE/COVARIANCE VAR

Under this method, sometimes called "analytic VAR," financial instruments are decomposed (or mapped) into delta equivalents[2] consisting of basic financial building blocks, or market factors. Once historical or other distributions for these market factors are specified, VAR and other measures are computed using standard statistical techniques. In most cases, historical data is used to build the variance/covariance matrix for the market factors, making this aspect of the calculation dependent upon the time period selected. Over the past two years, data sets that provide distributions for many common market factors (for example RiskMetrics[3]) have become available, as have commercial software packages that perform VAR computations.

HISTORICAL VAR

Under this method, financial instruments are analysed over the number of days in the historical observation period (for example, 100 days), and the actual change that was experienced in the value of each financial instrument is calculated using the desired time horizon (for example, overnight). Note that while most users analyse financial instruments specifically, some

* *This article was first published in* Bank Accounting and Finance, *Vol. 10 (1996). This copyrighted material is reprinted with permission from Institutional Investor, Inc., 488 Madison Avenue, New York, New York 10022. The author would like to thank Frank Iacono for his valuable input.*

translate their financial instruments into equivalent building blocks or market factors and calculate the changes on these. Once the changes in value are calculated, each change is added to today's value for the financial instrument or its equivalent to produce an array of observations. As this replicates historical behaviour, the risk view depends upon the time period selected. To complete the calculation, the array is analysed statistically. For example, if there are 100 observations, the fifth lowest observation value would be the one-day 95% confidence interval VAR.

SIMULATION VAR

Under this methodology, the theoretical probability distribution of changes in value for each financial instrument or its equivalent is calculated for the desired time horizon (for example, over two weeks) as per the distribution parameters specified in the simulation. Typically, correlations and lognormal or other distributions are incorporated. The theoretical changes in values are then added to today's value for the financial instrument or its "equivalent" and arrayed as in the case of historical VAR to produce the desired confidence interval VAR. The process is often completed under varying sets of parameters.

Each type of VAR has its strengths and weaknesses. Variance/covariance VAR is the least computationally intensive and free data is available. However, it is based on normal or lognormal distributions so it misses fat-tailed behaviour[4] and does not properly incorporate options or other non-linear instruments. Historical VAR is the easiest to implement from a systems perspective and may be the easiest to explain to the non-mathematically inclined. However, its output depends heavily on the time period selected (simply stated, history must repeat itself). Simulation VAR can incorporate any joint distribution for the market factors, so offers the greatest flexibility for sensitivity analyses regarding market plus model issues, and fully captures non-linear instruments. However, it has the greatest systems, programming, and data needs.

Seven lessons about VAR

Beginning in 1994, dealers focused on implementing at least some VAR measure and devoted their resources to data, systems, and programming challenges. Risk-management software vendors took a similar approach, focusing primarily on the need to expand their systems to include at least one VAR alternative. At first, most implemented variance/covariance or historical VAR calculations. Larger corporations implemented VAR as well, with the goal of comparing the treasury area's performance versus an established internal benchmark. Some institutional investors and investment managers (particularly insurance companies, mutual funds, and "manager of managers") began to implement VAR over the past six to 12 months, with the goal of calculating risk-adjusted portfolio performance. Many smaller corporations, as well as pension funds, public funds, foundations, and endowments, have started to address VAR more recently.

To date and in general, the theoretical discussions of VAR far exceeded firms' actual practices[5]. This is due to the many practical issues that complicate and surround its implementation. However, valuable lessons have been learned, and these are being addressed as VAR approaches its third year of use in risk management. Seven lessons follow.

LESSON ONE

For instruments with non-linear price functions, variance/covariance VAR understates risk. The variance/covariance approach significantly understates risk for portfolios with options or financial instruments with non-linear price functions,[6] particularly during periods of large volatility or with large changes in the price of the underlying. Most dealers with significant non-linear exposures have implemented or are switching over to simulation-based VAR calculations for at least the non-linear books within their businesses. This presents aggregation issues regarding VARs calculated with different methods over different time horizons. Research is under way regarding risk management add-ons to a variance/covariance approach that better reflects non-linear risks.

LESSON TWO

Historical and simulation VAR can differ drastically. The historical VAR and simulation VAR approaches may produce vastly different results, especially when the historical period comprises a heavily trending market. This is due to the fact that the key variables in simulation VAR are computed according to the user's expectations or may be computed randomly and often differ substantially from those for the recent historical period. There are many types of simulation, each determined by the user's preferences and parameters. Monte Carlo simulations are the most common type of random simulations. To the degree random or user-specified expectations vary from trending market expectations, differences between the two approaches will be magnified. Note that the choice of simulation parameters is itself an important determinant of the VAR result, so some dealers and end users are beginning to stress-test the sensitivity of the VAR result to alternate sets of parameters. Appropriate stress tests vary and depend upon factors such as portfolio composition, holding period, risk appetite, systems capabilities, etc.

LESSON THREE

Mapping can impair VAR calculations. For large dealers and end users, historical VAR and simulation VAR[7] require vast quantities of data plus numerous pricing models. To enable calculation of VAR as models and databases are built or to reduce the total amount required, most VAR users have resorted to some degree of mapping financial instruments into equivalents and/or matrix pricing. This often results in significant differences between the risk/reward profile of the actual financial instrument and its mapped equivalent. Research is under way to learn the degree to which this impacts the VAR result, particularly in the case of non-diversified portfolios, heavily engineered instruments, exotic instruments, etc. I have reviewed several cases in which the VAR calculation was performed correctly, but the accuracy lost through mapping or matrix pricing produced misleading results for the actual portfolio.

LESSON FOUR

Poor assumptions about diversification can lead to flawed results. The variance/covariance approach requires mapping financial instruments into market factors that are contained in the matrix. To facilitate this process, entire instrument classes are often mapped into market indexes. For example, all domestic stocks may be mapped into the S&P 500 or all corporate bonds into a swap index. For several portfolios we have reviewed, mapping an undiversified portfolio into an assumed diversified portfolio produced misleading results. Research is under way to analyse the relationship between the quality of the VAR result after such mapping and varying degrees of diversification.

LESSON FIVE

Combining adjusted VARs from different time periods can be misleading. Many VAR users employ different time horizons for different trading areas or asset classes. For example, an overnight horizon is used for the forward foreign exchange positions, while a longer time horizon is used for real estate or illiquid/exotic financial instruments. To obtain a firmwide VAR statistic for a comparable time period, adjustments are made using statistical approximations such as the square root of time. To the degree that markets do not follow linear price behaviour and normal distributions (most markets do not) and to the degree that drift should be considered, misleading results will be produced by such approximations.

LESSON SIX

VARs may be less comparable than they appear. Performance measurement and capital allocation are common goals of VAR users. The desire is to allocate capital to areas that have the greatest performance with the least amount of risk. However, many financial instruments and markets are inefficient and have risk profiles that change over time. Thus, the VAR for highly liquid, diversified portfolios may be compared to the VAR for highly illiquid, undiversified portfolios, and results are often not comparable. Furthermore, two portfolios or business areas with equivalent VAR and return may have different risk tails, thus producing different expectations of loss outside of the confidence bands. Research is under way to see what can be learned from analysing the changes in VAR over time (that is, the first derivative with respect to time). Other research is studying the relationship between downside risk and the degree of diversification to determine how these risk dimensions should be incorporated into performance measurement and the capital allocation decision.

LESSON SEVEN

Accounting and economic measures may not mix. Many corporations use VAR in conjunction with a benchmark in the treasury area. For many, the goal is to manage the volatility of earnings. Two common problems arise with this approach. First, accounting realities may differ significantly from economic realities. To the degree that the benchmark is accounting-based and the VAR calculation is economic-based, this problem will be exacerbated. Second, earnings occur continuously and involve all business activities of the company, while VAR typically is based on a snapshot of selected activities of the corporation at a point in time. Both require adjustments in how VAR is employed.

Which VAR should you use?

VAR research to date primarily has involved portfolios of simple, highly liquid financial instruments such as Treasury strips, equity index options, and forward foreign exchange contracts. Our review of dozens of dealers' and end-users' risk-management techniques revealed vast differences not only in the type of VAR calculation but also in the VAR statistics produced. Variances in the VAR statistic ranged by as much as 14 times for the same portfolio, depending on the type of VAR calculation and the time horizon.[8] Large variances in VAR have been corroborated by others' research, particularly for portfolios that contain options.[9] Yet other research suggests that variances in VAR may be less significant for portfolios that do not contain options or other instruments with non-linear price behaviour, especially over one-day holding periods,[10] and that the length of sampling periods plays an important role.[11]

Which VAR methodology to select depends on several factors. Typically, dealers and end-users with complex portfolios set a goal of implementing a consistent, firmwide VAR that reflects their outlook preferences and the complexity of the portfolio. For portfolios with options or significant non-linear price behaviour, the historical VAR and simulation VAR produce superior results to the variance/covariance VAR. However, the systems, model, data, personnel, educational, and time requirements of the historical and simulation VARs often result in the use of variance/covariance VARs or multiple VAR methodologies on an interim basis. The choice between historical and simulation VAR resides largely with the user's outlook preferences and the desire to perform sensitivity analyses. Historical VAR is based on actual, past market experience whereas simulation VAR is based on the user's outlook and expectations. Full sensitivity analyses can be performed only on the latter.

Once the outlook preferences and the complexity of the portfolio are analysed and one or more VARs are selected, users must make decisions about several important dimensions of the calculation:

❑ the length of the VAR horizon (overnight, two weeks, longer),
❑ database,
❑ correlation assumptions,
❑ mathematical engine and quantitative approach,
❑ percentage of outcomes to be considered,
❑ other risk-management and risk-measurement tools combined with VAR.

THE LENGTH OF THE VAR HORIZON

VAR requires the firm to select a time horizon for analysing risk in the context of expected losses. For example, dealers often select overnight time horizons, while pension funds and corporations often select longer horizons.

One challenge in the selection of the time horizon is that while a model may produce adequate views of capital at risk on an overnight or weekly basis, it may produce inadequate risk views over time horizons of several months, a year, or longer. For example, the calculation of one-day or overnight VAR may be misleading for customised or exotic products that cannot be analysed, action decided upon, and liquidated in such a time frame. The 1995 Basle Amendment suggests that firms employ a single time horizon of two weeks (10 business days) for VAR calculations. This may be short relative to the life of many asset classes and other exposures and potentially too long for highly liquid instruments.

A second challenge is that while longer time horizons may be preferred for instruments such as illiquid, path-dependent options, some mathematical functions are inaccurate beyond small market moves. For example, many mathematical models are incapable of handling discontinuities such as market gapping or require linearity to produce accurate information, yet these are used in pricing models that are part of the VAR calculation. Over the past two years, dozens of dealers and end-users announced losses due to differences between estimated short-term profits and actual experience over longer time horizons. This suggests that firms should test the sensitivity of the VAR calculation to alternate assumptions regarding pricing models (see below) and time horizon.

For some firms, a third challenge is to compare and combine VARs calculated over alternate time frames and under different methods. As discussed above, the translation of long-horizon VARs into short-horizon VARs (and vice versa) typically assumes linearity, joint normal relationships (that is, that the square root of time is sufficient), or static relationships (that is, no drift), which may produce misleading results.

DATABASE

VAR requires data covering all relevant market factors and variables on which to perform the calculations. Vastly different risk views may be produced by alternate data sets. For example, during a recent 24-hour period, the 10-year US Treasury traded at as high a price as 103 for three hours but only at par for one hour. Thus, time of day (or intra-day data versus end-of-day data) can produce contrary risk views via VAR. Different risk views can also be created by the use of historical versus market-implied data. Note that historical end-of-day data is most often employed to calculate VAR, but the historical period selected varies significantly from firm to firm. Some firms employ the most recent 90-day time horizon while others use the past year at a minimum. Other firms expand the time horizon to capture periods of stressful market moves such as market crashes or dislocations. The proposed Basle Amendment suggests that firms employ a one-year minimum data set for VAR calculations.

Length of time is not the sole criterion to establish and test regarding the data set. As discussed, mapping procedures are a critical part of most VAR processes. Furthermore, sampling frequency and independence of data also can affect VAR significantly. For example, a one-year database comprised of 12 end-of-month data points may be no more relevant than a data set of 12 points selected through random chance. Alternately, theoretical mark-to-model prices for customised or illiquid instruments may be far from market prices at the time of transactions. Such data issues can cause unpleasant surprises, as experienced in 1994 by many mutual funds, pension funds, and municipalities that monitored engineered mortgage securities and/or inverse floaters at month-end based on theoretical values.[12]

Another decision regarding the data is whether to exclude certain data points. For example, should the data set include outlier events caused by onetime events, market gapping, or other dislocations? Such occurrences are often characterised as extreme but low-probability events. Recent examples are the devaluation of the Mexican peso, the 1987 stock market crashes, and commodity volatility during the Gulf War. Note that two databases, distinguished by inclusion of outlier events, are likely to produce different VAR calculations.

Yet another challenge is to determine whether an outlier event is an indication of structural change in the market. For example, fundamental change in the prepayment patterns for mortgage-based securities in the US occurred over the past few years, driven by mortgage broker activity and education of the home owner. Before the change, conventional wisdom dictated that a drop in interest rates had to prevail for two to three months before refinancing occurred. Subsequently, this refinancing lag shortened from months to weeks, and the mortgage market demonstrated new prepayment patterns during the rally that ended with the Federal Reserve's interest-rate hike in February 1994. Thus, use of historical prepayment data was misleading in predicting the expected life (and therefore return) of many mortgage securities.

Some firms employ data sets based on implied market information to reduce dependence on historical data. Whatever the data set, firms should stress-test the sensitivity of the VAR calculation not only to exclude any data points but also for sampling error and the use of specific historical periods and/or mark-to-model dependence. The goal is to determine whether alternate data sets drive large differences in the value of VAR for the same portfolio or exposures.

CORRELATION ASSUMPTIONS

VAR requires that the user decide which exposures are allowed to offset each other and by how much. For example, is the Japanese yen correlated to movements in the Italian lira or the Mexican peso? Is the price of Saudi Light correlated to movements in the price of natural gas? If so, by how much? VAR requires that the user determine correlations not only within markets (for example, US dollar currency underlyings versus US dollar commodity underlyings) but also across markets (for example, how do changes in the bond market in the US relate to changes in the equity market in Australia?). Note that mapping procedures have additional embedded correlation assumptions. For example, mapping individual stocks into the S&P 500 or fixed-income securities into the swap curve translate into the assumption that individual financial instruments move as the market overall. While this may be a reasonable assumption for well-diversified portfolios, it may not be reasonable for undiversified or illiquid portfolios.

Dealers, end users, regulators, and financial theorists espouse wildly different views on the topic of correlation relationships both within and across markets. For instance, pension funds have tackled correlation issues for decades in analysing strategic versus tactical allocation of assets. Pension funds with a lack of diversification across asset classes (for example, stocks versus bonds) or capital markets (for example, domestic versus foreign) may well be considered to be in violation of the prudent man standard of the Employee Retirement Income Security Act of

1974 (ERISA). Financial theory[13] demonstrated the value of diversification, both within and across markets, decades ago. While cross-border legal and netting risks may exist, these risks typically are managed and reserves are taken separately from market risks. Despite the use of separate reserves and risk calculations, the 1995 Basle Amendment allows only the extreme position of correlation within asset classes. For calculating VAR, the amendment assumes a correlation of 1 between long positions and a correlation of –1 between long and short positions. While this may be of little consequence for some relationships (for example, the correlation between strong currencies and interest rates in European Community countries), it is of huge consequence for others (for example, the correlation between the price of a restaurant stock in Sri Lanka and a Yankee bond issued by the Canadian telephone company). Not surprisingly, the rigid correlation methodology in the 1995 Basle Amendment raises VAR significantly relative to more common correlation assumptions.[14]

Additional challenges exist. What happens if a market breaks through its historical or implied trading pattern and violates the correlation assumption in place? A recent example is provided by the many currencies that previously displayed little or no historical correlation to the Mexican peso but made sympathy moves during the peso's devaluation. What happens if some temporary phenomenon alters correlations significantly? For example, barrier options on spreads (also known as knock-out or knock-in options) have been blamed for unexpected, high correlations during periods that market levels approach strike levels, with both the writers and the buyers of the barriers suspected of large trading volume to influence the outcome in their favour.

In CMRA's review of different approaches to VAR, some firms assumed that all cash flows were correlated across all markets, while others assumed a lower degree of correlation. Sophisticated mean-variance models, for example the one used to compute the RiskMetrics data set, allow correlation for all instruments across all markets that are covered. At the other extreme are models such as the 1995 Basle Amendment, which require correlation of 1 or –1, depending on what is least favourable to the VAR calculation.

MATHEMATICAL ENGINE AND QUANTITATIVE APPROACH

All VAR calculations require the use of mathematical models to value individual instruments (or their components or assumed equivalents) as well as to value the aggregate portfolio. Valuation variances produced by widely accepted models (termed mark-to-model risk) are well documented and the subject of numerous articles.[15] For example, the Black-Scholes versus Hull and White options models can produce differences of 5% or more in pricing, even when all input data and curve construction (that is, crossover from futures to cash, interpolation, extrapolation, etc) are identical. In addition, the selection of probability distribution(s)[16] in one model versus another varies from firm to firm and is a topic of great debate among theoreticians and practitioners alike.

While many dealers and end-users are well-versed in testing the behaviour of an individual position or portfolio given market moves (for example, what happens if interest rates rise or fall by one basis point or by 200 basis points?), they have only recently commenced testing the behaviour of individual positions or portfolios for changes in model assumptions. Given the increased pace of losses due to model risk (the risk that the market price will be different than that calculated theoretically by a model), firms should test the sensitivity of the VAR calculation to alternate mapping and model assumptions. The goal is to determine how much the risk picture changes if one changes either the underlying mathematical model or one or more assumptions regarding the data source, time of collection, curve creation, probability distribution, mathematical process, or other factors to reflect the VAR approaches described in the 1995 Basle Amendment, the RiskMetrics Technical Document, or other common VAR models. To the degree that other common models indicate an aggressive stance by the firm, an adjustment to the VAR calculation may be appropriate or a higher VAR factor may be appropriate to protect the firm's capital from a market-risk perspective. Such model-risk adjustments should be taken in addition to those for credit risk, market risk, liquidity risk, operations risk, or other standard risk reserves.

PERCENTAGE OF OUTCOMES TO BE CONSIDERED

The VAR methodology requires the firm to select the percentage of outcomes that will be used to determine the expectation of loss. For example, some firms calculate VAR under the requirement that the outcome or a worse outcome is expected approximately 1% of the time (often called a "99% confidence interval"). Others pose a lower requirement of expecting the outcome approximately 10% or 5% of the time. Perhaps due to the confidence interval terminology, some firms make the mistake of equating their VAR expectation to a certainty that the firm will not lose more than the stated amount. This is incorrect.

An important challenge in selecting the percentage of outcomes is to address the firm's need for an absolute loss limit. For example, a 95% confidence interval dictates that losses are expected to exceed the VAR limit at least once every three weeks. Users should address how large these losses may become through stress-testing and establish limits accordingly. Furthermore, users may wish to address the potential for cumulative losses, none of which exceed the VAR limit individually, to be greater than the risk appetite of the firm. What if the amount of the VAR limit is lost continuously over contiguous time horizons (for example, daily for an entire month)?

OTHER RISK-MANAGEMENT AND RISK-MEASUREMENT TOOLS COMBINED WITH VAR

Most users combine VAR with stress-testing to address questions such as "How much do I expect to lose the other 1% of the time?" As with VAR, the quality of the answer depends on the inputs, including the financial engineer's ability to select appropriate scenarios. Both the European currency crisis and the Gulf War demonstrated that predicting factors such as maximum volatility is difficult and that correlation relationships can change substantially during extreme market moves. The increasing complexity and optionality of many derivatives and engineered securities make relevant scenario selection even harder. Given such challenges, firms often resort to designing stress tests that analyse large historical market moves.

In CMRA's experience, portfolios do not necessarily produce their greatest losses during extreme market moves. Whether asset based or asset-plus-liability based, portfolios often possess Achilles' heels that require only small moves or changes between instruments or markets to produce significant losses. Stress-testing extreme market moves does little to reveal the greatest risk of loss for such portfolios. Furthermore, a review of a portfolio's expected behaviour over time may reveal that the same stress test that indicates a small impact today indicates embedded land mines with a large impact during future periods. This is particularly true of options-based portfolios that change characteristics due to time, rather than due to changes in the components of the portfolio. For this reason, it is paramount to employ stress-testing to reveal the following:

❑ For market variables or model assumptions that have a high likelihood of change, what is the impact of small and large changes on VAR?

❑ For variables or exposures considered to offset each other, how do alternate correlation assumptions affect VAR?

❑ How wide is the variance of results produced by other common VAR approaches compared to yours?

The Mexican peso devaluation in December 1994 illustrates the difficulty in using stress-testing to analyse crises. The devaluation and subsequent market dislocation caused a 30% drop in the value of holdings in five days, with average losses ranging between 15% and 50%. More than 400 funds and most emerging market derivatives portfolios held TELMEX stock, so they experienced significant, unexpected losses. How should such dramatic market moves be captured by the VAR calculation or other tests? In virtually all cases, the VAR calculation considered the likelihood of occurrence minuscule (far less than a 1% expectation) when analysing either historical or expected movements of the peso. In virtually all cases, firms' stress tests considered far less dramatic market moves. Today, firms remain divided about including such a low-probability event in future calculations. Firms are divided as well on the inclusion of the December 1994 peso move in historical data sets. In other words, the peso move is considered to be an outlier, so some firms remove it from their historical data sets when calculating VAR. Regardless of whether such moves are included, a valuable post mortem is to assume such an event occurred and to determine whether losses expected under VAR equal those incurred. Back-testing a firm's qualitative and quantitative risk-management approach for actual, extreme events (whether market dislocations or the actions of a rogue trader) often reveals the need to adjust reserves, increase the VAR factor, adopt additional policies/limits/controls/procedures, or expand risk calculations plus reporting.

The Mexican peso crisis was not a stand-alone event in terms of magnitude, suggesting the importance of such back-testing. At least one major market (not an emerging market) makes a 10 or more standard deviation move every year.

1. Risk management framework

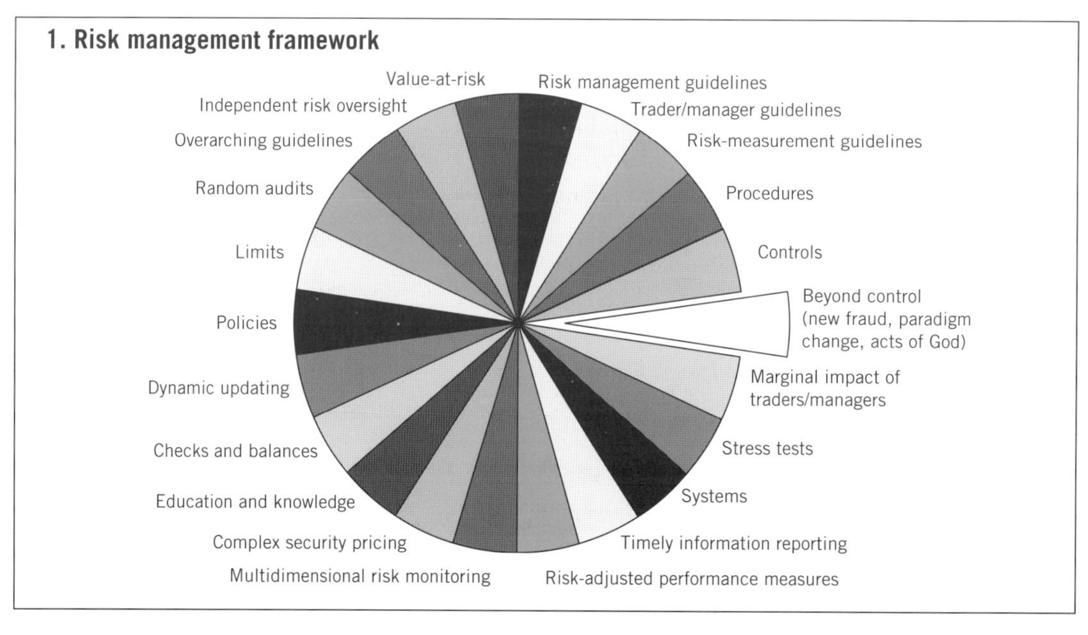

For example, there have been nine Hong Kong market declines greater than 20% and two more than 50% in the past 15 years. The devaluation of the Italian lira, the stock market crashes of 1987, and the oil shocks in the 1970s are further examples of market moves far beyond the 2- to 3-standard-deviation assumption used in most VAR calculations. In the case of the 1982–87 US bull market followed by stock market crash (508-point plunge on October 19, 1987), within six months the markets stabilised and in less than two years the markets returned to pre-crash levels.

Many risk variables such as political risk, personnel risk, regulatory risk, phantom liquidity risk, and others are difficult or impossible to capture through quantitative techniques. Yet as demonstrated by recent, well-publicised losses, such variables can cause significant risk. For this reason, VAR must be supplemented not only with stress-testing but also with prudent checks and balances, procedures, policies, controls, limits, random audits, appropriate reserves, and other risk measures (see Figure 1).

VAR in practice

Comparing five different variance/covariance, historical, and simulation VARs for a hypothetical portfolio consisting of Treasury strips plus S&P 500 equity index contracts and options shows some of the vagaries of VAR. Table 1 sets forth the portfolio as of May 25, 1995, comprised of long positions in 2-year and 30-year US Treasury strips[17] and a long position in the S&P 500 equity index contract plus long and short options on the same index. The net investment in the portfolio is $2 million.

Variance/covariance VAR is calculated once, using the JP Morgan RiskMetrics data set. Historical VAR is calculated twice, using 25-day and 100-day prior historical periods. Simulation VAR is calculated twice, using correlations and volatilities from the RiskMetrics data set (Simulation A) and from the 10 years prior (Simulation B). The results of the calculations appear in Table 2 and Figures 2 and 3.

The actual VAR statistics are set forth in Table 2 and may be interpreted as follows: under the

Table 1. The strip and equity index portfolio

Portfolio composition

Instrument	2-year strip	30-year strip	Total Portfolio
Yield (%)	5.91	6.85	
Price	89.12	14.94	
Face amount ($)	779,778	2,041,424	
Purchase amount ($)	694,964	305,036	1,000,000

Instrument	Jun 520	Jun 545	Sep 530	Dec 540	S&P 500	
Type	Put	Call	Call	Put	Long	
Strike v. market	+20	+45	+30	+40	0	
Price	1.95	0.60	14.90	18.45	528.59	
Number	4,157.4	–28,723.8	19,784.8	11,617.0	945.9	
Purchase amount ($)	8,107	(17,234)	294,793	214,335	499,999	1,000,000
Total portfolio						**2,000,000**

assumptions specific to the particular VAR calculation, there is a 1% (or 5%) expectation that the portfolio will suffer a loss greater than or equal to the statistic shown. Thus, under the assumptions made to perform historical VAR over a 250-day holding period and assuming a two-week holding period, there is a 1% expectation of loss equal to or exceeding 1.08% of the $2 million investment in the portfolio (that is, a loss greater than or equal to $21,600.)

The distributions for the VAR calculations are set forth in Figures 2 and 3. For both the 1% and 5% expectation of loss results, the alternate methods produce quite different results. Several observations may be made:

❑ In all cases, Simulation B produces much higher expected loss levels. This is due to the fact that all four other VAR calculations depend significantly upon a more recent historical period, whereas Simulation B is based upon correlations and volatilities drawn from a 10-year prior period.

❑ The 100-day and 250-day historical VAR calculations produce quite different downside and upside risk expectations. For example, the 1% expectation of loss for VAR in the case of the 100-day historical simulations is a single data point, consisting of the largest loss over a single overnight and over a single 10-day trading period. Furthermore, there is high autocorrelation in the data set. In other words, not only does a 1% probability consist of only 1 of the 100 observations, but there are only 10 distinct 10-day periods. During the 100-day and 250-day periods included in the historical VAR calculations, the value of Treasury strips largely appreciated. Had a period of interest rates been selected, the opposite result would have been produced. The danger in basing VAR estimates on direct historical observations, and over short data periods, is apparent - history must repeat itself for this method to provide an accurate expectation of future loss.

❑ The loss of the fat tails due to the non-linearity of both the options and the Treasury positions is clear when the variance/covariance VAR distribution is compared to all other results.

VAR: only one aspect of risk management

While firms typically select a single VAR measure, it is important to determine the degree to which the answer changes under different methods. Several important dimensions of VAR are now being researched and may provide insights into adjustments that may be practicable for various methods:

❑ the impact of time horizon;

❑ the impact of non-linearity;

❑ the degree of price opacity (reverse engineering complexity, illiquid underlyings, illiquid instruments, lack of historical data, etc);

❑ the degree of residual error (differences between the actual and the mapped portfolio, equivalents, etc);

REPORT CARD ON VAR: HIGH POTENTIAL BUT SLOW STARTER

Table 2. VAR results (%)

1-day VAR for the portfolio

	1%	5%
Variance/covariance	0.80	0.57
Simulation A	0.77	0.57
Simulation B	1.14	0.89
Historical – 250 days	1.08	0.74
Historical – 100 days	0.73	0.48

10-day VAR for the combined portfolio

	1%	5%
Variance/covariance	2.54	1.80
Simulation A	3.00	2.51
Simulation B	8.91	3.21
Historical – 250 days	2.89	2.56
Historical – 100 days	1.71	1.24

2. Distribution of one-day returns

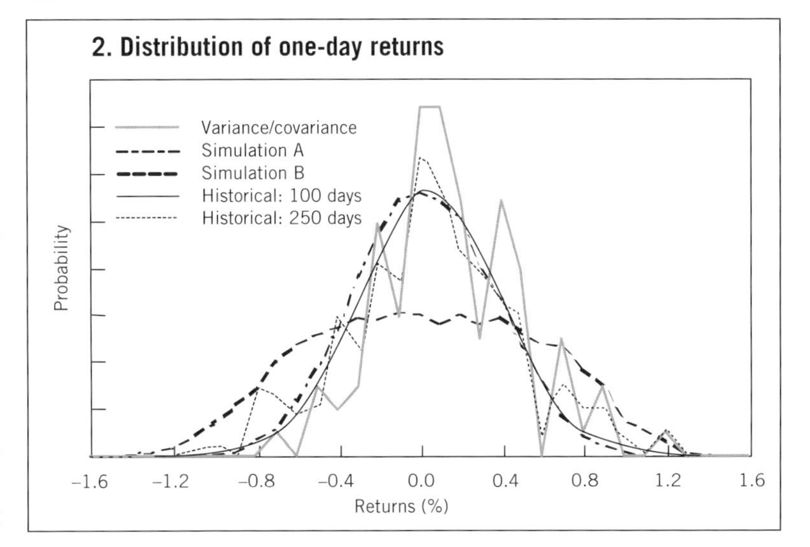

3. Distribution of two-week returns

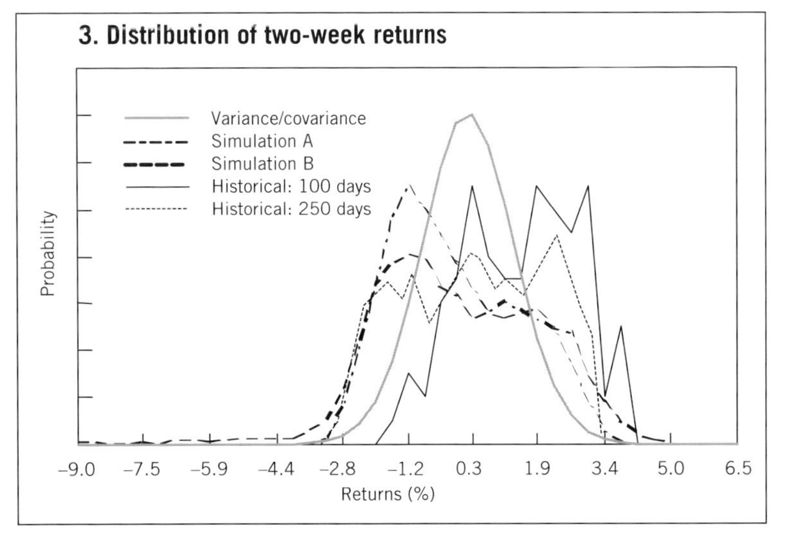

❑ the impact of diversification (whether it magnifies, dampens, or does not affect differences across VAR calculations);
❑ the impact of sampling issues (sufficiency of sample period, size, and breadth).

VAR, while an important advance in risk measurement, is only one aspect of an overall risk management programme. Different VAR methodologies and selection of the key decision factors for VAR are appropriate for different firms and depend upon many factors. These include the types of exposures, other qualitative and quantitative risk-management techniques employed, and the firm's risk appetite relative to its capital base. However, combined with the appropriate additional risk-management and risk measurement tools, VAR gets high marks.

1 *Mathematically, VAR quantifies the amount of expected loss based on the probability of certain market events occurring during a stated time period.*

2 *A delta equivalent is a linear estimate of a security's value based on its first derivative with respect to a specific factor or factors.*

3 *RiskMetrics is perhaps the most widely used of available data and assumes normal distributions.*

4 *Fat-tailed behaviour, also known as leptocurtosis, refers to distributions in which there is a broad range of values at the tails (for example, 1% of the time).*

5 *Charles Smithson of CIBC Wood Gundy summed it up very well in a recent discussion regarding VAR: "The talk to action ratio is very high."*

6 *Non-linear price functions exist not only for options, derivatives with exponential functions, and leveraged instruments but also when yields are mapped into prices (for example, basic bonds). For an example of how these affect VAR, see T. Styblo Beder, "VAR: Seductive but Dangerous",* Financial Analysts Journal, *September–October 1995; reprinted as Chapter 17 of the present volume.*

7 *It is possible to run a simulation VAR that uses variance/covariance data, such as RiskMetrics. This technique is illustrated in the section "VAR in Practice".*

8 *T. Styblo Beder, "VAR: Seductive but Dangerous."*

9 *J. V. Jordan and R. J. Mackay, "Assessing Value at Risk for Equity Portfolios: Implementing Alternative Techniques,"* Handbook of Firmwide Risk Management, *Beckstrom, Campbell, and Fabozzi, editors, 1996, as reported in* Risk, *January 1996. Differences of more than 10 times are set forth in this data.*

10 *D. Hendricks, "Evaluation of Value-at-Risk Models Using Historical Data,"* FRBNY Economic Policy Review, *April 1996; reprinted as Chapter 21 of the present volume.*

11 *Philippe Jorion, "Risk²: Measuring the Risk in Value at Risk,"* Financial Analysts Journal, *November/December 1996; reprinted as Chapter 23 of the present volume.*

12 *Learning from these mistakes, firms often limit the portion of their portfolio or overall exposure that is based on theoretical mark-to-model values or erratic/infrequent data points. In addition, firms often impose the requirement that risk management, audit, IRO, or custodian obtain outside pricing from a different dealer than the dealer from whom the customised or illiquid securities were purchased.*

13 *The seminal work by Markowitz.*

14 *T. Styblo Beder, "VAR: Seductive but Dangerous."*

15 *T. Styblo Beder, 1994, "Derivatives: The Realities of Marking to Model,"* Bank Accounting & Finance *4, pp. 4–12.*

16 *An assumption of anticipated or experienced market behaviour.*

17 *The market yield for each strip as of May 25, 1995, is stated on an actual/365 basis with semi-annual compounding. The price of each strip is stated as a percentage of face amount.*

19

Value at Risk –

New Approaches to Risk Management*

Katerina Simons
Federal Reserve Bank of Boston

Several common methods for calculating VAR are described. Important assumptions and methodological issues are discussed, illustrated by two step-by-step examples in which VAR is calculated for a single instrument. Varying assumptions about distributions and methods of calculating volatilities are found to produce quite different estimates. VAR is found to work best for frequently-traded instruments for which market values are easily available.

Managing risk has always been an integral part of banking. Recently, however, "risk management" has become a popular buzzword – the phrase appeared in the *American Banker* 72 times in 1990 and 325 times in 1995.[1] At the centre of the recent interest is an approach to risk management called value-at-risk (VAR). In the past two years it has been accepted by both practitioners and regulators as the "right" way to measure risk, becoming a *de facto* industry standard. Yet, the danger is that overreliance on VAR can give risk managers a false sense of security or lull them into complacency. After all, VAR is only one of many tools for managing risk, and it is based on a number of unrealistic assumptions. Moreover, there is no generally accepted way to calculate VAR, and various methods can yield widely different results.

This paper will review briefly the reasons for the new approaches and describe the Basle Market Risk Standard, which proposes the use of banks' internal VAR models to set appropriate capital levels to cover market risk in bank trading operations. The paper will describe several common methods for calculating VAR and highlight important assumptions and methodological issues. These issues will be illustrated by two step-by-step examples of calculating VAR for a single instrument. The paper concludes with a brief discussion of strengths and weaknesses of VAR.

Why a new approach?

Increased volatility in the financial markets since the 1970s has spurred new emphasis on risk management. Increased volatility first became apparent in the currency markets after the collapse of the Bretton Woods Agreement, followed, in short order, by interest rates and commodity prices. Figures 1a, 1b, and 1c overleaf depict examples of these volatility patterns.

Rapid advances in information technology have increased proprietary trading activity and heightened the emphasis on money management performance. At the same time, the growing complexity of financial products, particularly derivatives, has made it more difficult to evaluate and measure the risks taken by financial institutions, as accounting and disclosure rules have failed to keep pace with financial innovation. The use of derivatives has also increased linkages between markets. For example, a shock in the equity futures market of one country can be transmitted rapidly to the market for the underlying equities and perhaps to currency and equity markets of other countries as well.

The sharp rise in transaction volume in derivatives markets, coupled with several well-publi-

* *This paper was first published in the* New England Economic Review, *September–October 1996. The author thanks Peter Fortune, Richard Kopcke, and James O'Brien for helpful comments and Timothy Lin for able research assistance.*

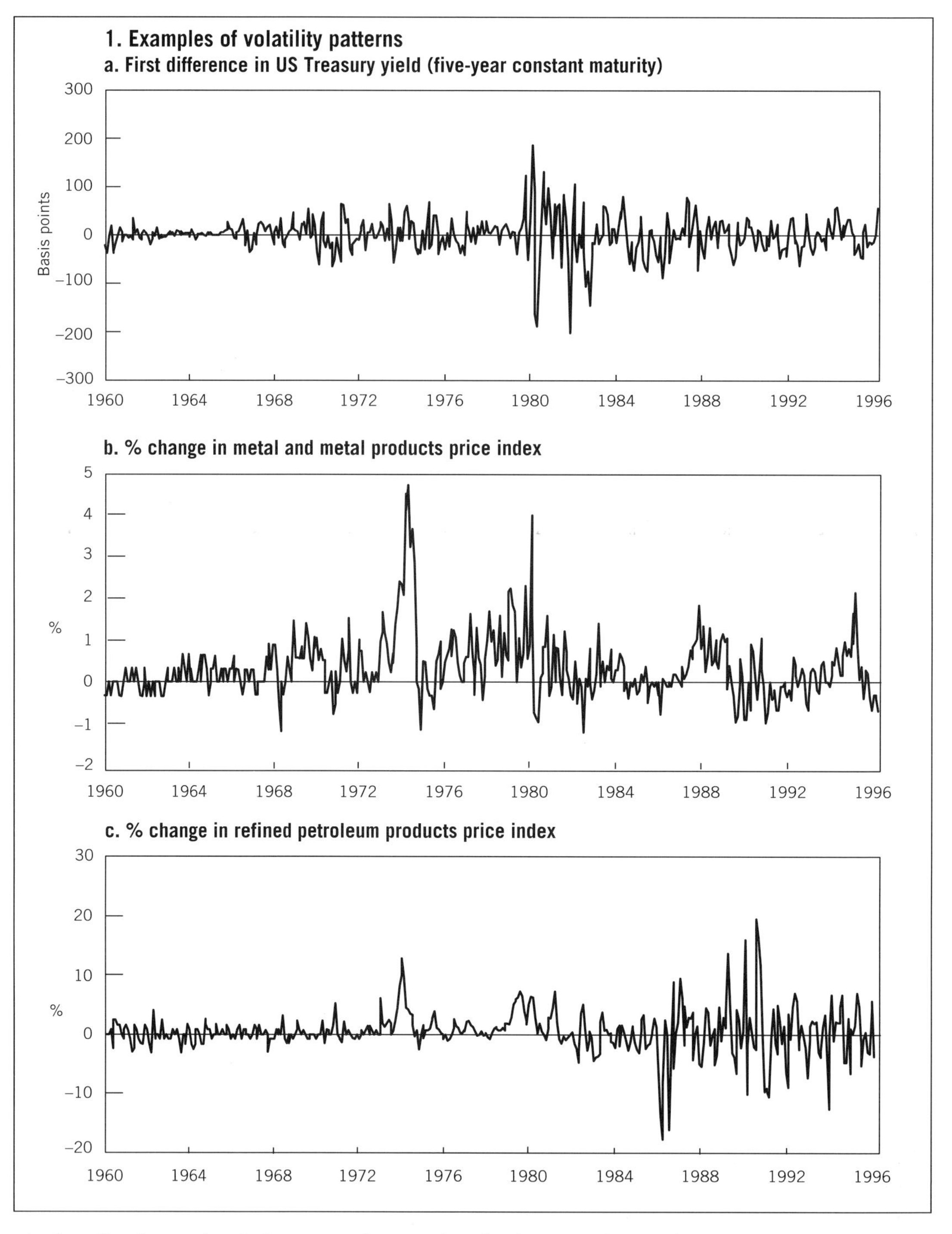

cised trading losses, has led to a new interest in an "objective" way of gauging the adequacy of capital. In their search, financial institutions turned in part to analytical tools introduced in derivatives markets, and VAR emerged as the favoured method for measuring risk. The 1993 study by the Group of Thirty, *Derivatives: Practices and Principles*, strongly recommends VAR analysis; that study's recommendations have been broadly accepted by the industry as the standard of "best practices".

Currently, derivatives techniques have spread to many instruments and their structures have become increasingly complex. More than 1,000 banks, non-financial corporations, insurance companies, mutual funds, and other asset managers use them to manage their risks. The availability of data on derivatives prices from the past decade gives a better empirical foundation to VAR analysis. The Bank for International Settlements (BIS) has allowed banks to use their own internal models of risk in setting capital requirements for market risk. The acceptable models must rely on VAR methodologies.

VAR has an intuitive appeal because it summarises the risk of the entire portfolio in a single number. Moreover, it expresses in dollar terms the major concern of risk management – the potential loss to portfolio value. VAR can be applied to many different instruments and can calculate and aggregate risk across instruments and types of assets.

VAR is applied primarily to market risk, though applications have recently been expanded to incorporate credit risk. VAR holds promise of combining all quantifiable risks across the business lines of an institution, yielding one firm-wide measure of risk.

What is VAR?

Essentially, VAR poses the question: "How much money might we lose over the next period of time?" Rephrasing it more precisely, "Over a given period of time with a given probability, how much could the value of the portfolio decline?" For example, if the given time is one week, the given probability 1%, and the value at risk $20 million, then we estimate that the odds that this portfolio will decline in value by more than $20 million within the next week are 1 in a 100.

To calculate VAR, one needs to choose a common measurement unit, a time horizon, and a probability. The common unit can be US dollars, German marks, or whatever currency the organisation primarily uses to do business. The chosen probability of loss usually ranges between 1–5%. The time horizon can be of any length, but it is assumed that the portfolio composition does not change during the holding period. The most common holding periods used are one day, one week, or two weeks. The choice of the holding period depends on the liquidity of the assets in the portfolio and how frequently they are traded. Relatively less liquid assets call for a longer holding period.

VAR and capital requirements for market risk

VAR models have been accepted by both practitioners and bank regulators as the state of the art in quantitative risk measurement. In its recent risk-based capital proposal, the Basle Committee on Banking Supervision endorsed the use of banks' VAR models to allocate capital for market risk. The Basle standard covers internationally active banks and applies only to their trading account. The proposal offers two alternatives: "standardised" and "internal models". US bank regulators favour the internal models approach, whereby the bank's own VAR model is used to set aside capital for market risk. The proposal has an implementation period of two years and will take effect in January 1998.

To be acceptable to regulators for the purposes of allocating capital, banks' internal models must meet certain qualitative and quantitative standards. In essence, qualitative standards relate to the institution's risk management function as a whole. They call for independent validation of the models by the bank or a third party; strong controls over inputs, data, and model changes; independence of the risk management function from business lines; full integration of the model into risk management; and, most important, director and senior management oversight of the risk management process.

Quantitative standards relate to specific features of the VAR model. They call for the use of a 1% probability level and a two-week holding period. In addition, the VAR thus found is to be multiplied by a factor of three. The multiplication factor is designed to allow for potential weaknesses in the modelling process and other non-quantifiable factors, such as incorrect assumptions about distributions, unstable volatilities, and extreme market movements.

Many practitioners, however, consider these standards too restrictive. They note that a holding period of two weeks is too long for many instruments, as traders get in and out of positions many times during a typical day. Moreover, a two-week holding period combined with a 1% probability safeguards against events that can be expected to occur only once in four years. This makes it difficult to validate the model within a reasonable period of time.

It should be noted that a few features of the proposal have been modified as a result of industry criticism. In particular, an earlier version of the proposal allowed the models to account for correlations of asset returns within, but not among, asset classes, such as equities, currencies, and bonds. Now, all correlations are allowed.

Parametric VAR

No consensus has been reached on the best way to implement VAR analysis. Most methodological issues revolve around estimation of the statistical distributions of asset returns. The main approaches are known as parametric (also known as the analytical or correlation method), historical, historical simulation, and stochastic simulation (also known as Monte Carlo).

Parametric VAR is based on the estimate of the variance-covariance matrix of asset returns, using historical time series of asset returns to calculate their standard deviations and correlations. The main assumption of the parametric VAR is that the distributions of asset returns are normal. This means that the variance-covariance matrix completely describes the distribution.[2]

The parametric approach can be summarised by the equation:

$$\sigma_p^2 = \sum (a_i \cdot \sigma_i)^2 + \sum_{i \neq j} \sum_{i \neq j} a_i \cdot a_j \cdot \rho_{ij} \cdot \sigma_i \cdot \sigma_j$$

where:

σ_p^2 = the volatility of portfolio returns,

a_i = the dollar amount of the portfolio share of the ith instrument,

σ_i^2 = the volatility of the ith instrument, and

ρ_{ij} = the correlation between the returns of the ith and the jth instruments.

The equation shows that portfolio risk, as expressed by its variance, is a function of the variance of the return on each instrument in the portfolio, as well as on the correlations between each pair of returns. This means that unless the returns in the portfolio are perfectly correlated (all ρ_{ij} = 1), the variance of the portfolio does not equal the simple sum of the variances of the individual positions. When the risk that any investment contributes to the portfolio is less than the risk of that investment alone because of diversification, the risk of the portfolio is less than the sum of the risks of its parts.

The best-known parametric VAR model is JP Morgan's RiskMetrics. JP Morgan has done much to advance the public understanding and acceptance of VAR analysis by making both the methodology and the data sets of volatility and correlation estimates for RiskMetrics publicly available on the Internet.

Table 1. Daily returns on a bond futures contract

Date	Futures prices	Daily return (%)
May 24, 1996 (Today)	110.0	
May 23, 1996	109.4063	0.524702
May 22, 1996	110.1563	–0.68085
May 21, 1996	109.5625	0.541928
May 20, 1996	109.7813	–0.171086
***	***	***
May 31, 1995	111.25	0.674157
May 30, 1995	111.125	0.112486

2. VAR for normally distributed futures returns

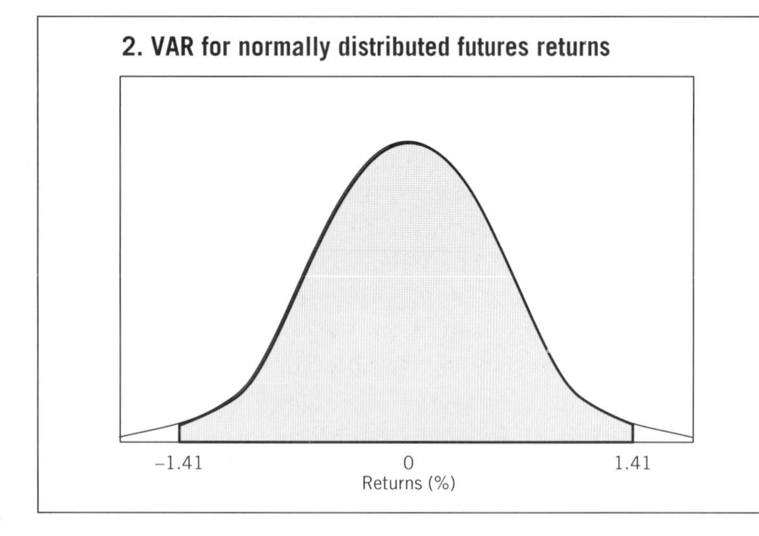

To illustrate the parametric approach we will calculate the VAR for one instrument – a Treasury bond futures contract.[3] In this example, we will estimate the VAR of a position consisting solely of a June 1996 Treasury bond futures contract purchased on May 24, 1996. The closing futures price for that day was 110. Since each Treasury bond futures contract is for the delivery of \$100,000 in face value of bonds, each \$1 change in the futures price results in a \$1,000 change in the value of the position. VAR is usually estimated in terms of returns, rather than prices. The return is calculated as:

$$R_t = \frac{P_t - P_{t-1}}{P_{t-1}} \cdot 100$$

where R is the daily return and P is the price of the instrument. The daily returns on the bond futures contract are shown in Table 1.

To calculate the one-day VAR of this position, we need to estimate the mean of the daily returns, and the volatility, as measured by the standard deviation. (Since the portfolio consists of only one instrument, we need not be concerned about correlations.) If these returns are governed by the normal distribution, then 95% of all returns will fall within 1.96 standard deviations of the mean return. Moreover, 98% of all returns will fall within 2.33 standard deviations of the mean return. The mean and the standard deviation in our case of Treasury future returns were found to be −0.00224% and 0.605074%, respectively. This means that 98% of all returns would fall between −1.41% and 1.41% and only 1% of returns will be lower than −1.4% (Figure 2).

To convert the negative return of 1.41% to a dollar amount, we recall that the futures price on May 24, the day for which we are calculating the VAR, was 110. From this we calculate a one-day VAR at the 1% probability level to be 1.41%/100 × 110 × \$1,000 or \$1,551.00. If the VAR estimate is correct, the daily loss on this position will exceed \$1,551.00 no more than one day out of a hundred.

Suppose that the risk manager decides that a one-day holding period is too short, and that a one-week holding period is more appropriate. If, in addition to normality, we assume that returns are serially independent, meaning that a return on one day does not affect the return on any other day, then the standard deviation increases proportionately with the square root of time. Thus, if the one-day standard deviation of returns is 0.605074%, the standard deviation for one week consisting of five trading days is $\sqrt{5} \times 0.605074$, or 1.3530%. This gives us a one-week VAR of $3,467.70 with a 1% probability level, which means that if we held the position for a week, we should not expect to lose more than $3,467.70 more often than in one week out of a hundred.

The two assumptions about the distribution of returns that underlie the parametric method - normality and serial independence - allow us to be very parsimonious in the use of data. Since volatilities and correlations are all we need to calculate the VAR at any confidence level for any holding period, it is unnecessary to have the historical returns themselves, which are used in the historical approach, as shown below.

Does volatility change over time?

In the preceding example, by calculating the volatility of the daily returns from a year of data, we implicitly assumed that the volatility of returns was constant throughout the year. However, volatility can change over time, sometimes quite abruptly, and it may make sense to pay more attention to the most recent observations in forecasting future volatility. For example, had we used only the last two months of returns, rather than a full year, we would have found the standard deviation to be 0.6513, rather than 0.605074, resulting in a VAR of $1,669.22, rather than $1,551.00. Clearly, the result would have been different still, had we used one month, six months, or five years of historical data on returns.

One popular way to estimate volatility is through exponential weighting of observations. This approach emphasises more recent observations at the expense of the more distant ones because the weights assigned to past observations decline with time. The volatilities and correlations are updated every day in accordance with the most recent data, as the earliest observation is dropped from the historical series and the newest one is added.

The formula for the standard deviation (σ) of the daily return (R) and mean return m with exponential weights based on a historical period of N days is:

$$\sigma = \sqrt{(1-\lambda)\sum_{i=1}^{N} \lambda^{i}(R_{N-i}-\mu)^{2}}.$$

The parameter λ is known as the decay factor; it determines how fast the weight on past observations decays. The higher the λ, the slower is the rate of decay and the more weight is given to the more distant observations.[4] One study (Hendricks 1996) estimated volatilities for a number of decay factors and historical periods of different length for 1,000 simulated foreign exchange portfolios and found significant differences in the resulting volatilities.

Table 2. Estimates of VAR using different decay factors

λ = 0.94 (rapid decay)		λ = 0.97 (slower decay)		λ = 0.99 (slowest decay)	
δ	VAR ($)	δ	VAR ($)	δ	VAR ($)
0.5829	1,494.04	0.5503	1,410.48	0.4011	1,028.44

To check if our VAR estimate is sensitive to a choice of decay factors, we estimate the 1% probability level VAR for our bond futures returns using three different decay factors for a period of 50 days. Table 2 shows these estimates.

In the time period chosen for our example, the volatility of the return on the Treasury bond futures was increasing over time. Thus, the lower the weight placed on the more distant observations, the higher the estimate of volatility.

The historical approach

The simplicity and convenience of the normal distribution are powerful inducements for its use in VAR analysis, but this does not necessarily make its use appropriate. Since the early work of Mandelbrot (1963) and Fama (1965), most empirical research into the statistical properties of asset returns has found systematic deviations from normality. In particular, many studies have found that distributions of asset returns tend to exhibit kurtosis; namely, they are more peaked around the mean and have fatter tails than the normal distribution. Moreover, some, though not all, asset returns tend to be skewed to the left; that is, more unusually large negative returns are present than would have been expected if returns were normal.

To see if these observations apply to our chosen example of the bond futures contract, we construct a frequency distribution of the daily returns between May 1995 and May 1996. The resulting histogram is shown in Figure 3 overleaf, with a normal distribution superimposed for comparison. The returns exhibit the typical pattern found in many asset returns: "fat tails" and left-skewness.

Fortunately, it is possible to calculate VAR without resorting to the assumption of normality, by using a simple historical method. This entails

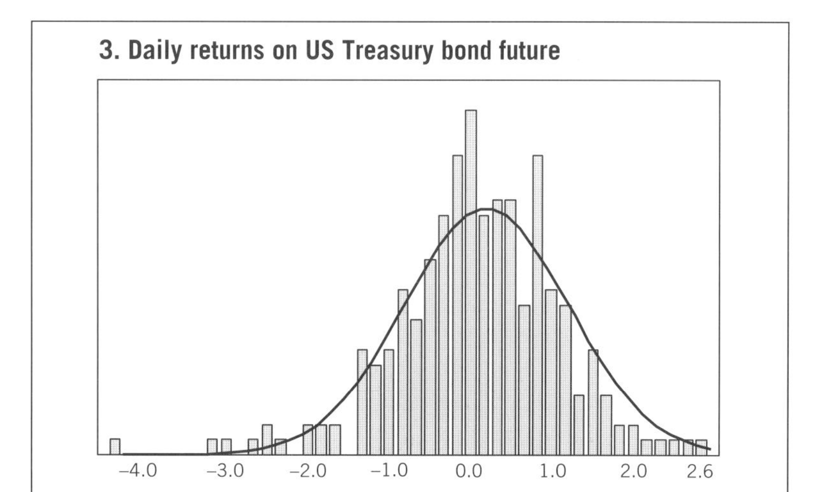

finding the lowest returns in the real historical data. To calculate VAR at the 1% probability level, we ranked the daily returns and identified the lowest 1% of returns. The first percentile return is –1.73%, giving us the daily VAR of 1.73%/100 × 110 × \$1,000= \$1,903.00, almost 23% greater than the \$1,551.00 calculated with the parametric approach.

If we want to recalculate the VAR for a different holding period without making the assumption of serial independence, we cannot simply multiply the daily VAR by the square root of time. Instead, we must recalculate all the returns for the new holding period, construct the new frequency distribution, and identify the appropriate percentiles.

The historical method has a number of advantages over the parametric method. First, it makes no explicit assumptions about the volatilities of returns and the covariances between them. Second, it makes no assumptions about the shape of the distributions themselves. In particular, it makes no assumption of normality. On the other hand, the historical approach lacks flexibility. Unlike the parametric method, it does not allow one to try different values for volatilities and correlations to test the sensitivity of VAR to these assumptions. In addition, it requires investors to obtain and maintain large amounts of actual, historical data. Long historical data series relevant for one's portfolio can be expensive or may not even exist. In contrast, the parametric approach requires just the parameters of distributions, if one is willing to delegate the estimation of those parameters to a third party.

Simulation approaches – from risk factors to VAR

Often, it is not appropriate to calculate VAR directly by estimating the probability distribution of returns on the instrument itself, as was done in the last example. If an institution has a large or complicated portfolio, it may be impossible or impractical to maintain historical data on all the instruments involved. Moreover, historical data do not exist for many instruments, particularly those that are customised. In those cases, the historical data set used to calculate the VAR will consist of returns not on the instruments themselves, but on their "risk factors", that is, other instruments or factors that influence their values. For example, for a domestic bond, the risk factor is the interest rate. For a bond denominated in foreign currency, the risk factors are the foreign interest rate and the exchange rate. For many equity derivatives, the main risk factor is the value of the S&P 500 index. For an S&P 500 option, the relevant risk factors are the value of the S&P 500 index, its volatility, the dividend yield on the index, and the risk-free interest rate.

In these cases, we can improve on the pure historical approach by using "historical simulation". Instead of looking at the volatility of the actual portfolio returns in the past, we will "simulate" the past portfolio returns by using the actual values of the risk factors and the *current* portfolio composition. Then, we can construct the empirical frequency distribution of the simulated portfolio returns by ranking them into percentiles and determining the VAR at the chosen confidence level.

STOCHASTIC SIMULATION IN SIX EASY STEPS

Historical simulation shares one disadvantage with the simple historical approach: a lack of flexibility to investigate different assumptions. However, instead of using the past values of the risk factors, we can model these factors explicitly by specifying the underlying distributions and their parameters. Using these distributions and parameters, we can generate thousands of hypothetical scenarios for the risk factors and determine the portfolio value for each scenario. As in the historical simulation, the resulting portfolio returns can then be used to construct the empirical frequency distribution and determine the VAR at the desired confidence level. This is the approach generally known as the Monte Carlo, or "stochastic simulation."

As an illustration of this approach, we will calculate the one-day VAR for a position consisting of one call option, which gives the holder the right, but not the obligation, to buy an asset for a certain price. In this example, we will calculate the VAR for a call option on the S&P 500 index –

a popular equity derivative traded on the Chicago Board of Trade. This particular option was bought on May 28, 1996 for $20.90 (the closing price for the contract on that day). The option expires on July 20, 1996 and gives the holder the right to buy the S&P 500 index for $670. (The actual value of the S&P 500 on May 28, 1996 was $674.9606.)

Finding the one-day VAR on May 28, 1996 involves the following six steps:

1. Calculate the daily returns on the S&P 500 and find the parameters of the normal distribution of returns.
2. Simulate returns on the S&P 500 for one day by generating random numbers from a normal distribution with the calculated parameters.
3. Use the simulated S&P 500 returns as input to calculate the simulated S&P 500 prices.
4. Use an option-pricing model to calculate the value of the call option at each simulated value of the S&P 500 index.
5. Calculate the one-day returns on holding the call option from the simulated call option prices.
6. Find the parameters of the distribution of call option returns and calculate the VAR.

The crucial part of this process is the transformation from the distribution of the S&P 500 to the distribution of the option values. In this example, the option was valued using the standard Black-Scholes model modified to value a stock index.[5] The formula is as follows:

$$c = Se^{-q(T-t)}N(d_1) - Xe^{-r(T-t)}N(d_2)$$

where d_1 and d_2 are given by:

$$d_1 = \frac{\ln(S/X) + (r - q + \sigma^2/2)(T-t)}{\sigma\sqrt{T-t}}$$

$$d_2 = d_1 - \sigma\sqrt{T-t}.$$

The notation is as follows:

c = the value of the call option;
S = the price of the S&P 500 index;
$T-t$ = the time left until the expiration of the option (in this case, 53 days);
q = the dividend yield of the S&P 500 (estimated to be 2% per year);
X = the strike price of the option (in this case, $670);
$N(x)$ = the cumulative probability distribution for a standardised normal variable (that is, the probability that such a variable will be less than x);
r = risk-free rate of interest, in this case, the federal funds rate, or 5.5% per year;
σ = volatility of the S&P 500 index.

4. Daily returns on simulated S&P 500 call premiums

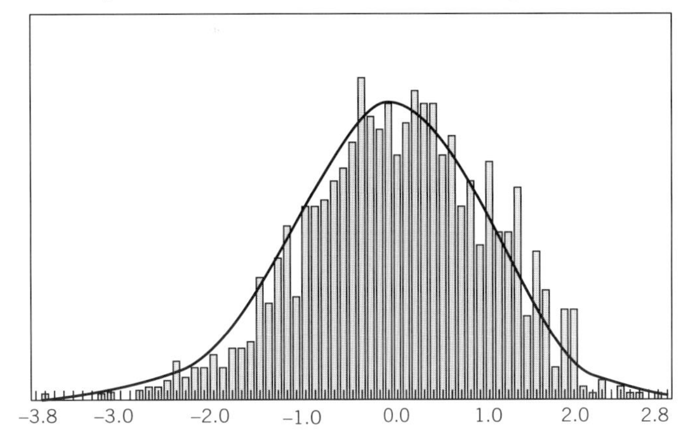

The distribution of the resulting simulated returns is depicted in Figure 4. To calculate VAR, we rank the returns into percentiles and identify the 1 percentile return. This happens to be −0.3787. The price of the call option on May 28, 1996 was 20.90. Every option contract on the S&P 500 is for $100 of the index. Thus, the dollar value of VAR for one contract is 0.3787 × 20.90 × $100 = $791.48. This means that the chance is 1 in 100 that we will lose more than $791.48 on the call option contract in one day.

It should be noted that, in this example, volatility was calculated from one year of data with all observations weighted equally. Of course, a longer or shorter historical period could be used along with various exponential weighting schemes to generate a different estimate of volatility of the S&P 500 index, which would result in a different VAR for the call option.

Conclusion

In many financial circles, the reputation of VAR stands as high as that of motherhood and apple pie. But, as with motherhood and apple pie, a good concept is not enough - good implementation is equally important. VAR analysis is a general framework that covers models with a wide variety of assumptions and methods of calculation, and, inevitably, it produces a wide variety of results. Our examples demonstrate that varying assumptions about distributions and methods of calculating volatilities produced quite different estimates.

VAR is a useful tool for risk management but it is not a panacea. One limitation is that it focuses on a single arbitrary point on the distribution of profits and losses, while it would be more useful to have a representation of the whole distribution. A second limitation of VAR is that it tells us little about how risks are to be measured in extreme market conditions. During market crises, correlations between asset prices break down, liquidity disappears, and price data may not be available at all. Modelling risk under such conditions would require some sense of the concentration of ownership of different securities, information that most market participants would be reluctant to disclose, for competitive reasons.

VAR is often put forward as the way to aggregate risks across the whole institution. While integrating disparate risks is the ultimate purpose of global risk management, the use of VAR for this purpose is problematic. VAR analysis works best for frequently traded instruments for which market values are easily available. VAR first took hold at the derivatives desks in the trading rooms of a few large banks, because they had both the expertise and the need to estimate and aggregate the market risks of many dissimilar instruments. From derivatives desks it spread to other trading desks, such as those for bonds and currency, and it is now beginning to be applied beyond trading to the broader arena of asset-liability management. However, many bank assets and liabilities, in particular deposits and loans, have long-term horizons and are not actively traded. Thus, they have poor or non-existent price data and marking them to market on a day-to-day basis would be both impractical and misleading. VAR has the same limitations for life insurance companies, because these institutions have long-term, non-traded liabilities. Other methods may prove superior to VAR as a global measure of risk. One alternative is a measure of how much one is willing to pay to eliminate risk, or the price of purchasing a guarantee to avoid a loss of a certain magnitude. VAR, which focuses on the distribution of possible losses, is only one element in the valuation of such a guarantee.

Overall, VAR constitutes a useful though limited family of techniques for measuring risk. It is most useful in measuring short-term risk of traded instruments in normal market conditions. An additional benefit is that its use has created a common language for discussions about risk, and it has prompted more dialogue about risk issues. However, successful risk management is a much broader task, which depends crucially on appropriate incentives and internal controls.

1 *See "New Risk Tests Win Fans - But Will They Work?",* American Banker, *February 7, 1996.*

2 *While a number of distributions other than normal can be completely described by their parameters, in VAR analysis the parametric approach usually refers to a normal distribution.*

3 *A futures contract is an agreement to buy or sell an asset at a certain time in the future for a certain price. A Treasury bond futures contract is traded on the Chicago Board of Trade and is the most popular long-term interest rate derivative.*

4 *See JP Morgan,* RiskMetrics Technical Document, *3rd ed. Chapter 2, Section 3 for details on the choice of decay factors. RiskMetrics currently uses a decay factor of 0.94 for all daily volatilities of the series it maintains. (Peter Zangari, JP Morgan, personal communication.)*

5 *The model for valuing options for non-dividend-paying stocks was developed by Black and Scholes (1973). The formula for valuing options on stock indexes paying dividends was derived by Merton (1973).*

BIBLIOGRAPHY

Black, F. and M. Scholes, 1973, "The Pricing of Options and Corporate Liabilities", *Journal of Political Economy* 81, pp. 637–54.

Fama, E., 1965, "The Behaviour of Stock Market Prices", *Journal of Business* 38, pp. 34–105.

Group of Thirty, 1993 *Derivatives: Practices and Principles*, Global Derivatives Study Group, Washington, DC.

Hendricks, D., 1996, "Evaluation of Value-at-Risk Models Using Historical Data", *Federal Reserve Bank of New York Economic Policy Review* April, pp. 39–70; reprinted as Chapter 21 of the present volume.

Mandelbrot, B., 1963, "The Variation of Certain Speculative Prices", *Journal of Business* 36, pp. 394–419.

Merton, R., 1973, "Theory of Rational Option Pricing", *Bell Journal of Economics and Management Science* 4, pp. 141–83.

20

Value-at-Risk

A New Methodology for Measuring Portfolio Risk*

Gregory P. Hopper
Morgan Stanley

This paper outlines the various methods used to calculate VAR. Simple examples are used to highlight the different methods of assessing VAR, and their respective strengths and weaknesses. Problems in implementation and interpretation are identified. Although much progress has been made in describing how volatilities change over time, not as much progress has been made in the description of time-varying co-variances. Thus, VAR numbers should be viewed with caution at this point.

Commercial banks, investment banks, insurance companies, non-financial firms, and pension funds hold portfolios of assets that may include stocks, bonds, currencies, and derivatives. Each institution needs to quantify the amount of risk its portfolio may incur in the course of a day, week, month, or year.

For example, a bank needs to assess its potential losses in order to set aside enough capital to cover them. Similarly, a company needs to track the value of its assets and any cash flows resulting from losses in its portfolio. An investment fund may want to understand potential losses on its portfolio, not only to allocate its assets better but also to fulfill its obligation to make set payments to investors. In addition, credit rating and regulatory agencies must be able to assess likely losses on portfolios as well, since they need to set capital requirements and issue credit ratings.

How can these institutions judge the likelihood and magnitude of potential losses on their portfolios? A new methodology called value-at-risk (VAR) can be used to estimate these losses. This paper describes the various methods used to calculate VAR, paying special attention to VAR's weaknesses.

What is value-at-risk?

VAR is an estimate of the largest loss that a portfolio is likely to suffer during all but truly exceptional periods. More precisely, the VAR is the maximum loss that an institution can be confident it would lose a certain fraction of the time over a particular period. Consider a bank with a portfolio of assets that would like to characterise its potential losses using VAR. For example, the bank could specify a horizon of one day and set the frequency of maximum loss to 98%. In that case, a VAR calculation might reveal that the maximum loss is $1 million. Thus, on average, in 98 trading days out of 100, the loss on the portfolio will not exceed $1 million over a one-day horizon. But on two trading days in 100, losses will, on average, exceed $1 million.

VAR can be used to assess the potential loss on a portfolio of assets generally. The user can specify any horizon and frequency of loss that fits his particular circumstances. But the method of calculating VAR depends not only on the horizon chosen but also on the kinds of assets in the portfolio. One method may yield good results with portfolios consisting of stocks, bonds, and currencies over a short horizon, but the same method may not work well over longer horizons such as a month or a year. If the portfolio contains derivatives, methods that differ from those used to analyse portfolios of stocks, bonds, or currencies may be needed.

**This paper was first published in the Federal Reserve Bank of Philadelphia Business Review, Sept/Oct (1996) pp.19–30.*

VAR for a single share of stock

Ultimately, we want to calculate VAR for a general portfolio of different assets, such as stocks, bonds, currencies, and options.[1] Let's focus on the simplest case first: a single stock. A portfolio consisting of one asset will allow us to consider the different methods for assessing VAR in a simple context. Then, we can generalise the discussion by considering how the calculation changes when the institution has a portfolio of many stocks, bonds, or currencies. Finally, we will consider how the inclusion of derivatives in the portfolio can dramatically change the methodology for calculating VAR.

RANDOMNESS IN THE STOCK MARKET

Let's consider a portfolio consisting of a single share of stock worth $1 at the beginning of trading today. We want to find the VAR over a one-day horizon at a 98% confidence level, that is, the largest one-day price drop we are likely to see during 98 of every 100 trading days. Since VAR is essentially a statement about the likelihood of losses on a stock, we need to characterise the unpredictability of daily changes in our stock's price.

One way to picture the unpredictability of our stock's return over one day is to imagine the stock market spinning a roulette wheel. Of course, this is a fiction, but a useful one: economists have found that stock returns have a random component.

Suppose there are 100 equally likely outcomes on the wheel, with each outcome corresponding to a specific percentage daily price change or daily return for our stock.[2] In general, positive and negative returns are included on the wheel. To determine the return over one day, the stock market spins the roulette wheel. If the wheel comes up with a return of 25%, our stock would be worth $1.25 at the end of the day. Alternatively, a spin of the wheel may generate a return of −25%, in which case our stock would be worth $0.75 at the end of the day. We can't say for sure what the daily return will be, but we know that it will be one of the outcomes on the wheel.

Finding the VAR for our $1 stock is particularly simple if we know the returns on the roulette wheel. Suppose we look at the outcomes on our roulette wheel and see that 98 of them involve returns no bigger than −30% while two outcomes have returns larger than −30%. Then we have found the VAR for our $1 stock: the VAR is $0.30 at a 98% confidence level. We can be confident that 98 days out of 100 our daily stock loss will be no bigger than $0.30. But two days out of 100, the daily loss may indeed exceed $0.30.

SUMMARY MEASURES OF RANDOMNESS

To find the VAR for our stock, we needed to know the 100 returns on the wheel. But how do we know what they are? Imagine that, every day, the market is spinning the wheel behind a curtain. We can't see the outcomes on the wheel, but we do know which daily returns were selected in the past – we can look them up in the newspaper. By categorising past daily returns, we should be able to infer the outcomes on the wheel. For example, if we saw that daily returns of 10% occurred on five trading days in 100, on average, we can assume that five outcomes on the wheel involve a 10% return. Similarly, if changes of −5% occurred on 10 trading days in 100, on average, a return of −5% must correspond to 10 outcomes on the wheel. By continuing this analysis, we can associate price changes with all outcomes on the wheel. Then we will have reconstructed the wheel that the economy spins daily. Using our reconstructed wheel, we can easily find the VAR.

A simpler way to do this reconstruction is to summarise the 100 returns on the wheel by using two numbers: the average return and the volatility of the returns. Elementary statistics teaches that if the returns follow a certain pattern, called the normal, or bell-shaped, distribution, then all the outcomes on the wheel can be summarised by these two numbers.

We can estimate the average return as an equally weighted average of past daily returns selected by the roulette wheel, returns, that again, could be looked up in the newspaper. For technical reasons, analysts often don't perform this calculation but assume instead that the average return is zero.[3] The second number, the volatility[4], tells us how much the return is likely to deviate from its average value for any particular spin. The volatility, then, measures the capacity of the roulette wheel to generate extreme returns, whether positive or negative, with respect to the average value of zero. The higher the volatility of the roulette wheel, the more it tends to select large returns. We can estimate the volatility as an equally weighted average of past squared returns. We could use the same returns we looked up in the newspaper; we only need to square each change.

Armed with the average return of zero and the

volatility of our stock's returns, we can find the VAR over a one-day horizon at the 98% confidence level by following a simple procedure. To calculate VAR for our stock, we need only multiply today's stock price of $1 times the square root of the volatility times a number corresponding to the 98% confidence level, called the confidence factor. The confidence factor is derived from the properties of the normal distribution. At the 98% confidence level, it equals 2.054.[5]

This procedure can be done on any day in the future as well. Let's assume that it is now tomorrow and the stock price is $0.95. If we wanted to calculate VAR, we would follow the same procedure as before but use a stock price of $0.95. We don't need to change the volatility or the confidence number: they don't vary from day to day. When VAR is calculated in this fashion, we are using a constant volatility method.

TIME-VARYING VOLATILITY

The problem with the constant volatility method is that substantial empirical evidence shows volatility is not constant from day to day but rather varies over time.[6] A look at a graph of the daily dollar return on the Deutschmark shows that volatility tends to cluster together (Figure 1). Notice that highly volatile times, characterised by large up-and-down swings in the exchange rate, tend to follow one another, while quiet periods, characterised by smaller up-and-down swings, tend to follow each other as well. For example, volatility seems to have been higher in 1991 than in 1990. A graph of the daily return on the S&P 500 confirms this impression for stock prices (Figure 2). The increase in volatility is particularly apparent after the stock market crash in 1987. Time-varying volatility seems to be a general feature of asset prices that is seen not only in currencies but also in stocks. Consequently, using the constant volatility method to calculate VAR could be very misleading.

What does time-varying volatility mean for our roulette wheel analogy? It means that the market behaves as if it is spinning a different roulette wheel each day. When the average return and the volatility don't vary from day to day, the returns on the wheel don't vary either. Thus, the market is spinning the same roulette wheel every day. But if the volatility is changing from day to day, the returns on the wheel must also be changing, which means that the market is spinning a different wheel each day.

If the market spins a different roulette wheel every day, VAR becomes more complicated.

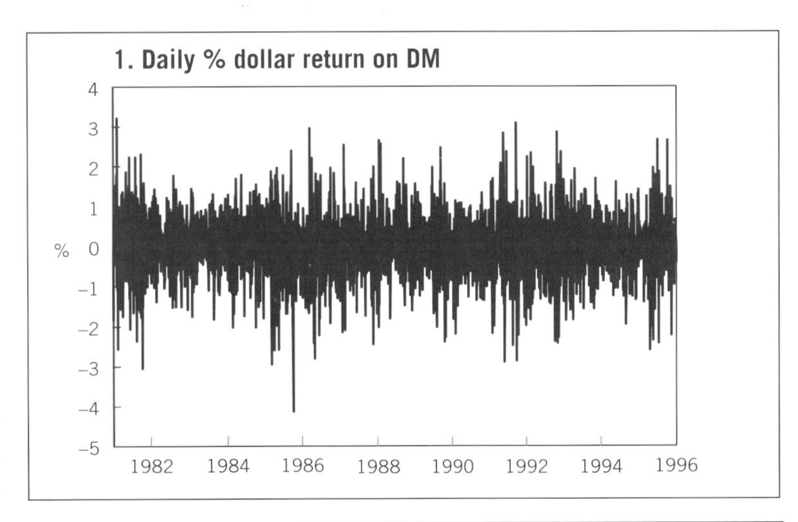

1. Daily % dollar return on DM

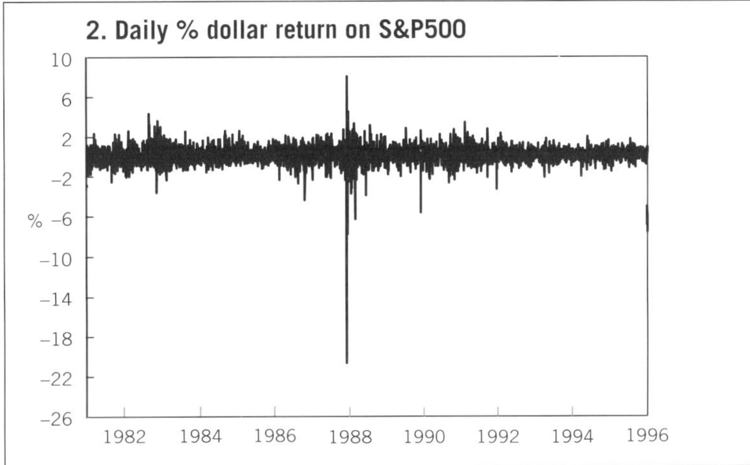

2. Daily % dollar return on S&P500

How do we know which returns will be on the wheel today? Equivalently, how do we know today's volatility? The most common solution to this problem was introduced in 1986 by economist Tim Bollerslev, who generalised work done by economist Robert Engle in 1982. Bollerslev's time-varying volatility technique, called the GARCH method, allows us to base our knowledge of today's roulette wheel on yesterday's wheel.

Bollerslev's GARCH technique estimates the volatility of today's roulette wheel using yesterday's estimate of volatility and the squared value of yesterday's return. If yesterday's return was large, in either a positive or negative direction, and yesterday's volatility was high, today's roulette wheel will tend to have a high volatility. Thus, today's spin of the wheel will tend to produce large returns as well. In this way, large returns, positive or negative, would tend to follow one another, leading to periods of high and low volatility as we saw in Figures 1 and 2.

How can we estimate today's volatility and find the VAR using Bollerslev's GARCH method? The daily volatility using GARCH turns out to be a weighted average of past squared returns, just as it was in the constant volatility case. The difference is that the constant volatility method weights past squared returns equally while Bollerslev's GARCH method weights recent squared returns more heavily than distant returns.

It is easy to calculate volatility using the constant volatility method. Bollerslev's GARCH method is much harder to implement: to find the right weight for each past squared return, we must employ a complicated, computer-intensive procedure. Once we have found today's volatility, we can multiply the confidence factor times the square root of today's volatility times today's stock price to find today's VAR. When we use Bollerslev's GARCH method, the confidence factor is the only number that does not change daily.

RISKMETRICS

Bollerslev's GARCH method has found widespread empirical support among financial economists, but the difficulty in estimating daily volatilities has slowed its adoption by many institutions engaged in risk management. To make the calculations easier, JP Morgan introduced RiskMetrics, a risk management system that includes techniques to approximate GARCH volatilities. Like Bollerslev's method, the RiskMetrics estimate of daily volatility involves a weighted average of past squared returns, with recent squared returns weighted more heavily. The RiskMetrics weights are chosen to produce daily volatility estimates similar to GARCH volatilities. The set of weights calculated by the RiskMetrics method is easier to compute and can be used for any asset in the portfolio. For example, the analyst would use the same set of weights to calculate volatilities of stocks, bonds, and currencies. Bollerslev's GARCH method, in contrast, requires the computation of different weights for each volatility calculation, and each set of weights is harder to calculate than they would be using the RiskMetrics method.[7]

OTHER METHODS

Two other methods of calculating volatility are sometimes used. The first method relies on recognising that pricing methods for options require the user to specify his estimate of the future volatility of an asset. For example, if a user wants to price an option on a stock using a method such as the popular Black-Scholes method, he must specify an estimate of the volatility of the stock over the life of the option.[8] Since option prices are observable in the marketplace, the market's view of volatility can be backed out of the option price using the Black-Scholes formula. Volatility estimates inferred from option prices in this way are called implied volatilities.

This method has two disadvantages that limit its appeal. First, options may not be traded on the particular asset of interest. Thus, implied volatility estimates may not be obtainable for some assets in the portfolio. Second, economists are unsure about whether implied volatility estimates are better than GARCH estimates of daily volatility.

The other method of estimating volatility is based on judgment. The user analyses the economic environment and forecasts volatility based on his subjective views. This method has limited appeal as well, since testing the validity of a subjective view is difficult.

VAR for a portfolio of assets

Up to this point, we have considered only how to calculate the VAR of a portfolio consisting of a single stock. Now let's look at a portfolio of two stocks. The principles we are about to discuss apply generally to a portfolio of many stocks, but we will consider just two stocks to make the ideas more clear.

As before, ultimately we want to find the volatility of the return on the portfolio. It's clear that the volatility of the portfolio should depend on the volatility of the return of each stock in the portfolio. So, we need to estimate the volatilities of the returns of both stocks. But stock returns may covary as well. For example, if the covariance between the stocks in a portfolio of two stocks is negative, then when one stock has a positive return, the other has a negative return, and vice versa. Thus, the two stocks dampen each other's swings in return, producing a portfolio whose volatility is lower than the volatility of each stock in the portfolio. Adding stocks to the portfolio would reduce the volatility further, provided that the additional stocks' returns are not highly positively correlated with the return of the initial portfolio. To account for this effect, we must also estimate the covariance between the stocks' returns. Once we know the stock returns' volatilities and covariances, we can calculate the volatility of the entire portfolio and find the VAR as before.

As an example of the calculation, suppose we have invested one dollar in stocks 1, 2, and 3. Then by an elementary statistical formula, the daily volatility of the portfolio would be volatility (portfolio) = volatility (stock 1) + volatility (stock 2) + volatility (stock 3) + 2.0 × covariance (stock 1,stock 2) + 2.0 × covariance (stock 1, stock 3) + 2.0 × covariance (stock 2, stock 3)

If the correlation between the daily returns of stocks 1, 2, and 3 was 1, we could sum the square root of the volatilities of each stock to get the square root of the volatility of the portfolio.[9] Thus, if correlations between all assets were 1, we could find the VAR of each asset separately and then sum them to get the VAR of the portfolio. But since correlations are in general not 1, we can't in general find the VAR of individual assets and sum them to get the VAR of the portfolio. Moreover, we can't find the VARs of asset classes such as stock and currency portfolios and sum them. We must account for the covariances between asset classes as well.

To calculate covariances between the assets' returns using the constant covariance method, we use an equally weighted average of the products of each stock's past daily returns. However, since economists have found evidence that covariances change over time, it may be advisable to estimate time-varying covariances using an extension of Bollerslev's GARCH method or the RiskMetrics GARCH approximation.[10]

What about derivatives?

Many portfolios have significant numbers of derivatives such as futures, options, and swaps, all of which are securities whose value is derived from the value of some other asset. Consider a derivative on our $1 stock. We know how to find the VAR of the stock over a one-day horizon at the 98% confidence level: we find the volatility of its return and multiply its square root by the product of today's stock price and the confidence factor. But how can we find the VAR of a derivative on this stock?

One method is to link the derivative to the underlying stock and use the standard VAR method. To do this, we use a derivative-pricing method, such as the Black-Scholes model, to calculate a number called delta, which gives us a way to translate the derivative portfolio into the stock portfolio. A derivative's delta tells us how the derivative's price changes when the stock price changes a small amount. For example, if the delta is 0.5, the derivative's price goes up half as much as the stock's price. For small price changes, a derivative with a delta of 0.5 behaves as if it is half a share of the $1 stock. So, using our estimate of the stock's volatility, we could calculate VAR as we did before: by multiplying $0.50 times the square root of the stock's volatility times the confidence factor.

A serious drawback to this method is that it works well only when stock price changes are small. For larger changes, delta itself can change dramatically, leading to inaccurate VAR estimates. In general, we need to account for how delta changes, considerably complicating the analysis.

To avoid this complication, risk managers often use an alternative method called Monte Carlo analysis. Using the volatility and covariance estimates for the derivatives' underlying assets as well as a derivative pricing tool such as the Black-Scholes method, risk managers construct a new roulette wheel. The new wheel will still have 100 numbers, but each number will correspond to a potential change in the derivative's price. The computer can then look at the largest loss the derivative will sustain for 98 of the outcomes. Let's suppose this loss is $0.01. Then the VAR of the derivative over a one-day horizon at the 98% confidence level is $0.01. Since RiskMetrics yields volatility and covariance estimates, Monte Carlo evaluation of derivative portfolios can be done under JP Morgan's system as well.[11]

Weaknesses of VAR

When properly used, VAR can give an institution an idea about the maximum losses it can expect to incur on its portfolio a certain fraction of the time, making VAR an important risk management tool. Using VAR calculations, an institution can judge how it should reallocate the assets in its portfolio to achieve the risk level it desires. But the VAR methodology is not without its weaknesses and, improperly used, may lead an institution to make poor risk management decisions. This can happen for two reasons: either the VAR is incorrectly calculated or the VAR is correctly calculated but irrelevant to the institution's real risk-management goals.

WHAT IS THE BEST METHOD FOR ESTIMATING VOLATILITY?

Bollerslev's GARCH method works better for currencies than it does for stock prices. Financial economists have found that stock volatility goes up more as a result of a large negative return than it does as a result of a large positive return. A weakness of Bollerslev's GARCH method is that GARCH volatility estimates don't depend on whether yesterday's return was positive or negative. Thus, this method can't allow for stock volatility's asymmetric response to past returns.

To account for this effect, financial economists have developed methods for estimating asymmetric volatilities.[12] These methods are important because they can give very different estimates of volatility for days following large stock returns than would the GARCH or RiskMetrics method. For small daily returns, Bollerslev's method, RiskMetrics, and the asymmetric volatility method yield similar one-day-ahead volatility predictions, leading a user to think, perhaps, that one model is as good as the others for daily volatility predictions. But for large daily returns, the one-day-ahead volatility predictions of these methods can be substantially different. If an asymmetric volatility method is appropriate for stock prices, both Bollerslev's method and RiskMetrics may understate one-day-ahead volatility whenever a large drop in stock prices occurred the previous day, thus producing a potentially substantial underestimate of daily VAR. Similarly, the GARCH or RiskMetrics method could overestimate the VAR after a large increase in stock prices.

Robert Engle and Victor Ng have provided evidence that a particular asymmetric volatility method well describes the volatility of Japanese stock returns and that GARCH methods can substantially underpredict volatility following large negative returns. Thus, VAR estimates of stock portfolios produced by GARCH or the RiskMetrics GARCH approximation should be viewed with caution if the calculations are done on days with large stock returns.

Although having the right method for calculating the volatilities of assets is important, correctly calculating the covariances between the returns on assets is also important. Unfortunately, not as much work has been done by financial economists to identify the right method for calculating covariances. To date, many methods have been proposed, but no consensus has yet emerged. Thus, we don't yet know for sure how we should handle covariances in portfolios. This uncertainty introduces the risk that any method we use may substantially underestimate or overestimate VAR. In particular, RiskMetrics commits the user to a special case of Bollerslev's GARCH method. Since we don't yet know whether Bollerslev's GARCH method is adequate in describing covariances, we should use even more caution in interpreting results whenever we have used covariances in our VAR calculations.

In the long run, the volatility estimates produced by GARCH methods tend, in general, to approach the values that the constant volatility method would have calculated. Thus, for horizons much longer than one day, using the constant volatility method to calculate VAR may be warranted.[13]

FREQUENCY OF LARGE RETURNS

Using either Bollerslev's GARCH model or the constant volatility method, we could find the VAR by assuming that the returns on the wheel follow a normal distribution. However, a substantial amount of evidence indicates that the normal distribution is inadequate because large daily returns, positive or negative, occur more often in the market than a normal distribution would suggest. One remedy is to use a different distribution for the price changes, one that generates more frequent large returns.[14] Alternatively, we could use statistical methods that assume the returns follow the normal distribution, but which remain valid even if this assumption is mistaken.

Whichever method we use, we are essentially looking at the past frequencies and magnitudes of returns and attempting to represent them on a reconstructed wheel. Even if we account for the non-normality of returns during this process, there is still a problem: we're going to put on the wheel only those returns we saw in the past with the frequency we saw in the past. So, if some potential negative returns are rare or have not yet occurred, we may under-represent them on the wheel, implying that the VAR will be underestimated.

STRUCTURAL SHIFTS IN THE ECONOMY

VAR may also be underestimated if the wheel the market is spinning suddenly changes in an unpredictable way because of a structural change in the underlying economy. For example, consider the European Exchange Rate Mechanism (ERM), which kept daily returns of major European currencies small. In 1993, in response to economic pressures, much larger returns were suddenly allowed. Thus, the volatility of the returns suddenly shot up faster than Bollerslev's GARCH method would have forecast based on past volatilities and returns. If we had calculated the VAR the day before the shift, we would have underestimated it because we would have used an estimate of the volatility that was too low. More subtly, since we never know when the economy may suddenly shift to higher or lower volatility as a result of a structural change, we will incorrectly estimate the VAR unless we explicitly account for this possibility.

Because of the problems caused by infrequent large returns and structural shifts in the economy, it seems prudent, then, to supplement statistical calculations of VAR with judgmental estimates. For example, an institution could have asked its economists to project the likely price effects if the ERM suddenly allowed larger price changes. These projections could be based on similar historical episodes, economic theory, and empirical experience. VAR estimates based on judgment could be generated for changes in central bank monetary regimes, political instability, structural economic changes, and other events that have either never happened before or happen infrequently.

LIQUIDITY OF THE ASSETS

VAR measures the maximum loss that an institution can expect a certain fraction of the time over a specific horizon. Losses are measured by assuming that the assets can be sold at current market prices. However, if a firm has highly illiquid asset - meaning that they cannot quickly be resold - VAR may underestimate the true losses, since the assets may have to be sold at a discount.

CREDIT RISK

Another potential problem for VAR is that the methods used to evaluate the assets in the portfolio may not properly treat credit risk. Suppose a bank buys a portfolio of derivatives from many different firms. The derivatives are valuable to the bank because they impose obligations on the firms. For example, one of the derivatives may oblige a firm to sell foreign currency to the bank at a price below the current market price, yielding a profit to the bank under some conditions, but oblige the bank to deliver foreign exchange at a below-market price under other conditions. Using the Black-Scholes method and a Monte Carlo simulation, which assume no derivative credit risk, the bank calculates a VAR of $5 million at a 98% confidence rate for a three-month horizon. But if some of the firms may default on their obligations, the true value of these derivatives is lower than would be estimated by the Black-Scholes method coupled with Monte Carlo analysis. Thus, the true value at risk is larger than $5 million. To account for this possibility when valuing derivatives, the bank should use a method that includes credit risk. For some applications, credit risk may be small enough to ignore, but, in general, users need to include credit risk analysis in their VAR methods.

IS VAR THE RIGHT METHODOLOGY?

In many situations, VAR may not be the correct risk management methodology. If we pick a specific loss such as $1 million, VAR allows us to estimate how often we can expect to experience this particular loss. For example, using VAR we might estimate that we will lose at least $1 million dollars on one trading day in 20, on average. During some 20-day periods, we might lose less than $1 million. During other 20-day periods, we might lose more than $1 million on more than one day. VAR tells us how often we can expect to experience particular losses. It doesn't tell us how large those losses are likely to be. In particular, in any 20-day period, there is always one day on which the worst loss is experienced. If we want to know the size and frequency of the worst loss, VAR provides no guidance.

One way of handling this is to use worst-case-scenario analysis (WCSA), proposed by Jacob Boudoukh, Matthew Richardson, and Robert Whitlelaw. (See Chapter 11). WCSA might show that on the day with the worst price change in a 20-day period, we can expect to lose at least $2.77 million 5% of the time, a number substantially bigger than $1 million. Thus, if a firm is interested in the size of a worst-case loss, VAR could underestimate it.

Conclusion

VAR is an important new concept in portfolio risk management. It gives the maximum loss that an institution can expect to lose with a certain frequency over a specific horizon, and it can be calculated by using a constant volatility or time-varying volatility method. There are, however, problems in implementation and interpretation. To implement VAR calculations, it is important to use the right method, especially under unusual circumstances such as stock market crashes. Although much progress has been made in describing how volatilities change through time, not as much progress has been made in the description of time-varying covariances. Thus, VAR numbers should be viewed with caution at this point.

Besides the problem of identifying the right method, VAR measures may mislead unless they properly account for liquidity risk, rare or unique events, and credit risk. Moreover, in many situations, it may not be the right risk-management concept. An institution might want to investigate an alternative such as worst-case-scenario analysis.

Despite the contribution that VAR can make

to a firm's understanding of the risks in its portfolio, these risks can be misunderstood if they are not communicated effectively to a management that understands the value and limitations of sophisticated financial technology. Poor management practices, which could lead to unauthorized trades, may also contribute to this misunderstanding. Thus, a firm should use VAR in the context of a broader risk-management culture, fostered not only by the firm's risk managers but also by its senior management.

Appendix A

PROS AND CONS OF USING RISKMETRICS AS A RISK MANAGEMENT TOOL

Pros

❑ Computationally convenient approximation to Bollerslev's GARCH method. Thus, will require relatively smaller investment in research and information systems.
❑ Not a proprietary system. The methodology is explained in detail in JP Morgan publications.
❑ JP Morgan publishes volatilities and correlations on a wide variety of assets free of charge.
❑ Substantial third-party software support.

Cons

❑ Commits user to a one-size-fits-all method: the GARCH method. This may be misleading for stocks, especially following large changes in stock prices. GARCH may also not describe covariances well.
❑ There is no consensus on how well GARCH models forecast volatility. Even if GARCH models forecast volatility well in a statistical sense, that is, make small forecast errors, they may not forecast well in an economic sense. For example, the RiskMetrics volatility estimate may not maximise profits even if it does forecast volatility well in a statistical sense.
❑ VAR may be the wrong methodology for the firm.

Appendix B

VAR AND CAPITAL REQUIREMENTS FOR MARKET RISK

In 1995, the Basle Committee on Banking Supervision at the Bank for International Settlements (Basle Committee) issued a proposal for comment entitled *Internal Model-Based Approach to Market Risk Capital Requirements*. This proposal would establish a VAR-based method of measuring banks' portfolio risk. In January 1996, the Basle Committee approved an approach that would allow banks to use their own internal risk management models or the Basle Committee's standard model. The internal risk management models would be subject, however, to qualitative and quantitative restrictions. US regulators are expected to implement this approach for nine or 10 of the largest US banks. Some examples of the restrictions the Basle Committee would impose on internal models are:

Quantitative criteria

❑ VAR must be computed daily using a horizon of 10 trading days.
❑ The confidence level should be set to 99%.
❑ Models should account for changing delta when computing VAR. In addition, VAR models should account for the impact of time-varying volatility on option prices.
❑ Banks may use covariances within and across asset classes.

1 *An option is a derivative security, ie its value is derived from the value of some other asset.*

2 *In reality, when economists imagine stock returns on a wheel, they think of the wheel as having an infinite number of outcomes so that all possible returns are represented. To simplify the discussion, I have used 100 outcomes on the wheel as an approximation to an infinite-outcome wheel.*

3 *Since the average return is estimated very imprecisely, it may pay to set it to zero to avoid corrupting the rest of the VAR analysis. For more discussion on setting the average return equal to zero, see the papers by Steven Figlewski (1995) and David Hsieh (1995).*

4 *To ease the exposition, I have defined the volatility to correspond to the statistical concept of variance. However, financial market participants usually use the term volatility to refer to the standard deviation, which is the square root of the variance.*

5 *From elementary statistics, 2.054 standard deviations leave 2% of the normal distribution in its left tail, which corresponds to stock losses occurring 2% of the time. If the confidence level were 95%, the confidence factor would be 1.65, because 1.65 standard deviations leave 5% of the normal distribution in the left tail.*

6 *The evidence suggests that volatility is time-varying for*

short horizons such as up to a week or 10 days. For longer horizons, the evidence for time-varying volatility is weaker. If a firm is interested in calculating VAR over a much longer horizon, the time-varying volatility may not be so important.

7 *Under the RiskMetrics method, a different set of weights is calculated for each of a series of 400 assets. The weights are then combined to yield a single composite set of weights that can be used for any asset in the portfolio.*

8 *For an explanation of this method, see the paper by Fischer Black and Myron Scholes.*

9 *The correlation between stock 1 and stock 2 is equal to the covariance between stock 1 and stock 2 divided by the product of the square roots of the volatilities of the two stocks.*

10 *For further discussion on covariance techniques, see the paper by Robert Engle and Kenneth Kroner and the 1990 paper by Tim Bollerslev.*

11 *For more detail on this process, see the RiskMetrics technical document. For an example of a related methodology, see the 1993 papers by David Hsieh.*

12 *The prototypical asymmetric volatility model is EGARCH. See the paper by Daniel Nelson.*

13 *See the paper by David Hsieh (1993a) for a discussion about when the constant volatility model may be appropriate.*

14 *For an example of this technique, see the paper by Daniel Nelson.*

BIBLIOGRAPHY

Black, F., and M. Scholes, 1973, "The Pricing of Options and Corporate Liabilities", *Journal of Political Economy* 81, pp. 637-59.

Bollerslev, T., 1986, "Generalized Autoregressive Conditional Heteroskedasticity", *Journal of Econometrics* 31, pp. 307-27.

Bollerslev, T., 1990, "Modelling the Coherence in Short-Run Nominal Exchange Rates: A Multivariate Generalised ARCH Model", *Review of Economics and Statistics* 78, pp. 498-505.

Boudoukh, J., M. Richardson, and Robert Whitelaw, 1995, "Expect the Worst", *Risk* 8, 9, pp. 100-01; reprinted as Chapter 11 of the present volume.

Engle, R.F., 1982, "Autoregressive Conditional Heteroskedasticity with Estimates of the Variance of UK Inflation", *Econometrica* 50, pp. 987-1008.

Engle R.F., and G. Lee, 1993a, "A Permanent and Transitory Component Model of Stock Return Volatility", Discussion Paper, University of California at San Diego.

Engle R.F., and G. Lee, 1993b, "Long Run Volatility Forecasting for Individual Stocks in a One Factor Model", Discussion Paper, University of California at San Diego.

Engle, R.F., and V.K. Ng, 1993a, "Measuring and Testing the Impact of News on Volatility", *Journal of Finance* 48, pp. 1749-78.

Engle, R.F., and K.K. Kroner, 1993b, "Multivariate Simultaneous Generalized Arch", Mimeograph, University of California at San Diego.

Figlewski, S., 1994, "Forecasting Volatility Using Historical Data", Working Paper, New York University.

Hopper, G., 1996, "Notes on the Estimation of a Bivariate GARCH Model for VaR Calculations on a Portfolio of the Yen and Deutschemark", Mimeograph, Federal Reserve Bank of Philadelphia.

Hsieh, D.A., 1993a, "Implications of Nonlinear Dynamics for Financial Risk Management", *Journal of Financial and Quantitative Analysis* 28, pp. 41-64.

Hsieh, D.A., 1993b, "Assessing the Market and Credit Risks of Long-Term Interest Rate and Foreign Currency Products", *Financial Analysts Journal*, July-August, pp. 75-9.

Hsieh, D.A., 1995, "Nonlinear Dynamics in Financial Markets: Evidence and Implications", *Financial Analysts Journal*, July-August, pp. 55-62.

Nelson, D.B., 1991, "Conditional Heteroskedasticity in Asset Returns: A New Approach", *Econometrica* 59, pp. 347-70.

JP Morgan, 1995, *RiskMetrics Technical Document*, 3rd edition, New York.

21

Evaluation of Value-at-Risk Models using Historical Data*

Darryll Hendricks
Federal Reserve Bank of New York

VAR techniques are becoming increasingly popular, but how well do they perform in practice? This paper applies VAR models to one thousand randomly chosen foreign exchange portfolios over the period 1983–94, using a number of different techniques. The results are then compared. Important differences emerge, though none of the approaches employed is found to be superior on every count.

Researchers in the field of financial economics have long recognised the importance of measuring the risk of a portfolio of financial assets or securities. Indeed, concerns go back at least four decades, when Markowitz's pioneering work on portfolio selection (1959) explored the appropriate definition and measurement of risk. In recent years, the growth of trading activity and instances of financial market instability have prompted new studies underscoring the need for market participants to develop reliable risk measurement techniques.[1]

One technique advanced in the literature involves the use of "value-at-risk" models. These models measure the market, or price, risk of a portfolio of financial assets – that is, the risk that the market value of the portfolio will decline as a result of changes in interest rates, foreign exchange rates, equity prices, or commodity prices. VAR models aggregate the several components of price risk into a single quantitative measure of the potential for losses over a specified time horizon. These models are clearly appealing because they convey the market risk of the entire portfolio in one number. Moreover, VAR measures focus directly, and in dollar terms, on a major reason for assessing risk in the first place – a loss of portfolio value.

Recognition of these models by the financial and regulatory communities is evidence of their growing use. For example, in its recent risk-based capital proposal (1996a), the Basle Committee on Banking Supervision endorsed the use of such models, contingent on important qualitative and quantitative standards. In addition, the Bank for International Settlements' Fisher report (1994) urged financial intermediaries to disclose measures of VAR publicly. The Derivatives Policy Group, affiliated with six large US securities firms, has also advocated the use of VAR models as an important way to measure market risk. The introduction of the RiskMetrics database compiled by JP Morgan for use with third-party VAR software also highlights the growing use of these models by financial as well as non-financial firms.

Clearly, the use of VAR models is increasing, but how well do they perform in practice? This paper explores this question by applying VAR models to 1,000 randomly chosen foreign exchange portfolios over the period 1983–94. We then use nine criteria to evaluate model performance. We consider, for example, how closely risk measures produced by the models correspond to actual portfolio outcomes.

We begin by explaining the three most common categories of VAR models – equally weighted moving average approaches, exponentially weighted moving average approaches, and historical simulation approaches. Although within these three categories many different

* *This paper was first published in the Federal Reserve Bank of New York Economic Policy Review, Vol.2 (1996). The author thanks Christine Cumming, Arturo Estrella, Beverley Hirtle, John Kambhu, Paul Kupiec, James Mahoney, Christopher McCurdy, Matthew Pritske and Philip Strahan for helpful comments and discussions.*

approaches exist, for the purposes of this article we select five approaches from the first category, three from the second, and four from the third.

By employing a simulation technique using these twelve VAR approaches, we arrived at measures of price risk for the portfolios at both 95% and 99% confidence levels over one-day holding periods. The confidence levels specify the probability that losses of a portfolio will be smaller than estimated by the risk measure. We then use nine criteria to evaluate the performance of the models. Although this article considers VAR models only in the context of market risk, the methodology is fairly general and could in theory address any source of risk that leads to a decline in market values. An important limitation of the analysis, however, is that it does not consider portfolios containing options or other positions with non-linear price behaviour.[2]

We choose several performance criteria to reflect the practices of risk managers who rely on VAR measures for many purposes. Although important differences emerge across VAR approaches with respect to each criterion, the results indicate that none of the twelve approaches we examine is superior on every count. In addition, as the results make clear, the choice of confidence level - 95% or 99% - can have a substantial effect on the performance of VAR approaches.

Introduction to VAR models

A VAR model measures market risk by determining how much the value of a portfolio could decline over a given period of time with a given probability as a result of changes in market prices or rates. For example, if the given period of time is one day and the given probability is 1%, the VAR measure would be an estimate of the decline in the portfolio value that could occur with a 1% probability over the next trading day. In other words, if the VAR measure is accurate, losses greater than the VAR measure should occur less than 1% of the time.

The two most important components of VAR models are the length of time over which market risk is to be measured and the confidence level at which market risk is measured. The choice of these components by risk managers greatly affects the nature of the VAR model.

The time period used in the definition of VAR, often referred to as the "holding period," is discretionary. VAR models assume that the portfolio's composition does not change over the holding period. This assumption argues for the use of short holding periods because the composition of active trading portfolios is apt to change frequently. Thus, this chapter focuses on the widely used one-day holding period.[3]

VAR measures are most often expressed as percentiles corresponding to the desired confidence level. For example, an estimate of risk at the 99% confidence level is the amount of loss that a portfolio is expected to exceed only 1% of the time. It is also known as a 99th percentile VAR measure because the amount is the 99th percentile of the distribution of potential losses on the portfolio.[4] In practice, VAR estimates are calculated from the 90th to 99.9th percentiles, but the most commonly used range is the 95th to 99th percentile range. Accordingly, the text charts and the tables in Appendix B report simulation results for each of these percentiles.

Three categories of VAR approaches

Although risk managers apply many approaches when calculating portfolio VAR models, almost all use past data to estimate potential changes in the value of the portfolio in the future. Such approaches assume that the future will be like the past, but they often define the past quite differently and make different assumptions about how markets will behave in the future.

The first two categories we examine, "variance-covariance" VAR approaches,[5] assume normality and serial independence and an absence of non-linear positions such as options.[6] The dual assumption of normality and serial independence creates ease of use for two reasons. First, normality simplifies VAR calculations because all percentiles are assumed to be known multiples of the standard deviation. Thus, the VAR calculation requires only an estimate of the standard deviation of the portfolio's change in value over the holding period. Second, serial independence means that the size of a price move on one day will not affect estimates of price moves on any other day. Consequently, longer horizon standard deviations can be obtained by multiplying daily horizon standard deviations by the square root of the number of days in the longer horizon. When the assumptions of normality and serial independence are made together, a risk manager can use a single calculation of the portfolio's daily horizon standard deviation to develop VAR measures for any given holding period and any given percentile.

The advantages of these assumptions, however, must be weighed against a large body of evidence suggesting that the tails of the distributions of daily percentage changes in financial market prices, particularly foreign exchange rates, will be fatter than predicted by the normal distribution.[7] This evidence calls into question the appealing features of the normality assumption, especially for VAR measurement, which focuses on the tails of the distribution. Questions raised by the commonly used normality assumption are highlighted throughout the chapter.

In the sections below, we describe the individual features of the two variance-covariance approaches to VAR measurement.

EQUALLY WEIGHTED MOVING AVERAGE APPROACHES

The equally weighted moving average approach, the most straightforward, calculates a given portfolio's variance (and thus, standard deviation) using a fixed amount of historical data.[8] The major difference among equally weighted moving average approaches is the timeframe of the fixed amount of data.[9] Some approaches employ just the most recent 50 days of historical data on the assumption that only very recent data are relevant to estimating potential movements in portfolio value. Other approaches assume that large amounts of data are necessary to estimate potential movements accurately and thus rely on a much longer time span - for example, five years.

The calculation of portfolio standard devia tions using an equally weighted moving average approach is

$$\sigma_t = \sqrt{\frac{1}{(k-1)}\sum_{s=t-k}^{t-1}(x_s-\mu)^2} \qquad (1)$$

where σ_t denotes the estimated standard deviation of the portfolio at the beginning of day t. The parameter k specifies the number of days included in the moving average (the "observation period"), x_s, the change in portfolio value on day s, and μ, the mean change in portfolio value. Following the recommendation of Figlewski (1994), μ is always assumed to be zero.[10]

Consider five sets of VAR measures with periods of 50, 125, 250, 500, and 1,250 days, or about two months, six months, one year, two years, and five years of historical data. Using three of these five periods of time, Figure 1 plots the time series of VAR measures at bi-weekly intervals for a single fixed portfolio of spot foreign exchange positions from 1983 to 1994.[11] As shown, the 50-day risk measures are prone to rapid swings. Conversely, the 1,250-day risk measures are more stable over long periods of time, and the behaviour of the 250-day risk measures lies somewhere in the middle.

EXPONENTIALLY WEIGHTED MOVING AVERAGE APPROACHES

Exponentially weighted moving average approaches emphasise recent observations by using exponentially weighted moving averages of squared deviations. In contrast to equally weighted approaches, these approaches attach different weights to the past observations contained in the observation period. Because the weights decline exponentially, the most recent observations receive much more weight than earlier observations. The formula for the portfolio standard deviation under an exponentially weighted moving average approach is

$$\sigma_t = \sqrt{(1-\lambda)\sum_{s=t-k}^{t-1}\lambda^{t-s-1}(x_s-\mu)^2}. \qquad (2)$$

The parameter λ, referred to as the "decay factor," determines the rate at which the weights on past observations decay as they become more

1. Value-at-risk measures for a single portfolio over time: equally weighted moving average approaches

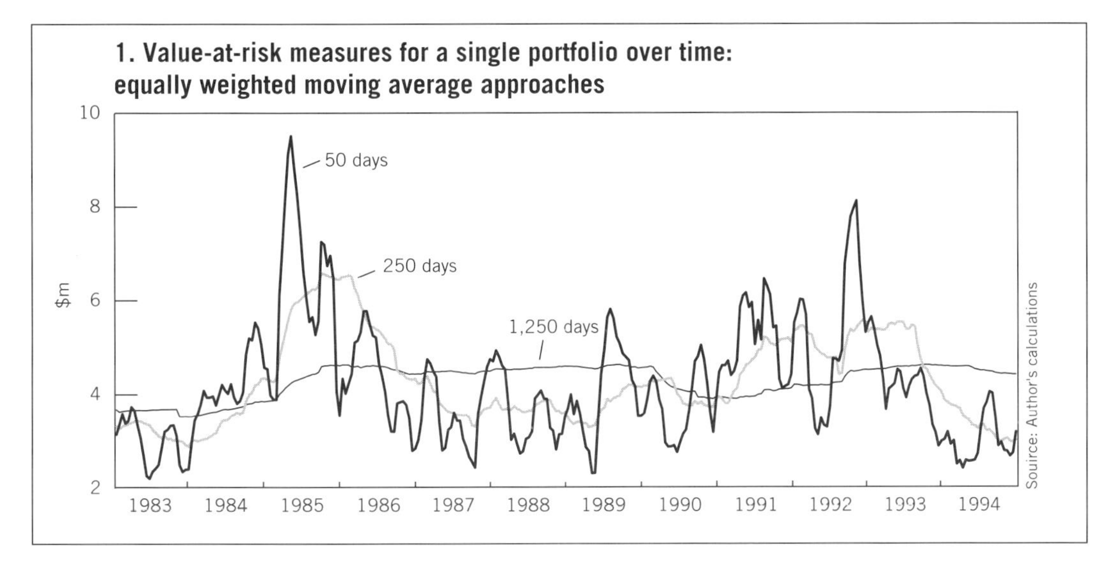

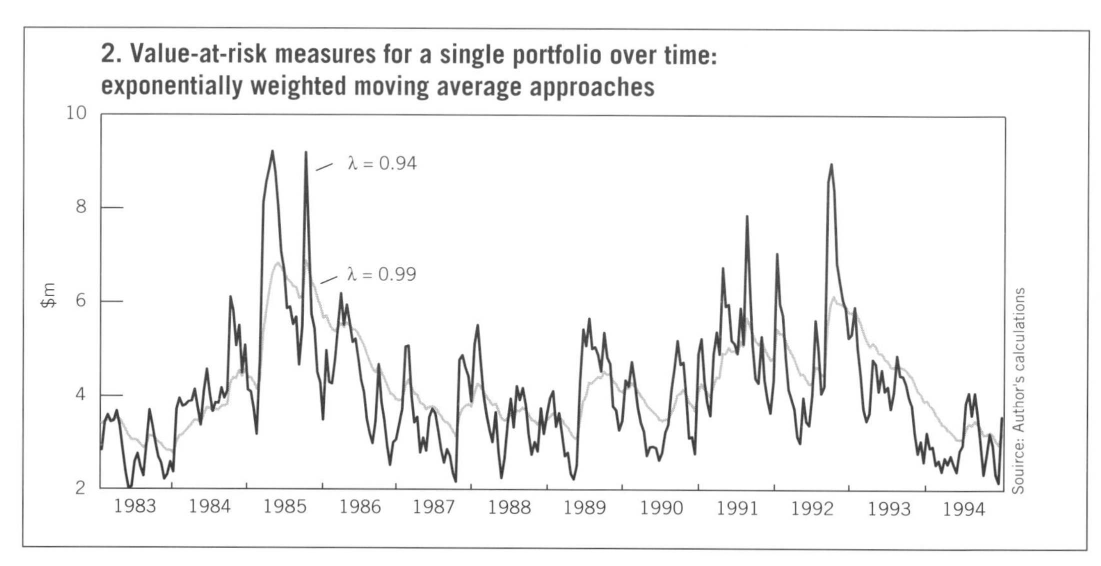

distant. In theory, for the weights to sum to one, these approaches should use an infinitely large number of observations k. In practice, for the values of the decay factor λ considered here, the sum of the weights will converge to one, with many fewer observations than the 1,250 days used in the simulations. As with the equally weighted moving averages, the parameter m is assumed to equal zero.

Exponentially weighted moving average approaches clearly aim to capture short-term movements in volatility, the same motivation that has generated the large body of literature on conditional volatility forecasting models.[12] In fact, exponentially weighted moving average approaches are equivalent to the IGARCH(1,1) family of popular conditional volatility models.[13] Equation 3 gives an equivalent formulation of the model and may also suggest a more intuitive understanding of the role of the decay factor:

$$\sigma_t = \sqrt{\lambda\sigma_{t-1}^2 + (1-\lambda)(x_{t-1}-\mu)^2} \qquad (3)$$

As shown, an exponentially weighted average on any given day is a simple combination of two components: the weighted average on the previous day, which receives a weight of λ; and yesterday's squared deviation, which receives a weight of (1 − λ). This interaction means that the lower the decay factor λ, the faster the decay in the influence of a given observation. This concept is illustrated in Figure 2, which plots time series of VAR measures using exponentially weighted moving averages with decay factors of 0.94 and 0.99. A decay factor of 0.94 implies a VAR measure that is derived almost entirely from very recent observations, resulting in the high level of variability apparent for that particular series.

On the one hand, relying heavily on the recent past seems crucial when trying to capture short-term movements in actual volatility, the focus of conditional volatility forecasting. On the other hand, the reliance on recent data effectively reduces the overall sample size, increasing the possibility of measurement error. In the limiting case, relying only on yesterday's observation would produce highly variable and error-prone risk measures.

HISTORICAL SIMULATION APPROACHES

The third category of VAR approach is similar to the equally weighted moving average category in that it relies on a specific quantity of past historical observations (the observation period). Rather than using these observations to calculate the portfolio's standard deviation, however, historical simulation approaches use the actual percentiles of the observation period as VAR measures. For example, for an observation period of 500 days, the 99th percentile historical simulation VAR measure is the sixth largest loss observed in the sample of 500 outcomes (because the 1% of the sample that should exceed the risk measure equates to five losses).

In other words, for these approaches, the 95th and 99th percentile VAR measures will not be constant multiples of each other. Moreover, VAR measures for holding periods other than one day will not be fixed multiples of the one-day VAR measures. Historical simulation approaches do not make the assumptions of normality or serial independence. However, relaxing these assumptions also implies that historical simulation approaches do not easily accommodate translations between multiple percentiles and holding periods.

Figure 3 depicts the time series of one-day 99th percentile VAR measures calculated through

3. Value-at-risk measures for a single portfolio over time: historical simulation approaches

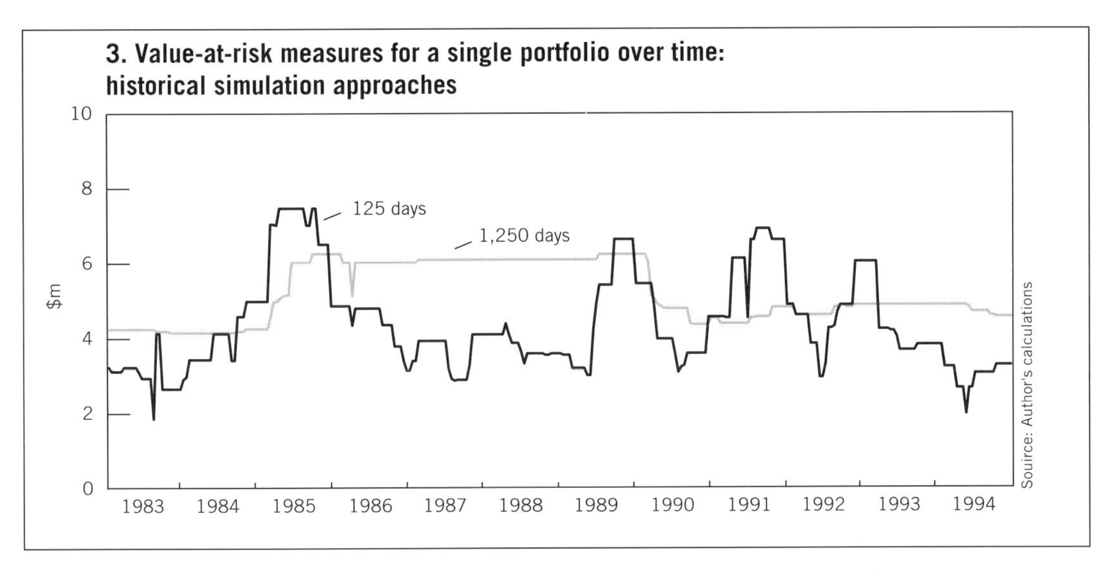

historical simulation. The observation periods shown are 125 days and 1,250 days.[14] Interestingly, the use of actual percentiles produces time series with a somewhat different appearance than is observed in either Figure 1 or Figure 2. In particular, very abrupt shifts occur in the 99th percentile measures for the 125-day historical simulation approach.

Trade-offs regarding the length of the observation period for historical simulation approaches are similar to those for variance-covariance approaches. Clearly, the choice of 125 days is motivated by the desire to capture short-term movements in the underlying risk of the portfolio. In contrast, the choice of 1,250 days may be driven by the desire to estimate the historical percentiles as accurately as possible. Extreme percentiles such as the 95th and particularly the 99th are very difficult to estimate accurately with small samples. Thus, the fact that historical simulation approaches abandon the assumption of normality and attempt to estimate these percentiles directly is one rationale for using long observation periods.

Simulations of VAR models

This section provides an introduction to the simulation results derived by applying 12 VAR approaches to 1,000 randomly-selected foreign exchange portfolios and assessing their behaviour along nine performance criteria (see Appendix A). This simulation design has several advantages. First, by simulating the performance of each VAR approach for a long period of time (approximately 12 years of daily data) and across a large number of portfolios, we arrive at a clear picture of how VAR models would actually have performed for linear foreign exchange portfolios over this time span. Second, the results give insight into the extent to which portfolio composition or choice of sample period can affect results.

It is important to emphasise, however, that neither the reported variability across portfolios nor variability over time can be used to calculate suitable standard errors. The appropriate standard errors for these simulation results raise difficult questions. The results aggregate information across multiple samples, that is, across the 1,000 portfolios. Because the results for one portfolio are not independent of the results for other portfolios, we cannot easily determine the total amount of information provided by the simulations. Furthermore, many of the performance criteria we consider do not have straightforward standard error formulas even for single samples.[15]

These stipulations imply that it is not possible to use the simulation results to accept or reject specific statistical hypotheses about these twelve VAR approaches. Moreover, the results should not in any way be taken as indicative of the results that would be obtained for portfolios including other financial market assets, spanning other time periods, or looking forward. Finally, this chapter does not contribute substantially to the ongoing debate about the appropriate approach to or interpretation of "back testing" in conjunction with VAR modelling.[16] Despite these limitations, the simulation results do provide a relatively complete picture of the performance of selected VAR approaches in estimating the market risk of a large number of linear foreign exchange portfolios over the period 1983–94.

For each of the nine performance criteria, Figures 4–12 provide a visual sense of the simulation results for 95th and 99th percentile risk measures. The vertical axis depicts a relevant range of the performance criterion under consideration (VAR approaches are arrayed horizontally across the chart). Filled circles depict the average results across the 1,000 portfolios, and the boxes drawn for each VAR approach depict the 5th, 25th, 50th, 75th, and 95th percentiles of the distribution of the results across the 1,000 portfolios.[17] In some charts, a horizontal line is drawn to highlight how the results compare with an important point of reference. Simulation results are also presented in tabular form in Appendix B.

MEAN RELATIVE BIAS

The first performance criterion we examine is whether the different VAR approaches produce risk measures of similar average size. To ensure that the comparison is not influenced by the scale of each simulated portfolio, we use a four-step procedure to generate scale-free measures of the relative sizes for each simulated portfolio.

First, we calculate VAR measures for each of the 12 approaches for the portfolio on each sample date. Second, we average the 12 risk measures for each date to obtain the average risk measure for that date for the portfolio. Third, we calculate the percentage difference between each approach's risk measure and the average risk measure for each date. We refer to these figures as daily relative bias figures because they are relative only to the average risk measure across the 12 approaches rather than to any external standard. Fourth, we average the daily relative biases for a given VAR approach across all sample dates to obtain the approach's mean relative bias for the portfolio.

Intuitively, this procedure results in a measure of size for each VAR approach that is relative to the average of all 12 approaches. The mean relative bias for a portfolio is independent of the scale of the simulated portfolio because each of the daily relative bias calculations on which it is based is also scale-independent. This independence is achieved because all of the VAR approaches we examine here are proportional to the scale of the portfolio's positions. For example, a doubling of the scale of the portfolio would result in a doubling of the VAR measures for each of the 12 approaches.

Mean relative bias is measured in percentage terms, so that a value of 0.10 implies that a given VAR approach is 10% larger, on average, than the average of all 12 approaches. The simulation results suggest that differences in the average size of 95th percentile VAR measures are small. For the vast majority of the 1,000 portfolios, the mean relative biases for the 95th percentile risk measures are between −0.10 and 0.10 (Figure 4a). The averages of the mean relative biases across the 1,000 portfolios are even smaller, indicating that across approaches little systematic difference in size exists for 95th percentile VAR measures.

For the 99th percentile VAR measures, however, the results suggest that historical simulation approaches tend to produce systematically larger risk measures. In particular, Figure 4b shows that the 1,250-day historical simulation approach is, on average, approximately 13% larger than the average of all 12 approaches; for almost all of the portfolios, this approach is more than 5% larger than the average risk measure.

Together, the results for the 95th and 99th percentiles suggest that the normality assumption made by all of the approaches, except the historical simulations, is more reasonable for the 95th percentile than for the 99th percentile. In other words, actual 99th percentiles for the foreign exchange portfolios considered in this article tend to be larger than the normal distribution would predict.

Interestingly, the results in Figures 4a and 4b also suggest that the use of longer time periods may produce larger VAR measures. For historical

4. Mean relative bias

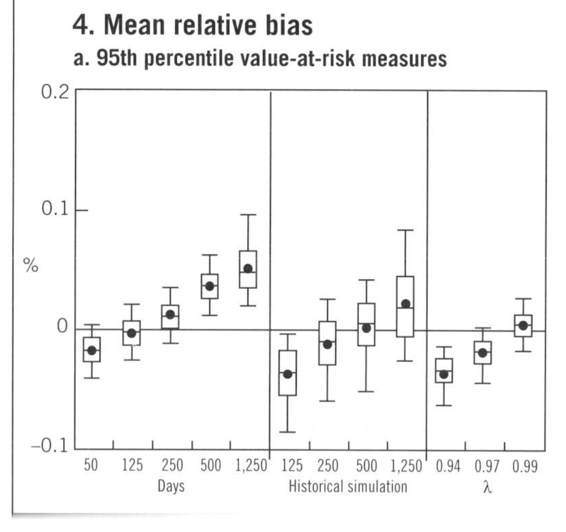

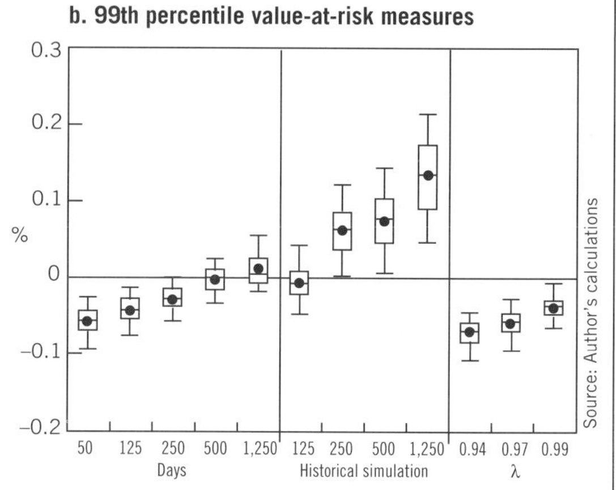

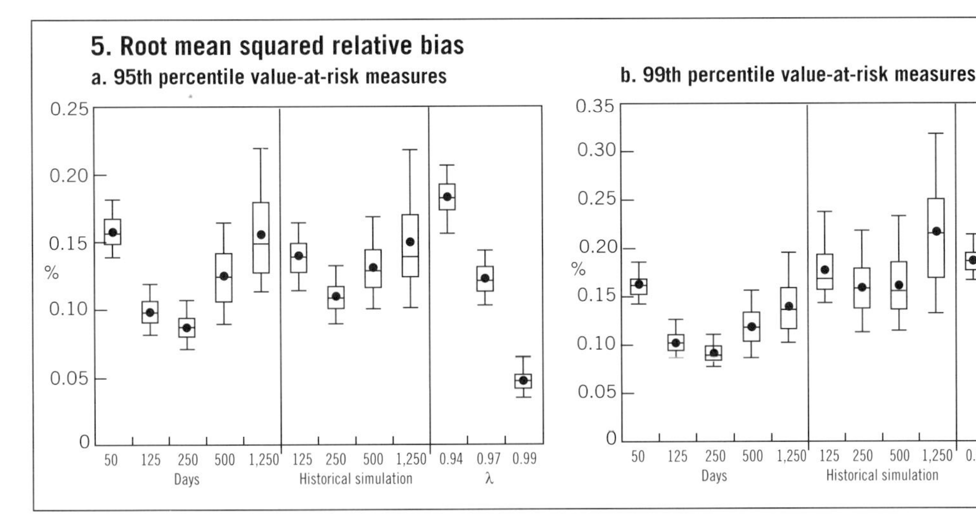

simulation approaches, this result may occur because longer horizons provide better estimates of the tail of the distribution. The equally weighted approaches, however, may require a different explanation. Nevertheless, in our simulations the time period effect is small, suggesting that its economic significance is probably low.[18]

ROOT MEAN SQUARED RELATIVE BIAS

The second performance criterion we examine is the degree to which the risk measures tend to vary around the average risk measure for a given date. This criterion can be compared to a standard deviation calculation; here the deviations are the percentage of deviation of the risk measure from the average across all 12 approaches. The root mean squared relative bias for each VAR approach is calculated by taking the square root of the mean (over all sample dates) of the squares of the daily relative biases.

The results indicate that for any given date, a dispersion in the risk measures produced by the different VAR approaches is likely to occur. The average root mean squared relative biases, across portfolios, tend to fall largely in the 10–15 % range, with the 99th percentile risk measures tending toward the higher end (Figures 5a and 5b). This level of variability suggests that, in spite of similar average sizes across the different VAR approaches, differences in the range of 30–50% between the risk measures produced by specific approaches on a given day are not uncommon.

Surprisingly, the exponentially weighted average approach with a decay factor of 0.99 exhibits very low root mean squared bias, suggesting that this particular approach is very close to the average of all twelve approaches. Of course, this phenomenon is specific to the 12 approaches considered here and would not necessarily be true of exponentially weighted average approaches applied to other cases.

ANNUALISED PERCENTAGE VOLATILITY

The third performance criterion we review is the tendency of the risk measures to fluctuate over time for the same portfolio. For each portfolio and each VAR approach, we calculate the annualised percentage volatility by first taking the standard deviation of the day-to-day percentage changes in the risk measures over the sample period. Second, we put the result on an annualized basis by multiplying this standard deviation by the square root of 250, the number of trading days in a typical calendar year. We complete the second step simply to make the results comparable with volatilities as they are often expressed in the marketplace. For example, individual foreign exchange rates tend to have annualised percentage volatilities in the range of 5–20%, although higher figures sometimes occur. This result implies that the VAR approaches with annualised percentage volatilities in excess of 20% (Figures 6a and 6b) will fluctuate more over time (for the same portfolio) than will most exchange rates themselves.

Our major observation for this performance criterion is that the volatility of risk measures increases as reliance on recent data increases. As shown in Figures 6a and 6b, this increase is true for both the 95th and 99th percentile risk measures and for all three categories of VAR approaches. This result is not surprising, and indeed it is clearly apparent in Figures 1-3, which depict time series of different VAR approaches over the sample period. Also worth noting in Figures 6a and 6b is that for a fixed length of observation period, historical simulation approaches appear to be more variable than the corresponding equally weighted moving average approaches.

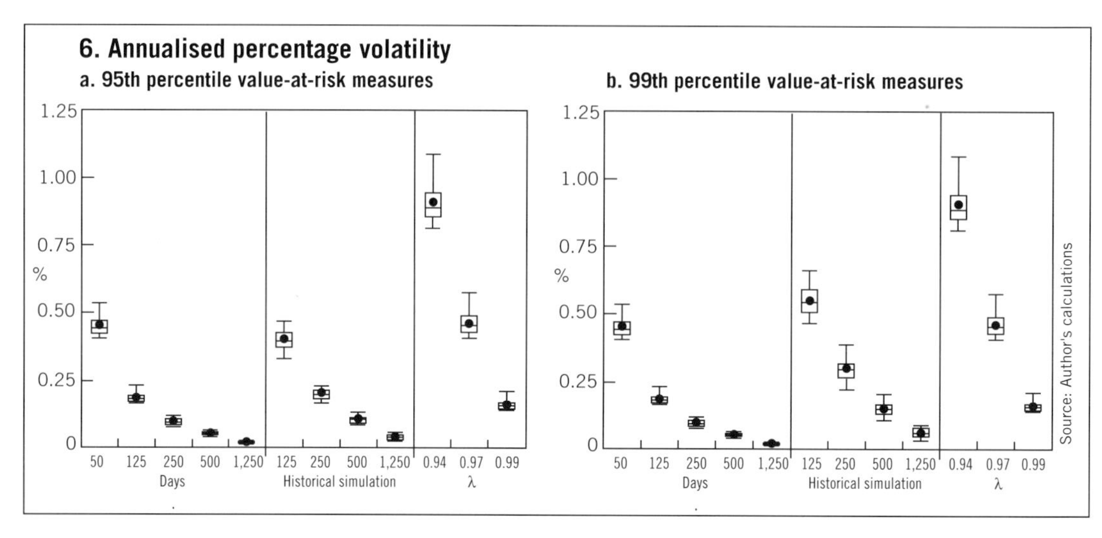

FRACTION OF OUTCOMES COVERED

Our fourth performance criterion addresses the fundamental goal of the VAR measures - whether they cover the portfolio outcomes they are intended to capture. We calculate the fraction of outcomes covered as the percentage of results where the loss in portfolio value is less than the risk measure.

For the 95th percentile risk measures, the simulation results indicate that nearly all 12 VAR approaches meet this performance criterion (Figure 7a). For many portfolios, coverage exceeds 95%, and only the 125-day historical simulation approach captures less than 94.5% of the outcomes on average across all 1,000 portfolios. In a very small fraction of the random portfolios, the risk measures cover less than 94% of the outcomes.

Interestingly, the 95th percentile results suggest that the equally weighted moving average approaches actually tend to produce excess coverage (greater than 95%) for all observation periods except 50 days. By contrast, the historical simulation approaches tend to provide either too little coverage or, in the case of the 1,250-day historical simulation approach, a little more than the desired amount. The exponentially weighted moving average approach with a decay factor of 0.97 produces exact 95% coverage, but for this approach the results are more variable across portfolios than for the 1,250-day historical simulation approach.

Compared with the 95th percentile results, the 99th percentile risk measures exhibit a more widespread tendency to fall short of the desired level of risk coverage. Only the 1,250-day historical simulation approach attains 99% coverage across all 1,000 portfolios, as shown in Figure 7b. The other approaches cover between 98.2 and 98.8% of the outcomes on average across portfolios. Of course, the consequences of such a shortfall in performance depend on the particular circumstances in which the VAR model is being used. A coverage level of 98.2% when a risk manager desires 99% implies that the VAR model misclassifies approximately two outcomes every year (assuming that there are 250 trading days per calendar year).

Overall, the results in Figures 7a and 7b support the conclusion that all 12 VAR approaches

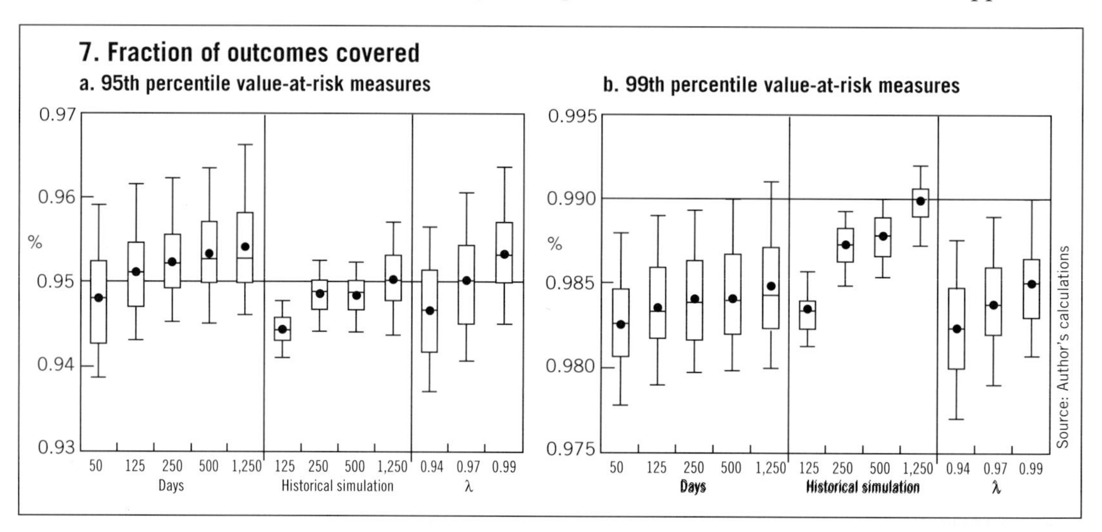

either achieve their desired levels of coverage or come very close to it on the basis of the percentage of outcomes misclassified. Clearly, the best performer is the 1,250-day historical simulation approach, which attains almost exact coverage for both the 95th and 99th percentiles, while the worst performer is the 125-day historical simulation approach, partly because of its short-term construction.[19] One explanation for the superior performance of the 1,250-day historical simulation is that the unconditional distribution of changes in portfolio value is relatively stable and that accurate estimates of extreme percentiles require the use of long periods. These results underscore the problems associated with the assumption of normality for 99th percentiles and are consistent with findings in other recent studies of VAR models.[20]

MULTIPLE NEEDED TO ATTAIN DESIRED COVERAGE

The fifth performance criterion we examine focuses on the size of the adjustments in the risk measures that would be needed to achieve perfect coverage. We therefore calculate on an ex post basis the multiple that would have been required for each VAR measure to attain the desired level of coverage (either 95% or 99%). This performance criterion complements the fraction of outcomes covered because it focuses on the size of the potential errors in risk measurement rather than on the percentage of results captured.

For 95th percentile risk measures, the simulation results indicate that multiples very close to one are sufficient (Figure 8a). Even the 125-day historical simulation approach, which on average across portfolios is furthest from the desired outcome, requires a multiple of only 1.04. On the whole, none of the approaches considered here appears to understate 95th percentile risk measures on a systematic basis by more than 4%, and several appear to overstate them by small amounts.

For the 99th percentile risk measures, most VAR approaches require multiples between 1.10 and 1.15 to attain 99% coverage (Figure 8b). The 1,250-day historical simulation approach, however, is markedly superior to all other approaches. On average across all portfolios, no multiple other than 1 is needed for this approach to achieve 99% coverage. Moreover, compared with the other approaches, the historical simulations in general exhibit less variability across portfolios with respect to this criterion.

The fact that most multiples are larger than one is not surprising. More significant is the fact that the size of the multiples needed to achieve 99% coverage exceeds the levels indicated by the normal distribution. For example, when normality is assumed, the 99th percentile would be about 1.08 times as large as the 98.4th percentile, a level of coverage comparable to that attained by many of the approaches (Figure 7b). The multiples for these approaches, shown in Figure 8b, are larger than 1.08, providing further evidence that the normal distribution does not accurately approximate actual distributions at points near the 99th percentile. More generally, the results also suggest that substantial increases in VAR measures may be needed to capture outcomes in the tail of the distribution. Hence, shortcomings in VAR measures that seem small in probability terms may be much more significant when considered in terms of the changes required to remedy them.

These results lead to an important question: what distributional assumptions other than normality can be used when constructing VAR measures using a variance-covariance approach? The

8. Multiple needed to attain 95% (99%) coverage

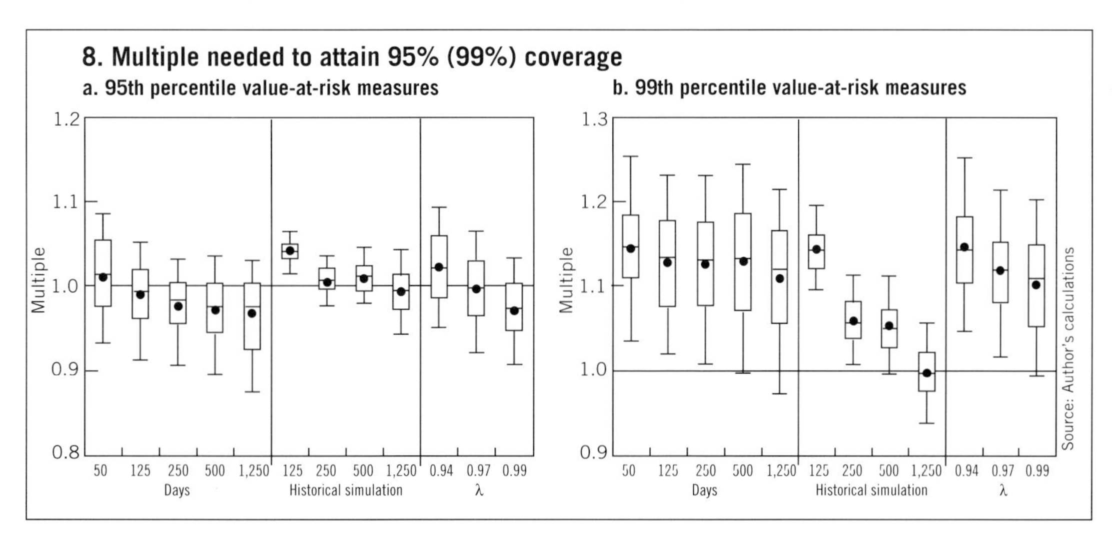

t distribution is often cited as a good candidate, because extreme outcomes occur more often under *t* distributions than under the normal distribution.[21] A brief analysis shows that the use of a *t* distribution for the 99th percentile has some merit.

To calculate a value-at-risk measure for a single percentile assuming the *t* distribution, the value-at-risk measure calculated with the assumption of normality is multiplied by a fixed multiple. As the results in Figure 8b suggest, fixed multiples between 1.10 and 1.15 are appropriate for the variance-covariance approaches. It follows that *t* distributions with between four and six degrees of freedom are appropriate for the 99th percentile risk measures.[22] The use of these particular *t* distributions, however, would lead to substantial overestimation of 95th percentile risk measures because the actual distributions near the 95th percentile are much closer to normality. Since the use of *t* distributions for risk measurement involves a scaling up of the risk measures that are calculated assuming normality, the distributions are likely to be useful, although they may be more helpful for some percentiles than for others.

AVERAGE MULTIPLE OF TAIL EVENT TO RISK MEASURE

The sixth performance criterion that we review relates to the size of outcomes not covered by the risk measures.[23] To address these outcomes, we measure the degree to which events in the tail of the distribution typically exceed the value-at-risk measure by calculating the average multiple of these outcomes ("tail events") to their corresponding VAR measures.

Tail events are defined as the largest percentage of losses measured relative to the respective VAR estimate - the largest 5% in the case of 95th percentile risk measures and the largest 1% in the case of 99th percentile risk measures. For example, if the VAR measure is $1.5 million and the actual portfolio outcome is a loss of $3 million, the size of the loss relative to the risk measure would be 2. Note that this definition implies that the tail events for one VAR approach may not be the same as those for another approach, even for the same portfolio, because the risk measures for the two approaches are not the same. Horizontal reference lines in Figures 9a and 9b show where the average multiples of the tail event outcomes to the risk measures would fall if outcomes were normally distributed and the VAR approach produced a true 99th percentile level of coverage.

In fact, however, the average tail event is almost always a larger multiple of the risk measure than is predicted by the normal distribution. For most of the VAR approaches, the average tail event is 30–40% larger than the respective risk measures for both the 95th percentile risk measures and the 99th percentile risk measures. This result means that approximately 1% of outcomes (the largest two or three losses per year) will exceed the size of the 99th percentile risk measure by an average of 30–40%. In addition, note that the 99th percentile results in Figure 9b are more variable across portfolios than the 95th percentile results in Figure 9a; the average multiple is also above 1.50 for a greater percentage of the portfolios for the 99th percentile risk measures.

The performance of the different approaches according to this criterion largely mirrors their performance in capturing portfolio outcomes. For example, the 1,250-day historical simulation approach is clearly superior for the 99th percentile risk measures. The equally weighted moving average approaches also do very well for the 95th percentile risk measures (Figure 7a).

9. Average multiple of tail event to risk measure

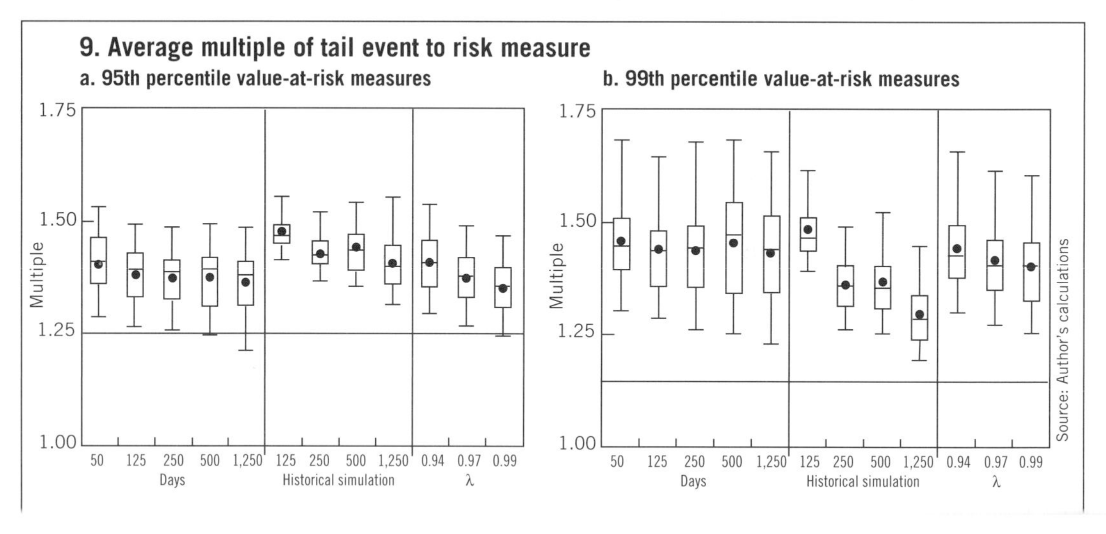

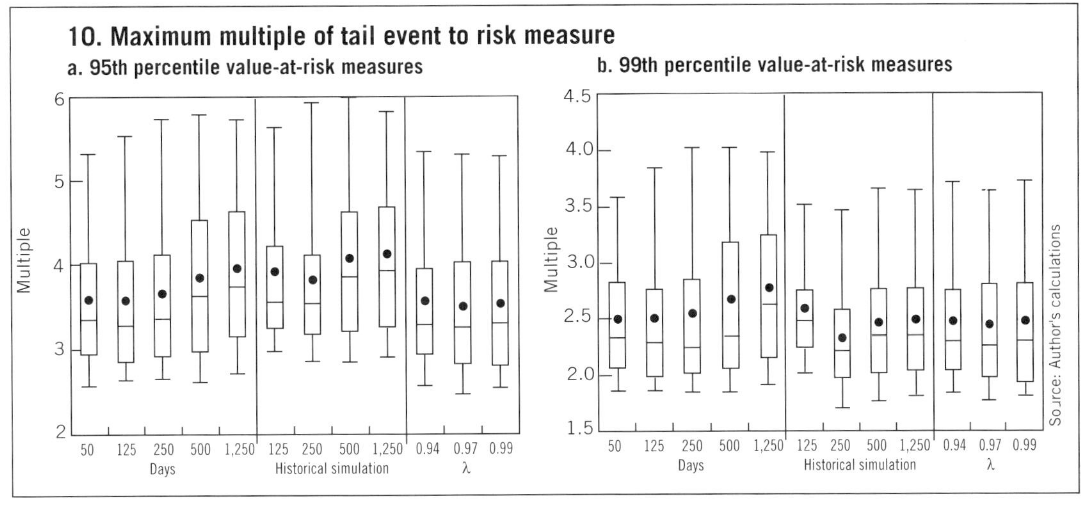

MAXIMUM MULTIPLE OF TAIL EVENT TO RISK MEASURE

Our seventh performance criterion concerns the size of the maximum portfolio loss. We use the following two-step procedure to arrive at these measures. First, we calculate the multiples of all portfolio outcomes to their respective risk measures for each VAR approach for a particular portfolio. Recall that the tail events defined above are those outcomes with the largest such multiples. Rather than average these multiples, however, we simply select the single largest multiple for each approach. This procedure implies that the maximum multiple will be highly dependent on the length of the sample period – in this case, approximately 12 years. For shorter periods, the maximum multiple would likely be lower.

Not surprisingly, the typical maximum tail event is substantially larger than the corresponding risk measure (Figures 10a and 10b). For 95th percentile risk measures, the maximum multiple is three to four times as large as the risk measure, and for the 99th percentile risk measure, it is approximately 2.5 times as large. In addition, the results are variable across portfolios – for some portfolios, the maximum multiples are more than five times the 95th percentile risk measure. The differences among results for this performance criterion, however, are less pronounced than for some other criteria. For example, unlike for many of the other performance criteria, the 1,250-day historical simulation approach is not clearly superior for the 99th percentile risk measure, although it exhibits lower average multiples (Figure 9b).

These results suggest that it is important not to view VAR measures as a strict upper bound on the portfolio losses that can occur. Although a 99th percentile risk measure may sound as if it is capturing essentially all of the relevant events, our results make it clear that the other 1% of events can in extreme cases entail losses substantially in excess of the risk measures generated on a daily basis.

CORRELATION BETWEEN RISK MEASURE AND ABSOLUTE VALUE OF OUTCOME

The eighth performance criterion assesses how well the risk measures adjust over time to underlying changes in risk. In other words, how closely do changes in the VAR measures correspond to actual changes in the risk of the portfolio? We answer this question by determining the correlation between the VAR measures for each approach and the absolute values of the outcomes. This correlation statistic has two advantages. First, it is not affected by the scale of the portfolio. Second, the correlations are relatively easy to interpret, although even a perfect VAR measure cannot guarantee a correlation of 1 between the risk measure and the absolute value of the outcome.

For this criterion, the results for the 95th percentile risk measures and 99th percentile risk measures are almost identical (Figures 11a and 11b). Most striking is the superior performance of the exponentially weighted moving average measures. This finding implies that these approaches tend to track changes in risk over time more accurately than the other approaches.

In contrast to the results for mean relative bias (Figures 4a and 4b) and the fraction of outcomes covered (Figures 7a and 7b), the results for this performance criterion show that the length of the observation period is inversely related to performance. Thus, shorter observation periods tend to lead to higher measures of correlation between the absolute values of the outcomes and the VAR measures. This inverse relationship supports the view that, because market behaviour

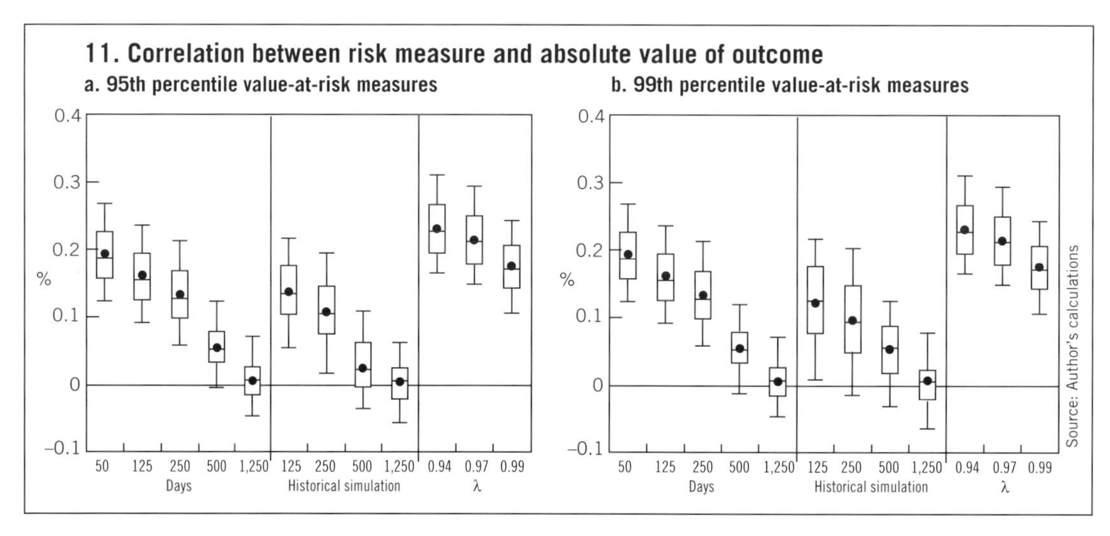

changes over time, emphasis on recent information can be helpful in tracking changes in risk.

At the other extreme, the risk measures for the 1,250-day historical simulation approach are essentially uncorrelated with the absolute values of the outcomes. Although superior according to other performance criteria, the 1,250-day results here indicate that this approach reveals little about actual changes in portfolio risk over time.

MEAN RELATIVE BIAS FOR RISK MEASURES SCALED TO DESIRED LEVEL OF COVERAGE

The last performance criterion we examine is the mean relative bias that results when risk measures are scaled to either 95% or 99% coverage. Such scaling is accomplished on an *ex post* basis by multiplying the risk measures for each approach by the multiples needed to attain either exactly 95% or exactly 99% coverage (Figures 8a and 8b). These scaled risk measures provide the precise amount of coverage desired for each portfolio. Of course, the scaling for each VAR approach would not be the same for different portfolios.

Once we have arrived at the scaled VAR measures, we compare their relative average sizes by using the mean relative bias calculation, which compares the average size of the risk measures for each approach to the average size across all 12 approaches (Figures 4a and 4b). In this case, however, the VAR measures have been scaled to the desired levels of coverage. The purpose of this criterion is to determine which approach, once suitably scaled, could provide the desired level of coverage with the smallest average risk measures. This performance criterion also addresses the issue of tracking changes in portfolio risk - the most efficient approach will be the one that tracks changes in risk best. In contrast to the correlation statistic discussed in the previous section, however, this criterion focuses specifically on the 95th and 99th percentiles.

Once again, the exponentially weighted moving average approaches appear superior (Figures 12a and 12b). In particular, the exponentially weighted average approach with a decay factor of 0.97 appears to perform extremely well for both 95th and 99th percentile risk measures. Indeed, for the 99th percentile, it achieves exact 99% coverage with an average size that is 4%

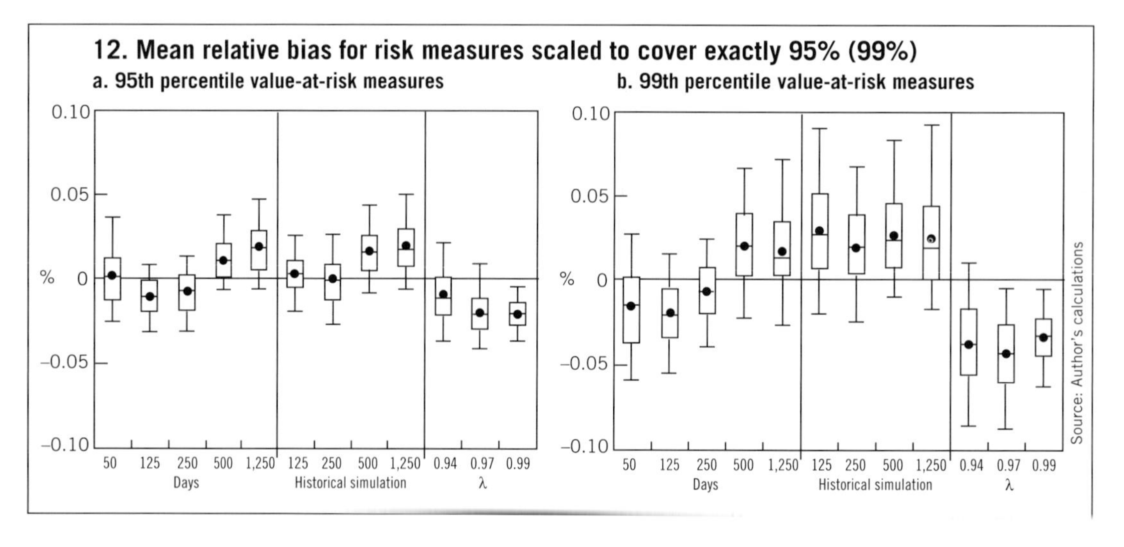

smaller than the average of all 12 scaled VAR approaches.

The performance of the other approaches is similar to that observed for the correlation statistic (Figures 11a and 11b), but in this case the relationship between efficiency and the length of the observation period is not as pronounced. In particular, the 50-day equally weighted approach is somewhat inferior to the 250-day equally weighted approach - a finding contrary to what is observed in Figures 11a and 11b - and may reflect the greater influence of measurement error on short observation periods along this performance criterion.

At least two caveats apply to these results. First, they would be difficult to duplicate in practice because the scaling must be done in advance of the outcomes rather than *ex post*. Second, the differences in the average sizes of the scaled risk measures are simply not very large. Nevertheless, the results suggest that exponentially weighted average approaches might be capable of providing desired levels of coverage in an efficient fashion, although they would need to be scaled up.

Conclusions

A historical examination of 12 approaches to VAR modelling shows that in almost all cases the approaches cover the risk that they are intended to cover. In addition, the 12 approaches tend to produce risk estimates that do not differ greatly in average size, although historical simulation approaches yield somewhat larger 99th percentile risk measures than the variance-covariance approaches.

Despite the similarity in the average size of the risk estimates, our investigation reveals differences, sometimes substantial, among the various VAR approaches for the same portfolio on the same date. In terms of variability over time, the VAR approaches using longer observation periods tend to produce less variable results than those using short observation periods or weighting recent observations more heavily.

Virtually all of the approaches produce accurate 95th percentile risk measures. The 99th percentile risk measures, however, are somewhat less reliable and generally cover only between 98.2 percent and 98.5 percent of the outcomes. On the one hand, these deficiencies are small when considered on the basis of the percentage of outcomes misclassified. On the other hand, the risk measures would generally need to be increased across the board by 10% or more to cover precisely 99% of the outcomes. Interestingly, one exception is the 1,250-day historical simulation approach, which provides very accurate coverage for both 95th and 99th percentile risk measures.

The outcomes that are not covered are typically 30 to 40% larger than the risk measures and are also larger than predicted by the normal distribution. In some cases, daily losses over the twelve-year sample period are several times larger than the corresponding VAR measures. These examples make it clear that VAR measures - even at the 99th percentile - do not "bound" possible losses.

Also clear is the difficulty of anticipating or tracking changes in risk over time. For this performance criterion, the exponentially weighted moving average approaches appear to be superior. If it were possible to scale all approaches ex post to achieve the desired level of coverage over the sample period, these approaches would produce the smallest scaled risk measures.

What more general conclusions can be drawn from these results? In many respects, the simulation estimates clearly reflect two well-known characteristics of daily financial market data. First, extreme outcomes occur more often and are larger than predicted by the normal distribution (fat tails). Second, the size of market movements is not constant over time (conditional volatility). Clearly, constructing VAR models that perform well by every measure is a difficult task. Thus, although we cannot recommend any single VAR approach, our results suggest that further research aimed at combining the best features of the approaches examined here may be worthwhile.

Appendix A

DATA AND SIMULATION METHODOLOGY

This paper analyses 12 VAR approaches. These include five equally weighted moving average approaches (50 days, 125 days, 250 days, 500 days, 1,250 days); three exponentially weighted moving average approaches (λ=0.94, λ=0.97, λ=0.99); and four historical simulation approaches (125 days, 250 days, 500 days, 1,250 days).

The data consist of daily exchange rates (bid prices collected at 4:00pm New York time by the Federal Reserve Bank of New York) against the US dollar for the following eight currencies: British pound, Canadian dollar, Dutch guilder, French franc, German mark, Italian lira, Japanese yen, and Swiss franc. The historical sample covers the period January 1, 1978, to January 18, 1995 (4,255 days).

Through a simulation methodology, we attempt to determine how each VAR approach would have performed over a realistic range of portfolios containing the eight currencies over the sample period. The simulation methodology consists of five steps:

Step 1: Select a random portfolio of positions in the eight currencies. this step is accomplished by drawing the position in each currency from a uniform distribution centred on zero. In other words, the portfolio space is a uniformly distributed eight dimensional cube centred on zero. [24]

Step 2: Calculate the VAR estimates for the random portfolio chosen in step one using the 12 VAR approaches in the sample(day 1,251 to day 4,255. In each case, we draw the historical data from the 1,250 days of historical data preceding the date for which the calculation is made. For example, the 50-day equally weighted moving average for a given date would be based on the 50 days of historical data preceding the given date.

Step 3: Calculate the change in the portfolio's value for each day in the sample(again, day 1,251 to day 4,255. Within the paper, these values are referred to as the ex post portfolio results or outcomes.

Step 4: Assess the performance of each VAR approach for the random portfolio selected in step 1 by comparing the VAR estimates generated by step 2 with the actual outcomes calculated in step 3.

Step 5: Repeat steps one through four 1,000 times and tabulate the results.

Appendix B

VALUE-AT-RISK SIMULATION RESULTS FOR EACH PERFORMANCE CRITERION

The nine tables below summarise for each performance criterion the simulation results for the 95th and 99th percentile risk measures. The value-at-risk approaches appear at the extreme left of each table. The first column reports the average simulation result of each approach across the 1,000 portfolios for the particular performance criterion. The next column reports the standard deviation of the results across the 1,000 portfolios, a calculation that provides information on the variability of the results across portfolios. To indicate the variability of results over time, the remaining four columns report results averaged over the 1,000 portfolios for four subsets of the sample period.

Table B1. Mean relative bias

	Entire sample period		1983–85	1986–88	1989–91	1992–94
	Mean across portfolios	Std dev across portfolios	Mean across portfolios	Mean across portfolios	Mean across portfolios	Mean across portfolios
Panel A: 95th percentile value-at-risk measures						
50 day equally weighted	–0.02	0.01	0.00	–0.05	0.01	–0.03
125 day equally weighted	0.00	0.01	0.00	–0.02	0.01	0.00
250 day equally weighted	0.01	0.01	–0.01	0.03	0.00	0.03
500 day equally weighted	0.04	0.02	0.01	0.08	–0.01	0.07
1,250 day equally weighted	0.05	0.03	0.08	0.06	0.05	0.01
125 day historical simulation	–0.04	0.03	–0.04	–0.06	–0.03	–0.04
250 day historical simulation	–0.01	0.03	–0.03	0.00	–0.02	0.00
500 day historical simulation	0.00	0.03	–0.02	0.05	–0.05	0.03
1,250 day historical simulation	0.02	0.03	0.05	0.03	0.02	–0.02
exponentially weighted (λ = 0.94)	–0.03	0.01	–0.02	–0.07	–0.01	–0.04
exponentially weighted (λ = 0.97)	–0.02	0.01	–0.01	–0.05	0.00	–0.02
exponentially weighted (λ = 0.99)	0.00	0.01	0.00	0.00	0.01	0.01
Panel B: 99th percentile value-at-risk measures						
50 day equally weighted	–0.05	0.02	–0.03	–0.09	–0.03	–0.06
125 day equally weighted	–0.04	0.02	–0.03	–0.06	–0.03	–0.04
250 day equally weighted	–0.03	0.02	–0.04	–0.01	–0.04	–0.01
500 day equally weighted	0.00	0.02	–0.02	0.04	–0.05	0.03
1,250 day equally weighted	0.01	0.03	0.04	0.02	0.01	–0.02
125 day historical simulation	–0.01	0.03	–0.03	0.00	0.01	0.00
250 day historical simulation	0.06	0.04	0.02	0.08	0.07	0.08
500 day historical simulation	0.08	0.04	0.04	0.11	0.05	0.11
1,250 day historical simulation	0.13	0.05	0.18	0.13	0.13	0.09
exponentially weighted (λ = 0.94)	–0.07	0.02	–0.05	–0.10	–0.05	–0.08
exponentially weighted (λ = 0.97)	–0.06	0.02	–0.04	–0.08	–0.04	–0.06
exponentially weighted (λ = 0.99)	–0.03	0.02	–0.03	–0.04	–0.04	–0.03

Table B2. Root mean squared relative bias

	Entire sample period		1983–85	1986–88	1989–91	1992–94
	Mean across portfolios	Std dev across portfolios	Mean across portfolios	Mean across portfolios	Mean across portfolios	Mean across portfolios
Panel A: 95th percentile value-at-risk measures						
50 day equally weighted	0.16	0.01	0.17	0.15	0.14	0.16
125 day equally weighted	0.10	0.01	0.10	0.10	0.08	0.11
250 day equally weighted	0.09	0.01	0.08	0.09	0.08	0.09
500 day equally weighted	0.13	0.02	0.13	0.13	0.08	0.13
1,250 day equally weighted	0.16	0.04	0.18	0.14	0.14	0.14
125 day historical simulation	0.14	0.02	0.15	0.13	0.13	0.14
250 day historical simulation	0.11	0.01	0.12	0.11	0.10	0.11
500 day historical simulation	0.13	0.02	0.14	0.13	0.10	0.14
1,250 day historical simulation	0.15	0.03	0.17	0.13	0.13	0.15
exponentially weighted (λ = 0.94)	0.18	0.01	0.20	0.17	0.17	0.19
exponentially weighted (λ = 0.97)	0.12	0.01	0.13	0.11	0.10	0.13
exponentially weighted (λ = 0.99)	0.05	0.01	0.05	0.04	0.04	0.05
Panel B: 99th percentile value-at-risk measures						
50 day equally weighted	0.16	0.01	0.17	0.16	0.14	0.16
125 day equally weighted	0.10	0.01	0.11	0.11	0.08	0.11
250 day equally weighted	0.09	0.01	0.09	0.09	0.09	0.09
500 day equally weighted	0.12	0.02	0.13	0.12	0.10	0.12
1,250 day equally weighted	0.14	0.03	0.16	0.13	0.13	0.14
125 day historical simulation	0.18	0.03	0.15	0.19	0.17	0.17
250 day historical simulation	0.16	0.03	0.14	0.15	0.16	0.16
500 day historical simulation	0.16	0.04	0.15	0.18	0.12	0.17
1,250 day historical simulation	0.22	0.06	0.24	0.20	0.19	0.19
exponentially weighted (λ = 0.94)	0.19	0.01	0.20	0.19	0.17	0.19
exponentially weighted (λ = 0.97)	0.13	0.01	0.14	0.13	0.11	0.13
exponentially weighted (λ = 0.99)	0.06	0.01	0.06	0.06	0.05	0.06

Table B3. Annualised percentage volatility

	Entire sample period		1983–85	1986–88	1989–91	1992–94
	Mean across portfolios	Std dev across portfolios	Mean across portfolios	Mean across portfolios	Mean across portfolios	Mean across portfolios
Panel A: 95th percentile value-at-risk measures						
50 day equally weighted	0.45	0.05	0.49	0.42	0.44	0.45
125 day equally weighted	0.19	0.03	0.18	0.19	0.17	0.20
250 day equally weighted	0.10	0.02	0.10	0.09	0.09	0.11
500 day equally weighted	0.05	0.01	0.06	0.05	0.05	0.05
1,250 day equally weighted	0.02	0.00	0.03	0.02	0.02	0.02
125 day historical simulation	0.40	0.04	0.38	0.39	0.40	0.41
250 day historical simulation	0.20	0.02	0.20	0.19	0.19	0.21
500 day historical simulation	0.10	0.01	0.11	0.09	0.10	0.10
1,250 day historical simulation	0.04	0.01	0.04	0.04	0.04	0.04
exponentially weighted ($\lambda = 0.94$)	0.91	0.09	0.94	0.88	0.89	0.94
exponentially weighted ($\lambda = 0.97$)	0.47	0.06	0.49	0.43	0.44	0.49
exponentially weighted ($\lambda = 0.99$)	0.16	0.03	0.18	0.14	0.15	0.17
Panel B: 99th percentile value-at-risk measures						
50 day equally weighted	0.45	0.05	0.49	0.42	0.44	0.45
125 day equally weighted	0.19	0.03	0.18	0.19	0.17	0.20
250 day equally weighted	0.10	0.02	0.10	0.09	0.09	0.11
500 day equally weighted	0.05	0.01	0.06	0.05	0.05	0.05
1,250 day equally weighted	0.02	0.01	0.03	0.02	0.02	0.02
125 day historical simulation	0.55	0.07	0.49	0.55	0.51	0.57
250 day historical simulation	0.30	0.05	0.27	0.28	0.27	0.31
500 day historical simulation	0.15	0.03	0.16	0.13	0.14	0.15
1,250 day historical simulation	0.06	0.02	0.06	0.05	0.06	0.06
exponentially weighted ($\lambda = 0.94$)	0.91	0.10	0.94	0.88	0.88	0.94
exponentially weighted ($\lambda = 0.97$)	0.47	0.06	0.49	0.43	0.44	0.49
exponentially weighted ($\lambda = 0.99$)	0.16	0.03	0.18	0.14	0.15	0.17

Table B4. Fraction of outcomes covered

	Entire sample period		1983–85	1986–88	1989–91	1992–94
	Mean across portfolios	Std dev across portfolios	Mean across portfolios	Mean across portfolios	Mean across portfolios	Mean across portfolios
Panel A: 95th percentile value-at-risk measures						
50 day equally weighted	0.948	0.006	0.948	0.947	0.949	0.948
125 day equally weighted	0.951	0.006	0.950	0.953	0.951	0.953
250 day equally weighted	0.953	0.005	0.946	0.960	0.950	0.956
500 day equally weighted	0.954	0.006	0.946	0.963	0.947	0.958
1,250 day equally weighted	0.954	0.006	0.954	0.959	0.954	0.950
125 day historical simulation	0.944	0.002	0.943	0.946	0.943	0.946
250 day historical simulation	0.949	0.003	0.943	0.955	0.945	0.952
500 day historical simulation	0.948	0.003	0.942	0.959	0.941	0.952
1,250 day historical simulation	0.951	0.004	0.951	0.956	0.951	0.945
exponentially weighted ($\lambda = 0.94$)	0.947	0.006	0.948	0.946	0.947	0.946
exponentially weighted ($\lambda = 0.97$)	0.950	0.006	0.950	0.950	0.950	0.950
exponentially weighted ($\lambda = 0.99$)	0.954	0.006	0.950	0.957	0.951	0.956
Panel B: 99th percentile value-at-risk measures						
50 day equally weighted	0.983	0.003	0.985	0.982	0.982	0.983
125 day equally weighted	0.984	0.003	0.984	0.984	0.982	0.984
250 day equally weighted	0.984	0.003	0.982	0.987	0.982	0.986
500 day equally weighted	0.984	0.003	0.981	0.989	0.981	0.987
1,250 day equally weighted	0.985	0.003	0.984	0.988	0.984	0.983
125 day historical simulation	0.983	0.001	0.983	0.985	0.982	0.984
250 day historical simulation	0.987	0.001	0.984	0.991	0.986	0.989
500 day historical simulation	0.988	0.001	0.985	0.991	0.986	0.990
1,250 day historical simulation	0.990	0.001	0.990	0.992	0.989	0.989
exponentially weighted ($\lambda = 0.94$)	0.982	0.003	0.984	0.981	0.982	0.983
exponentially weighted ($\lambda = 0.97$)	0.984	0.003	0.986	0.983	0.983	0.984
exponentially weighted ($\lambda = 0.99$)	0.985	0.003	0.985	0.986	0.983	0.986

Table B5. Multiple needed to attain desired coverage level

	Entire sample period		1983–85	1986–88	1989–91	1992–94
	Mean across portfolios	Std dev across portfolios	Mean across portfolios	Mean across portfolios	Mean across portfolios	Mean across portfolios
Panel A: 95th percentile value-at-risk measures						
50 day equally weighted	1.01	0.05	1.01	1.02	1.01	1.02
125 day equally weighted	0.99	0.04	1.00	0.98	0.99	0.98
250 day equally weighted	0.98	0.04	1.02	0.93	1.00	0.95
500 day equally weighted	0.97	0.04	1.02	0.90	1.02	0.93
1,250 day equally weighted	0.97	0.05	0.95	0.93	0.97	1.00
125 day historical simulation	1.04	0.01	1.05	1.03	1.05	1.03
250 day historical simulation	1.01	0.02	1.05	0.96	1.03	0.98
500 day historical simulation	1.01	0.02	1.06	0.94	1.06	0.99
1,250 day historical simulation	1.00	0.03	0.98	0.95	0.99	1.04
exponentially weighted ($\lambda = 0.94$)	1.02	0.05	1.01	1.03	1.02	1.03
exponentially weighted ($\lambda = 0.97$)	1.00	0.04	0.99	1.00	1.00	1.00
exponentially weighted ($\lambda = 0.99$)	0.97	0.04	0.99	0.95	0.99	0.96
Panel B: 99th percentile value-at-risk measures						
50 day equally weighted	1.15	0.06	1.11	1.19	1.19	1.14
125 day equally weighted	1.13	0.07	1.12	1.11	1.17	1.13
250 day equally weighted	1.13	0.07	1.17	1.06	1.20	1.11
500 day equally weighted	1.13	0.08	1.22	1.03	1.20	1.10
1,250 day equally weighted	1.11	0.08	1.12	1.04	1.13	1.17
125 day historical simulation	1.14	0.03	1.15	1.13	1.18	1.16
250 day historical simulation	1.06	0.03	1.11	0.99	1.12	1.04
500 day historical simulation	1.05	0.03	1.13	0.98	1.10	1.02
1,250 day historical simulation	1.00	0.04	1.00	0.94	1.01	1.04
exponentially weighted ($\lambda = 0.94$)	1.14	0.06	1.12	1.19	1.14	1.16
exponentially weighted ($\lambda = 0.97$)	1.12	0.06	1.09	1.15	1.15	1.12
exponentially weighted ($\lambda = 0.99$)	1.10	0.06	1.11	1.08	1.17	1.09

Table B6. Average multiple of tail event to risk measure

	Entire sample period		1983–85	1986–88	1989–91	1992–94
	Mean across portfolios	Std dev across portfolios	Mean across portfolios	Mean across portfolios	Mean across portfolios	Mean across portfolios
Panel A: 95th percentile value-at-risk measures						
50 day equally weighted	1.41	0.07	1.40	1.41	1.41	1.41
125 day equally weighted	1.38	0.07	1.39	1.35	1.39	1.39
250 day equally weighted	1.37	0.07	1.43	1.28	1.41	1.36
500 day equally weighted	1.38	0.08	1.46	1.24	1.43	1.34
1,250 day equally weighted	1.36	0.08	1.35	1.27	1.35	1.43
125 day historical simulation	1.48	0.04	1.47	1.45	1.49	1.50
250 day historical simulation	1.43	0.05	1.49	1.34	1.46	1.44
500 day historical simulation	1.44	0.06	1.53	1.29	1.48	1.43
1,250 day historical simulation	1.41	0.07	1.39	1.31	1.39	1.50
exponentially weighted ($\lambda = 0.94$)	1.41	0.07	1.39	1.42	1.41	1.42
exponentially weighted ($\lambda = 0.97$)	1.38	0.07	1.37	1.38	1.38	1.38
exponentially weighted ($\lambda = 0.99$)	1.35	0.07	1.38	1.30	1.38	1.34
Panel B: 99th percentile value-at-risk measures						
50 day equally weighted	1.46	0.12	1.48	1.45	1.48	1.47
125 day equally weighted	1.44	0.11	1.45	1.41	1.42	1.50
250 day equally weighted	1.44	0.13	1.49	1.34	1.44	1.50
500 day equally weighted	1.46	0.14	1.56	1.29	1.46	1.47
1,250 day equally weighted	1.44	0.14	1.43	1.31	1.39	1.55
125 day historical simulation	1.48	0.07	1.51	1.47	1.46	1.55
250 day historical simulation	1.37	0.07	1.44	1.28	1.37	1.41
500 day historical simulation	1.37	0.09	1.46	1.25	1.34	1.40
1,250 day historical simulation	1.30	0.10	1.28	1.20	1.25	1.40
exponentially weighted ($\lambda = 0.94$)	1.44	0.11	1.45	1.44	1.44	1.48
exponentially weighted ($\lambda = 0.97$)	1.42	0.11	1.43	1.40	1.41	1.45
exponentially weighted ($\lambda = 0.99$)	1.40	0.11	1.44	1.35	1.42	1.44

Table B7. Maximum multiple of tail event to risk measure

	Entire sample period		1983–85	1986–88	1989–91	1992–94
	Mean across portfolios	Std dev across portfolios	Mean across portfolios	Mean across portfolios	Mean across portfolios	Mean across portfolios
Panel A: 95th percentile value-at-risk measures						
50 day equally weighted	3.59	0.93	3.25	2.56	2.73	2.98
125 day equally weighted	3.59	0.98	3.01	2.54	2.56	3.09
250 day equally weighted	3.67	1.01	3.03	2.45	2.59	3.07
500 day equally weighted	3.86	1.08	3.25	2.33	2.66	3.04
1,250 day equally weighted	3.97	1.10	3.05	2.35	2.60	3.21
125 day historical simulation	3.91	1.02	3.13	2.84	2.78	3.49
250 day historical simulation	3.85	1.10	3.03	2.61	2.62	3.31
500 day historical simulation	4.09	1.16	3.35	2.44	2.73	3.30
1,250 day historical simulation	4.14	1.12	3.12	2.44	2.67	3.37
exponentially weighted ($\lambda = 0.94$)	3.58	0.99	3.16	2.55	2.75	3.03
exponentially weighted ($\lambda = 0.97$)	3.53	0.99	3.13	2.46	2.57	2.99
exponentially weighted ($\lambda = 0.99$)	3.55	0.96	3.03	2.40	2.55	2.96
Panel B: 99th percentile value-at-risk measures						
50 day equally weighted	2.50	0.61	2.26	1.83	1.91	2.08
125 day equally weighted	2.50	0.70	2.09	1.82	1.79	2.15
250 day equally weighted	2.56	0.73	2.11	1.75	1.81	2.14
500 day equally weighted	2.70	0.78	2.27	1.66	1.85	2.13
1,250 day equally weighted	2.77	0.77	2.14	1.67	1.81	2.24
125 day historical simulation	2.58	0.52	2.18	1.97	1.86	2.25
250 day historical simulation	2.34	0.57	2.00	1.66	1.72	2.02
500 day historical simulation	2.48	0.63	2.08	1.60	1.70	2.05
1,250 day historical simulation	2.49	0.65	1.89	1.54	1.63	2.02
exponentially weighted ($\lambda = 0.94$)	2.48	0.64	2.20	1.83	1.92	2.10
exponentially weighted ($\lambda = 0.97$)	2.46	0.66	2.18	1.76	1.79	2.08
exponentially weighted ($\lambda = 0.99$)	2.47	0.68	2.11	1.72	1.78	2.06

Table B8. Correlation between risk measures and absolute value of outcome

	Entire sample period		1983–85	1986–88	1989–91	1992–94
	Mean across portfolios	Std dev across portfolios	Mean across portfolios	Mean across portfolios	Mean across portfolios	Mean across portfolios
Panel A: 95th percentile value-at-risk measures						
50 day equally weighted	0.19	0.05	0.21	0.15	0.12	0.19
125 day equally weighted	0.16	0.05	0.17	0.13	0.07	0.14
250 day equally weighted	0.13	0.05	0.12	0.15	0.02	0.13
500 day equally weighted	0.06	0.04	0.01	0.07	0.05	0.05
1,250 day equally weighted	0.01	0.03	0.05	0.05	–0.04	–0.02
125 day historical simulation	0.14	0.05	0.16	0.11	0.04	0.12
250 day historical simulation	0.11	0.05	0.10	0.12	0.02	0.10
500 day historical simulation	0.03	0.04	0.00	0.06	0.03	0.01
1,250 day historical simulation	0.00	0.04	0.06	0.05	–0.03	–0.05
exponentially weighted ($\lambda = 0.94$)	0.23	0.05	0.26	0.18	0.15	0.24
exponentially weighted ($\lambda = 0.97$)	0.22	0.05	0.23	0.17	0.14	0.21
exponentially weighted ($\lambda = 0.99$)	0.17	0.04	0.17	0.15	0.09	0.17
Panel B: 99th percentile value-at-risk measures						
50 day equally weighted	0.19	0.04	0.21	0.15	0.12	0.19
125 day equally weighted	0.16	0.05	0.17	0.12	0.07	0.15
250 day equally weighted	0.13	0.05	0.12	0.15	0.02	0.13
500 day equally weighted	0.06	0.04	0.02	0.07	0.05	0.06
1,250 day equally weighted	0.01	0.04	0.06	0.04	–0.04	–0.02
125 day historical simulation	0.12	0.06	0.16	0.07	0.06	0.13
250 day historical simulation	0.10	0.07	0.10	0.09	0.01	0.12
500 day historical simulation	0.05	0.05	0.03	0.04	0.06	0.06
1,250 day historical simulation	0.01	0.04	0.05	0.04	–0.02	0.00
exponentially weighted ($\lambda = 0.94$)	0.23	0.05	0.26	0.18	0.15	0.24
exponentially weighted ($\lambda = 0.97$)	0.22	0.05	0.23	0.17	0.14	0.22
exponentially weighted ($\lambda = 0.99$)	0.17	0.04	0.17	0.15	0.09	0.17

Table B9. Mean relative bias for risk measures scaled to desired coverage levels

	Entire sample period		1983–85	1986–88	1989–91	1992–94
	Mean across portfolios	Std dev across portfolios	Mean across portfolios	Mean across portfolios	Mean across portfolios	Mean across portfolios
Panel A: 95th percentile value-at-risk measures						
50 day equally weighted	0.00	0.02	0.00	0.00	0.00	0.00
125 day equally weighted	–0.01	0.01	–0.01	0.00	0.00	–0.01
250 day equally weighted	–0.01	0.01	0.00	–0.01	0.00	–0.01
500 day equally weighted	0.01	0.02	0.02	0.01	–0.01	0.01
1,250 day equally weighted	0.02	0.02	0.01	0.01	0.01	0.02
125 day historical simulation	0.00	0.01	0.00	0.01	0.01	0.01
250 day historical simulation	0.00	0.02	0.01	0.00	0.00	–0.01
500 day historical simulation	0.02	0.02	0.03	0.01	0.00	0.02
1,250 day historical simulation	0.02	0.02	0.01	0.01	0.01	0.03
exponentially weighted (λ = 0.94)	–0.01	0.02	–0.02	–0.01	0.01	–0.01
exponentially weighted (λ = 0.97)	–0.02	0.01	–0.02	–0.02	–0.01	–0.02
exponentially weighted (λ = 0.99)	–0.02	0.01	–0.02	–0.02	–0.02	–0.02
Panel B: 99th percentile value-at-risk measures						
50 day equally weighted	–0.02	0.03	–0.03	0.02	0.00	–0.03
125 day equally weighted	–0.02	0.02	–0.03	–0.02	0.00	–0.02
250 day equally weighted	–0.01	0.02	0.00	–0.02	0.01	–0.01
500 day equally weighted	0.02	0.03	0.06	0.00	0.00	0.02
1,250 day equally weighted	0.02	0.03	0.04	–0.01	–0.01	0.03
125 day historical simulation	0.03	0.03	0.00	0.06	0.05	0.05
250 day historical simulation	0.02	0.03	0.02	0.00	0.05	0.02
500 day historical simulation	0.03	0.03	0.05	0.01	0.00	0.03
1,250 day historical simulation	0.03	0.04	0.04	–0.01	0.00	0.03
exponentially weighted (λ = 0.94)	–0.04	0.03	–0.05	0.01	–0.05	–0.04
exponentially weighted (λ = 0.97)	–0.04	0.02	–0.06	–0.01	–0.03	–0.05
exponentially weighted (λ = 0.99)	–0.03	0.02	–0.04	–0.03	–0.01	–0.04

1 *See, for example, the so-called G-30 report (1993), the US General Accounting Office study (1994), and papers outlining sound risk management practices published by the Board of Governors of the Federal Reserve System (1993), the Basle Committee on Banking Supervision (1994), and the International Organization of Securities Commissions (IOSCO) Technical Committee (1994).*

2 *Work along these lines is contained in Jordan and Mackay (1995) and Pritsker (1995).*

3 *Results for 10-day holding periods are contained in Hendricks (1995). This paper is available from the author on request.*

4 *The 99th percentile loss is the same as the 1st percentile gain on the portfolio. Convention suggests using the former terminology.*

5 *Variance-covariance approaches are so named because they can be derived from the variance-covariance matrix of the relevant underlying market prices or rates. The variance-covariance matrix contains information on the volatility and correlation of all market prices or rates relevant to the portfolio. Knowledge of the variance-covariance matrix of these variables for a given period of time implies knowledge of the variance or standard deviation of the portfolio over this same period.*

6 *The assumption of linear positions is made throughout the paper. Non-linear positions require simulation methods, often referred to as Monte Carlo methods, when used in conjunction with variance-covariance matrices of the underlying market prices or rates.*

7 *See Fama (1965), a seminal paper on this topic. A more recent summary of the evidence regarding foreign exchange data and "fat tails" is provided by Hsieh (1988). See also Taylor (1986) and Mills (1993) for general discussions of the issues involved in modelling financial time series.*

8 *The portfolio variance is an equally weighted moving average of squared deviations from the mean.*

9 *In addition, equally weighted moving average approaches may differ in the frequency with which estimates are updated. This paper assumes that all VAR measures are updated on a daily basis. For a comparison of different updating frequencies (daily, monthly, or quarterly), see Hendricks (1995). This paper is available from the author on request.*

10 *The intuition behind this assumption is that for most financial time series, the true mean is both close to zero and prone to estimation error. Thus, estimates of volatility are often made worse (relative to assuming a zero mean) by including noisy estimates of the mean.*

11 *Figures 1–3 depict 99th percentile risk measures and are derived from the same data used elsewhere in the paper (see Appendix A). For Figures 1 and 2, the assumption of normality is made, so that these risk measures are calculated by multiplying the portfolio standard deviation estimate by 2.33. The units on the y-axes are millions of dollars,*

but they could be any amount depending on the definition of the units of the portfolio's positions.

12 *Engle's (1982) paper introduced the autoregressive conditional heteroskedastic (ARCH) family of models. Recent surveys of the literature on conditional volatility modelling include Bollerslev, Chou, and Kroner (1992), Bollerslev, Engle, and Nelson (1994), and Diebold and Lopez (1995). Recent papers comparing specific conditional volatility forecasting models include West and Cho (1994) and Heynen and Kat (1993).*

13 *See Engle and Bollerslev (1986).*

14 *For obvious reasons, a 50-day observation period is not well suited to historical simulations requiring a 99th percentile estimate.*

15 *Bootstrapping techniques offer perhaps the best hope for standard error calculations in this context, a focus of the author's ongoing research.*

16 *For a discussion of the statistical issues involved, see Kupiec (1995). The Basle Committee's recent paper on backtesting (1996b) outlines a proposed supervisory backtesting framework designed to ensure that banks using VAR models for regulatory capital purposes face appropriate incentives.*

17 *The upper and lower edges of the boxes proper represent the 75th and 25th percentiles, respectively. The horizontal line running across the interior of each box represents the 50th percentile, and the upper and lower "antennae" represent the 95th and 5th percentiles, respectively.*

18 *One plausible explanation relies solely on Jensen's inequality. If the true conditional variance is changing frequently, then the average of a concave function (that is, the VAR measure) of this variance will tend to be less than the same concave function of the average variance. This gap would imply that short horizon VAR measures should on average be slightly smaller than long horizon VAR measures. This logic may also explain the generally smaller average size of the exponentially weighted approaches.*

19 *With as few as 125 observations, the use of actual observations inevitably produces either upward- or downward-biased estimates of most specific percentiles. For example, the 95th percentile estimate is taken to be the seventh largest loss out of 125, slightly lower than the 95th percentile. However, taking the sixth largest loss would yield a bias upward. This point should be considered when using historical simulation approaches together with short observation periods, although biases can be addressed through kernel estimation, a method that is considered in Reiss (1989).*

20 *In particular, see Mahoney (1995) and Jackson, Maude, and Perraudin (1995).*

21 *See, for example, Bollerslev (1987) and Baillie and Bollerslev (1989).*

22 *The degrees of freedom,* d, *are chosen to solve the following equation,*

$$a * z(0.99) = t(0.99,d) / \sqrt{\frac{d}{d-2}}$$

where a *is the ratio of the observed 99th percentile to the 99th percentile calculated assuming normality,* $z(0.99)$ *is the normal 99th percentile value, and* $t(0.99,d)$ *is the t-distribution 99th percentile value for d degrees of freedom. The term under the square root is the variance of the t-distribution with d degrees of freedom.*

23 *This section and the next were inspired by Boudoukh, Richardson, and Whitelaw (1995).*

24 *The upper and lower bounds on the positions in each currency are +$100 million and –$100 million, respectively. In fact, however, all of the results in the paper are completely invariant to the scale of the random portfolios.*

BIBLIOGRAPHY

Baillie, R. T., and T. Bollerslev, 1989, "The Message in Daily Exchange Rates: A Conditional-Variance Tale", *Journal of Business and Economic Statistics*, 7, pp. 297–305.

Bank for International Settlements, 1994, "Public Disclosure of Market and Credit Risks by Financial Intermediaries", Euro-currency Standing Committee of the Central Banks of the Group of Ten Countries [Fisher Report].

Basle Committee on Banking Supervision, 1994, Risk Management Guidelines for Derivatives.

Basle Committee on Banking Supervision, 1996a. Supplement to the Capital Accord to Incorporate Market Risks.

Basle Committee on Banking Supervision, 1996b. Supervisory Framework for the Use of "Backtesting" in Conjunction with the Internal Models Approach to Market Risk Capital Requirements.

Board of Governors of the Federal Reserve System, 1993, Examining Risk Management and Internal Controls for Trading Activities of Banking Organisations.

Bollerslev, T., 1987, "A Conditionally Heteroskedastic Time Series Model for Speculative Prices and Rates of Return", *Review of Economics and Statistics* 69, pp. 542–7.

Bollerslev, T., R.Y. Chou, and K.F. Kroner, 1992, "ARCH Modelling in Finance: A Review of the Theory and Empirical Evidence", *Journal of Econometrics* 52, pp. 5–59.

Bollerslev, T., R.F. Engle, and D.B. Nelson, 1994, "ARCH Models." In Robert F. Engle and D. McFadden, eds., *Handbook of Econometrics*. Vol. 4. Amsterdam: North-Holland.

Boudoukh, J., M. Richardson, and R. Whitelaw, 1995, "Expect the Worst", ***Risk*** 8, 9, pp. 100–1; reprinted as Chapter 11 of the present volume

Derivatives Policy Group, 1995, *Framework for Voluntary Oversight*.

Diebold, F.X., and J. A. Lopez, 1995, "Modelling Volatility Dynamics", Technical Working Paper no. 173, National Bureau of Economic Research.

Engle, R.F., 1982, "Autoregressive Conditional Heteroskedasticity with Estimates of the Variance of UK Inflation", *Econometrica* 50, pp. 987-1008.

Engle, R.F., and T. Bollerslev, 1986, "Modelling the Persistence of Conditional Variance", *Econometric Review* 5, pp. 1-50.

Fama, E.F., 1965, "The Behaviour of Stock Market Prices", *Journal of Business* 38, pp. 34-105.

Figlewski, S., 1994, "Forecasting Volatility Using Historical Data." Working Paper no. 13, New York University.

Group of Thirty Global Derivatives Study Group, 1993, *Derivatives: Practices and Principles*. Washington, DC [G-30 report].

Hendricks, D., 1995, "Evaluation of Value-at-Risk Models Using Historical Data," Federal Reserve Bank of New York. Mimeographed.

Heynen, R.C., and H.M. Kat, 1993, "Volatility Prediction: A Comparison of GARCH (1,1), EGARCH(1,1) and Stochastic Volatility Models", Erasmus University, Rotterdam. Mimeographed.

Hsieh, D.A., 1988, "The Statistical Properties of Daily Exchange Rates: 1974-1983." *Journal of International Economics* 13, pp. 171-86.

International Organisation of Securities Commissions' Technical Committee, 1994. *Operational and Financial Risk Management Control Mechanisms for Over-the-Counter Derivatives Activities of Regulated Securities Firms*.

Jackson, P., D.J. Maude, and W. Perraudin, 1995, "Capital Requirements and Value-at-Risk Analysis," Bank of England, Mimeographed.

Jordan, J.V., and R.J. Mackay, 1995, "Assessing VAR for Equity Portfolios: Implementing Alternative Techniques", Virginia Polytechnic Institute, Pamplin College of Business, Center for Study of Futures and Options Markets. Mimeographed.

JP Morgan, 1995, *RiskMetrics Technical Document*. 3d ed. New York.

Kupiec, P.H., 1995, "Techniques for Verifying the Accuracy of Risk Measurement Models." Board of Governors of the Federal Reserve System. Mimeographed.

Mahoney, J.M., 1995, "Empirical-based versus Model-based Approaches to Value-at-Risk." Federal Reserve Bank of New York. Mimeographed.

Markowitz, H.M., 1959, *Portfolio Selection: Efficient Diversification of Investments*. New York: John Wiley & Sons.

Mills, T.C., 1993, *The Econometric Modelling of Financial Time Series*. Cambridge, Cambridge University Press.

Pritsker, M.,1997, "Evaluating VAR Methodologies: Accuracy versus Computational Time", *Journal of Financial Services Research*, forthcoming; reprinted as Chapter 27 of the present volume

Reiss, R-D., 1989, *Approximate Distributions of Order Statistics*. New York: Springer-Verlag.

Taylor, S., 1986, *Modelling Financial Time Series*. New York: John Wiley & Sons.

US General Accounting Office, 1994. *Financial Derivatives: Actions Needed to Protect the Financial System*. GAO/GGD-94-133.

West, K.D., and D. Cho, 1994, "The Predictive Ability of Several Models of Exchange Rate Volatility", Technical Working Paper no. 152, National Bureau of Economic Research.

22

Bank Capital and Value-at-Risk*

Patricia Jackson, David J. Maude and William Perraudin
Bank of England; Birkbeck College and Centre for Economic Policy Research

To measure the risks involved in their trading operations, major banks are increasingly employing value-at-risk models. In an important regulatory innovation, the Basle Committee has proposed that such models be used in the determination of the capital that banks must hold to back their securities trading. This paper examines the empirical performance of different VAR models using data on the actual fixed income, foreign exchange and equity security holdings of a large bank. We examine how a bank applying the models would have fared in the past if the proposed rules had been in operation.

In the last decade, banks have greatly increased their holdings of traded assets such as bonds, equities, interest rate and equity derivatives, and foreign exchange and commodity positions. Their motive has been to make trading profits and to hedge exposures elsewhere in their banking portfolios. The swaps markets have been especially important in enabling banks to raise funds in a wider range of markets while avoiding mismatched portfolios.

The increase in the relative importance of trading risk in bank portfolios has obliged regulators to reconsider the system of capital requirements agreed in the 1988 Basle Capital Accord. The common framework for treating risk laid down by the 1988 Accord was designed primarily for limiting credit risk and had clear drawbacks in its treatment of trading risk. For example, short positions and holdings of government securities were not covered, although the latter were included in the UK. Also, while the counter-party risk of off-balance sheet positions was included, their position risk was not.

The capital charge imposed by the 1988 Accord was a minimum of 8% of private sector assets regardless of maturity and made no allowance for the volatility of different security prices. Thus, low-risk short-maturity private sector bonds were penalised much more than longer-dated corporate debt. In certain markets, this placed banks at a competitive disadvantage compared to securities firms for whom capital requirements, at least in the UK and US, allow for such risk in a more sophisticated way.

These problems led the European Commission and the Basle Supervisors' Committee to study alternative ways of treating trading book positions. The Commission's Capital Adequacy Directive (CAD), agreed to in 1993 and introduced at the beginning of 1996, established European Union minimum capital requirements for the trading books of banks and securities firms. The Basle Committee proposals are summarised in the Overview of the Amendment of the Capital Accord to Incorporate Market Risks (1996).

This and two earlier 1995 reports propose a system comprising two alternative ways of calculating trading book capital. Commercial banks would themselves decide whether they wished to be regulated under the so-called "standardised" or the "alternative" model proposed by Basle. G-10 supervisory authorities are to implement the two approaches by the end of 1997.[1]

* *This article was first published in the* Journal of Derivatives, *Vol. 4 (1997). This copyrighted material is reprinted with permission from Institutional Investor, Inc., 488 Madison Avenue, New York, New York 10022. The views expressed here are those of the authors and not necessarily those of the Bank of England. We thank Lina El-Jabel and Adrian Chalcraft for research assistance, Xavier Freixas, and Bank of England staff for valuable comments, and JP Morgan, Tokai Bank Europe and various other financial institutions for generously supplying us with data.*

Additive capital requirements

The CAD and the Basle standardised approaches are very similar. Heavily influenced by the systems of capital requirements operated by UK and US securities regulators, both systems require firms to hold capital equivalent to a percentage of their holdings in different asset categories, where the percentages are chosen to reflect the price volatilities of generic assets in the relevant categories.

An important drawback of both CAD and the Basle standardised approach is the additive nature of the capital required for broad asset categories.[2] The requirement is calculated market by market for equity, foreign exchange (FX) and interest rate risk, and then the separate requirements are summed. Thus, for example, the capital requirement for a long position in UK equities takes into account hedging in the same market but not, say, any offset from holding a short position in US equities. Nor does it take into account the benefits in diversification from holding long positions in both markets.[3]

The effect is to favour specialised market-makers at the expense of globally diversified banks. Banks that run global portfolios have therefore pressed the Basle Committee to consider approaches to capital requirements that do recognise the benefits of diversification.

Clearly, achieving this in a regime in which the supervisors set the percentage capital requirements and hedging allowances for different types of position would be extremely complex. But firms themselves have been developing methods of measuring the risk of given losses on a total portfolio, and these internal whole book or value-at-risk models have provided a way of making the problem tractable. Hence, it is possible to develop an alternative to the Basle standardised approach.[4]

The Basle alternative approach

In the Basle "alternative approach", rather than laying down percentage capital requirements for different exposures, regulators would establish standards for banks' in-house risk models. These models would then form the basis for the calculation of capital requirements. This has the key additional advantage of aligning the capital calculation with the risk measurement approach of the particular firm.

Using internal models to generate capital requirements is a radical change in approach, but supervisors have for some time been moving steadily in this direction. In the CAD and the Basle standardised method, it is recognised that only by employing the firms' internal models can some positions be correctly processed for inclusion in the capital calculation. This is particularly the case for options, but sensitivity models designed to convert large books of swaps into equivalent bond exposures and to assess the risk on foreign exchange books are also allowed.

This does, however, raise a number of issues for supervisors concerning the safeguards which should be put in place to ensure that the capital requirements generated are adequate. Basle has addressed this in several ways. One is to lay down standards for the construction of the models. For example, models must calculate the distribution of losses over a 10-day holding period using at least 12 months of data, and must yield capital requirements sufficient to cover losses on 99% of occasions.

Adopting general standards is necessary both to increase consistency between banks and to ensure that capital requirements really are adequate to the task. In theory, however, they might create inconsistencies between the regulatory model and the one that a firm uses for its own purposes. Typically, firms' VAR models use a 95% confidence interval and a 24-hour holding period. Basle will not, however, prescribe the type of model to be used.

Regulatory safeguards

As a *post hoc* check on the accuracy of the models under the proposed alternative Basle approach, the supervisors will carry out back testing, the comparison of actual trading results with model-generated risk measures. This may pose problems, first, because trading results are often affected by changes in portfolios in the period following the calculation of the VAR. Because of this, Basle has urged banks to develop the capability to perform back tests using the losses which would have occurred if the book had been held constant over a one-day period. Second, Kupiec (1995) argues that back testing requires a large number of observations in order to make a judgement about the accuracy of the model's estimate of the tail of the probability distribution.

Nevertheless, back testing and some kind of penalty are essential to provide incentives for firms to increase the accuracy of the models. The Basle proposals envisage that firms which do not meet the back testing criterion for accuracy should suffer additional capital charges.

As well as back testing, the system would

include the safeguard of an over-riding multiplier. More precisely, Basle is proposing that the capital requirement should be equivalent to the higher of (a) the current VAR estimate and (b) the average VAR estimate over the previous 60 days multiplied by three.

The incorporation of a multiplier has the advantage of making the system more conservative without distorting the treatment of trading books with different risk profiles. Of course, if the multiplier is too high, it could discourage firms from developing in-house models and lead them to select the standardised rather than the alternative approach, because, as mentioned above, banks themselves are free to choose which they adopt.

VAR analysis

What then is the nature of the "whole-book" or VAR models that will be used in capital requirement calculations by banks that take the Basle Committee's alternative approach? The typical VAR models developed by firms for their internal risk-management purposes attempt to measure the loss on a portfolio over a specified period (often the next 24 hours) that will be exceeded only on a given fraction of occasions (typically 1% or 5%). Two broad types of VAR analysis are employed.

First, under parametric VAR analysis, the distribution of asset returns is estimated from historical data under the assumption that this distribution is a member of a given parametric class. The most common procedure is to suppose that returns are stationary, joint normal, and independent over time. Using estimates of the means and covariances of returns, one may calculate the daily loss that will be exceeded with a given probability.

Second, the simulation approach to VAR analysis consists of finding, from a long run of historical data, the loss that is exceeded on a given percentage of the days in the sample. As a nonparametric procedure, the latter imposes no distributional assumptions.[5]

In this paper, we examine various aspects of VAR analysis and its use as an instrument of banking regulation from an empirical point of view. Using data on the equity, interest and FX rate exposure of a bank with significant trading activity, we compare the empirical performance of parametric and simulation-based VAR analysis. Even though the proposed Basle Accord Amendment does not specify which approach banks should use, the penalties envisaged for banks whose models fail to forecast loss probabilities accurately makes this an important question.[6]

We also look at the impact of window length (ie the length of returns data series used) and weighting factors for the returns. The alternative Basle system requires the use of at least one year of data, and we assess whether this appears sensible.

A finding of considerable practical significance is that adopting different approaches to estimating return volatility for reasonably well-diversified fixed-income portfolios makes little difference to the degree to which one can forecast the average size of price changes. The techniques one employs in calculating volatility can affect forecasting accuracy in a statistically significant way, but the improvements are not substantial enough to be economically significant. On the other hand, the various approaches to VAR modelling differ widely in the accuracy with which they predict the fraction of times a given loss will be exceeded. If this latter criterion is applied, simulation-based rather than parametric VAR techniques appear preferable.

Finally, we investigate the precise formula for required capital proposed in the Basle alternative approach. As mentioned above, the current proposal is that capital must exceed the maximum of (a) the previous day's VAR, or (b) three times the average VAR of the previous 60 days. It is interesting to ask, with our real-life books, how the scaling factor and the fact that one must take the maximum of two quantities affect the outcome.

Empirical analysis of VARs

TRADING BOOKS

In evaluating the different VAR techniques, we employ data on the trading book of a bank with significant trading exposure. From these data on sensitivities of the different assets in the book to given market movements, provided to us on condition of anonymity, one may deduce the amounts held by the bank in a number of asset categories.

The asset breakdown consists of 14 maturity "buckets" (ie intervals along the yield curve) for five different government bond markets (UK, US, Japan, Germany and France). The time buckets comprise four bands for maturities less than one year, annual bands for one to 10-year maturities, and a single band for maturities longer than 10 years.

Table 1 shows the breakdown of the four dif-

Table 1. Portfolio amounts of daily returns (£m)

	Ffr	£	$	¥	DM
Portfolio 1					
FX	-10.89	–	-46.02	4.31	40.95
3–12 month	24.04	56.82	-191.56	-590.78	462.35
2–5 year	-11.45	-336.42	83.13	1247.51	-139.10
6–10 year	-3.52	-14.62	69.96	-65.45	-144.32
11+ year	0.00	0.00	-3.19	5.52	-41.66
Portfolio 2					
FX	-5.95	–	5.72	-22.23	10.20
3–12 month	64.96	40.01	-135.10	-529.87	629.90
2–5 year	-130.29	-268.84	-33.18	1194.70	-178.89
6–10 year	19.39	11.17	0.93	-58.66	-107.47
11+ year	0.00	0.00	-2.71	5.20	-8.76
Portfolio 3					
FX	-9.86	–	33.50	-5.59	22.48
3–12 month	-237.72	105.39	4.56	-1314.62	11.69
2–5 year	43.46	-245.85	11.11	346.49	89.64
6–10 year	39.53	22.44	0.26	-58.31	-69.96
11+ year	0.00	-26.70	-2.72	4.75	-8.81
Portfolio 4					
FX	28.51	–	-132.10	11.84	-26.08
3–12 month	-11.00	2.22	-153.15	-341.36	-327.05
2–5 year	-160.38	13.88	24.53	357.72	559.87
6–10 year	179.83	-53.34	53.92	40.87	-398.86
11+ year	43.13	39.72	29.90	0.00	0.00
Equities	1.50	2.81	-37.69	6.06	8.24

Table 2. Standard deviations of daily returns

	Ffr	£	$	¥	DM
FX	6.32	–	10.74	10.00	6.63
< 3 months	0.90	0.48	0.31	0.22	0.25
3–6 months	1.09	0.86	0.53	0.34	0.45
6–9 months	1.31	1.32	0.83	0.53	0.67
9–12 months	1.49	1.76	1.16	0.70	0.88
1–2 years	2.63	3.33	2.09	1.30	1.72
2–3 years	3.62	4.42	3.10	1.95	2.27
3–4 years	4.59	5.53	4.13	2.67	2.93
4–5 years	5.58	6.57	5.15	3.43	3.50
5–6 years	6.65	7.55	6.14	4.36	4.06
6–7 years	7.99	8.55	7.13	5.62	4.97
7–8 years	9.36	9.80	8.13	6.73	6.19
8–9 years	10.15	10.97	9.08	7.66	7.34
9–10 years	10.40	12.05	9.94	8.43	8.53
11+ years	11.45	13.66	11.63	10.09	10.50
Equities	19.48	14.24	16.51	22.43	20.02

Note: standard deviations are annualised (multiplied by $\sqrt{250}$) and in %.

ferent books that we employed in our statistical analysis. The first three portfolios were held by the bank in three consecutive months. The foreign exchange exposure for a particular currency represents the total net sterling value of assets denominated in that currency. Hence, for example, if the bank acquires a 10-year DM-denominated bond, both the FX exposure and the six–10-year bond categories in the DM column of Table 1 increase.[7]

Two features of the data stand out. First, the degree to which the bank's fixed-income exposure fluctuates over relatively short periods of time is quite striking. This fact underlines the importance of banks satisfying capital requirements for market risk almost on a continuous basis. Thus, VAR models need to be run daily.

Second, the bank's net foreign exchange (FX) exposure is small except for the large short US dollar position in Portfolio 4. This suggests that the bank is systematically hedging the net FX risk in its trading book.[8] Other data in our possession suggest that the months we chose were fairly typical of the bank's general behaviour in that FX risk is systematically hedged while other exposures fluctuate considerably.

The main advantage of using actual books for the predominant bank trading risks is that it ensures that the pattern of risk exposures along the yield curve and between markets is realistic. The amount of exposure taken at different points on the yield curve and between markets clearly reflects a bank's investment decisions. Randomly generated portfolios are unlikely to be representative and it would be difficult to build stylised books which were representative without basing them on actual books.

Finally, most of our data on the bank's portfolio consisted of fixed-income investments in different currencies. Yet it is important to examine whether VAR analysis produces different results when applied to portfolios containing equities rather than just fixed-income and FX positions. The bank was kind enough to provide us with data on a single additional portfolio, which we label Portfolio 4, which contained equity exposures. The relatively small size of this equity book is typical of what most banks hold.

RETURNS DATA

The bond returns in our study are based on a time series of zero-coupon yield curves calculated by an investment bank (not the one that supplied us with portfolio data). From this, we calculate holding returns for the maturity categories on which we have portfolio data. For equities, we use the returns on the French CAC-40, the British FT-All Share, the German DAX, the US S&P Composite, and the Japanese Nikkei-225. Including equities and FX positions means that in total we are dealing with 79 different sources of risk. All returns are calculated as changes in log prices.

Throughout the analysis we take sterling to be the base currency and use data between July 1987 and April 1995. Table 2 shows the annualised sample standard deviations of the daily returns on our 79 different rates of return. The figures in Table 2 suggest that returns on fixed-income books are much less volatile than returns on books that include significant equity exposure, unless the fixed-income portfolio includes very long-dated securities. Even holdings heavily-weighted towards long-dated bonds will have relatively low average durations, and hence are likely to exhibit lower volatilities than portfolios that include equities or FX exposure.

Although the returns data cover the period July 1987 to April 1995, estimates of the VARs are made only for the period June 1989 through April 1995. Data from the earlier period are used in whole or in part (depending on the length of the data window) to construct the first VAR estimate. This means that it was not possible to compute a VAR estimate for the 1987 equity market crash, although the crash does appear in the past data when VAR estimates were calculated using a 24-month window.

PARAMETRIC VAR ANALYSIS

The first issue we wish to address in our empirical analysis is the sensitivity of parametric VAR analysis to the precise way in which the volatilities are estimated. The approach to volatility estimation typically used in VAR applications is to take a weighted average of the squared deviation from an estimate of the mean return using a window of lagged data. Thus, if r_t is the holding return at t, a typical estimator for $\sigma^2 = \mathrm{Var}(r_t)$ would be:

$$\hat{\sigma}_t^2 = \frac{1}{T-1}\sum_{i=0}^{T-1}\lambda_i\left(r_{t-T+i} - \bar{r}_t\right)^2 \qquad (1)$$

where

$$\lambda_i \in [0,1], \quad \sum_{i=0}^{T-1}\lambda_i / T = 1$$

and

$$\bar{r}_t \equiv \sum_{j=0}^{T-1} r_{t-T+j} / T.$$

In implementing the VAR models, we work out the returns for one-day or rolling 10-day holding periods on a given portfolio, and then calculate volatilities, tail probabilities and so on, using that single series. This approach yields results that are arithmetically identical to those one would obtain estimating a full covariance matrix for n individual asset return series, call it Σ, and then estimated the volatility of a portfolio with portfolio holdings, $a \equiv (a_1, a_2, \ldots, a_n)'$ by calculating the quadratic form, $a'\Sigma a$.

The latter approach is that taken by practitioners (including JP Morgan in its RiskMetrics system). It is clearly more efficient if one has many portfolios for which one wants the value-at-risk on a single date. When a large number of VAR calculations are required for a small number of portfolios on different dates, our approach is quicker.

Three choices must be made in implementing the parametric VAR described above, namely (a) the appropriate length for the lagged data "window," (T); (b) the weighting scheme to adopt, $(\lambda_0, \lambda_1, \ldots, \lambda_{T-1})$; and (c) estimating the mean using the sample mean,

$$\bar{r}_t \equiv \sum_{j=0}^{T-1} r_{t-T+j} / T$$

or setting it to zero as some empirical researchers have advocated.[9]

FORECASTING PERFORMANCE AND WINDOW LENGTH

Table 3 shows two ways of assessing the sensitivity of the VAR results to the choice of T. In the upper block of the Table, we show the mean absolute forecast error where we define the forecast error at period t as:

$$\left|\, |r_t - \bar{r}_t| - \hat{\sigma}_t \,\right|. \qquad (2)$$

Averaging the absolute forecast errors over the entire sample period yields a measure of the accuracy of the volatility estimates. Standard errors are reported in parentheses under each mean. They are calculated using the technique of Newey and West (1987) and hence are robust to complex patterns of time dependence. The standard errors give a very conservative impression

Table 3. Parametric VARs and window length

		3 months data	6 months data	12 months data	24 months data
Mean absolute forecast error					
Portfolio 1	Mean	26.71*	26.79	27.02	27.17
	Std err	(0.85)	(0.79)	(0.64)	(0.60)
	T-stat	–	[0.20]	[0.57]	[0.79]
Portfolio 2	Mean	17.26*	17.32	17.40	17.29
	Std err	(0.55)	(0.47)	(0.42)	(0.41)
	T-stat	–	[0.21]	[0.39]	[0.08]
Portfolio 3	Mean	5.43	5.42	5.44	5.40*
	Std err	(0.21)	(0.17)	(0.15)	(0.14)
	T-stat	[0.23]	[0.18]	[0.72]	–
Portfolio 4	Mean	77.12*	78.11	78.10	78.60
	Std err	(2.10)	(1.85)	(1.78)	(1.72)
	T-stat	–	[0.89]	[0.68]	[0.99]
Tail probabillities					
Portfolio 1		1.71	1.38	1.32*	1.32*
Portfolio 2		2.11	1.91	1.58	1.51*
Portfolio 3		1.58	1.32	1.45	1.25*
Portfolio 4		1.71	1.65	1.71	1.38*

Note: calculations employ equal weights ($\lambda_i = 1, \forall i$), zero means and daily returns. Forecast errors are multiplied by 10,000 for scaling. Newey-West standard errors are in parentheses. T-ratios are given for difference from lowest mean absolute error in the same row.
* Indicates lowest in row.

of the statistical significance of differences in mean forecast errors since means calculated under different assumptions are highly positively correlated, reducing the variability of the average difference. Hence, we also give the t-statistics for the difference between each mean absolute forecast error and the other means in the same row of the table. The t-statistics are again calculated using Newey-West techniques.

We tried working with various other measures of forecast accuracy. First, one may define the forecast error itself as

$$\left| \, |r_t - \bar{r}_t| - \hat{\sigma}_t \, \right|$$

and then employ the sample mean of these absolute differences. In this case, one is evaluating forecasts of the variance rather than the standard deviation. Since VAR calculations employ the latter, this is probably not appropriate.

Second, we experimented by using root mean squares of the forecast errors instead of simply means. The problem with this approach is that it attributes most weight in the comparison to outliers. We thought it better, therefore, to use means.

In the lower block of Table 3, we provide measures of the degree to which capital requirements based on different VAR models do indeed cover losses that occur with a given probability. Assuming normally distributed returns, one may deduce from the time series of estimated volatilities a corresponding series for what we shall call 1% cut-off points, meaning the loss that, according to the model, will be exceeded on average 1% of the time. More precisely, the cut-off points may be obtained by inverting the equation:

$$\text{Prob}\left[\sum_{n=1}^{N} r_{nt} a_n < -\gamma \middle| \sigma^2, \mu \right] = 0.01 \qquad (3)$$

for γ on a period-by-period basis. (In (3), a_n is the holding of the nth asset. Throughout our analysis, we shall normalise initial wealth to unity so that $\Sigma_{n=1}^{N} a_n = 1$.)

Inverting this equation yields:

$$\gamma \equiv -\mu - \Phi^{-1}(0.01)\sigma \qquad (4)$$

where $\Phi(\cdot)$ is the cumulative distribution function for a standard normal random variable. As a measure of the performance of different VAR models, the lower panel in Table 3 shows the proportion of actual portfolio returns that fall below the 1% cut-off points.

As one may see from the upper panel of Table 3, the mean absolute forecast errors are relatively insensitive to the length of the data window, although it is true in most cases that a short window yields slightly more accurate forecasts. On the face of it, the insensitivity is surprising since plots of the forecasts based on long or short windows look quite different (see Figure 1). Furthermore, comparisons of the forecasting

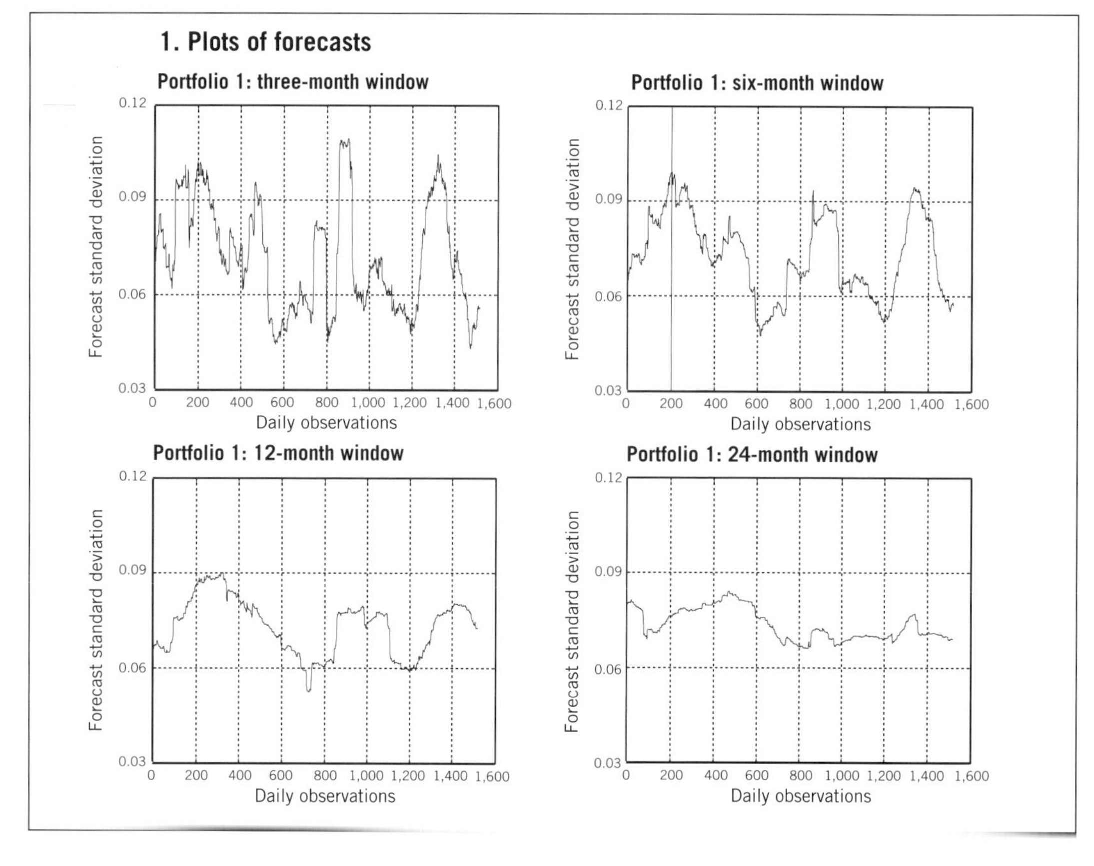

accuracy of different VAR techniques applied to individual exchange rate returns included in RiskMetrics (1995) suggest that different window lengths do make a difference (although not a large one).

In fact, the forecastability of volatilities and the sensitivity of the forecasts to different techniques depend very much on the return series in question. When we repeated the analyses reported in Table 3 using the return on a single exchange rate, as in RiskMetrics (1995), we found distinctly greater differences between the forecasting performances of different VAR techniques.

It is important to note, however, that using a different window size does significantly affect the tail probabilities shown in the lower part of Table 3, with the longest samples producing the best performance, in contrast to the results in the upper panel. In general, the figures in the table show that losses exceed the 1% cutoff points much more than 1% of the time, demonstrating the inaccuracy of the measures of tail probability implied by parametric VARs based on normal distributions. Hendricks (1996) reaches a similar conclusion in his study of VAR models applied to FX portfolio returns.

This is not surprising given the widely documented leptokurtosis of interest rates and stock returns. The results in Table 3 suggest that a longer data window helps to reduce the tail probability bias, however.

WEIGHTING SCHEMES

As mentioned before, a common procedure is to calculate variance estimates for VAR-type analyses using weighted squared deviations from an estimate of the mean. Rapidly declining weights mean that variance estimates are largely based on the last few observations, although information contained in more lagged observations is not totally ignored. The motivation for this approach is the widely recognised fact that financial market returns are conditionally heteroscedastic.[10]

A range of more or less complicated techniques has been developed to model this feature of financial returns. In particular, generalised autoregressive and conditionally heteroscedastic (GARCH) models are specifically designed for this purpose. Most implementations of VAR analysis have taken the simpler approach of estimating variances using the weighted average of squared deviations from the mean, with weights that decline exponentially as the lag length increases.

Table 4. Parametric VARs and exponential weights

		Equal weights	λ=0.97	λ=0.94
Mean absolute errors				
Portfolio 1	Mean	27.17	26.37	26.11*
	Std err	(0.60)	(0.84)	(0.94)
	T-stat	[1.67]	[1.33]	–
Portfolio 2	Mean	17.29	17.05	16.86*
	Std err	(0.41)	(0.53)	(0.60)
	T-stat	[1.08]	[1.26]	–
Portfolio 3	Mean	5.40	5.36	5.30*
	Std err	(0.14)	(0.19)	(0.22)
	T-stat	[0.71]	[1.03]	–
Portfolio 4	Mean	78.60	76.49	75.62*
	Std err	(1.72)	(1.98)	(2.15)
	T-stat	[2.18]	[1.61]	–
Tail probabillities				
Portfolio 1		1.32*	1.32*	1.72
Portfolio 2		1.51*	1.71	1.91
Portfolio 3		1.25*	1.45	1.45
Portfolio 4		1.38*	1.65	1.65

Note: calculations employ zero means, daily returns and a 24-month window. Forecast errors are multiplied by 10,000 for scaling. Newey-West standard errors are in parentheses. T-ratios are given for difference from lowest mean absolute error in the same row.
* Indicates lowest in row.

The weights are thus of the form:

$$\lambda_i \equiv T\frac{1-\lambda}{1-\lambda^{T-1}}\lambda_i \text{ for } i = 0,1,2,\ldots,T-1 \qquad (5)$$

for a constant $\lambda \in [0,1]$. Standard results on geometric series imply that $\Sigma_0^{T-1}\lambda_i = T$.

The upper panel of Table 4 shows mean absolute volatility forecast errors obtained using different weighting schemes. The calculations are carried out using daily returns with 24-month windows of lagged data and means fixed at zero. Once again, the volatility forecasts for the fixed-income and FX books are quite insensitive to the precise approach followed, although rapidly declining weights $\lambda = 0.94$ perform somewhat better for all four portfolios, and yield a statistically significant improvement in forecast accuracy for Portfolio 4.

The lower panel of Table 4 shows the tail probabilities for different weighting schemes. It is apparent that using weighting schemes with rapidly declining weights increases the upward bias in the tail probabilities. As with window length, there appears to be a trade-off in that weighting schemes may improve the degree to which the VAR calculations track time-varying volatilities (ie the mean absolute forecast errors may be reduced to some small degree), but the bias in the tail probabilities is exacerbated.

COMPARISON OF PARAMETRIC AND NON-PARAMETRIC VARS

Because non-parametric-based VARs do not yield a time series of volatility forecast errors, we

Table 5. Parametric and simulation VARs: tail probabilities

	3 months data	6 months data	12 months data	24 months data
Portfolio 1				
1-day return parametric	1.71	1.38	1.32	1.32
10-day return parametric*	1.78	1.05	1.32	1.05
1-day return simulation	1.71	0.79	1.38	0.92
10-day simulation**	3.69	1.97	2.30	1.78
Portfolio 2				
1-day return parametric	2.11	1.91	1.58	1.51
10-day return parametric*	0.79	0.72	0.99	0.92
1-day return simulation	1.78	0.99	1.18	1.18
10-day return simulation**	2.63	1.32	1.45	1.65
Portfolio 3				
1-day return parametric	1.58	1.32	1.45	1.25
10-day return parametric*	1.58	1.12	1.05	1.05
1-day return simulation	1.51	0.86	1.18	0.86
10-day return simulation**	3.09	1.32	1.58	1.18
Portfolio 4				
1-day return parametric	1.71	1.65	1.71	1.38
10-day return parametric*	1.12	1.12	1.18	0.92
1-day return simulation	1.38	0.72	1.38	0.92
10-day return simulation**	3.09	1.58	1.38	1.25

* Calculated by multiplying the one-day VAR estimate by √10 and comparing with the subsequent realised 10-day log returns.
** Calculated by estimating the VAR from the portfolio losses over 10-day periods and comparing these with the subsequent realised 10-day log returns.

restrict our comparison to the tail probabilities that the two kinds of model produce. Table 5 shows the results for data window lengths ranging from three to 24 months.

For the parametric approach, 10-day return tail probabilities were calculated by scaling up the one-day VAR estimates by √10 and then taking the fraction of observations for which the 10-day loss outturns exceed the implied cut-off level. The one-day tail probabilities are calculated as before.

For the non-parametric approach, 10-day return tail probabilities were calculated using 10-day portfolio losses to compute the VAR and then taking the fraction of observations for which the 10-day losses exceed the implied cut-off level. For the one-day tail probabilities, the VAR is computed using one-day portfolio losses and the result compared with the one-day losses. For both the parametric and the non-parametric approaches, the 10-day return losses were computed on a rolling basis by summing the log daily returns.

The results in Table 5 suggest that calculating the one-day and 10-day VAR cut-off points from short data windows is inadvisable in that the small sample biases are very substantial. For longer data windows, the non-parametric approach for the one-day returns consistently outperforms the parametric VAR model, in that the tail probabilities are matched more accurately. For the parametric approach, the tail probabilities computed using the different lag lengths consistently exceed the 1% level, reflecting the well-known non-normality of financial returns.

Looking at the 10-day returns, for some portfolios, the non-parametric approach appears to perform worse than the parametric VAR estimates. In general, the tail probability figures for 10-day returns serve to underline the statistical problems involved in attempting to deduce 10-day volatilities directly from estimates of one-day volatilities.

INCLUSION OF ESTIMATED MEANS

The last exercise we perform to assess the sensitivity of VAR analyses to different assumptions is to calculate mean absolute forecast errors for parametric VARs (a) with means estimated from lagged returns, and (b) with the means set to zero. Fixing the means at zero might seem an unconventional statistical procedure but the estimation error associated with badly determined mean estimates may reduce the efficiency of the estimated volatilities. (Figlewski (1997) makes a similar point in the context of return variance estimation.) If the true mean returns are, as seems likely, very close to zero, fixing them at this level could enhance the forecasts.

In fact, the results in Table 6 show that, for the particular books and return data we employ, the findings are mixed. The mean absolute forecast errors with means set to zero are in some cases lower and in some higher than in cases in which the means are freely estimated. With one-day returns, the differences are very small. With Portfolio 1, one-day return forecast accuracy is improved in a statistically significant way, but the gain appears economically insignificant.

CALCULATION OF VAR OVER 10-DAY PERIODS

We look at the effect of trying to estimate the VAR over a 10-day period. We did not have a sufficiently long run of data to estimate the VAR using returns calculated over non-overlapping 10-day periods (this would reduce the number of observations by a factor of 10). Hence, for the parametric approach we chose between using the VAR estimated for a 24-hour period grossed up by $\sqrt{10}$, or using overlapping returns based on rolling 10-day periods.

Because the use of overlapping data induces artificial autocorrelation in the series (which makes them appear smoother than they actually are), for the parametric approach we did not attempt to calculate the VAR using 10-day rolling returns. For the non-parametric approach, we calculate the VAR using portfolio losses calculated over rolling 10-day periods. As illustrated in Table 5, the 10-day VAR estimates using both the parametric and the non-parametric approaches are substantially biased. Moreover, the direction of the bias appears to be portfolio-dependent.

"SPIKE" LOSS PERIODS

An important question is whether the ability of parametric VAR analysis to "track" the time series behaviour of volatility enables it to outperform simulation-based VARs in predictions of large, "spike" losses in portfolio values. It is possible that even if parametric VARs do not yield lower mean absolute forecast errors, as we see above, they are better at picking out large market movements.

This issue is particularly important if VAR analysis is to be used for regulatory purposes, for the primary concern of regulators regarding trading book risks is that banks will be wiped out by sudden large losses that occur before action can be taken to reduce the riskiness of the bank's portfolio. To examine this issue, we split our sample period into six-month intervals, and identify, for each of our portfolios, the day within each period on which the largest loss occurs.

Before comparing the performance of the parametric and simulation-based VAR models, let us examine the composition of the spike portfolio losses. Table 7 provides detailed breakdowns of the constituent parts of each of these large value declines for Portfolio 4, which, as the reader may recall, contains equity as well as interest rate and FX risk.

As is apparent from Table 7, bond risk is the most important factor in generating large losses, serving as the dominant factor in eight out of 12 cases. FX risk is the most important factor in the remaining four cases. Table 1 shows that Portfolio 4 contains greater FX exposure than the other portfolios (in particular, a relatively large net US dollar position).

Table 6. Parametric VARs: sample mean inclusion – mean absolute forecast errors

			Sample mean	Zero mean
Portfolio 1	1-day return	Mean	27.30	27.17*
		Std err	(0.61)	(0.60)
		T-stat	[2.01]	–
	10-day return**	Mean	82.54	81.58*
		Std err	(2.44)	(2.46)
		T-stat	[0.95]	–
Portfolio 2	1-day return	Mean	17.31	17.29*
		Std err	(0.41)	(0.41)
		T-stat	[0.56]	–
	10-day return**	Mean	51.27	50.67*
		Std err	(1.34)	(1.38)
		T-stat	[0.86]	–
Portfolio 3	1-day return	Mean	5.39*	5.40
		Std err	(0.14)	(0.14)
		T-stat	–	[1.14]
	10-day return**	Mean	16.34*	16.38
		Std err	(0.45)	(0.49)
		T-stat	–	[0.23]
Portfolio 4	1-day return	Mean	78.53*	78.60
		Std err	(1.73)	(1.72)
		T-stat	–	[0.34]
	10-day return**	Mean	237.69	232.23*
		Std err	(7.23)	(7.65)
		T-stat	[1.68]	–

Note: equal weights, one-day returns, 24-month window. Forecast errors are multiplied by 10,000 for scaling. Newey-West standard errors are in parentheses. T-ratios are given for difference from lowest mean absolute error in the same row.
* Indicates lowest in row.
** Calculated by multiplying one-day VAR returns by $\sqrt{10}$.

It is surprising that the equity exposure creates no spike losses in the period of our sample. We were initially concerned that this result reflects the fact that large changes in equity values tend to be negative, and the largest equity exposure in Portfolio 4 is a short position in US equities.

As an experiment, we re-ran the VAR calculations assuming that the equity exposures (and the corresponding components of the FX exposures) are of opposite sign. Even with this change, none of the spike losses were attributable mainly to equity losses. One may therefore conclude that the relatively small size of the equity exposure is enough to make equity risk minimal, even though equity returns themselves are much more volatile than those on bond portfolios.[11]

Table 8 shows the capital requirement implied by the VAR estimates minus the actual loss sustained.[12] We term this quantity the capital surplus (+) or capital shortfall (–). As one can see, parametric and simulation-based VAR models perform somewhat differently.

Table 7. "Spike" losses – portfolio 4

Date		Ffr	£	$	¥	DM	Total
July 3, 1989	FX	0.13	–	-2.03	-0.01	-0.11	-2.02
	Bond	0.26	-0.09	-0.05	-1.61	-1.12	-2.61
	Equities	0.01	0.02	-0.12	0.04	0.09	0.03
	Total	0.39	-0.07	-2.20	-1.58	-1.14	-4.60
Feb 21, 1990	FX	0.01	–	-0.72	0.06	-0.02	-0.67
	Bond	1.35	0.02	0.04	0.46	-4.22	-2.36
	Equities	-0.01	-0.02	0.03	-0.16	-0.06	-0.23
	Total	1.34	0.00	-0.65	0.35	-4.30	-3.26
Aug 6, 1990	FX	-0.04	–	-0.87	0.05	0.04	-0.82
	Bond	-3.18	-0.32	-2.41	-1.47	2.99	-4.38
	Equities	-0.07	-0.07	0.98	-0.16	-0.39	0.29
	Total	-3.28	-0.38	-2.30	-1.58	2.64	-4.90
Feb 11, 1991	FX	-0.04	–	-0.56	0.04	0.06	-0.50
	Bond	0.75	-0.04	-0.13	-1.65	-1.38	-2.45
	Equities	0.01	0.04	-0.81	0.00	0.10	-0.66
	Total	0.73	-0.00	-1.50	-1.61	-1.23	-3.61
Sep 1, 1991	FX	-0.03	–	-2.08	0.11	0.06	-1.95
	Bond	0.35	-0.06	0.03	-1.09	-1.10	-1.88
	Equities	-0.00	-0.01	0.04	-0.03	-0.06	-0.05
	Total	0.32	-0.07	-2.01	-1.01	-1.10	-3.87
Nov 18, 1991	FX	-0.18	–	-1.35	0.09	0.15	-1.28
	Bond	-0.50	0.07	-0.04	-0.04	-0.14	-0.67
	Equities	-0.04	-0.04	-0.22	-0.15	-0.07	-0.52
	Total	-0.72	0.03	-1.60	-0.11	-0.06	-2.47
Sep 23, 1992	FX	0.09	–	0.03	-0.08	-0.17	-0.13
	Bond	-3.25	-0.05	-0.34	-0.06	-2.33	-6.02
	Equities	-0.00	-0.00	-0.02	0.00	0.03	0.01
	Total	-3.16	-0.05	-0.33	-0.14	-2.46	-6.15
Jan 5, 1993	FX	0.47	–	-3.14	0.26	-0.46	-2.87
	Bond	-0.30	-0.24	-0.13	0.06	-0.54	-1.15
	Equities	0.01	-0.01	0.08	-0.05	0.11	0.13
	Total	0.18	-0.25	-3.19	0.27	-0.89	-3.89
Apr 13, 1993	FX	0.09	–	-2.46	0.20	-0.11	-2.27
	Bond	0.31	0.06	-0.23	-0.81	-0.20	-0.88
	Equities	0.02	0.02	-0.06	0.22	0.06	0.26
	Total	0.42	0.08	-2.75	-0.40	-0.25	-2.89
Mar 1, 1994	FX	0.05	–	0.01	0.04	-0.03	0.07
	Bond	-1.51	-0.17	-1.07	-1.79	0.86	-3.68
	Equities	-0.03	-0.03	0.18	0.06	-0.08	0.09
	Total	-1.50	-0.20	-0.88	-1.69	0.75	-3.52
Jun 28, 1994	FX	0.00	–	0.58	-0.02	-0.01	0.55
	Bond	-0.23	-0.08	-0.78	-1.44	-3.15	-5.67
	Equities	0.01	0.01	0.09	0.08	0.10	0.29
	Total	-0.22	-0.07	-0.11	-1.37	-3.06	-4.82
Oct 3, 1994	FX	0.10	–	-0.07	0.09	-0.10	0.02
	Bond	-1.64	-0.06	-0.49	-1.19	-0.03	-3.42
	Equities	-0.02	-0.03	0.07	0.02	0.00	0.04
	Total	-1.57	-0.09	-0.49	-1.08	-0.13	-3.36

Note: figures are daily returns in percent.

Table 8. Model performance on "spike" loss dates

	Portfolio 1		Portfolio 2		Portfolio 3		Portfolio 4	
Model	Sim	VAR/Cov	Sim	VAR/Cov	Sim	VAR/Cov	Sim	VAR/Cov
Period 1	-1.63	-1.51	-0.49	-0.47	-0.06	-0.05	-0.81	-0.58
Period 2	-0.56	-0.64	-0.42	-0.43	-0.08	-0.10	0.05	-0.15
Period 3	-0.75	-0.89	-0.48	-0.54	-0.11	-0.13	-1.62	-1.95
Period 4	0.03	-0.08	-0.29	-0.39	-0.10	-0.12	-0.32	-0.53
Period 5	0.28	0.11	0.15	0.02	-0.09	-0.12	-0.62	-0.79
Period 6	-1.08	-1.34	-1.05	-1.22	-0.08	-0.16	0.79	0.58
Period 7	-1.81	-2.09	-1.39	-1.51	-0.75	-0.80	-3.19	-3.29
Period 8	0.04	-0.24	-0.31	-0.35	-0.01	-0.10	-0.34	-0.79
Period 9	0.40	0.15	-0.08	-0.10	0.16	0.06	0.66	0.13
Period 10	0.11	-0.08	0.06	0.00	0.04	-0.03	-0.54	-0.47
Period 11	-0.07	-0.10	-0.04	-0.04	0.03	0.01	-1.28	-1.40
Period 12	-0.16	-0.08	0.18	0.12	0.04	0.04	0.29	-0.09

Note: capital shortfall (–) or surplus (+) for the largest loss for each six-month period. Parametric approach uses zero mean. Figures are expressed in daily returns as percent.

2. Comparison of simulation and parametric-based VARs

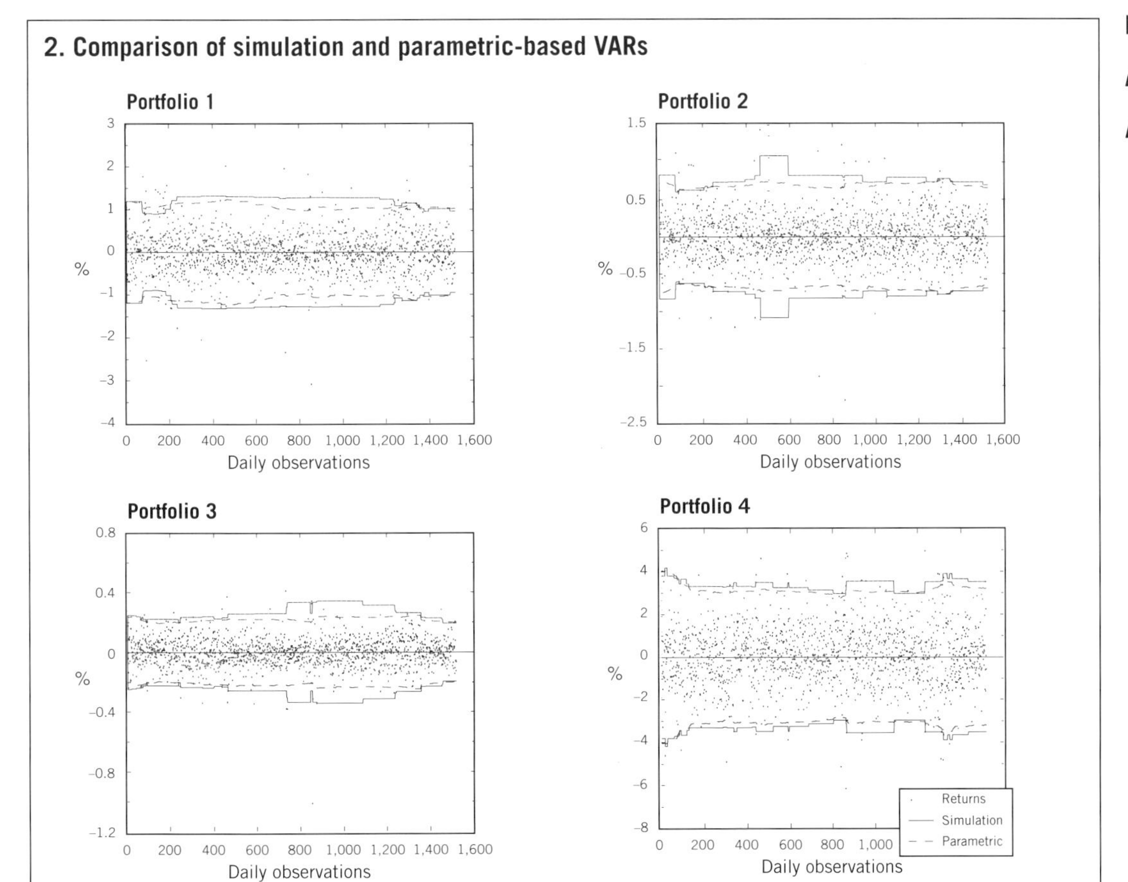

When capital is based on the simulation-based VAR model, the bank has a capital surplus on 16 of the 48 spike loss dates. When the parametric VAR model is used, the bank has a surplus on nine occasions. Whether the capital surplus is positive or negative, on most spike loss dates, the simulation-based VAR model implies a larger capital surplus than the parametric VAR.

The implication is that, although it does not exploit the conditional structure of volatility, the simulation-based VAR seems to do a somewhat better job of establishing appropriate capital requirements. Figure 2 illustrates this, using a 24-month window, for each of the portfolios.

BASLE ALTERNATIVE APPROACH TO CAPITAL CALCULATIONS

A final but important question is the amount of capital cushion that the proposed Basle alternative approach would deliver for actual books, given not only the 99% confidence level but also the multiplier of three. We look at this issue for our portfolios by comparing the capital requirement that would be generated by one part of the proposed two-stage test, namely, three times the 60-day average of the VARs calculated to cover a 10-day holding period using the parameters laid down by Basle. A bank would be required to hold capital equivalent to the greater of (a) this amount and (b) the VAR for the current book. With a multiplier of three, the first of these tests will "bite", unless the bank's current book is abnormally risky.

We compare the 10-day returns which would have been secured on our four portfolios over the period July 1989–April 1995 with the capital requirement based on three times the 60-day average of the daily VARs. (The Basle requirement would usually be calculated using the 60-day average for VARs for different books held on different days.) In performing the calculations, we used the parametric approach with a 24-month window of past returns data, equal weights, and a zero mean. We calculated the capital requirement implied by multipliers of 2.0 and 2.5 as well as 3.0.

None of the portfolios had a single loss outlier (losses which exceeded the capital requirement) when the multiplier was either 2.5 or 3. Three of the portfolios had a single (marginal) loss outlier for a multiplier of 2.0.

BASLE APPROACH TO BACK TESTING

The proposed alternative Basle approach envisages that banks will suffer increases in their capital requirements if, over a 250-day period, their

Table 9. Back testing results

Portfolio	1	2	3	4
Period 1	6	7	4	3
Period 2	4	7	5	3
Period 3	3	2	4	1
Period 4	4	5	4	4
Period 5	1	1	2	3
Period 6	2	1	0	7

Note: number of exceptions in each 250-day period.
Green zone = 0–4 exceptions.
Yellow zone = 5–9 exceptions.
Red zone = 10+ exceptions.

VAR models underpredict the number of losses exceeding the 1% cut-off point. Such losses are termed "exceptions". If a bank's VAR model has generated zero to four exceptions, it is said to be in the green zone; if five to nine, it is in the yellow zone; and if there are more than 10 exceptions, it is in the red zone. The capital requirement for banks whose models are in the yellow zone may be increased by regulators; if banks are in the red zone, the requirement would almost certainly be increased.

We ran backtests for all four of our portfolios, comparing the VAR figures calculated for one-day holding periods (again, using the parametric approach) with the actual return on each book. The number of exceptions for each portfolio over the different 250-day periods are set out in Table 9.

The results vary for different portfolios. For three of the six periods, if Portfolio 2 were held, the model would generate more than four exceptions. The highest number of exceptions is seven, which occurred twice for Portfolio 2 and once for Portfolio 4. According to the Basle guidelines, this would normally lead to an increase in the multiplier of 0.65, unless the supervisor could be persuaded that special factors had affected outcomes.[13]

The fact that the model moves from the green to the yellow zone so much from period to period underlines the difficulty of distinguishing between good and bad models using samples of a mere 250 observations. Our results suggest, however, that a grossly inaccurate model would be picked up by such back testing.

Conclusion

We have sought to provide practical analysis that is helpful to those contemplating the use of VAR models either for risk measurement within a bank or for regulatory control of bank risk-taking, relating our results to the recommendations and provisions of the alternative approach of the Basle Accord Amendment. A strength of our study is the use of data on the actual trading books of a bank active in a wide range of markets. Judgements about whether one approach dominates another seem to be sensitive to the kind of portfolios held. Studies that analyse VAR modelling on the basis of, for example, a single equity index or FX rate seem to us to be ill-advised, therefore, and it is important to look at realisticportfolios.

The main conclusions that emerge from the empirical section of our study are as follows. Simulation-based VAR techniques yield more accurate measures of tail probabilities than parametric VAR models. This arises from the severe non-normality of financial returns. We are not convinced by the common argument that mismeasurement by parametric VARs of the level of tail probabilities does not matter because they correctly rank different portfolios. Different asset returns will be more or less fat-tailed, leading to varying biases.

Parametric VAR analysis tracks the time series behaviour of volatility better, and appears to yield slightly superior volatility forecasts compared to non-parametric, simulation-based techniques (although the differences are generally not statistically significant). With reasonably well-diversified fixed-income books, however, the gains in forecasting accuracy are relatively slight. The parametric VAR models that yield the best forecasts have relatively short window lengths and large weighting factors. But such models are very poor at fitting the tails of return distributions, and capital requirements based on them tend to be too low.

What are the implications of the proposed amendment to the Basle Accord for banks? The amendment proposes that the value-at-risk calculated using VAR techniques should be scaled up by a factor of three. With such a high scaling factor, only extremely risky portfolios will ever fail to be covered.

Even so, the back testing provisions proposed by Basle are likely to affect banks quite significantly. Under the proposed amendment, if a bank's VAR model underpredicts the number of large losses, the capital requirement will be increased. A bank holding the portfolios we employ in this study would find its capital requirements adjusted fairly frequently if it uses the parametric approach.

1 *Jackson (1995) and Kupiec and O'Brien (1995) discuss risk measurement in the context of bank regulation.*

2 *Dimson and Marsh (1995) discuss at length the implications of the building block approach.*

3 *The UK securities regulators address this problem for equity positions by using a simplified Sharpe portfolio model, an approach not adopted by either CAD or Basle.*

4 *A systematic description of different approaches to VAR appears in Jackson (1995). The June 1996 VAR Supplement in* Risk *provides various practitioner perspectives on VAR.*

5 *The terminology used to distinguish these two forms of VAR analysis varies across authors in a somewhat confusing manner. For example, Laycock and Paxson (1995) refer to what we call parametric and simulation-based VARs as simulation and backtesting approaches, respectively. The former is also often referred to as the variance-covariance approach.*

6 *A significant omission in our study is that we do not consider the treatment of derivatives in VAR models.* Risk Management Guidelines for Derivatives *(1994) discusses some of the problems involved in the risk management of derivatives portfolios. Estrella (1995) argues that the standard approach of linearising non-linear claims such as options can cause problems.*

7 *Considering the exchange rate and foreign currency asset price risks separately is common among practitioners.*

8 *The exposures are the consolidated exposures for the bank and its securities companies, so this does not simply reflect the effect of the Bank of England's guideline on overnight FX exposures that applies to the bank.*

9 *See, for example, RiskMetrics (1995) p.66.*

10 *Some banks' VAR models, for example CSFB's Primerisk, apply different weighting schemes across asset categories. Lawrence and Robinson (1995) argue for asset-specific weighting schemes. We follow RiskMetrics in employing a uniform weighting scheme.*

11 *The more "spiky" and volatile nature of equities has been recognised by regulators, for instance, in the CAD building-block approach. Under the CAD, a single position in a ten-year government bond would carry a capital requirement of 2.4%, whereas a single position in an equity index would carry a charge of 8%. For a single equity, the charge would be 12%.*

12 *The capital "requirement" is the VAR for the whole book produced using a 99% confidence level. We do not incorporate in this calculation any other aspects of the Basle proposals such as the three times multiplier.*

13 *A supervisor can disregard the yellow zone if they believe there is a good reason for the poor performance unrelated to the model. However, the red zone can only be disregarded in extraordinary circumstances.*

BIBLIOGRAPHY

Basle Committee on Banking Supervision, 1995, *An Internal Model-Based Approach to Market Risk Capital Requirements*.

Basle Committee on Banking Supervision, 1996, *Overview of the Amendment to the Capital Accord to Incorporate Market Risks*.

Basle Committee on Banking Supervision, 1995, *Planned Supplement to the Capital Accord to Incorporate Market Risks*.

Basle Committee on Banking Supervision, 1994, *Risk Management Guidelines for Derivatives*.

Dimson, E., and P. Marsh, 1995, "Capital Requirements for Securities Firms", *Journal of Finance*, 3, pp. 821–51.

Estrella, A., 1995, "Taylor, Black and Scholes: Series Approximations and Risk Management Pitfalls", Federal Reserve Bank of New York Research Paper No. 9501, March.

Figlewski, S., 1997, "Forecasting Volatility Using Historical Data", Working Paper, New York University.

Hendricks, D., 1996, "Evaluation of Value-at-Risk Models Using Historical Data", *Federal Reserve Bank of New York Economic Policy Review* 1, pp. 39–69; reprinted as Chapter 21 of the present volume.

Jackson, P., 1995, "Risk Measurement and Capital Requirements for Banks", *Bank of England Quarterly Bulletin* 35, no 2, pp. 177–84.

JP Morgan, 1995, *RiskMetrics Technical Document*, 3rd edition, New York.

Kupiec, P.H., 1995, "Techniques for Verifying the Accuracy of Risk Measurement Models", *Journal of Derivatives*, Winter; reprinted as Chapter 24 of the present volume.

Kupiec, P.H., and J.M. O'Brien, 1995, "Recent Developments in Bank Capital Regulation of Market Risks", Federal Reserve Board, Finance and Economics Discussion Paper No. 95-51, December.

Lawrence, C. and G. Robinson, 1995, "How Safe Is RiskMetrics?", *Risk* 8, 1, pp. 26–32, reprinted as Chapter 8 of the present volume.

Laycock, M.S., and D.A. Paxson, 1995, "Capital Adequacy Risks: Return Normality and Confidence Intervals", Bank of England mimeo, presented at the Annual Meeting of the European Financial Management Association.

Newey, W.K., and K.D. West, 1987, "A Simple Positive Semi-definite, Heteroskedasticity and Autocorrelation Consistent Covariance Matrix", *Econometrica* 55, pp. 703–08.

23

Risk^2:

Measuring the Risk in Value-at-Risk*

Philippe Jorion
University of California, Irvine

There is risk even in value-at-risk, since VAR numbers are themselves affected by sampling variation, or "estimation risk". This paper lays out the statistical methodology for analysing estimation error in VAR and shows how to improve the accuracy of VAR estimates. With these limitations in mind, VAR is found to be an indispensable tool in controlling financial risks.

The need to improve control of financial risks has led to a uniform measure of risk called value-at-risk (VAR), which the private sector is increasingly adopting as a first line of defence against financial risks.

Regulators and central banks also provided the impetus behind VAR. The Basle Committee on Banking Supervision announced in April 1995 that capital adequacy requirements for commercial banks will be based on VAR.[1] In December 1995, the Securities and Exchange Commission issued a proposal that requires publicly-traded US corporations to disclose information about derivatives activity, with a VAR measure as one of three possible methods for making such disclosures. Thus, the unmistakable trend is toward more transparent financial risk reporting based on VAR measures.

VAR summarises the worst expected loss over a target horizon within a given confidence interval. VAR summarises in a single number the global exposure to market risks and the probability of adverse moves in financial variables. It measures risk using the same units as the bottom line - dollars. Bankers Trust, for example, revealed in its 1994 annual report that its daily VAR was an average of $35 million at the 99% confidence level over one day; this number can be readily compared to an annual profit of $615 million or total equity of $4.7 billion. On the basis of such data, shareholders and managers can decide whether they feel comfortable with a level of risk. If the answer is no, the process that led to the computation of VAR can be used to decide where to trim risk.

In addition to financial reporting, VAR can be used for a variety of other purposes, such as setting position limits for traders, measuring returns on a risk-adjusted basis, and model evaluation. Institutional investors are also embracing VAR as a dynamic method for controlling their exposure to risk factors, especially when many outside fund managers are involved. Non-financial corporations, especially those involved with derivatives, are also considering risk management systems centred around VAR. VAR provides a consistent measure of the effect of hedging on total risk, which is a significant improvement over traditional hedging programmes that typically focus only on individual transactions. No doubt these desirable features explain the wholesale trend toward VAR.

Current implementations of VAR, however, have not recognised the fact that VAR measures are only estimates of risk. VAR should be considered as a first-order approximation to possible losses from adverse financial risk. Although VAR is a vast improvement over no measure at all, VAR numbers cannot be taken at face value. A VAR figure combines existing positions with estimates of risk (including correlations) over the

* *This paper was first published in Financial Analysts Journal, November/December 1995.*

target horizon. If these estimates are based on historical data, they inevitably will be affected by "estimation risk"; thus value-at-risk also entails risk.[2]

Recognising the existence of estimation risk has several important consequences. For instance, users might want to set the confidence level, usually set arbitrarily, to a value that will minimise the error in VAR. Or, the statistical methodology might be guided by the need to minimise estimation error.

In addition, VAR should be reported with confidence intervals. For instance, a bank might announce that its VAR over the next day is \$35 million with a 95% confidence interval of \$32-38 million. A tight interval indicates relative confidence in the \$35 million estimate, particularly compared with a hypothetical interval of \$5 million–65 million. The latter would say that the VAR number is quite inaccurate – although not in the range of billions. The purpose of this chapter is to provide a formal framework for analysing estimation error in VAR and, more importantly, to discuss methods to improve the accuracy of VAR measures.

Measuring VAR

To formally define a portfolio's VAR, one first must choose two quantitative factors: the length of the holding horizon, and the confidence level. Both are arbitrary. As an example, the latest proposal of the Basle Committee defines a VAR measure using a 99% confidence interval over 10 trading days. The resulting VAR is then multiplied by a safety factor of three to arrive at the minimum capital requirement for regulatory purposes.

Presumably, the 10-day period corresponds to the time needed for regulators to detect problems and take corrective action. Presumably also, the choice of a 99% confidence level reflects the trade-off between the desire of regulators to ensure a safe and sound financial system and the adverse effect of capital requirements on bank profits. Different choices of horizon and confidence level will result in trivially different VAR numbers.

1. Measuring value-at-risk

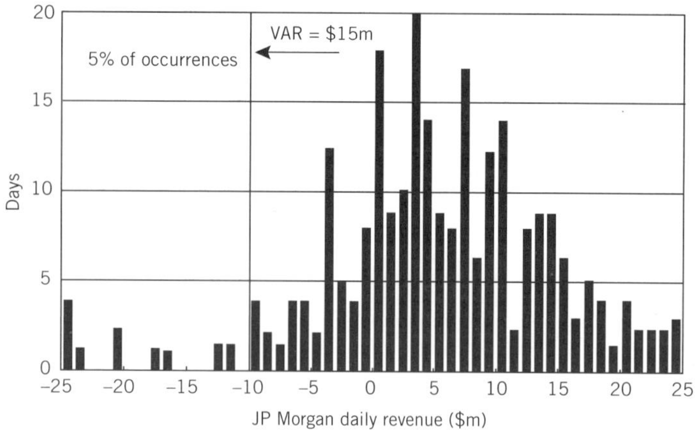

The significance of the quantitative factors depends on how they are to be used. If the resulting VARs are directly used for the choice of a capital cushion, then the choice of the confidence level is crucial. This choice should reflect the company's degree of risk aversion and the cost of a loss exceeding the VAR. Higher risk aversion, or greater costs, implies that a larger amount of capital should be available to cover possible losses, thus leading to a higher confidence level.

In contrast, if VAR numbers are used only to provide a company-wide yardstick to compare risks among different markets, then the choice of the confidence level is not very important. Assuming a normal distribution, disparate VAR measures are easy to convert into a common number.

To compute the VAR of a portfolio, define W_0 as the initial investment, and R as its rate of return. The portfolio value at the end of the target horizon is $W = W_0(1 + R)$. Define μ and σ as the annual mean and standard deviation of R, respectively, and Δt as the time interval considered. If successive returns are uncorrelated, the expected return and risk are then $\mu\Delta t$ and $\sigma\sqrt{\Delta t}$ over the holding horizon.

VAR is defined as the dollar loss, relative to what was expected; that is,

$$\begin{aligned} VAR &= E(W) - W^* \\ &= W_0(\mu - R^*) \end{aligned} \qquad (1)$$

where W^* is the lowest portfolio value at given confidence level c. Finding VAR is equivalent to identifying the minimum value, W^*, or the cutoff return, R^*.

VAR FOR GENERAL DISTRIBUTIONS

In its most general form, VAR can be derived from the probability distribution for the future portfolio value $f(w)$. At a given confidence level, c, we wish to find the worst possible realisation W^*, such that the probability of exceeding this value is c, where:

$$c = \int_{W^*}^{\infty} f(w)dw \qquad (2)$$

or such that the probability of a value lower than

W^* is $1-c$, where

$$1-c=\int_{-\infty}^{W^*} f(w)dw. \tag{3}$$

In other words, the area from $-\infty$ to W^* must sum to $1-c$, which might be, say, 5%. This specification is valid for any distribution, discrete or continuous, fat- or thin-tailed. As an example, in its 1994 annual report JP Morgan revealed that its daily trading VAR averaged $15 million at the 95% level over one day. This number can be derived from Figure 1, which reports the distribution of JP Morgan's daily revenues in 1994.

From Figure 1, we find the average revenue is about $5 million. Next, we have to find the observation (also called a quantile) such that 5% of the distribution is on its left side. There are 254 observations, so we need to find W^* such that the number of observations to its left is $254 \times 0.05=13$. This exercise yields W^* equal to –$10 million and a daily VAR of $15 million.

VAR FOR NORMAL DISTRIBUTIONS

If the distribution can be assumed to be normal, the computation can be simplified considerably. By using a multiplicative factor that is a function of the confidence level, VAR can be derived directly from the portfolio standard deviation.

First, map the general distribution $f(w)$ into a standard normal distribution $\Phi(\varepsilon)$ in which the random variable has a mean of zero and a standard deviation of 1. The cutoff return, R^*, can be associated with a standard normal deviate α such that

$$-\alpha=-\frac{\mu\Delta t-R^*}{\sigma\sqrt{\Delta t}}. \tag{4}$$

Then, VAR may be found in terms of portfolio value W^*, cutoff return R^*, or normal deviate α; that is,

$$\begin{aligned}1-c&=\int_{-\infty}^{W^*} f(w)dw\\&=\int_{-\infty}^{R^*} f(r)dr\\&=\int_{-\infty}^{-\alpha}\Phi(\varepsilon)d\varepsilon.\end{aligned} \tag{5}$$

To report VAR at the 95% confidence level, for example, the 5% left-tailed deviate from a standard normal distribution can be found from standard normal tables as 1.645. Once α is identified, VAR can be recovered as

$$\text{VAR}=W_0\times\alpha\sigma\sqrt{\Delta t}. \tag{6}$$

The key result is that VAR is associated with the standard deviation only.

For instance, for the JP Morgan example from Figure 1, the standard deviation of the distribution is $9.2 million. Therefore, the normal-distribution VAR is

$$\begin{aligned}\alpha(\sigma W_0)&=1.65\times\$9.2\text{ million}\\&=\$15.2\text{ million}.\end{aligned}$$

This number is very close to the VAR obtained from the general distribution, showing that the normal approximation provides a good estimate of VAR.

SIGMA-BASED VAR

Generally, this method applies to any probability function besides the normal, a convenient attribute because many financial variables have fatter tails (ie more extreme observations) than the normal distribution. Most notably, the stock market crash of October 1987 was a 20 standard deviation event - one that under a normal distribution should never have happened. This behaviour is particularly worrisome because VAR attempts to describe tail behaviour precisely.

One possible explanation is that volatility changes through time, increasing in times of greater than normal turbulence. A stationary model might then erroneously view large observations as outliers, when they are really drawn from a distribution with temporarily greater dispersion. Indeed, the recent literature on time-variation in second moments provides overwhelming evidence that variances on a variety of financial assets do change over time.[3]

Even controlling for time variation, however, residual returns still appear to be fat-tailed. One simple method to account for these tails is to model a Student's *t* distribution, which is characterised by an additional parameter, called "degrees of freedom" (v) that controls the size of tails. As v grows large, the distribution converges to a normal distribution.

Table 1 provides estimates of v for a number of daily price returns over the 1990–94 period. Typically, v is in the range of 4 to 8, which confirms the existence of fat tails.

Table 1. Estimates of degrees of freedom for the *t* distribution

Asset	Estimated parameter
US stocks	6.8
DM/$ exchange rate	8.0
DM/£ exchange rate	4.6
US long bond	4.4
US three-month T-Bill	4.5

To find the VAR under a t distribution, Equation 5 still applies, but Φ is replaced by the standard t distribution, and α by the appropriate $(1 - c)$ deviate. For example, for a t with ν equal to 6 at the 95% confidence level, α equals 1.943.

Thus, for many distributions, the dispersion can be summarised by one parameter, the standard deviation. This approach applies to most financial prices, stock prices, bond prices, exchange rates and commodities. Of course, it is inappropriate for strongly asymmetric distributions, such as positions in options. With large portfolios such as trading portfolios of commercial banks, however, the issue is one of fatness in tails, not asymmetry.

Evaluating VAR

So far, much of the analysis has been standard fare. What is less recognised, however, is the effect of estimation error. Indeed, all VAR measures are merely estimates. VAR measures are exact only when the underlying distribution is measured with an infinite number of observations. In practice, data are available for only a limited time period.

Various methods can be used to create VAR measures. "Historical-simulation" methods replicate the behaviour of the current portfolio over a sample of previous days. "Delta-normal" methods summarise risk factors by a variance-covariance matrix estimated from historical data. JP Morgan's RiskMetrics system, for instance, provides an application of the delta-normal method in which risk measures are time-varying. In each case, using different time periods will invariably lead to different measures of VAR. The issue is whether sampling variation leads to material changes in VAR.

This possibility is why sensitivity analysis of VAR is a useful exercise. Beder (1995), for instance, compares VAR results from different models. (See Chapter 17.) Risk was measured at a two-week (10-day) horizon at the 5% level for a \$1 million bond portfolio. Historical-simulation methods based on the previous 100 and 250 days yielded VARs of \$2,000 and \$17,000, respectively. The RiskMetrics method yielded a VAR of \$18,200. These discrepancies appear to be wide and unsettling.

Upon further inspection, the historical-simulation method using 100 days appears to have been inadequate because of the small number of effective observations: only 10 (100 historical observations divided by the horizon of 10 business days). Such a small sample size makes the 5% left tail of a distribution difficult to measure. Otherwise, the remaining measures of VARs are in line with each other.

This experiment demonstrates the need for a good understanding of the methodology behind VAR.

The question is whether discrepancies arise because of fundamental differences in methodologies, or simply because of sampling variation.

ESTIMATION ERROR IN QUANTILE-BASED VAR

For arbitrary distributions, the cth quantile can be empirically determined from the historical distribution as $\hat{q}(c)$. Of course, some sampling error is associated with the statistic. Kendall (1994), for instance, showed that the asymptotic standard error of the sample quantile, $\hat{q}$, is derived as

$$se(\hat{q}) = \sqrt{\frac{c(1-c)}{Tf(q)^2}} \qquad (7)$$

where T is the sample size and $f(.)$ is the probability distribution function evaluated at the quantile q. Kupiec (1995) pointed out that this standard error can be quite large and argued that this method does not provide "suitable benchmarks" for measuring VAR. In particular, the standard error increases markedly as the confidence level increases. In other words, the estimate grows increasingly unreliable farther into the left tail; that is the 1% quantile is less reliable than the 10% quantile.

This phenomenon is illustrated in Figures 2 and 3, where the expected quantile and two standard error intervals are plotted for the normal and Student distributions, respectively.

For the normal distribution, the 5% left-tailed interval is centred around 1.645. With T equal to

2. Confidence bands for sample quantile: normal distribution

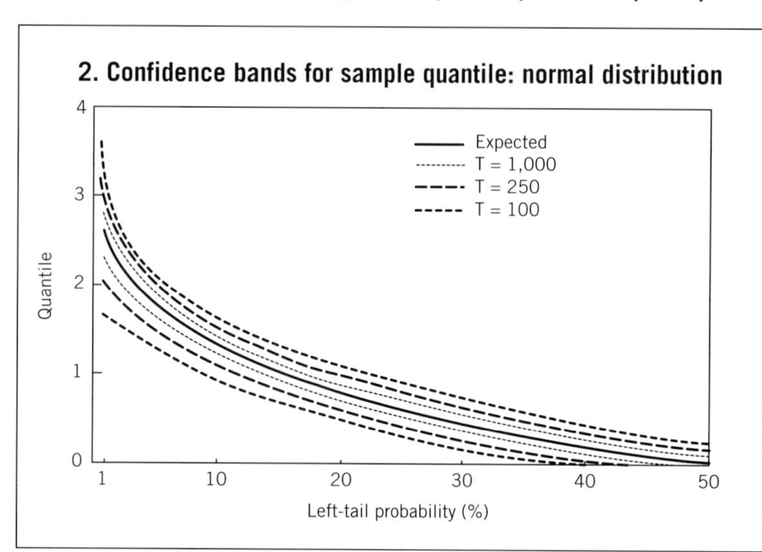

100, a two standard error confidence interval is 1.24 to 2.04, which is quite large. With 250 observations, which correspond to one year of trading days, the interval is still 1.38 to 1.91. With $T = 1{,}000$, the interval shrinks to 1.51 to 1.78. The interval widens substantially as one moves to more extreme quantiles. For instance, the same interval for the 1% quantile is 2.09 to 2.56 with T equal to 1,000. As expected, more imprecision is found in the extreme tails, which have fewer data points.

Contrast these results with Figure 3, which displays confidence bands for a *t* distribution with 6 degrees of freedom, typical of financial data. The figure shows that the α deviates are greater for the *t* distribution than for the normal distribution; confidence bands are also much wider. For instance, the 5% quantile has an expected value of 1.943 and a band of [1.33, 2.56] with $T = 100$. This interval is much wider than for the normal distribution.

These observations bring us back to an unresolved issue in the computation of VAR: the choice of the confidence level is completely arbitrary, especially since the Basle Committee has decided to multiply the VAR by another arbitrary factor, 3. Commercial banks now report their VARs with various incompatible parameters.[4] Given this arbitrariness, we might want to choose a level c that provides the best sampling characteristics.

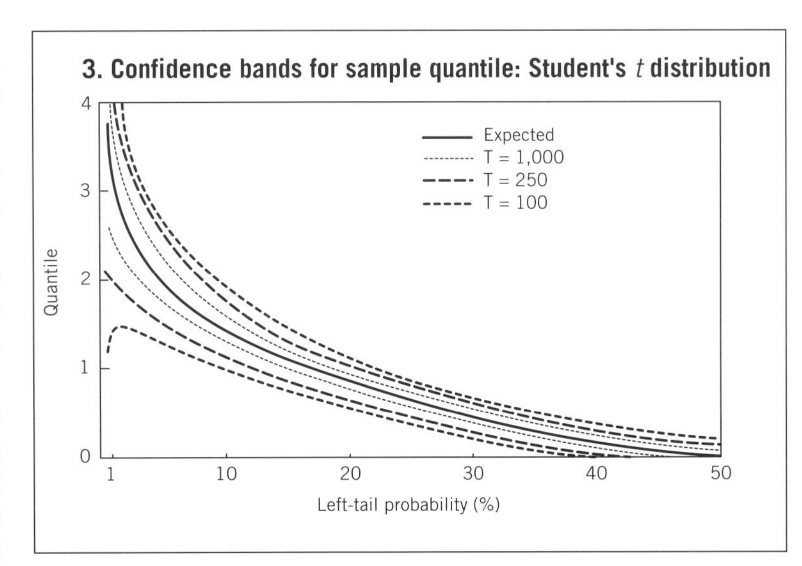

ESTIMATION ERROR IN SIGMA-BASED VAR

Additional precision might be gained by directly measuring the standard deviation, which can be multiplied by an appropriate scaling factor to obtain the desired quantile.

For the normal distribution, for instance, the VAR can be computed in two steps: first, compute the sample standard deviation, s; then, multiply the number by a scaling factor, $\alpha(c)$, to obtain the desired confidence level - say 1.645 for a 95% confidence level for a normal distribution.

Using this method, the standard error of the estimated quantile is

$$se(\alpha s) = \alpha \times se(s). \tag{8}$$

This method leads to substantial efficiency gains relative to using the estimated quantile. In the case of the normal distribution, for instance, we know that the sample standard deviation is a sufficient statistic for the dispersion and also is the most efficient; that is, it has the lowest standard error. Intuitively, this efficiency is explained by the fact that s uses information about the whole distribution (in terms of all squared deviations around the mean), but a quantile uses only the ranking of observations and the two observations around the estimated value.

For the normal distribution, we have an analytical formula for the standard error of s, which is

$$se(s|\Phi) = \sigma\sqrt{\frac{1}{2T}}. \tag{9}$$

Figure 4 displays the standard error of the estimated quantile using the two methods applied to a normal distribution with T equal to 250. As theory would suggest, the sample standard deviation method has uniformly lower standard errors and is, therefore, uniformly superior to the sample quantile method.

A similar adjustment can be made for the *t* distribution, for which the quantile can be estimated from the sample standard deviation. Without analytical results for se(s), however, simulations must be used to determine the advan-

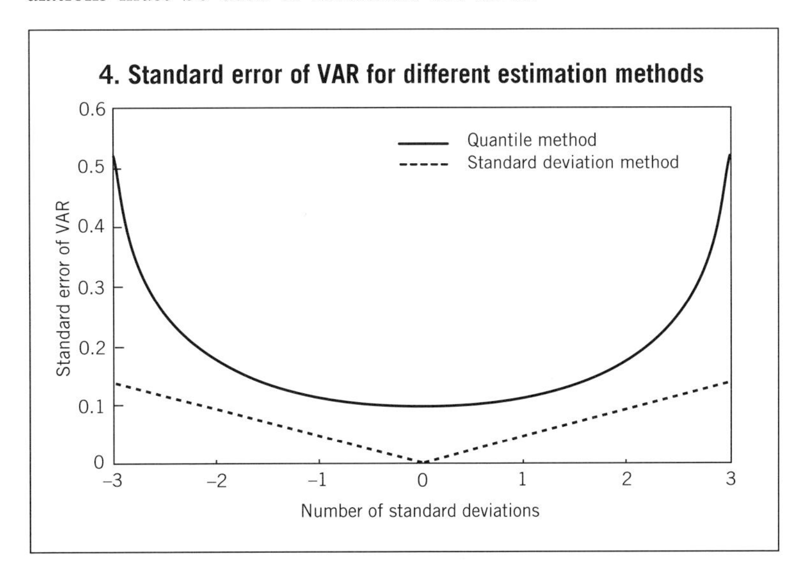

Table 2. VAR statistics: normal distribution

	T = 100			T = 250			T = 1,000			
	Simulation		Asymptotic	Simulation		Asymptotic	Simulation		Asymptotic	
Statistic	Average	Std error	std error	Average	Std error	std error	Average	Std error	std error	Exact
Std deviation (s)	0.998	0.071	0.071	0.999	0.045	0.045	1.000	0.022	0.022	1.000
VAR – Method 1										
Quantile (10%)	−1.278	0.166	0.171	−1.279	0.106	0.108	−1.281	0.053	0.054	−1.282
Quantile (5%)	−1.640	0.204	0.211	−1.662	0.133	0.134	−1.644	0.066	0.067	−1.645
Quantile (1%)	−2.332	0.339	0.373	−2.405	0.238	0.236	−2.323	0.116	0.118	−2.326
VAR – Method 2										
α(10%)s	−1.279	0.091	0.091	−1.280	0.058	0.057	−1.282	0.029	0.029	−1.282
α(5%)s	−1.641	0.117	0.116	−1.643	0.074	0.074	−1.644	0.037	0.037	−1.645
α(1%)s	−2.321	0.165	0.164	−2.323	0.105	0.104	−2.325	0.052	0.052	−2.326

Note: Averages and standard errors based on 10,000 replications. Underlying distribution is the standard normal distribution N(0,1). Asymptotic standard errror is analytically derived from exact parameters.

Table 3. VAR statistics: Student's *t* distribution

	T = 100			T = 250			T = 1,000			
	Simulation		Asymptotic	Simulation		Asymptotic	Simulation		Asymptotic	
Statistic	Average	Std error	std error	Average	Std error	std error	Average	Std error	std error	Exact
Std deviation (s)	1.216	0.128	na	1.221	0.084	na	1.224	0.044	na	1.225
VAR – Method 1										
Quantile (10%)	−1.439	0.217	0.222	−1.439	0.139	0.140	−1.440	0.069	0.070	−1.440
Quantile (5%)	−1.949	0.309	0.313	−1.977	0.200	0.198	−1.944	0.098	0.099	−1.943
Quantile (1%)	3.267	0.848	0.781	−3.362	0.567	0.494	−3.148	0.246	0.247	−3.143
VAR – Method 2										
α(10%)s	−1.430	0.151	na	−1.436	0.098	na	−1.439	0.050	na	−1.440
α(5%)s	−1.926	0.205	na	−1.934	0.132	na	−1.939	0.068	na	−1.943
α(1%)s	−3.118	0.329	na	−3.131	0.214	na	−3.138	0.110	na	−3.143

Note: Averages and standard errors based on 10,000 replications. Underlying distribution is a Student's *t* distribution with 5 degrees of freedom. Asymptotic standard errors are analytically derived from exact parameters.

tage of the s-based estimator over the usual quantile. Simulations are also useful for assessing the small-sample properties of these estimators.

COMPARISONS OF METHODS

Tables 2 and 3 describe VAR statistics from drawings from a normal and *t* distributions, respectively, using simulations based on 10,000 replications. Two methods are compared: Method 1 is based on the sample quantile and Method 2 is based on the sample standard deviation.

For Table 2 with one year of data (T = 250), for example, the standard errors of VAR estimated using the two methods are generally in close accordance with the asymptotic numbers but the standard deviation method is about twice as efficient as the quantile method. For instance, the standard error of the 95% VAR for Method 1 is 0.133, as compared with 0.074 for Method 2, an improvement of about 45%.

The advantage is also substantial for the *t* distribution. For instance, using the same parameters as before, the standard error of Method 1 is 0.200, as compared with 0.132 for Method 2, an improvement of about 35%. The advantage is even greater for quantiles farther in the tail, where the improvement is in the order of 60%.

In practical terms, substantial improvement in precision can be obtained by switching estimation technique. Bankers Trust, for example, reported a daily VAR of $35 million at the 99% level. Assuming this number came from the sample quantile based on one year of data from a *t* distribution, the associated confidence interval is [$24, $46] million – not particularly tight. In contrast, if the number were based on the sample standard deviation method, the interval would shrink to [$30, $40] million.

One remaining issue is whether the distributions underlying the simulations adequately represent empirical distributions of financial returns. Table 4 presents efficiency comparisons for an actual distribution: daily returns on the on-

Table 4. VAR statistics: Empirical distribution, daily return on 30-year bond, 1990–94

	T = 100		T = 250		T = 1,000		
	Simulation		Simulation		Simulation		
Statistic	Average	Std error	Average	Std error	Average	Std error	Exact
Std deviation (s)	0.610	0.061	0.612	0.039	0.612	0.020	0.613
VAR – Method 1							
Quantile (10%)	−0.754	0.121	−0.757	0.078	−0.758	0.038	−0.760
Quantile (5%)	−0.996	0.132	−1.010	0.078	−1.003	0.041	−1.007
Quantile (1%)	−1.631	0.463	−1.643	0.313	−1.524	0.086	−1.534
VAR – Method 2							
$\alpha(10\%)s$	−0.757	0.076	−0.759	0.049	−0.760	0.024	−0.760
$\alpha(5\%)s$	−1.002	0.101	−1.005	0.065	−1.006	0.032	−1.007
$\alpha(1\%)s$	−1.526	0.153	−1.530	0.098	−1.532	0.049	−1.534

Note: Averages and standard errors based on 10,000 replications. Empirical distribution is bootstrapped from actual distribution of daily returns on the current 30-year bond from 1990–94 (1,259 days).

the-run 30-year bond from 1990 to 1994. The distribution is free to take any form – fat-tailed, asymmetric, and so on. I took this distribution as the true distribution, then bootstrapped it – that is, sampled with replacement – to generate random drawings. As before, the table shows that the standard deviation method is much more efficient than the sample quantile method, with standard errors typically about one-third to two-thirds lower.

These results clearly indicate that estimation error in the estimated quantiles can be substantially reduced by using a multiple of the sample standard deviation. When the distribution is normal, the deviates can be obtained from a normal distribution table. In practice, when the tails appear to be too fat, a *t* distribution, from which deviates are readily available, can be fitted easily.[5]

Conclusions

The rapidly spreading use of VAR must be seen as a vast improvement over antiquated or non-existent risk management practices, some of which have caused financial disasters. One of the lessons of the Orange County, California, bankruptcy, for example, is that municipalities investing in the pool would have been more careful had the value-at-risk of their investment been clearly explained to them.[6] In addition, investors would not have had the excuse that they did not know what they were getting into, which would have limited the rash of lawsuits against third parties. This experience demonstrates why regulators now embrace VAR as a means of improving transparency and stability in financial markets.

The benefits of VAR should not, however, mask its shortcomings. Any VAR number is itself measured with some error, or estimation risk. Thus, understanding the statistical methodology is important in order to interpret VAR estimates. This interpretation would be made easier not only by reporting a single VAR number, but also by reporting a confidence band around it.

The main purpose of this chapter was to show the extent to which VAR is affected by estimation risk and also to make recommendations on how to measure quantiles. For the distributions considered here, estimating quantiles from a multiple of the sample standard deviation is far superior to estimating them directly from sample quantiles. Therefore recognising estimation error can lead to better measurement methods.

In the end, the greatest benefit of VAR may lie in the imposition of a structured methodology for thinking critically about risk. Financial institutions that go through the process of computing their VARs are forced to confront their exposure to financial risks and to set up a risk management function to supervise the front and back offices. Thus, the process of getting to VAR may be as important as the number itself. Nevertheless, VAR is undoubtedly here to stay.

1 *The Basle Committee consists of central bankers from a group of 10 countries. This committee sets minimum standards of capital requirements in member countries.*

2 *In addition, for complex portfolios involving positions in options that are difficult to price, VAR is also affected by "model risk," which results from differences in valuations that can be traced to different option valuation models. Another conceptual problem is that, especially over long horizons, VAR does not account for changing positions. Sound risk management practices typically decrease the size of positions in response to losses or increasing volatility, which decreases the worst loss relative to a static VAR measure. For further analysis of limitations of VAR methods, see Jorion (1996).*

3 *For a review, see, for instance Bollerslev, Chou and Kroner (1992). Time-series models that allow for time variation in risk can also capture structural changes as long as these do not occur too abruptly.*

4 *For instance, Bankers Trust uses a 99% level of confidence; Chemical Bank and Chase Manhattan, a 97.5% level; Citibank, a 95.4% level; and BankAmerica and JP Morgan a 95% level.*

5 *These simulations assumed that the underlying distribution was known. If the distribution is truly irregular because of, for example, heavy optionality in the portfolio, nonparametric methods such as kernel estimation can be used to provide estimates of the quantile and associated standard errors. These methods lead to improved precision by smoothing the distribution. See, for example, Sheather and Marron (1990).*

6 *For a description of the Orange County disaster, see Jorion (1995).*

BIBLIOGRAPHY

Beder, T. Styblo, 1995, "VAR.: Seductive but Dangerous," *Financial Analysts Journal*, September/October, pp. 12–24; reprinted as Chapter 17 of the present volume.

Bollerslev, T., R. Chou, and K. Kroner, 1992 "Arch Modeling in Finance: A Review of the Theory and Empirical Evidence," *Journal of Econometrics*, April/May, pp. 5–59.

Jorion, P., 1995, *Big Bets Gone Bad; Derivatives and Bankruptcy in Orange County*, San Diego Academic Press.

Jorion, P., 1996, *Value-at-Risk: The New Benchmark for Controlling Market Risk*, Chicago, Irwin.

Kendall, M., 1994, *Kendall's Advanced Theory of Statistics*, New York, Halstead Press.

Kupiec, P., 1995, "Techniques for Verifying the Accuracy of Risk Measurement Models," *Journal of Derivatives*, winter, pp. 73–84, reprinted as Chapter 24 of the present volume.

Sheather, S. and J. Marron, 1990, "Kernel Quantile Estimators," *American Statistical Association Journal*, June, pp. 410–16.

24

Techniques for Verifying the Accuracy of Risk Measurement Models*

Paul H. Kupiec

Board of Governors of the Federal Reserve System

Given their function both as internal risk management tools and as potential regulatory measures of risk exposure, it is important to quantify the accuracy of an institution's VAR estimates. This paper shows that the formal statistical procedures that would typically be used in performance-based VAR verification tests require large samples to produce a reliable assessment of a model's accuracy in predicting the size and likelihood of very low probability events. Verification test statistics based on historical trading profits and losses have very poor power in small samples, so it does not appear possible for a bank or its supervisor to verify the accuracy of a VAR estimate unless many years of performance data are available. Historical simulation-based verification test statistics also require long samples to generate accurate results: estimates of 0.01 critical values exhibit substantial errors even in samples as large as ten years of daily data.

This paper considers alternative statistical techniques that could be used to verify the accuracy of estimates of the tail values of the distribution of potential gains and losses for a portfolio of securities, futures, and derivative positions. These so-called reality checks have been advanced as a tool for determining the accuracy of risk exposure estimates generated by risk measurement models. Dealer banks and broker-dealers typically maintain internal risk measurement models that are used to estimate the daily global exposures generated by the institution's portfolio of financial assets and derivative obligations (see Group of Thirty [1993]). Risk exposures are typically quantified in terms of a "value-at-risk" estimate.

A VAR estimate corresponds to a specific critical value of a portfolio's potential one-day profit and loss probability distribution. Typically, a VAR estimate is defined to be a loss large enough so that the probability that the portfolio could post a larger loss is at most some specified value, like 1% or perhaps 5%. A VAR measure thus corresponds to a specific left-hand critical value of the portfolio's potential profit and loss distribution.

The Basle Bank Supervisors Committee proposes that critical value estimates from a bank's internal risk measurement model become the basis for a bank's market risk regulatory capital requirement. Its proposal defines VAR in terms of a two-week holding period (see Bank for International Settlements [1995]). Similarly, under a proposal by the Derivatives Policy Group

This paper was first published in The Journal of Derivatives, *Winter (1995), pp.73–84. This copyrighted material is reprinted (with minor amendments) with permission from The Journal of Derivatives, a publication of Institutional Investor, Inc. 488 Madison Avenue, New York 10022. The conclusions in this paper are those of the author and do not represent the views of the Federal Reserve Board, or any of the Federal Reserve Banks. The author is grateful to Cedomir Crnkovic, Greg Duffee, Mark Fisher, Bob Litterman, Jim O'Brien, Pat Parkinson, Matt Pritsker, and Larry Wall for useful discussions or comments on an earlier draft of this article.

(DPG), internal model risk exposure estimates could be used to establish capital guidelines for the derivatives activities of unregulated affiliates of US broker-dealers (see Derivatives Policy Group, (1995)).

Given their function both as internal risk management tools and as potential regulatory measures of risk exposure, it is important to quantify the accuracy of an institution's model-based risk exposure measures. Despite the importance of accuracy assessment, little research has considered the statistical techniques that would be appropriate for judging the quality of a financial institution's VAR estimates.[1]

The Group of Thirty "Derivatives" study (1995) suggests that institutions perform "reality checks" for judging model performance. Recommendation 8, for example, suggests that an institution's VAR estimates be compared against its portfolio's subsequent profit and loss outcomes, but it does not provide any detail regarding the formal statistics that facilitate the comparison. Similarly, the Basle Supervisors Committee recommends back testing as a means of verifying the accuracy of a bank's risk exposure estimates, but again the recommendation does not provide the details of the proposed verification test.

This paper derives the formal statistical properties of alternative statistics that can be used to verify the accuracy of a VAR estimate. The procedures use historical profits and losses on the institution's portfolio or historical simulation exercises to verify the accuracy of an institution's estimate of its potential loss exposure.

The results indicate that, unless a relatively long performance history or historical simulation data base is available, there are significant statistical difficulties surrounding verification of VAR estimates. The results have implications both for banks that wish to assess the accuracy of their internal risk measurement models as well as for supervisors who must verify the accuracy of an institution's risk measurement model and assign an appropriate market risk scaling factor under the Basle proposal.

Given the nature of internal model risk exposure estimates, performance-based verification tests should compare one-day potential loss estimates with one-day actual performance data. Although the one day horizon of comparison may be self-evident to an institution assessing the performance of its own internal risk measurement model, analysis suggests that the one-day horizon is equally appropriate for a supervisor attempting to verify an internal model-based capital charge.

Even when tests are based on daily performance comparisons, small sample test statistics have extremely poor power for detecting a model or institution that habitually underestimates potential loss amounts. If only a small history of performance is available, moreover, a model or institution can substantially underestimate the magnitude of its potential losses with little probability of detection either internally by the bank's risk management staff or externally by a supervisor using a performance-based verification test. Reliable performance-based verification techniques require a relatively long comparison sample period.

Verification schemes need not be based on historical performance. If the distributions of the underlying financial factors are stationary, loss exposure estimates can, in theory, be corroborated using the critical value estimates from simulations of the historical loss distribution of an institution's current portfolio. The results presented here show that historical simulation-based verification schemes also perform very poorly unless historical simulation sample sizes are large.

When potential loss distributions are fat-tailed, simulation-based critical value estimates exhibit significant biases and have standard errors of substantial magnitude, even in relatively large samples. The characteristics of simulation-based verification tests do not recommend their use either as a technique for estimating tail values or as a means of performing validation checks of risk exposure estimates.

Because reliable performance-based verification tests require significant amounts of data, the verification process is necessarily time-consuming. If a model is determined to be inaccurate, the model will be altered, the institution will begin accumulating a new performance data sample, and a substantial amount of time must elapse before the accuracy of the new model can be confidently accepted. Time considerations have implications for the VAR multiplication factor of the Basle proposal. If the magnitude of the factor is linked to statistical verification, in the event a bank's model is deemed inaccurate, the results suggest that the bank's VAR scaling factor should remain elevated for a significant time period.

The regulatory verification problem

Under the internal models proposal for setting market risk capital requirements, banks would use their internal risk measurement models to estimate the distribution of potential loss exposure associated with their trading portfolio positions.[2] Regulation would require banks to report an estimate of the size of the potential loss that would be exceeded less than 1% of the time in a two-week period. This loss estimate would, in effect, be an estimate of the 1% lefthand critical value of the trading account's two-week potential profit and loss distribution.

Market risk capital requirements would be some multiple - the "scaling factor" - of the loss associated with the 1% critical value reported by the bank. The scaling factor would (under the current version of the proposal) have a minimum value of 3, which would be increased if the supervisor concludes that a bank's risk measurement model is inaccurate.

Despite the central importance of model verification, there is no commonly accepted standard statistical approach for determining the accuracy of VAR estimates. A typical VAR model estimates potential changes in portfolio value by approximating the value changes for the component instruments as linear functions of the changes in their underlying pricing factors (eg default-free interest rates of different maturities). The coefficients of the pricing factors are derived from the coefficients in a Taylor series expansion of a theoretical pricing model. (See RiskMetrics Technical Document (1995)).

As VAR models are not statistical regression models, there is no ex ante measure of their goodness-of-fit. Presumably a model-based loss estimate could be considered accurate if a bank's actual losses do not frequently exceed its *ex ante* internal model-based critical value estimates, or if its loss estimates do not exceed the potential losses that would have been generated by the portfolio if it had been held by the bank through some historic period.

THE MONITORING HORIZON

The use of historical performance data to verify internal model-based estimates of long holding-period potential loss exposures is complicated by the endogenous nature of the portfolio's risk. (For a more detailed discussion, see Kupiec and O'Brien (1995)). Over the regulatory monitoring interval, the bank can and will adjust its trading risk exposure.

Any scheme that attempts to verify a long-horizon risk exposure estimate with actual portfolio profits and losses is comparing the risk estimate for a portfolio of fixed composition to the profit or loss performance generated by a series of portfolios that differ in composition. Indeed, even over a single day, an institution's risk profile can be significantly altered by intraday changes in positions. If intraday exposure changes are significant, verification tests should be based on performance calculated by re-marking the original portfolio to market.

Any true long-horizon risk exposure verification scheme would also have to be based on the long-horizon profits or losses generated by repricing the initial portfolio. Monitoring schemes based on historical performance are internally consistent only when they compare a portfolio's potential loss estimate with the same portfolio's actual performance.

A final consideration is the time period necessary to conduct meaningful verification analysis and detect under-reporting banks. The statistical analysis shows that relatively large sample sizes are necessary if verification tests are to have any power against important alternative hypotheses. The time necessary to accumulate a large enough sample of independent two-week horizons is too long to be useful for supervisory purposes. Thus, both data processing and statistical power considerations suggest one-day performance comparisons.

ALTERNATIVE STATISTICAL METHODS FOR REGULATORY MONITORING

If portfolio performance can be monitored, day-to-day profits and losses determine the outcome of a binomial event: either the bank's loss on trading activities is less than its *ex ante* estimate (a success), or the loss on trading activities exceeds the *ex ante* estimate (a failure). If daily forecasts are efficient, potential loss estimates are independent across days, and the performance data are distributed as a series of independent draws from a Bernoulli distribution. Because a supervisor has no knowledge of the parametric form of the bank's profit and loss distribution - and indeed there is good reason to believe that the form of the distribution changes depending on the composition of the bank's portfolio - the size of the differences between a bank's potential loss estimate and its actual gains or losses is not informative.

The null hypothesis - that the probability of a failure on any day is 1% - can be tested in a variety of ways.[3] The appropriate test depends on how the bank is being monitored and the performance comparison sample size available. If the bank is monitored continuously, and a single failure is observed, the supervisor can formally test the hypothesis that the bank's true failure rate is the 0.01 used for its reported VAR. An alternative approach is to monitor the bank at less frequent intervals, and test the null hypothesis using the proportion of failures observed in the monitoring period.

As an alternative to monitoring a bank's actual performance, the bank's loss estimates can be compared periodically to a simulated performance distribution. In this approach, the critical values of the bank's portfolio loss distribution are generated by historically simulating the day-to-day gains and losses the bank's current portfolio would have generated if it were held over some fixed historical time period. This verification technique is termed the historical simulation approach.

The internal verification problem

Institutions must also assess the accuracy of their risk measurement models. The task of assessing the accuracy of an institution's VAR estimates is statistically the same, whether the assessment is made by a supervisor or by an institution's risk management staff. Although an institution's internal staff could have better information about the parametric form of the potential profit or loss distribution, in verifying tail loss estimates it appears that such knowledge will have little additional value.

Verification tests can be constructed that use information about the parametric form of a portfolio's potential profit and loss distribution. For example, Crnkovic and Drachman (CD) (1995) use Kuiper's (1962) results to construct a goodness-of-fit measure for an estimate of the entire profit and loss distribution. Using a symmetric weighting function, CD specialise their goodness-of-fit measure into a test of the accuracy of a risk management model's tail probability estimates. Their weighting function places equal importance on the extreme profit and loss tail events. Using a weighting function that implicitly assumes the underlying distribution is symmetric, CD conclude from a Monte Carlo analysis that their testing procedure requires a minimum of 1,000 observations to be reliable.[4] If the symmetry assumption is discarded, the test would require additional data. Compared to CD's testing procedure, the VAR verification tests proposed in this study are computationally simpler and may be more accurate in smaller data sets.[5]

Consequently, even from the perspective of an institution's internal risk management staff, it is appropriate to construct VAR verification tests from the series of Bernoulli trial outcomes generated by a daily performance comparison. Alternatively, if a performance history is not available, an institution might attempt to verify its VAR estimate by comparing it to the critical value of the portfolio's simulated historical loss distribution.

Verification tests based on the time until first failure

In a performance-based verification scheme, the initial monitoring statistic of interest is the number of observations until a failure is observed. A subsequent section develops the verification tests required when analysing a monitoring period that covers multiple failures. Let $\tilde{T}$ be a random variable that denotes the number of days until the first failure is recorded. If p is the probability of a failure on any given day, the probability of observing the first failure on day V is given by:

$$\mathrm{Prob}\left(\tilde{T} = V\right) = p(1-p)^{V-1}. \tag{1}$$

$\tilde{T}$ has a geometric distribution with an expected value – the expected number of observations until the first failure is observed – of $1/p$. For example, when $p = 0.01$, the average time until the first failure is 100; when $p = 0.05$, the average time until failure is 20.

Given a realisation for $\tilde{T}$, we want to test that the underlying potential loss estimates are consistent with the null hypothesis. A hypothesis test can be constructed using the likelihood ratio (LR) test procedure. The Neyman-Pearson lemma establishes that the LR test is the uniformly most powerful against simple alternative hypotheses in this context.

Given a value for $\tilde{T}$, $\tilde{T}=V$, the LR statistic for testing the null hypothesis $p=p^*$ is given by $LR(V,p^*)$:

$$LR(V,p^*) = -2\log\left[p^*(1-p^*)^{V-1}\right] + 2\log\left[(1/V)(1-1/V)^{V-1}\right]. \tag{2}$$

Under the null hypothesis, $LR(V,p^*)$ has a chi-squared distribution with one degree of freedom.[6] The 5% critical value of this distribution is 3.841; that is, if the likelihood ratio exceeds 3.841, the null hypothesis that $p=p^*$ can be rejected at a 5% Type I error rate. The Type I error rate is the probability of incorrectly rejecting a true null hypothesis. Table 1 reports the two-sided acceptance regions for the 5% [TUFF (0.05)] and 10% [TUFF(0.10)] levels of the time until first failure (TUFF) test, for various null hypotheses. Notice that the non-rejection region grows larger as the null hypothesis values of

$p = p^*$ approach zero.

When testing the null hypothesis $p^* = 0.01$, the TUFF (0.05) critical values for V are $V = 6$ and $V = 439$. That is, if the first failure occurs before the seventh trading day, it can be concluded that $p > 0.01$. If the first failure occurs after the 438th trading day, it can be concluded that $p < 0.01$.

For a null hypothesis of $p^* = 0.05$, the TUFF (0.05) test critical values for V are: between 0 and 1 (an impossibility), and 87. The lower critical value implies that it is impossible to determine at the 5% level whether $p > 0.05$, because under the null hypothesis a failure occurs with 5% probability on the first draw. If V is greater than 87, it can be concluded at the 5% level that the loss estimates are consistent with a tail loss probability of less than 0.05.

The test of any null hypothesis for which p^* is 0.05 or larger will be associated with a TUFF (0.05) test non-rejection region that includes samples that realise a failure on the first observation. The implication is that the TUFF (0.05) test will reject these null hypotheses only when the true model error rate is smaller than 0.05. In other words, the TUFF (0.05) test does not have the ability to detect models with failure rates greater than 5%.

If the TUFF test Type I error rate is increased beyond the p^* value associated with the null hypothesis, the test can detect an alternative hypothesis for which $p > p^*$. For example, Table 1 reports the non-rejection region for the TUFF (0.10) test of $p^* = 0.05$. Notice that the TUFF (0.10) test will reject the null hypothesis if a failure is observed on the first observation.

The TUFF (0.05) test critical values reported in Table 1 indicate very large non-rejection regions for the null hypothesis where p^* is small. It may be somewhat surprising to observe that if the first failure occurs on the seventh trading day, the maximum likelihood estimate of p is (1/7) or 14.3%, and yet a null hypothesis of $p^* = 0.01$ cannot be rejected by the TUFF (0.05) test. Despite the fact that the LR test criterion generates the most powerful test using data on the time until the first failure, the substantial size of the region over which the null hypothesis cannot be rejected is an indication that the test statistic has a poor ability to distinguish among a wide range of interesting alternative hypotheses.

Table 2 reports the Type II error rates for selected TUFF (0.05) test values. A Type II error is the probability of accepting a false null hypothesis. For example, if the null hypothesis is $p^* = 0.01$, a Type II error is the probability of accepting the null hypothesis $p^* = 0.01$, when in fact the probability of a failure on any single observation is different from 0.01.

Table 1. Critical values for the TUFF test

Null hypothesis probability p^*	Non-rejection region for V 0.05 Type I error	Non-rejection region for V 0.10 Type I error
0.005	$11 < V < 879$	$21 < V < 729$
0.010	$6 < V < 439$	$10 < V < 364$
0.015	$4 < V < 292$	$7 < V < 242$
0.020	$3 < V < 219$	$5 < V < 182$
0.025	$2 < V < 175$	$4 < V < 145$
0.030	$2 < V < 146$	$3 < V < 121$
0.035	$2 < V < 125$	$3 < V < 103$
0.040	$1 < V < 109$	$3 < V < 90$
0.045	$1 < V < 97$	$2 < V < 80$
0.050	$V < 87$	$2 < V < 72$

V is the number of observations until the first failure is recorded.

Table 2. Selected Type II error rates for the TUFF (0.05) test

Null hypothesis probability	Alternative hypothesis	Type II error rate
$p^* = 0.010$	$p = 0.015$	0.898
$p^* = 0.010$	$p = 0.020$	0.868
$p^* = 0.010$	$p = 0.030$	0.808
$p^* = 0.010$	$p = 0.040$	0.751
$p^* = 0.010$	$p = 0.050$	0.698
$p^* = 0.025$	$p = 0.030$	0.908
$p^* = 0.025$	$p = 0.040$	0.884
$p^* = 0.025$	$p = 0.050$	0.857

The Type II error rate is the probability of accepting the false null hypothesis using a 5% level TUFF test when the specific alternative hypothesis is true.

The Type II error rate depends on the true underlying value of p that generates the data. The larger the true probability, the smaller the probability of committing a Type II error.

The error rates reported in Table 2 show that there is a very high probability that the null hypotheses $p^* = 0.01$ or $p^* = 0.025$ could be accepted by the TUFF (0.05) test even when a bank's true tail probability is far in excess of the null hypothesis value being tested. The high Type II error probabilities indicate that the TUFF test has very poor power characteristics.[7]

For example, Table 1 shows that if the first failure is observed between the 7th and 438th observation, the null hypothesis $p^* = 0.01$ cannot be rejected by the TUFF (0.05) test. Yet if the portfolio's true probability of experiencing a loss worse than the reported 1% level is $p^* = 0.02$, Table 2 shows that 86.8% of the time the TUFF (0.05) test would accept the false null hypothesis.

The difficulty of distinguishing between very small alternative VAR values (eg 0.01 and 0.02) may at first glance appear to be a point of academic interest with little practical significance. In

Table 3. Trade-off between Type I and Type II error rates for the TUFF test

Level of tests (Type I error)	Acceptance region	Type II error probability when true $p = 0.02$
0.05	$6 < V < 439$	0.868
0.10	$10 < V < 364$	0.784
0.15	$15 < V < 319$	0.722
0.20	$20 < V < 287$	0.651
0.25	$24 < V < 262$	0.598

fact, such small differences can have substantial economic importance.

Consider a fat-tailed probability distribution often used to model financial asset prices, such as the Student's *t* distribution. The 0.01 critical value of a *t* distribution with one degree of freedom is −31.82. The 0.02 critical value from the same distribution is −15.89. In this situation, a 0.02 cumulative probability tail loss underestimates the 99% VAR value by 100%. The particularly troubling aspect is that it would be virtually impossible for the regulatory authority or the bank's internal risk management staff to detect even such a gross underestimate using the TUFF (0.05) test.

Although the one degree of freedom *t* distribution is (intentionally) a dramatic illustration of the problem, the qualitative point of the example is general: slight differences in the cumulative probability attached to a VAR estimate can translate into substantial differences in potential loss amounts.

The TUFF (0.05) test Type II error rates can be reduced by accepting a greater probability of incorrectly rejecting a true null hypothesis. Table 3 reports the null hypothesis acceptance regions and the corresponding Type II error rates for the alternative $p = 0.02$ for the TUFF test of $p^* = 0.01$ under various Type I error rates. The Type II error rates reported show that the TUFF test of the null hypothesis $p^* = 0.01$ has poor power against the alternative $p = 0.02$ even for large Type I error rates.

The analysis suggests that the TUFF statistic has poor ability to distinguish reliably between alternative underlying values for the tail probability associated with a VAR estimate. Although the TUFF test is logically the first test to employ when initially undertaking a performance-based monitoring scheme, its power is limited by the small sample sizes for which it applies.

Performance tests based on proportion of failures

Continued monitoring beyond an observed failure will clearly add information that can be used to verify potential loss estimates. Provided the null hypothesis is not rejected, there are alternative ways to analyse additional performance data.[8]

Tests based only on the time between failures are inherently inefficient because they ignore information about the total number of failures that have occurred since monitoring began. When the TUFF test cannot reject the null hypothesis, verification tests should be based on the proportion of failures in the sample.

The probability of observing x failures regardless of order in a sample of size n is:

$$\text{binomial}[n, x](1 - p)^{n-x} p^x \tag{3}$$

where binomial $[n, x]$ signifies the binomial coefficient for n objects taken x at a time, and p is the probability of a failure on any one of the independent trials. The likelihood ratio test of the null hypothesis is again the uniformly most powerful test for a given sample size.

The LR test statistic is given by:

$$\begin{aligned} &-2\log\left[(1 - p^*)^{n-x}(p^*)^x\right] \\ &+2\log\left[(1 - [x/n])^{n-x}(x/n)^x\right] \end{aligned} \tag{4}$$

where p^* is the probability of a failure under the null hypothesis, n is the sample size, and x is the number of failures in the sample. We will call the test given in (4) the PF (proportion of failures) test. Under the null hypothesis, $p = p^*$, the PF test has a chi-squared distribution with one degree of freedom. For the specialised case of a single failure in a sample size of n, the PF test is mathematically identical to the TUFF test. Given this equivalence, this test also has the same poor power properties described at length earlier.

In a daily monitoring scheme, the PF test is used to compare the total number of failures observed to the total accumulated sample size. Table 4 enumerates the critical values of n (the sample size rejection regions) that are associated with alternative values for x (the number of observed failures) for testing alternative null hypotheses using the PF (0.05) test.

For example, assume that six failures are observed in a monitoring period. The values in Table 4 indicate that the null hypothesis $p^* = 0.01$ can be rejected if there are fewer than 241 days in the monitoring period. In other words, it would require six failures in less than one year to reject $p^* = 0.01$. Using the same six-failure example, the null hypothesis $p^* = 0.05$ would be rejected by the performance data if the monitoring period covers fewer than 50 days.

Instead of following the continuous monitoring scheme, it might be more convenient to collect a sample of performance-generated Bernoulli outcomes and perform a verification test for a fixed sample size. Table 5 reports the critical number of failures that correspond to PF (0.05) tests for alternative sample sizes and null hypotheses.

Like the TUFF test, the PF test has poor power characteristics in small samples. That is, in small samples the null hypothesis acceptance regions are large, so there is a significant probability that one will accept the null hypothesis when it is false. Table 6 reports the Type II error rates that correspond to selected PF (0.05) hypothesis testing situations. Notice that large sample sizes are required to reduce the PF (0.05) test Type II error rates.[9]

Because Type I and Type II error rates are inversely related, the power of the PF test could also be improved at the expense of increasing the Type I error rate in a reduced sample size, but the trade-off may not be acceptable in many circumstances. For example, suppose a supervisor wants to design a scheme that requires only one year of data and would detect at least 75% of all banks that attempt to report critical value estimates that are twice the 1% regulatory requirement. Such a scheme would allow a bank to record three or fewer failures in a 255-day trading year and still be deemed to meet the regulatory criterion by the supervisor's verification test.

The Type I error rate associated with this rule is about 75%.[10] This implies that in order to catch 75% of the banks under-reporting their potential loss exposures, the supervisor must be willing to falsely accuse of under-reporting 75% of all banks that are reporting accurately. As this example makes concrete, the trade-off between Type I and Type II errors is not very favourable even in samples as long as a year.

Table 4. Maximum sample size (n) for which the null hypothesis $p = p^*$ is rejected by a PF (0.05) test

Number of failures	$p^*=0.01$	$p^*=0.02$	$p^*=0.03$	$p^*=0.04$	$p^*=0.05$
x = 1	6	3	–	–	–
x = 2	34	17	11	9	–
x = 3	75	38	26	19	16
x = 4	125	63	42	32	26
x = 5	180	91	61	46	37
x = 6	240	121	81	61	49
x = 7	302	152	102	77	62
x = 8	367	184	124	93	75
x = 9	434	218	146	110	88
x =10	503	253	169	127	102

For example, if two failures are observed in a sample and the sample size is less than or equal to 34, the null hypothesis p*=0.01 can be rejected at the 5% level.

Table 5. Non-rejection regions for PF (0.05) test for alternative sample sizes

Null hypothesis	Non-rejection region		
probability p^*	for x,n = 255 days	for x,n = 510 days	for x,n = 1,000 days
0.010	x < 7	1 < x < 11	4 < x < 17
0.025	2 < x < 12	6 < x < 21	15 < x < 36
0.050	6 < x < 21	16 < x < 36	37 < x < 65
0.075	11 < x < 28	27 < x < 51	59 < x < 92
0.100	16 < x < 36	38 < x < 65	81 < x < 120

x is the number of failures that could be observed in a sample size equal to the specified number of trading days without rejecting the indicated null hypothesis at the 5% level of the PF test.

Table 6. Type II error rates for the PF (0.05) test

Null hypothesis	Alternative hypothesis	Type II error rate n = 255	n = 510	n = 1,000
p* = 0.010	p = 0.011	0.976	0.949	0.930
p* = 0.010	p = 0.020	0.749	0.557	0.218
p* = 0.010	p = 0.030	0.355	0.101	0.003
p* = 0.010	p = 0.040	0.113	0.008	0.000
p* = 0.025	p = 0.028	0.920	0.941	0.928
p* = 0.025	p = 0.030	0.898	0.901	0.844
p* = 0.025	p = 0.040	0.674	0.523	0.237
p* = 0.025	p = 0.050	0.374	0.154	0.014
p* = 0.050	p = 0.055	0.944	0.913	0.899
p* = 0.050	p = 0.060	0.905	0.819	0.729
p* = 0.050	p = 0.075	0.639	0.329	0.102
p* = 0.050	p = 0.100	0.147	0.009	0.000
p* = 0.075	p = 0.083	0.915	0.903	0.846
p* = 0.075	p = 0.100	0.669	0.478	0.186

The Type II errror rate is the probability of accepting the indicated false null hypothesis when the specific alternative hypothesis is true using the PF test with a sample size = n.

Verification schemes based on historical simulation

As an alternative to verification tests based on historical profit and loss performance, it is sometimes suggested that historical simulations can be used as a validation technique. Given a portfolio, it is possible to calculate the daily changes in value the portfolio would have experienced if it had been held over some prior period. The daily changes in portfolio value that would have resulted from the historical day-to-day changes in market prices and interest rates could be used to construct a sample histogram. From such a histogram, 1% (or 5%) critical value loss estimates could be determined. A comparison of a VAR estimate with such a simulation-based critical value loss estimate could be the basis of a verification test.

Such an approach assumes that the statistical processes that generate asset price changes are stationary over time. An appealing quality of this approach is that it does not make explicit assumptions about the underlying covariance structures among asset price changes. The historical volatilities and correlations are automatically captured in the historical simulation exercise.

The drawback of such an approach is the large sampling errors associated with their empirical critical value estimates. Historical simulation-based frequency distributions are estimates of the true underlying distribution and consequently are subject to estimation error. In many cases, very large samples are necessary to reduce the sampling error associated with the critical value estimates for very small (or very large) cumulative probability values.

It is possible to derive a theoretical approximation for the variance of the critical value from a sample frequency distribution. Let X_p correspond to the p% critical value of a probability density f(x), so that the integral from negative infinity to X_p equals p%. It can be shown (see Kendall and Stuart [1960]) that the variance of an estimate of X_p, from a sample of size n is approximately equal to:

$$\mathrm{Var}(X_p) \approx p(1-p) / \left[n f(X_p)^2\right]. \tag{5}$$

For example, the standard error of the estimate of the 0.01 critical value from a sample of size n from a normal distribution with a variance of σ^2 is approximately $3.7689\ \sigma\ n^{-1/2}$. The standard error of the estimate of the 0.05 critical value from this sample is approximately $2.1304\ \sigma\ n^{-1/2}$.

These examples illustrate the general property that the standard errors of critical value estimates from sample histograms increase as the cumulative tail probability associated with the critical value declines. The importance of sampling error in historical simulation-derived estimates of critical values can be illustrated more concretely using Monte Carlo experiments. In our experiments, 10,000 independent samples of various sizes are drawn from known underlying probability distributions. For each of the 10,000 samples, a sample histogram is constructed, and important critical values - the 0.01, 0.05, and 0.10 cumulative probability critical values - are estimated. From these estimates, sampling distributions are constructed for the alternative critical value estimates. The process is repeated for alternative underlying distributions.

Table 7 reports the simulation results for the standard normal distributions for sample sizes of 100, 250, 500, 1,000, and 2,500 observations. Table 8 reports parallel results for the Student's *t* distribution with eight degrees of freedom. Table 9 reports results for a *t* distribution with two degrees of freedom. The progression of distributions from Table 7 through Table 9 includes distributions with increasingly large tail probability weights in their theoretical density functions.

The empirical results reported in Tables 7–9 illuminate some clear patterns of interest. As the sample size increases, on average, the bias in critical value estimates decreases. The results also show clearly that the standard error of a critical value estimate increases as the cumulative probability associated with the critical value estimate decreases.

Consistent with the theoretical approximation, the standard errors of critical value estimates decline as the sample sizes used to generate the critical value estimates are increased. Similarly, as the sample size increases, the range of critical value estimates recorded for any critical value level declines.

A very important pattern is visible in the results for the *t* distribution:

❑ the bias of 0.01 and 0.05 critical value esti-

Table 7. Accuracy of historical simulation-based critical value estimates for a standard normal distribution for a sample of size n

Statistic	Theoretical value	n = 100	n = 250	n = 500	n = 1,000	n = 2,500
0.01 Critical value	−2.326	−2.148	−2.256	−2.285	−2.307	−2.317
Standard deviation		0.309	0.209	0.159	0.116	0.074
Minimum value		−3.658	−3.157	−2.910	−2.828	−2.595
Maximum value		−1.212	−1.393	−1.755	−1.867	−1.987
0.05 Critical value	−1.645	−1.594	−1.624	−1.634	−1.638	−1.643
Standard deviation		0.203	0.130	0.094	0.066	0.042
Minimum value		−2.469	−2.136	−2.008	−1.910	−1.808
Maximum value		−0.899	−1.119	−1.289	−1.401	−1.489
0.10 Critical value	−1.282	−1.254	−1.271	−1.275	−1.278	−1.280
Standard deviation		0.177	0.107	0.077	0.053	0.034
Minimum value		−1.865	−1.727	−1.579	−1.476	−1.440
Maximum value		−0.705	−0.811	−0.989	−1.082	−1.140

The estimates are based on the results from 10,000 sample histograms simulated in S-Plus.

Table 8. Accuracy of historical simulation-based critical value estimates for a *t* distribution with eight degrees of freedom for a sample of size n

Statistic	Theoretical value	n = 100	n = 250	n = 500	n = 1,000	n = 2,500
0.01 Critical value	–2.896	–2.636	–2.787	–2.834	–2.867	–2.884
Standard deviation		0.528	0.366	0.276	0.203	0.128
Minimum value		–6.898	–4.749	–4.229	–3.832	–3.469
Maximum value		–1.338	–1.794	–1.814	–2.279	–2.390
0.05 Critical value	–1.859	–1.803	–1.839	–1.848	–1.855	–1.857
Standard deviation		0.270	0.176	0.125	0.090	0.057
Minimum value		–3.111	–2.649	–2.367	–2.303	–2.092
Maximum value		–1.000	–1.178	–1.333	–1.550	–1.636
0.10 Critical value	–1.397	–1.372	–1.387	–1.391	–1.395	–1.395
Standard deviation		0.202	0.132	0.092	0.065	0.041
Minimum value		–2.237	–1.926	–1.735	–1.709	–1.566
Maximum value		–0.680	–0.882	–1.046	–1.169	–1.252

The estimates are based on the results from 10,000 sample histograms simulated in S-Plus.

Table 9. Accuracy of historical simulation-based critical value estimates for a *t* distribution with two degrees of freedom for a sample of size n

Statistic	Theoretical value	n = 100	n = 250	n = 500	n = 1,000	n = 2,500
0.01 Critical value	–6.965	–6.235	–6.725	–6.774	–6.881	–6.933
Standard deviation		3.357	2.201	1.571	1.142	0.715
Minimum value		–64.393	–31.651	–22.241	–14.128	–11.064
Maximum value		–1.601	2.785	–3.475	–4.242	–4.821
0.05 Critical value	–2.919	–2.845	–2.887	–2.903	–2.914	–2.918
Standard deviation		0.738	0.460	0.333	0.233	0.148
Minimum value		–7.770	–5.193	–4.517	–3.987	–3.613
Maximum value		–1.153	–1.668	–1.863	–2.190	–2.433
0.10 Critical value	–1.886	–1.862	–1.874	–1.879	–1.882	–1.885
Standard deviation		0.390	0.248	0.174	0.121	0.079
Minimum value		–4.273	–3.016	–2.611	–2.377	–2.165
Maximum value		–0.786	–1.081	1.367	–1.425	–1.594

The estimates are based on the results from 10,000 sample histograms simulated in S-Plus.

mates increases as the underlying distribution becomes more leptokurtotic (fat-tailed); and

❑ the standard error of the 0.01 critical value estimates (and to a lesser degree, the 0.05 critical value estimates) increases markedly as the underlying distribution becomes more leptokurtotic. The 0.01 critical value estimates for the *t* distribution with two degrees of freedom exhibit strong bias and standard errors that are very large (relative to underlying theoretical critical values) even in sample sizes as large as 2,500 – a sample size equivalent to almost 10 years of daily data.

These simulation results suggest that historical simulation-based critical value estimates for 0.01 (and 0.05) cumulative probabilities may suffer from significant biases and are subject to large sampling variation. When the underlying distribution has fat tails, historical simulation-based critical value estimates for the 0.01 level are remarkably unreliable even in large samples.

The bias and variations exhibited by historical simulation-based 0.01 critical value estimates suggest that they are not very reliable estimates of potential losses. As a consequence, they are not suitable benchmarks for comparisons with alternative internal model-generated potential loss estimates. This analysis does not support the use of historical simulations for validation exercises.

Conclusion

The statistical results reported here suggest that simple performance-based VAR verification tests require large samples to produce a reliable accuracy assessment. Small sample reality check statistics based on historical trading profits and losses have very poor power against even substantially larger alternative tail probabilities.

The results indicate that there are significant statistical difficulties surrounding the verification of VAR estimates even in performance samples as long as a year. It does not appear possible for a bank or its supervisor to verify the accuracy of a VAR estimate unless a long model performance history is available.

Historical simulation-based reality check statistics also require long historical sample periods to generate accurate results. Historical simulation-based estimates of 0.01 critical values exhibit substantial bias and retain substantial sampling errors even in samples as large as 10 years of daily data.

1 *RiskMetrics Technical Document (1995) provides an abbreviated discussion of model verification issues. Crnkovic and Drachman (1995) propose a measure of the goodness-of-fit for an entire estimated potential profit and loss distribution.*

2 *As the DPG recommendations do not include a mandatory regulatory capital requirement for the unregulated affiliates of SEC-regulated broker-dealers, our discussion focuses on verification problems for bank regulators.*

3 *The null hypothesis of independence could also be tested, but we do not perform such tests in this paper.*

4 *Such a weighting function may not be appropriate. In historical financial data, the occurrence of extreme losses is more common than the occurrence of an extreme gain. This underlying asymmetry will be compounded by a concentration of option positions in an institution's portfolio. See Kupiec and O'Brien (1995) for further discussion.*

5 *A formal comparison of these testing techniques is a topic for future research.*

6 *The chi-squared distribution result is true asymptotically. Monte Carlo simulation results indicate that the critical values of the chi-squared distribution provide good approximations in this setting.*

7 *The power of a statistical test is defined to be 1 minus the Type II error probability for a given alternative hypothesis.*

8 *If the null hypothesis is rejected, and the risk measurement system is altered to correct the detected inaccuracy, performance data from the new model constitute a new data series distinct from the performance data produced by the prior model. The verification process will begin again, and a new set of performance data will accumulate with time.*

9 *For each null analysed, the first reported Type II error rate is calculated for a relatively local alternative hypothesis: an alternative that is 110% of the null. This comparison is included because a 0.01 difference between the null and the alternative is a relatively small difference if the null is 0.1; it is a very large difference if the null is 0.01. The results show that, for all sample sizes, the power against local alternatives declines as the p-value under the null hypothesis shrinks toward 0.*

10 *The Type I error rate must be calculated by evaluating the LR test and calculating the corresponding chi-squared probability.*

BIBLIOGRAPHY

Bank for International Settlements, 1995, *An Internal Model-Based Approach to Market Risk Capital Requirements*, Basle Committee on Banking Supervision, April.

Crnkovic, C., and J.Drachman, 1995, *A Universal Tool to Discriminate Among Risk Measurement Techniques*, Corporate Risk Management Group, JP Morgan & Co Inc., New York, September 26.

Derivatives Policy Group, 1995, *A Framework for Voluntary Oversight*, New York, March.

Group of Thirty, 1993, *Derivatives: Practices and Principles*, Washington, DC, July.

JP Morgan, 1995, *RiskMetrics Technical Document*, 3rd edition, New York.

Kendall, M.G., and A. Stuart, 1960, *The Advanced Theory of Statistics*, London: Charles Griffin &Co.

Kuiper, N.H., 1962, *Proceedings of the Koninklijke Nederlandse Akademie van Wetenschappen*, Ser.A Vol. 63, pp.38-47.

Kupiec, P., and J. O'Brien, 1995, "The Use of Bank Trading Risk Measurement Models for Regulatory Capital Purposes", FEDS Working Paper No. 95-11, Federal Reserve Board.

SELECTING AND IMPROVING VAR METHODOLOGIES: NEW RESEARCH

Introduction

Andrew Smith
KPMG

This section links recent research on two general themes - how to improve VAR modelling, and how to choose the right VAR approach. It contains the most mathematically challenging articles of the whole book, so it may not be particularly clear to readers with developing quantitative skills. If the papers seem too difficult, save them for the future, and move straight on to Section IV.

VAR is a simple concept, but it becomes progressively more complex as we start applying it to real situations. Statistical analysis is a poorly understood science with an astonishing ability to mislead the casual user. The overall profit and loss probability distribution is really a massive multi-dimensional statistical problem in any large financial or non-financial firm - so correlations are generally far more important than volatilities. Unfortunately, financial market correlations show little evidence of stationary behaviour,[1] making estimation difficult.

In computing VAR, a breakdown in correlation patterns can lead to much higher losses than the model would imply; statistical sampling theory implies not only that it can be difficult to forecast parameters for the VAR model, but also that the VAR figure itself can be very unstable over short periods.

The lack of stationary behaviour within financial markets exacerbates this effect, which is one reason why regulators emphasise the importance of stress and scenario testing. And, whilst VAR is a scale for risk rather than an absolute measure, normal distribution confidence levels often do not provide sufficient accuracy in the presence of leptokurtic (fat-tailed) distributions.

Does VAR provide all the information about risk that firms need? In most organisations, the need for more sophisticated VAR applications stems from their increasing exposure to non-linear products such as options and CMOs. However, simple VAR approaches only cover linear risks.

And whilst it is interesting to know (statistically) potential loss, it would be even better to know how it can arise. This "inversion" of the multi-dimensional probability distribution can be very difficult to achieve.

In any case, there are several different ways of calculating VAR, and each method has its supporters and detractors. It can be very difficult to strike the correct balance between speed, accuracy and complexity and relate it to the particular needs of any one instrument, portfolio or entity.

Despite all these issues, VAR continues to be a popular risk measurement tool. The objective of VAR implementation is to focus on the good, whilst "managing out" the weaker aspects and ensuring a clear understanding of its limitations.

The papers in Section III are set out in two streams following the key strands of the chapter. The reader will find a range of mathematical sophistication within the material, but the starting hurdle is set pretty high! The material below has been designed to support the reader through each paper.

Improvements in VAR

As a firm of professional risk management consultants, one of the questions KPMG is frequently asked is "which VAR model should we choose - RiskMetrics, Historical Simulation (which KPMG refers to as Historical Data Evolution [HDE] for reasons that will be rather arcane to non-statisticians[2]) or Monte Carlo?" The normal response is to ask whether the client has considered any of the other approaches available. Several papers in this section discuss alternative VAR models. A good start is "Beyond VAR and Stress Testing" by Julian Shaw, which provides a non-mathematical introduction to many VAR issues whilst introducing two interesting approaches: using "skew" and "kurtosis" to generate a fitted probability distribution, and enhancing the speed of Monte Carlo through Latin Hypercube sampling and updating the gamma profile.

In essence, Shaw's article suggests and promotes "robust" and/or "non-parametric" approaches to solving the statistical problem that VAR presents. The material on correlation and the central limit theorem is particularly interesting. Nevertheless, the proposed solution is relatively complex, and the reader may wish to balance potential extra accuracy against the use of a "standard" variance-covariance approach, together with non-parametric distributional inequalities such as those in Abramowitz and Stegun (1972). Most statisticians would intuitively expect the central limit theorem to hold well for the size and nature of the statistics associated with a VAR calculation, so the evidence that it does not is very interesting. The problem probably lies in the variability of covariances, particularly in stress situations. This is what causes the leptokurtosis to persist.[3]

"Principals of Risk..." by Jon Frye demonstrates the use of principal components. This method has great power for single currency interest rate problems due to the apparent elimination of the correlation difficulty, but it is not easy to generalise to large-scale VAR because of the requirement to forecast correlations between the principal components of different markets. Other viewpoints favour a non-independent, but algebraically orthogonal, factor[4] approach. This has the merit that the factors are both stable and known to the user. It also offers a highly efficient method for including spread risks within a VAR model.

Nevertheless, both principal and components and factor methods achieve a significant dimensional reduction in the VAR problem, and both are "full curve" models. The dimensional reduction allows efficient computation, whilst the full curve approach should be acceptable under the BIS Capital Accord Supplement, although it appears that fewer than six time buckets are present for the yield curve.

Perhaps the most interesting article in this section is "Quadratic Maximum Loss" by Gerold Studer and HJ Lüthi. Although the advanced mathematical content makes it a challenging read, the paper has several particularly interesting features. Readers will find a clear explanation of the difference between VAR, a confidence level on the profit and loss distribution, and what the article calls maximum loss, the largest loss within a region as defined by confidence levels on the underlying stochastic variables. This is an approach which allows both the maximum loss and its source to be established for quadratic portfolios (ie including a static gamma description). The approach is a semi-dynamic gamma concept. An "average" static gamma can be computed across the distribution within the maximum loss hyper-ellipsoid.

KPMG tends to prefer Monte Carlo as the best approach to VAR in a sophisticated institution. This is somewhat heretical, given the widespread belief that Monte Carlo is too slow to be practical. However, experience with clients has shown that valuable insights can be achieved through a combination of parallel computation, factorisation, portfolio splitting (into linear, quadratic and non-linear components), and time efficient valuation algorithms as well as through optimisation of the Monte Carlo algorithm itself. Note that a high precision answer is not critical for VAR Monte Carlo, unlike derivative pricing. So 1,000 scenarios, possibly only 500,[5] would probably suffice for the BIS Capital Accord Supplement standards.

Much recent research in this area has focused on low discrepancy sequences (LDS). These are deterministic sets of numbers that fill a (multi-dimensional) space relatively uniformly rather than randomly, as in true Monte Carlo. They often generate faster scenarios than Monte Carlo and can offer faster convergence. In "Scrambled Nets for Value-at-Risk calculations," Art Owen and Domingo Tavella introduce a new LDS method that demonstrates good performance in low dimensional problems. Unfortunately, VAR is usually required in very high dimensional situations and, as yet, it appears that Monte Carlo continues to outperform all LDS.

The final paper in the stream proposing improvements to VAR modelling is "Value-at-Risk – Proposals on a Generalisation" by Michael Schröder. This paper shows what might be achieved if the profit and loss probability distribution is known, but of more interest is the author's discussion on investor utility. For realistic multi-dimensional portfolios it is, of course, theoretically possible to compute the overall profit and loss distribution, given valuation formulas and the statistics of the relevant stochastic variables. However, this process would be relatively inefficient, particularly for non-linear products.

VAR model selection

The second stream of articles in Section III considers VAR model selection and implementation. Several VAR models are compared and discussed, and the papers are highly complimentary to the material introduced above.

"Value-at-Risk: Implementing a Risk Measurement Standard" by Christopher Marshall and Michael Siegel reports the results of a comparative study of the figures generated by several RiskMetrics algorithms, attempting to analyse the differences into model and "systems risks" categories. The differences in respect of FRAs and swaps (and options thereon), probably arise from different yield curve interpolations. It is worth re-emphasising the authors' conclusion that treating software as a deterministic black box is unwise.

"Evaluating Value-at-Risk Methodologies: Accuracy versus Computational Time," by Matt Pritsker is worthy of considerable attention. Pritsker compares the performance (in this article, the balance between accuracy and computational time) of six relatively common VAR models: delta, delta-gamma-delta, delta-gamma-minimisation, delta-gamma Monte Carlo, modified grid Monte Carlo and full Monte Carlo. The paper includes a good description of the models and provides an excellent perspective on the computational considerations involved in implementing any of the Monte Carlo approaches.

Overall, the author favours, albeit in the context of a relatively small test, the delta-gamma Monte Carlo approach for entities with product mixes of an intermediate level of sophistication - a conclusion which many would support in conjunction with splitting a portfolio into delta (linear) delta-gamma (semi-linear) and true non-linear components. The extended results suggest that four of the six models, delta-gamma Monte Carlo, full Monte Carlo, delta-gamma, and delta, provide superior results. Choosing the right one depends on the user's individual needs.

Although this section emphasises issues surrounding VAR model selection, readers should not get the impression that choice of a particular model is all important - it isn't! Using the model(s) that are selected wisely is far more important. Any reasonably sophisticated institution should have access to at least two models and should make a point of evaluating the differences between them on a regular basis.

The reader who has followed all the material presented in this section will recognise that the mathematics involved is relatively advanced and, consequently, unlikely to be understood by all senior managers. So how can firms ensure that they are making the most of their VAR calculations?

Risk information must have certain fundamental qualities: it must be complete; it must be timely; it must be relevant to the style of business being undertaken and it must be genuinely useful to the people to whom it is addressed.

It is essential that managers understand the strengths and weaknesses of the chosen VAR model. Realise that more than one model may be useful. And realise that there is little point in developing a sophisticated VAR model without developing an equally strong stress and scenario testing regime.

Significant VAR elements have not yet been fully explored from either a theoretical or a practical business standpoint. Over the next few years, it would be good to see new research addressing the incorporation into VAR of spread risks as well as funding and liquidity risks and issues surrounding the aggregation of market and credit risks. While these are issues that KPMG routinely address at present, we would certainly appreciate some thoughtful alternative views.

Finally, while technical research is vital if VAR is to serve as the primary measure of market risk for business firms and for regulators, we cannot overstate our belief that VAR methodologies must be grounded in the business processes of the firms that employ them to measure market risks. While mathematical correctness is a necessary condition, it is not in itself sufficient to ensure the analytical soundness of any VAR application. That can only be achieved when sound quantitative approaches are combined with equal measures of market/product knowledge and a comprehensive understanding of each firm's unique business requirements.

1 *Stationary distributions do not change with time. Differences from one period to another only arise as sampling issues.*

2 *HDE is in fact a single sample taken over a particular historical period. It is not a simulation - an* ex-ante *model which sets out possible outcomes given a set of core assumptions.*

3 *and, requires sophisticated VAR models to address the non-normal modelling problem head on.*

4 *Principal components (PCs) and factors are concepts from multivariate statistics. Their relative similarities and subtle differences can cause statisticians to become quite passionate. For this book, it will suffice to say that: (orthogonal, independent) PCs are a special case of (o,i) factor theory - they are both vectors; (o,i) PCs arise from maximisation of*

the trace (the sum of the diagonals) of a quadratic form: vector times symmetric matrix times vector; (o,i) factors arise from the minimisation of the off-diagonal elements of the quadratic form; normally the number of (o,i) factors chosen is less than the number of PCs. Where the number is the same, (o,i) PCs and (o,i) factors are identical. Readers can also choose to have other factors, for example, orthogonal but not statistically independent - as suggested above.

5 *This is a very different paradigm to derivative pricing, where 10,000 or even 1 million scenarios are common.*

BIBLIOGRAPHY

Abramovitz, M., and I.A. Stegun, 1965, *Handbook of Mathematical Functions*, Dover Publications, New York.

25

Beyond VAR and Stress Testing

Julian Shaw
NatWest Markets

Conventional value-at-risk fails to provide realistic estimates of the probabilities of precisely the events in which we are most interested, ie extremes and in particular extreme losses. *Stress testing is an* ad hoc *alternative which does not repair the defects of VAR. This paper exposes the egregious assumptions of conventional VAR and outlines a practical alternative methodology.*

Value-at-risk (VAR) is the z in the following proposition: Given a holding period of x days and a confidence level of y%, find the VAR z which satisfies the following condition: With our current portfolio, over the next x trading days with probability at least y% we will lose no more than $z, assuming no change in portfolio composition during that period.

Symptomatic of the confusion reigning in the risk management world is the fact that x ranges from 1 to 250 and y ranges from 95 to 98 and beyond in different firms.

It seems obvious (to me at least) that risk management departments should focus on the risk of *extreme* events. By definition, a 95% confidence level will be exceeded at least once a month on average - it is forecasting what will happen *on those days* that is the point of risk management. If there is to be a single confidence level it should be set much higher, certainly to the equivalent of no more than one trading day per year, ie 99.6%. In any case we really want to approximate the *entire* P&L distribution, not just one confidence level.

Conversely I favour holding periods which approximate the time it would take to neutralise the position, albeit under adverse conditions. This depends on the specific market and the portfolio but one day seems reasonable for many markets, 10 trading days seems sufficient for all but the most illiquid markets and one year seems absurdly long. We really want a methodology which allows us to *specify* any holding period, so that we can adjust it to suit the portfolio we are evaluating.

What is wrong with VAR?

The essential problem with conventional VAR is neither the confidence level nor the holding period, both of which can be adjusted, but rather the method by which it is typically computed. This relies on the following proposition:

Assume that the changes in the risk factors are multivariate normal where
σ_i is the standard deviation of F_i and
ρ_{ij} is the correlation coefficient for changes in F_i versus changes in F_j (Assumption 1)
Assume that portfolio value is driven by K factors F_i, and that we can approximate the change in portfolio value ΔPFVal as the sum of the sensitivity to each factor times the change in the factor, ie:

$$\Delta \text{PFVal} = \sum \left(\delta_{F_i} * \Delta F_i\right) \qquad \text{(Assumption 2)}$$

Then ΔPFVal is normally distributed too with standard deviation σ given (in matrix form) by

$$\sigma^2 = \left[\delta_{F_i}\right] * \left[\text{COV}_{ij}\right] * \left[\delta_{F_i}\right]'$$

where $\text{COV}_{ij} = \rho_{ij} * \sigma_i * \sigma_j$.

Thus, assuming a mean return of approximately zero, y-percentile VAR can be estimated as NORMSINV (y) * σ.[1] For example, 95-percentile VAR is 1.64 * σ and 98-percentile VAR is 2.05 * σ. Indeed any confidence level VAR can be estimated from σ.

The only justification for computing VAR with this algorithm is that it is *easy*. It does *not* provide a good estimate of what we really need, which is realistic estimates of the probabilities of extreme losses. The proposition is correct but the assumptions are wrong when applied to typical financial markets.

Assumption 1 is wrong

It is well known that changes in financial time series have much fatter tails than would be the case if they were normally distributed. As has been pointed out many times, assuming a normal distribution for equity returns, the crash of October 1987 was a greater than 20σ event and hence would only be expected once every many millions of years!

There is a lot of faith in the risk management world in the applicability of the central limit theorem. This says roughly that the sum of a number of distributions tends toward normality, even if the individual distributions are not normal.[2] Hence it is hoped that portfolio returns will tend to normality even though the individual components are not normal, and that returns over longer periods will be normal even though daily returns are not normal.

But neither is necessarily true. We examined the returns of a test portfolio from Cox (1995). This portfolio is long 5% Nikkei 225 index, short 10% S&P 500, long 15% DAX, long 20% FTSE-100 and short 30% CAC40. It has net zero exposure, the absolute values of the exposures sum to 80% and it is continually readjusted to maintain them. Whereas Cox considered three years of bi-weekly data, we consider 10 years of daily data for the same portfolio. The returns have much fatter tails than those of a normal distribution with the same mean and standard deviation, as shown in Figure 1.

1. Long and short equity portfolio: all data

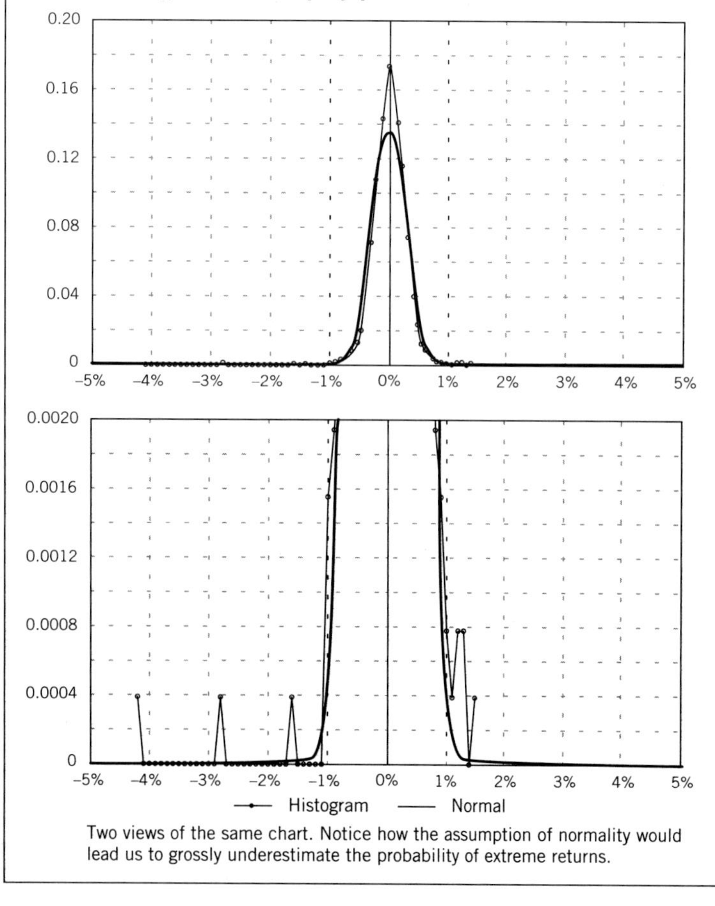

Histogram — Normal

Two views of the same chart. Notice how the assumption of normality would lead us to grossly underestimate the probability of extreme returns.

Nor is it true that returns over longer periods are necessarily closer to normality than returns over shorter periods. As Ray points out, three month changes in US three-month bills have been even less normal than one day changes in the same instruments (Ray, 1993).

One reason for the disappointing lack of normality is that portfolio components do not have fixed correlations and there is serial correlation between returns in different periods. Because the normal distribution is familiar this leads to the hypothesis that returns are normal but with *changing* standard deviation, so returns are only *conditionally* normal. Various volatility estimation techniques are used, ranging from simple sample standard deviation models, to exponential weighting (such as RiskMetrics) or more sophisticated GARCH techniques[3] to estimate the variance of this hypothesised continually changing normal distribution. Volatility changes *do* account for some of the fatness in the tails of return distributions but not enough, especially at the extremes as the following argument shows:[4]

We seem to see a 20%+ fall in the S&P500 about once every 60 years, or every 15,000 trading days. This implies that *if* the annualised volatility were constant, it would have to be approximately SQRT(250) * – 20%/(NORMSINV (1/(60 * 250))); ie 83%. If volatility is not constant this implies that volatility would have to be even higher than 83% on some days – but predicted volatilities never get that high (typically they are around 20%) except ... the day *after* a crash!

As Jackwerth and Rubinstein (1996) observe, options traders seem to have learned a lesson from the crash of '87. Although traders have always continually revised their at-the-money option implied volatilities, since the crash they have also charged a hefty implied volatility premium for out-of-the-money options giving rise to the volatility "smile". This means that the risk-neutral probabilities of 3 and 4 standard deviation declines are respectively 10 and 100 times more likely than under the assumption of lognormality. So options traders do not believe that (log) returns are conditionally normal, let alone unconditionally normal. Some day risk analysts may learn the same lesson.

Actually most people in risk management *do* know that returns have fat tails, but they do not know what to do about it. This has led to some feeble suggestions for coping with the problem. The regulators' knee-jerk reaction is to load VAR estimates by some *ad hoc* multiple but this is just fudging.

One authority on risk management justifies the use of 98-percentile VAR with the following argument: if there are two unimodal distributions and one has fatter tails then it must also have a thinner peak and the density functions must cross somewhere. Empirically, for financial time series that place is located around the 98th percentile, so the 98-percentile VAR should be computed and reported assuming normality[5] (*even though this misleads naive management into underestimating the probability of the more extreme events they are really interested in!*)

At the conclusion of a technical paper which assumes normality, another author approvingly quotes the Federal Reserve Board as follows:

"Assuming a normal distribution, the probability of experiencing a four standard deviation event is approximately ... once in 130 years. In practice, however, such unusual market movements are seen in most major markets on average almost every year".

She concludes: "Clearly, there is much more to risk management than calculating VAR" (Bagg, 1996) but she does not explain what that "more" is. If VAR (computed as specified above) cannot give reliable estimates of the consequences of financial events that occur as often as *once a year*, then what *is* it good for?

Assumption 2 is wrong

Assumption 2 says that the effects of changes in the risk factors are *linear* in each variable and *orthogonal*, ie the total effect of a number of changes is just the sum of the individual effects.

For portfolios which incorporate derivatives (which means the global portfolios of every major investment bank) this is wrong. The value of such portfolios is not linear in the market risk factors (that is the point of derivatives!) and may not even be monotonic in them. The maximum loss could occur at any point, not necessarily at some combination of extreme changes in the risk factors.

A more subtle point is that the effects of changes are not orthogonal – the effect of changing the value of the underlying security and changing the implied volatility is not simply the sum of effects of the two individual changes. Note that the commonly used "greek" approximation

$$
\begin{aligned}
\Delta \text{ Portfolio Value} \sim\; & \delta * \Delta S \\
+\; & \gamma * (\Delta S)^2 \\
+\; & \theta * \Delta T \\
+\; & \kappa * \Delta\sigma \\
+\; & \rho * \Delta r
\end{aligned}
$$

which expresses changes in derivative portfolio value in terms of delta, gamma, theta, kappa and rho is non-linear in changes in the value of the underlying only (because of the gamma term) and it assumes orthogonality. (It is a poor global approximation anyway for many derivative portfolios.)

Some claim that in practice the linear approximation to derivatives risk is good enough. But this is not true when the effects of large moves are considered. Figure 2 shows the P&L of a simple derivatives portfolio as a function of the price underlying security. Clearly no linear (or quadratic function for that matter) will be a good global approximation to a P&L like this.

Is this example unreasonable? I do not believe it is. Real derivative portfolios are not random collections of derivative positions – they are *managed* by traders who keep their portfolios locally hedged. Delta neutral (and delta-gamma neutral) portfolios are the rule, not the exception. However, contrary to the implicit assumption of those who feed delta equivalents into their VAR computations, these portfolios are not riskless!

Also it is perfectly natural to compare the risk of a derivative business with the risks of vanilla businesses – indeed the point of VAR as compared to the old *ad hoc* greek and other market-specific risk measures is that it can express the risks of

2. A simple derivatives portfolio and its "greek" approximations

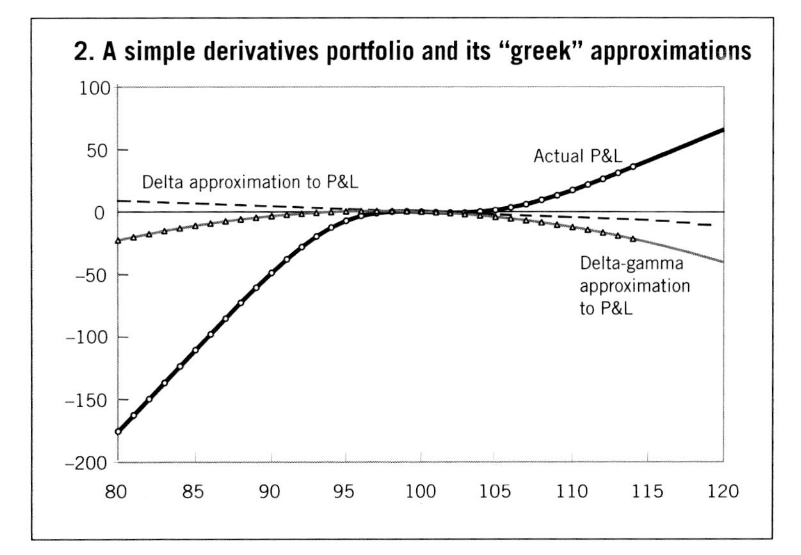

diverse businesses *commensurately*. If risk management cannot realistically estimate the risks of derivative businesses, then it is not doing its job.

Correlation is bunk!

A more subtle problem with the assumption of multivariate normality concerns the use of correlation as the measure of association between risk factor changes.

Implicit in the use of correlation is the assumption that the relationship between a pair of risk factors F_i and F_j can be summed up by one number, the (linear) correlation coefficient ρ_{ij}. An approximate characterisation of ρ_{ij} is that if the $\langle F_i , F_j \rangle$ observations are plotted on a scatter diagram and an ellipse drawn around them, then ρ_{ij} is approximately...

$$\pm[1.0 - (\text{minimum width of the ellipse}) / (\text{maximum width of the ellipse})]$$

where the sign is plus if the ellipse leans to the right and minus if it leans to the left. Thus the skinnier the ellipse, the higher the absolute value of the correlation.

A precise characterisation of ρ_{ij} is that it is the square root of the fraction of the variation in F_j that is explained by the ***straight line*** of best fit drawn through the graph of F_j versus F_i where "best" means minimising the sum of the squared error terms.

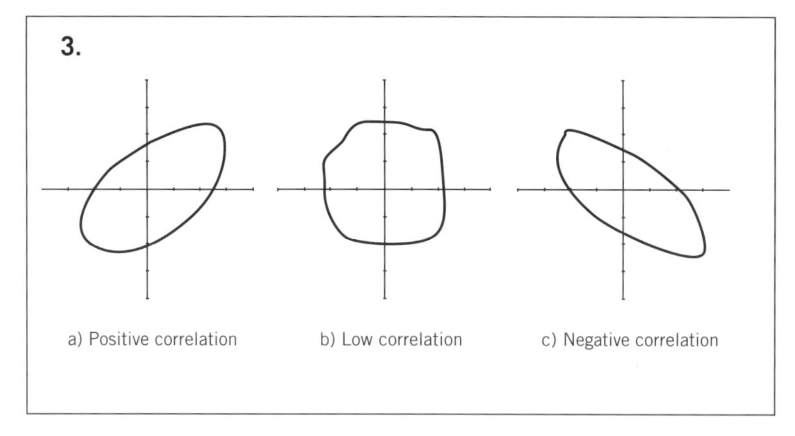

3.

a) Positive correlation b) Low correlation c) Negative correlation

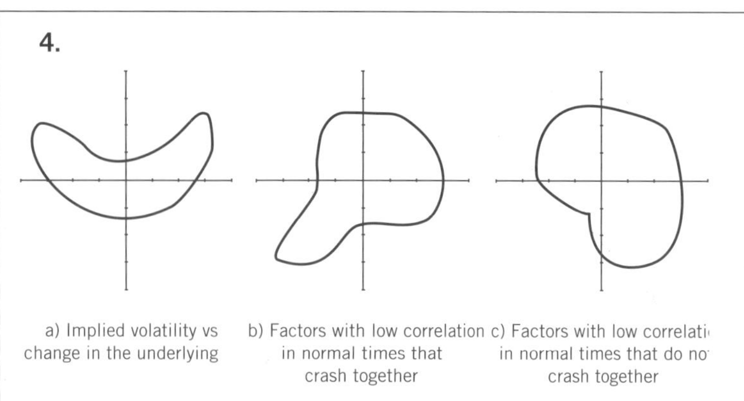

4.

a) Implied volatility vs change in the underlying b) Factors with low correlation in normal times that crash together c) Factors with low correlation in normal times that do not crash together

Our fundamental objection to correlation of *any type* is that it assumes that a relationship between two factors can be summed up by one number. A (linear) correlation coefficient will only capture relationships of the types indicated in Figure 3.

A little thought about financial factors reveals that this does not include all the relationships of interest in financial simulation. For example, we know that there is a relationship between changes in implied volatility and changes in the corresponding underlying security. In general, a big move up or down in the underlying security tends to be associated with a rise in implied volatility. This non-linear relationship might be represented in Figure 4a.

For another example, consider equity indexes around the globe. Under normal market conditions the correlation is only moderate, but given a very large move the correlation is extreme. While the crash of the S&P500 alone in October 1987 was improbable enough under the hypothesis of normally distributed changes, the simultaneous crashes of all the major equity markets was even more astronomically improbable, given the hypothesis of multivariate normality and the typical correlations between equity markets.

The true relationship is better represented by Figure 4b. Again, there is a relationship, but it is non-linear. Ordinary linear correlation estimated over a typical time period will overestimate the actual effect of small moves and greatly underestimate the effect for big moves.

Finally there might be financial variables which have low conventional correlation but rarely crash together. Figure 4c illustrates this situation.

For yet another example, consider Bookstaber's example of stocks versus treasuries versus junk bonds (Chew, 1994). In normal times junk bond prices are primarily driven by rates and hence correlate with treasuries. But when equities crash, junk debt is driven by equities. These relationships are indicated in Figure 5.

Implementation problems of VAR

The fundamental problems with conventional VAR computation discussed above are compounded by the shortcuts which are required to make conventional VAR "practical".

Typically the variance/covariance methodology uses historical data (possibly with additional data such as implied volatilities) to estimate an underlying multivariate normal distribution. This is not easy, since there are thousands of risk factors to consider in computing firmwide VAR but typically only about 2,500 days or 10 years of data. So even if the world were multivariate normal, the error in estimating all the correlations would be huge – especially if they are time-varying.

Variance/covariance VAR modellers have two ways of coping with the multiplicity of risk factors. The first is to reduce the number of factors by using factor models. For example, changes in the yields of all bonds are modelled as combinations of shifts in a few key rates. For another example, implied volatilities of all maturities are assumed to move by some deterministic function of changes in three month implied volatility (for example, the square root of time).

These cures can be worse than the disease because many factor models fail to pick up the risks of *typical* trading strategies which can be the greatest risks run by an investment bank. According to naive yield factor models, huge spread positions between on-the-run bonds and off-the-run bonds are riskless! According to naive volatility factor models, hedging one year (or longer dated) implied volatility with three month implied volatility is riskless, provided it is done in the "right" proportions – ie the proportions built into the factor model! It is the *rule*, not the exception, for traders to put on spread trades which defeat factor models *since they use factor type models to identify richness and cheapness!*

The second method used by variance/covariance VAR modellers to cope with the multiplicity of factors is explicitly or implicitly to set huge numbers of the correlations between factors to zero – for example, by estimating the VAR of a firm's total portfolio as the square root of the sum of the squares of sub-portfolio VARs. The standard deviation of the firm's total P&L is therefore estimated to be the square root of the sum of the squares of the firm's fixed income risk, equity risk, FX risk and so on.

On average these correlations are close to zero, but in extremes risk factors tend to move together. If there is a huge move in equities, there is likely to be a large move in interest rates too. They might go down (as in 1987) or they might go up (as in the minicrash of 1989) but it is very likely there will be some kind of extreme move in rates. This fact is contradicted by VAR implementations which explicitly or implicitly set such correlations to zero.

What is wrong with stress testing?

Stress testing is often suggested as a "complementary" methodology to value-at-risk, which fails to provide reasonable estimates of the probability of extreme losses because of the assumptions incorporated in its method of computation. In practice stress testing is used as a band-aid for poor VAR. Despite the methodologies of VAR proponents, VARs *are* the right numbers to ask for because, if correctly computed, they take into account the joint probability distribution of changes in risk factors and the diversification of exposures to these factors in portfolios.

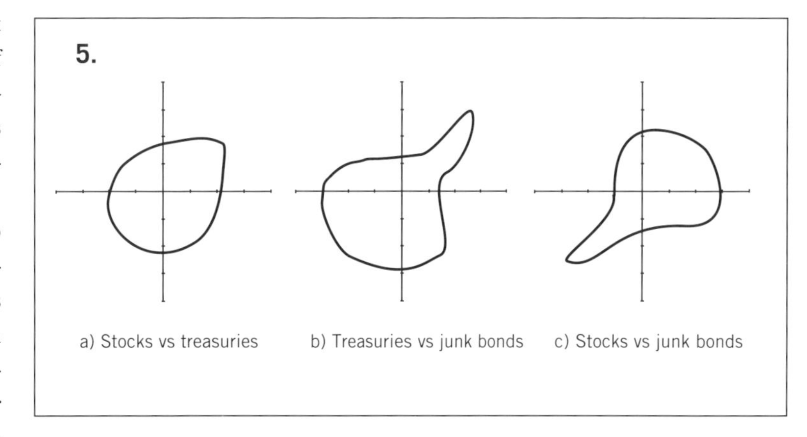

There are various ways of performing stress testing, but in general hypothetical extreme scenarios are created and corresponding hypothetical P&Ls are computed. The two obvious questions are:

- ❑ Where do the scenarios come from? and
- ❑ What should we do with the results?

One method is to dream up global scenarios But dreaming up multiple *global* scenarios which include all the changes in the thousands of risk factors to which a typical investment bank is exposed is hard, since there are so many changes to consider. If a hypothesis is that the Deutschmark sharply appreciates against the dollar, what is the hypothesis about, say, the Austrian Schilling and the Dutch guilder, or the yen or the Dax, or interest rates, and so on and so on?

Another method is to generate many *local* scenarios, and so consider a few risk factors at a time. For example, given an FX option portfolio, we might compute the hypothetical P&L for each currency pair under a variety of exchange rate and implied volatility scenarios. The problem then is how to amalgamate the results. One way is to simply add the worst case results for each of the sub-portfolios for the portfolio as a whole. But this obviously ignores the portfolio effect and fails to reward cross hedging.

Does this matter? *Yes it does!* Both these factors can be critical to risk adjusted return, and traders' whole approach to trading. Cross hedging, spreading and diversification are the *modus operandi* of traders. Cross hedging Austrian Schilling or Dutch guilder risk with positions in Deutschmarks is certainly not riskless but it is certainly not as risky as the sum of individual naked positions, which is a vast and useless overestimate. Risk management methodologies which cannot provide realistic estimates of the risks of such commonplace strategies are not adding value.

Artificial scenarios in general have the problem that, since there is no probability measure associated with them, they are not very useful in controlling risk as opposed to just limiting the loss under those scenarios we happen to think up. This is the problem with Taleb's alternative to conventional VAR (Taleb, 1997). Taleb says that risk managers should prepare "a list of associated crisis scenarios without unduly attaching probabilities to the array of events, until such time as we can show a better grasp of probability of large deviations...". He does not say when that time will come, nor does he explain what one should do with these scenarios. In any case their usefulness is contradicted by his dictum that "nothing predictable can be truly harmful".

An alternative approach is to use global scenarios from history to create a time series of hypothetical P&Ls. This would let us calculate the amounts that we would have made or lost daily over, say, the last 10 years if we had held our current portfolio. This immediately provides some useful information such as the worst losses we would have experienced. As we shall see, with some analysis, we can get the VAR estimates which we really needed all along.

Obviously a *purely* historical approach cannot encompass risks that we know exist but which have not yet manifested themselves and are hard to quantify - the prospect that an exchange rate which is now pegged will be allowed to float, for example. What we want is a method for incorporating this extra information into a realistic VAR system to get *conditional* VAR.

Large-scale market risk simulation

We have attacked conventional VAR and stress testing but what do we propose to put in their place? The simple but hardly straightforward answer is *simulation*. In theory, we can simply take a large set of scenarios which we think characterises the joint distribution of risk factor changes, compute the P&L under each scenario and then sort the P&Ls to constitute our estimate of the entire P&L distribution. We can then simply read off or interpolate any confidence level VAR we wish.

If the changes in risk factors happen to be multivariate normal and our exposures to them are linear, we would get the same answer for portfolio VAR as we do when we use the matrix multiplication short cut, apart from simulation error. However, the exposures to the risk factors no longer have to be linear and orthogonal. We now have the freedom to chose any multivariate distribution we like.

Another way to compute VAR is to create a time series of the simulated P&L of today's portfolio under the historical changes and then apply econometric analysis to this time series to estimate tomorrow's P&L distribution. Again, we would expect that if the joint distribution is normal and our exposures are linear, our VAR estimates should approximate VAR computed by the standard short cut - but we are not forced to assume either multivariate normality or linear exposures to the risk factors.

These freedoms give rise to two big problems:

PROBLEM 1

Computational and software feasibility. In many cases revaluing a portfolio thousands of times is not computationally feasible, either because it contains too many instruments or, as with path-dependent options, because the valuation algorithms are too slow. Also, building software capable of revaluing every instrument in the total portfolio of an investment bank is an enormous task. Fortunately, as we will see, it is also an unnecessary one.

PROBLEM 2

Methodology. If we are going to use an alternative joint distribution of risk factor changes where are we going to get it from? Alternatively, if we are going to use raw history and then analyse the simulated P&L time series, what precisely are we going to do?

Computational and software complexity of market risk management

Before we start proposing many thousands of revaluations to compute VAR by simulation, let us consider the work required to produce the one revaluation that every investment bank does daily.

Typically there are hundreds, if not thousands, of portfolios of thousands of securities organised by currency, product type, bank division and trader. They are managed by a plethora of computer systems, ranging from large commercial or in-house systems to spreadsheets.

Each of these systems contains static data defining the securities, plus descriptions of the portfolios of the positions in these instruments held by the bank. At the end of the day (or more frequently) each system takes a subset of the world's market data and uses it to mark its books to market. The profit or loss of each book, trader, division and the entire firm is then computed.

The simple-minded approach to simulation is to pull all the transactions into a central database and replicate all the various mark-to-market systems in the risk management system. The cost of building such a system, reconciling it with the various front office systems and continually updating it to cope with new products would be monstrous.

It is true that we do not require great accuracy in the VAR number itself but this is no great saving, since small errors in the values of underlying instruments can lead to large errors in the P&L and therefore large errors in VAR estimates. And any discrepancy in valuation between the front office system and the risk management system will lead to loss of confidence in risk estimates.[6]

Typical commercial VAR systems which use simulation either only attempt to value restricted classes of instruments or try to do the whole lot and fail. Note that these "implementation" problems are usually left out of risk management texts but *this is where global risk management projects get stuck* – they take so long replicating existing systems that they never get around to risk management for more than vanilla products. Even if the software feasibility problem is solved, the systems run into computational feasibility problems if more than conventional VAR computation is attempted. Their software is too slow to revalue portfolios the many times that simulation-based VAR requires.

Another dream is that all businesses within a firm will use the *same* front office system, and that the risk management system can be built on top of this. But no single system as yet in existence adequately handles all markets; each business quite rightly wants the system which best serves its own trading needs.

Constructing the global P&L approximation function

Our solution to the computational and software feasibility problems is to construct a Global P&L Approximation Function (GPLAF) from the outputs of the firm's existing front office systems. The two requirements of a GPLAF are that it is fast to compute (so that we can recompute it many thousands of times in our P&L simulations) and that it provides a good approximation *globally*, ie it gives a reasonable approximation to the firm's P&L (even ±20% would be acceptable) over a wide range of risk factor changes. Note that this behaviour is the opposite of typical "greek" approximations, which are unnecessarily good for small changes in risk factors but can be poor approximations for large changes.

Most front office systems already implicitly specify a P&L approximation function in the form of sensitivities (deltas, PVBPs, key rate durations, option greeks and so on), from which a P&L approximation function can be strung together. So why not use this? This is appropriate for some well behaved portfolios, even though it was only designed to apply for small changes of risk factors.

But generally the classic greek approximation for derivative portfolio value is not good enough to use as a global approximation, because of the inherent properties of derivative portfolios and because of the way traders use the greeks. As we remarked earlier, using classic dynamic hedging techniques for hedging derivative portfolios, option traders typically keep their greeks as flat as possible – which means they are well hedged for small moves, but not necessarily for large ones.

The first step in constructing the GPLAF is to identify the factors which drive each of the subportfolio's P&L. This is a much harder task than might be imagined, and where risk managers who actually understand the strategies that the traders are employing are invaluable.

The next step is to construct P&L approximations for each of the subportfolios. The GPLAF will simply be the sum of the approximation functions for the P&Ls of the individual portfolios. Again, this is a task best performed in conjunction with individual risk managers who know what the front end systems under their supervision can deliver.

Given that any decent front end system can generate "what-if" P&L scenarios; we can construct a GPLAF which interpolates and extrapolates from these scenarios. This is a generalisation of the implicit P&L approximation used in conventional VAR, where the effects of individual risk factors are extrapolated from the effects of small moves, eg 1bp.

6. P&L of portfolio of exotic options

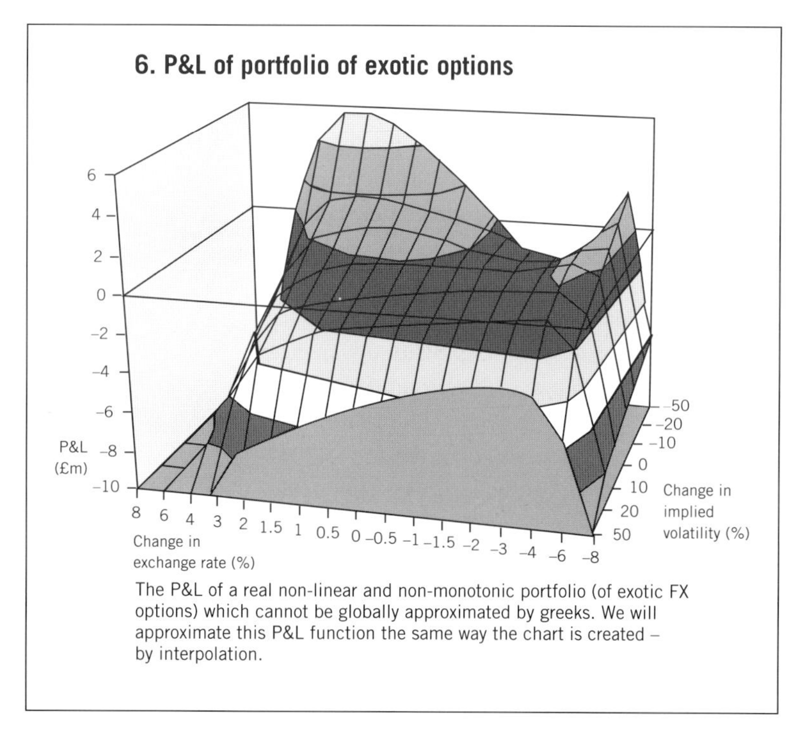

The P&L of a real non-linear and non-monotonic portfolio (of exotic FX options) which cannot be globally approximated by greeks. We will approximate this P&L function the same way the chart is created – by interpolation.

Our generalisation is to approximate total P&L as a sum of interpolations from vectors of scenarios (where there is little interaction between risk factors) or matrices (where there is interaction between two factors, such as changes in volatility and the value of the underlying security). Computing these vectors and matrices is overhead (performed by the individual front office systems) and the simulation itself just interpolates and sums these values. Interpolation is an extremely fast process and huge numbers of *approximate* simulations are feasible.

What about interactions between three or more factors? We could extend our method to allow interpolation and extrapolation from three or higher dimensional arrays, but the number of grid points in an n-dimensional space with k points per dimension is k^n, so we want to avoid this since the overhead threatens to become infeasible. In the case of higher dimensional complex interactions between risk factors or uncertainty over what the important risk factors really are, a more automated approach can be taken.

Elucidating and approximating the effects of large numbers of variables on some output variable from examples is a classic problem of artificial intelligence. A front end system can be required to revalue portfolios under a number of scenarios of changes in the valuation inputs. These scenarios can be chosen using Latin Hypercube techniques or their generalisations (see below). Then artificial intelligence techniques can be used to create a quick approximation function which has "learned" the relationships between the inputs and the output – the P&L. For example, abductive inference techniques generate networks of polynomials, which approximate the output as a function of the input (Drake and Yim, 1997).

Of course, no matter what approximation scheme we use it is always possible to come up with a pathological P&L function which will defeat it. Suppose there are only, say, 60 risk factors affecting a P&L and there is one combination of up moves and down moves that will bankrupt the firm. The number of combinations of up and down moves that would have to be checked to be certain of finding the disaster combination is 2^{60}, that is, $\sim 10^{36}$, which is clearly infeasible. Even in the Black-Scholes formula there are interactions between all the input variables.

Fortunately, however, serious interactions between risk factors tend to be limited (in particular to interactions between implied volatility and the price of the underlying security) because more complex interactions tend to make the securities unprofitable to hedge.

The details of how to implement this scheme

7. Two-dimensional linear interpolation and extrapolation

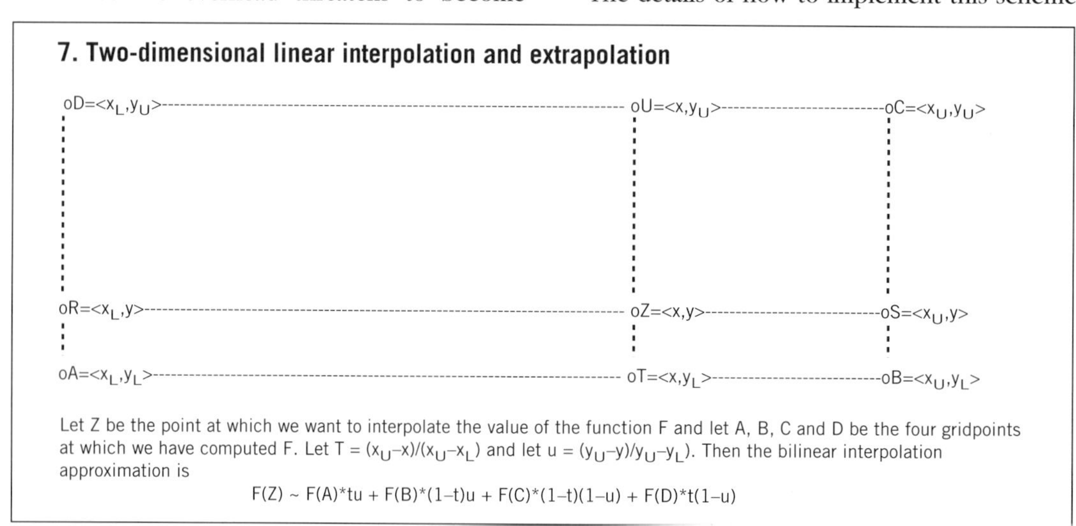

Let Z be the point at which we want to interpolate the value of the function F and let A, B, C and D be the four gridpoints at which we have computed F. Let $T = (x_U-x)/(x_U-x_L)$ and let $u = (y_U-y)/y_U-y_L)$. Then the bilinear interpolation approximation is

$$F(Z) \sim F(A)*tu + F(B)*(1-t)u + F(C)*(1-t)(1-u) + F(D)*t(1-u)$$

may vary between sub-portfolios but the goal is always the same – a fast-to-compute function which is a good global approximation to the P&L. These functions can be programmed on spreadsheets and provide a real-time approximation to P&L with live data feeds, which can then be verified against actual P&L, especially on days with moves of a reasonable size.

This scheme has several advantages. It is software efficient – we do not try to replicate existing software. It is also computationally efficient – we do not end up demanding impossible numbers of complete revaluations. And, crucially for any global risk management project, it is also *organisationally* efficient – we make maximal use of our talent in the frontlines of risk management, we can incrementally reconcile each piece of our global approximation function with results from the traders' own software, and we can incrementally improve our approximation as computing power and algorithms in the various front-office systems improve.

Once we have a function which gives a good approximation of the firm's P&L with any combination of risk factor changes, how are we going to use it? As we saw earlier, the classic method is to create a huge sample which approximately characterises the joint distribution of tomorrow's risk factor changes, apply the GPLAF to this sample and sort the results. An alternative approach is to simulate the P&L that we would have observed over time and perform analysis on this simulated P&L time series to predict the distribution of tomorrow's P&L.[7] Let us consider each strategy in turn.

Estimating and simulating the joint distribution of risk factor changes

How does one estimate the joint distribution of hundreds, if not thousands of risk factors? Our short cut is to assume that the correlation "structure" remains constant. Estimating time varying correlations is an attempt (fraught with estimation risk) to compensate for the inaccuracy of the initial linear correlation hypothesis, a hypothesis we have discarded. We will avoid explicitly estimating the correlation structure and instead use a sampling technique which ensures that our sample has a structure similar to that of the historical data, but we will allow the individual risk factor distributions to vary over time.

ESTIMATING INDIVIDUAL RISK DISTRIBUTIONS

Using historical data we want to parameterise the individual distributions in the sense that we want to fit simple, smooth probability distributions that are more realistic than the classic normal or lognormal distributions. Details of several families of such distributions have been published. In particular, Ramberg, Tadikamalla, Dudewicz and Mykytka (1979) have created a parametric fitting family which is particularly simple and fast to sample from. Given any specified mean μ, variance σ^2, skew and kurtosis (within bounds), they show how to construct a distribution from their family which has almost exactly the same moments.

Of course there are alternatives to RTDM. Rachev et al in a number of papers report excellent results fitting Weibull and double Weibull (two Weibull distributions pasted together in the middle) distributions to many financial time series including very fat tailed unconditional distributions, such as the dollar/Bulgarian Lev exchange rate. (Chobanov, Mateev, Mittnik and Rachev, 1996).

An obvious strategy is to use one of these distributions fitted to our historical data, but in doing so we would throw away any temporal information in the data. Although we have criticised techniques such as GARCH because they assume conditional normality, they do seem to have some power. On average, when they predict a high volatility the returns are in fact more dispersed.

We would like to make use of such predictions without swallowing the normality assumption. We can use GARCH or (even better) implied volatility if it is available or any other volatility predictor in a non-parametric way by plotting actual historical moves versus the volatility predicted for that day. We should see the historic distribution widening out as the predicted volatility increases. In that case a sensible strategy is to fit a function not to the entire history of historical changes but instead to those changes which occurred when predicted volatility was near its current predicted level.

As an example of our method, in Figures 8–11 overleaf we consider the dollar/sterling exchange rate, to which we have fitted double Weibull distributions conditional on either implied volatility or GARCH predicted volatility.

So far we have modelled each of the individual risk factor distributions. How can we use them for multivariate simulation?

An efficient simulation method which preserves correlation structure

It is well known that the variance of an estimate

8. $/£ January 1988–April 1996 daily log returns:

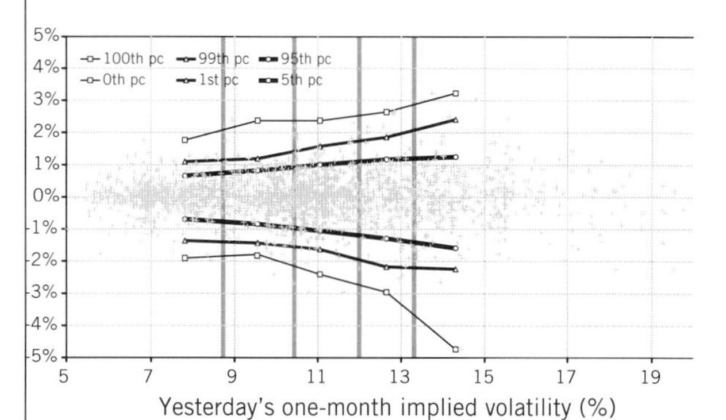

In this chart each + represents the actual move in the $/£ exchange rate versus yesterday's one-month implied volatility. We divide yesterday's implied volatility into five quintiles. The boundaries of these quintiles are indicated by the shaded vertical lines in the chart. For each quintile we compute the 0th, 1st, 5th, 95th, 99th and 100th percentile actual moves for all the points for which yesteday's implied volatility belonged to the quintile. We have plotted these percentiles at points in the middle of each quintile, ie, at the 10th, 30th, 50th, 70th and 90th percentiles of yesterday's implied volatility. We then join the corresponding percentile moves with straight lines.
As one would hope, the percentiles fan out as yesterday's implied volatility increases and we can use this chart to estimate the distribution of tomorrow's move *given the current level of the indicator* without assuming conditional normality and without explicitly specifying a transformation between implied volatility and one-day realised volatility.

10. $/£ January 1988–April 1996 daily log returns

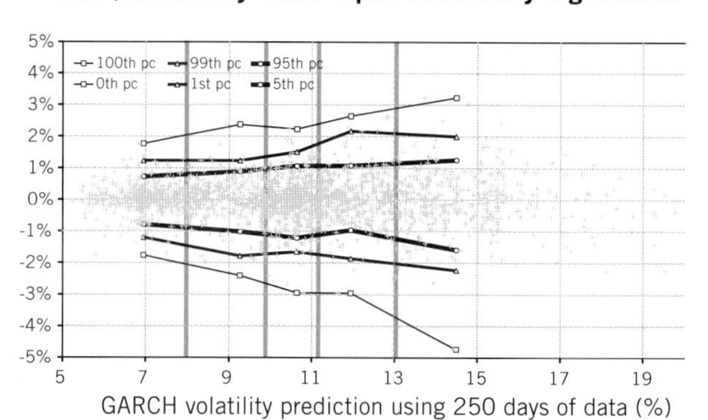

This chart is similar to Figure 8 except that now GARCH is used as the volatility indicator instead of implied volatility. In general, if we have a choice as we do for $/£ we would use implied volatility as our indicator in preference to GARCH since it has better predictive power (Jorion, 1995). However, implied volatility is unavailable for most financial time series so we will illustrate our approach to modelling a distribution conditional on the level of a volatility indicator with GARCH as the indicator.

9. $/£ January 1988–April 1996 daily log returns:
all data

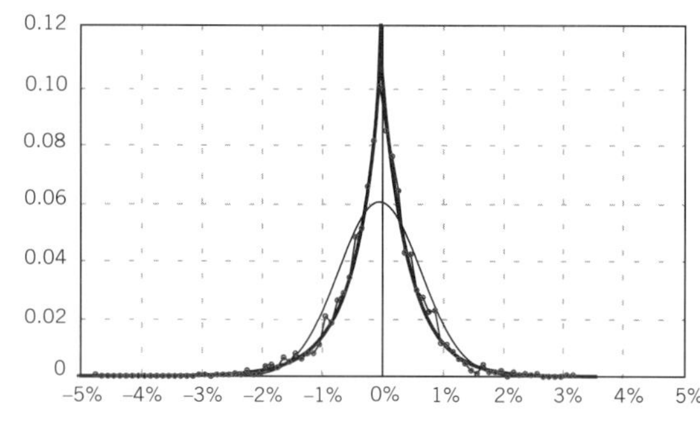

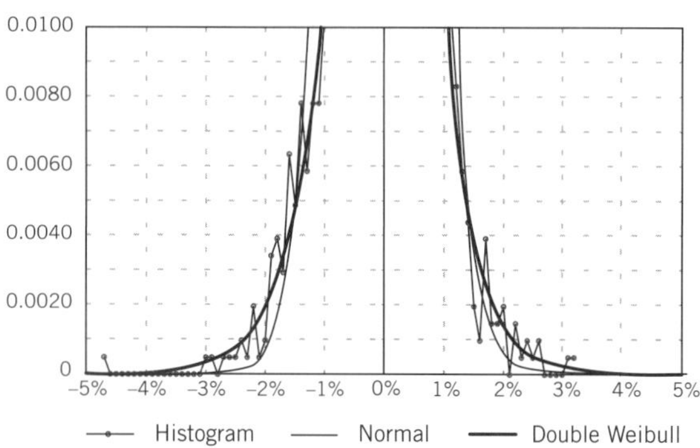

Two views of the same chart in which a Double Weibull distribution is fitted with maximum likelihood to the unconditional changes in the $/£ exchange rate. The normal distribution with the same mean and standard deviation as the data is also plotted for comparison. Note that the Double Weibull distribution with its taller thinner peak and fatter tails fits the data much better.

11. $/£ January 1988–April 1996 daily log returns
First quintile by GARCH volatility forecast using last 250 days' data

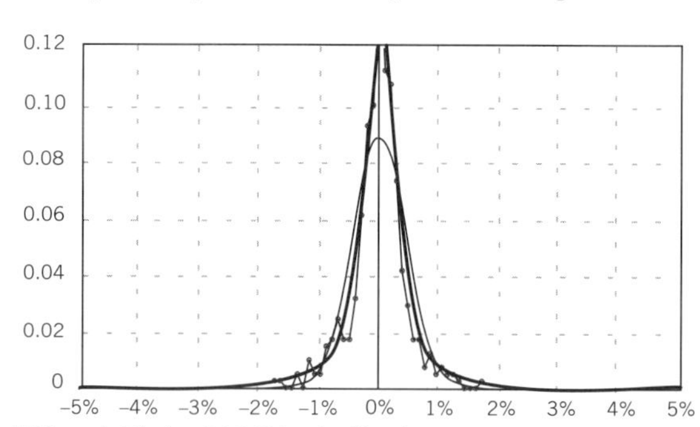

Fifth quintile by GARCH volatility forecast using last 250 days' data

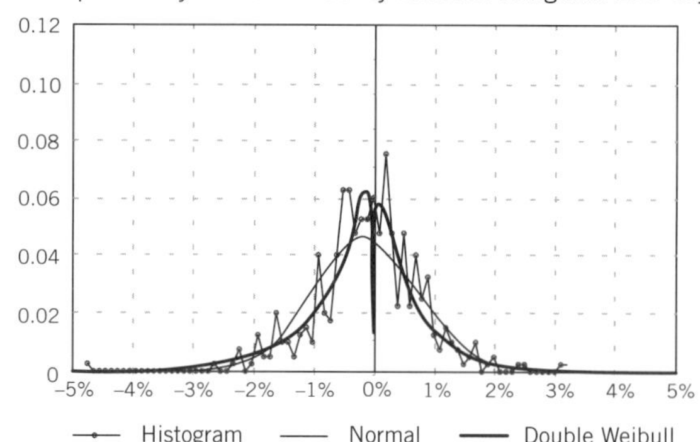

The top chart shows our fit to $/£ *conditional on* the GARCH volatility estimate being in the *first* quintile of its range. The lower chart is our fit to the same series conditonal on the GARCH volatility esimate being in the *fifth* quintile of its range.

of an average provided by Monte Carlo sampling decreases in proportion to the inverse of the square root of the number of trials to improve the accuracy of the estimate by a factor of 10, the number of trials must be increased by a factor of 100. A simple technique which greatly speeds up convergence is stratified sampling. In this technique, if N simulations are required the cumulative probability range interval [0,1] is sliced into M equal size buckets and N/M simulations are performed in each bucket. This avoids the clustering which occurs with naive sampling.

In a naive generalisation of stratified sampling to multivariate simulation, if we wanted each of the K variables to be individually stratified M ways we would end up with M^K buckets, which is infeasible since we have a lot of variables. A feasible alternative is Latin Hypercube sampling, in which samples are drawn in such a manner that each variable is *individually* stratified, as illustrated in Figure 12. Obviously when K is large the sampling is very sparse even when a large number of samples is taken, simply because there is so much ground to cover.

Fortunately, as Stein shows, this not a problem if the function to be evaluated is approximately *additive* (linear in each variable and orthogonal in the individual variables) in which case a Latin Hypercube scheme will work well. In particular if the function is exactly additive then the variance of the average of that function decreases in proportion to the inverse of N itself, a huge improvement over the unstratified technique (Stein 1987).

Typical option portfolios are not additive so we cannot expect to achieve the full speedup, but we can concentrate our sampling effort on the worst behaved ones.

Latin Hypercubes can be generalised to Orthogonal Arrays in which the samples are chosen so that we are stratifed in each pair or triple of dimensions, not just each dimension individually (Owen 1994), (Tang 1993). Orthogonal arrays in turn can be generalised to (t,m,s) nets (Owen).

Remember that we want our simulation not only to be efficient but also to preserve the "correlation structure" of our empirical multivariate distribution. So we need to do it without destroying our stratification.

To justify our choice of technique let us first consider some methods for multivariate simulation that will not solve our problem. Every simulation text shows how to sample from a correlated multivariate normal distribution;

12. A Latin Hypercube sample
with N = 6 and K = 2 for X distributed uniformly on the unit square

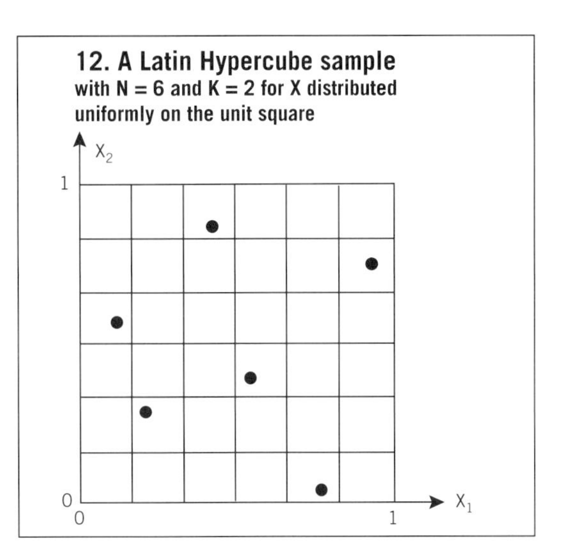

indeed it is usually the only multivariate technique given. The trick is to apply the Cholesky decomposition of the correlation matrix to independent normal samples to get a correlated multivariate sample, a technique developed by Scheuer and Stoller (1962). This is no good to us for several reasons - we reject the assumption of normality, we do not want linear correlation and applying the Cholesky decomposition would destroy stratification of the individual variables.

Hull discards both the normality assumption and the assumption that the individual distributions are of the same form. This requires that rank correlation replace linear correlation, and Hull shows how to create a sample with approximately the same rank correlation matrix by using the standard Cholesky decomposition technique and mapping the actual distributions onto normal distributions percentile by percentile (Hull, 1977). Independently, Iman and Connover (1982) use a similar technique, except that their samples have a Latin Hypercube stratification. This is better but, as discussed earlier, we cannot adequately represent the relations between factors by any correlation coefficient.

Stein's algorithm, by contrast, gives us almost everything we want (see Appendix). It creates a sample which is both hypercube stratified and has approximately the same distribution (not just the same rank correlation matrix) as the joint distribution when the sample is large.

The key idea is that the initial sampling is only to obtain a correct correlation structure. These samples are replaced by their ranks and then discarded. In turn the ranks are used to force stratification in each dimension simultaneously, and the correlation between the stratification intervals is determined by the original sample.

In our application of Stein's algorithm, our initial sampling is from the empirical joint distribution of risk factor changes so that is where our correlation structure comes from. However, our inverse cumulative distribution functions F_{k-1} will be the distributions we have estimated or fitted to the distributions of the individual risk factor changes.

Analysis of simulated univariate P&L

In this alternative approach, let us start by implicitly assuming that the set of historical changes in the risk factors is the best estimate of tomorrow's joint distribution of changes in risk factors. Each combination of risk factor changes observed historically is assumed to be equally likely tomorrow (and implicitly any combination of changes not observed in the history has probability zero). The corresponding simulated P&Ls can then be sorted to obtain a complete estimate of the P&L distribution. The effects of historical crises on the portfolio can also be noted.

This process is worth carrying out because it is simple, easily understood and reveals interesting information such as the maximum simulated loss, but it does discard temporal information in the simulated returns. We know that financial markets change over time and we can see changes in the volatility of the simulated P&L over time – but this information is lost if we just sort the P&Ls. The obvious solution is to use econometric methods on the simulated P&L time series to improve our estimate of tomorrow's P&L distribution.

We have already massaged the raw historical risk factor changes to obtain a better estimate of the joint distribution of those changes. Our alternative route is to use the raw historical data to generate a raw simulated P&L times series and then massage this P&L series to improve our estimate of tomorrow's P&L distribution.

An advantage of modelling individual risk factor changes is that they are usually, if not normal, at least unimodal, whereas there is no reason why the P&L of portfolios which contain derivatives should be either. The other advantage of modelling the individual risk factor changes is that extra information such as implied volatilities is often available, which can easily be incorporated into our estimates of the individual risk factor return. But there is no direct way of incorporating such information into the estimates of our P&L distribution. The big disadvantage of modelling the individual risk factor changes is that we have to explicitly deal with correlation structure, which we can avoid by simulating the historical P&L distribution directly.

So if we are going to model the P&L distribution directly, we must be prepared to model a complicated albeit univariate distribution. However, univariate distributions are much easier to deal with than multivariate distributions and we can use non- or semi-parametric methods on the simulated P&L to incorporate extra information.

We suggest four techniques for improving on simple historical simulation through analysis of the simulated P&L time series:

❑ *Parametric use of P&L volatility forecasts* Take the simple simulated P&Ls, divide each P&L by the corresponding GARCH or other forecast of the volatility for that particular day, then multiply them all by today's GARCH volatility forecast to get adjusted P&Ls. Then take these sorted adjusted P&Ls as our P&L distribution forecast. This normalises each day's P&L by its forecast volatility to get a time series of P&L expressed in units of the standard deviation of the forecast volatility.[8]

❑ *Non-parametric use of P&L volatility forecasts* Take the simple simulated daily P&Ls and use GARCH or any other technique to estimate the time varying parameters of the simulated P&L given its time series to date. We can then use non-parametric methods to estimate P&L percentiles given the level of the GARCH forecast.

For example, given that the GARCH volatility forecast is, say, in the 4th quintile (of all such forecasts that would have been made given the simulated P&Ls to that date) we would look at the observed percentiles of simulated P&L on the days that the forecast was in the 4th quintile of forecasts. These P&L percentiles would be our estimate of the P&L distribution. This non-parametric use of volatility forecasts is appropriate when the P&Ls are skewed or otherwise deviate from normality.

❑ *Apply extreme value theory to the P&L series to estimate the (albeit unconditional) probability of extreme losses* (Longin, 1997).

❑ *Generalisation to other factors* We can generalise this and analyse the effect on P&L of various factors, not just forecast volatility. Conceptually the idea is to make a scatter diagrams of the (simulated historical) P&Ls versus changes in the factor and find the ones that are associated with big losses – exploratory data analysis is a fancy name for this. Then if we have a view on what these factors will be tomorrow we can use that to forecast P&L percentiles.

This can be automated and hundreds or even thousands of factors considered using artificial intelligence techniques. The "factors" can be arbitrarily complex – the value of a basket of European currencies against the dollar, for example. It is also worth noting that the effects of these factors incorporate historical correlates, so if we plot the effect of, say, dollar interest changes versus our simulated P&L, we are seeing the effect of all the changes that have been historically associated with dollar interest rates as well.

This is the key to the method's effectiveness. It is easy to tabulate the effects of individual risk factors moving in isolation but not very informative since the portfolio effect is not seen. It is also easy to tabulate the P&Ls of various arbitrarily chosen scenarios but, once again, the scenarios are confined to a few factors at a time, the portfolio effect is not seen.[9] Using our method we can discover complex scenarios which have the biggest effects on our P&L taking the correlation structure into account. This transforms VAR from a static number into a tool for understanding the dynamics of our portfolios.

Appendix

Stein's algorithm (1987)

Suppose there are K factors in the multivariate distribution we want to simulate, and that we want to create N Latin Hypercube stratified samples from the distribution.

First, draw a sample of N unstratified K-vectors from the distribution. From these vectors construct an $N \times K$ matrix Y in which the ijth element $Y(i,j)$ is the jth element from the ith sample. Define another $N \times K$ matrix R in which the ij-th element $R(i,j)$ is the rank within the jth column of Y of the element $Y(i,j)$.

From R, define a third $N \times K$ matrix Y^* in which the ijth element

$$Y^*(i,j) = F_k^{-1}\{[R(i,j) + e_{ij} - 1]/N\}$$

where e_{ij} is a uniform $[0,1]$ variate and F_k^{-1} is the inverse cumulative distribution function for the kth factor.

The rows of Y^* constitute the Latin Hypercube stratified sample we require.

1 NORMSINV *and other capitalised functions in this paper are the standard Excel functions but note that* NORMSINV(x) *incorrectly returns –500,000 when* $x < 10^{-7}$. *If you really want to use the normal distribution for extremes you should use Moro's algorithm (Moro, 1995).*

2 *Actually it says that the sum of a number of distributions tends toward a stable distribution of which the Normal distribution is only one member. For example a sum of Cauchy distributions (which are very fat tailed) is Cauchy, not Normal.*

3 *GARCH stands for Generalised Auto Regressive Conditional Heteroskedasticity. For an introduction see Alexander (1996). For an in-depth survey see Bollerslev, Chou and Kroner (1992).*

4 *The assumption of conditional normality is common but not essential when using GARCH techniques. For example the sterling-Deutschmark exchange rate is modelled as a conditional Student's* t *distribution in Pesaran & Robinson (1993). Since Student's* t *is a fat-tailed distribution this is promising for risk management applications, though for equities and other assets which are more likely to melt down than melt up we would prefer an* asymmetric *fat-tailed distribution.*

5 *I swear I heard this rationale given by a prominent speaker at a conference on risk management.*

6 *It is a function of risk management to check front-office software but checking software is much different and easier that creating an industrial strength replica of it.*

7 *This strategy was suggested independently by Barone-Adesi and Giannopoulos.*

8 *This idea, at least when applied to individual risk factors, is due to Jan Kwiatkowski of BZW*

9 *In the case of multivariate normal world with linear sensitivities our method would correspond to Garman's "VaR Delta" (Garman, 1996).*

BIBLIOGRAPHY

Alexander, C., 1996, "Volatility and Correlation Forecasting" in *The Handbook of Risk Management*, John Wiley.

Bagg, J., 1996, "Risk Management - Taking the Wider View," *International Derivative Review*, June, pp. 12-14

Barone-Adesi, G., and Giannopoulos, K., Undated, "A Simplified Approach to the,Conditional Estimation of Value at Risk", Manuscript, University of Alberta, City University and University of Westminster.

Bollerslev, T., Chou, R. and Kroner, K., 1992, "ARCH modeling in finance", **Journal of Econometrics** 52, pp. 5-59.

Chew, L., 1994 "Shock Treatment", *Risk*, 7, 9, pp. 63-70.

Chobanov G., P. Mateev, S. Mittnik and S. Rachev., 1996, "Modeling the Distribution of Highly Volatile Exchange Rate Time Series", Lecture Notes in Statistics 115: Athens Conference on Applied Probability and Time Series, Volume II: Time Series Analysis, Springer.

Cox, E., 1995, "Magic and Regulation", *Risk* 8, 3, pp. 50-4.

Drake, K. and R. Yim, 1997, "Abductive Information Modeling Applied to Financial Time Series", in Caldwell, Randall, B., *Nonlinear Financial Forecasting - Proceedings of the First INFFC*, Finance and Technology Publishing, Haymarket, VA.

Garman, M., 1996, "Improving on VAR," *Risk* 9, 5, pp. 61-3; reprinted as Chapter 13 of the present volume.

Hull, J.C., 1977, "Dealing with Dependence in Risk Simulations", *Operational Research Quarterly*, 28, No. 1, ii, pp. 201-13.

Iman, R.L. and W.J. Connover, 1982, "A Distribution-Free Approach to Inducing Rank Correlation Among Input Variables", *Communications in Statistics Part B - Simulation and Computation* 11, pp. 311-34.

Jackwerth, J. and M. Rubinstein, 1996, "Recovering Probability Distributions from Option Prices," *Journal of Finance*, LI, No 5, pp. 1611-31.

Jorion, P., 1995a, "Predicting Volatility in the Foreign Exchange Market", *Journal of Finance* 50, pp. 507-28.

Longin, F., 1997, "From Value at Risk to Stress Testing: The Extreme Value Approach", CERESSEC Working Paper 97-004.

Moro, B., 1995, "The Full Monte", *Risk* 8, 2, pp. 57-8.

Owen, A., 1994, "Lattice Sampling Revisited: Monte Carlo Variance of Means over Randomized Orthogonal Arrays", *Annals of Statistics* 22, 2, pp. 930-45.

Owen, A., Undated, "Randomly Permuted (t,m,s)-Nets and (t,s)-Sequences", Manuscript, Stanford University.

Pesaran, B. and G. Robinson, 1993, "The European Exchange Rate Mechanism and the Volatility of the Sterling-Deutschmark Rate", *The Economic Journal*, 103, No 421, pp. 1418-31.

Ray, C., 1993, *The Bond Market*, Business One Irwin, Homewood Illinois.

Ramberg, J., P. Tadikamalla, E. Dudewicz and E. Mykytka, 1979, "A Probability Distribution and Its Uses in Fitting Data," *Technometrics* 21, No. 2, pp. 201-14.

Scheuer, E. and D. Stoller, 1962, "On the Generation of Random Normal Vectors", *Technometrics* 4, pp. 278-81.

Stein, M., 1987, "Large Scale Properties of Simulations Using Latin Hypercube Sampling", *Technometrics* 29, No. 2, pp.143-51.

Taleb, N., 1997, "Against VAR," *Derivatives Strategy*, pp. 20-6.

Tang, B., 1993, "Orthogonal Array-Based Latin Hypercubes", *Journal of the American Statistical Association*, 88, No. 424, Theory and Methods pp. 1392-7.

26

VAR Analytics:

Portfolio Structure, Key Rate Convexities, and VAR Betas*

Thomas S.Y. Ho, Michael Z.H. Chen and Fred H.T. Eng
Global Advanced Technology Corporation

This paper describes a new approach to determining the value-at-risk of a portfolio and using the VAR numbers to manage risks. It begins with grouping the holdings by type of risk. These holdings are "blocks" that define the portfolio structure. The VAR numbers for the entire portfolio (the total risk) and for all the blocks are then calculated. These results show how the VAR numbers of the blocks "roll up" to the total risk. Finally, we calculate the marginal contribution of risk from each of the blocks (called VAR betas) and the scenarios that result in the losses measured by VAR.

Many researchers discuss various VAR methodologies. Beder (1995), Crnkovic and Drachman (1995), Kupiec (1995) and RiskMetrics-Technical Document (1995) are some examples. Yet, few papers say how risk managers should use the VAR numbers to analyse portfolio risks and how such analysis relates to risk management. We address these topics.

The absence of discussion on the analysis of VAR numbers may be the result of the widespread use of Monte Carlo simulations. Monte Carlo simulation methodology is computer-intensive, so the methodology cannot be easily used to calculate the blocks of a portfolio.

We use the delta-gamma approach, which can identify the option risks in a portfolio and can calculate the VAR numbers efficiently. Wilson (1994) describes the delta-gamma approach in a general context. The appropriate measures of the "gamma" of interest rate-contingent claims are called key rate convexities. Key rate convexities capture the price change of any interest rate-contingent claim when the security is hedged along the yield curve (on the delta basis). Hence, key rate convexity measures the second-order risk of any movements of the yield curve.

We show that second-order risk can be complicated even though the security can be quite simple. This second-order measure is important for a portfolio with options or with a combination of exchange rate and market risks.

The grouping of holdings by risk type has been discussed elsewhere, in the Basle test, for example. We propose a more formal structure and application of the marginal contributions of risks from the basic building blocks of the portfolio to each higher level of the portfolio. As a result, risk managers can take risk management actions.

We use the Basle test portfolio to demonstrate this procedure. It has over 100 securities, including many derivatives, both option-embedded and option-free. The portfolio is allocated in five currencies, and in equity, interest rate and currency types, with long and short positions. It is exposed to over 110 risk sources. We show that our methodology can be implemented for such a portfolio relatively easily.

Portfolio structure

One useful approach to the organisation of a

* *This paper was first published in the Journal of Portfolio Management, Vol. 23 (1996). This copyrighted material is reprinted with minor amendments with permission from Institutional Investor, Inc. 488 Madison Avenue, New York, New York 10022. The authors thank Mark Abbott, Hanya Marie Kim, Magnus Nystrom, and Tony Persson for their comments.*

Table1. Portfolio building blocks

Portfolio evaluation date May 30, 1995

Currency	Asset	Market value by assets (Skr)	Market value by currencies (Skr)	Total market value (Skr)
				−3,771,365,237.04
DM			−8,029,512,802.05	
	Equity	207,413,697.67		
	Interest rate	−8,820,409,119.72		
	Foreign exchange	583,482,620.00		
Ffr			11,874,907,355.40	
	Equity	171,906,626.36		
	Interest rate	10,675,260,729.04		
	Foreign exchange	1,027,740,000.00		
£			−4,526,830,517.34	
	Equity	197,266,694.30		
	Interest rate	−4,136,817,211.64		
	Foreign exchange	−587,280,000.00		
¥			12,862,868,409.32	
	Equity	143,010,038.87		
	Interest rate	11,838,938,370.45		
	Foreign exchange	880,920,000.00		
$			−15,952,797,682.36	
	Equity	165,273,815.63		
	Interest rate	−14,212,698,157.99		
	Foreign exchange	−1,905,373,340.00		

portfolio is to group the holdings by type of risk. The portfolio structure consists of "blocks", and a portfolio can be constructed from these smaller building blocks. In turn, each block may be constructed from sub-blocks. These sub-blocks may then be constructed from smaller blocks, until these blocks reach the smallest units, the basic building blocks.

To assure that the portfolio structure is well defined, we require that every security of a portfolio be allocated to only one basic building block. The purpose of constructing a portfolio structure is to identify the sources of risk to a portfolio. For effective risk management, we need to measure the risk exposure from the basic building blocks and to "roll up" to the total risk of the portfolio.

1. Market value of the positions by currency and asset type

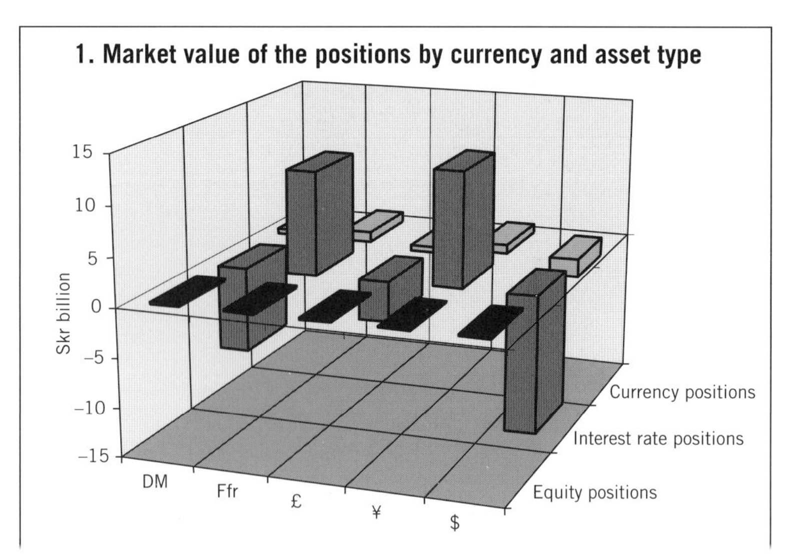

Once this is done, the portfolio structure can reveal the interactions of the risks across the portfolio, specifying the natural hedges in the portfolio, the effect of diversification, and the major sources of risk.

The highest level of the blocks is the currency block. In a global portfolio, we assign all the securities by the currency of their payments. Some structured products may have several currencies in their payments. In these cases, we may break up the structured products into several securities and allocate each of the securities to the appropriate currency blocks.

Each currency block is built from three asset blocks: equity, interest rate, and foreign exchange. All securities are then assigned, according to their main sources of risk, to one of these three asset types. We use the sample portfolio of the Basle test to illustrate this portfolio structure. Table 1 presents the portfolio in terms of its building blocks.

When the blocks of the portfolio are constructed, we can then calculate the market value for each of the blocks. Calculation of the market values makes it is possible to identify distribution of the investments across the sources of risk.

An example of these procedures can be seen in Table 1, which shows the market valuation of each of the blocks. The result shows that the total portfolio value is a short position of Skr3,771,365,237.

Figure 1 depicts the distribution of the assets across the five currencies translated into Swedish krona. The results indicate that the portfolio holds significant positions in interest rate products, and large short positions in dollars and Deutschmarks, while it is long in the French franc and the yen. It is incorrect to conclude, however, that the portfolio is exposed to mostly interest rate risks. The total exposure will depend on the volatilities and correlations of all risk sources.

For most securities, it is usually quite clear which basic building block they should be assigned to. Most problems in assignment are likely to arise from derivatives. Let us consider some examples here.

Currency swaps are exchanges of payments in different currencies. In this case, the payments of a currency swap are assigned to two different currencies. This means each payment is an interest rate asset. Long-dated stock options are sensitive to both interest rate and equity risks, but usually equity risks dominate interest rate risks, so the stock option will be considered "equity."

VAR risk measures: key rate convexities

The VAR measure in this analysis is defined as the maximum loss for a 99% level of statistical confidence, with a 10-day time horizon. VAR can be calculated or analysed by using different methodologies, including delta-normal, non-linear (delta-hedged residual risk), delta-gamma, and vega measures.

Delta-normal assumes that the loss is related to the risk of the delta hedge position. The delta hedge position is calculated by the price sensitivity to each risk source. For an interest rate security, we use key rate durations. Key rate durations are the securities' sensitivity to each of the key rates' local shifts of the spot rates in the government curve or the swap curve.

Ho (1992) describes the precise construct of the key rate durations. He shows that the sum of the key rate durations is the effective duration. Therefore, key rate duration is a risk measure that decomposes the effective duration to the interest rate-contingent claim's sensitivities along the yield curve. McCoy (1995) shows that a portfolio that has zero key rate durations is exposed to negligible yield curve risks.

This analysis does not use a bucket approach for the cashflows. This is because the key rate durations provide a consistent framework to calculate the deltas for both option and non-option securities. The risk of option-embedded bonds or securities with option risk can be accurately measured in KRDs and not by the bucket approach.

Non-linear risk is the residual risk of the securities net of the linear risk (or the delta-normal risk). It is the risk that the position has when it is delta-hedged. By definition, combining the linear and the non-linear risks gives us the total risk.

This does not mean that the sum of the VARs of the delta-normal and non-linear measures gives the VAR of the total risk. This is because the scenarios of the largest loss for delta-normal measure, non-linear risk, and total risk can all be different.

Following from the definition of non-linear risk, we generally expect option-free securities to have little non-linear risk. For options, the non-linear risk would be the time decay or the convexity (gamma) risk.

To measure the total risk of a security, we use a delta-gamma methodology, which looks at the delta and the gamma of a security. For interest rate risks, we use key rate durations and key rate convexities. The portfolio delta and gamma (or key rate duration and key rate convexity) are the market-weighted delta and gamma of each security in the portfolio.

Key rate convexity is defined as the second-order Taylor expansion of the price (or value) of an interest rate-contingent claim, where the independent variables are the key rates. Let P be the price of the interest rate-contingent claim, and let r_i be the ith key rate, for $i = 1, 2,\dots,n$. Then, the ith key rate duration is defined as:

$$KRD\ (i) = -(dP/dr_i)/P. \qquad (1)$$

Similarly, the key rate convexity for the simultaneous change of the ith and jth key rates is defined as:

$$KRC\ (i,j) = (d^2P/dr_i dr_j)/P. \qquad (2)$$

Clearly, key rate convexities of a security can be represented by a symmetric matrix of dimension n. It can be shown in a straightforward manner that the sum of the key rate convexities equals the convexity. Also, the weighted-average sum of each key rate convexity across all the securities in a portfolio equals the portfolio key rate convexity. That is, the property of the key rate convexity is similar to that of the key rate duration.

Key rate convexities of a security are numerically estimated. Figure 2 depicts the key rate convexities of an at-the-money cap with a five-year tenor, six-month reset. This result shows that the key rate convexities of a cap can be represented

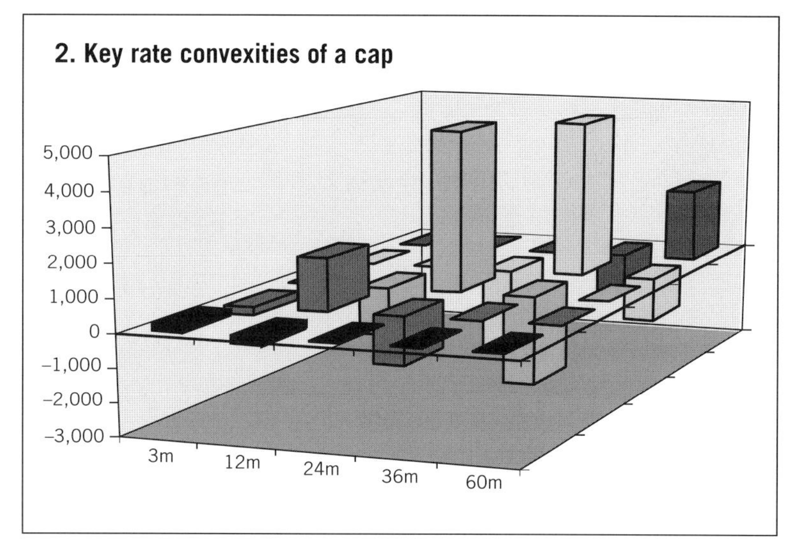

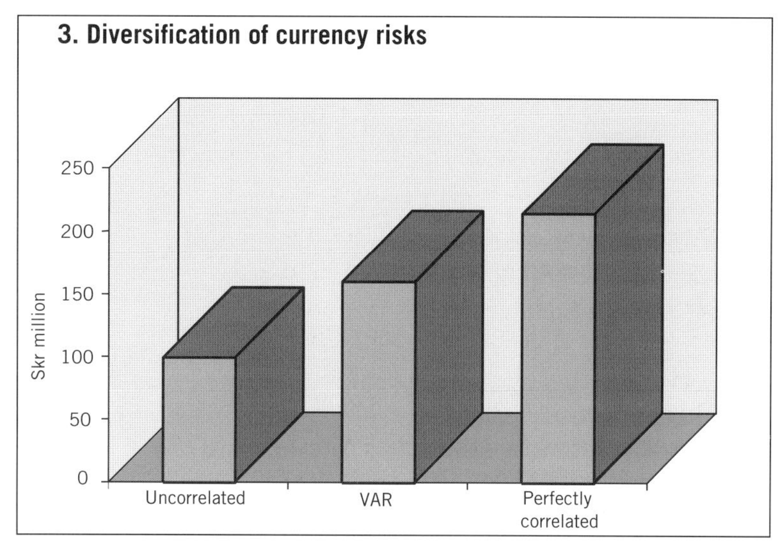

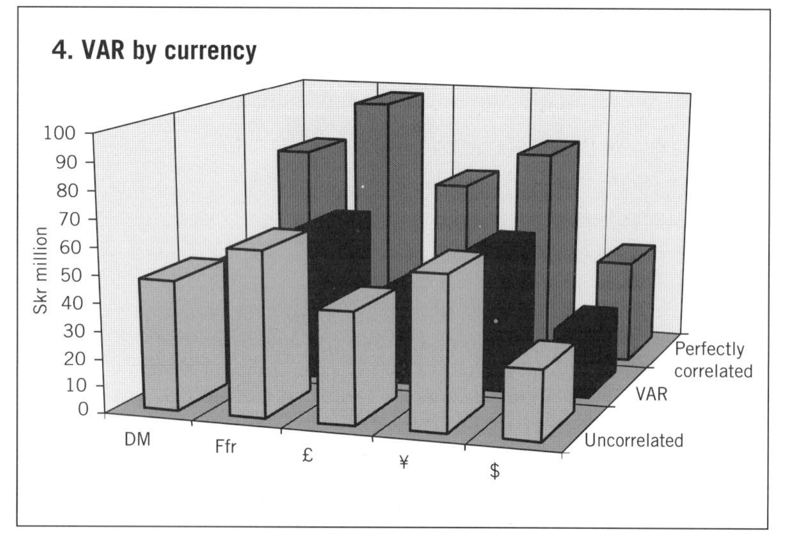

by a symmetric tridiagonal matrix with positive elements along the diagonal and negative elements off the diagonal. That is, a cap is exposed more to the yield curve twist movement than the parallel movement when the cap is delta-hedged.

According to the Taylor Expansion, we have the following approximate equation:

$$\Delta P / P = -\sum_i KRD(i) \times \Delta r_i + 0.5 \sum_{ij} KRC(i,j) \Delta r_i \Delta r_j. \quad (3)$$

Equation (3) enables us to search for the largest loss within a 99% confidence level of the yield curve movements, or the change of the key rates, given their correlations.

Delta-gamma has a number of advantages over the Monte Carlo simulation approach. We discuss them later.

Risk attributions

The total risk is the VAR number for the whole portfolio, taking all currency, interest rate, and equity risks into account. The extent of the risks depends on the domestic investor's point of view. The total risk shows the risk exposure of the whole portfolio.

To manage the risks, it is important to analyse the building blocks of the risks that roll up to the total risk. To do this, we calculate the VAR for the currency blocks. If all the currencies were perfectly correlated, the total risk would be equal to the sum of the VARs of all the currency blocks, when we assume that the non-linear risk and the cross-currency positions are small. On the other hand, if all the currencies are independent, then the VAR of the total risk would be the square root of the sum of the squares of the currency blocks. By comparing the VAR for the total risk under those two different assumptions, perfect correlation and no correlation, we can identify the impact of diversification of risks.

Figure 3 shows the diversification effect of the currency risks on the Basle test portfolio.

Next, we analyse the building blocks of risk for each currency block. This is accomplished by comparing the risk of each currency block, assuming perfect correlation and no correlation with the asset types. This way, we can identify the effectiveness of the diversification across the asset types the same way we looked at the impact of diversification for the portfolio as a whole.

Figure 4 depicts the diversification effect of the assets across the currencies. The results show that the VAR is similar to the uncorrelated case and significantly less than the perfectly correlated case. Note that the VAR can be less than the uncorrelated case because of the short positions in the portfolio. Kao and Kallberg (1994) also discuss a similar risk measure, which they call "concentration risk".

Table 2. "Rolling up" of VAR measures

Portfolio evaluation date May 30, 1995

Currency	Asset	Market value by assets (Skr)	Market value by currencies (Skr)	Total market value (Skr)
				159,974,656.72
DM			97,312,519.60	
	Equity	13,064,580.25		
	Interest rate	37,286,460.28		
	Foreign exchange	96,868,567.40		
Ffr			57,282,779.24	
	Equity	14,486,806.00		
	Interest rate	38,248,864.05		
	Foreign exchange	44,290,663.77		
£			35,710,835.11	
	Equity	10,685,478.93		
	Interest rate	32,124,946.43		
	Foreign exchange	23,107,028.34		
¥			52,360,478.59	
	Equity	12,089,772.07		
	Interest rate	14,795,327.20		
	Foreign exchange	52,651,722.16		
$			25,108,297.89	
	Equity	6,870,186.93		
	Interest rate	22,957,735.70		
	Foreign exchange	2,956,407.24		

The rolling up of the VAR measures of the Basle portfolio is shown in Table 2, which presents the VAR numbers for all the building blocks. This way, we can compare the VAR and the market value of each block. We have shown that the total risk is Skr159,974,656. This means, at a 99% confidence level, the portfolio would not lose more than 4.24% if it is left unchanged for the next 10 days.

Figure 5 depicts the distribution of the VARs. The results show that there is significant risk exposure to the equity risks, even though the equity market value is relatively small.

In risk measurement, the Basle test considers two other risk measures. First, the non-linear risk assesses the impact of options even if the portfolio is delta-hedged. This risk is reported in Table 3 overleaf. Second, the Basle test requires the VAR of each asset type assuming that the currency risks are hedged. These numbers are reported in Table 2 labelled "Market Value by Asset".

Thus far, we have calculated the VAR of each of the blocks of the portfolio. That is, we have related the composition of the lowest level of the portfolio structure, the basic blocks, to the portfolio VAR numbers. Consequently, we can calculate the change in VAR numbers of the portfolio for an increase in value of each basic block by a unit. The unit "alpha" may be 1% of the market value of the basic block in the portfolio value. This marginal contribution of risk is called VAR beta of the ith basic block.

When the VAR beta is negligible, we can conclude that the basic block risk is well-diversified or hedged by other blocks. When the VAR beta is negative, the basic block is providing a hedge of the portfolio risk. Finally, when the VAR beta is positively large, the basic block contributes significant risks to the portfolio. In risk management, we should rank the VAR betas of the portfolio to determine the main contributors to the total portfolio risk.

It is straightforward to show that the sum of the VAR betas is alpha times the VAR number when the portfolio has no options or other non-linear risks. In other words, the sum of VAR betas is the alpha of delta-normal VAR. This result enables risk managers to identify the constituents of the VAR number.

5. VAR by assets

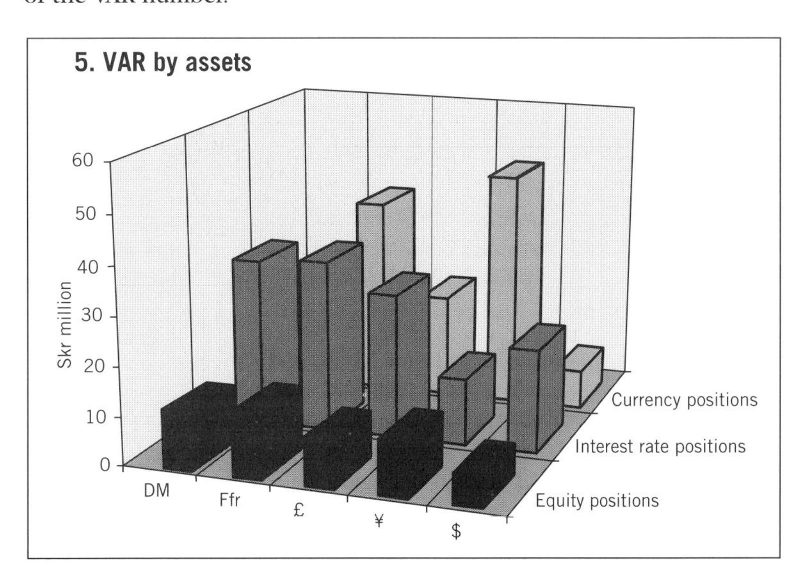

Table 3. VAR with delta hedging

Portfolio evaluation date May 30, 1995

Currency	Asset	Market value by assets (Skr)	Market value by currencies (Skr)	Total market value (Skr)	Delta-normal (Skr)
				(3,771,365,237.04)	
DM			(8,029,512,802.05)		
	Equity	207,413,697.67			13,064,580.25
	Interest rate	(8,820,409,119.72)			36,982,892.51
	Foreign exchange	583,482,620.00			26,240,827.60
Ffr			11,874,907,355.40		
	Equity	171,906,626.36			14,486,777.48
	Interest rate	10,675,260,729.04			37,326,375.08
	Foreign exchange	1,027,740,000.00			44,290,663.77
£			(4,526,830,517.34)		
	Equity	197,266,694.30			10,685,110.97
	Interest rate	(4,136,817,211.64)			31,896,956.22
	Foreign exchange	(587,280,000.00)			23,107,028.34
¥			12,862,868,409.32		
	Equity	143,010,038.87			12,089,772.07
	Interest rate	11,838,938,370.45			14,800,453.31
	Foreign exchange	880,920,000.00			52,651,722.16
$			(15,952,797,682.36)		
	Equity	165,273,815.63			6,870,169.86
	Interest rate	(14,212,698,157.99)			23,458,545.87
	Foreign exchange	(1,905,373,340.00)			0.00

VAR betas can be calculated for all the VAR numbers, not merely for the total risk VAR. In so doing, we can better understand how the increase in a position leads to the increase of risk in all portfolio blocks. In general, the impact is higher, the lower the block level to which the position belongs. The effect lessens as we "roll up" the risk of the total portfolio. This risk reduction is the result of diversification. The VAR betas can reveal the effect of diversification and hedging as the portfolio structure is analysed.

Comparing Monte Carlo approach to delta-gamma approach

For VAR measures, the non-linear risks are measured in a relatively short time horizon (for example, 10 days). For this reason, a second-order approximation using gamma or convexities should be adequate for most portfolios. VAR also assumes normal distribution of risk sources in most cases.

For these reasons, delta-gamma methodology should be a better alternative over Monte Carlo simulations for the VAR calculations, and thus improve upon the accuracy for Basle Committee testing purposes. In comparison with Monte Carlo simulations, the delta-gamma methodology has the following advantages:

❑ *Accuracy* When we need to identify the non-linear risks of a portfolio with many risk sources, it can take a considerable number of simulations to provide the confidence level of 99%. Typically, in a multicurrency portfolio, there are more than 50 risk sources. For each yield curve, the movements should be modelled by five to ten key rate movements.

To determine the non-linear risks, we need to search for the largest loss under the constraints of the confidence interval. Suppose we need 100 simulations to search for the largest loss, for a 50-risk source portfolio. The total number of simulations would be huge. If we were to apply a Monte Carlo random sampling approach to, for example, a sample size of 1,000, the sampling would in general be very inadequate. The delta-gamma approach provides the exact answer analytically.

❑ *Identification of the scenarios* There is the problem of accurate identification of maximum-loss scenarios. Monte Carlo simulation provides an approximate maximum potential number. When there are many significantly different scenarios that give similar potential losses, then Monte Carlo simulations will fail to identify all the scenarios. Therefore, we cannot use Monte Carlo simulation results to manage risk without more careful research into other hidden risks that have not been identified by the random (and possibly sparse) sampling.

The delta-gamma method, in fact, identifies all the local maximums and the scenarios that lead to these local maximums. Therefore, delta-gamma methodology can be used for determining effective risk management strategies.

❑ *Consistent risk management framework* Our

adjusted delta-gamma approach solves the problem of maintaining a consistent risk management framework. Consistency is a serious issue under traditional Monte Carlo sampling. If each testing of a security's risk is made under separate random samplings, it is almost impossible for the interest rate paths that are used to be the same. Thus, the risk measure of a security will vary substantially from test to test, solely because of the randomness of the sample space. This lack of consistency is especially crucial in such VAR measures as the 1% likelihood, which can be rendered inaccurate due to this inconsistency of paths.

Traditionally, this lack of consistency in sampling was dealt with by fixing the Monte Carlo paths, so that each risk test is performed on the same basis. However, the deficiency of this approach is evident: the paths are no longer random.

❑ *Additivity of portfolio risk* The gamma, or convexities, of a portfolio is the weighted sum of the gamma, or convexities, of its constituents. This property gives the risk manager a straightforward way to calculate the non-linear risks of the portfolio. Moreover, the risk manager can easily devise risk management strategies by identifying the portfolio's gamma or convexity.

In contrast, the non-linear risk calculated by the Monte Carlo simulation is not additive. That means the non-linear risk of the portfolio is not the (weighted) sum of the non-linear risks of the bonds or swaps.

Conclusion

We discuss the structure of portfolio and use of a risk attribution procedure so that we can "roll up" the risks from the basic level to total risk. We also suggest that the delta-gamma approach is a better alternative to the Monte Carlo simulation methodology.

When the delta-gamma methodology fails, it is because the bond or security cannot be approximated by duration and convexity. We must note that in principle (proven theoretically), all securities' model prices are "smooth" functions of interest rates. This means they can all be approximated by durations and convexities, given a sufficiently short investment time horizon. (A 10-day horizon is considered short.)

A security for which a horizon cannot be approximated by duration and convexities must be considered "exotic." In this case, one must question the robustness of the model of such a security.

There are methodologies to check the validity of using duration and convexity to approximate the changes in a security value. One way is to calculate the third-order term of the Taylor expansion. When securities fail the validity test, we should examine the risk exposure of these securities more carefully.

We provide an approach to analyse the risk exposure of a portfolio by systematically measuring the risks of the basic blocks to the total portfolio. By employing this technique, risk managers can better implement risk management strategies.

BIBLIOGRAPHY

Beder, T. Styblo, 1995, "VAR: Seductive but Dangerous", *Financial Analysts Journal*, September/October 1995, pp. 12–24; reprinted as Chapter 17 of the present volume.

Crnkovic, C. and J. Drachman, 1995, "A Universal Toll to Discriminate Among Risk Measurement Techniques." Corporate Risk Management Group, JP Morgan & Co, Inc., New York, September 26.

Ho, T., 1992, "Key Rate Durations: Measures of Interest Rate Risks", *Journal of Fixed Income*, September 1992, pp. 29–44.

JP Morgan, 1995, *RiskMetrics Technical Document*, 3rd edition, New York.

Kao, D-L., and Jarl G. Kallberg, 1994 "Strategies for measuring and managing risk concentrations in loan portfolios", *Journal of Commercial Lending*, January 1994, pp. 18–27.

Kupiec, P., 1995, "Techniques for Verifying the Accuracy of Risk Measurement Models", *Journal of Derivatives*, Winter 1995, pp. 73–84.

McCoy, W., 1995 "Bond Dynamic Hedging and Return Attribution: Empirical Evidence", *Journal of Portfolio Management*, Winter 1995, pp. 93–101.

Wilson, T., 1994 "Plugging the gap", *Risk* 7 no 10, pp. 74–80.

Evaluating Value-at-Risk Methodologies:

Accuracy versus Computational Time*

Matt Pritsker
Board of Governors of the Federal Reserve System

Recent research has shown that different methods of computing value-at-risk (VAR) generate widely varying results, suggesting that the choice of VAR method is very important. This paper examines six VAR methods, and compares their computational time requirements and their accuracy when the sole source of inaccuracy is errors in approximating non-linearity. Simulations using portfolios of foreign exchange options show fairly wide variation in accuracy and unsurprisingly wide variation in computational time. When the computational time and accuracy of the methods are examined together, four methods are found to be superior to the others. The paper also presents a new method for using order statistics to create confidence intervals for the errors and errors as a percentage of true value at risk for each VAR method. This makes it easier to interpret the implications of VAR errors for the size of shortfalls or surpluses in a firm's risk-based capital.

New methods of measuring and managing risk have evolved in parallel with the growth of the OTC derivatives market. One of these measures, known as value-at-risk (VAR), has become especially prominent, and now serves as the basis for the most recent BIS market risk-based capital requirement. VAR is usually defined as the largest loss in portfolio value that would be expected to occur due to changes in market prices over a given period of time in all but a small percentage of circumstances.[1] This percentage is referred to as the confidence level for the VAR measure.[2] An alternative description of VAR is the amount of capital the firm would require to absorb its portfolio losses in all but a small percentage of circumstances.[3]

VAR's popularity is because of its conceptual simplicity and flexibility. It can be used to measure the risk of an individual instrument, or an entire portfolio. It is also potentially useful for short-term management of the firm's risk. If VAR figures are available on a timely basis, then an organisation can increase its risk if VAR is too low, or decrease its risk if VAR is too high.

While VAR is conceptually simple, it must be reasonably accurate if it is to be of any use, and must be available sufficiently quickly for it to be acted upon. This will typically involve a trade-off between accuracy and computational time, since the most accurate methods may take unacceptably long amounts of time to compute, while the methods that take the least time are often the

* *This is an edited version of a paper due to appear in the* Journal of Financial Services Research, *December 1997, Vol. 1, Issue 2. It is reprinted with permission from Kluwer Academic Publishers. The views expressed in this paper reflect those of the author and not those of the Board of Governors of the Federal Reserve Sytem, or other members of its staff. The author thanks Ruth Wu, Jim O'Brien, Phillipe Jorion, Vijay Bhasin, Paul Kupiec, Pat White and Chunsheng Zhou for their help and asistance. All errors are the responsibility of the author.*

least accurate. The purpose of this paper is to examine the trade-offs between accuracy and computational time in six different VAR methods and so to highlight the different methods' respective strengths and weaknesses.

The importance of accurate VAR figures is clear, since the most recent Basle market risk capital proposal sets capital requirements based on firm's own internal VAR estimates. And recent evidence on the accuracy of different methods has not been encouraging; different methodologies tend to generate widely varying results, suggesting that the choice of method is very important. The differences appear to be due to different methods for imputing the distribution of the factor shocks (Hendricks (1996), Beder (1995)),[4] and also because of differences in the treatment of instruments whose pay-offs are non-linear functions of the factors (Marshall and Siegel (1997)).[5]

The trade-offs between accuracy and computational time are most acute when portfolios contain large holdings of instruments whose payoffs are non-linear in the underlying risk factors - VAR is especially difficult to compute for this type of portfolio. However, while the dispersion of VAR estimates for non-linear portfolios has been documented, there has been relatively little publicly-available research comparing the accuracy of the various methods. Moreover, the results that have been reported are often portfolio-specific, and reported only in dollar terms. This makes it hard to compare results across the VAR literature; it also makes it difficult to relate results to the capital charges under the BIS market-risk based capital proposal. And while there has been little information on the methods' standards of accuracy, even less has been published on their computational feasibility.

This paper's contribution is that it considers the balance between accuracy and computational time for portfolios that exclusively contain non-linear instruments. It also provides a statistically rigorous and easily interpretable method for gauging the accuracy of VAR estimates, both in dollar terms, and as a percentage of true VAR even though true VAR is not known.

Before proceeding, it is useful to summarise our empirical results. We examined accuracy and computational time in detail, using simulations on test portfolios of foreign exchange options. In terms of accuracy, the results varied widely. One method (delta-gamma-minimisation) consistently overstated VAR by very substantial amounts. The other methods fall into two groups – simple methods (delta, and delta-gamma-delta), and relatively complex (delta-gamma Monte Carlo, modified grid Monte Carlo, and Monte Carlo with full repricing). The simple methods were generally found to be less accurate than the complex methods and there were substantial differences in performance as a whole.

Not surprisingly, the results on computational time favoured the simple methods. However, one of the complex methods (delta-gamma Monte Carlo), takes a relatively short time to compute, and produces some of the most accurate results. As a whole, this method appears the best for the portfolios considered here. However, we were still able to detect a tendency to overstate or understate true VAR for about 25% of the 500 randomly-chosen portfolios from simulation exercise 2. When VAR was over- or understated, a conservative estimate of the average magnitude of the error was about 10% of true VAR, with a standard deviation of about the same amount.

In addition, we found from simulation 1 that all VAR methods except Monte Carlo with full repricing generated large errors as a percentage of VAR for deep out-of-the-money options with a short time to expiracy. Although VAR for these options is typically very small, the best way to capture the risk for portfolios with a large concentration of them may be to use Monte Carlo with full repricing.[6]

Methods for measuring VAR

It is useful to begin our analysis of VAR with its formal definition. Throughout this paper, we will follow current practice and measure VAR over a fixed span of time (normalised to one period) in which positions are assumed to remain fixed. Many firms set this span of time to be one day. This is long enough for risk to be worth measuring, and is short enough for the fixed position reasonably to approximate the firm's one-day or overnight position for risk management purposes.

A formal definition of VAR requires some notation. Denote $V(P_t, X_t, t)$ as the value of portfolio V at time t with instruments X_t and instrument prices P_t and denote $\Delta V(P_{t+1} - P_t, X_t, t)$ as the change in portfolio value between period t and $t+1$. The cumulative density function of $\Delta V(P_{t+1} - P_t, X_t, t)$ conditional on X_t and time t information I_t is:

$$G(k, I_t, X_t) = \text{Probability}\left(\Delta V(P_{t+1} - P_t, X_t) \leq k \middle| I_t\right).$$

This allows the inverse cumulative density func

tion for $\Delta V(P_{t+1} - P_t, X_t)$ to be defined as:

$$G^{-1}(u, I_t, X_t) = \inf\{k : G(k, I_t, X_t) = u\}.$$

VAR for confidence level u is defined in terms of the inverse cumulative density function of ΔV:

$$VAR(u, I_t, X_t) = G^{-1}(u, I_t, X_t).$$

In words, VAR at confidence level u is the largest loss that is expected to occur except for a set of circumstances with probability u.[7] This is equivalent to defining VAR at confidence level u as the uth quantile of the distribution of $\Delta V(P_{t+1} - P_t, X_t)$ given I_t. The definition of VAR highlights its dependence on the function G^{-1} which is a conditional function of the instruments X_t and the information set I_t.[8]

VAR attempts, either implicitly or explicitly, to make inferences about $G^{-1}(u, I_t, X_t)$ in a neighbourhood near confidence level u. In a large portfolio G^{-1} depends on the joint distribution of potentially tens of thousands of different instruments. This makes it necessary to make simplifying assumptions in order to compute VAR.

These usually take three forms. First, the dimension of the problem is reduced by assuming that the price of the instruments depend on a vector of factors f that are the primary determinants of changes in portfolio value.[9] This allows changes in portfolio value to be expressed as $\Delta V(\varepsilon_{t+1}, X_t, t)$ where $\varepsilon_{t+1} = f_{t+1} - f_t$. Second, $\Delta V(\varepsilon_{t+1}, X_t, t)$ is usually approximated instead of being calculated explicitly. Finally, convenient functional forms are often assumed for the distribution of ε_{t+1}.

Each of these simplifying assumptions is likely to introduce errors in the VAR estimates. The first assumption induces errors if an incorrect or incomplete set of factors is chosen; the second assumption introduces approximation error; and the third assumption introduces error if the wrong distribution of ε_{t+1} is chosen. The first and third sources of error are model error, while the errors of the second type are errors of approximation. Because model error can take so many forms, we choose to abstract from it here by assuming that the factors have been chosen correctly, and the distribution of the factor innovations is correct. This allows us to focus on the errors induced by the approximation used in each VAR method, and to get a clean measure of these errors. In future work, I hope to incorporate model error in the analysis and examine whether some methods of computing VAR are robust to certain classes of model errors.

Different methods of computing VAR are distinguished by their simplifying assumptions. The methodologies considered here fall into two broad categories. The first are delta and delta-gamma methods, which typically make assumptions that lead to analytic or near analytic tractability for the VAR computation. The second group use Monte Carlo simulation to compute VAR. They are capable of producing very accurate VAR estimates, but they are not analytically tractable, and they are very time and computer-intensive.

DELTA AND DELTA-GAMMA METHODS

The delta and delta-gamma methods typically make the distributional assumption that changes in the factors are distributed normally conditional on today's information:

$$(\varepsilon_{t+1} | I_t) \sim N(0, \Sigma).$$

They differ principally in their approximation of change in portfolio value. The delta method approximates the change in portfolio value using a first order Taylor series expansion in the factor shocks and the time horizon over which VAR is computed[10]:

$$\Delta V(\varepsilon_{t+1}, X_t) \approx \delta^T \varepsilon_{t+1} + \theta$$

$$\text{where } \delta = \left. \frac{\partial V(\varepsilon_{t+1}, X_t, t)}{\partial \varepsilon_{t+1}} \right|_{\{\varepsilon_{t+1}=0\}}$$

$$\theta = \left. \frac{\partial V(\varepsilon_{t+1}, X_t, t)}{\partial t} \right|_{\{\varepsilon_{t+1}=0\}}$$

Delta-gamma methods approximate changes in portfolio value using a Taylor series expansion that is second order in the factor shocks and first order in the VAR time horizon:

$$\Delta V(\varepsilon_{t+1}, X_t) \approx \delta^T \varepsilon_{t+1} + .5 \varepsilon_{t+1}^T \Gamma \varepsilon_{t+1} + \theta$$

$$\text{where } \Gamma = \left. \frac{\partial V(\varepsilon_{t+1}, X_t, t)}{\partial \varepsilon_{t+1} \partial \varepsilon_{t+1}^T} \right|_{\{\varepsilon_{t+1}=0\}}$$

At this juncture it is important to emphasise that the Taylor expansions and distributional assumptions depend on the choice of factors. This choice can have an important impact on the ability of the Taylor expansions to approximate nonlinearity[11], and may also have an important impact on the adequacy of the distributional assumptions.

For a given choice of factors, the first-order approximation and distributional assumption used in the *delta* method[12] imply $\Delta V(\varepsilon_{t+1}, X_t) \sim N(\theta, \delta' \Sigma \delta)$. So calculating VAR using this method only requires calculating the inverse cumulative density function of the normal distribution. In this case, elementary calculation shows VAR at confidence level u is

$$\theta + \Phi^{-1}(u)\sqrt{\delta'\Sigma\delta}$$

where Φ^{-1} is the inverse of the cumulative density function of the normal distribution.

The delta method's main virtue is its simplicity, which means that VAR can be computed very rapidly. However, its linear Taylor series approximation may be inappropriate for portfolios whose value is a non-linear function of the factors. The normality assumption is also suspect, since many financial time series are fat tailed.[13] The delta-gamma approaches attempt to improve on the delta method by using a second-order Taylor series to capture the non-linearities of changes in portfolio value. Some of the delta-gamma methods also allow for more flexible assumptions on the distribution of the factor innovations.

Delta-gamma methods have some advantages over the delta method since they offer a more flexible functional form for capturing non-linearity.[14] However, a second order approximation is still not capable of capturing all of the non-linearities of changes in portfolio value.[15] In addition, the non-linearities that are captured come at the cost of reduced analytic tractability relative to the delta method. The reason is that changes in portfolio value using the second order Taylor series expansion are not approximately normally distributed, even if the factor innovations are.[16] This loss of normality makes it more difficult to compute the G^{-1} function than in the delta method. Two basic fixes are used to try to overcome this difficulty. The first abandons analytic tractability and approximates G^{-1} using Monte Carlo methods; the second, by contrast, attempts to maintain analytic or near-analytic tractability by employing additional distributional assumptions.

Many VAR papers refer to the delta-gamma method. But in this paper, the description is inappropriate, since we are examining the performance of no fewer than three delta-gamma methods in detail, as well as discussing two recent additions to them. So instead of the usual terminology, we will use names that describe how the methods are implemented.

The first approach is the *delta-gamma Monte Carlo* method.[17] Under this approach, a large number of realisations of ε_{t+1} are drawn from its distribution[18] and for each realisation $\Delta V(\varepsilon_{t+1}, I_t, X_t)$ is computed according to the second order delta-gamma Taylor series approximation. The empirical cumulative density function of the resulting series of ΔVs is an approximation of the cumulative density function G. The value of $\Delta V(\varepsilon_{t+1}, I_t, X_t)$ corresponding to the uth percentile of the empirical distribution is the estimate of VAR. If the second order Taylor approximation is exact, then this estimator will converge to true VAR as the number of Monte Carlo draws approaches infinity.

The next approach is the *delta-gamma-delta* method, so-called because it is a delta-gamma based method that maintains most of the simplicity of the delta method. It does so by making the distributional assumption that ε_{t+1} and the unique elements of $\varepsilon_{t+1}\varepsilon_{t+1}^{T}$ are uncorrelated and normally distributed shocks to portfolio value with portfolio sensitivities corresponding to the elements of δ and Γ that they multiply in the second order Taylor series expansion.[19] For example, if V is a function of one factor, then the shocks to V are ε_{t+1} and ε_{t+1}^{2}, and their assumed distribution is:

$$\begin{bmatrix} \varepsilon_{t+1} \\ \varepsilon_{t+1}^{2} \end{bmatrix} \sim N\left(\begin{bmatrix} 0 \\ \sigma^2 \end{bmatrix}, \begin{bmatrix} \sigma^2 & 0 \\ 0 & 2\sigma^4 \end{bmatrix}\right).$$

The mean and covariance matrix in the above expressions are correct if $\varepsilon_{t+1} \sim N(0,\sigma^2)$, but the assumption of normality cannot possibly be correct[20], and should instead be viewed as a convenient assumption that simplifies the computation of VAR. Under this distributional assumption $\Delta V(\varepsilon_{t+1}, X_t) \sim N(\theta + .5\Gamma\sigma^2, \delta^2\sigma^2 + .5\Gamma^2\sigma^4)$.[21] Analogous to the delta method, G^{-1} and hence VAR, is simple to calculate in the delta-gamma-delta approach. In this example VAR is equal to

$$\theta + .5\Gamma\sigma^2 + \Phi^{-1}(u)\sqrt{\delta^2\sigma^2 + .5\Gamma^2\sigma^4}.$$

The calculation of VAR for a large number of factors proceeds along similar lines.[22]

The next delta-gamma approach is the *delta-gamma-minimisation* method.[23] It maintains the assumptions that ε_{t+1} is normally distributed, and that changes in portfolio value are well approximated quadratically. It then finds that value of ε_{t+1} that creates the greatest loss in portfolio value subject to the constraint that ε_{t+1} lies within a sphere centred at 0 that contains $1-u\%$ of the probability mass of the distribution of ε_{t+1}. In mathematical terms, this VAR estimate is the solution to the minimisation problem:

$$\text{VAR} = \min_{\varepsilon_{t+1}} \delta^{T}\varepsilon_{t+1} + .5\varepsilon_{t+1}^{T}\Gamma\varepsilon_{t+1}$$

$$\text{such that } \varepsilon_{t+1}^{T}\Sigma^{-1}\varepsilon_{t+1} \le c^{*}(1-u,k)$$

where $c^*(1-u,k)$ is the u% critical value of the central chi-squared distribution with k degrees of freedom; ie $1-u$% of the probability mass of the central chi-squared distribution with k degrees of freedom is below $c^*(1-u,k)$.

This approach makes a very strong but not obvious distributional assumption to identify VAR. The distributional assumption is that the value of the portfolio outside of the constraint set is lower than anywhere within the constraint set. If this assumption is correct, and the quadratic approximation for changes in portfolio value is exact, then the VAR estimate would exactly correspond to the uth quantile of the change in portfolio value. Unfortunately, there is little reason to believe that this key distributional assumption will be satisfied and it is realistic to believe that this condition will be violated for a substantial (ie non-zero) proportion of the shocks that lie outside the constraint set.[24] This means the probability of the realisations for which losses exceed VAR is less than u%. In other words, VAR is overstated.

In extreme cases the overstatement could be very large. For example, suppose ΔV has the same cumulative density function as a $N(0,1)$ variable, but that the lowest value of ΔV occurs for a factor shock that lies within the 95% constraint set. In this case, estimated VAR would be minus infinity at the 5% confidence level, while true VAR would be -1.645. This is an extreme example, but it does illustrate the point that this method is capable of generating large errors. It is more likely that at low levels of confidence, as the amount of probability mass outside the constraint set goes to zero, the estimate of VAR remains conservative but converges to true VAR (conditional on the second order approximation being exact). This suggests the delta-gamma-minimisation method will produce better (that is, less conservative) estimates of VAR when the confidence level u is small.

The advantage of the delta-gamma-minimisation approach is that it does not rely on the incorrect joint normality assumption used in the delta-gamma-delta method, and does not require the large number of Monte Carlo draws required in the delta-gamma Monte Carlo approach. Whether these advantages offset the errors induced by this approach's conservatism is an empirical question.

The sections that follow examine the accuracy and computational time requirements of the delta-gamma Monte Carlo, delta-gamma-delta, and delta-gamma-minimisation methods. For completeness we will also mention two additional delta-gamma methods. The first was recently introduced by Peter Zangari of JP Morgan (1996), and parameterises a known distribution function so that its first four moments match the first four moments of the delta-gamma approximation to changes in portfolio value. The cumulative density function of the known distribution function is then used to compute VAR. We will refer to this method as the *delta-gamma-Johnson* method because the statistician Norman Johnson introduced the distribution function that is used.

The second approach calculates VAR by approximating the uth quantile of the distribution of the delta-gamma approximation using a Cornish-Fisher expansion. This approach is used in Fallon (1996) and Zangari (1996). This approach is similar to the first except that a Cornish-Fisher expansion approximates the quantiles of an unknown distribution as a function of the quantiles of a known distribution function and the cumulants of the known and unknown distribution functions.[25] We will refer to this approach as the *delta-gamma-Cornish-Fisher* method.

Both of these approaches have the advantage of being analytic. Their key distributional assumption is that matching a finite number of moments or cumulants of a known distribution with those of an unknown distribution will provide adequate estimates of the quantiles of the unknown distribution. They are both likely to be less accurate than the delta-gamma Monte Carlo approach (with a large number of draws) since the Monte Carlo approach implicitly uses all of the information on the CDF of the delta-gamma approximation while the other two approaches throw some of this information away. In addition, as we will see below, the delta-gamma Monte Carlo method (and other Monte Carlo methods) can be used with historical realisations of the factor shocks to compute VAR estimates that are not tied to the assumption of conditionally normally distributed factor shocks. It would be very difficult to relax the normality assumption for the delta-gamma-Johnson and delta-gamma-Cornish-Fisher methods because without these assumptions the moments and cumulants of the second order Taylor series for ΔV would be unknown and very hard to compute.

MONTE CARLO METHODS

The next set of approaches for calculating VAR are based on Monte Carlo simulation. This works by using a series of random draws of the factor shocks (ε_{t+1}). These shocks, combined with some approximation method, are used to generate a random series of changes in portfolio value (ΔV). The empirical cumulative density function of the changes in portfolio value, $\hat{G}$, is then used as a proxy for G, and $\hat{G}^{-1}(u)$ is the corresponding estimate of VAR at confidence level u.

Monte Carlo approaches have the potential to improve on the delta and delta-gamma methods because they can allow for alternative methods of approximating changes in portfolio value and they can allow ε_{t+1} to have a non-normal distribution. The Monte Carlo methodologies considered here allow for two methods for approximating change in portfolio value and two methods of parameterising the distribution of ε_{t+1}. These approaches can be combined.

The first approximation method is the *full Monte Carlo* method.[26] This uses exact pricing for each Monte Carlo draw, thus eliminating errors from approximations to ΔV. Since this method involves no approximation error, $\hat{G}$, the full Monte Carlo estimate of G converges to G in probability as the sample size grows provided the distributional assumptions are correct. Consequently, $\hat{G}^{-1}(u)$ converges in probability to true value-at-risk at confidence level u. Because this approach produces good estimates of VAR for large sample sizes, the full Monte Carlo estimates are a good baseline against which to compare other methods. The downside is that this approach can be very time-consuming, especially if analytic solutions for some asset prices do not exist.

The second approximation method is the *grid Monte Carlo* approach.[27] Here, a grid of realisations for ε_{t+1} (for N factors, this would involve an N dimensional grid) is created, and the change in portfolio value is calculated exactly for each node of the grid. To make approximations using the grid, for each Monte Carlo draw, the factor shocks should lie somewhere on the grid, and changes in portfolio value for these shocks can be estimated by interpolating from changes in portfolio value at nearby nodes. This interpolation method is likely to provide a better approximation than either the delta or delta-gamma methods because it places fewer restrictions on the behaviour of the non-linearity, and because it becomes ever less restrictive as the mesh of the grid is increased.

As we will see below, grid Monte Carlo methods suffer from a curse of dimensionality problems, since the number of grid points grows exponentially with the number of factors. To avoid the dimensionality problem, we will model the change in the value of an instrument by using a low order grid combined with a first order Taylor series. The grid captures the effects of factors that generate the most non-linear value changes, while the first order Taylor series captures the effects of factors that generate less non-linear changes.[28]

There are two basic approaches that can be used to make the Monte Carlo draws. The first approach is to draw realisations of ε_{t+1}. This approach relaxes the normality assumption but is likely to introduce some error because the true distribution of ε_{t+1} is probably unknown. The second approach is to make the Monte Carlo draws via a historical simulation approach (also known as bootstrapping). In this approach, draws of ε_{t+1} are simulated from historical realisations of ε that are believed to be draws from the same conditional distribution as ε_{t+1}. This will require that past realisations of ε are observable, and it will probably require observability of the past factor realisations.[29] It will also be necessary to make some assumptions that link the stochastic process that generated draws of ε historically to the process that generates the draws for time period $t+1$.[30] The main advantage of this approach is that even when the true distribution of ε_{t+1} is not known, it may still be possible to make draws from it. The disadvantage is that there may not be enough historical data to make the draws, or there is no past time-period that is sufficiently similar to the present for the historical draws to provide information about the future distribution of ε_{t+1}.

The historical simulation approach will not be compared with other Monte Carlo approaches in this paper. It is hoped that this will be the topic of further research.

Measuring the accuracy of VAR estimates

Estimates of VAR are generally not equal to true VAR, and thus should ideally be accompanied by some measure of estimator quality such as statistical confidence intervals or a standard error estimate. This is typically not done for delta and delta-gamma based VAR estimates, since there is no natural method for computing a standard error or constructing a confidence interval.

In Monte Carlo estimation of VAR, anecdotal evidence suggests that error bounds are typically not provided, but that error is controlled somewhat by making Monte Carlo draws until the VAR estimates do not change significantly in response to additional draws. This procedure may be inappropriate for VAR calculation since VAR is likely to depend on extremal draws which are made infrequently. Put differently, VAR estimates may change little in response to additional Monte Carlo draws, even if the VAR estimates are poor.

Although error bounds are typically not provided for full Monte Carlo estimates of VAR, it is not difficult to use the empirical distribution from a sample size of N Monte Carlo draws to form confidence intervals for Monte Carlo VAR estimates (we will form 95% confidence intervals). Given the width of the interval, it can be determined whether the sample of Monte Carlo draws should be increased to provide better VAR estimates. The confidence intervals that we will discuss have the desirable properties that they are non-parametric (ie they are valid for any continuous distribution function G), based on finite sample theory, and are simple to compute. There is one important requirement: the draws from the distribution of ε_{t+1} must be independently and identically distributed (i.i.d.).

The confidence intervals for the Monte Carlo estimates of VAR can also be used to construct confidence intervals for the error and percentage error from computing VAR by other methods. These confidence intervals are extremely useful for evaluating the accuracy of both Monte Carlo and other methods of computing VAR. The use of confidence intervals should also improve on current practices of measuring VAR error. The error from a VAR estimate is often calculated as the difference between the estimate and a Monte Carlo estimate. This difference is an incomplete characterisation of the VAR error, since the Monte Carlo estimate is itself measured imperfectly. The confidence intervals give a more complete picture of the VAR error because they take the errors from the Monte Carlo into account.[31]

Table 1 provides information on how to construct 95% confidence intervals for Monte Carlo estimates of VAR for VAR confidence levels of one and five per cent. To illustrate the use of the table, suppose one makes 100 i.i.d. Monte Carlo draws and wants to construct a 95% confidence interval for VAR at the 5% confidence level (apologies for using confidence two different ways). Then, the upper right column of Table 1 shows that the largest portfolio loss from the Monte Carlo simulations and the 10th largest portfolio loss form a 95% confidence interval for the VAR. The parentheses below these figures restate the confidence bounds in terms of percentiles of the Monte Carlo distribution. Hence, the first percentile and 10th percentile of the Monte Carlo loss distribution bound the 5th percentile of the true loss distribution with 95% confidence when 100 draws are made. If the spread between the largest and 10th largest portfolio loss are too high, then a tighter confidence interval is needed and this will require more Monte Carlo draws. Table 1 provides upper and lower bounds for larger numbers of draws and for VAR confidence levels of 1% and 5%. As one would expect, the table shows that as the number of draws increase, the bounds, measured in terms of percentiles of the Monte Carlo distribution, tighten so that with 10,000 draws, the 4.57th and 5.44th percentile of the Monte Carlo distribution bound the 5th percentile of the true distribution with 95% confidence.

Table 1. Non-parametric 95% confidence intervals for Monte Carlo VAR figures

Number of draws	VAR confidence level 1%		VAR confidence level 5%	
	Lower bound	Upper bound	Lower bound	Upper bound
100	–	–	1	10
	–	–	(1%)	(10.%)
300	1	11	8	23
	(0.33%)	(3.67%)	(2.7%)	(7.7%)
500	1	10	15	35
	(0.2%)	(2.0%)	(3.0%)	(7.0%)
1,000	4	17	37	64
	(0.4%)	(1.7%)	(3.7%)	(6.4%)
10,000	81	120	457	544
	(0.81%)	(1.2%)	(4.57%)	(5.44%)
50,000	456	545	2,404	2,597
	(0.912%)	(1.09%)	(4.81%)	(5.19%)
100,000	938	1,063	4,865	5,136
	(0.938%)	(1.063%)	(4.865%)	(5.136%)
250,000	2,402	2,599	12,286	12,715
	(0.9608%)	(1.0396%)	(4.9144%)	(5.086%)
500,000	4,862	5,139	24,698	25,303
	(0.9742%)	(1.0278%)	(4.9396%)	(5.0606%)
1,000,000	9,805	10,196	49,573	50,428
	(0.9805%)	(1.0196%)	(4.9573%)	(5.0428%)

Notes: Columns (2)–(3) and (4)–(5) report the index of order statistics that bound the first and fifth percentile of an unknown distribution with 95% confidence when the unknown distribution is simulated using the number of i.i.d. Monte Carlo draws indicated in column (1). If the unknown distribution is for changes in portfolio value, then the bounds form a 95% confidence interval for value at risk at the 1% and 5% level. The figures in parentheses are the percentiles of the Monte Carlo distribution that correspond to the order statistics. For example, the figures in columns (4)–(5) of row (1) show that the 1st and 10th order statistic from 100 i.i.d. Monte Carlo draws bound the 5th percentile of the unknown distribution with 95% confidence. Or, as shown in parenthesis, with 100 i.i.d. monte-carlo draws, the 1st and 10th percentile of the Monte Carlo distribution bound the 5th percentile of the true distribution with 95% confidence. No figures are reported in columns (2)–(3) of the first row because it is not possible to create a 95% confidence interval for the first percentile with only 100 observations.

Table 1 can also be used to construct confidence intervals for the error and percentage errors from computing VAR using Monte Carlo or other methods. Details on how the entries in Table 1 were generated and details on how to construct confidence intervals for percentage errors are contained in Appendix A.

Computational considerations

Risk managers often indicate that the complexities of various VAR methods limit their usefulness for daily computation. The purpose of this section is to investigate and provide a very rough framework for categorising the complexity of various ways of calculating VAR. VAR computations are segregated into two basic types: the first involves approximating the value of the portfolio and its derivatives; the second involves estimating the parameters of the distribution function of ε_{t+1}.

We will not consider the second type here since information should already be available when VAR is to be computed, but we will consider the first type of computation. This type can be further segregated into two groups - *complex* computations that involve the pricing of an instrument or the computation of a partial derivative such as δ or Γ, and *simple* computations that involve relatively straightforward computations such as linear interpolation or using the inputs from complex computations to compute VAR.[32] For the purpose of this paper we assume that a single simple computation is involved each time the portfolio is repriced using simple techniques. We will also assume that, once delta and gamma have been calculated, computing VAR requires one simple computation. This is a strong assumption, but it is probably not very important because the bulk of the computational time is not driven by the simple computations, but by complex computations.

We will also make some assumptions about the number of complex computations required to price an instrument. In particular, we will assume that the pricing of an instrument requires a single complex computation no matter how the instrument is actually priced. This assumption is clearly inappropriate for modelling computational time in some circumstances,[33] but it is made here to abstract away from the details of the actual pricing of each instrument.

The amount of time that is required to calculate VAR depends on the number and complexity of the instruments in the portfolio, the method that is used to calculate VAR, and the amount of parallelism in the firm's computing structure. To illustrate these points in a single unifying framework, let V denote a portfolio whose value is sensitive to N factors, and contains a total of I different instruments. An instrument's complexity depends on whether its price, δ and Γ have closed form solutions, and on the number of factors used to price the instrument. For purposes of simplicity, we will assume that δ and Γ have closed form solutions for either all instruments or no instruments, and present results for both of these extreme cases. To model the other dimension of complexity, let I_n denote the number of different instruments whose value is sensitive to n factors.[34] It follows that the number of instruments in the portfolio is $I = \Sigma_{n=1}^{N} I_n$.

In order to calculate δ or Γ for the portfolio, it is necessary to calculate δ or Γ for individual instruments and then combine the results. We assume the number of computations required to calculate δ analytically for an instrument with n factors is n, and the number of numerical computations required is $2n$. Similarly, to calculate Γ for an instrument with n factors analytically requires $n(n+1)/2$ computations and the number of numerical calculations is $3n + 2n(n-1)$.[35, 36] This implies that the number of complex computations required for the delta approach is:

$$\#\text{Delta} = \begin{cases} \sum_{n=1}^{N} I_n n & \text{if analytical calculations} \\ \sum_{n=1}^{N} I_n 2n & \text{if numerical calculations} \end{cases}.$$

Similarly, the number of complex computations required for all of the delta-gamma approaches is equal to[37]:

$$\#\text{Delta-Gamma} = \begin{cases} \sum_{n=1}^{N} I_n n(n^2+3n)/2 & \text{if analytical calculations} \\ \sum_{n=1}^{N} I_n (2n^2+3n) & \text{if numerical calculations} \end{cases}.$$

The grid Monte Carlo approach prices the portfolio using exact valuation at a grid of factor values and prices the portfolio at points between grid values using some interpolation technique (such as linear). For simplicity, we will assume that the grid is computed for k realisations of each factor. This then implies that an instrument that is sensitive to n factors will need to be repriced at k^n grid points. This means that the number of complex computations that is required is:

$$\#\text{Grid Monte Carlo} = \sum_{n=1}^{N} I_n k^n.$$

The number of computations required for the grid Monte Carlo approach is growing exponentially in n. For even moderate sizes of n, the number of computations required to compute VAR using grid Monte Carlo is very large, so it will be desirable to modify the grid Monte Carlo approach. We will do this by using a method we will call the modified grid Monte Carlo approach. The derivation of this method is outlined in the Footnotes. It involves approximating the change in instrument value as the sum of the change in instrument value due to the changes in a set of factors that are allowed to enter non-linearly, plus the sum of change in instrument value due to other factors that are allowed to enter linearly. For example, if m factors are allowed to enter non-linearly, and each factor is evaluated at k values, then the change in instrument value due to the "non-linear" factors is approximated on a grid of points using linear interpolation on k^m grid points while all other factors are held fixed. The change in instrument value due to the other $n-m$ factors is approximated using a first order Taylor series while holding the "non-linear" instruments fixed.

The number of complex computations required for one instrument using the modified grid Monte Carlo approach is k^m+n-m if the first derivatives in the Taylor series are computed analytically, and $k^m+2(n-m)$ if they are computed numerically. Let $I_{m,n}$ denote the number of instruments with n factors that have m factors that enter non-linearly in the modified grid Monte Carlo approach. Then, the number of complex computations required in the modified grid Monte Carlo approach with a grid consisting of k realisations per factor on the grid is:

$$\#\text{Modified Grid Monte Carlo} = \begin{cases} \sum_{n=1}^{N}\sum_{m=1}^{n} I_{m,n}\left[k^m+n-m\right] & \text{if analytical calculations} \\ \sum_{n=1}^{N}\sum_{m=1}^{n} I_{m,n}\left[k^m+2(n-m)\right] & \text{if numerical calculations} \end{cases}.$$

Finally, the number of computations required for the exact pricing Monte Carlo approach (labelled Full Monte Carlo) is the number of draws made times the number of instruments that are repriced:

$$\#\text{Full Monte Carlo} = \text{NDRAWS}\sum_{n=1}^{N} I_n.$$

Only one simple computation is required in the delta approach and in most of the delta-gamma approaches. The number of simple computations in the grid Monte Carlo approach is equal to the expected number of linear interpolations that are made. This should be equal to the number of Monte Carlo draws. Similarly, the delta-gamma Monte-Carlo approach involves simple computations because it only involves evaluating a Taylor series with linear and quadratic terms. The number of times this is computed is again equal to the number of times the change in portfolio value is approximated.[38]

In order for us to obtain a better indication of the computational requirements for each approach, let us consider a sample portfolio with 3,000 instruments, where 1,000 are sensitive to one factor, 1,000 are sensitive to two factors, and 1,000 are sensitive to three factors. We will implement the modified grid Monte Carlo approach with only one "non-linear" factor per instrument. Both grid Monte Carlo approaches will create a grid with 10 factor realisations per factor considered.[39] Finally, 300 Monte Carlo draws will be made to compute VAR. The number of complex and simple computations required to compute VAR under these circumstances is provided in Table 2.

Table 2. Numbers of complex and simple computations for VAR methods

VAR method	# complex computations	# simple computations
Delta	6,000	1
Delta-gamma-delta	23,000	1
Delta-gamma-minimisation	23,000	1
Delta-gamma-Monte Carlo	23,000	300
Grid Monte Carlo	1,110,000	300
Modified grid Monte Carlo	33,000	300
Full Monte Carlo	900,000	0

Notes: The table illustrates the number of complex and simple computations required to compute VAR using different methods for a portfolio with 3,000 instruments. 1,000 instruments are sensitive to one factor; 1,000 instruments are sensitive to two factors; and 1,000 instruments are sensitive to three factors. The distinction between simple and complex computations is described in the text.

The computations in the table are made for a small portfolio which can be valued analytically. Thus, the results are not representative of true portfolios, but they are indicative of some of the computational burdens imposed by the different techniques.[40] The most striking feature of the table is the large number of complex computations required in the grid and Monte Carlo approaches, as against the relatively small number in the delta and delta-gamma approaches. The grid approach involves a large number of computations because the number of complex computations for each instrument is growing exponentially in the number of factors to which the instrument is sensitive.

For example, an asset that is sensitive to one factor is priced 10 times, while an asset that is sensitive to three factors is priced 1,000 times. Reducing the mesh of the grid will reduce the number of computations significantly, but it will still be substantial. If the mesh of the grid is reduced by half, 155,000 complex computations are required for the grid approach. The modified grid Monte Carlo approach ameliorates the curse of dimensionality problem associated with grid Monte Carlo in a more satisfactory way by modelling fewer factors on a grid. This will definitely affect the accuracy of the method, but it should very significantly improve on computational time when pricing instruments that are sensitive to a large number of factors.

The full Monte Carlo approach requires a large number of computations because each asset is priced 300 times. However, the number of calculations needed increases only linearly in the number of instruments and does not depend on the number of factors, so for large portfolios, Monte Carlo may involve a smaller number of computations than some grid based approaches.

The delta and delta-gamma approaches require a much smaller number of calculations because the number of complex computations required increases only linearly in the number of factors per instrument for the delta method and only quadratically for the delta-gamma methods. As long as the number of factors per instrument remains moderate, the number of computations involved in the delta and delta-gamma methods should remain relatively low.

An important additional consideration is the amount of parallelism in the firm's process for computing VAR. Table 2 shows that a large number of computations are required to calculate VAR for all the methods examined here. If some of these computations are split among different trading desks throughout the firm and then individual risk reports are funneled upward for a firmwide calculation, the amount of time required to compute VAR could potentially be smaller than implied by the gross number of complex computations. For example, if there are 20 trading desks and each one takes an hour to calculate its risk reports, it may take another hour to combine the results and generate a VAR number for the firm - a total of two hours. But if all the computations are done by the risk management group, it may take 21 hours to calculate VAR, by which point the figure may be irrelevant to the firm's day-to-day operations.[41]

It is conceptually possible to perform all of the complex computations in parallel for the various methods we are discussing. However, the effort will be rather more involved for the grid and Monte Carlo approaches since individual desks need a priori knowledge of the grid points so they can value their books, and they may also need a priori knowledge of the Monte Carlo draws so that they can value their books at the draw points.[42]

Empirical analysis

Two simulation exercises were conducted to evaluate the accuracy of different VAR methods; computational time was examined in a separate analysis. All simulations computed VAR in dollar units for portfolios of European foreign exchange options priced using the Black–Scholes model. Exchange rates and interest rates were treated as stochastic pricing variables; their covariance matrix was extracted using the RiskMetrics regulatory data set.[43] Implied volatility was treated as fixed. Estimates of VAR were computed using the methods described above, and all of the partial and second and cross-partial derivatives used in the delta and delta-gamma methods were computed numerically.[44] All of the Monte Carlo methods used 10,000 draws to compute VAR.

SIMULATION EXERCISES 1 AND 2

Simulation exercise 1 examined VAR for positions in a single option that were either long or short a dollar/French franc call or put that delivered Ffr1 million if exercised. For each option position, VAR was calculated for a set of seven evenly-spaced moneynesses that ranged from 30% out of the money to 30% in the money, and for a set of 10 evenly spaced maturities that ranged from .1 years to 1.0 years.

Simulation exercise 2 examined VAR for 500 randomly-chosen portfolios of foreign exchange rate options. The moneyness of each option chosen was as in simulation 1. The maturity of the options ranged from 18 days to 1 year. Each option's underlying exchange rate was chosen randomly from among the exchange rates between the currencies of Belgium, Canada, Switzerland, the US, Germany, Spain, France, the UK, Italy, Japan, the Netherlands, and Sweden. The probability that the exchange rate between a currency pair was chosen was proportional to the amount of turnover in the OTC foreign exchange derivatives market relative to the other currency pairs considered. The measures of turnover are on Table 9-G of the *Central Bank Survey of Foreign Exchange and Derivatives Market Activity 1995*. Additional details on the simulations are contained in Appendix B.

THE EMPIRICAL ACCURACY OF THE METHODS

Results from simulation 1 for positions in the long call option for VAR at the 1% confidence level are presented in Figures 1–5 and in Table 3; results for other option positions will be selectively discussed, but not formally presented in order to save space.[45] Figure 1 presents plots of estimated VAR against moneyness and time to expiration for all six methods. The VAR estimates are qualitatively similar and for five methods range from a low near 0 for deep out of the money options to a high near $3,500. However, the delta-gamma minimisation method generates substantially higher estimates, suggesting it grossly overstates VAR. This is consistent with its predicted bias.

Figures 2 and 3 plot the upper and lower bounds respectively of a 95% confidence interval for the error made using each VAR estimate. Figures 4 and 5 plot the upper and lower bounds of 95% confidence intervals for the percentage errors associated with each estimator.[46]

These confidence intervals are derived in Appendix A and are useful for hypotheses testing. If a confidence interval contains 0, the null of no error cannot be rejected at a 5% significance level. If the interval is bounded above by 0 (ie if the upper bound of the confidence interval is below 0), the null hypothesis of no error is rejected in favor of the estimate understating true VAR, and if the interval is bounded below by zero (ie if the lower bound of the interval is above zero), the null of the no error is rejected in favour of VAR being understated.

The upper bound confidence intervals in Figures 2 and 4 are almost always above zero, showing that VAR is rarely understated for long call option positions. However, Figures 3 and 5 show that the delta and delta-gamma-delta methods overstate VAR for at or near the money call options. This is not surprising; the value of a call option declines at a decreasing rate in the underlying, and the delta method does not account for this, so overstatement of VAR should be expected. The problem should be especially acute for at the money options where delta declines the most rapidly in the underlying.

The delta-gamma-delta method appears to be similar; its strange distributional assumptions do not improve much on the results from the delta method.The delta-gamma minimisation method also overstates VAR, but by very large amounts. By contrast, Figures 2–4 show the confidence intervals for the errors from the delta-gamma Monte Carlo method and delta-gamma-delta methods usually contain 0. The exception is for long call options that are deep out of the money and close to expiration. This should not surprise us since these options have low values, large exchange rate deltas, and their only risk is that option prices could decline. Since they have large deltas, but the option prices cannot decline much further, the dynamics of the option prices must be highly non-linear; a factor not adequately captured by any of the methods except full Monte Carlo. However, the delta-gamma Monte Carlo and modified grid Monte Carlo do a much better job with these non-linearities than do the delta and delta-gamma-delta methods.

The results for the *short call option* positions (not presented) for VAR at the 1% confidence

1. 1% quantile VAR estimates by VAR method, moneyness and time to expiration

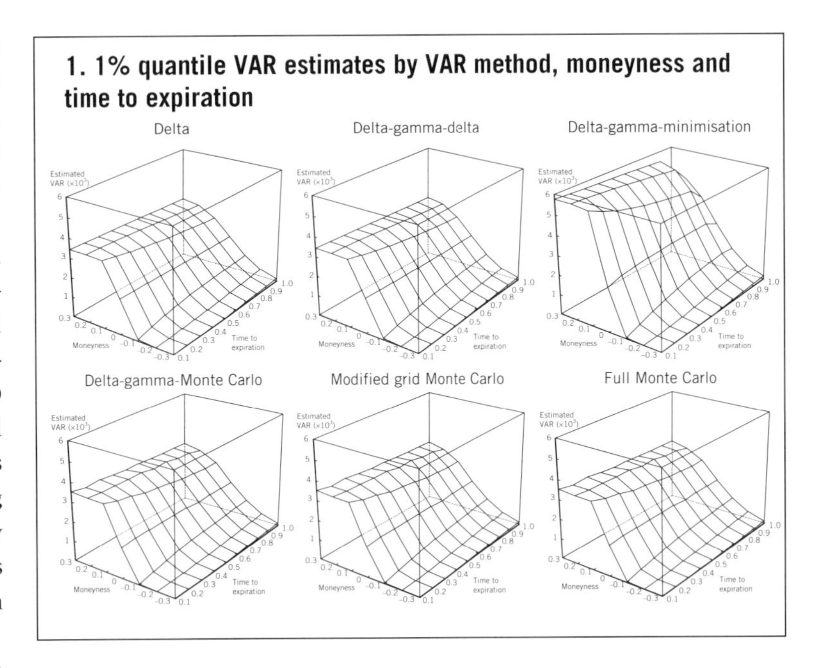

2. Upper bound errors in 1% quantile VAR estimates by VAR method, moneyness and time to expiration

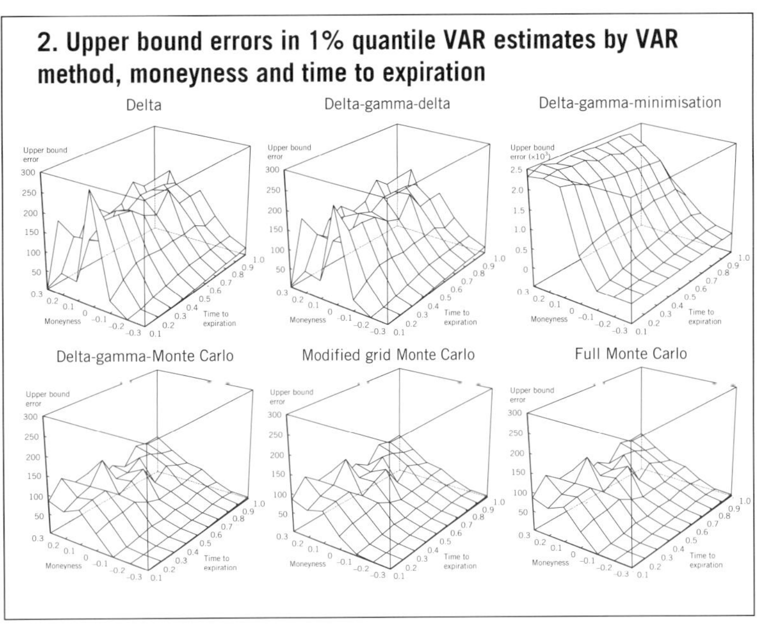

3. Lower bound errors in 1% quantile VAR estimates by VAR method, moneyness and time to expiration

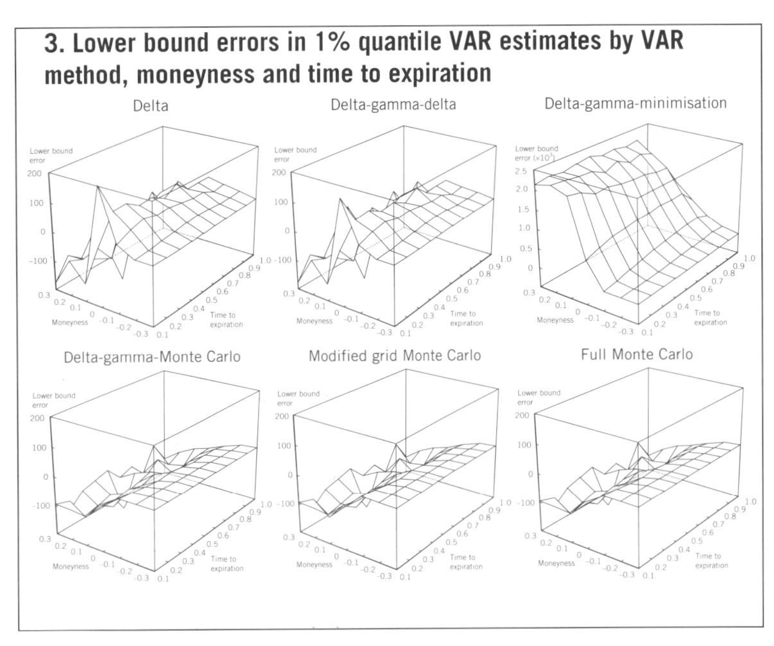

4. Upper bound 95% confidence interval for %ERRS: 1% quantile VAR estimates by VAR method, moneyness and time to expiration

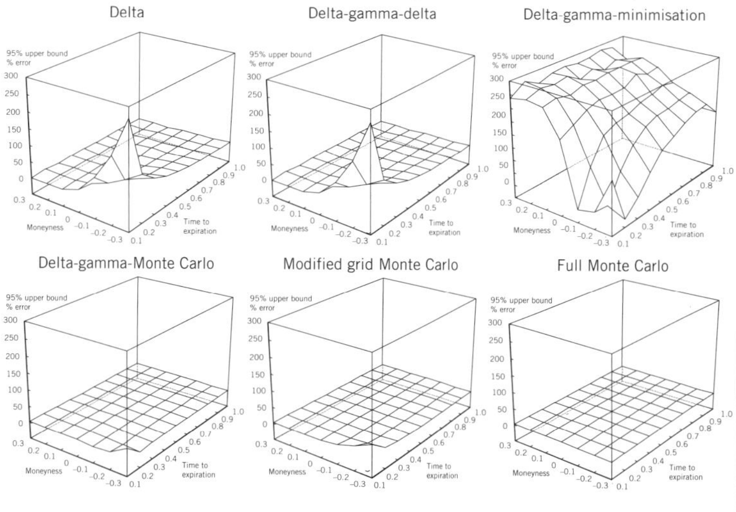

5. Lower bound 95% confidence interval for %ERRS: 1% quantile VAR estimates by VAR method, moneyness and time to expiration

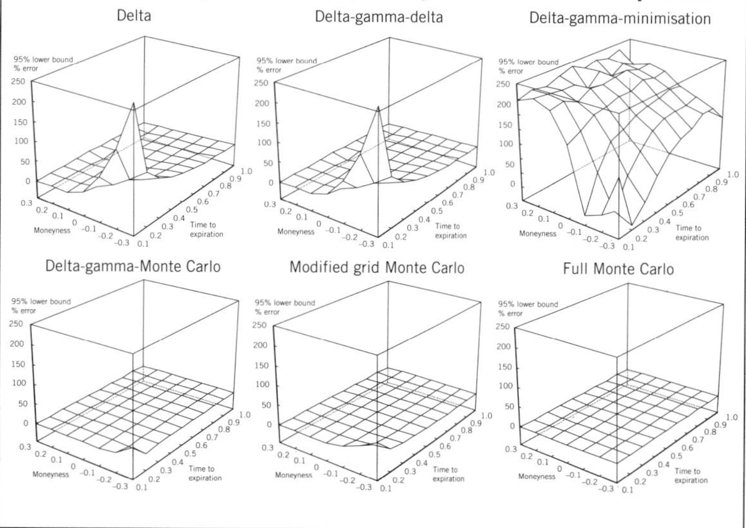

Notes for figures

Figures 1–5 present results on the properties of six different methods of computing VAR for 70 different option positions. Each position consists of a long position in one call option on the dollar/French franc exchange rate and delivers Ffr1 million if exercised. The 70 option positions vary by moneyness and time to expiration. Seven moneynesses are examined; they range from 30% out of the money to 30% in the money by increments of 10%. Ten maturities are examined; they range from 0.1 years to one year in increments of 0.1 years. The VAR methods that are considered are the delta, delta-gamma-delta, delta-gamma-minimisation, delta-gamma Monte Carlo, modified grid Monte Carlo, and full Monte Carlo methods.

Figure 1 presents estimates of VAR at the 1% quantile; ie the figure plots estimates of the 1% quantile of the distribution of the change in option value over a one-day holding period. Let U and L be upper and lower bounds of a 95% confidence interval for the error made when using VAR estimate $\hat{VAR}$ to compute VAR, and let U% and L% be upper and lower bounds of a 95% confidence interval for the percentage error made when using $\hat{VAR}$ to compute VAR.[54] Figures 2, 3, 4, and 5 present graphs of U, L, U%, and L% respectively for 1% quantile VAR estimates. For those options where U or U% is below zero, $\hat{VAR}$ understates VAR with probability exceeding 95%. A very conservative estimate of the amount by which VAR is understated is U, and a very conservative estimate of the amount by which VAR is understated as a percent of true VAR is U%.[55] Similarly, for those options where L or L% is above zero, $\hat{VAR}$ overstates VAR with 95% confidence. Very conservative estimates of the amount of understatement and percentage understatement are L and L%.

level are qualitatively similar. The delta and delta-gamma-delta methods tend to understate VAR for near the money options, because the exchange rate delta is increasing in the underlying exchange rate, and the delta method does not take this into account. The delta-gamma-minimisation method continues to substantially overstate VAR. Finally, the delta-gamma Monte Carlo method and the modified grid Monte Carlo method overstate VAR slightly for deep out of the money options with a short time to maturity.

Table 3 provides a large amount of supplemental information on the results in Figures 1–5. For those portfolios where a VAR method was statistically detected overstating VAR, panel A presents the proportion (FREQ) of portfolios for which VAR was overstated, and the mean and standard deviation (STD) of this overstatement using three measures of overstatement[47], LOW, MEDIUM, and HIGH. LOW is the most optimistic measure of error and HIGH is the most pessimistic. LOW and HIGH are endpoints of a 95% confidence interval for the amount of overstatement; MEDIUM is always between LOW and HIGH and is the difference between a VAR estimate and a full Monte Carlo estimate.

Panel B provides analogous information to panel A but uses the methods in Appendix A to scale the results as a percentage of true VAR. This allows us to make comparisons of results across the VAR literature and to interpret them in terms of risk-based capital. For example, let us suppose risk based capital charges are proportional to estimated VAR, and a firm uses the delta method to compute VAR and to determine its risk based capital, and its entire portfolio is a long position in one of these call options. In these (extreme) circumstances, for 62.86% of the long call option positions, VAR at the 1% confidence level would be overstated, and the firms risk based capital would exceed required capital by an average of 24.66% (LOW) to 30.50% (HIGH) with a standard deviation of about 45%, meaning that for some portfolios risk based capital could exceed required capital by 100%.

It is important to exercise caution when interpreting these percentage results; the errors in percentage terms should be examined with the errors in levels. For example, for the long call option positions, the largest percentage errors occur for deep out of the money options. Since VAR (based on full Monte Carlo estimates) and estimates of VAR errors in levels are low for these options, a large percentage error is not important unless these options are a large part of a firm's portfolio.

Panels C and D are analogous to A and B but present results for understatement of VAR. Panels E and F present results on those VAR estimates for which its error was statistically indistinguishable from 0. In this case, LOW and HIGH are endpoints of a 95% confidence bound for the error, which can be negative (LOW) or positive (HIGH). Medium is computed as before. The purpose of panels E and F is to give an indication of the size of error for those VAR errors which were statistically indistinguishable from 0. The panels show percentage errors for VAR estimates which were statistically indistinguishable from 0, probably ranged within plus or minus 3% of VAR.

The mean and standard deviation of the errors conditional on under- or overstatement provide useful information on different VAR method's implications for capital adequacy, but can be misleading when trying to rank them.[48] To further compare the methods, panels A and B report two statistical loss functions, Mean Absolute Error (MAE), the average absolute error for each VAR method, and Root Mean Squared Error (RMSE), the average squared errors for each VAR method.[49] The errors in these loss functions are computed using the Monte Carlo draws from the full Monte Carlo method. This means that they are not meaningful for the full Monte Carlo method, but are for other methods.

Table 3 confirms basic features of the figures. The delta-gamma-minimisation method overstates VAR by very large amounts; and the delta and delta-gamma-delta methods tend to overstate VAR for the long call option positions, and to underestimate it for short option positions (not shown). The table also shows that the frequency of under- and over-statement is much lower for the delta-gamma Monte Carlo and modified grid Monte Carlo methods than for other methods. Finally by all three error measures, the statistical loss functions in Table 3 show the best method is delta-gamma Monte Carlo, followed by modified grid Monte Carlo, delta-gamma-delta, delta, and delta-gamma-minimisation.

The results in Table 4 are analogous to Table 3, but are provided for simulation exercise 2.[50] Based on the frequency of under- or over-statement, the delta-gamma Monte Carlo and modified grid Monte Carlo methods under- or overstate VAR for about 25% of portfolios, at the 1% confidence level. This is about half the frequency of the delta or delta-gamma-delta methods. Despite the large differences in frequency of under- or over-statement, the statistical loss functions across the four methods are much more similar than in Table 3. The increased similarity between the methods may be because, on a portfolio-wide basis, the errors that delta or delta-gamma-delta methods make for long gamma positions in some options is partially offset by the errors made for short gamma positions in other options. Closer inspection of the results (not shown) revealed more details about the similarity of the loss functions. Roughly speaking, for the portfolios where the delta-gamma Monte Carlo and grid Monte Carlo methods made large errors, the other methods made large errors too. But for the portfolios where the delta and delta-gamma-delta methods made relatively small errors, the delta-gamma Monte Carlo and modified grid Monte Carlo methods often made no errors.

Thus, in Table 4, the superior methods are superior mostly because they make fewer small errors. This shows up as a large difference in frequency of errors, but relatively small differences in the statistical loss functions. Because of the smaller differences in the statistical loss functions, the rankings of the methods are a bit more blurred, but still roughly similar: the delta-gamma Monte Carlo and modified grid Monte Carlo methods have similar accuracies that are a bit above the accuracies of the other two methods. Importantly, the best methods in simulation exercise 2 over- or understated VAR for about 25% of the portfolios considered by an average amount of about 10% of VAR with a standard deviation of the same amount.

To summarise, the rankings of the methods in terms of accuracies are somewhat robust across the two sets of simulations. The most accurate methods are delta-gamma Monte Carlo and modified grid Monte Carlo, followed by delta-gamma-delta and then delta, and then (far behind) delta-gamma-minimisation. Although our results on errors are measured in terms of percentage of true VAR, and are relatively easy to interpret, they still have the shortcoming that they are specific to the portfolios we generated. A firm, in evaluating the methods here, should repeat the comparisons of these VAR methods using portfolios that are more representative of its actual trading book.

Empirical results: computational time

In order to examine computation time, a simulation exercise was conducted in which VAR was computed for a randomly chosen portfolio of 50 foreign exchange options using all six VAR methods. The results are summarised in Table 5. The time for the various methods was increasing in

Table 3. Summary statistics for simulation exercise 1: Long call, 1% quantile VAR estimates

A. OVERSTATEMENT OF VAR

VAR method	Error measure	Mean	STD	FREQ	MAE	RMSE
Delta	LOW	37.13	37.33	62.86	23.34	41.75
	MEDIUM	61.96	55.07	62.86	38.95	65.72
	HIGH	83.57	75.69	62.86	52.53	89.39
Delta-gamma-delta	LOW	28.36	29.18	61.43	17.42	31.89
	MEDIUM	51.48	47.02	61.43	31.62	54.64
	HIGH	71.94	67.30	61.43	44.19	77.21
Delta-gamma-minimisation	LOW	1,043.26	868.29	95.71	998.55	1,327.92
	MEDIUM	1,102.26	913.93	95.71	1,055.02	1,400.84
	HIGH	1,152.28	952.66	95.71	1,102.89	1,462.70
Delta-gamma Monte Carlo	LOW	0.00	0.00	2.86	0.01	0.07
	MEDIUM	0.00	0.00	2.86	0.02	0.14
	HIGH	0.00	0.00	2.86	0.03	0.25
Modified grid Monte Carlo	LOW	0.34	0.72	10.00	0.03	0.25
	MEDIUM	0.51	1.02	10.00	0.05	0.36
	HIGH	0.62	1.20	10.00	0.06	0.43
Full Monte Carlo	LOW	0.00	0.00	0.00	0.00	0.00
	MEDIUM	0.00	0.00	0.00	0.00	0.00
	HIGH	0.00	0.00	0.00	0.00	0.00

B. OVERSTATEMENT AS % OF VAR

VAR method	Error measure	Mean	STD	FREQ	MAE	RMSE
Delta	LOW	24.66	45.82	62.86	15.50	41.25
	MEDIUM	27.69	45.53	62.86	17.40	42.25
	HIGH	30.50	45.20	62.86	19.17	43.23
Delta-gamma-delta	LOW	22.41	44.88	61.43	13.76	39.32
	MEDIUM	25.36	44.60	61.43	15.58	40.21
	HIGH	28.12	44.25	61.43	17.28	41.10
Delta-gamma-minimisation	LOW	47.62	15.15	95.71	45.63	48.89
	MEDIUM	52.09	16.20	96.71	49.92	53.37
	HIGH	56.19	17.17	95.71	53.87	57.48
Delta-gamma Monte Carlo	LOW	16.29	14.66	2.86	0.55	3.74
	MEDIUM	16.99	14.49	2.86	0.63	3.85
	HIGH	17.57	14.30	2.86	0.73	3.99
Modified grid Monte Carlo	LOW	12.71	15.14	10.00	1.27	6.25
	MEDIUM	14.23	14.70	10.00	1.42	6.47
	HIGH	15.59	14.25	10.00	1.56	6.68
Full Monte Carlo	LOW	0.00	0.00	0.00	0.00	0.00
	MEDIUM	0.00	0.00	0.00	0.00	0.00
	HIGH	0.00	0.00	0.00	0.00	0.00

C. UNDERSTATEMENT OF VAR

VAR method	Error measure	Mean	STD	FREQ
Delta	LOW	0.00	0.00	0.00
	MEDIUM	0.00	0.00	0.00
	HIGH	0.00	0.00	0.00
Delta-gamma-delta	LOW	0.00	0.00	0.00
	MEDIUM	0.00	0.00	0.00
	HIGH	0.00	0.00	0.00
Delta-gamma-minimisation	LOW	0.00	0.00	1.43
	MEDIUM	0.00	0.00	1.43
	HIGH	0.00	0.00	1.43
Delta-gamma Monte Carlo	LOW	0.22	0.26	4.29
	MEDIUM	0.44	0.50	4.29
	HIGH	0.78	0.89	4.29
Modified grid Monte Carlo	LOW	0.00	0.00	0.00
	MEDIUM	0.00	0.00	0.00
	HIGH	0.00	0.00	0.00
Full Monte Carlo	LOW	0.00	0.00	0.00
	MEDIUM	0.00	0.00	0.00
	HIGH	0.00	0.00	0.00

D. UNDERSTATEMENT AS % OF VAR

VAR method	Error measure	Mean	STD	FREQ
Delta	LOW	0.00	0.00	0.00
	MEDIUM	0.00	0.00	0.00
	HIGH	0.00	0.00	0.00
Delta-gamma-delta	LOW	0.00	0.00	0.00
	MEDIUM	0.00	0.00	0.00
	HIGH	0.00	0.00	0.00
Delta-gamma-minimisation	LOW	3.48	0.00	1.43
	MEDIUM	4.88	0.00	1.43
	HIGH	6.53	0.00	1.43
Delta-gamma Monte Carlo	LOW	2.08	1.13	4.29
	MEDIUM	3.48	1.14	4.29
	HIGH	5.40	1.95	4.29
Modified grid Monte Carlo	LOW	0.00	0.00	0.00
	MEDIUM	0.00	0.00	0.00
	HIGH	0.00	0.00	0.00
Full Monte Carlo	LOW	0.00	0.00	0.00
	MEDIUM	0.00	0.00	0.00
	HIGH	0.00	0.00	0.00

E. VAR ERRORS STATISTICALLY EQUAL TO 0

VAR method	Error measure	Mean	STD	FREQ
Delta	LOW	−92.69	62.79	37.14
	MEDIUM	17.35	50.95	37.14
	HIGH	109.71	50.12	37.14
Delta-gamma-delta	LOW	−92.46	62.56	38.57
	MEDIUM	17.15	50.82	38.57
	HIGH	108.71	49.47	38.57
Delta-gamma-minimisation	LOW	−0.77	0.65	2.86
	MEDIUM	−0.26	0.27	2.86
	HIGH	0.07	0.04	2.86
Delta-gamma-Monte Carlo	LOW	−60.79	50.41	92.86
	MEDIUM	0.02	0.58	92.86
	HIGH	51.58	40.71	92.86
Modified grid Monte Carlo	LOW	−64.64	50.85	90.00
	MEDIUM	−1.90	2.40	90.00
	HIGH	51.29	39.41	90.00
Full Monte Carlo	LOW	−56.48	50.98	100.00
	MEDIUM	0.00	0.00	100.00
	HIGH	47.88	41.42	100.00

F. VAR ERRORS STATISTICALLY EQUAL TO 0 AS % OF VAR

VAR method	Error measure	Mean	STD	FREQ
Delta	LOW	−2.88	1.89	37.14
	MEDIUM	0.64	1.70	37.14
	HIGH	3.62	1.83	37.14
Delta-gamma-delta	LOW	−2.88	1.88	38.57
	MEDIUM	0.63	1.67	38.57
	HIGH	3.59	1.78	38.57
Delta-gamma-minimisation	LOW	−2.50	0.72	2.86
	MEDIUM	−0.48	0.71	2.86
	HIGH	0.90	0.85	2.86
Delta-gamma-Monte Carlo	LOW	−3.22	0.82	92.86
	MEDIUM	−0.09	0.24	92.86
	HIGH	2.63	0.77	92.86
Modified grid Monte Carlo	LOW	−3.14	1.04	90.00
	MEDIUM	0.04	0.43	90.00
	HIGH	2.79	0.58	90.00
Full Monte Carlo	LOW	−3.01	0.98	100.00
	MEDIUM	0.00	0.00	100.00
	HIGH	2.60	0.75	100.00

Notes: For VAR at the 1% confidence level, for long call option positions (from simulation 1), the table provides summary statistics on six methods for computing VAR using three measures of VAR error or percentage error. The option positions are long one call option in one of 70 dollar/French franc options that deliver Ffr1 million if exercised. The options vary by moneyness and time to expiration. For each group of option positions, the table reports the proportion (FREQ) for which VAR was overstated, understated, or statistically indistinguishable from zero. For positions classified as over- or understated, the Mean and Standard Deviation (STD) of over- or understatement are computed for three measures of error, LOW (an optimistic measure of error), MEDIUM (a less optimistic measure of error), and HIGH (a pessimistic measure of error). LOW and HIGH are the endpoints of a 95% confidence interval for the amount of over- or understatement. For positions classified as statistically indistinguishable from zero, LOW and HIGH are endpoints of a 95% confidence interval for VAR error. For all positions MEDIUM is always between LOW and HIGH, and measures error as the difference between a VAR estimate and full Monte Carlo estimate or as the difference between a VAR estimate and full Monte Carlo as a percentage of full Monte Carlo. A VAR estimate was classified as either under- or overstated if the 95% confidence interval for its error was bounded below or above by 0 respectively, and was statistically indistinguishable from 0 if the 95% confidence interval for its error contained 0. To rank the VAR methods two statistical loss functions are reported, Mean Absolute Error (MAE), and Root Mean Squared Error (RMSE). These loss functions were computed using an optimistic measure of error (LOW), a pessimistic measure (HIGH), and a middle range measure (MEDIUM). The loss function results in panel A are computed based on the levels of errors, the loss function results in panel B are computed based on the errors as a % of true VAR.

Table 4. Summary statistics for simulation exercise 2

A. OVERSTATEMENT OF VAR

VAR method	Error measure	Mean	STD	FREQ	MAE	RMSE
Delta	LOW	9,285.98	13,829.98	22.60	5,158.24	12,983.17
	MEDIUM	14,143.25	15,827.45	22.60	7,820.36	16,638.92
	HIGH	18,271.80	18,308.28	22.60	10,480.18	20,712.29
Delta-gamma-delta	LOW	9,348.09	14,306.30	21.20	4,773.82	12,692.74
	MEDIUM	14,491.12	16,174.45	21.20	7,341.28	16,265.99
	HIGH	18,856.94	18,615.27	21.20	9,893.22	20,284.14
Delta-gamma-minimisation	LOW	414,981.5	356,880.8	100.00	414,981.5	547,333.1
	MEDIUM	421,121.9	361,356.2	100.00	421,121.9	554.907.2
	HIGH	426,591.5	365,546.4	100.00	426,591.5	561,786.9
Delta-gamma Monte Carlo	LOW	15,236.24	19,463.43	11.60	3,954.29	12,482.32
	MEDIUM	20,912.81	21,023.91	11.60	5,545.61	15,394.13
	HIGH	25,865.86	23,197.04	11.60	7,200.20	18,764.70
Modified grid Monte Carlo	LOW	14,640.18	19,397.77	12.00	3,932.56	12,460.24
	MEDIUM	20,357.90	20,898.54	12.00	5,541.86	15,374.71
	HIGH	25,500.28	23,054.59	12.00	7,229.88	18,785.42
Full Monte Carlo	LOW	0.00	0.00	0.00	0.00	0.00
	MEDIUM	0.00	0.00	0.00	0.00	0.00
	HIGH	0.00	0.00	0.00	0.00	0.00

B. OVERSTATEMENT AS % OF VAR

VAR method	Error measure	Mean	STD	FREQ	MAE	RMSE
Delta	LOW	7.55	8.46	22.60	3.57	8.01
	MEDIUM	11.10	8.95	22.60	5.34	9.96
	HIGH	14.31	9.18	22.60	7.24	12.22
Delta-gamma-delta	LOW	7.27	8.85	21.20	3.07	7.05
	MEDIUM	10.84	9.36	21.20	4.72	8.93
	HIGH	14.05	9.61	21.20	6.49	11.10
Delta-gamma-minimisation	LOW	204.36	59.53	100.00	204.36	212.86
	MEDIUM	214.85	62.05	100.00	214.85	223.63
	HIGH	224.50	63.97	100.00	224.50	233.44
Delta-gamma Monte Carlo	LOW	10.36	11.64	11.60	2.19	6.63
	MEDIUM	14.22	12.25	11.60	3.08	8.07
	HIGH	17.64	12.52	11.60	4.01	9.64
Modified grid Monte Carlo	LOW	9.97	11.82	12.00	2.18	6.65
	MEDIUM	13.82	12.42	12.00	3.07	8.09
	HIGH	17.27	12.68	12.00	4.01	9.66
Full Monte Carlo	LOW	0.00	0.00	0.00	0.00	0.00
	MEDIUM	0.00	0.00	0.00	0.00	0.00
	HIGH	0.00	0.00	0.00	0.00	0.00

C. UNDERSTATEMENT OF VAR

VAR method	Error measure	Mean	STD	FREQ
Delta	LOW	10,478.12	15,896.63	29.20
	MEDIUM	15,835.58	18,672.39	29.20
	HIGH	21,749.17	21,870.54	29.20
Delta-gamma-delta	LOW	10,340.84	16,138.02	27.00
	MEDIUM	15,811.71	18,963.82	27.00
	HIGH	21,835.36	22,266.65	27.00
Delta-gamma-minimisation	LOW	0.00	0.00	0.00
	MEDIUM	0.00	0.00	0.00
	HIGH	0.00	0.00	0.00
Delta-gamma Monte Carlo	LOW	16,567.30	19,208.84	13.20
	MEDIUM	23,634.26	21,539.65	13.20
	HIGH	31,816.39	24,380.80	13.20
Modified grid Monte Carlo	LOW	16,736.45	19,209.47	13.00
	MEDIUM	23,837.82	21,549.07	13.00
	HIGH	32,075.74	24,389.10	13.00
Full Monte Carlo	LOW	0.00	0.00	0.00
	MEDIUM	0.00	0.00	0.00
	HIGH	0.00	0.00	0.00

D. UNDERSTATEMENT AS % OF VAR

VAR method	Error measure	Mean	STD	FREQ
Delta	LOW	6.37	8.92	29.20
	MEDIUM	9.69	9.43	29.20
	HIGH	13.74	9.95	29.20
Delta-gamma-delta	LOW	5.67	6.98	27.00
	MEDIUM	8.97	7.34	27.00
	HIGH	12.99	7.73	27.00
Delta-gamma-minimisation	LOW	0.00	0.00	0.00
	MEDIUM	0.00	0.00	0.00
	HIGH	0.00	0.00	0.00
Delta-gamma Monte Carlo	LOW	7.49	7.96	13.20
	MEDIUM	10.81	8.21	13.20
	HIGH	14.86	8.51	13.20
Modified grid Monte Carlo	LOW	7.54	7.89	13.00
	MEDIUM	10.86	8.14	13.00
	HIGH	14.93	8.43	13.00
Full Monte Carlo	LOW	0.00	0.00	0.00
	MEDIUM	0.00	0.00	0.00
	HIGH	0.00	0.00	0.00

E. VAR ERRORS STATISTICALLY EQUAL TO 0

VAR method	Error measure	Mean	STD	FREQ
Delta	LOW	−7,035.28	7,256.65	48.20
	MEDIUM	−155.78	4,747.76	48.20
	HIGH	6,010.55	5,747.92	48.20
Delta-gamma-delta	LOW	−6,896.76	6,904.83	51.80
	MEDIUM	−287.25	4,330.18	51.80
	HIGH	5,633.43	5,374.26	51.80
Delta-gamma-minimisation	LOW	0.00	0.00	0.00
	MEDIUM	0.00	0.00	0.00
	HIGH	0.00	0.00	0.00
Delta-gamma-Monte Carlo	LOW	−5,872.74	5,580.88	75.20
	MEDIUM	−19.14	2,639.36	75.20
	HIGH	5,249.76	4,947.50	75.20
Modified grid Monte Carlo	LOW	−5,922.22	5,606.95	75.00
	MEDIUM	−77.73	2,636.13	75.00
	HIGH	5,161.39	4,810.13	75.00
Full Monte Carlo	LOW	−6,140.43	4,897.27	100.00
	MEDIUM	0.00	0.00	100.00
	HIGH	5,469.60	4,576.15	100.00

F. VAR ERRORS STATISTICALLY EQUAL TO 0 AS % OF VAR

VAR method	Error measure	Mean	STD	FREQ
Delta	LOW	−3.53	1.98	48.20
	MEDIUM	−0.03	1.78	48.20
	HIGH	3.06	1.74	48.20
Delta-gamma-delta	LOW	−3.58	1.88	51.80
	MEDIUM	−0.08	1.65	51.80
	HIGH	2.99	1.60	51.80
Delta-gamma-minimisation	LOW	0.00	0.00	0.00
	MEDIUM	0.00	0.00	0.00
	HIGH	0.00	0.00	0.00
Delta-gamma-Monte Carlo	LOW	−3.48	1.24	75.20
	MEDIUM	0.02	0.89	75.20
	HIGH	3.08	1.12	75.20
Modified grid Monte Carlo	LOW	−3.51	1.22	75.00
	MEDIUM	−0.01	0.93	75.00
	HIGH	3.05	1.19	75.00
Full Monte Carlo	LOW	−3.54	0.85	100.00
	MEDIUM	0.00	0.00	100.00
	HIGH	3.07	0.69	100.00

Notes: For VAR at the 1% confidence level, for 500 randomly chosen portfolios of options (from simulation 2), the table provides summary statistics on six methods for computing VAR using three measures of VAR error or percentage error. For each group of option positions, the table reports the proportion (FREQ) for which VAR was overstated, understated, or statistically indistinguishable from zero. For positions classified as over- or understated, the Mean and Standard Deviation (STD) of over- or understatement are computed for three measures of error, LOW (an optimistic measure of error) MEDIUM (a less optimistic measure of error), and HIGH (a pessimistic measure of error). LOW and HIGH are the endpoints of a 95% confidence interval for the amount of over- or understatement. For positions classified as statistically indistinguishable from zero, LOW and HIGH are endpoints of a 95% confidence interval for VAR error. For all positions MEDIUM is always between LOW and HIGH, and measures error as the difference between a VAR estimate and full Monte Carlo estimate or as the difference between a VAR estimate and full Monte Carlo as a percentage of full Monte Carlo. A VAR estimate was classified as either under - or overstated if the 95% confidence interval for its error was bounded below or above by 0 respectively, and was statistically indistinguishable from 0 if the 95% confidence interval for its error contained 0. To rank the VAR methods two statistical loss functions are reported, Mean Absolute Error (MAE), and Root Mean Squared Error (RMSE). These loss functions were computed using an optimistic measure of error (LOW), a pessimistic measure (HIGH), and a middle range measure (MEDIUM). The loss function results in panel A are computed based on the levels of errors, the loss function results in panel B are computed based on the errors as a percentage of true VAR.

Table 5. Results on computational time

VAR method	Computation time (seconds)	# complex computations	# simple computations
Delta	.076	504	1
Delta-gamma-delta	1.17	3,300	1
Delta-gamma-minimisation	1.27	3,300	1
Delta-gamma-Monte Carlo	3.88	3,300	10,000
Modified grid Monte Carlo	32.29	804	10,000
Full Monte Carlo	66.27	10,000	0

Notes: The table presents information on the time required, and the computational complexity involved, for computing VAR for a portfolio that contained 50 European exercise foreign exchange options using six different methods of computing VAR. Forty-eight of the options were mapped to five risk factors in RiskMetrics and two options were mapped to six risk factors.

the number of complex computations, as expected, with the exception of the modified grid Monte Carlo method. The different results for the modified grid Monte Carlo method are not too surprising since the complexity of the programming to implement this method is likely to have slowed it down.[51] The delta method took .07 seconds, the delta-gamma-delta method required 1.17 seconds, the delta-gamma-minimisation method required 1.27 seconds, the delta-gamma Monte Carlo method required 3.87 seconds, the grid Monte Carlo method required 32.29 seconds, and full Monte Carlo required 66.27 seconds. This translates into .003 hours per VAR computation for a portfolio of 10,000 options using the delta method, .065 hours using the delta-gamma-delta method, .07 hours using the delta-gamma-minimisation method, .215 hours using the delta-gamma Monte Carlo method, 1.79 hours using the modified grid Monte Carlo method, and 3.68 hours using full Monte Carlo. Of course, the relative figures are more important than the literals since these figures depend on the computer technology at the Federal Reserve Board. The results on time that are reported here were computed using Gauss for Unix on a Sparc 20 workstation.

Accuracy versus computational time

This paper investigated six methods of computing VAR in terms of both accuracy and computational time. The results for full Monte Carlo were the most accurate, but also took the longest time to compute. The next most accurate methods were the delta-gamma Monte Carlo and modified grid Monte Carlo methods. Both attained comparable levels of accuracy, but the delta-gamma Monte Carlo method is faster by more than a factor of 8. The next most accurate methods are the delta-gamma-delta and delta methods. These methods are faster than the delta-gamma Monte Carlo methods by a factor of 3 and 51 respectively. Finally, the delta-gamma-minimisation method is slower than the delta-gamma-delta method and is the most inaccurate of the methods.

Based on these results, the delta-gamma-minimisation method seems to be dominated by other methods which are both faster and more accurate. Similarly, the modified grid Monte Carlo method is dominated by the delta-gamma Monte Carlo method since the latter method has the same level of accuracy but is quicker to estimate. The remaining four methods cannot be strictly ranked. However, full Monte Carlo seems too slow a method of calculating VAR, while the delta-gamma Monte Carlo method is reasonably fast (.215 hours per 10,000 options), and produces amongst the next most accurate results both for individual options, as in simulation 1, and for portfolios of options as in simulation 2. So it appears that the best of the methods considered here is delta-gamma Monte Carlo.

Conclusion

Methods of computing VAR need to be both accurate and available on a timely basis. There is likely to be an inherent trade-off between these objectives since more rapid methods tend to be less accurate. This paper has investigated the trade-off between accuracy and computational time, and has also introduced a method for measuring the accuracy of VAR estimates based on confidence intervals from Monte Carlo with full repricing. The confidence intervals allow us to quantify VAR errors both in monetary terms and as a percentage of true VAR, even though true VAR is not known. This lends a capital adequacy interpretation to VAR errors for firms that choose their risk based capital based on VAR.

To investigate the trade-off between accuracy and computational time, this paper investigated six methods of computing VAR. The accuracy of the methods varied fairly widely. When examining accuracy and computational time together, two methods were dominated because other methods were at least as accurate and required a smaller amount of time to compute. Of the undominated methods, the delta-gamma Monte Carlo method was the most accurate of those that required a reasonable amount of computational time. Other advantages of the delta-gamma Monte Carlo method is that it allows the assumption of normally distributed factor shocks to be relaxed in favour of alternative distributional assumptions including historical simulation. Also, the delta-gamma Monte Carlo method can be implemented in a parallel fashion across the firm, so that delta and gamma matrices can be computed for each trading desk, and then the results can be aggregated for a firmwide VAR computation.

While the delta-gamma Monte Carlo method produces among the most accurate VAR estimates, it still frequently produced errors that were statistically significant and economically large. For 25% of the 500 randomly-chosen portfolios of options in simulation exercise 2, it was detected over- or under-stating VAR by an average of 10% with a standard deviation of the same amount; and for deep out of the money options in simulation 1, its accuracy was poor. More importantly, its errors when actually used are likely to be different than those reported here for two reasons. First, the results reported here abstract away from errors in specifying the distribution of the factor shocks, these are likely to be important in practice. And secondly, firms' portfolios contain additional types of instruments not considered here, and many firms have hedged positions, while the ones used here are unhedged.

In order to better characterise the methods' accuracies and computational time, it is important to do the type of work performed here using more realistic factor shocks, and firm's actual portfolios. This paper has begun the groundwork to perform this type of analysis.

Appendix A

NON-PARAMETRIC CONFIDENCE INTERVALS

The confidence intervals derived in this section draw on a basic results from the theory of order statistics. To introduce this result, let $X_{(1)} < X_{(2)}, \ldots < X_{(N)}$ be order statistics from N i.i.d. random draws of the continuous random variable X with unknown distribution function G, and let ξ_p represent the pth percentile of G. The result in the following proposition illustrates how a confidence interval for the pth percentile of G can be formed from order statistics. The proof of this proposition is from the 2nd Edition of the book *Order Statistics* by Herbert A. David.

PROPOSITION 1 For $r < s$,

$$\mathrm{Prob}\left(X_{(r)} < \xi_p < X_{(s)}\right) = \sum_{i=r}^{s-1} \binom{N}{i} p^i (1-p)^{N-i}$$

PROOF:

$$r < s \Rightarrow \mathrm{Prob}\left(X_{(r)} < \xi_p\right)$$
$$= \mathrm{Prob}\left(X_{(s)} \le \xi_p\right) + \mathrm{Prob}\left(X_{(r)} < \xi_p < X_{(s)}\right)$$
$$\Rightarrow \mathrm{Prob}\left(X_{(r)} < \xi_p < X_{(s)}\right)$$
$$= \mathrm{Prob}\left(X_{(r)} \le \xi_p\right) - \mathrm{Prob}\left(X_{(s)} \le \xi_p\right)$$
$$= \sum_{i=0}^{N-r} \binom{N}{r+i} p^{r+i} (1-p)^{N-r-i} - \sum_{j=0}^{N-s} \binom{N}{s+j} p^{s+j} (1-p)^{N-s-j}$$
$$= \sum_{i=r}^{s-1} \binom{N}{i} p^i (1-p)^{N-i}.$$

Q.E.D.

CONFIDENCE INTERVALS FROM MONTE CARLO ESTIMATES.

To construct a 95% confidence interval for the pth percentile of G using the results from Monte Carlo simulation, it suffices to solve for an r and s such that:

$$\sum_{i=r}^{s-1} \binom{N}{i} p^i (1-p)^{N-i} \ge .95$$

and such that:

$$\sum_{i=r+1}^{s-1} \binom{N}{i} p^i (1-p)^{N-i} \le .95.$$

Then the order statistics $X_{(r)}$ and $X_{(s)}$ from the Monte Carlo simulation are the bounds for the confidence interval. In general, there are several r and s pairs that satisfy the above criteria. The confidence intervals contained in Table 1 impose the additional restriction that the confidence interval be as close to symmetric as possible about the pth percentile of the Monte Carlo distribution, ie r and s were chosen so that

$$p - \frac{r}{N} \approx \frac{s}{N} - p.$$

No more than two r and s pairs can satisfy all three criteria. In circumstances where there were two r and s pairs to choose from, one has been chosen at random.

Finally, since VAR at confidence level p corresponds to the pth percentile of some unknown distribution, the above results make it possible to create confidence intervals for value at risk based on the Monte Carlo results.

CONFIDENCE INTERVALS FOR VAR ERRORS

The bounds from the above Monte Carlo confidence intervals can be used to form confidence intervals for the errors from a VAR estimate. More specifically, let X_T denote true value at risk, and let X_H and X_L denote bounds such that

$$\mathrm{Prob}(X_L \le X_T \le X_H) = .95.$$

From the analysis above we know we can find these bounds. Given these bounds, let $\hat{X}$ be any other estimate of value at risk. It then follows that:

$$\text{Prob}\left(\hat{X} - X_L \geq \hat{X} - X_T \geq \hat{X} - X_H\right) = .95.$$

Therefore, $\hat{X} - X_L$ and $\hat{X} - X_H$ form upper and lower bounds for a confidence interval for the error when using VAR estimate $\hat{X}$.

The magnitude of the VAR errors made in any particular portfolio depends on the size of the positions in the portfolio. Therefore, in "small" portfolios, all methods may generate small VAR errors, and thus appear similar when in fact the methods are very different. The problem is the VAR errors need to be appropriately scaled when comparing the methods. Perhaps the best way to scale the errors, for purposes of comparison, is to scale the errors as a percentage of true VAR, ie to examine VAR percentage errors. The construction of confidence intervals for VAR Percentage Errors is discussed below.

CONFIDENCE INTERVALS FOR VAR PERCENTAGE ERRORS

The bounds from the above Monte Carlo confidence intervals can be used to form confidence intervals for the percentage errors made when using various methods of computing value at risk. To create this confidence interval requires some notation:

Let X_T denote the true value-at-risk, and let A denote the indicator function

$$A = 1_{\{L \leq X_T \leq H\}},$$

where L and H are bounds such that $H > L > 0$.[52]

Similarly, let $\hat{X}$ be an estimator of value-at-risk, with percentage error denoted by $\%\text{err}\,\hat{X}$ where

$$\%\text{err}\,\hat{X} = 100\frac{\hat{X} - X_T}{X_T},$$

and let A^* be the indicator function:

$$A^* = 1_{\{L^* \leq \%\text{err}\,\hat{X} \leq H^*\}}.$$

Where:

$$H^* = \sup\left(100\frac{\hat{X} - L}{L}, 100\frac{\hat{X} - L}{H}\right),$$

and

$$L^* = \inf\left(100\frac{\hat{X} - H}{H}, 100\frac{\hat{X} - H}{L}\right).$$

L^* and H^* are bounds for the percentage error in calculating value at risk using $\hat{X}$. The probability that $\hat{X}$ is in these bounds is given by the following proposition:

PROPOSITION 2 If L and H are greater than 0, and bound true value-at-risk with probability q, then L^* and H^* bound $\%\text{err}\,\hat{X}$ with probability greater than q.

PROOF: In mathematical terms, the proposition says

$$\text{Prob}(A = 1) = q, \Rightarrow \text{Prob}(A^* = 1) \geq q.$$

The main part of the proof involves showing that $\{A = 1\} \Rightarrow \{A^* = 1\}$. If this is true it follows that:

$$\text{Prob}\left(A^* = 1 \middle| A = 1\right) = 1.$$

Furthermore,

$$\begin{aligned}\text{Prob}(A^* = 1) &= \text{Prob}\left(A^* = 1 \middle| A = 1\right)\text{Prob}(A = 1)\\ &+ \text{Prob}\left(A^* = 1 \middle| A = 0\right)\text{Prob}(A = 0)\\ &\geq \text{Prob}\left(A^* = 1 \middle| A = 1\right)\text{Prob}(A = 1) = q.\end{aligned}$$

To prove $\{A = 1\} \Rightarrow \{A^* = 1\}$, suppose that $A = 1$, ie:

$$0 < L < X_T < H.$$

By algebra it follows that:

$$\frac{\hat{X} - L}{X_T} > \frac{\hat{X} - X_T}{X_T} > \frac{\hat{X} - H}{X_T}. \tag{1}$$

There are three cases to consider:

Case 1: $\hat{X} > H$ and $A = 1$: In this case, all terms in (1) are positive. If the first term in the inequality is multiplied by a positive number greater than 1, and the last term is multiplied by a positive number less than 1, the inequalities will still hold. Since $X_T/L < 1$ and $X_T/H > 1$, multiplying terms 1 and 3 by these respectively shows:

$\hat{X} > H$ and $A = 1 \Rightarrow$

$$\frac{\hat{X} - L}{L} > \frac{\hat{X} - X_T}{X_T} > \frac{\hat{X} - H}{H}.$$

Case 2: $\hat{X} < L$ and $A = 1$: In this case all terms in (1) are negative. If the first term in (1) is multiplied by a positive number less than 1, and the last term is multiplied by a positive number greater than 1, the inequalities will still hold. Since $X_T/H < 1$ and $X_T/L > 1$, multiplying terms 1 and 3 by these respectively shows: $\hat{X} < L$ and $A = 1 \Rightarrow$

$$\frac{\hat{X} - L}{H} > \frac{\hat{X} - X_T}{X_T} > \frac{\hat{X} - H}{L}.$$

Case 3: $L < \hat{X} < H$ and $A = 1$: In this case, the first term in (1) is positive and the last is negative. Therefore if the first term in (1) is multiplied by a positive number greater than 1, and the last term is multiplied by a positive number greater than 1, then the inequalities will still hold. Since $X_T/L > 1$, multiplying terms 1 and 3 by this shows: $\hat{X} < H$ and $A = 1 \Rightarrow$

$$\frac{\hat{X} - L}{L} > \frac{\hat{X} - X_T}{X_T} > \frac{\hat{X} - H}{L}.$$

Inspection shows that in cases 1–3 the upper bound corresponds to the formula for H^* and the lower bound corresponds to the formula for L^*. Therefore, $\{A = 1\} \Rightarrow \{A^* = 1\}$ and thus the proposition is proved.

It immediately follows that if L and H are bounds of a 95% confidence interval for a Monte Carlo estimate of value at risk, then L^* and H^* bound the percentage error of the value at risk estimate with confidence exceeding 95%.

Appendix B

Details on simulations 1 and 2

Details on data Factor volatilities, correlations, and exchange rates used in the simulations were extracted from JP Morgan's RiskMetrics database for August 17, 1992. Eurointerest rates for the same date were provided by the Federal Reserve Board. The implied volatilities that were used to price each option were the one-day standard deviations of (df/f) from RiskMetrics, where 100(df/f) represent percentage changes in the relevant exchange rates.[53]

Details on simulation 2 Simulation 2 generated 500 random portfolios of foreign exchange options. The number of options in each portfolio ranged from 1 to 50 with equal probability. For each option, the amount of foreign currency that was delivered if exercised was chosen from a uniform distribution with support from 1 to 11 million foreign currency units. Whether an option was a put or a call and whether the portfolio was long or short the option was chosen randomly and with equal probability.

To choose the exchange rate pairs for the options, define each option's home currency as the currency in which its price is denominated and its foreign currency as the currency it delivers if exercised. Similarly, define the home currency in a financial center as the national currency in the center's physical location and define a foreign currency as a currency other than the home currency. For many home currencies, Table 9-G of the *Central Bank Survey of Foreign Exchange and Derivatives Market Activity* provides information on the amount of turnover in the derivatives market broken down by foreign currency. The amounts of relative turnover in the home and foreign currencies of all currencies considered in the simulation were used as the probability function to generate the home and foreign currency pairs in the simulation with the exception of the dollar. Because the VAR measurements here are measured in dollars, in all currency pairs where the dollar was chosen as the foreign currency, they have been switched and the dollar made the home currency.

Appendix C

Details on delta-gamma methods

The delta-gamma methods are based on the second order Taylor series expansion for changes in portfolio value:

$$\Delta V \approx \delta^T \varepsilon_{t+1} + .5\varepsilon_{t+1}^T \Gamma \varepsilon_{t+1} + \theta$$

where

$$\varepsilon_{t+1} \sim N(0, \Sigma).$$

Applying the change of variables $u = \Sigma^{-.5}\varepsilon_{t+1}$, yields:

$$\Delta V \approx \delta^T \Sigma^{.5} u + .5 u^T \Sigma^{.5} \Gamma \Sigma^{.5} u + \theta.$$

This simplifies further by making the substitutions:

$$PDP' = \Sigma^{.5} \Gamma \Sigma^{.5},$$
$$u^* = P^T u$$

and

$$\delta^{*T} = \delta^T \Sigma^{.5} P$$

where P is a matrix of orthonormal eigenvectors of $\Sigma^{.5}\Gamma\Sigma^{.5}$ and D is a diagonal matrix of the corresponding eigenvalues. These substitutions imply:

$$\Delta V \approx \delta^{*T} u^* + .5 u^{*T} D u^* + \theta,$$

where $u^* \sim N(0, I)$.

After the substitutions, ΔV only depends on the elements of u_i^* and $(u_i^*)^2$ for $i = 1, \ldots N$. This allows the delta-gamma-delta method to be applied to the transformed system, which only involves $2N$ shocks. Without the transformation the number of shocks required for the delta-gamma-delta method would generally be $N + N(N + 1)/2$.

This transformation is also useful for the delta-gamma-minimisation method. The delta-gamma-minimisation method computes VAR as the solution to the transformed minimisation problem:

$$VAR = \min_{u^*} \delta^{*T} u^* + .5u^{*T} Du^* + \theta,$$

such that $u^{*T}u^* \leq c^*(1-u,k)$, where $c^*(1-u,k)$ is the $u\%$ critical value for the central chi-squared distribution with k (= number of factors) degrees of freedom.

Because D is diagonal, this transforms the minimisation in the delta-gamma-minimisation method to a very simple quadratic programming problem that can be solved by standard methods.

The diagonality of D in the transformed system is also useful for reducing the computations required to use the delta-gamma Monte Carlo method. Without the diagonality, the number of computations required to evaluate the quadratic term in the Taylor series expansion grows quadratically with the number of factors. After the transformation, the number of computations grows linearly with the number of factors. Therefore, if the transformed expression for ΔV is used for computing Monte Carlo iterations, it has promise to reduce the computational time required to perform the Monte Carlo.

1 *Barry Schacter, currently at Chase, maintains and periodically updates a bibliography of VAR literature on the Internet. It is located at http://pw2.netcom.com/bschacht/varbibilio.html*

2 *If a firm is expected to lose no more than $10 million over the next day except in 1% of circumstances, then its VAR for a one-day horizon at a 1% confidence level is $10 million.*

3 *Boudoukh, Richardson, and Whitelaw (1995) propose a different measure of capital adequacy. They suggest measuring risk as the expected largest loss experienced over a fixed period of time - the expected largest daily loss over a period of 20 days, for example.*

4 *Hendricks (1996) examined 12 different estimates of VAR and found that the standard deviation of their dispersion around the mean of the estimates is between 10 and 15%, indicating that it would not be uncommon for the VAR estimates be considered to differ by 30 to 50% on a daily basis. Beder (1995) examined eight approaches to computing VAR and found that the low and high estimates of VAR for a given portfolio differed by a factor that ranged from 6 to 14. See Chapters 17 and 21 of this book.*

5 *Marshall and Siegel (1997) asked a large number of VAR software vendors to estimate VAR for several portfolios. The distributional assumptions used in the estimations were presumably the same, since all of the vendors used a common set of correlations and standard deviations provided by RiskMetrics. Despite common distributional assumptions, VAR estimates varied especially widely for non-linear instruments, suggesting that differences in the treatment of non-linearities drive the differences in VAR estimates. For portfolios of foreign exchange options, which we will consider later, Marshall and Siegel found that the ratio of standard deviation of VAR estimate to median VAR estimate was 25%. See Chapter 28 of this book.*

6 *It is possible to combine Monte Carlo methods so that VAR with full repricing is applied to some sets of instruments, while other Monte Carlo techniques are applied to other options.*

7 *Some treatments decompose ΔV into a deterministic component (for a single option it would be $\theta\Delta t$) and a random component and then define VAR at confidence level u as the u'th quantile of the random component. This treatment is less appealing than the approach here because, from a risk management and regulatory perspective, VAR should measure a firm's capital adequacy, which is based on its ability to cover both the random and deterministic components of changes in V. An additional reason to prefer the approach in this paper is that the deterministic component is itself measured with error since it typically is derived using a first order Taylor series expansion in time to maturity.*

8 *All of the information on the risk of the portfolio is contained in the function $G(.)$; a single VAR estimate uses only some of this information. However, as much of the function $G(.)$ as is desired can be recovered using VAR methods by computing VAR for whatever quantiles are desired. The accuracy of the methods will vary based on the quantile.*

9 *Changes in the value of an instrument are caused by changes in the factors and by instrument-specific idiosyncratic changes. In well-diversified portfolios, only changes in the value of the factors should matter since idiosyncratic changes will be diversified away. If a portfolio is not well diversified, these idiosyncratic factors need to be treated as factors.*

10 *The general expression for the second term of the Taylor series is $\theta\Delta t$, where Δt is the time horizon for which VAR is computed. In our case this horizon has been normalized to one time period. Therefore, the second term in our first order expansion appears as θ.*

11 *To illustrate the impact of factor choice on a first order Taylor series's ability to capture non-linearity, consider a three year bond with annual coupon c and principal 1\$. Its price today is*

$B = cp(1) + cp(2) + (1 + c)p(3)$.

Where the $p(i)$ are the respective prices of zero coupon bonds expiring i years from today. If the factors are the zero coupon bond prices, then the bond price is clearly a linear function of the factors, requiring at most a first order Taylor series. If instead the factors are the one, two and three year zero coupon interest rates z_1, z_2, and z_3 (RiskMetrics provides information on zero coupon interest rates as factors, but not on zero coupon bond prices), then the expressions for δ and Γ are:

$$\delta = \begin{bmatrix} -ce^{(-z_1)} \\ -2ce^{(-2z_2)} \\ -3(1+c)e^{(-3z_3)} \end{bmatrix}$$

and

$$\Gamma = \begin{bmatrix} ce^{(-z_1)} & 0 & 0 \\ 0 & -4ce^{(-2z_2)} & 0 \\ 0 & 0 & -9(1+c)e^{(-3z_3)} \end{bmatrix}.$$

The example shows that the second set of factors requires a Taylor series of at least order 2 to capture the non-linearity of changes in portfolio value.

12 *Allen (1994) refers to the delta method as the correlation method; Wilson (1994) refers to this method as the delta-normal method.*

13 *The assumption that ε_{t+1} has mean 0 is appropriate over short time intervals such as a day or a week.*

14 *Anecdotal evidence suggests that many practitioners using delta-gamma methods set off diagonal elements of Γ to zero in practice.*

15 *Estrella (1995) highlights the need for caution in applying Taylor expansions by showing that a Taylor series expansion of the Black-Scholes pricing formula in terms of the underlying stock price diverges over some range of prices. However, a Taylor series expansion in (log stock price) does not diverge.*

16 *Changes in portfolio value in the delta method are approximated using linear combinations of normally distributed random variables. These are distributed normally. The delta gamma method approximates changes in portfolio value using the sum of linear combinations of normally distributed random variables and second order quadratic terms. Because the quadratic terms have a chi-square distribution, the normality is lost.*

17 *This approach is one of those used in Jordan and Mackay (1995). They make their Monte Carlo draws using a historical simulation or bootstrap approach.*

18 *This distribution need not be normal.*

19 *If V is a function of two factors, then the shocks are ε_1, ε_2, ε_1^2, ε_2^2, and $\varepsilon_1\varepsilon_2$.*

20 *If two random variables are uncorrelated and normally distributed, then they are independent. ε_{t+1} and ε^2_{t+1} are obviously not independent, thus they cannot be jointly normally distributed.*

21 *The computation of portfolio variance in the delta-gamma-delta approach is contained in the RiskMetrics Technical Document, third edition, page 137.*

22 *When there are N true factors, and no elements in the Γ matrix are restricted to be zero, the number of factors that are used in the delta-gamma-delta approach is $N^2 + 3N/2$. For moderate size N, this becomes unwieldy, and inelegant. When this approach is implemented later in the paper the problem is transformed so that only 2N factors are required to compute VAR. Details of this transformation are contained in Appendix C.*

23 *This approach is discussed in Wilson (1994).*

24 *Here is one simple example where the assumption is violated. Suppose a firm has a long equity position. Then, if one vector of factor shocks that lies outside the constraint set involves a large loss in the equity market, generating a large loss for the firm, then the opposite of this vector lies outside the constraint set too, but is likely to generate a large increase in the value of the firm's portfolio. A positive proportion of the factor shocks outside the constraint set are near the one in the example, and will also have the same property.*

25 *The order of the Cornish-Fisher expansion determines the number of cumulants that are used.*

26 *This method is referred to as Structured Monte Carlo in RiskMetrics-Technical Document, third edition.*

27 *Allen (1994) describes a grid Monte Carlo approach used in combination with historical simulation. Estrella (1995) also discusses a grid approach.*

28 *Suppose H is a financial instrument whose value depends on two factors, f_1, and f_2. In addition suppose H is highly non-linear in f_1 and nearly linear in f_2. Define ε_1 as the change in f_1 over the next period and ε_2 as the change in f_2. Then the change in H between today and tomorrow is an implicit function of the change in the factors and can thus be written as $\Delta H(\varepsilon_1,\varepsilon_2)$. If ΔH was approximated on a grid using 10 values of ε_1 and 10 values of ε_2 then the grid would contain 100 points and just computing the points on the grid would be computationally intensive. Instead, changes due to ε_1 are modelled on a grid and changes in value due to ε_2 are modelled using a first order Taylor series. More specifically:*

$$\begin{aligned} \Delta H(\varepsilon_1,\varepsilon_2) &= \Delta H(\varepsilon_1,0) + \left[\Delta H(\varepsilon_1,\varepsilon_2) - \Delta H(\varepsilon_1,0)\right]. \\ &\approx \Delta H(\varepsilon_1,0) + \Delta H_2(\varepsilon_1,0)\varepsilon_2 \\ &\approx \Delta H(\varepsilon_1,0) + \Delta H_2(0,0)\varepsilon_2 \end{aligned}$$

where

$$\Delta H(\varepsilon_1,0) = \frac{\partial}{\partial \varepsilon_2}\Delta H(\varepsilon_1,\varepsilon_2)\bigg|_{\varepsilon_2=0}$$

A first order Taylor series expansion of the term in square brackets generates the second line in the above chain of approximations from the first. The third line follows from the second under the auxiliary assumption that $\Delta H(\varepsilon_1,0) \approx \Delta H_2(0,0)$, ie the third line follows if the partial derivative of ΔH with respect to ε_2 is not very sensitive to the level of ε_1. The third line expresses ΔH as the sum of two functions. The first can be approximated using interpolation on a grid of values of ε_1. The second term is a first order Taylor series in ε_2. The reasoning in the above approximation also applies if ε_1 and ε_2 are vectors of changes in a set of factors. However, the restriction that generates line 3 from line 2 has more bite when there are more factors. In the implementation of the grid approach used in this paper, ΔH is modelled using one non-linear factor per instrument while allowing all other factors to enter linearly via the first order Taylor expansion.

29 *If the factors are observable, then* ε_t *is observable since* $\varepsilon_t = f_t - f_{t-1}$. *If* ε_t *is not observable, then the factors are not observable, and* ε *must be imputed some other way. This would invariably require some strong distributional assumptions that would undermine the advantages of using historical simulation in the first place.*

30 *It is important that the correct conditional distribution is used when making draws of* ε, *ie if today is considered a highly volatile period, then draws of* ε *should be made from a volatile historical period.*

31 *It is fortunate that confidence intervals can be constructed from a single set of* N *Monte Carlo draws. An alternative Monte Carlo procedure for constructing confidence intervals would involve computing standard errors for the Monte Carlo estimates by performing Monte Carlo simulations of Monte Carlo simulations, a very time-consuming process.*

32 *The distinction made here between single and complex computations is somewhat arbitrary. For example, when closed form solutions are not available for instrument prices, pricing is probably more computationally intensive than performing the minimisation in the delta-gamma minimisation method. On the other hand, the minimisation is more complicated than applying the Black-Scholes formula, but applying Black-Scholes is treated as complex while the minimisation method is treated as simple.*

33 *If the portfolios being considered contain some instruments that are priced analytically while others are priced using 1 million Monte Carlo draws, the computational burdens of repricing the two sets of instruments are very different and some allowance has to be made for this.*

34 *100 identical options is one instrument, five options at different strike prices are five different instruments.*

35 *Each time a price is calculated, one complex computation is assessed. Thus, it is assumed that* $2n$ *complex computations are required to compute* δ *because the numerical approximation for*

$$\frac{\partial f(x)}{\partial x} = \frac{[f(x+h) - f(x-h)]}{2h},$$

requires two repricings per factor. Similarly, we assume that

$$\frac{\partial^2 f(x)}{\partial x^2} = \frac{[f(x+h) + f(x-h) - 2f(x)]}{4h^2}$$

requires two repricings per factor and that

$$\frac{\partial^2 f(x,y)}{\partial x \partial y} = \frac{[f(x+h,y+h) + f(x-h,y-h) - f(x-h,y+h) - f(x+h,y-h)]}{4h^2}$$

requires four repricings per factor. For some instruments there are other methods of computing δ *and* Γ. *This will change the number of complex computations.*

36 *The figures on numbers of complex computations for* Γ *presume that all of elements of the* Γ *matrix are computed. If some elements are restricted to be zero, this will substantially reduce the number of complex computations.*

37 *Although the number of complex computations required to compute* Γ *analytically is smaller than the number required to compute it numerically, the analytical expressions for the second derivative matrix may be so complicated that it is faster to compute* Γ *numerically than analytically.*

38 *Evaluating the quadratic terms could be time consuming if the number of factors is large since the number of elements in gamma is of the order of the square of the number of factors. However, as shown in Appendix C, it is possible without loss of generality to transform the gamma matrix in the delta-gamma Monte Carlo approach so that the gamma matrix only contains non-zero terms on its diagonal. With this transformation the order of the number computations in this approach is the number of factors times the number of Monte Carlo draws.*

39 *For example, in the regular grid Monte Carlo approach, for instruments that are priced using three factors, the grid contains 1,000 points. In the modified grid Monte Carlo approach, the grid will always contain 10 points.*

40 *The relative number of complex computations required using the different approaches will vary for different portfolios; ie for some portfolios grid Monte Carlo will require more complex computations while for others full Monte Carlo will require more complex computations.*

41 *A potential problem with this parallel approach is that it removes an element of independence from the risk management function, and raises the question of how much independence is necessary and at what cost?*

42 *Similarly, it is possible to generate Monte Carlo draws of the factor shocks, and then for each Monte Carlo draw, approximate* ΔV *for the portfolio by adding together estimates of change in portfolio value for different parts of the portfolio. For example, a second order Taylor expansion can be used to approximate the change in the value of some instruments while full repricing can be used with other instruments.*

43 *The number of RiskMetrics risk factors typically exceeded the number of pricing variables. For example, if a bank based in the United Kingdom measures VAR in pounds sterling, and writes a four-month Deutschmark-denominated put on the Deutschmark/French franc exchange rate, the variables which affect the sterling value of the put are the Deutschmark/French franc exchange rate, the dollar/Deutschmark rate, and four-month interest rates in France and Germany. RiskMetrics does not provide explicit information on the correlation between these variables. Instead, these variables must be expressed as functions of the factors on which riskmetrics does provide information. In this case, the RiskMetrics exchange rate factors are the sterling/Deutschmark, dollar/French franc and sterling/dollar exchange rates. The four-month interest rates are constructed by interpolating between the three and six-month rates in each country. This adds two interest rate factors per country, for a total of seven factors.*

44 *It is important to emphasise that the gamma matrix used in the VAR methods below is a matrix of second and cross-partials of the change in portfolio value due to a*

change in the factors.

45 *These additional results are available from the author upon request.*

46 *The error of VAR estimate* $\hat{VAR}$ *is* $\hat{VAR} - VAR$, *and its percentage error is its percentage error as* $(\hat{VAR} - VAR)/VAR$.

47 *True overstatement is not known since VAR is measured with error.*

48 *Suppose one VAR method makes small and identical mistakes for 99 portfolios, and makes a large mistake for one portfolio, while for the same portfolios the "other" method makes no mistakes for 98 portfolios, and makes one small mistake and one large mistake. Clearly the "other" method produces strictly superior VAR estimates. However, conditional on making a mistake, the "other" method has a larger mean and variance than the method which is clearly inferior.*

49 *Mean Absolute Error (MAE) and Root Mean Squared Error (RMSE) can be computed from mean, standard deviation, and frequency of under- and overstatement. Errors that are statistically indistinguishable from 0 are treated as 0 and not included. The formulas for the loss functions are:*

$$MAE = MU*FREQU + MO*FREQO,$$

$$RMSE = \sqrt{(MU^2 + STDU^2)*FREQU + (MO^2 + STDO^2)*FREQU}$$

where MU, STDU, *and* FREQU *are mean, standard deviation, and frequency of understatement respectively and* MO, STDO, *and* FREQO *are mean, standard deviation, and frequency of overstatement respectively.*

50 *There are no three dimensional figures for simulation exercise 2 because the portfolios vary in too many dimensions.*

51 *For example, to price change in portfolio value from a grid for each option, a shock's location on the grid needed to computed for each Monte Carlo draw and each option. This added considerable time to the grid Monte Carlo method.*

52 *The assumption that the Monte Carlo lower bound for VAR is greater than 0 is important. The assumption is reasonable for most risky portfolios. If it is not true for a given number of Monte Carlo draws, but trueVAR is believed greater than zero, then additional Monte Carlo draws should eventually produce a lower bound that is greater than 0. If it is not possible to produce a lower bound that is greater than 0, then it will not be possible to create meaningful bounds for the percentage errors, but it will be possible to create bounds for the actual errors.*

53 *For options on some currency pairs RiskMetrics does not provide volatility information. For example, the variance of the French franc/Deutschmark exchange rate is not provided. To calculate this standard deviation from the data provided by RiskMetrics, let* $F = \$/Ffr$, $D = \$/DM$, *and let* $G = Ffr/DM$. *It follows that:*

$$G = D / F$$
$$\ln(G) = \ln(D) - \ln(F)$$
$$dG / G = dD / D - dF / F$$
$$VAR(dG / G) = VAR(dD / D) + VAR(dF / F) - 2*Cov(dD / D, dF / F).$$

VAR (dG/G) *can be computed in RiskMetrics since all the expressions on the right hand side of the last expression can be computed using RiskMetrics.*

54 U *and* V *are chosen so that*

$$Prob(U \geq \hat{VAR} - VAR \geq L) \geq .95,$$

and U% *and* L% *are chosen so that*

$$Prob\left(U\% \geq \frac{\hat{VAR} - VAR}{VAR} \geq L\%\right) \geq .95.$$

55 *The amount of understatement and percentage understatement are at least as big as* U *and* U% *respectively with*

BIBLIOGRAPHY

Allen, M., 1994, "Building A Role Model", *Risk* 7, 8: pp. 73–80.

An Internal Model-Based Approach to Market Risk Capital Requirements, 1995, Basle Committee on Banking Supervision.

Beder, T. Styblo, 1995, "VAR: Seductive but Dangerous", *Financial Analysts Journal*, September, pp. 12–24; reprinted as Chapter 17 of this book.

Boudoukh, J., M. Richardson and R. Whitelaw, 1995, "Expect the Worst", *Risk* 8, 9, pp. 100–1.

Central Bank Survey of Foreign Exchange and Derivatives Market Activity 1995, 1996, Bank for International Settlements.

Chew, L., 1994, "Shock Treatment", *Risk* 7, 9, pp. 63–70.

David, H.A., 1981, *Order Statistics*, 2nd Edition, John Wiley and Sons, Inc., New York.

Estrella, A., 1995, "Taylor, Black and Scholes: Series Approximations and Risk Management Pitfalls", Research Paper No. 9501, Federal Reserve Bank of New York.

Fallon, W., 1996, "Calculating Value-at-Risk", Mimeo, Columbia University.

Hendricks, D, 1996, "Evaluation of Value-at-Risk Models Using Historical Data", *FRBNY Economic Policy Review*, pp. 39–69; reprinted as Chapter 21 of the present volume.

Hull, J., 1993, *Options, Futures, and other Derivative Securities*, 2nd Edition, Prentice-Hall, Englewood Cliffs.

Jordan, J.V. and R.J. Mackay, 1995, "Assessing Value at Risk for Equity Portfolios: Implementing Alternative

Techniques", Mimeo, Center for Study of Futures and Options Markets, Pamplin College of Business, Virginia Polytechnic.

JP Morgan, 1994, *RiskMetrics - Technical Document*.

JP Morgan, 1995, *Enhancements to RiskMetrics*.

JP Morgan, 1995, *RiskMetrics - Technical Document*. Third Edition.

Lawrence, C. and G. Robinson, 1995, "Liquid Measures", *Risk* 8, 7, pp. 52-4.

Makarov, V.I., 1993, "Risk Dollars: The Methodology for Measuring Market Risk Within Global Risk Management", Mimeo, Chase Manhattan Bank, N.A.

Marshall, C. and M. Siegel, 1997, "Value at Risk: Implementing a Risk Measurement Standard", *Journal of Derivatives* Spring, pp. 91-111; reprinted as Chapter 28 of the present volume.

Wilson, T., 1994, "Plugging the Gap", *Risk* 7, 10, pp. 74-80.

Zangari, P., 1996, "A VAR Methodology for Portfolios that Include Options", *RiskMetrics Monitor*, 1st quarter, pp. 4-12.

Zangari, P., 1996, "How Accurate is the Delta-Gamma Methodology?", *RiskMetrics Monitor*, 3rd quarter, pp. 12-29.

Value-at-Risk: Implementing a Risk Measurement Standard*

Chris Marshall and Michael Siegel
National University of Singapore; Massachusetts Institute of Technology

Research cites differences in models as an important impediment to developing a value-at-risk standard. This paper considers discrepancies in a model's implementation in software and how they too affect the establishment of a risk measurement standard. Different leading risk management system vendors were given an identical portfolio of instruments of varying complexity, and were asked to assess the value at risk according to one common model, JP Morgan's RiskMetrics. We analysed the VAR results on a case-by-case basis and in terms of prior expectations from the structure of financial instruments in the portfolio, as well as prior vendor expectations about the relative complexity of different instrument classes. This research indicates the extent to which one particular model of risk can be effective, independent of the model's detailed implementation and use in practice.

In the wake of several high-profile failures of risk management, there have been widespread calls for better quantification of the financial risks facing corporations and financial services firms. Prominently featured in this clamour for a standardised risk measure is value-at-risk, or VAR, as it is commonly known.

VAR is defined as the expected minimum loss of a portfolio over some time period for some level of probability. For instance, a decision-maker might state that a firm's daily VAR is \$100,000 with 95% probability; this means that, over the coming day, there is only a 5% chance that a loss will be greater than \$100,000.

VAR's popularity is based on aggregation of several components of firmwide market risk into a single number. It also focuses on a major concern of senior managers: the potential for significant loss in a firm's portfolio of assets.

In its various forms, VAR has gained strong support from industry and regulatory bodies such as the Group of Thirty, the Bank of International Settlements, and the European Union. The European Union's Capital Adequacy Directive makes the VAR of the market risk in a bank's trading book one input in calculation of its capital reserve requirements. For banks in the Group of Ten countries, the Basle committee on banking supervision is proposing allocating risk capital according to banks' internal VAR models.

Proponents of VAR believe it will replace or at least complement less standardised techniques such as asset/liability management and stress testing. If so, it may well be that regulators, auditors, shareholders, and management will finally be speaking a common language with respect to risk.

While the concept of VAR is straightforward,

* *This paper was first published in the* Journal of Derivatives, *Spring (1997). This copyrighted material is reprinted with permission from Institutional Investor, Inc., 488 Madison Avenue, New York, NY10022. Many individuals and organisations contributed to this study. First and foremost is MIT's Finance Research Center. Additional funding for one of the researchers was also provided by Harvard Business School's Division of Research. Jacques Longerstaey and Scott Howard of JP Morgan were supportive throughout the project. Peter Kempthorne at MIT and James McKenney and Peter Tufano at Harvard Business School provided assistance on a number of technical issues. Thanks also to the risk management systems vendors who gave of their time and gathered much of the data from which this report is produced.*

its implementation is not. There are a variety of models and model implementations that produce very different estimates of risk for the same portfolio. Previous studies have focused on the way differences between models cause variation in VAR. This study instead considers how differences in implementation of the same model produce variation in estimated VAR.[1]

These issues are critical for practitioners; divergence in models and implementations leads to uncertainty in the mind of the user as to the meaning of the VAR estimates. This uncertainty creates a real risk that the VAR estimates are used inappropriately.

To understand the importance of this risk in the estimation of VAR, we developed a test portfolio that we gave to a number of leading risk management software vendors, all of whom advertised that they use the same model of risk, JP Morgan's RiskMetrics. We obtained from them their estimates of the portfolio's VAR. The portfolio is described in the appendix.

Previous research

This work builds on research describing different models of VAR, most notably, Beder's [1995] comparison of simulation and parametric models of VAR, and, more recently, Hendricks' [1996] comparison of random foreign exchange portfolios using different VAR models over multiple dates.

Beder applies eight different approaches to three hypothetical portfolios, and finds VAR results that vary by a factor of 14 for more complex portfolios. She explains this by noting VAR's extreme sensitivity as the model's choice of parameters, data, assumptions, and methodology.

Hendricks compares 12 value-at-risk models on 1,000 relatively simple randomly chosen foreign exchange portfolios. Using nine criteria to evaluate model performance, he finds less variation in results than does Beder, reflecting the less complex portfolios he uses. He notes that the different models generally capture the risk that they set out to assess and tend to produce risk estimates that are similar in average size.

Our study differs from previous research in two critical respects. First, our intent is not to compare different models, but rather to understand the importance of the real-world implementation and use of just one of these models. Second, our study focuses on different commercially available systems used by different individuals rather than specially constructed test systems used by the same individual. We suggest that this provides a more realistic test of the use and interpretation of systems' results.

Models of VAR and implementation risk

There are a variety of models that may be used to estimate value-at-risk. Some risk management systems allow user-defined simulations, or use scenario-based models to calculate VAR (Marshall and Siegel (1996). These techniques, and the circumstances in which they and the tools that implement them are most appropriate, are described elsewhere (see Leong (1996)).

The most widely used technique to calculate VAR uses historical covariances between different generic risk factors to assess the effect of shocks on a portfolio whose positions can be mapped to those risk factors. That is, the risks for the specific assets are expressed in terms of a set of exposures to the generic risk factors.[2] One such parametric model is JP Morgan's RiskMetrics. Given its widespread use, we believe it is timely to ask to what extent this particular model provides a lingua franca for the risk measurement.

Updated daily across the Internet, the RiskMetrics correlations and volatilities of standard prices and rates (foreign exchange, interest rates, equities, and commodities) allow users to assess their aggregate financial market risks (in terms of VAR) over a given time period consistently across different instrument classes.[3] And, in an effort to make use of the data sets transparent, JP Morgan has also made public the detailed model by which these volatilities and correlations are calculated and the manner in which instruments should be mapped to these standard rates and prices (see Guldimann (1995)).

While this model has been criticised as making overly simplistic assumptions, models are invariably compromises between usability on the one hand and accuracy on the other. RiskMetrics focuses on usability, providing a relatively simple and transparent tool (see Longerstaey and Zangari (1995)).[4]

Despite the popularity of RiskMetrics, the question remains whether this or any other model now available can constitute a standard independent of the details of the model's implementation and use. This is no new notion. It is Till Guldimann, one of the architects of RiskMetrics, who observed that "risk measurement and management continues to be as much a craft as it is a science," and that "no amount of sophisticated analytics will replace experience and professional judgement in managing risks." (1995, p. 1).

The formal model is not, and may never be, a complete description of the precise implementation of the model in every circumstance, because of the potentially infinite variety of instruments and the number of markets with varying institutional and statistical attributes. That a model is incomplete implies that decisions are left to the systems developer who chooses to implement the model and the systems user who interprets the inputs and outputs. It is these decisions that we suspect lead to variation in the outputs of the different systems, even though they use the same formal model.[5]

Unlike Beder and Hendricks, who focus on variation caused by a diversity of models, which we call model risk, we are concerned with the variation caused by a diversity of implementations of the same model, ie implementation risk. We measure implementation risk by considering the variation in results between implementations of the same model.[6]

We believe that a necessary condition for the use of any model as a potential standard is that it involves limited or at least quantifiable implementation risk. This is especially important in the case of VAR, where the typical user of the VAR results may not be a specialist in financial models and systems, and therefore might take model outputs at face value, partially oblivious to model risk and almost totally unaware of implementation risk.

Our research goals are fourfold:

❑ To assess the variation of VAR estimates produced by different commercial implementations of the same model of value-at-risk.

❑ To assess how such variation is dependent on the nature of the instrument class.

❑ To compare these results with vendors' and researchers' prior expectations of the difficulty of evaluating VAR for different instrument classes.

❑ To understand the importance of implementation risk in the provision of any potential standard for risk measurement.

Research design

RESEARCH PARTICIPANTS AND PROCESS

When we began this study, there were 17 vendors known to incorporate JP Morgan's RiskMetrics model into their assessments of value-at-risk, and all were asked to participate in the study. The vendors completing VAR estimates for all or part of the test portfolio are: Algorithmics, Brady, C*ATS Software, Dow Jones/Telerate, Financial Engineering Associates, Infinity, Price Waterhouse, Renaissance, Softek, True Risk, and Wall Street Systems.

The test portfolio summarised in the appendix was designed to assess the capabilities of all the tools and to produce instructions describing the parameter settings to be used in the test. When VAR estimates were returned, they were compared and analysed, and feedback was given to the vendors regarding any major discrepancies.[7]

In many cases, vendors asked to change their results; the new results and explanations of the changes are incorporated in the final report. Results were analysed case-by-case in terms of several prior hypotheses. A complete analysis was given to vendors describing all the results.

To encourage vendor participation, no details of a vendor's particular results are revealed.

RISK ASSESSMENT

The task facing vendors involves several elements. The first relates to inputs. Most critical is the test portfolio, which describes positions in various instrument classes, including government bonds, interest rate swaps, money market deposits, foreign exchange forwards, forward rate agreements, foreign exchange options, and interest rate options. Vendors were also given identical RiskMetrics data sets.

Second, vendors were asked to produce outputs of one-day, 95% confidence, dollar value-at-risk (VAR) estimates of interest rate, foreign exchange, and total risk for each instrument class in the test portfolio as of 10.30 am EST, September 27, 1995. We also asked vendors to produce VAR estimates for the same portfolio using non-parametric models, such as Monte Carlo and historical simulation.

The final element of the risk assessment task was the parameter settings, as described in Table 1 overleaf.

The vendor construction of VAR estimates can be broken into a number of basic steps, each of which presents an opportunity for implementation risk. First, vendors calculate the market-to-market/marked-to-model positions in the portfolio. These are then mapped onto a series of generic risk factors. Examples of risk factors are zero-coupon interest rates at different maturities, and spot exchange rates for a variety of currencies, as well as equity indexes and commodity rates. Finally, the covariance matrix for these risk factors, as supplied by us, is used to project these

Table 1. Benchmark parameterisation

Parameter	Parameter Description	Parameter Value
Decision-making horizon	The time it is assumed to take to neutralise or liquidate a position	One day
Initial valuation of position	Marked-to-market value in $. In the case of exchange-traded instruments, this is the last price on September 26.	Participants are strongly encouraged to use the end-of-day prices provided in the spreadsheet.
Confidence level	Probability associated with the occurrence of a given loss within the decision-making horizon.	95%
Forward rates and prices	Discounting of future cash flows.	For each market, a term structure of zero-coupon yields is provided.
Diversification	Assumption about diversification across assets.	Consistent with the RiskMetrics methodology recognising complete diversification within and across different asset classes.
Volatilities and correlations	Expected comovement of different instrument classes.	Participants should use the enclosed RiskMetrics data sets and assume that these covariances are constant.
Instrument mapping	Equivalent portfolio in terms of RiskMetrics underlying instrument classes.	Participants should perform the mapping in accordance with the RiskMetrics methodology. If this is not possible,participants should define and make explicit what seems to them a reasonable mapping.
Derivative pricing	Assumed relation between instrument and underlying assets.	Delta valuation (not incorporating any higher-order moments, such as gamma).
Estimation technique	Technique (eg user-defined simulation, RiskMetrics parametric, implied volatilities) used to calculate the 95% percentile.	Parametric using the RiskMetrics data sets.

mapped risk exposures into a single aggregate VAR estimate.

RESEARCH ISSUES

Gaining the cooperation of the vendors was a major challenge. Some vendors were busy with software releases; others were reluctant to commit to a project that might reveal awkward discrepancies. One vendor reasoned that VAR was such a relatively small part of its system's total functionality that any cross-tool survey based on VAR could not do the firm justice. In light of these challenges, one of the more impressive aspects of the study is that we obtained as extensive cooperation as we did - securing the involvement of a large proportion of the major risk management systems vendors.

The size of the sample is nevertheless clearly limited and limiting. To make up for this, we triangulated the quantitative results with prior structural analysis of the portfolio and with vendor expectations regarding the complexity of different instrument classes. We worked through several iterations of estimates from vendors - one vendor gave us three different iterations of VAR results; several others gave us two iterations - which minimised user risks, implementation errors, and user errors in the results.

User risk is the risk of different users using the same model and tool to produce different results for the same task. Implementation errors or user errors occur when developers or users make assumptions that are inconsistent with those made elsewhere in the model, in the model's implementation in software, or in its use.

Testing vendors' systems rather than end-users' systems allowed us to mitigate user risk and user errors, since it is reasonable to assume that a vendor knows how to use its system in the manner in which it is designed (thus mitigating user risk), and is less likely to make inconsistent assumptions (mitigating user errors). Consequently, the remaining variation in the VAR results provides us with an estimate of the magnitude of implementation risk.

These risk estimates are still subject to two potential biases. First, it is likely that implementation risk is underestimated, because we believe that vendors may have taken extra care with their results. After all, it was clear to vendors that the results (and any discrepancies) would be made public, although without attribution. The second bias is present in all empirical tests: specifically, that implementation risk may be overestimated, because real money was not at stake, and therefore the usual organisational safeguards such as back-office reconciliation, P&L, and audit were not in place.

Pre-empirical analysis

STRUCTURAL ANALYSIS OF THE PORTFOLIO

One of the easiest ways to understand derivative instruments is in terms of basic building blocks,

Table 2. Instrument structure

Instrument class	Risk equivalence to other instruments or calculations	Description
Zero-coupon bond	Z	A single payment at a specified future date. A single cash flow is mapped to one or two risk factors in the parametric model.
Government bond	$(Z_1, Z_2, Z_3, ...)$	A series of fixed coupon payments at periodic intervals, followed by a payment of the principal at the maturity. This can be represented as a series of zeros.
Money market note	MM = Z	Equivalent to a zero-coupon bond with a near-term maturity (within one year).
Floating-rate note (FRN)	FRN	A single floating-coupon payment with a short-term maturity.
Interest rate swap	$(MM_1, MM_2, MM_3, ..., FRN_1, FRN_2, FRN_3, ...)$	An exchange of a series of floating-rate payments and fixed-rate payments.
Forward rate agreement (FRA)	(MM_1, MM_2)	A means of locking in a forward interest rate. It is equivalent to being short a money market instrument and long a longer-maturity money making instrument.
Spot currency	SP	A spot position in a particular currency.
Foreign exchange forward (FXF)	FXF = (SP, MM1)	Can be interpreted as a spot position plus a money market instrument in a different currency.
Foreign exchange option	(Delta, FXF)	Assessing the delta requires a valuation model that relates the sensitivity of the value of the option to the underlying itself. Using delta mapping, the risk of an option is assessed as if the option were a position of delta units of the underlying.
Interest rate caps and floors	$(Delta_1, Z_1, Delta_2, Z_2, Delta_3, Z_3, ...)$	IR caps and floors effectively constitute a portfolio of options

such as money markets, forwards, and options (Smith (1993); Smithson (1987)). Different instrument classes in the test portfolio are also structurally related, providing clues as to the source of the additional variation in the risk assessments caused as new building blocks are pieced together to form more complex instrument classes.

The structural model of the instruments in Table 2 suggests (but does not necessarily imply) a similar structure for the standardised variation of VAR results across the different instrument classes. According to error analysis, when we build a new combination instrument out of two simpler instruments - for example, making a foreign exchange forward out of a spot currency position plus a foreign money market instrument - we expect the variation of the combination instrument's risk estimates to be both greater than the variation of the component instruments' risk estimates and less than the sum of the components' risk estimate variations. This is a result of the uncertainty (reflected in the standardised variation of instrument class VAR estimates) in estimating VAR for each of the component instruments, which increases the uncertainty in estimating VAR for the composite.

While some instrument classes are structurally equivalent to combinations of other instrument classes, individual positions in these combination instrument classes are not equivalent to specific positions in the component instrument classes. Hence, these structural relationships for the expected variability of VAR results across implementations for different instrument classes in the test portfolio provide us with only a proximate ordering.

With these caveats in mind, the structural relationships among the standardised deviations (SDev) of the different instrument classes are hypothesised:

1. SDev (money markets) < SDev (government bonds).
2. SDev (money markets) < SDev (interest rate swaps).
3. SDev (money markets) < SDev (FRAs).
4. SDev (FX options) < SDev (interest rate caps and floors).
5. SDev (FRAs) < SDev (interest rate swaps).
6. SDev (money markets) < SDev (FX forwards).

Because of the limited number of data points, we calculate relative standard deviation as the sample standard deviation of estimated risk exposures across different vendors divided by the sample median. This ordering provides us with an ordinal metric of the structural complexity of a particular instrument class that we will later compare with the implementation risk of that instrument class.

VENDOR EXPECTATIONS

We also asked that vendors express the degree of difficulty they had in evaluating the VAR of a particular instrument class (1-low effort through 7-high effort). The results are in Table 3 overleaf. To preserve anonymity, we identify vendors by

Table 3. Perceived complexity of instrument class

Vendor	Bonds	Swaps	MM deposits	FX forwards	FRAs	FX options	IR caps and floors
B	3	5	2	1	4	6	7
D	3	5	2	2	2	4	7
F	5	4	1	3	3	7	6
G	4	5	1	2	3	6	7
J	6	4	6	5	4	3	6
Mean	4.2	4.6	2.4	2.6	3.2	5.2	6.6

letters (A through J) and vendors' implementations by "letter-number" combinations (eg A.1 is the first of vendor A's implementations).

Non-linear instruments such as options, particularly interest rate caps and floors, were perceived to be the most complex. The simplest instrument classes are those with the smallest number of cash flows, such as money markets, FX forwards, and, to some extent, FRAs. We expected that the perceived complexity of VAR estimation for an instrument class would be positively related to the variation across vendors' VAR estimates for that instrument class.

Results

Going from the instrument classes least susceptible to implementation risk to those most susceptible, we describe vendors' estimates of VAR. Then, we make use of the extensive feedback from the vendors to suggest likely causes for any variation in vendors' results (see Marshall and Siegel (1996)). This feedback helped to mitigate the limitations of the small sample size.

FX FORWARDS

Table 4 describes results for foreign exchange forwards. The first thing to note is the similarity of all the parametric results. There are no major outliers. This suggests how easy it is for firms to map forward payments in different currencies to spot-plus-forward payments of the domestic currency. This is confirmed by users' descriptions of the task of estimating VAR for FX forwards.

Table 4. VAR of FX forward portfolio

RiskMetrics-based VAR	Interest rate risk	FX risk	Total VAR
B	48,446	442,524	426,288
D	na	na	437,379
E	47,000	441,000	426,000
F	48,817	441,988	425,677
G	46,605	440,845	425,189
J.1	47,352	441,729	425,363
Mean	47,644	441,617	427,649
Median	47,352	441,729	425,839
Standard deviation	949	698	4,784
Standard deviation/median (%)	2	0	1

Table 5. FX forward valuations

FX forwards	B	F	J	Std dev/mean (%)
Valuation	3,125,651	3,174,940	3,080,118	1.5
VAR	426,288	425,677	425,363	0.1
Implicit standard deviation (%)	8.3	8.1	8.4	1.5

Nevertheless, there is some variation across vendors' VAR estimates. Much of this can be accounted for by differences in their valuation of the forward positions in the portfolio upon which VAR is based. Mark-to-model valuation is known to be challenging in its own right.[8]

Because there is approximately a linear relationship between the valuation of an instrument and its risk assessment in dollars, if the VAR calculation introduces implementation risk beyond that introduced by differences in valuation, it will be seen in the extent to which the variation (as a percentage of the mean) of vendors' VAR estimates exceeds the variation of the vendors' valuations.[9]

This is tested in Table 5, which shows valuations and VAR estimates from three vendors that provided both. The rightmost column shows the standard deviation divided by the mean of the data in each table row. It suggests the extent to which different systems produce similar estimates for the same task (such as valuation or VAR assessment).

The implicit standard deviation of the distribution of value is defined as:

$$\text{Implicit standard deviation (\%)} = \frac{\text{VAR}}{1.65 \times \text{value}}.$$

We use this definition to "back out" the estimated standard deviation of returns for this asset class that the vendor is using to compare VAR from the valuation figure it reports.

This suggests that the VAR variation is almost certainly the result of variation in valuations, at least for this subsample. Curiously, this conflicts with the greater variation of the interest rate risk estimates in the broader sample compared with those of FX risk, since FX risks are generally most sensitive to variations in valuation.

To summarise, FX forwards appear to have minimal sensitivity to the precise choice of assumptions made. Despite a small number of data points, this is strongly borne out by our results, with very small (although non-zero) discrepancies between systems. What variation there is appears entirely the result of differences in valuations. We can conclude that for FX forwards RiskMetrics VAR becomes a highly effective standard with quite limited implementation risk.

MONEY MARKET DEPOSITS

Money markets are ranked by vendors as much like FX forwards in their relative complexity. Vendors also believe money market deposits to be among the least sensitive of the "linear" instrument classes (ie those that do not involve options) to the precise choice of assumptions made. Consequently, we would expect a standard model to have few difficulties in producing consistent results.

For the most part this is the case. Table 6 shows the only outlier of note as system A. A's estimate, while consistent with some simulation-based results obtained for the same portfolio, is lower than that of all the other parametric estimates. Although we have no evidence concerning A's valuation, we suspect that its VAR and that of J (also lower than most of other estimates) are caused by lower valuations for the portfolio's holdings of money market instruments.

This is also suggested by the relative importance of FX risk as a component of total VAR. When A is eliminated, the relative standard deviations of interest rate risk, FX risk, and total VAR decrease to 6%, 2%, and 2%, respectively. This is then only slightly larger than the results for FX forwards, which are structurally similar.

Some of the vendors provided the valuations of the money market positions in Table 7. The similarity of the relative standard deviation of the valuations to that of the VAR estimates suggests that among these systems most of, if not all, the variation in the VAR estimate comes from differences in the valuations, although these vendors show less variation in their estimates than do many of the others in the sample.

So, while valuation may be the predominant source of variation in VAR for these vendors, other VAR-specific factors may be responsible for some of the variation in the other vendors' estimates of VAR. To reiterate, money markets involve small implementation risk, somewhat greater than that for FX forwards.

Table 6. VAR of money market portfolio

RiskMetrics-based VAR	Interest rate risk	FX risk	Total VAR
A	3,018	498,586	498,425
B	2,739	673,558	673,101
D	na	na	668,690
E	3,000	674,000	673,000
F	2,729	673,554	673,034
G	2,741	672,060	671,626
H.1	na	na	671,060
J.1	2,554	640,454	639,968
Mean	2,797	638,702	646,113
Median	2,740	672,807	671,343
Standard deviation	179	69,891	60,720
Standard deviation/median (%)	7	10	9

Table 7. Money market valuations

Money market deposits	B	F	H.1	J	Std dev/ mean (%)
Valuation	48,758,258	48,750,860	48,750,575	46,408,239	2.4
VAR	673,101	673,034	671,060	639,968	2.4
Implicit std dev (%)	0.8	0.8	0.8	0.8	2.4

FORWARD RATE AGREEMENTS (FRAs)

For FRAs, like the structurally similar money markets, we see a fairly wide range (10%) in the VAR estimates (Table 8). This variation is also reflected in the slightly higher complexity ranking that vendors give the instrument class. Unlike the case for money markets, there are no clear outliers, and no obvious clustering around a particular estimate. As for FX forwards and money markets, because there are only two cash flows to map, there should be a limit to the effect of one potential source of variation, namely, different mapping assumptions.

Table 9 shows valuations from two vendors. The two valuations available suggest that valuation is partly responsible for variation in the VAR estimates.

To summarise, FRAs look much like money market deposits in the case of VAR estimation.

Table 8. VAR of FRA portfolio

RiskMetrics-based VAR	Interest rate risk	FX risk	Total VAR
B	93,485	15,527	88,452
D	na	na	81,099
E	91,000	16,000	86,000
F	73,411	18,225	71,706
G	72,430	17,956	69,934
J.1	83,301	17,610	76,612
Mean	82,725	17,064	78,967
Median	83,301	17,610	78,856
Standard deviation	9,712	1,218	7,534
Standard deviation/median (%)	12	7	10

Table 9. FRA valuations

FRAs	F	J	Std dev/mean (%)
Valuation	1,212,273	1,242,093	2.4
VAR	71,706	76,612	6.6
Implicit standard deviation (%)	3.6	3.7	4.4

Implementation risk appears greater for FRAs than it does for forwards and money markets. Compared to money markets, there are some indications that valuation is less the driving factor in the variation of VAR estimation for FRAs.

GOVERNMENT BONDS

Table 10 provides results for government bonds. First, note that there is little difference in the components of risk, but there is significant variation in the aggregate VAR assessment. Second, most of the variation in the aggregate results comes from two outliers (vendors C and H.1), neither of whom break their VAR into FX and interest rate components. The narrow range of VAR estimates is not surprising, as bonds are relatively simple instruments.

Although we are unable to ascertain why two systems' results are outliers, we note that these results are compatible with the non-parametric simulation results obtained from other vendors. Also, one of the tools, C, is a pre-release piece of software. When these outliers are removed, the standard deviation/median estimate decreases to less than 1%.

This is in spite of different assumptions made by this reduced sample of vendors regarding a number of issues, such as:

❑ Rather than taking the RiskMetrics approach of maintaining the portfolio's vertex variance under the mapping, vendors E and J maintained vertices' basis point sensitivities. This results in a slightly different mapping. (The term "vertex" in VAR terminology refers to the specific prices and rates used as risk factors, such as Treasury yields at one year, five years, and so on).

❑ Use of different day count schemes: we suggested that vendors use the day count conversions of the exchanges where the products are traded. In some cases, however, the vendors did not implement these particular parameter settings. The choice of day count is thought to be most likely to make a difference for very short-term bonds and money market deposits. Nevertheless, we have evidence that the magnitude of the effect is usually on the order of a fraction of a percentage point in the VAR estimate.

❑ Interest rate calculations: different exchanges and markets have slightly different conventions regarding yield calculation. Unlike the day count effect, this effect seems to cause greater discrepancies as the maturity of the instrument increases.

❑ Small differences in valuation dates. E's numbers are calculated as of October 2, 1995, not September 27.

❑ Holidays and weekend adjustments: theoretically, settlement and reset dates should be adjusted if they fall on weekends or holidays. To do this requires significant calculation as it implies keeping a record of holidays in multiple markets and adjusting for leap years. Most of the vendors believed this to have little effect and since there was a range of implementations on this issue, the data largely confirm this.

Many of these issues also affect the other instrument classes. We note them here because of vendor results specific to government bonds.

Vendors' valuations are shown in Table 11. Although not all the valuations are available, the fact that the VAR estimates vary much more than the valuations suggests that variation in valuations only partially accounts for the variation in VAR. Even when the H.1 outlier is eliminated, although valuation becomes relatively more important as a cause of variation in the VAR estimates, it still causes only half the variation in the VAR results. The variation not accounted for by valuations is probably due to a combination of the factors we have discussed.

To summarise, implementation risk is generally small for bonds using the RiskMetrics model, but significant outliers do exist. Valuation differences account for at most half of the variation in the VAR results, with the remaining variation believed to be caused by differences in mapping and other factors. Bonds appear to become more complex, and thus more likely to produce outliers in VAR, as the number of coupons increases.

Table 10. VAR of bond portfolio

RiskMetrics-based VAR	Interest rate risk	FX risk	Total VAR
B	1,171,322	4,191,516	3,808,750
C	na	na	5,490,568
D	na	na	3,802,820
E	1,158,000	4,127,000	3,754,000
F	1,190,421	4,211,048	3,824,799
G	1,175,013	4,192,618	3,809,410
H.1	na	na	4,823,042
J.1	1,174,177	4,191,972	3,806,757
Mean	1,173,787	4,182,831	4,140,018
Median	1,174,177	4,191,972	3,809,080
Standard deviation	11,550	32,280	652,762
Standard deviation/median (%)	1	1	17

Table 11. Bond valuations

Money market deposits	B	F	H.1	J	Std dev/ mean (%)
Valuation	357,008,500	357,823,842	344,739,857	357,284,825	1.8
VAR	3,808,750	3,824,799	4,823,042	3,806,757	12.4
Implicit std dev (%)	0.7	0.7	0.8	0.6	14.2

INTEREST RATE SWAPS

The swaps results in Table 12 present a major contrast with those for bonds, with much greater variation in the VAR estimates; ie there is higher implementation risk. Systems A and G are outliers, but taking them out of the sample does not eliminate the relative standard deviation, which decreases to about 8%. G's estimates are based on its assumption that all the fixed legs and all the floating legs of the swap should contribute to the interest rate risk component of the swap; other vendors assume that all the fixed legs but only the first floating leg should contribute to interest rate risk. The RiskMetrics technical document argues that the remaining floating legs of a swap do not contribute to interest rate risk, because if interest rates change then so too do the forward rates used to value the leg, and the remaining floating legs will revalue to par.

All the vendors have widely different allocations to FX risk. We believe that this is due to differences in valuation, as spot FX risk is a direct function of the instrument's net present value. Several vendors believe the VAR of the swap is especially sensitive to the swap's valuation (ie more than the other linear instruments).

Table 13 shows the vendor's valuations. We see much greater variation in the valuations of swaps than in bond valuations, but a similar variation in the VAR estimates. This suggests that while estimation of VAR for swaps is of similar difficulty as VAR estimation of bonds, swaps valuation poses greater difficulties. For swaps, it appears that about half the variation in VAR estimates is the result of variation in the valuations.

To summarise, the choice of whether to map one or multiple floating legs contributes most to variation in the swap VAR, with much of the remaining variation caused by discrepancies in the valuations. Presumably, like bonds, the large numbers of cash flows for some swaps mean that mapping differences may be responsible for some additional variation.

Table 12. VAR of swap portfolio

RiskMetrics-based VAR	Interest rate risk	FX risk	Total VAR
A	398,519	221,048	438,680
B	326,574	133,688	315,177
D	na	na	303,502
E	304,000	129,000	307,000
F	327,133	128,595	315,322
G	40,503	218,050	205,770
H.1	na	na	250,058
J.1	328,278	152,008	317,796
Mean	287,501	163,732	306,663
Median	326,854	142,848	311,089
Standard deviation	125,192	44,083	66,648
Standard deviation/median (%)	38	31	21

Table 13. Swap VAR and valuations

Money market deposits	B	F	H.1	J	Std dev/ mean (%)
Valuation	14,021,377	13,638,989	13,915,596	15,416,977	5.6
VAR	315,177	315,322	250,058	317,796	11.0
Implicit std dev (%)	1.4	1.4	1.1	1.3	10.9

FOREIGN EXCHANGE OPTIONS

There are two commonly-used parametric approaches to calculate VAR for options. The first, so-called delta valuation, suggested by the RiskMetrics model, estimates the VAR of the option assuming a constant delta (ie a constant value for the option premium's sensitivity to changes in the price of the underlying instrument). The second approach, full valuation, values the option at different levels of the underlying prices and rates. Both approaches are limited, being linear approximations to a non-linear relation between generic risk factors and option value.

For the non-linear instruments, we include a number of non-parametric results of non-parametric models including full valuation (F), Monte Carlo simulation (H.3), historical simulation (H.2), structured Monte Carlo simulation based on the 95th percentile (J.2), and structured Monte Carlo simulation based on a multiple (1.65) of the standard deviation (J.3). See Table 14.

Table 14. VAR of the FX option portfolio

RiskMetrics-based VAR		Interest rate risk	FX risk	Total VAR
B		30,127	873,329	889,609
E		29,000	927,000	943,000
G		160	501,770	501,811
J.1		21,730	725,883	718,846
Mean		20,254	756,996	763,317
Median		25,365	799,606	804,228
Standard deviation		13,903	190,213	198,829
Standard deviation/median (%)		55	24	25
Simulation-based VAR				
F	Full valuation	576	2,111,045	2,111,349
H.3[1]	MC 1-month	26,010	575,033	577,059
H.3	MC 3-month	21,019	670,837	672,422
H.3	MC 6-month	19,807	850,223	848,537
H.3	MC 1-year	15,966	767,962	709,081
H.3	MC 2-year	16,164	753,054	759,248
H.3	MC 5-year	13,943	936,381	951,471
J.2	RM strct MC %	29,865	706,973	na
J.3	RM strct MCSD	31,560	764,556	na
Mean[2]		20,028	893,567	929,174
Median		20,413	766,259	781,738
Standard deviation		9,079	438,792	490,972
Standard deviation/median (%)		44	57	63

1 In one case, vendor H.3 provided us with different results estimated using the same methodology (eg, historical simulation) but using different data sets. In accordance with our definition of a model as "a system of postulates and data," these are considered distinct models.
2 All simulation-based VAR statistics (mean, median) include the median estimate obtained from the parametric results. The reason for this is to obtain an assessment of model risk, and as the parametric results present an alternative model of risk, they are included as an indicator of model risk.

Table 15. FX option valuations

FX forwards	F	H.3	J	Std dev/mean (%)
Valuation	−1,261,177	−873,053	−1,578,703	29
VAR	2,111,349	734,165	718,846	67
Implicit standard deviation (%)	−101.5	−51.0	−27.6	63

Obviously these results do not tell us anything about implementation risk, but as with the studies by Hendricks (1996) and Beder (1995) they do suggest the magnitude of implementation risk relative to model risk. The first thing to notice about the FX options results is that using the parametric model of RiskMetrics is no guarantee to producing consistent results. The parametric results too have significant variation. This should be seen as reinforcing many vendors' concerns about using a parametric model assumes constant sensitivity of the derivative value with respect to the underlying rates (delta).

For far-out-of-the-money options, this might be a reasonable assumption, but in a more general portfolio such as we have here, the assumption breaks down. In general, however, FX options appear less sensitive to these assumptions than do interest rate caps and floors.

The choice of a different risk model such as full valuation versus delta valuation versus simulation incorporating vega and gamma risks appears to have a massive impact on the VaR estimation. This is well illustrated in F's very different full valuation-based VAR estimate. Like all options, FX options are highly sensitive to the choice of volatilities used.

The second observation is that the non-parametric results vary more than the parametric results, suggesting that model risk is greater than implementation risk for this instrument class. The wide variation in valuation, shown in Table 15, appears to explain the variation in VAR results only partly. This variation is surprising, because all three vendors used the Garman-Kohlhagen model for valuation of FX options.

Table 16. VAR of the IR option portfolio

RiskMetrics-based VAR	Interest rate risk	FX risk	Total VAR
B	286,411	274,505	416,722
G	288,393	512,586	616,145
J.1	292,223	263,864	416,523
Mean	289,009	350,318	483,130
Median	288,393	274,505	416,722
Standard deviation	2,954	140,628	115,194
Standard deviation/median (%)	1	51	28
Simulation-based VAR			
F Full valuation	4,429	300,128	296,890
H.2 Historical simulation	438,426	181,996	455,960
H.3 MC 1-month	255,996	229,227	347,301
H.3 MC 3-month	354,898	192,398	401,068
H.3 MC 6-month	332,272	205,440	387,729
H.3 MC 1-year	253,044	163,249	297,497
H.3 MC 2-year	219,222	143,821	263,300
H.3 MC 5-year	163,818	135,485	212,941
J.2 RM strct MC %	615,177	269,237	na
J.3 RM strct MCSD	618,431	266,218	na
Mean	322,191	214,700	342,156
Median	288,393	205,440	347,301
Standard deviation	183,097	56,844	79,878
Standard deviation/median (%)	63	28	23

To summarise, FX options are non-linear in their dependence on the underlying risk factors used in RiskMetrics. Consequently, they are very sensitive to the precise assumptions made in the system and the model.

INTEREST RATE CAPS AND FLOORS

Perhaps the most conspicuous result for interest rate caps and floors is the closeness of the parametric interest rate risk estimates (see Table 16). This is surprising, as nearly all the other instrument classes show more variation in estimating interest rate risks than in FX risk estimates. This may of course be a feature of this small data set. Also surprising is that two of the three parametric estimates are very close in the FX risks and total VAR. Neither we, nor vendor G, know why G's results are so different.

Less surprisingly, there is also extensive model variation, particularly in the interest rate risk estimates. For interest rate caps and floors, most of the discrepancies seem to be due to the choice of model, followed by variation in the valuation of the portfolio.

Vendors were repeatedly dubious about the effectiveness of parametric methods for interest rate caps and floors because of the significance of the non-delta risks. The added complexity of the interest rate caps and floors is also seen in vendor use of additional models of interest rate term structure. Combining these models of itself adds to complexity and increases the likelihood of user and implementation error. Despite the very small number of data points, but consistent with those concerns, interest rate options appear to have the highest implementation risk of all the instruments considered in this test portfolio.

The valuations shown in Table 17 are much more similar to each other than the valuations for FX options are. Variation in valuations appears responsible for a smaller part of the variation in VAR than it is for FX options (less than a third). This suggests that the risk assessment of interest rate caps and floors is more complex than that of FX options, even though the valuation appears easier.

To summarise, model and implementation

Table 17. Valuations of the IR option portfolio

FX forwards	B	F	H.1 and H.2	H.3	J	Std dev/mean (%)
Valuation	14,404,289	15,295,900	13,915,596	13,458,349	13,370,796	6
VAR	416,722	296,890	455,960	322,399	416,523	18
Implicit standard deviation (%)	1.8	1.2	1.9	1.5	1.9	20

risks are more similar for interest rate options, and generally larger than for any other instrument class in the portfolio. Valuation is less obviously a cause of variation in VAR results than it is for FX options.

COMPARATIVE ANALYSIS OF AGGREGATE TOOL RESULTS

The vendors also produced assessments of VAR for the complete portfolio using RiskMetrics parametric techniques. We asked that vendors assume diversification of all risks both across, and within, different instrument classes, ie a complete portfolio effect over all positions in all risk classes.[10]

The aggregate results appear in Table 18. Note the wide range of results even for the RiskMetrics-based results. For the non-linear portfolio, this variation is very large. Most of the variation results from F's use of the full valuation assumption in its otherwise parametric assessment of the non-linear positions.[11] With F's non-linear estimates removed, the parametric variation (described by the standard deviation/median) decreases to 11% and 13% for the non-linear and aggregate portfolios, respectively. Most of this variation reflects the importance of the bonds in the aggregate portfolio, and thus may even underestimate the difficulties in estimating the aggregate VAR.

It is also very interesting to note that the variation caused by using different implementations of the RiskMetrics model, even with F removed, is similar in magnitude to that caused by using different models. For the linear portfolio, the implementation risk is actually greater than the model risk. One potential explanation for the small variation in the non-parametric compared to parametric estimates may lie in the fact that more vendors (seven) were involved in producing the different parametric estimates than in producing the different simulation-based estimates (two). This might have caused vendors to recalibrate their model results to be more consistent, thus reducing the variation of the model VARs.

Also surprising is that variation at the aggregate level is of a similar magnitude to that of the instrument classes. This suggests that implementation risk may have systematic components, with diversification of implementation differences across asset classes having less of an effect on the total variation than might be expected. One explanation for this result might be that different implementations exhibit systematic biases for particular instruments to a greater extent than do different models.[12]

Less surprisingly, non-linear instruments show consistently greater model risks than do linear instruments. When F's estimates are included, the same is true of implementation risks. When F's estimates are removed, we have the curious result that the implementation risk may actually be larger for the linear portfolio than for the non-linear portfolio.

CORROBORATION OF RESEARCHER EXPECTATIONS

Our expectations are largely corroborated in the results:

1. SDev (money markets) (9%) < SDev (government bonds) (17%) TRUE
2. SDev (money markets) (9%) < SDev (interest rate swaps) (21%) TRUE

Table 18. Aggregate VAR estimates

RiskMetrics-based VAR	Linear portfolio	Non-linear portfolio	Entire portfolio
B	4,246,678	786,767	3,848,254
C	5,410,794	na	na
D	4,236,783	na	na
E	2,989,000	na	na
F	4,225,722	2,071,517	6,141,525
G	4,327,583	906,713	4,764,070
J.1	4,092,468	747,521	3,832,917
Mean	4,218,433	1,128,130	4,646,692
Median	4,236,783	846,740	4,306,162
Standard deviation	702,638	632,560	1,087,510
Standard deviation/median (%)	17	75	25
Simulation-based VAR			
H.2 Historical simulation	4,824,224	na	na
H.3 MC 1-month	3,707,069	578,636	3,491,719
H.3 MC 3-month	3,698,294	742,004	3,344,544
H.3 MC 6-month	4,293,514	896,789	3,799,679
H.3 MC 1-year	3,811,267	786,138	3,296,188
H.3 MC 2-year	3,546,585	790,756	3,018,187
H.3 MC 5-year	4,097,556	969,585	3,338,785
Mean	4,026,912	801,521	3,513,699
Median	3,954,412	790,756	3,344,544
Standard deviation	421,447	124,458	420,653
Standard deviation/median (%)	11	16	13

3. SDev (money markets) (9%) < SDev (FRAs) (10%) TRUE
4. SDev (FX options) (25%) < SDev (interest rate options) (28%) TRUE
5. SDev (FRAs) (10%) < SDev (interest rate swaps) (21%) TRUE
6. SDev (money markets) (9%) < SDev (FX forwards) (1%) FALSE

Obviously with such small samples, there is a large confidence interval around these estimates of variation. There are also a number of important caveats to remember when using this heuristic ordering; we mentioned them earlier. These prevent us from expecting a definitive structural relation in the variation of the estimates. Nevertheless, these results are suggestive and bolster the study's external validity.

CORROBORATION OF VENDOR EXPECTATIONS

We plotted vendors' prior perceptions of the difficulty of performing the risk assessment of a particular instrument class against the relative standard of the VAR estimates of the sample to see if there were any relationship (see Figure 1). There is a clear correlation.

This should not be interpreted as a casual connection, but rather that both variables are actually proxies for a more fundamental metric of complexity associated with each instrument class. Nevertheless, the validation of both the researchers' and the vendors' prior expectations does enhance confidence in the general validity of the data, despite the small size of the sample.

1. Perceived complexity versus implementation risk

Implementation risk (standard deviation of VAR, %)

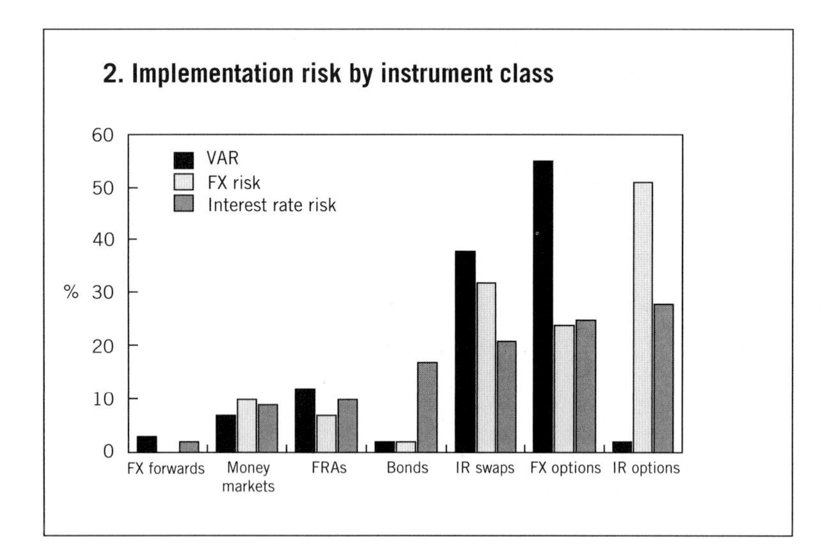

2. Implementation risk by instrument class

Conclusion

Our first goal was *to assess the variation in VAR estimates produced by different commercial implementations of the same model of value-at-risk*. We find that in no case do any two systems' implementations of the same model or two different models produce precisely the same estimate of VAR for the same instrument class. For some instrument classes, vendors' VAR estimates exhibit extensive differences. This suggests that, despite the formal and public nature of the extensive RiskMetrics model, some important decisions regarding assumptions still have to be made by users and systems developers.

It also argues that a naïve view of risk assessment systems as straightforward implementations of models is incorrect. Although software is deterministic (ie given a complete description of all the inputs to the system, it has well-defined outputs), as software and the embedded model become more complex, from the perspective of the only partially knowledgeable user, they behave stochastically. This also justifies our use of elementary probability analysis in understanding the results produced by the systems.

Perhaps the critical insight of our work is that as models and their implementations become more complex, treating them as entirely deterministic black boxes is unwise, and leads to real implementation and model risks (see Perrow (1985)).

Our second goal was *to assess how variation is dependent on the nature of the instrument class*. The evidence shows that the extent of this variation in VAR estimates is related to the complexity of the instrument.[13] Instrument classes with more complex structures generally produce greater variation in VAR estimates. The extent of variation in VAR (and thus the importance of implementation risks) for each instrument class is shown in Figure 2.

The efficacy of the RiskMetrics model for each instrument class in summarised below

FX FORWARDS

The data suggest that the VAR variation is almost certainly the result of variation in valuations. This is consistent with the vendors' beliefs that FX forwards are the least sensitive of all the instrument classes to the precise choice of assumptions made. Despite a small number of data points, this is strongly borne out by our results, with very small (although non-zero) discrepancies between systems. What variation there is appears entirely the result of differences in valuations. We can conclude that for FX forwards, more than for any other instrument class in the test portfolio, the RiskMetrics VAR is an effective standard with limited implementation risk.

MONEY MARKETS

Money markets are well suited to the RiskMetrics model, although not to the same extent as FX forwards. Money markets thus involve a small but insignificant implementation risk, greater than that for forwards, but less than for all other instrument classes.

FORWARD RATE AGREEMENTS

FRAs look much like money market deposits in the ease of VAR estimation. Unlike for money markets, there are some indications that valuation is less the driving factor in the evaluation of VAR estimation. Hence, implementation risk appears greater for FRAs than for forwards and money markets but less than that for bonds and swaps.

GOVERNMENT BONDS

While implementation risk is generally small for bonds using the RiskMetrics model, significant outliers do exist. Valuation accounts for at most half of the variation in the VAR results, with the remaining variation believed to be caused by differences in mapping and other factors. Bonds appear to become more complex and thus more likely to produce outliers in VAR as the number of coupons increases.

INTEREST RATE SWAPS

The choice of whether to map one or multiple floating legs contributes most to variation in the swap VAR, with much of the remaining variation caused by discrepancies in the valuations. As for bonds, the large numbers of cash flows for some swaps mean that mapping differences may also be responsible for some additional variation.

FX OPTIONS

FX options are non-linear in their dependence on the underlying risk factors used in RiskMetrics. Consequently, they are very sensitive to the precise assumptions made in the system and the model. Implementation risks for FX options are higher than for any linear instrument.

INTEREST RATE CAPS AND FLOORS

Variation in valuations appears responsible for a small part of the variation in VAR than it is for FX options. This suggests that the risk assessment of interest rate options is more complex than that of FX options, even though the valuation appears easier. Implementation risks are more similar for interest rate options, and larger than for any linear instrument class. Valuation is less obviously a cause of variation in VAR results than it is for FX options.

AGGREGATE PORTFOLIO

The variation caused by using different implementations of the RiskMetrics model, even with the main outlier removed, is similar in magnitude to that caused by using different models. Surprisingly, variation at the aggregate level is of a magnitude similar to that of any of the component instrument classes. This suggests that implementation risk may have systematic components, with diversification across asset classes having less of an effect on the total variation than might be expected. With F's estimates included, non-linear instruments show, as one might predict, greater implementation risks than linear instruments.

Our third goal in performing this study was *to compare these results with the prior expectations of the vendors and those of the researchers*. For the most part, comparisons confirm our hypothesis that the complexity of the instrument is a key determinant of implementation risk. The results also suggest the importance of developing metrics of portfolio complexity as a means to understand and therefore manage model and implementation risk.

Our final research goal was *to understand the importance of implementation risk in the provision of any potential standard for risk measurement*. Implicit in this study is our assumption that a necessary condition for a model to be a standard is that it involves limited or at least quantifiable implementation risk. The data suggest that RiskMetrics provides a useful benchmark for FX forwards, money markets, and FRAs. It is somewhat less useful for bonds and swaps, and it has major weaknesses dealing with non-linear instruments such as FX options and interest rate caps and floors. Discrepancies in FX risk seem to be caused by variation in valuation, but other significant factors also appear to affect variation in interest rate risk assessment. Variations in valuation occur for most instrument classes, which suggests that a benchmark model for value-at-risk may be most useful in conjunction with a benchmark model for valuation.

We note that where implementation risks reflect genuine disagreement among similarly competent vendors about the appropriate implementation of a model, they are not necessarily a threat to the accurate measurement of the total financial risk of a portfolio, provided users can obtain estimates of its magnitude. Multiple implementations may provide a useful variety of perspectives on the complex task of risk assessment.

Given our estimates of implementation-induced variation, we can adjust the market risk-based VAR estimate to include implementation risks. Such an adjustment takes advantage of the fact that VAR is, in essence, an estimate of a parameter of a distribution and, like all estimates, subject to noise. By matching the extent of the noise to the magnitude of the variation induced by implementation risk, we can estimate the proxy distribution that might give rise to such noise. This in turn allows us to estimate the true VAR, combining both market and implementation risks.

Finally, to reiterate, as financial instruments become more complex, so too do the models and the associated software implementations required to value them and assess their risk. Our results suggest that implementation risk should be an important concern of any user of a value-at-risk model, particularly in the case of more complex instruments. This is all too often forgotten by managers.

Future research

While this study provides research methods, a framework, and preliminary results for understanding implementation risk, it is inevitably limited by its small sample size. The most effective way to estimate model and implementation risk is through a larger-scale empirical survey of risk assessment/valuation models and their implementations. Weston and Cooper (1996) in The Bank of England survey make an early attempt to do this for banks' internal valuation models.

The development of such a wide-ranging survey would have other effects. Because of secrecy and competitiveness, there are few resources available in the financial services industry for a relatively unbiased assessment and comparison of models and systems. Vendors were able to use even our relatively small-scale study to help them validate their own models and systems; several vendors produced multiple iterations of VAR estimates based on our feedback. In addition, other vendors and risk management system developers have since requested that test portfolio as a means to validate their implementations. This suggests a real need for independent advice on complex financial models and their implementations.

It is our hope that this study establishes a foundation geared to fulfilling that need and to cataloguing, sensitivity analysis, and comparative analysis of such complex financial models, as well as pointing the way toward a more systematic management of firms' financial models, their implementations, and their use.

Appendix

TEST PORTFOLIO GIVEN TO VENDORS

Exchange rates versus $1

DM	1.4413002	Ffr	4.9718098
IL	1,605.1364	¥	101.10201

Government bonds

Currency	Instrument	Price – clean	Maturity	Coupon (%)	Amount (local currency – LC)	Amount ($)
Ffr	BTAN	101.88	Aug 12, 1997	7.25	300,000,000	60,340,200
Ffr	BTAN	103.88	Apr 12, 2000	7.75	450,000,000	90,510,300
Ffr	OAT	102.33	Oct 25, 2005	7.75	–165,000,000	–33,187,110
Ffr	OAT	77.29	Oct 25, 2025	6.00	172,000,000	34,595,048
DM	Schatz	103.18	May 20, 1997	6.38	125,000,000	86,727,250
DM	Bobl	104.16	Mar 15, 2000	6.50	75,000,000	52,036,350
DM	Bund	109.53	Jul 22, 2002	8.00	48,000,000	33,303,264
DM	Bund	87.18	Jan 4, 2024	6.25	25,000,000	17,345,450
IL	BTP	98.8	Oct 1, 1996	9.00	–5,000,000,000	–3,115,000
IL	BTP	98.08	Apr 1, 2000	10.50	10,000,000,000	6,230,000
¥	JGB	114.303	Sep 20, 2004	4.60	–2,500,000,000	–24,727,500
$	Treasury	99.95317	Jul 31, 1997	5.88	–10,000,000	–10,000,000
$	Treasury	100.03125	Jul 31, 2000	6.13	15,000,000	15,000,000
$	Treasury	101.54688	May 15, 2005	6.50	25,000,000	25,000,000

Interest rate swaps

Currency	Receive	Value (LC) incl. acc. int.	Roll frequency	Maturity	Next settle	Current fixed	Fixed rate (%)	Floating rate (%)	Amount (LC)	Amount ($)
Ffr	Floating	–2,256,800	6M	Jun 30, 1997	Dec 31, 1995	6.29	7.40	7.00	125,000,000	25,141,750
Ffr	Fixed	11,412,000	6M	Sep 30, 1999	Sep 30, 1995	6.825	8.00	6.75	225,000,000	45,255,150
DM	Fixed	5,247,000	6M	Jun 15, 2000	Dec 15, 1995	6.04	7.50	5.63	75,000,000	52,036,350
DM	Floating	55,000	3M	Apr 1, 2005	Oct 1, 1995	7.015	6.75	5.85	52,500,000	36,425,445
IL	Fixed	1,203,000,000	6M	Jun 1, 1997	Dec 3, 1995	10.905	12.50	10.50	55,000,000,000	34,265,000
¥	Fixed	309,332,000	6M	Jul 1, 1999	Jan 3, 1996	1.87	3.50	2.25	5,000,000,000	49,455,000
$	Fixed	4,073,000	3M	Mar 30, 2000	Sep 29, 1995	6.385	8.02	5.25	55,000,000	55,000,000
$	Floating	45,000	3M	Mar 30, 1996	Sep 29, 1995	5.809	5.25	4.60	15,000,000	15,000,000

FX forwards

Buy	Sell	Value (buy currency)	Value date	Forward rate	Contract rate	Buy amount (LC)	Buy amount (LC)
$	Ffr	0	Dec 29, 1995	4.92	4.92	30,000,000	147,600,000
DM	Bfr	–180,000	Jun 28, 1996	20.594	20.7	35,000,000	724,500,000
DM	$	–69,000	Sep 30, 1995	1.4255	1.43	45,000,000	31,468,531
$	¥	3,058,000	Dec 29, 1995	99.1	89	30,000,000	2,670,000,000
$	IL	–11,000	Mar 29, 1996	1,643.75	1,650	3,000,000	4,950,000,000

Money market deposits

Currency	Instrument	Value (LC)	Maturity	Basis	Current yield	Contract rate (%)	Amount (LC)	Amount ($)
DM	Demand deposit	55,077,000	Oct 30, 1995	30/360	4.06	5.75	55,000,000	38,159,990
IL	Demand deposit	5,002,071,000	Dec 31, 1995	30/360	10.43	10.60	5,000,000,000	3,115,000
¥	Demand deposit	512,075,000	Mar 31, 1996	30/360	0.46875	5.31	500,000,000	4.945,500

Forward rate agreements

Currency	Instrument	Value (LC)	Maturity	Value date	Current yield (%)	Contract rate (%)	Amount (LC)	Amount ($)
Ffr	Bought	583,000	Mar 30, 1996	Sep 28, 1995	6.40	6.92	225,000,000	45,255,150
DM	Sold	56,000	Mar 15, 1996	Dec 15, 1995	4.00	4.30	75,000,000	52,036,350
DM	Sold	62,000	Aug 3, 1996	May 3, 1996	4.00	4.60	42,000,000	29,140,356
¥	Bought	80,881,000	Mar 15, 1996	Dec 15, 1995	0.59	2.75	15,000,000,000	148,365,000
$	Sold	237,000	Jun 1, 1996	Jan 2, 1996	5.77	6.25	100,000,000	100,000,000

FX options

Instrument	Base	Premium (%)	Maturity	Volatility (%)	Optioned	Strike	Amount (LC)	Amount ($)
Buy call	$	3.57 per$	Dec 30, 1995	15	¥	100 ¥/$	45,000,000	45,000,000
Buy put	$	0.44 per $	Oct 16, 1995	15	DM	1.46 DM/$	55,500,000	55,500,000
Sell call	$	6.18 per $	Nov 30, 1995	15	DM	1.5 DM/$	77,500,000	77,500,000
Buy call	DM	2.50 per ¥	Mar 30, 1996	15	¥	68 ¥/DM	95,000,000	65,912,710
Sell put	DM	0.20 per DM	Feb 17, 1996	15	Ffr	3.6 Ffr/DM	85,000,000	58,974,530

Interest rate caps and floors

Currency	Instrument	Premium (bp)	Volatility (%)	Maturity	Value date	Strike (%)	Amount (LC)	Amount ($)
DM	Buy cap 6M	0.07	17.0	Jul 8, 1996	Jan 8, 1996	5.00	75,000,000	52,036,350
DM	Sell floor 6M	173	16.7	Jan 5, 2004	Jan 8, 1996	5.00	110,000,000	76,319,980
Ffr	Sell floor 6M	14.8	23.0	Sep 3, 1998	Mar 3, 1996	4.50	250,000,000	50,283,500
Ffr	Sell cap 6M	36.9	22.6	Sep 3, 1998	Mar 3, 1996	8.75	250,000,000	50,283,500
¥	Buy floor 6M	1,521.3	41.6	Apr 11, 2000	Oct 11, 1995	5.25	10,000,000,0000	98,910,000

1 *The term, "model" denotes a system of postulates and data, together with a means of drawing dynamic inferences from them. This definition is taken from the model management literature. See, for example, Little [1970]. For a more recent perspective on financial models, see Derman [1996] and Merton [1994].*

2 *While inevitably a simplification since real instruments' behaviour only proximately matches linear combinations of generic risk factors, mapping techniques have the important advantage that they avoid the need to track correlations and volatilities of the huge number of individual instruments' values.*

3 *Internet address: http://www.J.P.Morgan.com/RiskMetricsTM.*

4 *Lawrence and Robinson [1995] criticise some of the RiskMetrics assumptions, such as its choice of a 95% confidence interval, the assumption of normal distributions for returns, and its decision to ignore information in implied volatilities. Our test of this model probably underestimates the extent of implementation risk involved in more complex models.*

5 *That different model and system developers make different assumptions does not imply that they are in error. Rather, an assumption's "correctness" is really an evolving social contract, based on accepted practice. Assumptions also differ from errors; we use the term, "error," to describe inconsistencies between assumptions within the same model or implementation.*

6 *Ours is a narrow definition of model risk. The term sometimes denotes the broader set of risks occasioned by the need to use theoretical models for valuation and hedging.*

7 *Vendors were informed of the median and the standard deviation of the sample of VAR results by instrument class.*

8 *The difficulties in model-based valuation are discussed in Beder [1994] and Weston and Cooper [1996].*

9 *"Linear relationship" is a simplification because it describes the relation between VAR and valuation at the level of individual cash flows, not at the level of aggregations of cash flows, ie real portfolios. For variation differences, recall that:*

$$\text{VAR} = 1.65 \times \text{standard deviation of changes in value} \times \text{value}$$

$$\therefore \frac{\partial \text{VAR}}{\partial \text{value}} = 1.65 \times \text{standard deviation of value changes}$$

If the implementation introduces no variation beyond that caused by variation in valuations, then variation in VAR (δVAR) *should be linearly related to variation in value* (δvalue):

$$\delta\text{VAR} = \frac{\delta\text{VAR}}{\delta\text{value}}\delta\text{value}$$

$$\therefore \frac{\delta\text{VAR}}{|\text{VAR}|} = 1.65 \times \text{standard deviation of value changes} \times \frac{\delta\text{value}}{|\text{VAR}|}$$

$$\therefore \frac{\delta\text{VAR}}{|\text{VAR}|} = 1.65 \times \text{standard deviation of value changes} \times \frac{|\text{value}|}{|\text{VAR}|} \times \frac{\delta\text{value}}{|\text{value}|}$$

$$\therefore \frac{\delta\text{VAR}}{|\text{VAR}|} = \frac{\delta\text{value}}{|\text{value}|}$$

10 *This is as suggested in Guldimann [1995], but contrary to the proposal outlined in "Public Disclosure of Market and Credit Risks by Financial Intermediaries" [1994], which allows for the diversification of risks only within and not across difference instrument classes.*

11 *Other parametric implementations of the RiskMetrics model use a delta valuation assumption. This brings up a subtle issue: when does model risk become implementation risk? The reality is that there is a continuum of decisions regarding assumptions made by modellers and systems developers.*

12 *A natural corollary of this is that users are well advised to combine the results from different models to increase the accuracy of the VAR results, rather than using different implementations of the same model. See Batchelor and Dua [1995] for a discussion. This goes against much of the drive toward integration of models and systems, particularly across the front- and back-office, since for more complex instruments such integration may actually increase model and implementation risks.*

13 *To some extent, this clashes with the work of Beder [1995], who finds little systematic behaviour in the errors according to different methodologies. Her comparisons are across models rather than implementation, however, which presumably introduces a great deal of additional variation in the results.*

BIBLIOGRAPHY

Batchelor, R., and P. Dua, 1995, "Forecaster Diversity and the Benefits of Combining Forecasts", *Management Science*, 41, 1, pp. 68-75.

Beder, T. Styblo, 1994, "The Realities of Marking to Model", *Bank Accounting and Finance*, 7, 4, pp. 4-12.

Beder, T. Styblo, 1995, "VAR: Seductive but Dangerous," *Financial Analysis Journal*, September-October, pp. 12-24; reprinted as Chapter 17 of the present volume.

Derivatives: Practices and Principles, 1993, Group of Thirty.

Derman, E., 1996, "Model Risk", *Risk* 9, 5, pp. 34-7; reprinted as Chapter 12 of the present volume.

Hendricks, D., 1996, "Evaluation of Value at Risk Models using Historical Data", *Federal Reserve Bank of New York Economic Policy Review*, April, pp. 39-69; reprinted as Chapter 22 of the present volume.

Lawrence, C., and G. Robinson, 1995, "How Safe is RiskMetrics?" *Risk*, 8, 1, pp. 26-9; reprinted as Chapter 8 of the present volume.

JP Morgan, 1995, *RiskMetrics Technical Document*, 3rd edition, New York.

Leong, K., 1996. "The Right Approach", *Risk*, Special Supplement on Value-at-risk, June, pp. 9-14; reprinted as Chapter 5 of the present volume.

Little, J.D.C., 1970, "Models and Managers: The Concept of a Decision Calculus", *Management Science*, 16, 8, pp. 466-485.

Longerstaey, J., and P. Zangari, 1995, "A Transparent Tool", *Risk*, 8, 1, pp. 30-2; reprinted as Chapter 9 of the present volume.

Marshall, C.L., and M. Siegel, 1996, "Get IT into your System", *Risk*, Special Supplement on Value-at-risk, pp. 26-32.

Merton, R.C., 1994, "Influence of Mathematical Models in Finance on Practice: Past, Present and Future", *Phil. Trans. R. Soc. Lond.*, 347, pp. 451-463.

Perrow, C., 1985, *Normal Accidents: Living with High-Risk Technologies*, Basic Books, New York.

Public Disclosure of Market and Credit Risks by Financial Intermediaries (Fisher Report), 1994, Eurocurrency Standing Committee of the Central Banks of the Group of Ten Countries, Bank for International Settlements, 1994.

Smith, D.J., 1993, "The Arithmetic of Financial Engineering". In *The New Corporate Finance: Where Theory Meets Practice*. McGraw-Hill, New York, pp. 401-10.

Smithson, C.W., 1987, "A Lego Approach to Forwards, Futures, Swaps and Options", *Midland Corporate Finance Journal*, 4, 4, pp. 16-29.

Weston, S., and S. Cooper, 1996, "Bank Checks", Risk 9, 2, pp. 23-7.

29

Principals of Risk

Finding VAR through Factor-Based Interest Rate Scenarios

Jon Frye
NationsBanc-CRT

This paper considers the factor-based approach to calculating VAR. It begins with a principal components analysis of the yield curve, including a shift factor that allows rates to rise or fall and a twist factor that allows the curve to steepen or flatten. Combining these factors produces specific yield curve scenarios, which are then used to estimate hypothetical portfolio profit or loss. The greatest loss among these scenarios provides a rapid VAR figure that tends towards a conservative estimate of the nominal percentile of the loss distribution.

This paper describes a method of assessing the value-at-risk (VAR) of portfolios containing interest rate-sensitive instruments. The factor based scenario method calculates profit or loss for the entire portfolio under several specially-constructed hypothetical interest rate scenarios that in turn derive from a principal components analysis of the yield curve. The VAR estimate equals the greatest loss that results in any of the scenarios.

This method has several advantages over other VAR strategies. First, options can be included in its analysis without modifications. Options can provoke very misleading results in VAR calculations that linearise profit as a function of market variables. Secondly, it is quick - unlike methods that depend on extensive simulation; a VAR estimate is of little use unless it arrives in time to allow the portfolio to be adjusted. Third, the method provides a useful summary of the types of risk facing a portfolio. It is easy to spot that it is sensitive to, say, rising interest rates or a steepening yield curve. Fourth, it identifies whether an additional trade will increase or decrease risk, which can help hedge strategies. Finally, the method allows the straightforward aggregation of risks across portfolios maintained and valued on different computer systems. The response to a given scenario of the combined portfolio is simply the sum of each portfolio's individual response.

The factor-based scenario method is not foolproof and the user must judge its suitability for particular circumstances. But it works well for an important portfolio class - those that display a concave response to changing market prices, such as portfolios dominated by short positions in standard options. The negative gamma of such positions creates particular risk control issues.

In this paper we consider four alternative measures of VAR in a single underlying market. We then consider the factor-based scenario method and the statistical technique of principal components analysis (PCA). PCA is placed in the more familiar context of regression analysis, the steps used to convert the generic results of PCA into specific scenarios useful for risk control. Finally, we examine how the factor-based scenario method performs when it is applied to randomly-generated sample portfolios and to an actual trading portfolio.

The author wishes to thank Mark Bennett, Bill DeRonne, John Fuqua, Doug Huggins, Carol Lobbes, George McClintick, Ivan Marcotte, Mike O'Neill and Tim Weithers for their extensive comments on earlier versions, and many others at NationsBanc-CRT and the Chicago Risk Management Workshop for their helpful observations and suggestions. The views expressed reflect those of the author, not NationsBanc, and the errors are his.

Measuring risk in a single market

VAR is usually defined as a specific percentile of a distribution of loss over a specific length of time. We will consider a one-day, 99th percentile VAR:

$$P[\text{one-day loss} > \text{VAR}] = 1\%.$$

Suppose we seek VAR for a portfolio tied to only a single market price. Figure 1 depicts a delta-hedged short position in a short-term, out-of-the-money call option on a Treasury Bond futures contract. Possible changes to the futures price have been stated in standard deviations.

Let us consider four different VAR calculations: Monte Carlo simulation, historical simulation, variance-covariance, and the factor-based scenario method.

The Monte Carlo approach randomly selects a hypothetical movement for the bond futures price and then values the portfolio. Many such hypothetical valuations reveal a distribution of profit and loss. The 99th percentile of the loss distribution provides the VAR estimate.

This approach has some significant drawbacks. It might take minutes of computer time to value a portfolio of fixed income instruments. Even if several machines are devoted to risk calculations, they can complete only a few hundred calculations in the allotted production cycle. This relatively low number of simulations does not allow for the accurate estimation of the higher percentiles of the loss distribution. The loss that might occur one time in a thousand – one day in four years, on average – would be estimated quite inaccurately, even though it is of considerable importance. Second, the result of a Monte Carlo simulation is a random number that depends on random inputs. In a trading situation where a position may need adjustment, decision making is not enhanced by the thought that a second run might produce a different result! And Monte Carlo results may be difficult to interpret and communicate when dissimilar random scenarios result in nearly the same loss.

1. Profit and loss of hedged short call

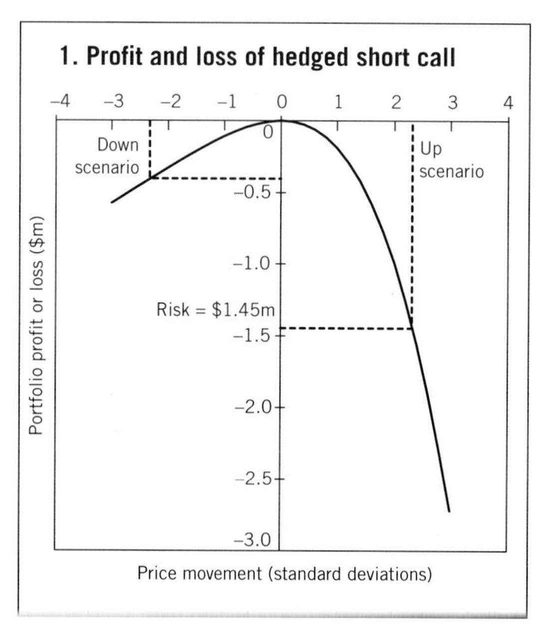

One way of speeding the calculation and making it non-random is to use actual historical price movements rather than simulated movements – the last 100 days of price changes, perhaps. This caps the number of simulation runs, but again it cannot provide good estimates of high percentiles of the loss distribution.

Perhaps the most frequently discussed way of calculating VAR is the variance-covariance method. This technique approximates the portfolio's response by a process called mapping, in which a position's risk is represented as quantities of standardised instruments. These respond linearly to underlying markets and have no optionality; essentially, the portfolio response is approximated by a linear function.

But if the portfolio has a non-linear response to market variables, as in Figure 1, this approach can produce very misleading results. In particular, it assigns zero risk to a delta-hedged short option position. But far from having zero risk, this position would lose a considerable amount of money if there are big market moves. It is exactly this sort of position that risk controllers must limit to avoid large losses when the market moves strongly.

The factor-based scenario method, by contrast, first devises the scenarios, generally with reference to the quantiles of the normal distribution. It may try scenarios at various levels of intensity such as ±2.33 standard deviations, ±4 standard deviations, and ±6 standard deviations. (A different limit applies to each set of scenarios.) For the portfolio in Figure 1 there is only one "factor," the price of the T-Bond contract. The portfolio is then revalued under each scenario. Figure 1 shows valuations under the up 2.33 SDs and down 2.33 SDs scenarios.

In cases such as this, when only one market affects the portfolio, the factor-based scenario method simply shocks that market up and down by a fixed number of standard deviations. Here the portfolio is a delta-hedged short position in a short-term, out-of-the-money call option on Treasury Bond futures. Such a position is unaffected by a very small movement in the underlying market but tends to lose money in large moves up or down. In particular, the portfolio loses money under both the up scenario (underlying price up 2.33 standard deviations) and the down scenario (underlying price down 2.33 standard deviations). The greatest loss among the scenarios, $1.45 million, provides the VAR estimate. This estimate corresponds to the 98.999999994 percentile because of the small chance that the price might fall enough to produce a $1.45 million loss. (This ignores the existence of daily limits on futures price movements.)

The factor-based scenario method performs a complete revaluation of the portfolio under each of the hypothetical scenarios it selects. In this way it resembles the Monte Carlo method more strongly than the variance-covariance approach. Yet the scenario method produces its result much more quickly than Monte Carlo because the number of revaluations it employs is small – two in this case.

Something is lost in this otherwise favourable bargain: the resulting estimate does not exactly equal the 99th percentile of the loss distribution. This is partly because the T-Bond futures price is not normally distributed; for example, it tends to rise by 2.33 standard deviations more than 1% of the time. Even treating the market as normal, the factor-based estimate understates the 99th percentile loss. That is because there is a 1% chance that the price rises by more than 2.33 standard deviations (causing a loss greater than $1.45 million), and in addition there is a 0.000000006% chance that price falls by more than 6.4 standard deviations (this occurs to the left beyond Figure 1 and also causes a loss greater than $1.45 million). Where the 0.01 quantile was sought, the 0.01000000006 quantile was found. Should the portfolio show the same loss under both the up scenario and the down scenario, the resulting estimate represents the 98th percentile of loss rather than the 99th percentile. The actual 99th percentile loss would correspond to 2.58 standard deviations (two-tailed 1%) rather than 2.33 standard deviations (one-tailed 1%), a 9.7% error. The chance of this degree of error occurring is the price the user must pay for the factor-based scenario method's other advantages for a portfolio of hedged short options in a single market.

It is easy to construct portfolios where the estimation error is large. The simplest is when the portfolio is long a put and long a call, as in Figure 2. Valued at either the up scenario or the down scenario, this portfolio makes money, so the scenario method sets VAR equal to $0, despite what can be seen in the diagram. If the profit function tends to have important interior minima such as this, the scenario method is not appropriate and the remainder of this paper assumes the portfolio at hand lacks interior minima.

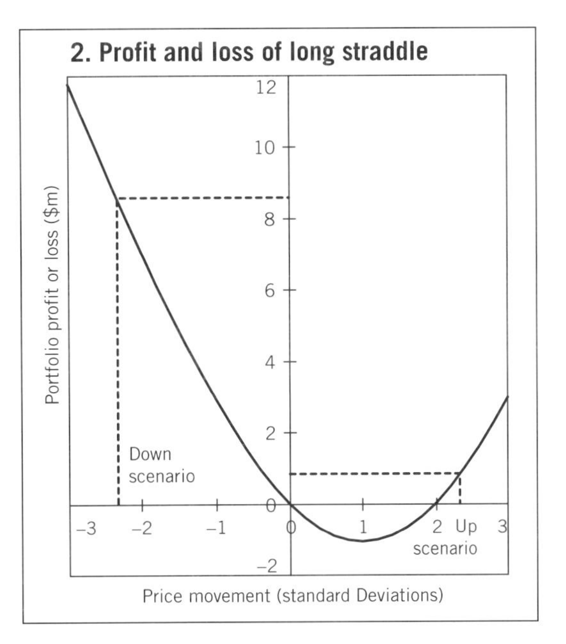

Interest rate scenarios and principal components analysis

The commonest yield curve scenarios posit a shift of a given number of basis points at all maturities. However, portfolio value usually depends on the steepness of the yield curve as well as its overall level. This in turn might lead to additional scenarios: curve steepening, curve flattening, and curve rising and steepening. More scenarios might be devised to reveal the risk of more complicated positions, and so forth. Unfortunately, this *ad hoc* process quickly loses contact with the probabilities revealed in interest rate data.

The factor-based scenario method is much more rigorous in deriving interest rate scenarios. Movements in the yield curve are seen as stemming from several underlying factors. As Litterman and Scheinkman (1991) have argued, the factors are identified through multivariate statistical technique of principal components analysis (PCA). PCA results in an explicit statement of the factors themselves, and supplies the associated standard deviations to measure each component's relative. The first principal component has the greatest effect on the data and the greatest standard deviation; the other principal components follow in turn.

The first few principal components of the data represent the most typical movements of the yield curve. The first principal component appears similar to a level shift factor. This corresponds to the intuition that the most important event affecting the yield curve on a given day is whether yields generally are rising or falling. The second, less important, component appears similar to a curve steepening factor, which allows the yield curve to pivot steeper or flatter. The third principal component allows intermediate-term yields to rise (fall) while both short-term and long-term rates fall (rise).

Nothing about PCA is intrinsically difficult. Still, it is unfamiliar even to market participants familiar with statistical regression. PCA is usually taught in multivariate statistics courses where most of the applications are drawn from social sciences such as psychology rather than finance. Different texts on PCA do not even agree on the meanings of some key terms. The geometric intuition imparted by some texts may not seem relevant. Nonetheless, PCA has direct relevance to the problem at hand because it reduces the apparent complexity of interest rate instruments while retaining their essential richness. Anyone acquainted with linear regression can understand and interpret the results of PCA.

Table 1. Sample of mean-adjusted changes in interest rates (basis points)

	3m	6m	1y	2y	3y	4y	5y	7y	10y	30y
Jan 4, 89	6.0	3.5	4.7	2.8	0.7	0.6	0.1	–0.2	–0.9	–1.0
Jan 5, 89	19.8	7.4	8.1	7.3	8.6	6.8	6.4	6.6	5.6	2.3
Jan 6, 89	–10.4	0.3	5.7	1.0	0.9	0.5	–0.3	–2.1	–2.1	–4.1
Jan 9, 89	0.2	2.3	–0.4	–5.1	–1.8	–1.3	–1.1	0.1	–0.7	–0.5
Jan 10, 89	–8.2	–5.9	–4.4	–1.6	–1.1	–0.9	0.2	–0.2	–0.4	–0.3
Jan 11, 89	7.6	3.5	1.3	2.9	–1.8	–0.4	–0.7	–0.2	0.1	0.4
Jan 12, 89	–1.4	–7.0	–13.7	–7.8	–7.6	–8.5	–8.6	–10.9	–9.3	–8.1
Jan 13, 89	–6.7	–8.6	–9.0	–7.0	–8.1	–9.6	–9.7	–10.3	–8.2	–8.6
Jan 17, 89	4.4	5.7	3.0	2.8	2.8	1.6	0.9	0.1	0.3	0.7
Jan 18, 89	–13.5	–5.3	–7.3	–4.3	–3.8	–4.8	–5.0	–5.7	–6.5	–5.2

Table 2. Selected results from principal components analysis

Principal components loadings

	PC1	PC2	PC3	PC4	PC5	PC6	PC7	PC8	PC9	PC10
3m	0.21	–0.57	0.50	0.47	–0.39	–0.02	0.01	0.00	0.01	0.00
6m	0.26	–0.49	0.23	–0.37	0.70	0.01	–0.04	–0.02	–0.01	0.00
12m	0.32	–0.32	–0.37	–0.58	–0.52	–0.23	–0.04	–0.05	0.00	0.01
2y	0.35	–0.10	–0.38	0.17	0.04	0.59	0.56	0.12	–0.12	–0.05
3y	0.36	0.02	–0.30	0.27	0.07	0.24	–0.79	0.00	–0.09	–0.00
4y	0.36	0.14	–0.12	0.25	0.16	–0.63	0.15	0.55	–0.14	–0.08
5y	0.36	0.17	–0.04	0.14	0.08	–0.10	0.09	–0.26	0.71	0.48
7y	0.34	0.27	0.15	0.01	0.00	–0.12	0.13	–0.54	0.00	–0.68
10y	0.31	0.30	0.28	–0.10	–0.06	0.01	0.03	–0.23	–0.63	0.52
30y	0.25	0.33	0.46	–0.34	–0.18	0.33	–0.09	0.52	0.26	–0.13

Sample of principal component scores

	PC1	PC2	PC3	PC4	PC5	PC6	PC7	PC8	PC9	PC10
Jan 4, 89	4.6	–7.4	0.0	0.1	–1.9	–0.1	0.8	0.1	0.0	–0.3
Jan 5, 89	23.6	–11.8	5.9	6.9	–5.0	–0.8	–0.9	–1.4	–0.8	–0.3
Jan 6, 89	–1.9	1.5	–10.7	–6.2	2.4	–1.8	–0.5	–0.3	–0.3	0.7
Jan 9, 89	–3.1	–1.3	3.1	–2.1	1.3	–2.7	–1.8	–1.2	0.5	–0.4
Jan 10, 89	–6.1	8.8	–3.1	0.3	1.2	0.4	0.1	–0.3	0.7	0.3
Jan 11, 89	3.0	–6.8	3.8	1.2	–1.4	1.3	2.7	0.4	–0.5	–0.2
Jan 12, 89	–26.7	–1.7	1.3	6.8	1.9	1.5	–0.4	1.4	0.4	1.0
Jan 13, 89	–27.0	0.5	–3.2	1.8	0.2	1.4	0.1	0.1	–1.1	0.9
Jan 17, 89	6.6	–5.7	0.7	–0.3	1.2	0.7	–0.8	0.9	–0.1	0.0
Jan 18, 89	–18.1	6.4	–6.8	–1.5	5.1	0.9	–0.6	0.6	0.6	–0.4

Principal component standard deviations

PC1	PC2	PC3	PC4	PC5	PC6	PC7	PC8	PC9	PC10
17.49	6.05	3.10	2.17	1.97	1.69	1.27	1.24	0.80	0.79

Principal components results

In this section we consider the PCA results produced by standard software. The data consists of 1,543 daily observations at 10 points along the yield curve: six and one quarter years (1/89 through 3/95) of daily changes in constant-maturity US Treasury yields (in basis points) observed at tenors of 3, 6 and 12 months and 2, 3, 4, 5, 7, 10, and 30 years.

The first step in the analysis removes the downward drift of interest rates – about 200 basis points (less than 0.2 basis points per day) at each point on the curve over the sample period. The mean of each adjusted series is zero. (This has no effect on the results produced by standard statistical packages, but facilitates the analogy to regression analysis presented below.) Table 1 shows the mean-adjusted data for the first 10 dates.

Several statistical software packages offer PCA. Any of them will produce a wealth of results that include the loadings[1] of each principal component, the factor scores, and each component's standard deviation.

Table 2 presents selected PCA results for the interest rate data, and shows the loadings of all ten principal components arising from the analysis of the ten points on the yield curve. The first three characterise typical movements of the yield curve as understood by market participants. PC1 causes every interest rate to rise, PC2 causes the yield curve to steepen, and PC3 causes one-year to five-year rates to fall while both long-term and short-term rates rise. Thus the first few principal components correspond to the traders' instinctive felings about how the market moves on a daily basis.

The factor scores restate each day's yield curve movement as a combination of the movements of principal components. For example, Table 1 shows that on January 5, 1989 all interest rates rose and that short-term rates rose more than long-term rates. Table 2 restates this movement as a combination of factors: PC1 enters with a large positive score (the curve shifts up) and PC2 enters with a large negative score (the curve flattens). The scores of the first two principal components shown in Table 2 have nearly as much information as all 10 data points which are shown in Table 1.

The standard deviations of the 10 factor score

series determine their ordering. In Table 2, the volatility of the scores of PC1 exceeds that of any other component, the volatility of the scores of PC2 exceeds that of any component except PC1, and so forth. The squares of the standard deviations - the variances of the components - have an interesting property. The sum of the variances of the components equals the sum of the variances of the original data. The total variance in the original data is thus

$$17.49^2 + 6.05^2 + 3.10^2 + 2.17^2 + ... = 367.9$$

and the proportion of this data explained by the first factor is $17.49^2/367.9 = 83.1\%$. The proportion explained by the first two principal components is

$$(17.49^2 + 6.05^2)/367.9 = 93.1\%.$$

Since all 10 of the components explain 100% of the variation in the original data, the principal component scores provide an exact restatement of each day's activity that is equivalent to the original data. The principal components description is simpler though, because most of the variance in the original data concentrates in the first few principal components. A movement in the first principal component explains movement at all points of the yield curve and explains as much of that movement as possible.

Analogy to linear regression analysis

A comparison with regression analysis explains the previous statement. In regression, there is a dependent variable that ideally should be explained with the independent variable. Most interest centres on the regression coefficient and on R^2. The least-squares procedure maximises R^2 by minimising the sum of the squares of the errors produced by the regression equation.

Intuitively, PCA "makes up" the data on the right hand side of the regression equation. Instead of beginning with known data, PCA finds the data that provides the best fit. If there is just one day of yield curve data to understand, the best explanation would be the data itself. The statistical puzzle that PCA solves is how to find the best explanatory variable for all days in the sample period.

Continuing the analogy to regression analysis is revealing. It is helpful to think of PCA as operating by iteration. The iteration begins with a guess: the uniform-shift variable [1,1,1,1,1,1,1,1,1,1]. This variable serves on the right-hand side of each of $N = 1,543$ regression equations. Each regression separately estimates its coefficient to minimise the sum of squared errors within that regression. The total of the N sums of squared errors from these regressions measures the overall explanatory power of the independent variable. A good explanatory variable will produce a lower cumulated sum than a poor one. One can imagine the iterative procedure improving on the uniform shift variable until no further improvement is possible. *The cumulated sum of squared errors reaches its minimum when the explanatory variable equals the first principal component*[2]; no other variable explains the data as well as the first principal component. Starting with nothing, PCA finds the optimal independent variable.[3]

Continuing the regression analogy, *the coefficients that arise from the N regressions on the first principal component equal the factor scores as produced by PCA*. For example, regressing the data for January 5, 1989 on the PC1 column of the loadings matrix results in a regression coefficient of 23.6 - the factor score for PC1 that appears in Table 2 for January 5, 1989. One could say that the market on that day experienced 23.6 "units" of PC1. The restatement of market movement provided by the factor scores has the character of a regression relationship where the components play the role of the explanatory variables and the factor scores play the role of regression coefficients.

Finally, *the standard deviation of the set of coefficients that arise from the N regressions equals the standard deviation of the first principal component*. Any day's coefficient estimates how strongly the first component affects that day's interest rate movements. The standard deviation of the 1,543 coefficients tells the volatility of the component as revealed by the data. In the case of PC1, the standard deviation equals 17.49. Thus we can say that on January 5, 1989 PC1 took the unusual value of $23.6/17.49 = 1.35$ standard deviations.

If asked to write down the explanatory variable that best explains daily variation in the yield curve, many practitioners would choose a level shift in which all rates rise or fall by the same amount. The first principal component of the yield curve data improves on the intuitive idea that "all rates go up or down by the same amount" to provide a calibrated and non-uniform shift in rates.

Though the first principal component gives the best single explanation of daily movements, it leaves some variation unexplained. The remaining variation can act as data in a second set of N regressions. The best explanatory variable for these regressions equals the second principal component. The second principal component of the yield curve data improves on the intuitive idea "the yield curve tends to steepen or flatten" to provide a precise quantification of the relationships along the curve as it steepens or flattens.

Taken together, the first two principal components explain over 93% of the variation in the original data, and hence give an accurate impression of yield curve movements on most days. Since these two factors provide an approximate description of the historical data, it is natural to use them to develop an idea of the sorts of yield curve movements that may arise in the future. Combinations of the principal components produce yield curve scenarios that in turn reveal a portfolio's interest rate.

From components to scenarios

In this section, four scenarios are derived from the first two principal components. No formal statistical test can judge whether two components adequately capture yield curve movements. Instead, we pursue the practical test that the resulting scenarios are rich enough to reflect both the movement of individual interest rates and the movement of various spreads between interest rates. To capture the variation of certain spreads, 16 scenarios produced from the first four components are necessary, and this is the model finally adopted.

Table 3 shows the calculation of the shift factor and the twist factor, the two building blocks for four scenarios. Shift equals the standard deviation of PC1 times the loadings of PC1, and Twist equals the standard deviation of PC2 times the loadings of PC2. Thus the shift factor moves the 30-year yield by $17.49 \times 0.25 = 4.4$ basis points, and the twist factor moves the 30-year yield by $6.05 \times 0.33 = 2.0$ basis points. Table 3 shows the resulting scenarios as combinations of shift and twist. In the UpUp scenario, both factors operate in the positive direction. The yield of a 30-year instrument rises by $(4.4 + 2.0) \times 2.33 = 14.9$ basis points, where ± 2.33 standard deviations corresponds to the 1st and 99th percentiles of a normal distribution. Repeating the calculation of scenario UpUp for each point on the curve, all yields rise, though long-term yields rise more than short-term yields. In the UpDn scenario, all yields rise, but short-term yields rise more than long-term yields; the 30-year yield rises by $(4.4 - 2.0) \times 2.33 = 5.6$ basis points.

Table 3. Construction of two factors and four scenarios (basis points)

Yield curve factors

	3m	6m	1y	2y	3y	4y	5y	7y	10y	30y
Shift	3.6	4.6	5.6	6.2	6.3	6.3	6.2	5.9	5.4	4.4
Twist	–3.5	–3.0	–1.9	–0.6	0.1	0.8	1.0	1.6	1.8	2.0

Yield curve scenarios (2.33 SDs)

	3m	6m	1y	2y	3y	4y	5y	7y	10y	30y
UpUp	0.3	3.7	8.6	12.9	15.0	16.7	16.8	17.5	17.0	14.9
UpDn	16.4	17.6	17.5	15.8	14.5	12.9	12.2	9.9	8.4	5.6
DnUp	–16.4	–17.6	–17.5	–15.8	–14.5	–12.9	–12.2	–9.9	–8.4	–5.6
DnDn	–0.3	–3.7	–8.6	–12.9	–15.0	–16.7	–16.8	–17.5	–17.0	–14.9

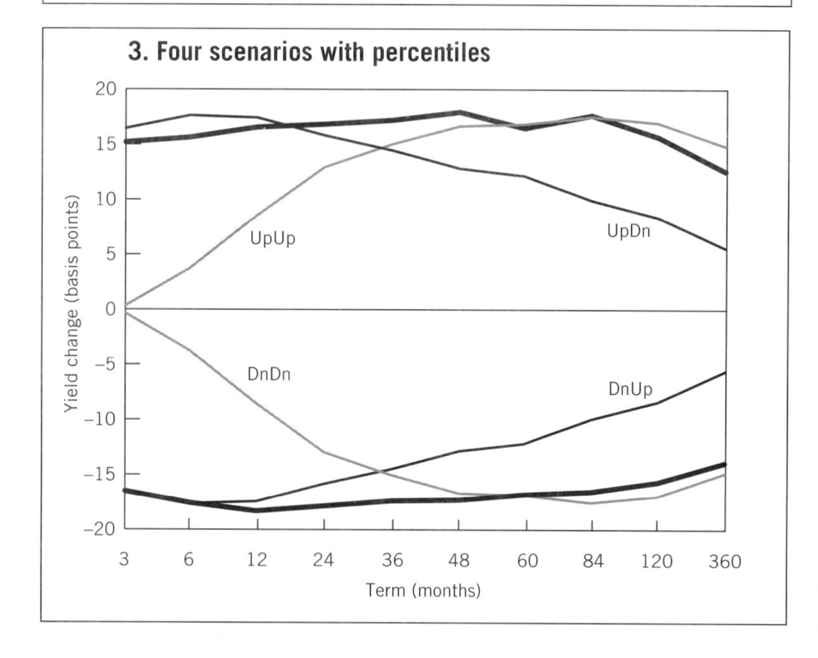

3. Four scenarios with percentiles

Figure 3 shows the 1st and 99th percentiles of the data. The two bold lines correspond to the 1st and 99th percentiles of the historical sample. For example, the 99th percentile of the three-month rate equals 15.2 basis points. The four other lines denote the four scenarios based on the shift and twist factors. The factor-based scenarios move the curve by an amount approximately equal to the 99th (or 1st) percentile.

The three-month rate rises by more than 15.2 basis points on just one day in a hundred. By contrast, scenario UpDn (interest rates generally move higher while the yield curve flattens) moves the three-month rate higher by 16.4 basis points. Thus one of the scenarios approximates the 99th percentile at the three-month point on the curve. The same is true at every point of the curve: the amount of movement represented by the 1st or 99th percentile is approximated by one of the four scenarios. If this were the only test of adequacy – that a set of scenarios reflects broad overall movements in interest rates – the two-factor, four-scenario model would appear to pass. However, if the portfolio to be analysed responds to differences between rates, it is preferable to check the modelling of spreads along the curve.

Scatterplots appear to provide the most insight in investigating the adequacy of two factors needed to explain spreads along the yield curve. Figure 4 compares the daily changes in the three-month yield and the six-month yield to four points corresponding to the four factor-based scenarios. For example, the scenario DnUp moves the three-month rate down 16.4 basis points and moves the six-month rate down 17.6 basis points; it appears as the lowest of the four scenario points on the graph. A polygon connects the four scenario points. Historical changes in three-month and six-month yields appear as + signs.

Many data points lie outside the polygon. The outliers tend to clump along the broad sides of the polygon rather than at the points in the first and third quadrants. So the scenario points reflect the cases where the three-month and six-month rates rise together or fall together, but fail to adequately reflect cases where the rates move in different directions. While the first two principal components describe the broad movements of the yield curve, they fail to describe movements in the six-month/three-month interest rate spread. This suggests adding a third or fourth factor.

The third factor, Bow-1, equals PC3 times its standard deviation. Adding that to shift and twist results in eight scenarios. Each of the previous four scenarios gives rise to two offspring, one in which Bow-1 rises and one in which Bow-1 falls. Adding Bow-2 (PC4 times its standard deviation) results in the 16 scenarios displayed in Figure 5, along with the market data of Figure 4. Eight of the scenario points define the periphery subject to stress, and eight others lie within the area. (The latter are not wasted; they appear on the periphery of scatterplots involving other points on the curve.) The resulting polygon appears to adequately contain the historical data on three-month and six-month rates, and a similar conclusion follows from inspection of each of the other 44 scatterplots involving pairs of variables.

Figure 6 displays the loadings of the first four principal components, which can be interpreted as features of daily changes on the yield curve. The sum of the squares of the loadings of each principal component equals one. The scale of any one loading therefore lacks direct interpretation.

PC1 appears as nearly a uniform shift and PC2

4. Four scenarios for three-month and six-month rates

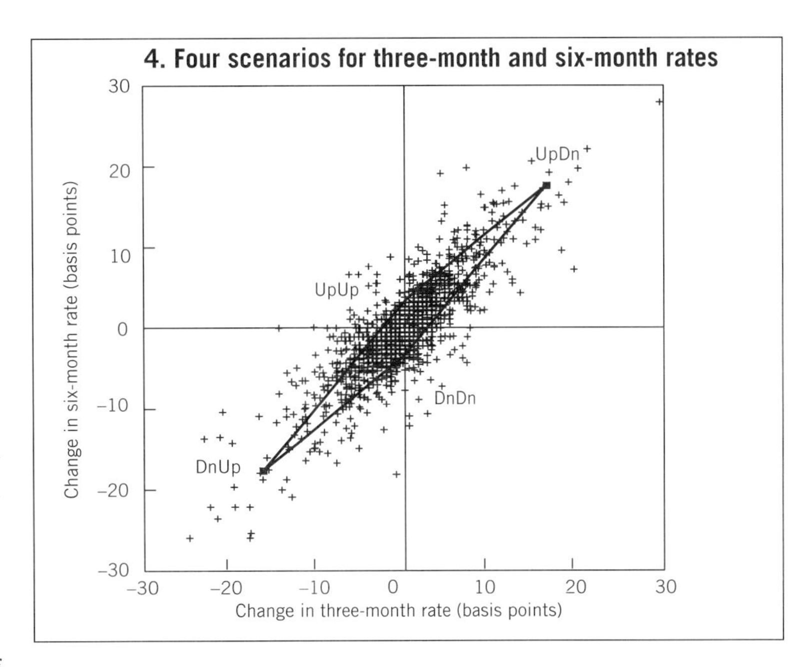

5. Sixteen scenarios for three-month and six-month rates

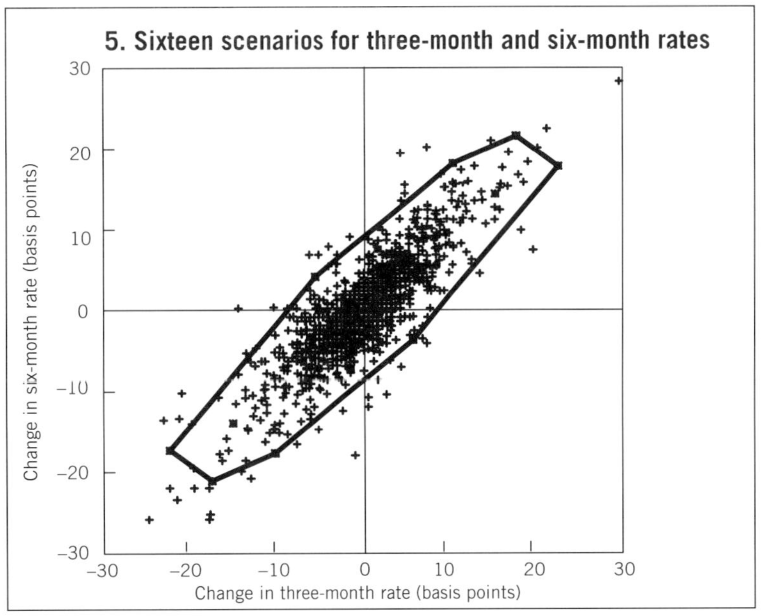

6. First four principal components

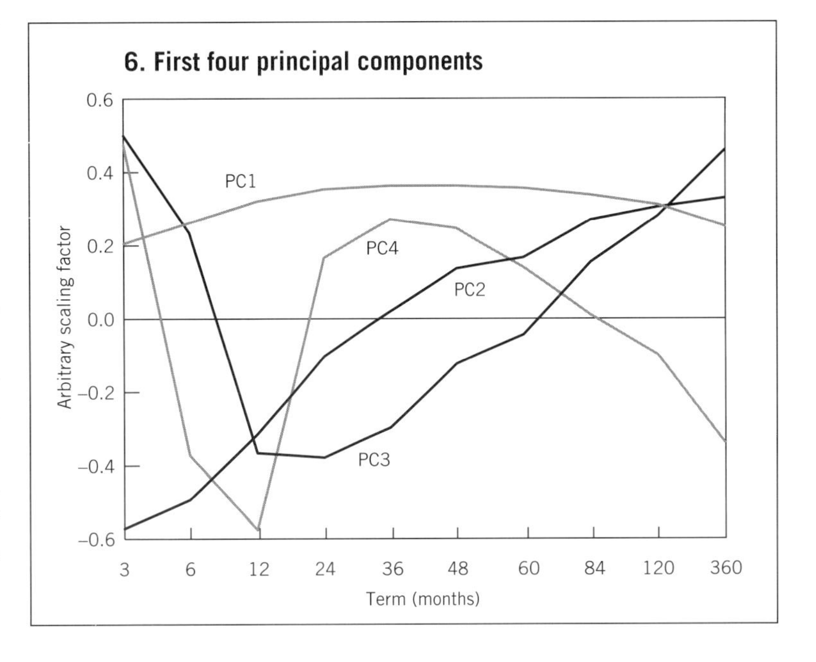

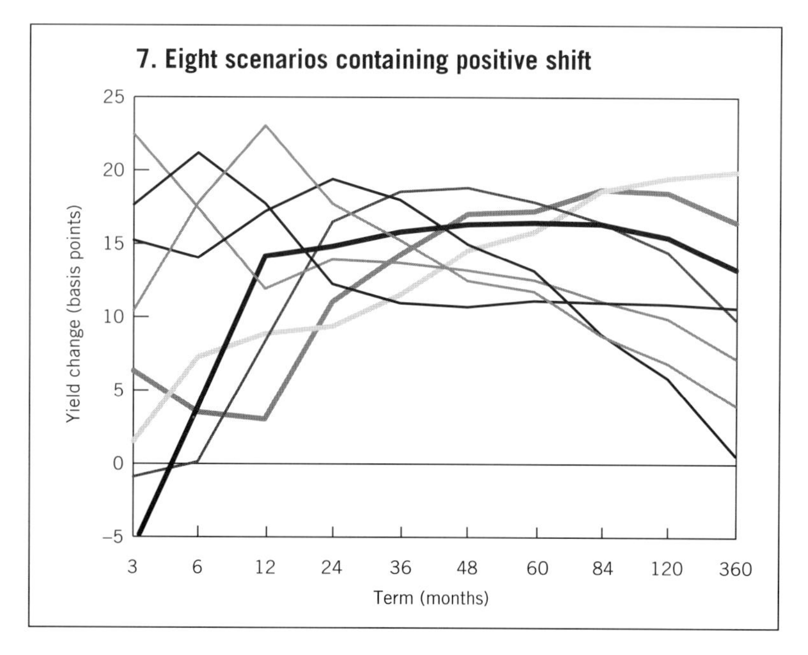

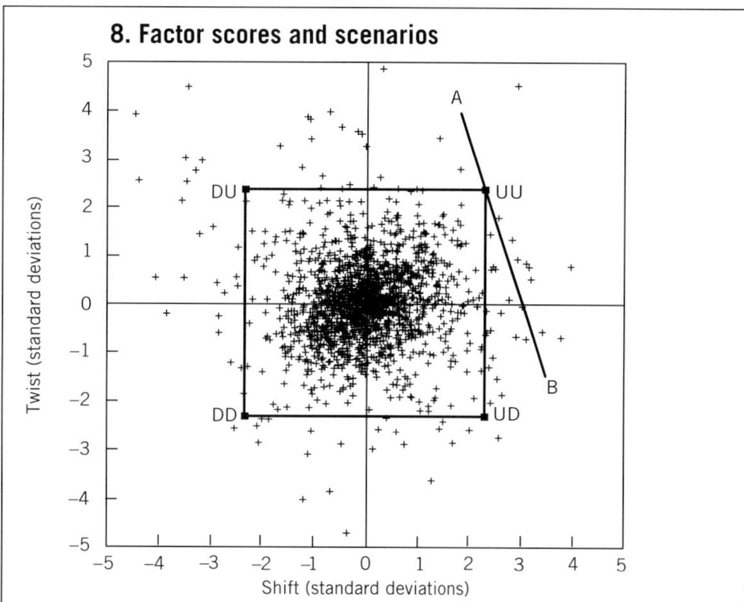

appears as nearly a linear twist. PC3 allows the short end of the yield curve to steepen (flatten) while the long end flattens (steepens). PC4 introduces contrast between the three-month and the six-month, and between the one-year and the two-year points on the curve. As seen in Figures 4 and 5, these contrasts provide an improvement in explaining some spreads that may have significance for certain portfolios.

Figure 7 shows eight of the 16 scenarios that stem from the first four factors. These eight contain the shift factor operating in the positive direction. The other eight scenarios would appear as mirror opposites of these. The message of Figure 7 is simply that the scenarios resulting from the first four factors display a very wide range of yield curve movements, demonstrating the richness of the scenarios produced by the factor-based method. Even if a portfolio contains long and short positions and depends on spreads and subtle interrelations on the yield curve, its risks should be revealed by one or another of these scenarios.

Non-option portfolios

Most of the issues that affect the accuracy of the factor-based scenario method make themselves felt within simple portfolios that do not contain options. Still, the factor-based method approximates the percentile of loss observed in historical data. The error of approximation tends to be one of overstatement – the conservative result from the perspective of most users of risk control. For example, using 2.33 standard deviations to construct scenarios tends to result in a VAR estimate greater than the 99th percentile of the loss distribution.

The basic conservatism of the factor-based method stems from the interaction of three competing influences. In isolation, the first two influences would lead to an understatement of risk, the third to an overstatement:

(a) The factors may have a non-normal distribution with fat tails. A factor would exceed 2.33 standard deviations in more than 1% of cases. Other things being equal, this influence would cause the factor-based estimate of VAR to understate risk.

(b) The portfolio may depend on factors of higher order than those used in constructing the scenarios. Scenarios based only on the first four factors would underestimate the risk of such a portfolio.

(c) The portfolio may depend on two or more of the first four factors.

The last situation occurs in the majority of cases and warrants further exploration. To simplify the discussion, assume that only two factors matter, shift and twist, and that they have a bivariate normal distribution. Figure 8 displays the scatterplot of the factor scores for the 1,543 days of data and the four scenario points.

If the portfolio in question responds linearly to the two factors, within the region of a rectangle such as that in Figure 8, the portfolio will achieve its maximum loss at a corner. Suppose the greatest loss occurs at point UU. The linearity of the profit function implies the set of points at which loss is equal to that at UU will appear as a straight line through UU.

Consider three cases. In the first, a portfolio depends only on the shift factor and not on the twist factor. Its loss will exceed the loss at point

UU only if the factor score for shift exceeds 2.33 – that is, only if the data point appears to the right of the vertical line passing through point UU. The probability that this occurs equals 1% under the normality assumption. Therefore the portfolio loss that arises from scenario UU will represent the 99th percentile loss. Second, consider a portfolio that depends only on the twist factor. Its loss will exceed that at point UU only if the factor score for twist exceeds 2.33 and the point appears above the horizontal line through UU. Again, the probability equals 1% and the portfolio value at point UU will again represent the 99th percentile loss. Finally, consider a portfolio that depends on both shift and twist. It will have a loss greater than at point UU only if the combination of shift and twist results in a point located above a line such as AB in Figure 8. A slanted line such as AB is further, on average, from the centre of the distribution than either the horizontal or vertical line through UU and isolates less of the probability space. The probability that a point will be above AB is less than 1%, so the value at UU represents a percentile of the loss distribution above the 99th percentile. The factor-based method therefore tends to overstate risk for portfolios that depend on more than one factor.

Figure 9 examines the practical importance of these three sources of estimation error. Each point in Figure 9 represents a randomly-generated portfolio of fixed income instruments.[4] Each portfolio was subjected to two experiments. The daily P&L was simulated for each of the 1,543 days of data – the 99th percentile of the distribution of these losses establishes the horizontal position of the point. Then the VAR of the portfolio was estimated by the factor-based scenario method. The portfolio was valued under each of the sixteen scenarios (eight of which appear in Figure 7), and the greatest loss among these establishes the vertical position of the point. When a point lies on the 45° line, the factor-based scenario method has succeeded in estimating the 99th percentile of the loss distribution for that portfolio.

Figure 9 makes several points. First, understatements of risk are few and small. This serves the risk control function by protecting against unpleasant surprises. Qualitatively, the conservatism introduced by influence (c), above, tends to dominate the influences of (a) and (b). Second, the factor-based scenario method tends to greater accuracy (as a fraction of the 99th percentile historical risk) for the portfolios that have greatest risk. This partly reflects the fact that the most risky portfolio will tend to respond to the most volatile factor rather than to a combination of several factors. Third, the average overstatement of risk (20.2%) and the variation in its overstatement (standard deviation = 15.7%) are within a range that senior managers (if not traders) may find acceptable. When options enter the picture they tend to absorb some, but generally not all, of this inherent conservatism.

9. Risk estimate and 99th percentile loss

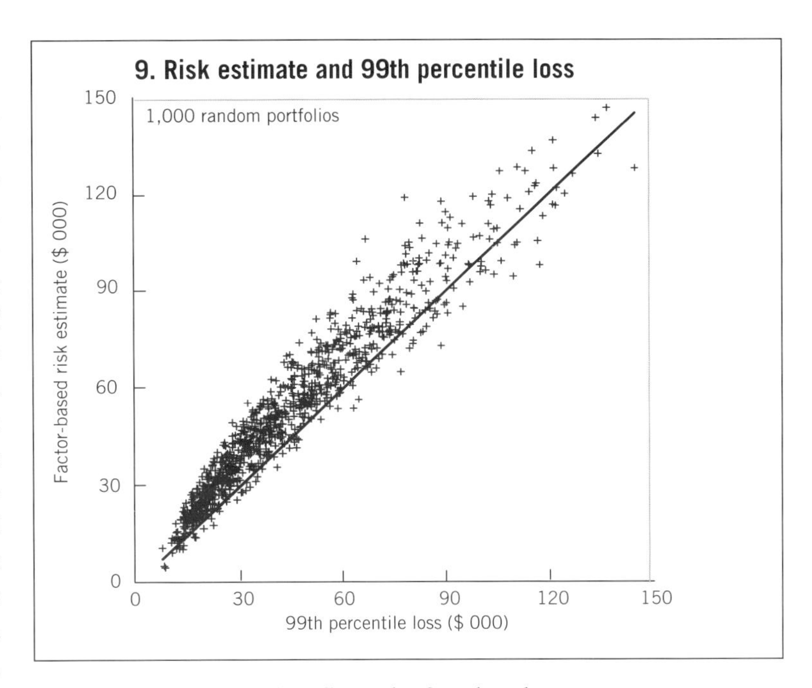

Portfolios containing options

Introducing options adds two elements to the analysis. First, option values depend on an additional parameter, volatility, and changes in volatility can affect portfolio value just as much as changes in interest rates. For the factor-based method, this adds one or more dimensions to those already identified. The resulting scenarios combine an interest rate shift and a volatility shift.

Second, options on fixed-income instruments have a much more non-linear response to interest rates than swaps, bonds, or futures. The non-linear response of options presents two challenges to the accuracy of the factor-based scenario method. Both challenges were met in the one-market environment. The most important issue is the potential that large losses might occur between scenario points. Through a variety of means the user can gain confidence that this is not the case for the portfolio at hand. Take as a representative portfolio the options held by an institutional participant in the fixed-income option market.[5] The portfolio reflects various market-making, hedging, and position-taking

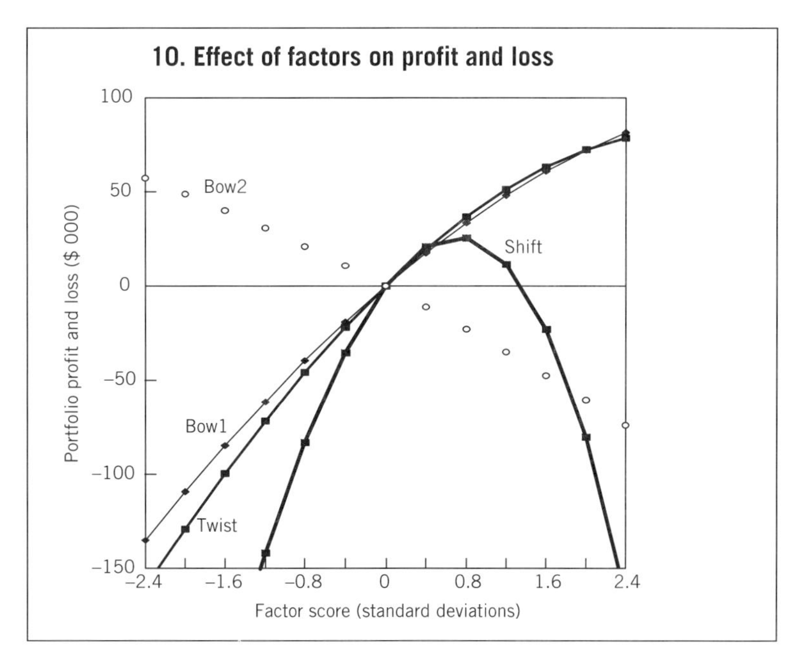

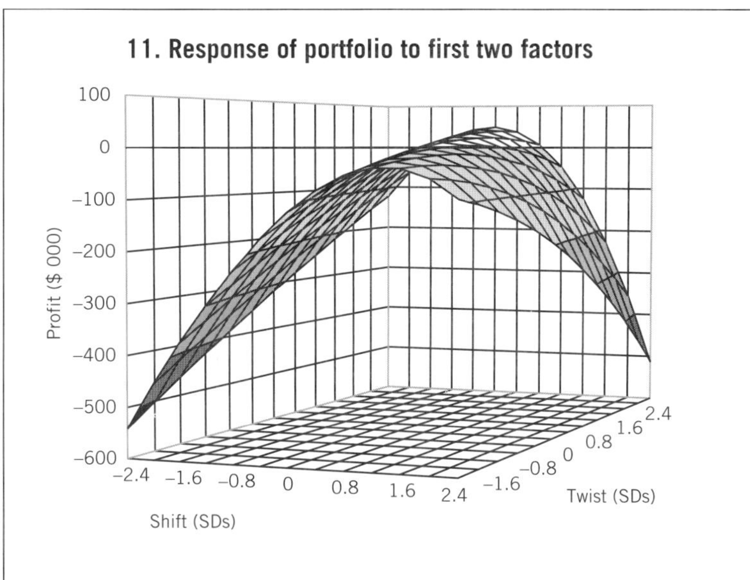

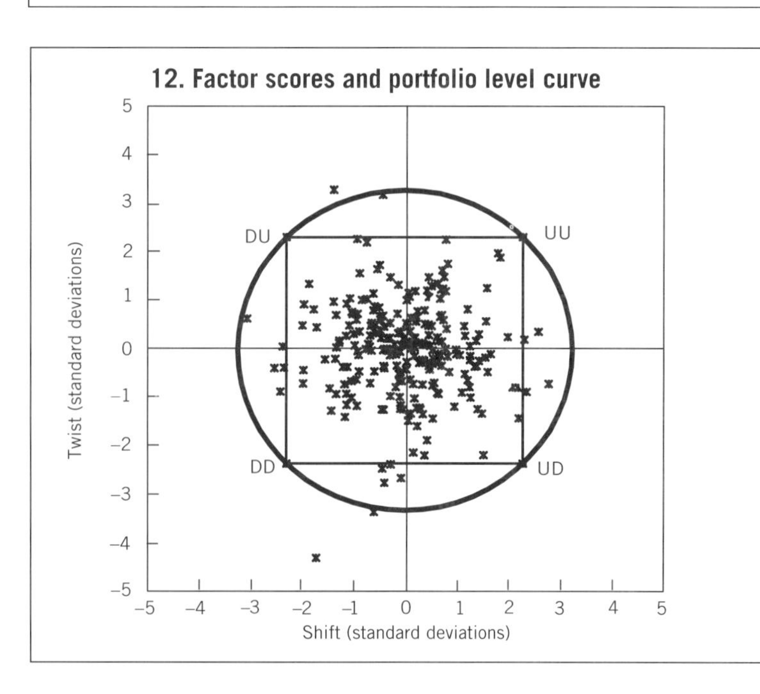

activities and contains options on 13 contracts of Treasury Bond futures, Treasury Note futures, and Five-Year Treasury futures. Just over $100 billion of securities underlay the options of this portfolio. To focus on the issue of non-linearity, a hedging set of T-Bond, T-Note, and Five-Year futures was included to minimise the maximum loss under any scenario.[6]

Figure 10 shows the portfolio profit and loss response to independent movements of each of the four factors. Each factor score is allowed to have an independent effect on the representative portfolio. Concavity is most apparent for the shift factor but is present for all factors. As any factor is adjusted through a range of values, the greatest loss occurs at one of the endpoints of the range.

The shift line shows the outcome when the shift factor score takes on various values (measured in standard deviations), while the other factors remain fixed. The portfolio is evidently long shift in that it tends to make money when shift has a small positive score. However, a large absolute shift score, either positive or negative, results in a loss. One can see that the portfolio is more sensitive to shift than any other factor and least sensitive to Bow-2. Most important, the response to each factor has concave curvature. On each plotted line, just as for a short option straddle, the maximum loss in any region occurs at one of the endpoints of the region.

Figure 11 shows the portfolio's concave profit surface as a function of the first two factors. The four corners of the floor of the diagram correspond to the four corners of the rectangle in Figure 8. The concavity of the surface implies that the greatest loss on a rectangular region occurs at one of the corners, specifically the corner where both shift and twist decline. This corresponds to scenarios beginning DD. The portfolio has the character of a short straddle and can also experience large losses in the diagonally opposite case of scenarios beginning UU.

The second challenge, implicit in the concavity of the profit surface, is that multiple areas of factor space may contribute to the probability that the loss will exceed the VAR estimate. This is analogous to the situation of Figure 1, in which the portfolio suffered a loss exceeding VAR both when the price rose 2.33 standard deviations and when the price fell 6.4 standard deviations. In the four-factor case, Figure 10 suggests the position could lose more than VAR given a sufficiently large movement in any of the four factors.

This might seem to imply the potential for a large understatement of risk, but such is not the case. Consider the story told by Figure 12 for a hypothetical portfolio in the two-factor case. Data points illustrate the probability density of the factor scores and a level curve represents the profit of a hypothetical portfolio. This portfolio experiences the same loss at every scenario point and at every point along the cir~~ular line connecting the scenario points. Loss at any point outside the circle will be greater than at the scenario points. Inspection shows few such points; for normally distributed factors the probability outside the circle is 0.5%. Despite the potential for the movement of either factor to cause loss exceeding VAR, the estimate remains conservative.

Intuitively, the curvature of the level curve causes it to miss the high-density areas between it and the square connecting the scenario points. It seems that the profit function cannot conform closely enough to the square to result in an understatement of risk, despite the chance for extreme movement of either factor to trigger a loss greater than VAR.

The level curve of a portfolio with a concave profit function might look also like that in Figure 13. Clearly, the probability outside such a curve exceeds the probability above the tangent line AB. That tangent line is the level curve of a linearly responding portfolio. Though the VAR estimate for linear portfolios was found to be conservative in Figures 8 and 9, introducing options might reduce confidence in the estimate.

A historical simulation of the representative portfolio provides evidence that the factor-based scenario method estimate remains conservative, nonetheless. Figure 14 shows the distribution of profit and loss for 300 out-of-sample days of interest rate history, the 99th percentile loss, and the factor-based scenario VAR estimate. The distribution resembles that for a short options position – many small profits and some large losses. The VAR estimate appears conservative relative to this test.

The factor-based scenario method can provide many benefits in estimating VAR: it produces a quick, easily interpreted result that is valid for option-intensive portfolios with negative gamma. However, it cannot guarantee accuracy for any type of portfolio sensitive to any set of risk factors. Generally the method works best when the portfolio appears to depend on a small number of factors, as with portfolios of fixed income instruments within a particular country or for spot foreign exchange risk among major countries. At the other extreme, a portfolio of options on individual stocks might be a poor candidate for factor-based VAR estimation if, for example, the spread between two gold stocks has a strong effect on profit; such a spread relationship might require many principal components to model adequately. Note that both the nature of the position and the statistical properties of market variables must be taken into any assessment of appropriateness.

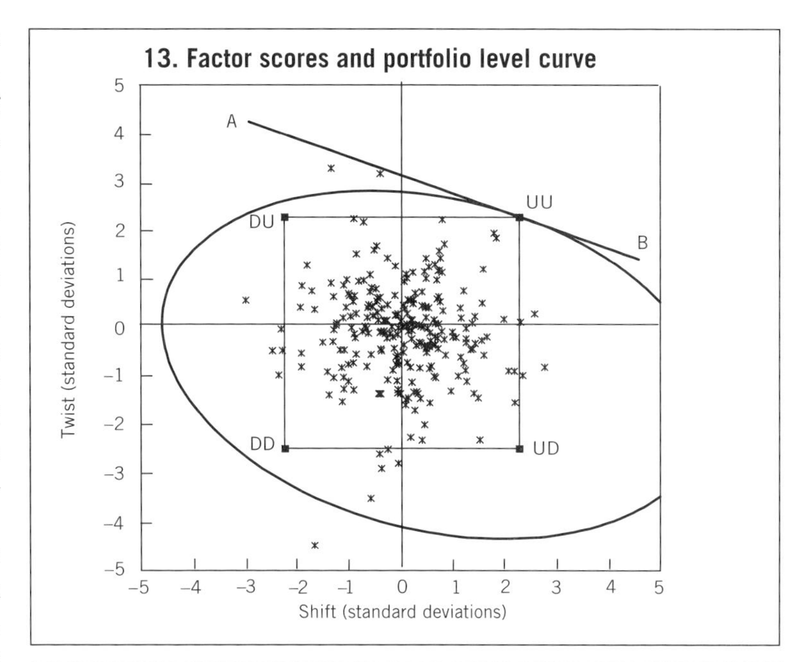

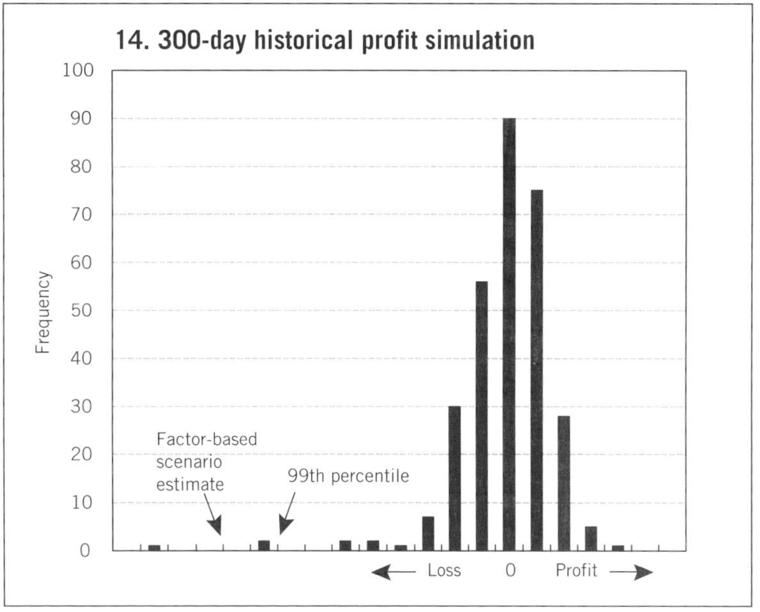

Conclusion

For portfolios of fixed income instruments dominated by short options positions, the factor-based scenario method tends to produce conservative estimates of VAR. The method chooses a set of interest rate scenarios and values the portfolio under each. The greatest loss that comes about under any scenario serves as the VAR estimate.

The scenario that produces the greatest loss characterises the market movement most dangerous for the portfolio.

Each scenario combines factors, referred to here as shift, twist, Bow-1, and Bow-2. Shift appears as a nearly uniform increase (or decrease) in yields at all points of the yield curve. Twist appears as a pivoting of the yield curve where long-term rates rise (or fall) relative to short-term rates. Bow-1 and Bow-2 induce more complex movements. In each scenario, each factor operates in either the positive direction or the negative direction.

The statistical technique of principal components analysis determines the factors. Principal components analysis can be viewed as equivalent to a regression study that finds optimal independent variables. The first principal component represents the most typical movement of the yield curve. Multiplying by its standard deviation produces the shift factor. The other factors have similar definitions.

Basing the scenarios on 2.33 standard deviations (corresponding to 99% confidence for a normal distribution), the risk estimate tends to overstate the 99th percentile of the loss distribution. That is because the factor-based scenario method tends to overstate risk for portfolios that depend on more than one factor - and most portfolios depend on multiple factors.

Appendix A

PROOF OF A DUALITY BETWEEN PCA AND REGRESSION ANALYSIS

Given: an N^*p matrix of mean-adjusted (the column means equal 0) data, Y.
Define: an arbitrary, normal p^*1 vector x (that is, $x'x = 1$).
Then: The cumulated sum of squares from N independent regressions of the rows of Y on x reaches its minimum when x equals the first principal component of the data Y.

Proof: Let Y_i' symbolise the ith row of the matrix Y. The ith regression takes the form

$$Y_i = \hat{a}\,x + e_i$$

where $\hat{a}$ is the regression coefficient and e_i is a p^*1 vector of residuals. Minimising $e_i'e_i$ subject to $x'x = 1$ implies

$$\hat{a} = Yi'\,x.$$

A row vector of regression residuals is then $Y_i' - Y_i'xx'$ and the Nxp matrix of residuals from all regressions is $Y - Yxx'$. The cumulated sums of squares from all regressions equals

$$\begin{aligned} CumSSE &= trace((Y - Yxx')\,(Y - Yxx')') \\ &= trace(YY - Yxx'Y') \\ &= trace(YY') - trace(x'Y'Yx) \\ &= trace(YY') - N\,x'Sx \end{aligned}$$

where $S = Y'Y/N$ is the variance-covariance matrix of Y. By definition, among all normal vectors x, the first principal component of Y maximises $x'Sx$. Therefore $CumSSE$ reaches its minimum when x is chosen as the first principal component.

Appendix B

MATHEMATICAL DEFINITION OF PRINCIPAL COMPONENTS

Most multivariate statistics texts provide an introduction to principal components analysis. A background in statistics and matrix algebra is helpful in exploring this topic.

Let Y be an N^*p matrix of data.

The first principal component of Y is the p^*1 vector x_1 that maximises the variance of $x_1'y$ subject to $x_1'x_1 = 1$.

The second principal component of Y is the p^*1 vector x_1 that maximises the variance of $x_2'y$ subject to $x_2'x_2 = 1$ and $x_2'x_1 = 0$.

The other principal components are defined similarly. It can be shown that the principal components equal the eigenvectors of S, the variance-covariance matrix of Y. Therefore,

$$S = PD^2P'$$

where P is a matrix having the eigenvectors of S as its columns and D^2 is a diagonal matrix of the eigenvalues of S in decreasing order from left to right. In the terminology of this article, the columns of P are the principal components loadings and the columns of PD are factors shift, twist, etc.

1 *This article defines "loading" as an element of an eigenvector of the covariance matrix. Some software packages may use the same word to mean an element of an eigenvector of the* correlation *matrix, a correlation between a data series and a component, or an element of an eigenvector times the square root of its associated eigenvalue. To resolve uncertainty, note that the sum of the squares of the elements of an eigenvector equals 1.*

2 *For proof, see Appendix A.*

3 *Up to a multiplicative factor. Constraining the sum of the squares of the loadings to equal 1.0 results uniquely in the first principal component.*

4 *The quantity of a security is a random normal with mean zero and standard deviation equal to $10,000,000 divided by duration. Therefore, all securities have the same expected dollar risk.*

5 *Changes have been made to safeguard proprietary information.*

6 *The hedge does not insulate the portfolio from movements in futures contracts or factors.*

BIBLIOGRAPHY

Beckstrom, R., and A. Campbell, eds, 1995, *An Introduction to VAR*. C*ATS Software.

Hendricks, D., 1996, "Evaluation of Value-at-Risk Models Using Historical Data", *Federal Reserve Bank of New York Economic Policy Review* 2, no. 1 pp. 39–69; reprinted as Chapter 22 of the present volume

Jordan, J.V., and R.J. Mackay, 1995, "Assessing Value-at-Risk for Equity Portfolios: Implementing Alternative Techniques", Working Paper, Center for Study of Futures and Options Markets, Virginia Polytechnic Institute.

JP Morgan, 1994, *RiskMetrics Technical Document*, New York.

Litterman, R. and J. Scheinkman, 1991, "Common Factors Affecting Bond Returns", *Journal of Fixed Income* 1, pp. 54–61.

Morrison, D.F., 1976, *Multivariate Statistical Methods*, McGraw Hill.

Pritsker, M., 1997, "Evaluating Value at Risk Methodologies: Accuracy versus Computational Time", *Journal of Financial Services Research*, forthcoming; reprinted as Chapter 27 of the present volume.

30

Scrambled Nets for Value-at-Risk Calculations

Art Owen and Domingo Tavella
Stanford University and Align Risk Analysis

This paper explores the performance of a new low discrepancy sequence when applied to the computation of the standard deviation of two very simple, low dimensional value-at-risk problems. The new sequence is constructed by a hybrid, known as scrambled nets, of Monte Carlo and quasi-Monte Carlo methods. Scrambled nets are as efficient as the deterministic quasi-Monte Carlo methods, but unlike them, they also allow for data-based estimation of accuracy. We present a detailed comparison of Monte Carlo, Sobol sequences and scrambled nets. In the examples we consider, scrambled nets appear to be at least as accurate as Sobol sequences and require of the order of one fiftieth as many function evaluations as Monte Carlo sequences. Standard errors estimated for the values at risk are less than one tenth of 1% of the estimated VAR.

The value-at-risk of a financial contract may be represented by a suitable multiple of the standard deviation of the contract value. The value of a financial contract is a function of a number of underlying stochastic variables, such as forward rates or indexes. When the value of the contract is linear in the underlying variables, the standard deviation of the contract value can be computed from the covariance matrix of the underlying variables. In cases where the contract value is a non-linear function of the underlying variables, simulation techniques are widely used to estimate the standard deviation.

There are two types of simulation approach – Monte Carlo methods and quasi-Monte Carlo methods. The former are characterised by rates of convergence that are independent of the dimension. The latter have superior asymptotic convergence rates, though the superiority is dimensionally-dependent, and error estimation is more difficult.

This paper aims to explore the effectiveness of a new type of quasi-random sequence, the Randomised Quasi-Monte Carlo (RQMC) sequence, in VAR problems. We have selected two simple financial contracts for study: a zero coupon bond and an interest rate cap. We have deliberately chosen low-dimensional problems as a first step in investigating (RQMC) for VAR problems. Some high-dimensional Quasi-Monte Carlo (QMC) simulations have been used in financial problems elsewhere. See, for instance, Paskov and Traub (1995) and Caflisch and Morokoff (1996).

Risk manager's summary

This paper describes improvements on Monte Carlo methods for estimating VAR. Improved estimates of VAR are possible, meaning that VAR can be estimated with greater accuracy. Of course this does not mean reducing the actual level of risk: no sampling technique can do that!

In the numerical examples, we find that scrambled nets are more accurate than plain Monte Carlo. In fact it would require a simulation about 50 times as long in plain Monte Carlo to get the same accuracy as we found with scrambled nets. The practical impact of this for some risk managers may simply be that it saves some computer time. But others may be able to calculate VAR for more portfolios or under more scenarios than they would be able to using other methods.

Another way to express this difference is that the VAR estimate will differ from the true VAR by less under randomised quasi-Monte Carlo than it will under Monte Carlo. The estimate can be higher or lower than the truth with either method. But, using the same number of runs, the error will tend to be greater under ordinary Monte Carlo than with randomised quasi-Monte Carlo. In our examples, a factor of 50 in variance translates into a factor of $\sqrt{50} \doteq 7$ in errors. The VAR error under Monte Carlo would then be about seven times as large.

The quasi-Monte Carlo and randomised quasi-Monte Carlo methods were of about equal accuracy. But randomised quasi-Monte Carlo has one advantage: the accuracy of the VAR can be estimated by comparing replicates. So risk managers can decide if the simulation should be larger, or if it could be smaller. Under ordinary quasi-Monte Carlo, by contrast, there is no principled way of estimating the accuracy of a VAR result from the data used to produce it.

But it must be stressed that any improvement is dependent on the model being simulated and the portfolio whose value is being assessed. So the performance ratio could be higher or lower than 50 on another problem. There are some theoretical and empirical reasons to expect that the randomised quasi-Monte Carlo results should never be much, if any, worse than ordinary Monte Carlo.

Value-at-risk

The value of the financial contracts we consider is determined by the term structure of interest rates. We characterise the term structure of interest rates by correlated stochastic processes $B_i(t, t+t_i)$, $i = 1, \ldots, I$. The quantity $B_i(t, t+t_i)$ denotes the value of an account continuously reinvested in zero coupon bonds of maturity $t+t_i$.

We can think of B_i as the value of a "constant maturity" zero coupon bond. The correlated stochastic processes are governed by

$$\frac{dB_i}{B_i} = \mu_i dt + \sigma_i dW_i \qquad (1)$$

where the μ_i are drift parameters determined from arbitrage constraints, the σ_i are volatilities, and the W_i are correlated Wiener processes.

The value of the kth financial contract at time t is a function

$$Y_k = Y_k(t) = g_k\big(B_1(t, t+t_1), \ldots, B_I(t, t+t_I)\big) \qquad (2)$$

of some or all of the B_i.

The financial contract's VAR is a suitable multiple of the standard deviation of Y_k.

We characterise the US term structure over 20 years by five stochastic processes. The bond we consider is a zero coupon bond with a 20-year maturity. The cap is a 20-year cap with semi-annual caplets and a cap rate close to the initial value of the forward rate.

Monte Carlo simulation

A simulation approach to this problem is as follows: the risk manager generates six independent uniformly distributed random variables, makes a polar transformation to normally distributed random variables, induces the means, variances and correlations appropriate to interest rate fluctuations over seven days, and then computes the resulting value of the derivative, subsuming the function g_k from equation (2). This is repeated independently, many times, and the mean and standard deviation of the resulting histogram is reported.

Figure 1 shows such a histogram for the cap. This histogram shows some "shoulders" which may represent caplets moving in or out of the money, though we should caution that this effect is quite subtle and may not be statistically significant. The histogram for the bond is similar, but more nearly normally distributed.

Let n be the number of simulations used. Let U_i, $i = 1, \ldots, n$ be n vectors of $d = 6$ uniform random variables. That is $U_i = (U_{i1}, \ldots, U_{i6})$ and all of the U_{ij} are independent $U[0,1]$ random variables. Let Y_i be the value of the instrument over seven days, and let f be the function that turns uniform

1. Histogram of cap values after seven days

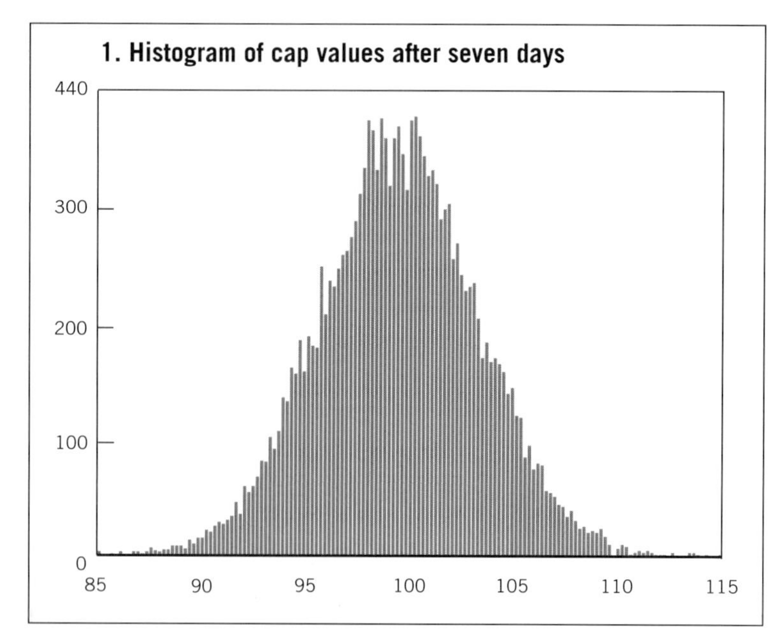

random variables into Gaussian random variables, induces means, variances and correlations, computes new interest rates and then finds the instrument's value.

Then $Y_i = f(U_i)$, the estimated mean is

$$\overline{Y} = \frac{1}{n}\sum_{i=1} Y_i$$

and the estimated standard deviation is

$$s_y = \sqrt{\frac{1}{n}\sum_{i=1}^{n}\left(Y_i - \overline{Y}\right)^2} \quad (3)$$

or perhaps

$$s_y^* = \sqrt{\frac{1}{n-1}\sum_{i=1}^{n}\left(Y_i - \overline{Y}\right)^2}. \quad (4)$$

The difference between s_y and s_y^* is not important for large n, in MC simulation. It can matter for RQMC simulation as described below, where s_y is to be preferred, at least for large n.

Standard statistical methods can be used to form approximate confidence intervals for these estimates. For example $\overline{Y} \pm 1.96 s_y \sqrt{n}$ is an approximate 95% confidence interval for μ. Approximate confidence intervals for σ are less widely known. Miller (1986) mentions some. The bootstrap (see Efron and Tibshirani [1993]), the jackknife (see Miller [1974]) or nonparametric likelihood ratio methods (see Owen [1990]) can also be used.

Quasi-Monte Carlo

The value $\overline{Y}$ is estimating a six fold integral

$$\mu = \int_{[0,1]^6} f(U)dU$$

and the value s_y is estimating

$$\sigma = \sqrt{\int_{[0,1]^6}\left(f(U) - \mu\right)^2 dU}$$

$$= \sqrt{\int_{[0,1]^6}\left(f(U)\right)^2 dU - \left(\int_{[0,1]^6}\left(f(U)\right)dU\right)^2}.$$

Therefore if these six-dimensional integrals can be done more accurately than by Monte Carlo simulation, the VAR can be calculated more quickly or more accurately. Quasi-Monte Carlo (QMC) integrals are a promising way to get better answers.

In QMC n vectors $U_1, \ldots, U_n$ are carefully constructed for use as above. Under Monte Carlo (MC), the points U_i tend to have some clumps and to leave some open spaces. Under QMC, the points U_i are constructed to have a much more even distribution.

Niederreiter (1992) gives an excellent account of Quasi-Monte Carlo methods. They can certainly be much more accurate than Monte Carlo methods, though it is still a research issue to determine what sort of integrands can be better integrated by QMC and for what value of n the improvement can be seen.

The QMC methods considered in this paper are known as (t,s)-sequences and (t,m,s)-nets. Their properties and some constructions are given by Niederreiter (1992). Some details are summarised below.

A drawback of deterministic QMC methods is that there is no practical way of estimating their accuracy from the values $Y_i = f(U_i)$.

Randomised QMC

By carefully randomising a QMC method, it is possible to produce random points $U_1, \ldots, U_n$ that are individually uniformly distributed on $[0,1]^d$ while avoiding the clumps and gaps of simpler random points.

Owen (1995) describes several such methods, including randomised (t,m,s)-nets and (t,s)-sequences. These are constructed by taking the (t,m,s)-net or (t,s)-sequence and scrambling their digits (in some base $b \geq 2$) at random. If the unscrambled points were a (t,m,s)-net or (t,s)-sequence, then the resulting points are still a (t,m,s)-net or (t,s)-sequence respectively.

Moreover, the resulting points $U_1, \ldots, U_n$ individually have the uniform distribution over $[0,1]^d$.

This uniformity makes $\overline{Y}$ an unbiased estimator of μ. By reducing the gaps and clusters among the U_i, the variance of $\overline{Y}$ is usually smaller under randomised QMC (RQMC) than it would be under MC. Carefully stated and proved theorems on this point are given in Owen (1997a). In summary, the RQMC variance divided by the MC variance typically tends to zero as n tends to infinity. For finite n the QMC variance can never be much larger than the MC variance, and the largest ratios are obtained at quite implausible integrands. The improvements in RQMC are greatest for integrands that are well approximated by sums of smooth (or at least coarse) functions of small dimension.

Surprisingly, randomising nets can improve their accuracy for integration problems. Owen (1997b) shows that for smooth integrands the variance of randomised net estimates is eventually of order $n^{-3}(\log n)^{d-1}$, yielding an error rate that is better by a factor of $n^{-1/2}$ than the one for unrandomised nets.

For an estimate of the uncertainty, take $r > 1$ independent replications of the scrambled net.

The results $\overline{Y}_j$, $j = 1, \ldots, r$ can be averaged to get $\overline{\overline{Y}}$. An unbiased estimate of the variance of $\overline{\overline{Y}}$ is

$$\frac{1}{r(r-1)} \sum_{j=1}^{r} \left(\overline{Y}_j - \overline{\overline{Y}} \right)^2 .$$

Because r is not necessarily large the denominator $r(r-1)$ may be significantly better than r^2. That is equation (4) is preferred to equation (3) for a small number r of independent replicates.

Owen (1997a) describes another method of constructing variance estimates. Instead of using r independently scrambled nets, a single large net is split into r equal length pieces. When this is done carefully, each of the pieces is also a net. Then $\overline{\overline{Y}}$ estimated this way is simply the average of all of the Y values seen. Splitting one net into r subnets will usually make $\overline{\overline{Y}}$ more accurate than using equally many function values taken from r independently randomised nets.

It will also usually be the case that the variance estimates obtained by using r pieces of a net are biased. On the average, over randomisations, this estimate overstates the true sampling variance of the statistic of interest, providing conservative estimates of uncertainty.

This section has described estimation of an average, not a standard deviation, even though standard deviations are of more importance here. The section on bias in standard deviations below considers the bias issues that arise when considering such statistics. For statistics such as the standard deviation, this bias is not ordinarily detrimental.

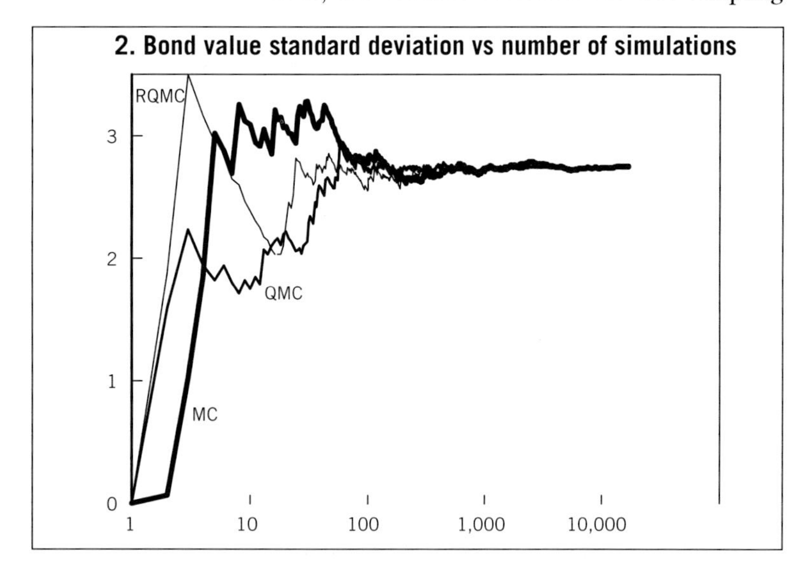

2. Bond value standard deviation vs number of simulations

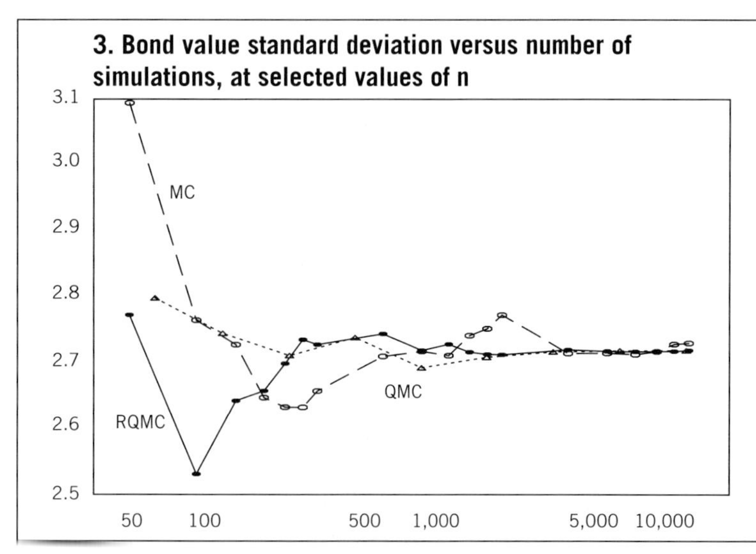

3. Bond value standard deviation versus number of simulations, at selected values of n

Bond example

The bond we consider is a zero coupon bond with a 20 year maturity. The value of this bond in seven days depends on the treasury curve as described above. We simulated via historically determined distributions, using MC, QMC and RQMC.

The MC method used independent identically distributed observations. The QMC method used was a Sobol sequence. The RQMC method used was a scrambled (t,m,s)-net, specifically a (0,5,6)-net in base 7. This net has $7^5 = 16807$ points in it, and is in fact the first 16807 points of a (0,6)-sequence in base 7. For comparison, 16807 MC and Sobol points were also used, though using only the first $2^{14} = 16384$ Sobol points might be preferable, since they are generated in base 2.

Figure 2 shows the running standard deviation s, based on the first n points of each series. The number of input points n is plotted on a logarithmic scale.

It is hard to discern the patterns in Figure 2 because the later points are so close together and the earlier points are erratic. Figure 3 shows the same running standard deviations for $n = \lambda 7^m$ for integers λ and m for which $49 \leq n \leq 16807$. By dropping points with $n < 49$, the vertical scale of the plot can be refined. When using the first n points of a randomised (t,s)-sequences in base b, it is best to use $n = b^m$ for some power m or λb^m for integer λ. Thus the points plotted are the best ones for RQMC accuracy.

In plots like Figure 2, it can appear that two methods are settling down to different answers. Sometimes this is an optical illusion, at least for MC. In MC plots, consecutive points on the curve are typically in the order of $1/n$ apart while they are in the order of $1/\sqrt{n}$ away from the true answer.

So two different MC plots can appear to have settled down to different answers, simply because the fluctuations within a curve are no guide to the error of the estimate at the end of the curve. Of course this could also arise if there were problems in the random number generator as reported by Paskov and Traub (1995). By spacing the points out nearly equally on the logarithmic scale, the fluctuations in the MC curve of Figure 3 are of a magnitude comparable to the error in the curve.

With RQMC the answers within a curve like Figure 2 also fluctuate by an amount of the order of $1/n$, but the errors in the estimate at points $n = \lambda b^m$ for large enough n (and smooth f) are of the order of $1/n\sqrt{n}$ (times logarithmic factors).

Thus with RQMC the fluctuations due to taking $n = \lambda b^m + 1$ can result in much greater error than taking $n = \lambda b^m$. For QMC the fluctuation in adding a point can be within logarithmic factors of the error magnitude.

It is possible to estimate the accuracy of the RQMC answer by independent repetitions. As we have already seen, there are reasons to prefer splitting the single series into subseries and treating them as repetitions. The original $7^5 = 16807$ RQMC points were split into seven data sets of $7^4 = 2401$ consecutive observations. The same was done for the MC points. Figure 4 shows trajectories like the ones in Figure 3, for the seven data subsets generated by each method. Since the QMC points are Sobol points, there is no reason to consider them in groups of size equal to a power of seven. A better comparison is to split the first $2^{14} = 16384$ Sobol points into eight groups of $2^{11} = 2048$ points.

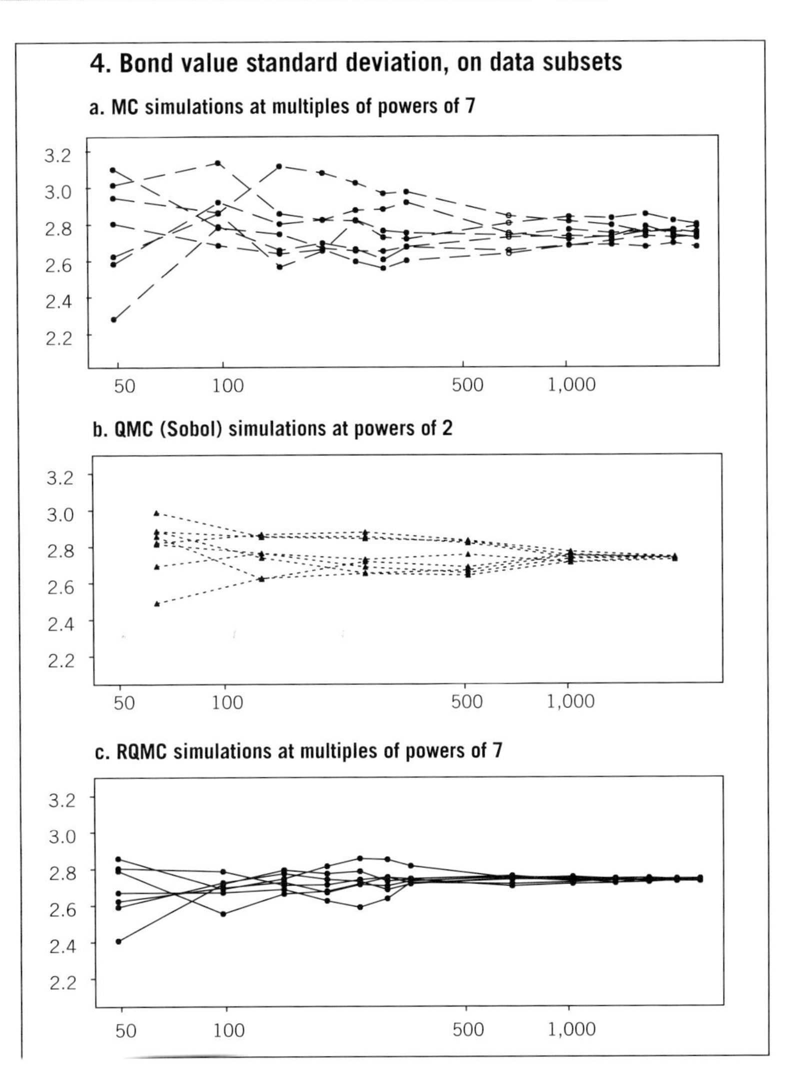

It is clear from Figure 4 that the running standard deviations from the QMC and RQMC points settle down much faster than the ones from MC points. The RQMC points appear to be slightly better than the QMC ones.

The mean of the seven values of the RQMC points at $n = 2401$ is $\bar{s} = 2.7366$. All empirical values are given to five significant figures, except for a few of them, referred to as approximate. The standard deviation of all 16,807 RQMC values is 2.7367. The standard deviation of the 7 RQMC values is 0.0058684. This allows us to estimate the sampling standard deviation of $\bar{s}$ by $0.0058684/\sqrt{7} = 0.0022180$. Adding plus or minus two of these standard errors to the estimate gives the interval (2.7322, 2.7411).

The MC points can be analysed in several ways, but for comparison we apply the same method as used for the RQMC points. The mean of the standard deviations from the seven data subsets is 2.7469. The standard deviation of them is 0.041770 and the corresponding interval is (2.7153, 2.7785).

The variance of the MC values is just over 50 times as large as the RQMC points, indicating that for this problem at least, RQMC has made a big improvement. Roughly speaking, comparable accuracy could be obtained with $50 * 2401 \doteq 120{,}000$ MC simulations as with 2401 RQMC simulations. Theory suggests that the efficiency ratio is even more favourable to RQMC for the actual sample size of 16,807. As mentioned above there is reason to believe that the variation among the RQMC points overestimates their true variation, and hence the ratio might well be larger than 51.

The MC interval contains the RQMC interval and is approximately 7.1 times as wide. The centre of the MC interval does not lie inside the RQMC interval, and there is no reason to expect that it should. Similarly, the standard deviation of all 16807 MC points is 2.7474 which is not in the RQMC interval, and neither is there any reason to expect that it should be in that interval. The standard deviation of the first 16384 Sobol points is 2.7366, and using all 16807 points only changes the final digit to 9 from 6. The QMC value is well within the RQMC interval, but the QMC method does not provide an interval of uncertainty.

Cap example

This section considers an interest rate cap related to the bond of the previous section.

The cap is a 20-year cap with semi-annual caplets and a cap rate close to the initial value of the forward rate. The value of the cap depends on the same interest rates as the bond and, as one would expect, it is negatively correlated with the bond.

5. Cap value standard deviation versus number of simulations, at selected values of n

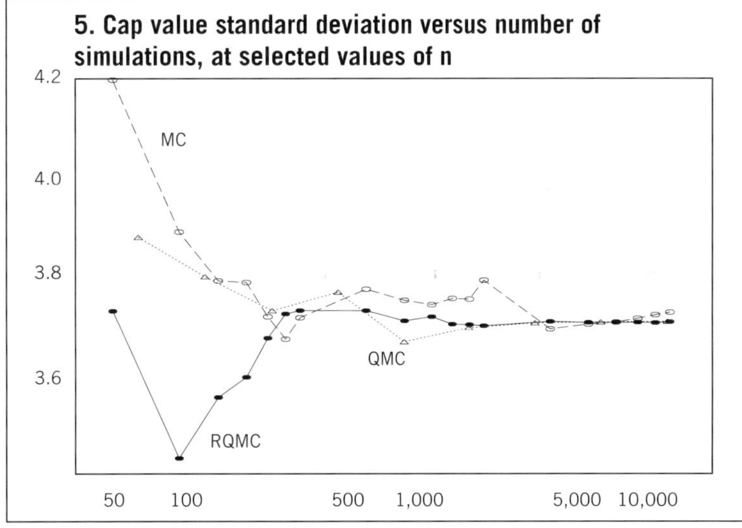

6. Cap value standard deviation, on data subsets

a. MC simulations at multiples of powers of 7

b. QMC (Sobol) simulations at powers of 2

c. RQMC simulations at multiples of powers of 7

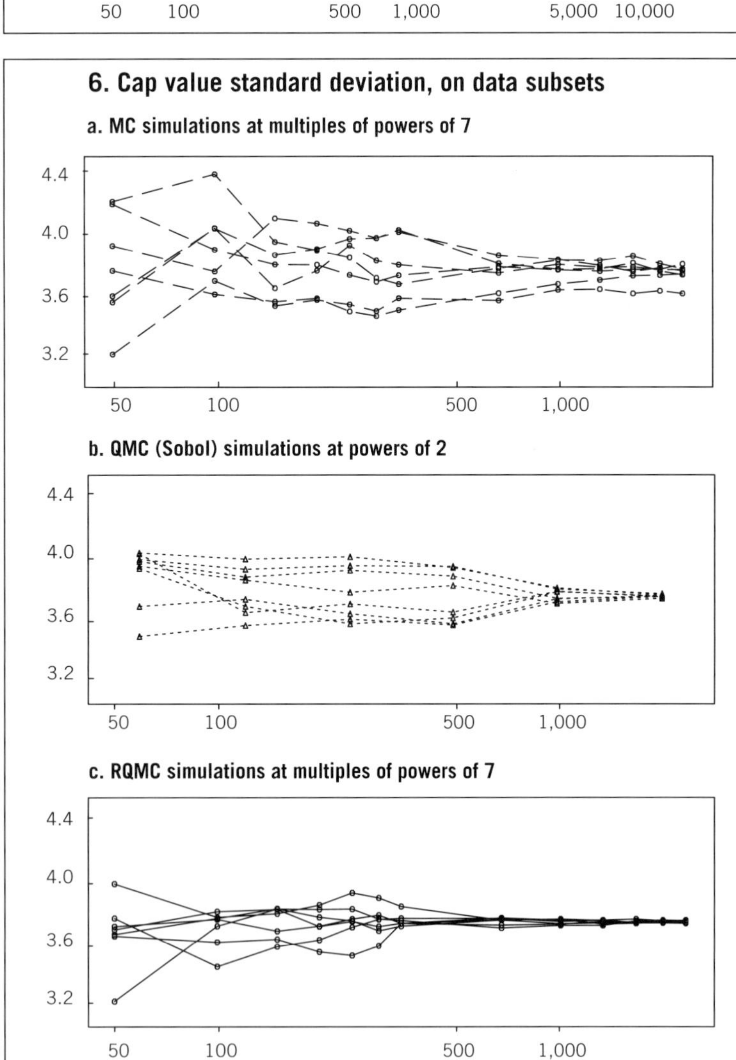

The analysis of the cap data is the same as used for the bond data. Figures 5 and 6 are the same as Figures 3 and 4, with cap values substituted for bond values. Once again, the QMC and RQMC points show much more rapid convergence than the MC points, and the RQMC points appear slightly better than the QMC ones.

For RQMC the mean of the seven data subset values is 3.7194, the standard deviation among them is 0.0075330 and the plus or minus two standard error interval is (3.7137, 3.7251). For MC the mean of the seven data subset values is 3.7374, the standard deviation among them is 0.062510 and the interval is (3.6902, 3.7847). The ratio of variances is approximately 69, in favour of the RQMC method. The QMC value based on the first 16384 observations is 3.7202.

Conclusions

For both VAR problems considered here, the Monte Carlo method was much slower to converge to the answer than either the QMC or RQMC methods. The QMC method appeared in the plots to be somewhat slower than RQMC, while the RQMC method allowed data-based estimates of the uncertainty in the VAR.

The standard deviation of the bond value over seven days was estimated to be 2.7367%. To this number we can attribute a sampling standard deviation of about 0.0022%, a relative error smaller than one part in a thousand. The standard deviation of the cap value over seven days was estimated to be 3.7194% with a sampling standard deviation of about 0.0028%.

In this case the RQMC method appeared to be about 70 times better than MC judged by efficiency. A ratio like this depends on the target function and the sample size. Theory says that as the sample size goes to infinity for a fixed integrand, this ratio does too.

For fixed n one can construct integrands for which the RQMC variance is higher than the MC variance, but that ratio cannot be large. On other integrands one has no reason to expect QMC methods to be much better than RQMC methods, because RQMC methods are themselves QMC methods. More details of this theory are given below and in the Bibliography.

Statistical issues

We now address some statistical questions that arise in this paper. First we consider the differences that arise in simulation based estimation of a standard deviation, as opposed to estimation of a mean. Then we consider why the usual practice of dividing by $n-1$ instead of n can in fact be harmful in RQMC simulations.

BIAS IN STANDARD DEVIATIONS

The description of RQMC and MC above assumed that the risk manager was interested in the average $\mu = E(Y)$, whereas in VAR calculations the risk manager is interested in the standard deviation $\sigma = \sqrt{V(Y)}$. It is well known that

$$\bar{Y} = \frac{1}{n}\sum_{i=1}^{n} Y_i$$

is unbiased for μ under MC and this is also true under RQMC. Under MC s_y^{*2} is unbiased for σ^2, while both s_y and s_y^* have some bias as estimators of σ.

We now consider whether this bias is important, and what happens with RQMC. Let us consider the situation where the risk manager wants to estimate a smooth function $g(\mu)$ by $g(\bar{Y})$. For non-linear functions g, there is usually some bias in this estimate. Simple Taylor expansion arguments show that the bias is

$$E\left(g\left(\bar{Y}\right)\right) - g(\mu) \doteq g''(\mu)V\left(\bar{Y}\right)/2$$

and that the variance is

$$V\left(g\left(\bar{Y}\right)\right) \doteq g'(\mu)^2 V\left(\bar{Y}\right)$$

where g' and g'' are the first two derivatives of g.

These both hold for MC and for RQMC. The squared error in $g(\bar{Y})$ is its variance plus the square of its bias. Because $V(\bar{Y})$ tends to zero as n increases, for large n the contribution of the bias squared ordinarily becomes negligible compared to the variance, for both MC and RQMC. Any exceptions involve special cases with $g'(\mu)$ equal or nearly equal to zero or $g''(\mu)$ infinite or extremely large.

Because $V(\bar{Y})$ tends to zero faster under RQMC than under MC, the bias becomes negligible more quickly under RQMC than under MC.

The standard deviation is not of the form $g(E(Y))$ but it is of the form $g(E(Y),E(Y)^2)$ and we estimate it by $g(\bar{Y}, \bar{Y}^2)$ where

$$\bar{Y}^2 = (1/n)\sum_{i=1}^{n} Y_i^2.$$

The same analysis applies except that the Taylor expansions have to become bivariate ones.

So, for either MC or RQMC, and large enough n, the bias ordinarily becomes negligible.

WHICH IS BETTER – S OR S*?

Should one estimate a standard deviation by s or by s^*? The ratio s/s^* is equal to

$$\sqrt{(n-1)/n} \doteq 1 - 1/(2n)$$

Therefore the choice of estimator makes a relative difference of roughly $1/2n$ in the value of the answer. For large enough n and MC sampling the issue is moot, because the estimate itself will differ from the truth by a larger amount of order $1/\sqrt{n}$.

For one of the data subsets, $1/2n$ is $1/2*2401$ or approximately 0.0002 for each of the seven replicates. This results in a relative difference of less than 0.5% of the confidence interval width for each MC example.

Because RQMC is usually more accurate than MC, the difference between s and s^* can matter. In the examples the difference between using these two methods is approximately equal to 3% of the width of the intervals. For most purposes this is negligible, but in other settings the difference could be important.

As n goes to infinity, for smooth functions, the RQMC variance eventually decreases proportionally to n^{-3} times logarithmic factors. By the argument above the error in s is ordinarily of order $n^{-3/2}$, times logarithmic factors. Therefore the difference between s and s^* is eventually larger than the error in s, and so s is to be preferred for large enough n.

Why is it that the argument about bias in standard deviations above does not also apply to s^*? The reason is that s^* is not expressible as a function $g(\bar{Y}, \bar{Y}^2)$, since it also depends on n. We can write $s^* = g(\bar{Y}, \bar{Y}^2, 1/n)$ with $\sigma = g(E(Y), E(Y^2), 0)$ for an appropriate function g but we cannot eliminate the effect of n.

Randomised (t,m,s)-nets and (t,s)-sequences

This section presents some background on (t,m,s)-nets and (t,s)-sequences based on Niederreiter (1992), and their randomisation based on Owen (1995, 1997a, 1997b.) For this section, we follow the conventions of using s to denote the dimension of the input space, and of integrating over the half open space $[0,1)^s$.

DEFINITIONS FOR NETS

Let $d = s \geq 1$ and $b \geq 2$ be integers. An *elementary interval* in base b is a hyperrectangular "cell" of the form

$$E = \prod_{j=1}^{s}\left[\frac{c_j}{b_j^{k_j}}, \frac{c_j+1}{b_j^{k_j}}\right)$$

for integers k_j, c_j with $k_j \geq 0$ and $0 \leq c_j < b^{k_j}$. The cell E has volume b^{-r} where $r = \sum_{j=1}^{s} k_j$.

Let $m \geq 0$ be an integer. A finite sequence of points X_i, $i = 1, \ldots, b^m$ from $[0,1)^s$ is a $(0,m,s)$-net in base b if every elementary interval E in base b of volume b^{-m} has exactly one of the points. That is, every elementary interval that "should" have one point of the sequence does have one point of the sequence.

This is a very strong form of equidistribution and by weakening it somewhat, constructions for more values of s and b become available. Let $t \leq m$ be a nonnegative integer. A finite sequence of b^m points from $[0,1)^s$ is a (t,m,s)-net in base b if every elementary interval in base b of volume b^{t-m} contains exactly b^t points of the sequence. Elementary intervals that "should" have b^t points do have b^t points, though elementary intervals that "should" have one point might not.

For $t \geq 0$, an infinite sequence $(X_i)_{i \geq 1}$ of points from $[0,1)^s$ is a (t,s)-sequence in base b if for all $k \geq 0$ and $m \geq t$ the finite sequence

$$(X_i)_{i=kb^m+1}^{(k+1)b^m}$$

is a (t,m,s)-net in base b.

The advantage of a (t,s)-sequence is that if the first b^m points are not found to be sufficient for an integration problem, another b^m points can be found that also form a (t,m,s)-net and tend to fill in places not occupied by the first net. If one continues to the point of having b such (t,m,s)-nets, then taken together they comprise a $(t,m+1,s)$-net.

For the case $s = 6$ in this paper, we used a $(0,5,6)$-net in base 7 obtained from the first $7^5 = 16807$ points of $(0,6)$-sequence in base 7, and a $(8,14,6)$-net in base 2 obtained from the first $2^{14} = 16384$ points of a $(8,6)$-sequence in base 2.

In the former, elementary intervals in base 7 of volume $7^{-5} = 1/16807$ each contain one point, and in the latter, elementary intervals in base 2 of volume $2^{8-14} = 1/64$ each contain $2^8 = 128$ points. The $(0,6)$-sequence in base 7 is a randomised version of a Faure (1982) sequence and the $(8,6)$-sequence in base 2 is a Sobol (1967) sequence.

PROPERTIES OF NETS

The theory of (t,m,s)-nets and (t,s)-sequences is given in Niederreiter (1992). A famous result of the theory is that integration over a (t,m,s)-net can attain an accuracy of order $O(\log(n)^{s-1}/n)$ while using (t,s)-sequences worsens this slightly to $O(\log(n)^s/n)$. These results hold for integrand of bounded variation in the sense of Hardy and Krause.

For large s, it takes unrealistically large n for these rates to be clearly better than $n^{-1/2}$ but in examples they seem to outperform simple Monte Carlo. The construction of (t,m,s)-nets and (t,s)-sequences is also described in Niederreiter (1992).

Here we remark that for prime numbers s a construction by Faure (1982) gives $(0,s)$-nets in base s and Niederreiter extended the method to prime powers s. See Niederreiter (1992) for details.

SCRAMBLING NETS

Owen (1995) describes a scheme to randomise (t,m,s)-nets and (t,s)-sequences. The points are written in a base b expansion and certain random permutations are applied to the coefficients in the expansion. The result is to make each permuted X_i uniformly distributed over $[0,1)^s$ while preserving the (t,m,s)-net ot (t,s)-sequence structure of the ensemble of X_i.

Let X_i^j denote the jth component of the ith point in a (t,m,s)-net in base b. Now write $X_i^j = \sum_{k=1}^{\infty} x_{ijk} b^{-k}$ where x_{ijk} is an integer between 0 and $b-1$ inclusive. The scrambled version of X_i^j is to be $U_i^j = \sum_{k=1}^{\infty} u_{ijk} b^{-k}$ with u_{ijk} described below.

To scramble the first component, X_1^1 through X_n^1, replace each x_{i11} by $u_{i11} = \pi(x_{i11})$, where π is a randomly drawn permutation from the $b!$ possible permutations of digits 0 through $b-1$. This may be visualised as chopping the cube $[0,1)^s$ into b slices along the X^1 axis and scrambling them. Then take each of those b slices, slices it into b pieces and scrambles the pieces as before. This has the effect of permuting the second digit x_{i12}. Continue in this way, using b^{k-1} independent random permutations for the kth base b digit of X_i^1, for $k = 1,2,3, \ldots$. The other components X_i^j for $j = 2,3, \ldots, s$ are scrambled the same way, independently of each other and of the first component. In practice one can usually stop scrambling after step k where b^{-k} is small compared to the floating point precision used.

One result of applying all those permutations is that each U_i individually has the uniform distribution on $[0,1)^s$, and so the sample estimate $n^{-1}\sum_{i=1}^{n} f(X_i)$ is unbiased for $\int f(X)dX$. Furthermore, if the original X_i are a (t,m,s)-net then so are the U_i and the result of scrambling a (t,s)-sequence is another (t,s)-sequence.

On some test integrands in Owen (1995), the randomised nets appeared to be somewhat more accurate than their unrandomised counterparts. A theoretical confirmation of this appears in Owen (1997b), including an explanation due to Hickernell.

For any integrand f in $L^2[0,1)^s$ the variance of $\hat{I}$ under scrambled net integration is eventually smaller than any positive multiple of $1/n$, along a sequence of the form $n = \lambda b^m$ $1 \le \lambda < b$, $0 \le m$. See Owen(1997a). For smooth enough f, this variance is $O(n^{-3}(\log n)^{s-1})$ leading to typical errors of order $n^{-3/2}(\log n)^{(s-1)/2}$ in probability. This is superior to the rate $n^{-1}(\log n)^{s-1}$ obtained for unrandomised nets. See Owen (1997b). The former rate describes the average case over randomisation for a fixed function. The latter describes the worst case over integrands for a fixed sequence of points, but there is reason to believe that a typical fixed function will have the same rate, only a better constant. Thus scrambling can improve asymptotic accuracy as well as allow data based estimation of attained accuracy.

Hickernell (1996) has studied the rate achieved by the worst case integrand (of bounded variation), averaged over randomisations of nets and finds a rate of $O(n^{-1}(\log n)^{(s-1)/2})$ for randomised (0,m,s)-nets. This rate is a factor of $n^{-1/2}$ worse than the asymptotic rate for scrambled nets on smooth integrands. Thus if one picks the integrand pessimistically after observing how the net was randomised, one loses the asymptotic advantage of scrambling the nets.

BIBLIOGRAPHY

Caflisch, R.E., and W. Morokoff, 1996, "Quasi-Monte Carlo Computation of a Finance Problem", Technical Report CAM Report 96-16, Department of Mathematics, UCLA.

Efron, B.M., and R.J.Tibshirani, 1993, *An Introduction to the Bootstrap*, Chapman and Hall.

Faure, H., 1982, "Discrépance de suites associées à un système de numération (en dimension s)", *Acta Arithmetica*, Vol. 41, pp. 337-51.

Hickernell, F.J., 1996, "The mean square discrepancy of randomised nets", Technical Report MATH-112, Department of Mathematics, Hong Kong Baptist University.

Miller, R.G., 1974, "The Jackknife - a Review", *Biometrika*, Vol. 61, pp.1-15.

Miller, R.G., 1986, *Beyond ANOVA, Basics of Applied Statistics*, Wiley.

Niederreiter, H., 1992, *Random Number Generation and Quasi Monte Carlo Methods*, SIAM, Philadelphia, PA.

Owen, A.B., 1990, "Empirical Likelihood Ratio Confidence Regions", *Annals of Statistics*, Vol. 18, pp.19-120.

Owen, A.B., 1995, "Randomly Permuted (t,m,s)-nets and (t,s)-sequences", pp.299-317 in *Monte Carlo and Quasi-Monte Carlo Methods in Scientific Computing* (H Niederreiter and PJS Shiue, eds), Springer-Verlag: New York.

Owen, A.B., 1997i, "Monte Carlo Variance of Scrambled Equidistribution Quadrature", *SIAM Journal of Numerical Analysis*, Vol. 34, forthcoming.

Owen, A.B., 1997ii, "Scrambled Net Variance for Integrals of Smooth Functions", *Annals of Statistics,* Vol. 25, forthcoming.

Paskov, S., and J. Traub, 1995, "Faster Evaluation of Financial Derivatives", *Journal of Portfolio Management*, 22, 1, pp. 113-120.

Sobol, I.M., 1967, "The Distribution of Points in a Cube and the Accurate Evaluation of Integrals" (in Russian), *Zh. Vychisl. Mat. I Mat. Phys.*, Vol. 7, pp. 784-802.

The Value-at-Risk Approach: Proposals on a Generalisation

Michael Schröder
Centre for European Economic Research (ZEW) GmbH

Value-at-risk is becoming increasingly common as a risk measurement tool. The approach, however, has both theoretical and practical shortcomings. This paper aims to overcome some of the difficulties encountered with standard VAR measures, using a special measure of shortfall risk to extend and improve VAR. Return distributions and shortfall measures are calculated for portfolios including option strategies. Though VAR is held constant across the resulting return distributions, quite different valuations of risk arise depending on the shortfall measure used for the comparison.

The importance of controlling the risks of banking operations is becoming increasingly understood. International organisations and professional associations are busy developing new concepts of measuring and controlling risk, with the aim of achieving a global standard in risk control. The well-publicised problems experienced by some banks and industrial companies in handling financial derivatives have further stressed the need for efficient control mechanisms.

The Basle Committee on Banking Supervision is responsible for the development of internationally-accepted standards and measures of bank regulation. In its publication *Amendment to the Capital Accord to incorporate Market Risks* (1996), the Committee emphasised the importance of internal risk models to measure the risk of banks' trading books. These models are developed by banks themselves and adjusted for specific applications.

The so-called value-at-risk (VAR) approach has an important role to play in measuring the risk potential of the trading book. The Basle Committee itself recommends VAR as a suitable method for risk measurement, and gives detailed instructions about the conditions necessary for its application.[1]

We believe that VAR has certain shortcomings - it lacks a sound theoretical foundation and does not differentiate between different attitudes to risk. In this paper we show that the VAR approach is interpretable as a special measure of shortfall risk. Using the shortfall approach it is straightforward to develop a generalised VAR approach that eliminates the methodology's main weaknesses. The generalised VAR approach is suitable for all kinds of risk-averse investors. It also widens the applications for VAR in the fields of performance measurement and capital allocation.

Problems with VAR

VAR is a general method of measuring risk. Its usual application is to measure the risks of bank trading books. VAR is the value of the potential loss of a capital investment that is exceeded by only a given very small probability (1% or 5%). VAR therefore indicates an exceptionally high loss.

The mathematical formula for VAR is as follows:

$$\Pr(R \le VAR) = \alpha$$
$$\Leftrightarrow F(VAR) = \alpha$$
$$\Rightarrow VAR = F^{-1}(\alpha).$$

The cumulative distribution function $F(R)$ indi-

I would like to thank Peter Albrecht for helpful comments and suggestions.

cates the probability (Pr) that the portfolio return (R) is less than a given value (α). Calculating VAR, the value of α is given exogenously. Usual values for the confidence level α are 1% or 5%. VAR then gives the return that is exceeded on average in (1 – α)% of all time periods.

The Basle Committee uses VAR to calculate the capital requirements for the trading operations of banks. For that purpose VAR is multiplied by the investment volume. The resulting amount gives the loss potential in local currency. In some articles this amount is called "value-at-risk". In this paper portfolios are represented only by their return distribution, and so VAR means a specific return value. The required capital for trading operations proposed by the Basle Committee is the amount of potential loss multiplied by three. The multiplication is chosen to account for the inherent "model risk" due to insufficient experience using the VAR approach.

In order to calculate VAR, it is necessary to have an estimation of the return distribution. Figure 1 illustrates graphically the calculation of VAR. In this example VAR is -4.24%. Left of VAR the area below the curve is equal to a probability of 5%. This means that portfolio returns less than -4.24 will on average occur with a probability of 5%.

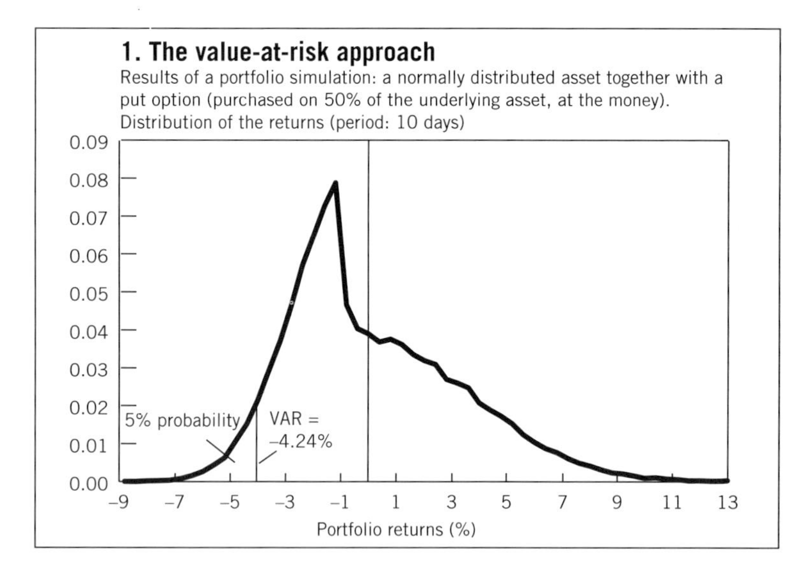

1. The value-at-risk approach

Results of a portfolio simulation: a normally distributed asset together with a put option (purchased on 50% of the underlying asset, at the money). Distribution of the returns (period: 10 days)

It is usually assumed that returns of stock- and bond-indices are approximately normally distributed.[2] Portfolios combining different stock- and bond-indices are then also approximately normally distributed. In this case VAR is easily calculated as the 1%- or 5%-quantile of the normal distribution with the properly chosen mean and standard deviation.

Controlling risk is a very important task if the portfolio contains a considerable amount of financial derivatives. Assuming that the returns of their underlying assets are normally distributed, the price of the options included in the portfolio can be calculated using the well known Black-Scholes formula.

In the rest of this paper simulation results are often used to give examples for the VAR approach. It is therefore necessary to describe in detail how the simulations have been constructed.[3] Figure 1 shows the return distribution of a portfolio that contains the normally distributed asset and a put option purchased on 50% of the underlying asset. The strike price of the put option is adjusted to the price of the underlying asset after each period (rolling hedge using at the money put options). The holding period of the options is 10 days, according to the Basle Committee's recommendations for the calculation of VAR. The return distributions are calculated from the portfolio values of 50,000 periods. Every distribution or calculated parameter refers to a period of 10 days.

Using VAR alone to compare the risk of two or more portfolios can be highly misleading. The two distributions in Figure 2 have only one characteristic number in common: the VAR value calculated with a confidence level of 5%. In both cases VAR is equal to -4.87%. That is, both portfolios have the characteristic that the return falls short of -4.87% with a probability of 5%. Table 2 compares important characteristic numbers of the two return distributions. The first distribution described in Table 2 is a simulated normal distribution. The mean return for a period of 10 days is 0.396% (approximately 10% annualised) and the standard deviation is 3.4. The second distribution contains a normally distributed asset (mean: 0.396%, standard deviation: 5) and put options purchased on 50% of the underlying asset.[4] Due to the costs of the put option the mean return (= 0.359%) is now slightly below the mean return of the normal distribution.

Table 1. The simulations

1. Normal distribution (= distribution of the underlying asset)	
(a) Number of periods	50,000
(b) Mean return (annualised)	10%
(c) Standard deviation (annualised)	from 3 to 25

2. Strategy with put options	
(a) Strike price of the put options	at the money (depending on the price of the underlying asset)
(b) Holding period	10 days (= time to maturity of the option)
(c) Rolling hedge	a new put option is purchased after 10 days
(d) Part of the underlying asset on which put options are purchased	50%
(e) Proportion (asset:put option)	1:1
(f) Interest rate	5%
(g) Volatility (= annualised standard deviation)	from 3 to 25 (depending on the volatility of the underlying asset)

One important difference between the two distributions is the skewness. Table 2 compares the quantiles of the distributions. The portfolio containing put options is skewed to the right. Below the VAR the probability of a loss is smaller than compared to the normal distribution. Choosing a VAR-confidence level of 1% instead of 5%, the portfolio containing the put options has a smaller VAR than the normal distribution; with a VAR-confidence level of 10% the normal distribution exhibits a smaller VAR, however. Below the VAR the portfolio with put options has not only a smaller loss probability but also a smaller average loss. The loss below the VAR is on average 5.8%. The normal distribution, however, has an average loss of 6.2% left to the VAR value.

It is a major shortcoming of the VAR approach that it considers only loss probabilities but not the possible amount of any losses. VAR can therefore have undesirable effects on the construction of portfolios, because a portfolio which aims at risk avoidance does not necessarily have a smaller capital requirement than a more aggressive one.

The concept of shortfall risk

The concept of shortfall risk refers to the possibility that a portfolio may fall short of a desired minimum return. Other expressions for the same concept are downside risk and lower partial moments. The term lower partial moments (lpm) means that in the concept of shortfall risk statistical moments are calculated below the desired minimum return.

Figure 3 gives an illustration of the shortfall risk concept. Before calculating the lower partial moments it is necessary to fix the minimum return, which will often have a value of 0%, or be equal to a current money market interest rate. Another possible choice is the required return for liabilities. Insurance companies may prefer to choose their competitors' return as the minimum return for calculating shortfall risk. In Figure 3 the desired minimum return is fixed arbitrarily at +1%.

The lower partial moments are calculated for that part of the return distribution below the minimum return. The returns above the minimum return are desired by the investor and are therefore not used to calculate the risk measures. Investors often criticise the use of variance or standard deviation as measures of risk because negative and positive returns are equally used in the calculation. But with shortfall risk only undesirable returns are used to calculate risk. Shortfall risk therefore best reflects investors' concerns about risk levels.

2. Two distributions with the same VAR

1. normal distribution, 2. portfolio with put options (purchased on 50% of the underlying asset, at the money).

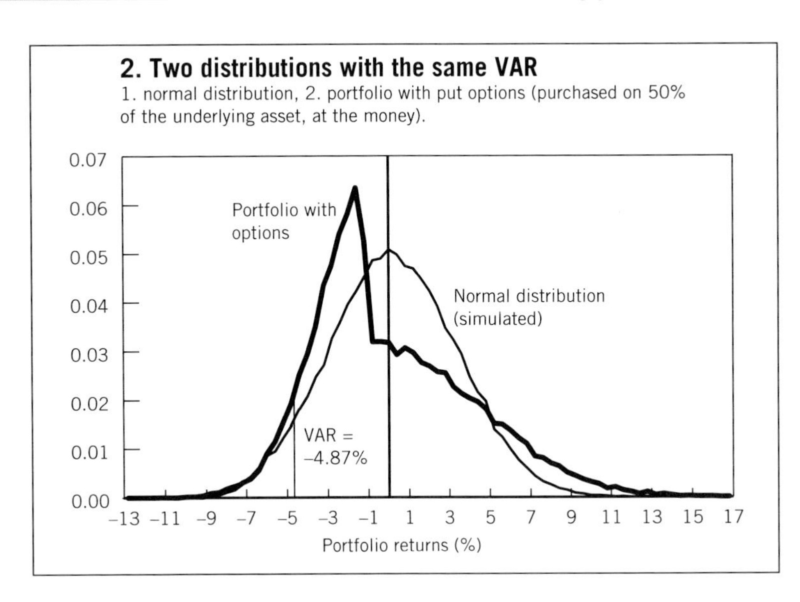

Table 2. Statistical characteristics of the two distributions

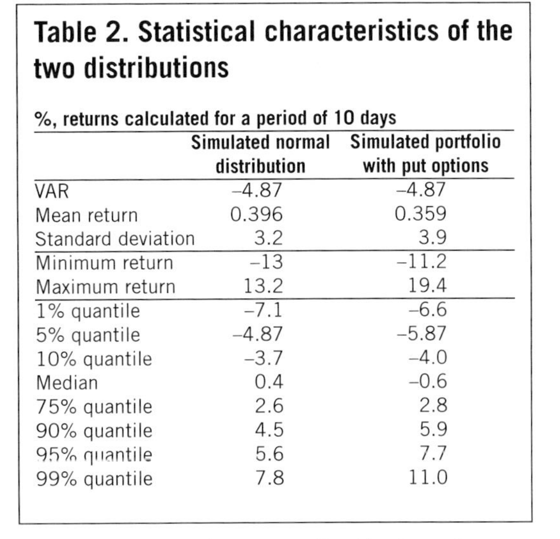

%, returns calculated for a period of 10 days

	Simulated normal distribution	Simulated portfolio with put options
VAR	–4.87	–4.87
Mean return	0.396	0.359
Standard deviation	3.2	3.9
Minimum return	–13	–11.2
Maximum return	13.2	19.4
1% quantile	–7.1	–6.6
5% quantile	–4.87	–5.87
10% quantile	–3.7	–4.0
Median	0.4	–0.6
75% quantile	2.6	2.8
90% quantile	4.5	5.9
95% quantile	5.6	7.7
99% quantile	7.8	11.0

Using options the return distribution of a portfolio will become skewed to the right or left. In such cases it is necessary to use lower partial moments because the standard deviation will indicate a misleading amount of risk, either too small (using call options) or too high (using put options).

3. The shortfall risk approach

Same portfolio as Figure 1

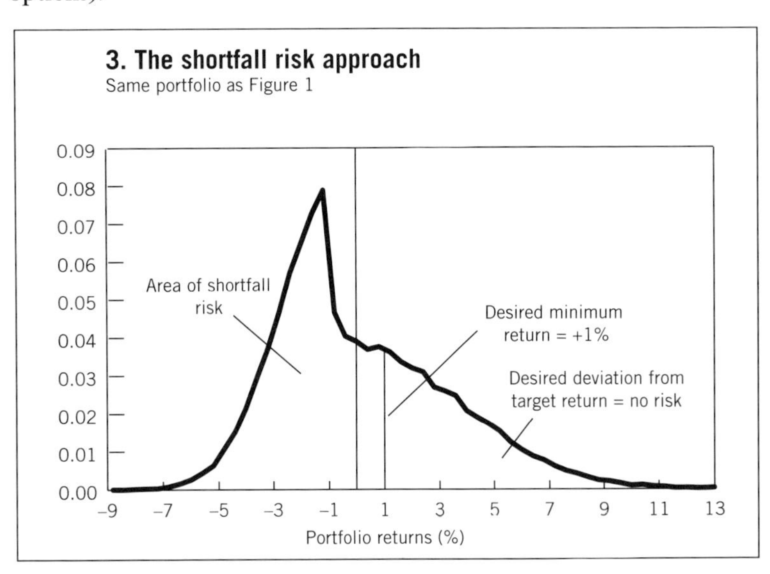

The general formula for the calculation of lower partial moments is as follows:

$$lpm_n(z) = \int_{-\infty}^{z} (z - R)^n dF(R).$$

Lower partial moments are calculated as the integral of the weighted return distribution (=F(R)) from minus infinity to the minimum return z. The weights (z – R) are always positive and are set to the nth power. In case of n = 0 the lower partial moment is the integral of the unweighted return distribution. lpm_0 is therefore equal to the cumulative distribution function F at the return R = z.

Using VAR as minimum return to calculate lpm_0, it is straightforward to express the similarity between the two concepts:

$$\begin{aligned} lpm_0 &= F(z) \\ &= \Pr(R \le z) \\ &= \Pr(R \le VAR) \\ &= F(VAR) \\ \Rightarrow VAR &= F^{-1}(lpm_0). \end{aligned}$$

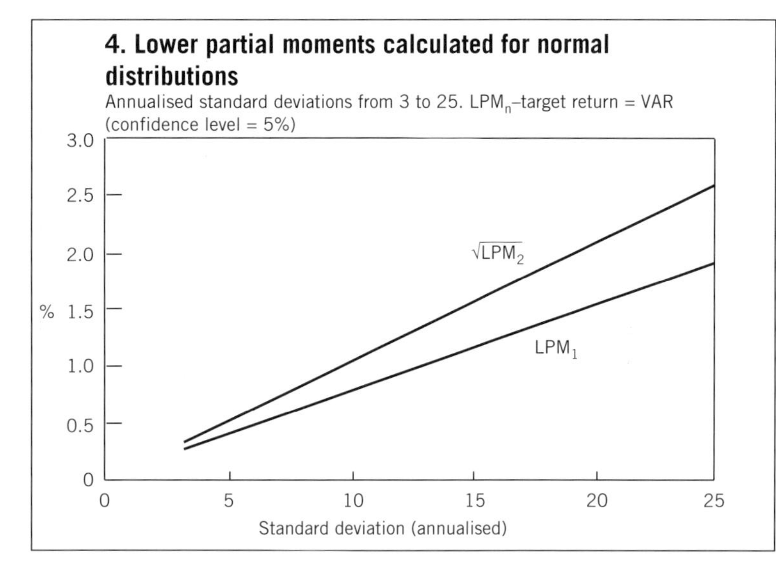

4. Lower partial moments calculated for normal distributions
Annualised standard deviations from 3 to 25. LPM_n–target return = VAR (confidence level = 5%)

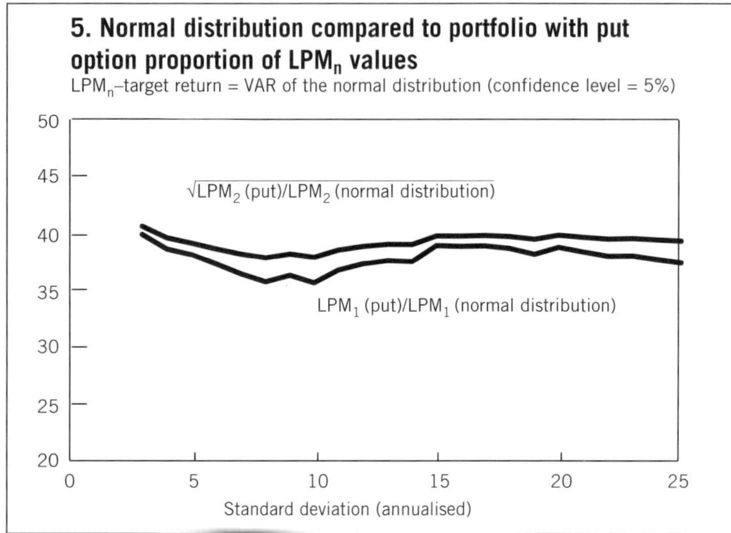

5. Normal distribution compared to portfolio with put option proportion of LPM_n values
LPM_n–target return = VAR of the normal distribution (confidence level = 5%)

The formulas showing lpm_0 and VAR are directly related via the cumulative distribution function. Fixing VAR lpm_0 gives the probability to fall short of the VAR value. Fixing the probability lpm_0, the corresponding VAR can be calculated.

The other lower partial moments are calculated choosing n = 1, 2, 3, etc. In the case n = 1 the lower partial moment is called target shortfall and it gives the expected loss below the minimum return. If, for example, lpm_1 is equal to 1%, then the deviation from the minimum return to the left is 1% on average. In case of n = 2 the differential between the portfolio return and the minimum return is squared. The resulting target semivariance (= lpm_2) is therefore calculated similarly to the variance.

Figures 4 and 5 illustrate the differences between lpm_n-measures. Figure 4 shows values of lpm_1 and the square root of lpm_2 calculated for different normal distributions. The normal distributions all have the same mean return (10% annualised), but different standard deviations. The graphs start with a standard deviation of 3, and end with a standard deviation of 25. The minimum return necessary for the calculation of the lower partial moments is fixed to the VAR values of each normal distribution given a confidence level of 5%. As can be seen, the lpm_2 value is always above the corresponding lpm_1 value. Normal distributions with higher standard deviation also exhibit higher values for the lower partial moments.

Figure 5 shows the ratios of the lower partial moments between a portfolio with put options and the corresponding normal distribution. The normal distribution chosen is therefore the same as the distribution of the underlying asset of the portfolio with put options. The minimum return for the calculation of the lpm values is equal to the VAR value of the normal distribution (confidence level = 5%). Figure 5 shows that the lpm values of the two portfolios are of quite different magnitude. The lpm_1 values of the portfolio with put options are only 38% of the lpm_1 values of the normal distribution and the analogous ratios to the square root of lpm_2 values are approximately 39%. These results demonstrate the big amount of possible risk reduction using the implemented hedging strategy with put options.

Lower partial moments can and should be used as a measure of risk instead of the standard deviation. Using lower partial moments means that a suitable degree of n has to be chosen. Fortunately, the concept of shortfall risk has a sound foundation in economic decision theory. Instead of the well known μ/σ criterion from

Markowitz a μ/lpm_n criterion is used.[5] The decision problem is the same: find all combinations of assets that minimise portfolio risk given a specific portfolio return. The result is an efficient frontier in the μ/lpm_n-space.[6]

The shape of the utility function of the investor, especially the degree of risk aversion, determines which shortfall measure should be chosen. If the utility function can be characterised by only a positive first derivative ($U' > 0$), then lpm_0 is the suitable risk measure. If the investor is risk averse so that the first derivative of the utility function is positive and the second derivative is negative ($U' > 0$, $U'' < 0$), the investor should choose lpm_1 as the measure of risk. If the investor is still more risk averse ($U' > 0$, $U'' < 0$, $U''' > 0$), he or she should choose lpm_2.[7]

The concept of shortfall risk makes no assumptions about the return distribution.[8] Therefore the shortfall risk approach is a generalisation of the Markowitz approach. As the requirement of normally distributed returns is a considerable restriction using the Markowitz approach in practice, lower partial moments are not only an improvement in theory but also in practice.[9]

The assumption of normally distributed returns is completely inappropriate for portfolios containing a considerable amount of options. But the shortfall approach is applicable to any kind of return distribution. And the specific level of the investor's risk aversion is taken into account in choosing the minimum return and the suitable lower partial moment.

A generalised VAR approach

The concept of shortfall risk gives a decision-theoretic foundation to the VAR approach. It is straightforward to develop a generalised VAR approach using lower partial moments. VAR is the same kind of measure as is lpm_0. Therefore VAR is suitable as a measure of risk for all investors with $U' > 0$. The use of lpm_n-measures ($n > 0$) is the basis for the development of generalised VAR measures that explicitly take risk aversion into account.

Instead of choosing a probability (or confidence level) to calculate VAR, the value of a general integral (S_n) has to be given:

$$S_n = \int_{-\infty}^{VAR_n} (VAR_n - R)^n dF(R).$$

Then the integral can be solved to the generalised VAR_n value. In case of $n = 0$ S_0 is equal to the confidence level of the usual VAR. S_1 can be interpreted as the expected deviation to the left of the VaR_n value. In case of $n > 1$, the meaning of S_n is more difficult to interpret. To make the choice of S_n easier it may be useful to look at the S_n values of a suitable normal distribution. We describe how this could work below. Some examples are added for further illustration.

S_n can take any real value. In the following example a normal distribution is used, which has the same mean return and the same VAR_0 value as the distribution of a portfolio with put options. Now the integrals S_1 and S_2 are calculated using this normal distribution. The upper boundary of the integral is the value of VAR_0, calculated with given confidence levels of 1%, 5% and 10% respectively. Given these values of S_1 and S_2, VAR_1 and VAR_2 can be calculated for the distribution of the portfolio containing put options.

Figures 6 and 7 show some examples. In Figure 6 the graphs show the VAR_0 values (= the usual VAR) and the VAR_2 values of the portfolio with put options. The values of S_2 are calculated

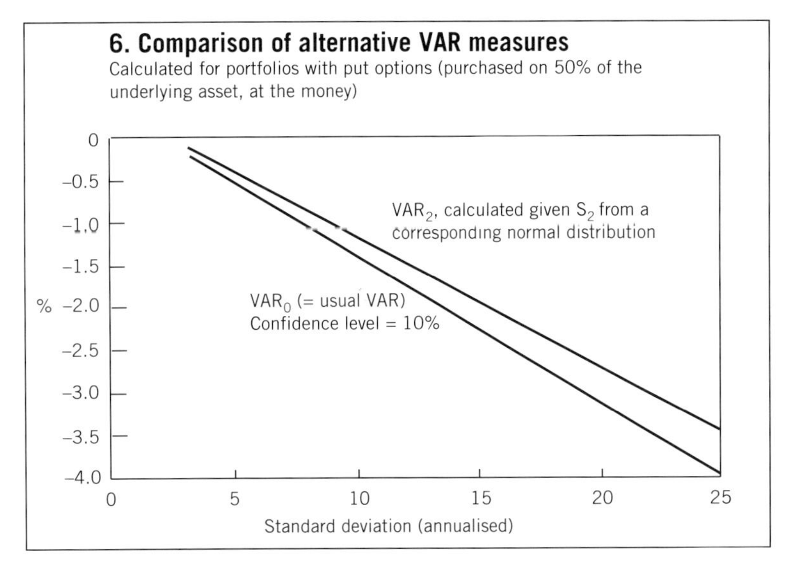

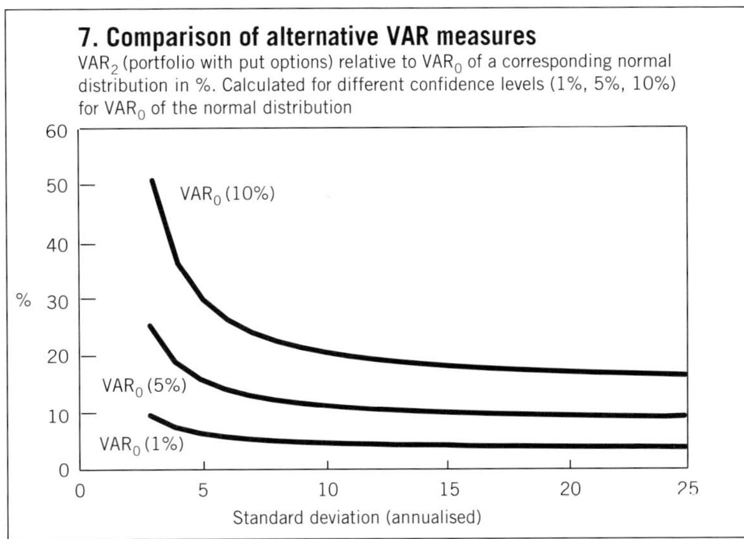

as described above, using a corresponding normal distribution. The VAR_2 is significantly smaller than VAR_0. This means that now the relatively defensive portfolio with the put options also has a smaller VAR_2 value than the corresponding normal distribution.[10]

Figure 7 shows the reduction using S_2 instead of S_0. The graphs are based on the ratio $(1 - VAR_2/VAR_0)*100\%$. For each chosen confidence level (S_0 = 1%, 5% or 10%) the results are very similar: The largest reduction of VAR reveals portfolios with low standard deviation. But for all relatively defensive portfolios the use of VAR_1 or VAR_2 instead of VAR_0 could reduce capital requirements significantly.

Lower partial moments as a risk management tool

The usual VAR measure (VAR_0) will probably be the most important tool for public risk control in the future. Not only does the Basle Committee recommend VAR for internal risk models but there are also commercial software products that facilitate the use of VAR in a bank's day-to-day business.[11]

There are also sound theoretical arguments why VAR is suitable for public risk control: VAR or equivalently lpm_0 are the least restrictive shortfall risk measures possible. They are a suitable risk measure for all investors having a utility with a positive first derivative. Risk averting behaviour is not a necessary condition.

But using VAR as a bank's only internal risk measure may be inadequate. One of the major tasks of risk management is the optimal allocation of capital. The Sharpe ratio is a well known measure to evaluate the performance of portfolios. The Sharpe ratio is directly derived from the Capital Asset Pricing Model (CAPM) and is equal to the slope of the efficient frontier in case of the market portfolio. In mathematical terms the Sharpe ratio divides the mean return less the riskless interest rate by the standard deviation of the portfolio returns. The result is therefore equal to the risk adjusted mean return of the portfolio and can be used to rank the performance of different portfolios.

But there is an important requirement for the successful use of the Sharpe ratio: the returns of the portfolio have to be normally distributed, at least approximately. The Sharpe ratio is therefore not an appropriate performance measure for portfolios containing options. The reason why portfolio returns have to be normally distributed is the use of the standard deviation in the denominator.

Using the lower partial moments as measures of risk as described above, modified Sharpe ratios can be constructed that are suitable to any return distribution.[12] The modified Sharpe ratios SR_1 and SR_2 defined below use lpm_1 and lpm_2 as measures of risk.[13] Therefore SR_1 and SR_2 take into account correctly deviations from the normal distribution. The formulas for SR_1 and SR_2 are as follows:

$$SR_1 = \frac{\mu - r}{lpm_1}$$

$$SR_2 = \frac{\mu - r}{\sqrt{lpm_2}}$$

where:

μ = average portfolio return

r = riskless interest rate.

Figures 8 and 9 illustrate the importance of the choice of the correct risk measure. Figure 8 shows Sharpe ratios of a normal distribution and of a portfolio containing put options. The graphs start with a standard deviation of the normal dis-

8. Comparison of Sharpe ratios

1. normal distribution, 2. portfolio with put options (purchased on 50% of the underlying asset, at the money). Corresponding distributions have equal mean and equal VAR_0

Normal distribution

Portfolio with put options

%

Standard deviation (annualised)

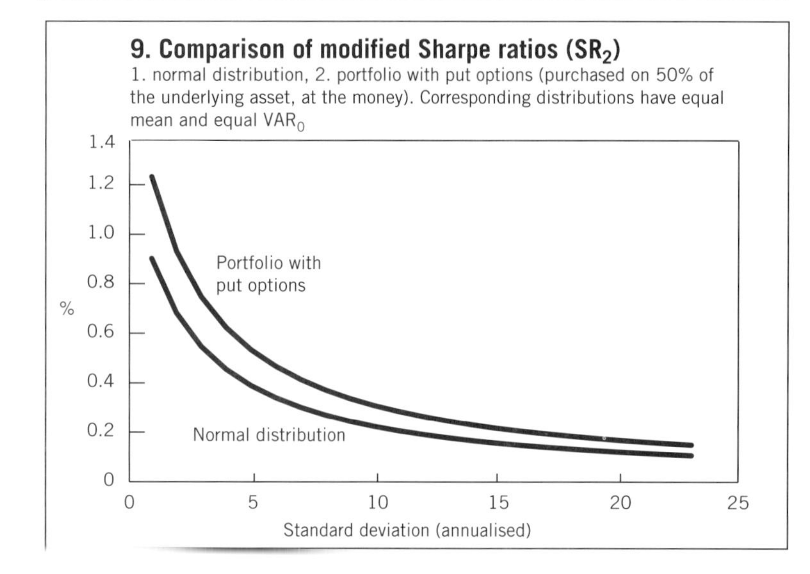

9. Comparison of modified Sharpe ratios (SR_2)

1. normal distribution, 2. portfolio with put options (purchased on 50% of the underlying asset, at the money). Corresponding distributions have equal mean and equal VAR_0

tribution (= distribution of the underlying asset in the second portfolio) of 3 and end with a value of 25. Both distributions have the same mean return and the same VAR_0 at a confidence level of 1%. The portfolio without options seems to outperform the other one. But using the standard deviation overestimates the risk of the partly insured portfolio: the standard deviation does not take into account that the portfolio is skewed to the right. As a consequence the risk-adjusted return of this portfolio seems to be relatively small.

Figure 9 shows the correct values for the risk adjusted performance of the two portfolios using SR_2 as performance measure. In this example the minimum return to calculate lpm_2 is the VAR_0 value using a confidence level of 1%. Now the portfolio containing put options has the higher risk adjusted performance because it has taken into account the fact that losses are less severe than compared to the normal distribution.

A ratio often used in risk management is the so-called Rorac (Return On Risk Adjusted Capital). Rorac is defined as the mean return of a portfolio divided by the usual VAR.[14] Rorac is therefore similar to a Sharpe ratio using VAR_0 as the risk measure in the denominator. Due to the use of VAR_0 to calculate Rorac this performance measure is inadequate if the risk manager is risk averse. A risk averse risk manager would do better to use lpm_1 or lpm_2 to calculate the risk adjusted performance.

The importance of the modified Sharpe ratios in risk management are the induced incentives to construct defensive portfolios. Portfolios insured using, for example, put options will have a higher risk adjusted return compared to more aggressive portfolios with the same unadjusted return (= mean return – riskless interest rate). Using lpm_2 this effect is more pronounced than using lpm_1. Using only VAR_0 as risk measure as in case of RORAC the skewness of the return distribution is not taken into account. Then there is no incentive to construct portfolios that are relatively defensive (skewed to the right). If the bank´s management is risk averse and has a preference for relatively defensive portfolios then lpm_1 or lpm_2 should be used as measure of risk in calculating the risk adjusted performance of portfolios.

$\frac{\bar{r}}{VAR}$ = RAROC

1 *Basle Committee on Banking Supervision (1996), Part B.*

2 *It is assumed that the continously compounded return has a normal distribution. Then the simple discrete return follows a lognormal distribution.*

3 *Table 1 summarises the assumptions underlying the simulations.*

4 *See Table 1 for a detailed description of the hedging strategy.*

5 *See Bawa and Lindenberg (1977) and Harlow and Rao (1989).*

6 *Under the condition:* $n > 0$. *See Bawa and Lindenberg (1977).*

7 *See Bawa (1978) and Fishburn (1977).* LPM_0 *is the general risk measure. It is applicable to all utility functions* ($u' > 0$). *The analogue in the theory of decisions under uncertainty is the 1. order Stochastic Dominance rule.* LPM_1 *and* LPM_2 *are more special than* LPM_0. *They are applicable if the investor is risk averse.* LPM_1 *and* LPM_2 *are analogous to the 2. and 3. order Stochastic Dominance rule, respectively.*

8 *Lower partial moments are applicable as generalised safety-first rules to any return distribution. In this application lower partial moments are only an approximation to the true solution. If the return distribution belongs to the two-parameter location-scale family (eg the t distribution, stable distribution) then lower partial moments give the exact solution to safety-first problems. See Bawa (1978) and Harlow and Rao (1989).*

9 *Alternatively it could be assumed that the utility function of the investor is quadratic. Much less restrictive and therefore much more common is the assumption of normally distributed asset returns. In this case the utility function can have any shape.*

10 *Using the method to calculated* VAR_n *as described in the text the* VAR_n *values of the normal distribution are the same for all* n. *That means the procedure described takes into account only deviations relative to the normal distribution.*

11 *See, for example, the software tool RiskMetrics from JP Morgan.*

12 *See Zimmermann (1994) and Albrecht, Maurer and Stephan (1995). Bawa and Lindenberg (1977) derive a generalised CAPM using lower partial moments instead of the standard deviation as risk measure. They assume that the target return is equal to a riskless interest rate* r. *The generalised CAPM under the assumption that the target rate can take any value is derived in Harlow and Rao (1989).*

13 *The investor can fix any target rate to calculate the lower partial moments. The risk adjusted performance of the portfolio and the ranking of different portfolios therefore depend on the* LPM_n *measure chosen and on the target return.*

14 *See Bürger (1995), p. 250.*

BIBLIOGRAPHY

Albrecht, P., R. Maurer, and T.G. Stephan, 1995, "Shortfall-Performance rollierender Wertsicherungsstrategien" *Finanzmarkt und Portfolio Management*, 9, pp. 197-209.

Basle Committee on Banking Supervision, 1994, "Public Disclosure of Market and Credit Risks by Financial Intermediaries", Basle.

Basle Committee on Banking Supervision, 1996, "Amendment to the Capital Accord to incorporate Market Risks", Basle.

Bawa, V.S., 1978, "Safety First, Stochastic Dominance, and Optimal Portfolio Choice", *Journal of Financial and Quantitative Analysis*, 13, pp. 255-71.

Bawa, V.S. and E.B. Lindenberg, 1977, "Capital Market Equilibrium in a Mean-Lower Partial Moment Framework", *Journal of Financial Economics*, 3, pp. 189-200.

Bürger, P., 1995, "Risikocontrolling - Optimaler Einsatz von Handelslimiten im derivativen OTC-Geschäft", Rudolph, Bernd (Hrsg.): *Derivate Finanzinstrumente*, Stuttgart, pp. 241-59.

Fishburn, P.C., 1977, "Mean-Risk Analysis with Risk Associated with Below-Target Returns", *American Economic Review*, 67, pp. 16-126.

Harlow, W.V., 1991, "Asset Allocation in a Downside-Risk Framework", *Financial Analysts Journal*, September/October, pp. 28-40.

Harlow, W.V. and R.K.S. Rao, 1989, "Asset Pricing in a Generalised Mean-Lower Partial Moment Framework: Theory and Evidence", *Journal of Financial and Quantitative Analysis*, 24, 3, pp. 285-311.

JP Morgan, 1995, *RiskMetrics Technical Document*, 3rd edition, New York.

Lee, W.Y. and R.K.S. Rao, 1988, "Mean Lower Partial Moment Valuation and Lognormally Distributed Returns", *Management Science*, 34, 4, pp. 446-53.

Zimmermann, H., 1994, "Reward-to-Risk", *Finanzmarkt und Portfolio Management*, 8, 1, pp. 1-6.

32

Quadratic Maximum Loss

Gerold Studer and H-J Lüthi
Swiss Federal Institute of Technology, Zurich

Regulatory authorities such as the BIS require institutions to use both value-at-risk models and stress testing. This paper aims to build a bridge between the two methods by examining the concept of maximum loss. In contrast to VAR, which depends on holding periods and confidence levels, ML has a supplementary degree of freedom known as a trust region. ML represents the worst case over such a trust region, and the calculation therefore identifies the worst case scenario for a portfolio.

The methodological discussion about the measurement of market risk has become an important topic in many financial institutions over the last few years. This is mainly because of two reasons. First, the volume of highly non-linear instruments (ie whose payoff does not linearly depend on market rates) has increased. Second, correlations among market parameters may influence the diversification effect and either reduce or increase a portfolio's overall risk. The consequence is that simple answers to the question "what is the risk of the portfolio?" no longer exist. This has also been realised by the regulatory authorities; the Bank for International Settlements, for example, requires that both value-at-risk (VAR) models and stress tests are used.

Maximum loss aims to build a bridge between these two methods. The problem with stress testing is that it has no methodological foundation: finding an appropriate set of scenarios is more of an art than a science. The maximum loss approach can be understood as a systematic way of identifying a portfolio's black holes without ignoring the correlations between the risk factors. For non-linear portfolios, this method gives much greater insight than a new risk figure alone.

Before going into detail, some notations must be clarified: changes of market rates such as commodity prices, foreign exchange rates, equity indices, interest rates are represented by risk factors $\omega_1, \ldots, \omega_M$ (ie, $\omega_i = 0$ corresponds to the actual value of market rate i). The risk factors are assumed to be random variates: for a time interval of length t (holding period of the portfolio), $\omega = (\omega_1, \ldots, \omega_M)$ is multinormally distributed with mean 0 and covariance matrix Σ_t. The risk factor space Ω is the set of all possible outcomes of the risk factors ω.

The effect of a change in the risk factors ω can be determined by repricing the portfolio. The change in portfolio value – called profit and loss is denoted $v(\omega)$; the definitions imply that $v(0) = 0$.

Concept of maximum loss

DEFINITION OF MAXIMUM LOSS

Maximum loss (ML) is defined as the maximum loss that can occur over some holding period t if the risk factors are restricted to a given set A_t, where it will be assumed that A_t is a closed set with confidence level

$$\Pr(\omega \mid \omega \in A_t) = \alpha.$$

This definition looks similar to the definition of VAR as the expected maximum loss over some time interval for some level of probability (Beckstrom and Campbell 1995). However, there is one important difference: whereas for calculating VAR the distribution of P&L has to be known (and whose determination is the crucial point in all VAR methods), ML is directly defined in the risk factor space Ω. The mathematical definition of maximum loss is:

$$\begin{aligned} ML &= \min \ v(\omega) \\ &\text{s.t. } \omega \in A_t;\ \text{where } \Pr(A_t) = \alpha \end{aligned} \quad (1)$$

1. Modelling maximum loss

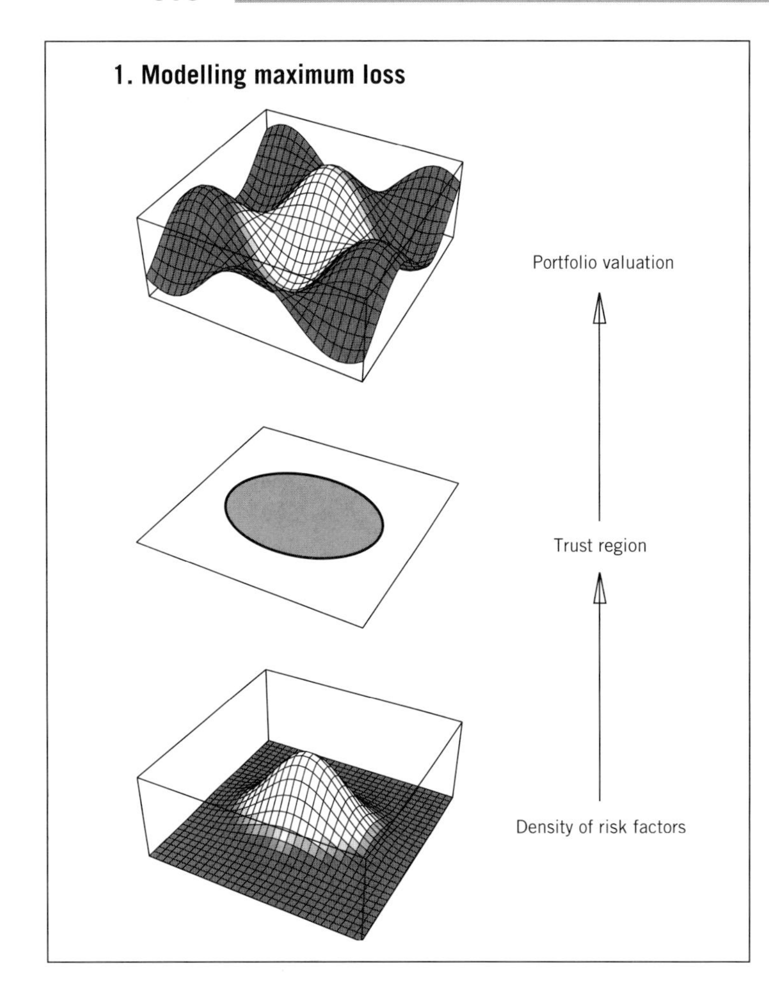

In contrast to VAR, which only depends on the holding period t and the confidence level α, ML has a supplementary degree of freedom, called trust region A_t; any closed set in the risk factor space Ω with probability α is a valid trust region, and ML represents the worst case over such a trust region, as explained in Figure 1.

MODELLING TRUST REGIONS

Trust regions are primarily defined with the help of the risk factor density $f_t(\omega)$. In the following, the construction for normally distributed risk factors $\omega \sim N(0,\Sigma_t)$ is explained. The joint density function of ω is

$$f_t(\omega) = \frac{1}{(2\pi)^{M/2}\sqrt{\det \Sigma_t}} \exp\left(-\frac{1}{2}\omega^T \Sigma_t^{-1} \omega\right) \quad (2)$$

The goal is to find a trust region A_t which covers a probability of α and includes the scenario $\omega = 0$ (today's state of the world). One possibility is to search for a constant c such that

$$\Pr\left(\omega \middle| f_t(\omega) \geq c\right) = \alpha. \quad (3)$$

This makes sense since $f_t(\omega)$ attains its maximum at $\omega = 0$ and leads to the trust region of minimal volume. By eliminating the constants, the problem is reduced to the following: find c_α such that

$$\Pr\left(\omega \middle| \omega^T \Sigma_t^{-1} \omega \leq c_\alpha\right) = \alpha. \quad (4)$$

Write

$$\omega^T \Sigma_t^{-1} \omega = \omega^T U^{-1} U^{-T} \omega = \left(U^{-T}\omega\right)^T \left(U^{-T}\omega\right) \quad (5)$$

where $\Sigma_t = U^T U$ is the Cholesky decomposition of the covariance matrix. But

$$\begin{aligned} \mathrm{Var}\left(U^{-T}\omega\right) &= E\left[\left(U^{-T}\omega\right)\left(U^{-T}\omega\right)^T\right] \\ &= U^{-T}\,\mathrm{Var}(\omega)\,U^{-1} \\ &= U^{-T}U^T U U^{-1} \\ &= 1. \end{aligned} \quad (6)$$

Hence

$$\left(U^{-T}\omega\right) \sim N(0,1) \quad (7)$$

and therefore $\omega^T\Sigma_t^{-1}\omega = \Sigma_{i=1}^M X_i^2$, where X_i are independent standard normal variates. Thus, $\omega^T\Sigma_t^{-1}\omega$ is χ^2 distributed with M degrees of freedom. Consequently, a valid trust region is obtained by choosing:

$$A_t = \left\{\omega \middle| \omega^T \Sigma_t^{-1} \omega \leq c_\alpha\right\} \quad (8)$$

where c_α is the α-quantile of a χ_M^2 distribution. This is the equation of an ellipsoid centred at the origin.

Supplementary conditions might eventually be introduced to further restrict the trust region; for example, by respecting triangular relationships of foreign exchange rates (Studer 1995).

RELATIONSHIP BETWEEN VAR AND ML

Compared to VAR, maximum loss is a conservative risk measure. In fact, it can be shown (Studer 1995) that the following relation holds for every portfolio:

$$\mathrm{ML} \leq \mathrm{VAR}. \quad (9)$$

Of course, this is only true (and meaningful) if both calculations refer to the same model, ie the P&L function $v(\omega)$, the confidence level α and the holding period t are identical. Furthermore, two other conditions must be satisfied – the change in portfolio value $v(\omega)$ is a continuous function, and the joint density $f_t(\omega)$ is strictly positive on Ω (but not necessarily normal).

However, (9) does not depend on the choice of trust region. Figure 2 shows how different choices of trust regions A_t can produce different values of ML. Take a portfolio consisting of one

2. Different choices of trust regions

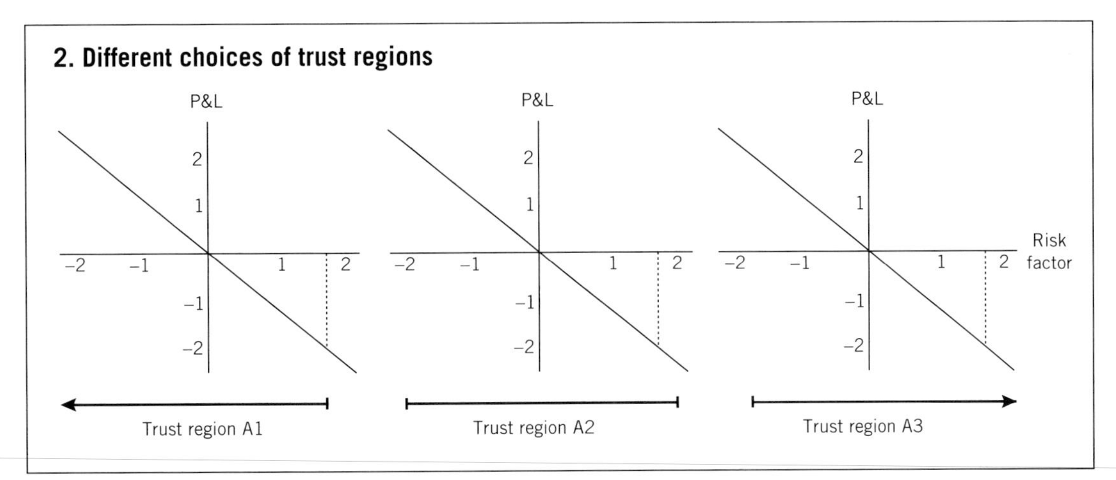

linear instrument; the underlying risk factor has a standard normal distribution, the confidence level is $\alpha = 95\%$.

VAR of this portfolio is −1.64; ML however is heavily dependent on the choice of the trust region.

- if trust region $A1 = [-\infty, 1.64]$ is chosen: $ML_{A1} = -1.64$.
- if trust region $A2 = [-1.96, 1.96]$ is chosen: $ML_{A2} = -1.96$.
- if trust region $A3 = [-1.64, \infty]$ is chosen: $ML_{A3} = -\infty$.

Nonetheless, the relation $ML \leq VAR$ holds in any case. It will be shown below that *for linear portfolios with normally distributed risk factors* it is always possible to adjust the confidence level $\tilde{\alpha}$ of ML, such that the choice

$$A_t = \left\{ \omega \middle| \omega^T \Sigma_t^{-1} \omega \leq c_{\tilde{\alpha}} \right\}$$

leads to $ML = VAR$.

LINEAR PORTFOLIOS

Delta-normal VAR is a methodology for calculating analytically the risk of a portfolio with normally distributed risk factors $\omega \sim N(0, \Sigma_t)$ and *linear* P&L function $v(\omega) = a^T \omega$. If these two conditions hold, it is also possible to derive an analytical expression for ML:

$$ML = \min a^T \omega \quad \text{s.t. } \omega^T \Sigma_t^{-1} \omega \leq c_\alpha \tag{10}$$

where the standard choice of trust region is used. Defining the functions $f(\omega) = a^T \omega$ and $g(\omega) = \omega^T \Sigma_t^{-1} \omega - c_\alpha$, the problem can be rewritten as

$$ML = \min f(\omega) \quad \text{s.t. } g(\omega) \leq 0. \tag{11}$$

Since $f(\omega)$ and $g(\omega)$ are convex functions, the solution ω^* must satisfy the Kuhn–Tucker conditions:

$$\nabla f(\omega^*) = -\lambda \nabla g(\omega^*) \tag{12}$$

$$\lambda g(\omega^*) = 0 \tag{13}$$

$$\lambda \geq 0 \tag{14}$$

Equation (12) implies that $a = -2\lambda \Sigma_t^{-1} \omega^*$, and therefore $\lambda \neq 0$. It follows that

$$\omega^* = -\frac{1}{2\lambda} \Sigma_t a. \tag{15}$$

Considering formula (13) this results in

$$\frac{1}{\lambda} = \frac{2\sqrt{c_\alpha}}{\sqrt{a^T \Sigma_t a}}.$$

Hence, (15) defines to find the worst case scenario

$$\omega^* = -\frac{\sqrt{c_\alpha}}{\sqrt{a^T \Sigma_t a}} \Sigma_t a \tag{16}$$

and the corresponding loss is

$$ML = -\sqrt{c_\alpha} \sqrt{a^T \Sigma_t a}. \tag{17}$$

This expression is very similar to delta-normal VAR, ie

$$-z_\alpha \sqrt{a^T \Sigma_t a}$$

the only difference lies in the scaling level factor: c_α is the α-quantile of a χ^2 distribution with M degrees of freedom , whereas z_α is the α-quantile of a standard normal distribution. Contrarily to VAR, ML depends on the number of risk factors used in the model (see Table 1).

However, the choice of a different confidence level $\tilde{\alpha} \neq \alpha$ such that

Table 1. Relation ML/VAR for different dimensions M

	M=2	M=5	M=10	M=50
α=90.0%	1.67	2.37	3.12	6.20
α=95.0%	1.49	2.02	2.60	5.00
α=97.5%	1.39	1.83	2.31	4.31
α=99.0%	1.30	1.67	2.07	3.75

$$\sqrt{c_{\tilde{\alpha}}} = z_\alpha$$

leads to identical values for both measures. Since all quantities of (16), except the constant c_α, are known from the calculation of delta-normal VAR, it is possible to determine the worst case scenario ω^* in every delta-normal VAR implementation without additional costs.

Maximum loss for quadratic portfolios

As is the case for VAR, there is no analytic expression of ML for quadratic P&L functions $v(\omega) = \frac{1}{2}\omega^T G\omega + g^T\omega$. However, it is possible to calculate efficiently a solution to the problem

$$ML = \min \tfrac{1}{2}\omega^T G\omega + g^T\omega \quad \text{s.t. } \omega^T \Sigma_t^{-1}\omega \le c_\alpha \tag{18}$$

where G is a symmetric $M \times M$ matrix, g a M-dimensional vector and c_α the α-quantile of a chi-square distribution with M degrees of freedom (see above).

An interesting approach to calculating VAR of a quadratic portfolio numerically is described in Rouvinez (1997).

THE LEVENBERG -MARQUARDT ALGORITHM
The solution to (18) can be calculated numerically by the Levenberg-Marquardt algorithm (Fletcher, 1987), which is usually used in restricted step methods in non-linear optimisation. The algorithm cannot directly be applied to (18); the ellipsoidal trust region has first to be transformed into a sphere. Since Σ_t is a covariance matrix and therefore positive semidefinite, its Cholesky decomposition

$$\Sigma_t = U^T U \tag{19}$$

can be calculated. Writing

$$\omega = U^T\hat{\omega} \tag{20}$$

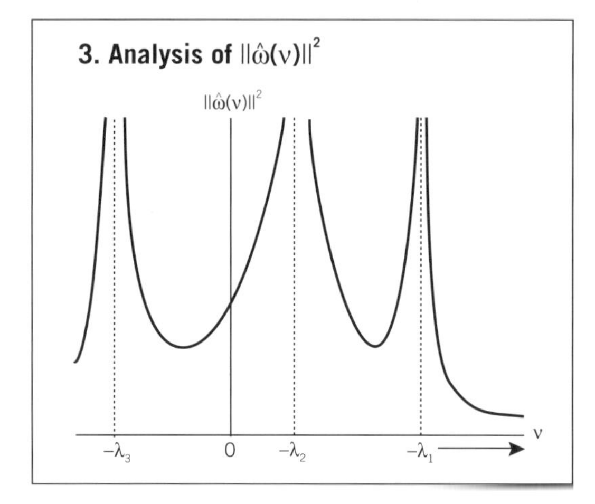

3. Analysis of $||\hat{\omega}(v)||^2$

we get an equivalent formulation to (18):

$$ML = \min \tfrac{1}{2}\hat{\omega}^T\hat{G}\hat{\omega} + \hat{g}^T\hat{\omega} \quad \text{s.t. } \hat{\omega}^T\hat{\omega} \le c_\alpha \tag{21}$$

where $\hat{g} = Ug$ and $\hat{G} = UGU^T$. Again, the objective function is quadratic, but this time the constraint represents a sphere, centred at the origin. The following theorem builds the basis of the solution process:

THEOREM 1: $\hat{\omega}$ is a *global* solution to (21) if and only if there exists $v \in \mathbb{R}$ such that

$$(\hat{G} + v\mathbb{1}) \text{ is positive semidefinite,} \tag{22}$$

and the following conditions hold:

$$(\hat{G} + v\mathbb{1})\hat{\omega} = -\hat{g} \tag{23}$$
$$v(c_\alpha - \hat{\omega}^T\hat{\omega}) = 0 \tag{24}$$
$$v \ge 0. \tag{25}$$

Furthermore, if v exists, it is unique.

The proof of this theorem is given in Fletcher (1987). The key idea behind the Levenberg-Marquardt algorithm is to make a one-dimensional search for v. Suppose for a moment we would have an orthonormal basis of eigenvectors of $\hat{G}: \beta = \{\hat{e}_1, \ldots, \hat{e}_M\}$ with corresponding eigenvalues $\lambda_1 \le \ldots \le \lambda_M$ (β exists because $\hat{G}$ is symmetric). We can express the vectors $\hat{g}$ and $\hat{\omega}$ in this new basis: $\hat{g} = \Sigma_{i=1}^M \alpha_i \hat{e}_i$ and $\hat{\omega} = \Sigma_{i=1}^M \beta_i \hat{e}_i$, where the coefficients β_i are the unknowns. (23) implies that

$$\beta_i = -\frac{\alpha_i}{\lambda_i + v}, i = 1, \ldots, M.$$

Therefore, $\hat{\omega}$ can be seen as a function of v and

$$\left\|\hat{\omega}(v)\right\|^2 = \sum_{i=1}^{M}\left(\frac{\alpha_i}{\lambda_i + v}\right)^2. \tag{26}$$

This is a positive, decreasing function with $\lim_{v\to\infty} ||\hat{\omega}(v)||^2 = 0$. Conditions (22) and (25) imply that $v \ge \max(-\lambda_1, 0)$. This situation is represented in Figure 3.

Depending on v, two cases have to be distinguished:

(a) $v = 0$: $\hat{G}$ is positive semidefinite by (22). From (23) we conclude that $\hat{\omega} = -\hat{G}^{-1}\hat{g}$ is the global solution to (21).

(b) $v > 0$. Let $0 < v_1 < v_2$ be two candidates for v. (23) implies that $\omega_i = -(\hat{G} + v_i 1)^{-1}\hat{g}, i = 1,2$. From (26) we know that $||\hat{\omega}_1||^2 > ||\hat{\omega}_2||^2$. Thus, we can apply a bisectionning method to find that value of v which satisfies (24), ie, $||\hat{\omega}(v)||^2 = c_\alpha$.

Obviously, neither the eigenvectors $\hat{e}_i$ of $\hat{G}$ nor its eigenvalues λ_i are needed to implement such a bisectionning algorithm. In fact, it is possible to implement the algorithm such that it solves the problem in polynomial time:

THEOREM 2: The number of arithmetic operations required for calculating the global solution to (21) is bounded by a polynomial in

- p: number of digits of the solution $\hat{\omega}$ requested
- L: bit-length of entry data ($\hat{G}$, $\hat{g}$, c_α: rationals)
- M: dimension of problem.

Elements of the proof are given in Vavasis (1991). It is important to note that this is the only nonconvex global optimisation problem for which a polynomial time algorithm is known. Technical details of the implementation are described in Dennis and Schnabel (1996).

EXAMPLE

The portfolio showed in Figure 4 will be used in the sequel to illustrate the concepts of maximum loss. It is an equity portfolio, where the risk factors $\omega_1, \ldots, \omega_7$ each represent an equity index. The points in Figure 4 show the P&L for the risk factors moving up or down 1 and 2 standard deviations. The solid lines display the best fitting quadratic functions to these points. It is obvious that the P&L function of this portfolio can reasonably be approximated by a quadratic approximation (which is, however, different from the second order Taylor series expansion using local sensitivities).

The Levenberg-Marquardt algorithm, applied to this example for a confidence level of $\alpha = 90\%$, gives the worst case scenario ω^*:

Risk Factor 1 = –2.796
Risk Factor 2 = –1.711
Risk Factor 3 = –3.395
Risk Factor 4 = –2.200
Risk Factor 5 = –2.494
Risk Factor 6 = –1.766
Risk Factor 7 = –0.844,

and a total loss of 2,786.36 units. Note that the correlation structure forces risk factors 2, 6 and 7 to move into the profitable region in order to maximise the overall loss of the portfolio.

The worst case scenario ω^* does not only tell us for which changes of market parameters the portfolio is most exposed, it is also an important information for the risk manager who has to reduce the overall risk of the portfolio. We found above that the relation $ML \leq VAR$ holds for every portfolio. Hence, restructuring the portfolio in order to ameliorate the situation for ω^* does not only reduce ML (ie force it towards 0), but at the same time it also reduces VAR.

4. Risk profiles of test portfolio

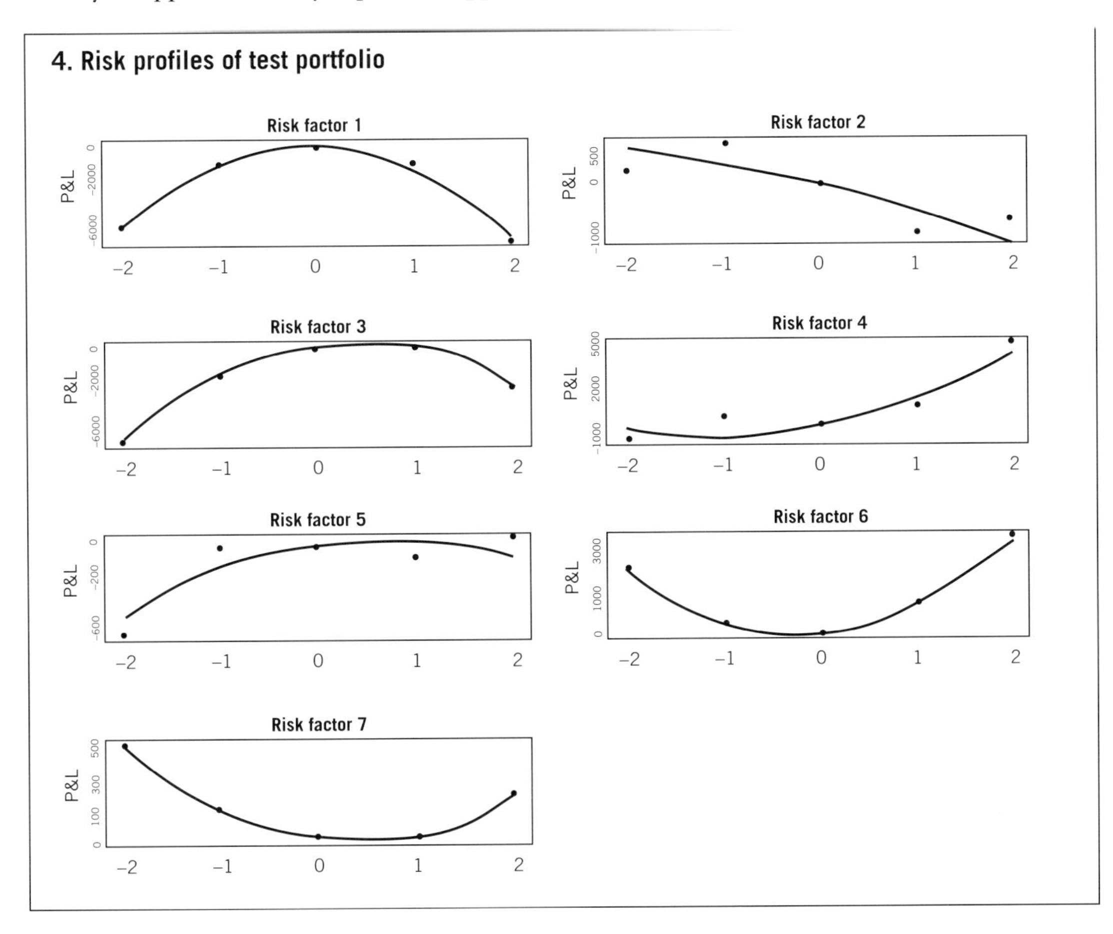

Portfolio characterisation

EXPANDING TRUST REGIONS

A repetitive calculation of ML gives insights into a portfolio that goes far beyond a simple worst case identification. The Levenberg-Marquardt algorithm described in chapter allows us to determine the value of the maximal loss as well as to identify the worst case scenario. If this calculation is repeated for several confidence levels α, a list of MLs and scenarios can be constructed. Table 2 sets out the results of the test portfolio.

The procedure has the following geometric interpretation: increasing α from 0 to some upper limit means expanding the trust region from a single point to the final ellipsoid (see Figure 5). Such a sequence of scenarios defines a path which starts at the origin (ie, $\omega = 0$) and follows the worst possible route (see Figure 6).

Table 2. Repetitive calculation of ML for test portfolio

α	ML	Risk Factor 1	Risk Factor 2	...	Risk Factor 7
⋮	⋮	⋮	⋮	...	⋮
88%	-2,688.49	-2.727	-1.671	...	-0.825
89%	-2,735.55	-2.761	-1.690	...	-0.834
90%	-2,786.36	-2.796	-1.711	...	-0.844
91%	-2,841.72	-2.834	-1.733	...	-0.855
⋮	⋮	⋮	⋮	...	⋮

5. Expanding trust regions

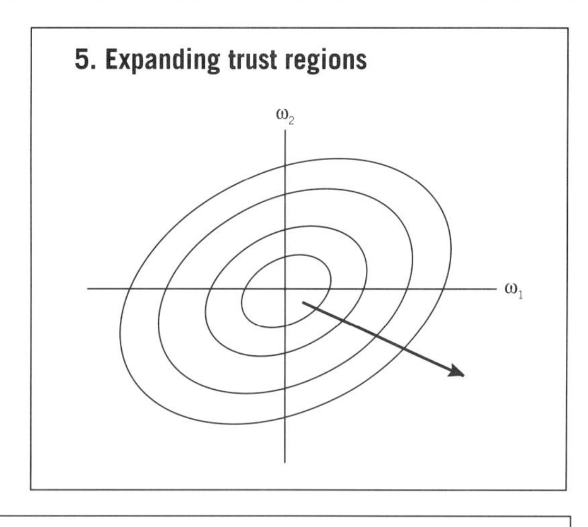

6. ML and MP paths of test portfolio

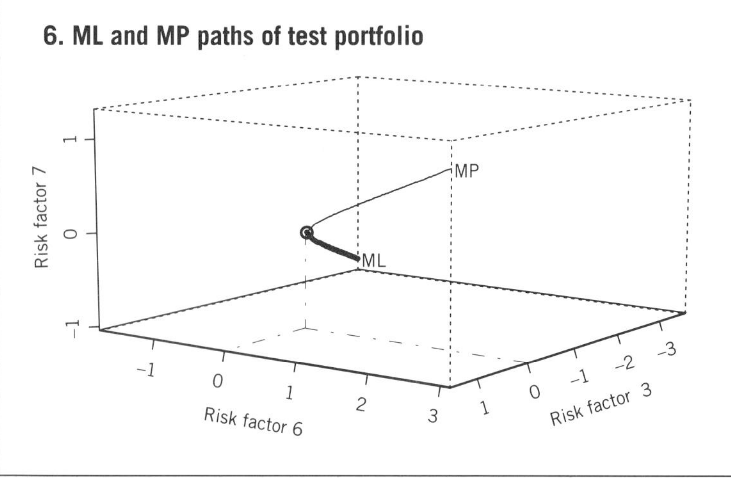

To obtain a path which is smooth, it is necessary to solve the minimisation problems many times for different levels of α. However, the number of minimisations may be reduced by using the results of a sensitivity analysis (Studer and Lüthi 1996) together with some interpolation scheme.

MAXIMUM LOSS ON AN ELLIPSOID

If the matrix G in problem (18) is positive definite (ie all curvatures are positive), the optimisation problem has an unique stationary point which is the strict global minimum. Consequently, the path will stop at this point as soon as it is reached. However, it might be interesting to see how the path would evolve if we restricted the minimisation to the surface of the expanding trust region. This is equivalent to the problem

$$\text{ML} = \min \tfrac{1}{2}\omega^{T} G \omega + g^{T}\omega \qquad \text{s.t. } \omega^{T} \textstyle\sum_{T}^{-1} \omega = c_{\alpha} \tag{27}$$

where the inequality has been replaced by an equality. To solve this problem, the ellipsoid is first transformed into a sphere, which leads to the following formulation

$$\text{ML} = \min \tfrac{1}{2}\hat{\omega}^{T} \hat{G} \hat{\omega} + \hat{g}^{T}\hat{\omega} \qquad \text{s.t. } \hat{\omega}^{T}\hat{\omega} = c_{\alpha}. \tag{28}$$

The following theorem shows how problem (28) can be solved using the Levenberg-Marquardt algorithm:

THEOREM 3: For every $\kappa > \max(\lambda_1, 0)$, where λ_1 is the lowest eigenvalue of $\hat{G}$, the two problems

$$\min \tfrac{1}{2}\hat{\omega}^{T}\left(\hat{G} - \kappa \mathbb{1}\right)\hat{\omega} + \hat{g}^{T}\hat{\omega} \qquad \text{s.t. } \hat{\omega}^{T}\hat{\omega} = c_{\alpha} \tag{29}$$

and

$$\min \tfrac{1}{2}\hat{\omega}^{T}\left(\hat{G} - \kappa \mathbb{1}\right)\hat{\omega} + \hat{g}^{T}\hat{\omega} \qquad \text{s.t. } \hat{\omega}^{T}\hat{\omega} \le c_{\alpha} \tag{30}$$

have an identical solution $\hat{\omega}^{*}$.

PROOF

The matrix $(\hat{G} - \kappa \mathbb{1})$ is not positive semidefinite. To satisfy equation (22) of theorem 1, we must have $\nu \ge \kappa > 0$. Hence, $\|\hat{\omega}\|^2 = c_{\alpha}$ must hold to fulfill condition (24). Since ν is unique (see theorem 1), it follows that the two problems (29) and (30) have identical solutions.

The fact that $\hat{\omega}^{T}\hat{\omega} = c_{\alpha}$ implies that

$$\tfrac{1}{2}\hat{\omega}^T\left(\hat{G}-\kappa\mathbb{1}\right)\hat{\omega}+\hat{g}^T\hat{\omega}=\tfrac{1}{2}\hat{\omega}^T\hat{G}\hat{\omega}+\hat{g}^T\hat{\omega}-\tfrac{1}{2}\kappa c_\alpha$$

therefore, the solution of (30) is also solution to (28). To be able to apply this theorem, a lower bound of λ_1 must be known, which can be obtained by using Gershgorin discs.

Of course, the ideas developed so far can also be applied to the profit side of the portfolio. Inverting the sign of the objective function of (28) leads to the problem

$$\begin{aligned} MP = -\min\; & -\tfrac{1}{2}\hat{\omega}^T\hat{G}\hat{\omega}-\hat{g}^T\hat{\omega} \\ \text{s.t. } & \hat{\omega}^T\hat{\omega}=c_\alpha \end{aligned} \tag{31}$$

and allows us to find the path of MP.

EXPECTED PROFIT AND LOSS ON AN ELLIPSOID

Are ML and MP sufficient to judge the quality of a portfolio? The answer is no: a study of nothing but the extremes gives no indication about what has to be expected in a typical case. Similar to ML and MP, we can also calculate the expected profit and loss on the ellipsoid: as before, the ellipsoid is first transformed into a sphere, which changes the P&L function to $\hat{v}(\hat{\omega})=\tfrac{1}{2}\hat{\omega}^T\hat{G}\hat{\omega}+\hat{g}^T\hat{\omega}$. Then, the expected value (EV) on the sphere is (see Studer and Lüthi 1996)

$$E\left(\hat{v}(\hat{\omega})\middle|\hat{\omega}^T\hat{\omega}=c_\alpha\right)=\frac{c_\alpha}{2}\frac{Tr(\hat{G})}{M} \tag{32}$$

where $Tr(\hat{G})=\Sigma_{i=1}^{M}\hat{G}_{i,i}$. Although this quantity is easy to calculate, it gives important information about the portfolio: plotting the value of (32) for increasing α leads to the EV path. The paths of the test portfolio we discussed above are shown in Figure 7: the absolute value of ML highly exceeds MP - and for every value of α. Since the expected value is negative and decreasing, it must be concluded that the portfolio has bad risk characteristics.

Coping with non-linearity

In the previous chapters, it has always been assumed that a quadratic P&L function $v(\omega)$ was given. Such a function can, for example, be obtained by using Taylor series expansions $v(\omega)=\delta^T\omega+\tfrac{1}{2}\omega^T\Gamma\omega+o(\|\hat{\omega}\|^2)$. For many financial instruments, local sensitivities (δ,Γ) can be obtained directly from the valuation models (Hull, 1993). However, such local approximations are only valid for small changes in ω - in our model for short holding periods t or small confidence levels α.

QUADRATIC APPROXIMATION

For large moves of the risk factors ω, local approximations can lead to tremendous errors. In practice, so-called risk profiles such as those shown in Figure 4 are used to analyse the structure of P&L functions $v(\omega)$: a set of scenarios $O=\{\omega^{(1)},\ldots,\omega^{(n)}\}$ is defined and the portfolio is fully repriced for each of them separately; the resulting P&Ls are denoted $P=\{\xi^{(1)},\ldots,\xi^{(n)}\}$. From the sets O and P, a quadratic approximation $v(\omega)=\tfrac{1}{2}\omega^TG\omega+g^T\omega+c$ can be constructed by minimising the sum of the squared errors (ie method of least squares):

$$\begin{aligned} \min\; & \sum_{i=1}^{n}\left(\tfrac{1}{2}\omega^{(i)T}G\omega^{(i)}+g^T\omega^{(i)}+c-\xi^{(i)}\right)^2 \\ \text{s.t. } & G\in R^{M\times M},\text{ symmetric} \\ & g\in\mathbb{R} \\ & c\in R. \end{aligned} \tag{33}$$

The solution to problem (33) can be determined by solving the normal equation

$$S^TSx=S^T\xi \tag{34}$$

where S is the scenario matrix

$$S=\begin{matrix}\omega^{(1)}\\ \omega^{(2)}\\ \vdots\\ \omega^{(n)}\end{matrix}\begin{pmatrix}\tfrac{1}{2}\omega_1^2 & \omega_1\omega_2 & \cdots & \omega_1\omega_M & \tfrac{1}{2}\omega_2^2 & \omega_2\omega_3 & \cdots & \tfrac{1}{2}\omega_M^2 & \omega_1 & \cdots & \omega_M & 1\\ \cdots & & & & & & & & & & \cdots & 1\\ \cdots & & & & & & & & & & \cdots & 1\\ & & & & & & \ddots & & & & & \vdots\\ \cdots & & & & & & & & & & \cdots & 1\end{pmatrix} \tag{35}$$

which is a

$$n\times\left(\frac{M(M+3)}{2}+1\right)$$

matrix; row i contains the various products of the components of scenario $\omega^{(i)}$. The vector

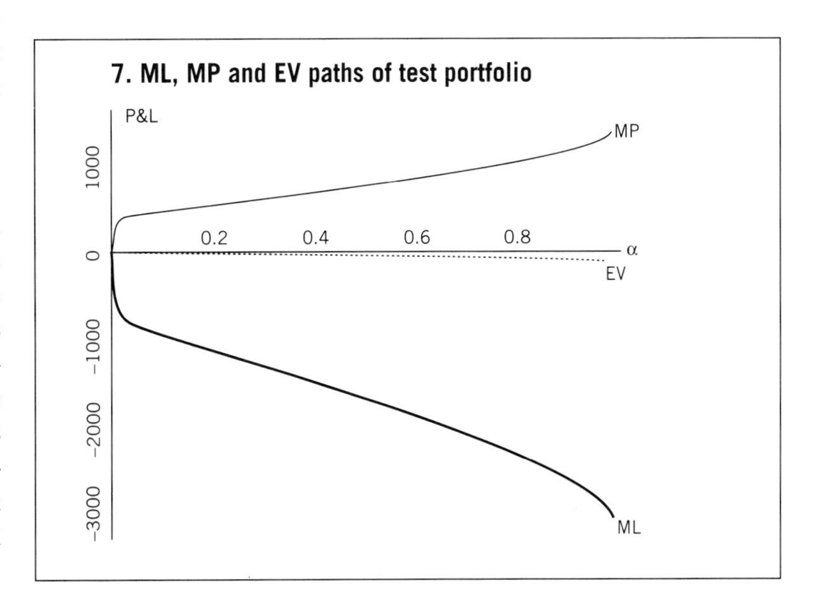

7. ML, MP and EV paths of test portfolio

8. Nonquadratic P&L function with calculated paths

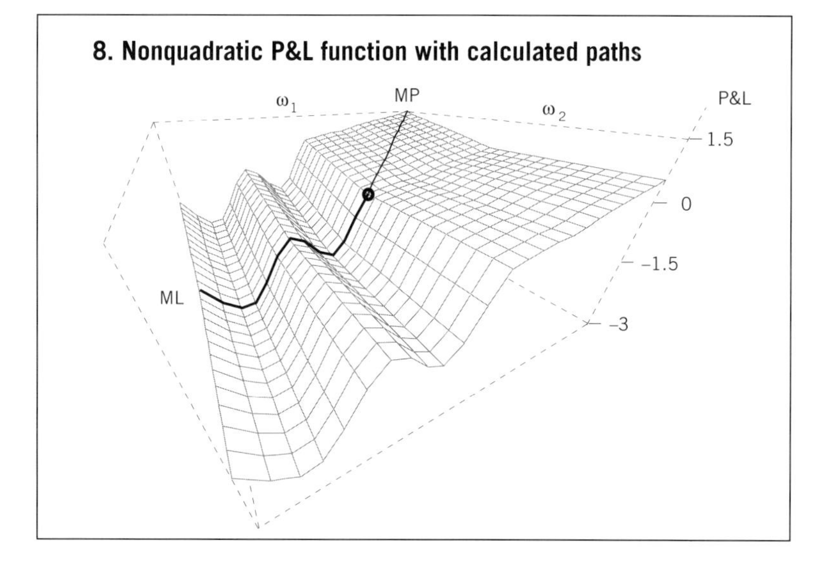

9. Characteristics of nonquadratic P&L function

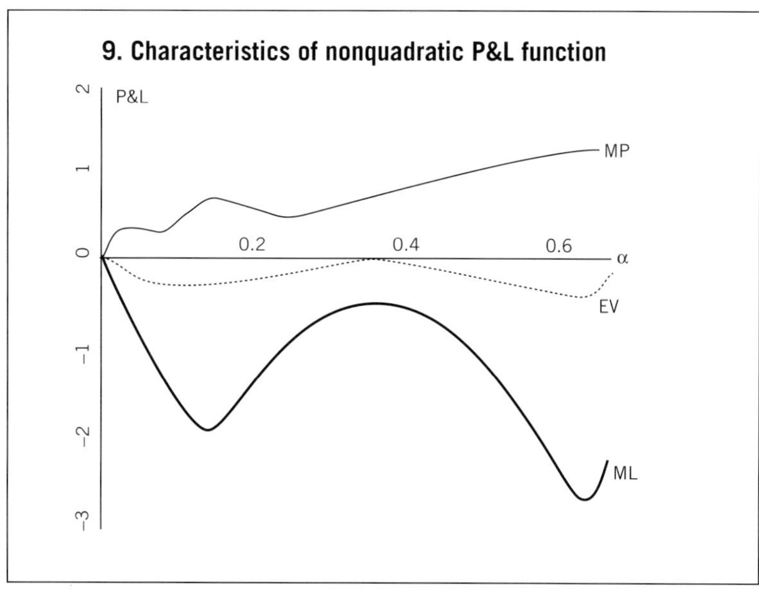

$$\xi = \left(\xi^{(1)},\ldots,\xi^{(n)}\right) \tag{36}$$

holds the P&Ls of each scenario. Finally, x is the vector of the unknowns:

$$x = \left(G_{1,1};G_{1,2};\ldots;G_{1,M};G_{2,2};G_{2,3};\ldots;G_{M,M};g_1;\ldots;g_M;c\right) \tag{37}$$

it has

$$\left(\frac{M(M+3)}{2}+1\right)$$

elements.

Note that the newly introduced constant c can simply be added to the previous results.

DYNAMIC WEIGHTING

The least squares method above leads to quadratic approximations with best fit to the *entire* scenario set O. However, if we seek ML *on* the surface of a specific ellipsoid (ie for a fixed level α) we can utilise better approximations by weighting the scenarios adequately: the scenarios $\omega^{(i)}$ lying close to the α-ellipsoid (ie $\omega^{(i)T}\Sigma_t^{-1}\omega^{(i)} \approx c_\alpha$) get a higher weight than those lying far away. Hence, for scenario $\omega^{(i)}$ the weight $\upsilon_i(\alpha)$ is set to:

$$\upsilon_i(\alpha) = \frac{1}{1+\beta\left|\omega^{(i)T}\Sigma_t^{-1}\omega^{(i)} - c_\alpha\right|^\gamma} \tag{38}$$

where β, $\gamma > 0$ are parameters which control the smoothness with respect to α. If $\Theta(\alpha)$ denotes the diagonal weighting matrix (ie $\Theta_{i,i}(\alpha) = \upsilon_i(\alpha); \Theta_{i,j}(\alpha) = 0$ if $i \neq j$), then the normal equation (34) becomes

$$S^T\Theta(\alpha)Sx(\alpha) = S^T\Theta(\alpha)\xi \tag{39}$$

where the solution $x(\alpha)$ defines the parameters $G(\alpha)$, $g(\alpha)$ and $c(\alpha)$. Thus, for every value of α, a new P&L function $v(\omega,\alpha) = \frac{1}{2}\omega^T G(\alpha)\omega + g(\alpha)^T\omega + c(\alpha)$ is defined. Hence, the paths of ML, MP and EV can be calculated with the methods described above. This way, it is possible to analyse portfolios, which are not necessarily quadratic, by using a family of quadratic approximations. Figure 8 shows a two-dimensional, highly non-linear P&L surface $v(\omega)$.

Figure 9 displays the results of the dynamic approximation technique. Note that this method produces exact results for quadratic functions.

IMPLEMENTATION

The following sequence of steps needs to be set up in order to implement the dynamic approximation technique:

❑ **1** Given are a set of scenarios $O = \{\omega^{(1)}, \ldots, \omega^{(n)}\}$ with respective P&Ls $P = \{\xi^{(1)}, \ldots, \xi^{(n)}\}$, as well as the risk factor covariance matrix Σ_t for a holding period of t days.

❑ **2** Calculate the Cholesky decomposition $\Sigma_t = U^T U$.

❑ **3** Use O and P to fill up the scenario matrix S and the P&L vector ξ according to (35) and (36).

❑ **4** For $\alpha = 0\%, \ldots, 99\%$

(a) Calculate the weight $\upsilon_i(\alpha)$ of each scenario $\omega^{(i)}$ by formula (38). Let Θ be the diagonal matrix built up of the elements $\upsilon_i(\alpha)$.

(b) Solve the normal equation (39) for $x(\alpha)$.

(c) According to (37) the vector $x(\alpha)$ holds the elements of the symmetric matrix $G(\alpha)$, the vector $g(\alpha)$, as well as the constant $c(\alpha)$, which define the quadratic function

$$v(\omega,\alpha) = \tfrac{1}{2}\omega^T G(\alpha)\omega + g(\alpha)^T\omega + c(\alpha).$$

(d) Use the Cholesky decomposition to

transform the ellipsoidal problem (18) to a spherical one (21) $\hat{g} = Ug(\alpha)$ and $\hat{G} = UG(\alpha)U^T$.

(e) Determine the maximum loss

$$ML = \min \tfrac{1}{2}\hat{\omega}^T\hat{G}\hat{\omega} + \hat{g}^T\hat{\omega} + c(\alpha)$$
$$\text{s.t. } \hat{\omega}^T\hat{\omega} = c_\alpha$$

by the Levenberg–Marquardt algorithm (c_α is the α-quantile of a χ^2 distribution with M degrees of freedom, where M is the number of risk factors).

(f) To get the worst case scenario, transform the result back into the original coordinates: $\omega = U^T\hat{\omega}$

(g) Find MP and the corresponding scenario by inverting the sign of the objective function [see (31)] and repeating the previous two steps.

(h) Calculate the expected value EV by (32).

❑ 5 Plot the ML, MP and EV paths.

This gives just the general structure of the algorithm. Practical implementations should take into account the various possibilities to reduce the computational costs. So is it advisable to use sparse matrix structures for the scenario matrix S and the weighting matrix Θ. Moreover, the quantity $\omega^{(i)T}\Sigma_t^{-1}\omega^{(i)}$ needs to be evaluated only in the first iteration of step 4. This way, the maximum loss analysis can be performed for high-dimensional portfolios within a short time.

One point remains to be specified: what scenarios should the set O contain? A naive answer would be to cover the whole scenario space with a regular grid and to valuate the portfolio at every point of this grid. However, if k points were chosen on every axis, this would require k^M portfolio repricings, which is computationally not practicable for portfolios with many risk factors. Since O is used to construct the M-dimensional quadratic function

$$v(\omega) = \tfrac{1}{2}\omega^TG\omega + g^T\omega + c$$

the set O needs at least

$$\left(\frac{M(M+3)}{2} + 1\right)$$

elements to determine G, g, and c uniquely. In order to approximate the mixed term coefficients $G_{i,j}$; $i \neq j$, the set O must include scenarios whose components ω_i and ω_j are not simultaneously 0. On the other hand, the product $\omega_i\omega_j$ reaches its extreme values among all scenarios $(\omega_i,\omega_j) \in [-l_i,l_i]\times[-l_j,l_j]$ at the corner points $[\pm l_i,\pm l_j]$. Thus, it seems reasonable to choose scenarios which lie on the diagonals to estimate the effect of the mixed terms (see Figure 10).

10. Choice of scenarios

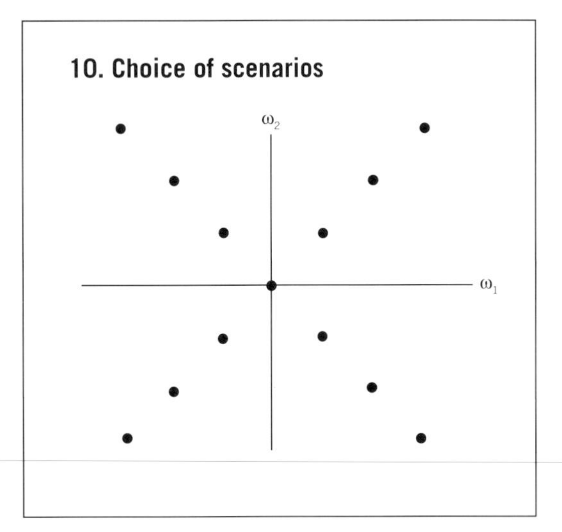

The repetition of this construction for all $\binom{M}{2}$ combinations of $i \neq j$ with k different points per diagonal leads to a total number of $(kM[M-1]+1)$ scenarios. Nonetheless, this number may be reduced: if it is known in advance that some of the risk factors ω_i and ω_j have no cross effects, the corresponding element $G_{i,j}$ can be set to 0 a priori (in such cases, however, it might become necessary to choose scenarios lying directly on the axis ω_i (and/or ω_j) in order to ensure that the scenario matrix S is of full rank).

It remains to be mentioned that the scenarios should be chosen within a meaningful range: formula (8) restricts ω_i to the interval

$$\left[-\sqrt{c_\alpha}\sqrt{(\Sigma_t)_{i,i}}, \sqrt{c_\alpha}\sqrt{(\Sigma_t)_{i,i}}\right].$$

Moreover, the parameters β and γ of the weighting function (38) need to be adapted to the number k of scenarios per diagonal to assure reasonably smooth functions $v(\omega,\alpha)$ with respect to α (eg $\beta = 100$ and $\gamma = 2$ for $k = 6$).

Conclusion

Maximum loss is, first of all, a methodology to determine systematically the worst possible outcome. It respects correlations between risk factors by choosing adequate trust regions. The result of a maximum loss analysis is not simply a loss figure: each calculation also identifies the worst case scenario. This scenario not only describes the most dangerous combination of market parameters, it is also helpful for risk managers who aim to reduce a portfolio's risks: an improvement of the portfolio for the worst case scenario reduces ML and VAR as well, since ML and VAR are interrelated.

QUADRATIC MAXIMUM LOSS

Portfolios with quadratic P&L functions can be analysed with an efficient algorithm. This allows a repetitive calculation for trust regions of different sizes (ie for different confidence levels). This way, a complete ML path can be constructed which, in some sense, displays the dynamic behaviour of the risk. Likewise, the positive outcomes can be investigated and lead to the MP path. Together with the path of the expected value, these three paths form the basis for a risk characterisation of portfolios.

The use of quadratic approximations instead of Taylor series expansions leads to the idea of dynamic approximations: each element of a given set of scenarios is weighted accordingly to its distance to the trust region which is actually investigated, and the calculations of ML, MP and EV are restricted to the surface of this trust region. As a consequence, the analyses can be expanded to a much broader class of P&L functions than quadratic ones alone.

BIBLIOGRAPHY

Beckstrom, R., and A. Campbell, 1995, *An Introduction to VAR* C*ATS Software Inc., Palo Alto.

Basle Committee on Banking Supervision, 1996, *Amendment to the Capital Accord to Incorporate Market Risks.*

Dennis, J.E., and R.B. Schnabel, 1996, *Numerical Methods for Unconstrained Optimisation and Non-linear Equations*, Prentice-Hall, Englewood Cliffs.

Fletcher, R., 1987, *Practical Methods of Optimisation*, 2nd edition John Wiley & Sons, Chichester.

Hull, J.C., 1993, *Options, Futures and other Derivative Securities*, Prentice-Hall, Englewood Cliffs.

Rouvinez, C., 1997, "Going Greek with VAR", *Risk* 10, 2, pp. 57–65.

Studer, G., 1995, "Value-at-Risk and Maximum Loss Optimisation", RiskLab. Technical Report, Zurich.

Studer, G., and H.-J. Lüthi, 1996, "Quadratic Maximum Loss for Risk Measurement of Portfolios", RiskLab: Technical Report, Zurich.

Vavasis, S.A., 1991, *Non-linear Optimisation, Complexity Issues*, Oxford University Press, New York.

33

The Value-at-Risk of a Portfolio of Currency Derivatives under Worst-Case Distributional Assumptions

Douglas Costa and Matthew Page
Susquehanna Investment Group

Standard value-at-risk definitions are based on strong assumptions about the joint distribution of underlying prices and their correlations. However, there is no reliable way to estimate this joint distribution where large losses may occur. This paper proposes a VAR measure of a portfolio of currency derivatives under worst-case distributional assumptions. The worst-case measure eliminates the risk that VAR will be underestimated due to inaccurate pricing assumptions

Let L be the loss on a given portfolio of currency derivatives over the next 10 business days. The value-at-risk (VAR) of the portfolio is the 99th percentile of L.[1]

Because of the non-linear dependence of an option's value on the underlying price, the standard "greeks" (ie instantaneous partial derivatives such as delta) give useable estimates of L only for small changes in the underlying price. For example, consider the sale of an overnight low-delta put. The VAR of this deal can be calculated by simply revaluing the put with the underlying price down 2.33 standard deviations. A delta-gamma approximation would grossly underestimate the loss on the put that would accompany this drop in the underlying price. Since large changes in the underlying price typically produce large P/L swings, low-order Taylor series approximations of L are likely to break down in the cases which are most important in VAR estimation. In order to estimate VAR accurately, the portfolio must be revalued under a number of different spot price realisations.

Currency derivatives portfolios can be partitioned into "books" by currency pair. In estimating the VAR of the entire portfolio, the question of how to aggregate risks across these books is crucial. If the portfolio includes cross-rate deals, the sum of the local VARs may be a loss that could only occur with inconsistent spot prices.

Suppose, for example, that one buys dollars against Deutschmarks, sells dollars against yen, and buys Deutschmarks against yen in the forward market. Assuming that 10-day changes in spot rates are normally distributed, the local VARs of the three deals correspond to the following events: Deutschmark/dollar down 2.33 standard deviations, yen/dollar up 2.33 standard deviations, and yen/Deutschmark down 2.33 standard deviations. Using the sum of the local VARs as a global VAR is equivalent to the assertion that the probability of the intersection of these three events is 1%. The occurrence of an arbitrage opportunity of this magnitude would constitute a major breakdown in the global banking system, an event whose probability is, we

We are very grateful to Steve Zucker for many insights and examples that have shaped the approach proposed here. We are also grateful for comments from Barry Belkin, Scott Brown, Darrell Duffie, Steve Elkins, Peter Glynn, Dan Heitner, Kai Huang, Brian Kanaga, John Lehoczky, Bob O'Brien, Craig Peters, Pat Schiedler, Walter Stromquist, Tsu Yao and Jeff Yass. We thank Scott Brown and Walter Stromquist for computational assistance.

hope, much less than 1%! In any case, such risks are outside the scope of this paper.

In the standard simulation approaches, the spot price realisations are drawn from an assumed joint distribution. The most commonly-used distributions are the multivariate lognormal and the historical distribution. In both cases, the estimated VAR depends heavily on the assumed distributions. The VAR measure proposed here overcomes this correlation-dependence by implicitly using the worst-case correlations for each portfolio.

VAR depends on the joint distribution of the underlying exchange rates. Given a univariate distribution for each exchange rate, consider the set of all joint distributions whose marginal distribution for each exchange rate is the corresponding univariate distribution. We propose an heuristic algorithm to estimate an upper bound on the VAR over this set of joint distributions.

The setup

We assume that there are three sources of risk for a currency derivatives portfolio, listed in order of importance: spot exchange rates, implied volatilities, and interest rates. We will make further assumptions about the distributions of these state variables below. We assume there is no credit risk.

We enumerate the currencies represented in the portfolio as $0, 1, \ldots, N$. For the portfolios that we are considering, N is typically between 15 and 25. For $0 \leq i \leq N$ and $0 \leq j \leq N$, let $S_{ij}(t)$ denote the spot price of one unit of currency j in units of currency i at time t. The time horizon h is assumed to be 10 business days. Let $S_{ij} = S_{ij}(h)$, $S_i = S_{0i}$, $\mathbf{S}_t = [S_1(t), \ldots, S_N(t)]$, and $\mathbf{S} = \mathbf{S}_h$. We assume that there are no riskless arbitrage opportunities at $t = 0$ or $t = h$. It follows that $S_{ik} = S_{ij} \cdot S_{jk}$ for all (i,j,k). In particular, we have $S_{ij} \cdot S_{ji} = S_{ii} = 1$ for all (i,j). For $i = 1, \ldots, N$ and $t \geq 0$, we assume that

$$dS_i(t) = \mu_i\left[t, S_i(t)\right]dt + \sigma_i(t)S_i(t)dB_i(t)$$

where $B_i(t)$ is a standard Brownian motion. It follows from Ito's lemma that all of the $S_{ij}(t)$ are diffusion processes of this form. Let $F_i(s)$ be the cumulative distribution function of S_i.

We assume that a valuation model will be available for every product in the portfolio. In consideration of the runtime constraint, we will use the following benchmark. On our 166 megahertz Pentium processor, a single evaluation of the Black-Scholes formula takes about 1.7×10^{-5} seconds. Revaluing a portfolio of 10^4 standard options, therefore, takes about 0.17 seconds.

Let $r_i(t) = r_i(t,u)$ be the instantaneous forward interest rate function for currency i at time t. Letting $r_i = r_i(h,h)$, we assume that interest rates at $t = h$ are determined by the following one-factor model:

$$r_i(h,u) = r_i + r_i(0,u) - r_i(0,h) \text{ for all } u > h.$$

Let $\mathbf{r}_t = [r_0(t), \ldots, r_N(t)]$.

Let Π_{ij} be the subportfolio of all deals whose boundary conditions (ie exercise value and barrier conditions) depend only on S_{ij}. For any expiration $T > 0$ of a deal in Π_{ij}, we assume that we can observe at $T = 0$ the market price of a European option to exchange at $t = T$ one unit of currency j for an amount of currency i equal to the current forward exchange rate (ie an at-the-money option). Let $\phi_{ij}(T)$ be the Black-Scholes implied volatility of such an option. Let $\sigma_{ij}(t) = \sigma_{ij}(t,u)$ be the instantaneous forward volatility function for $S_{ij}(u)$ at time t. We assume that $\sigma_{ij}(0,u)$ is consistent with $\phi_{ij}(T)$ in the following sense:

$$\phi_{ij}^2(T) = \frac{1}{T}\int_0^T \sigma_{ij}^2(0,u)du.$$

We define the $(N+1) \times (N+1)$ matrix $\sigma_t = [\sigma_{ij}(t)]$.

Let M be the number of *multi-pair* deals, whose boundary conditions depend on more than one of the S_{ij} (eg basket options). We assume that the risk of the multi-pair deals is small relative to the risk of the single-pair deals in the portfolio. For $1 \leq i \leq M$, let $f_i(t, \mathbf{S}_t, \sigma_t, \mathbf{r}_t)$ be the value, in units of currency 0, of the ith multi-pair deal at time t.

Let $V_{ij}(t,s,v,r,f)$ be the net value, in units of currency i, of all deals in Π_{ij} at time t, given that $S_{ij}(t) = s$, $\sigma_{ij}(t) = v(t)$, $r_i(t) = r(t)$, and $r_j(t) = f(t)$. Let $V_{ij}(s) = V_{ij}[h, s, \sigma_{ij}(0), r_i(0), r_j(0)]$. Let

$$V_t = V(t, \mathbf{S}_t, \sigma_t, \mathbf{r}_t) =$$

$$\sum_{i=0}^{N}\sum_{j=1}^{i} S_{0i}(t)V_{ij}\left[t, S_{ij}(t), \sigma_{ij}(t), r_i(t), r_j(t)\right] + \sum_{i=1}^{M} f_i(t, \mathbf{S}_t, \sigma_t, \mathbf{r}_t).$$

The loss whose 99th percentile is the focus of this paper is given by $L = V_0 - V_h$.

The effect of distributional assumptions

The joint distribution of $\mathbf{S}$ determines how exposures in different currency pairs are aggregated. The correlation matrix is an important feature of the joint distribution. The correlations assumed in a simulation can have a dramatic effect on VAR estimates. For example, suppose $S_1(0) = S_2(0) = 100$ and we are long one unit of currency 1 and short one unit of currency 2. In this case, the loss function is given by $L = S_1 - S_2$. Assuming that $\mathrm{var}(S_1) = \mathrm{var}(S_2) = \sigma^2$, we have

$$\sigma_L^2 = \mathrm{var}(L) = 2\sigma^2\left[1 - \mathrm{corr}(S_1 S_2)\right].$$

If S_1 and S_2 are jointly normally distributed with mean (100,100), then L is also normal and $\mathrm{VAR} = 2.33\sigma_L$. Taking $\sigma = 1$, Figure 1 shows VAR as a function of the correlation.

If the correlation is 0.9, for example, VAR is 1.04. But if the correlation is only 0.6, VAR doubles to 2.08!

As a more extreme example, suppose we sell an exotic option which pays one unit of currency 0 if $S_1 - S_2 \geq 2.08$ and zero otherwise. The only possible values of L are 1 and 0. If the actual correlation is 0.6 and a simulation is run under the assumption that the correlation is 0.9, the probability of observing a positive loss is of the order of 10^{-6}!

Historical correlation coefficients between spot rates can be far from stationary. The correlation structure depends on central bank policy, the political and economic environment, upcoming elections, and many other factors. Both hedgers and speculators tend to trade more when the correlation structure is less clear, so the risks are typically greater when the correlations cannot be estimated reliably. Therefore, VAR measures that assume a fixed correlation matrix tend to be least reliable at the riskiest times.

Motivated by the potentially misleading effects of correlation assumptions, we have developed a VAR algorithm that makes worst-case assumptions about the joint distribution.

The univariate distributions

The estimation of VAR does require assumptions about the univariate distribution of each foreign currency in the portfolio. For example, the short sale of one unit of currency 1 is a deal with theoretically unlimited losses. Any meaningful estimate of the VAR of this deal will depend on assumptions about the distribution of S_1. We will propose one way of estimating $F_i(s)$ for $i = 1, \ldots, N$.

Letting

$$X_i(t) = \ln\left[\frac{S_i(t+h)}{S_i(t)}\right]$$

we assume that $X_i(t)$ and $X_i(u)$ are independent and identically distributed whenever $|t - u| > h$. The first step is to construct piecewise-linear

1. VAR versus correlation

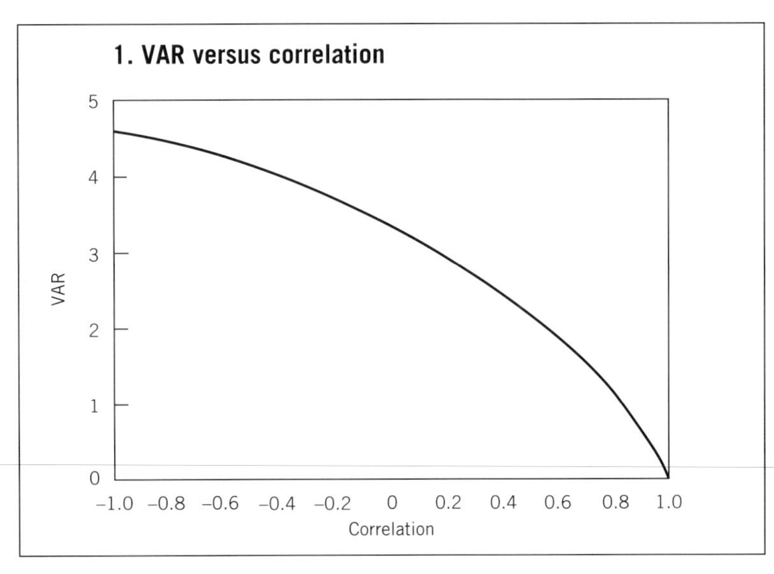

interpolations of the empirical distributions of the X_i. The problem with using the empirical distribution to measure risk is that there is no probability outside the sample range, where large losses are likely to occur. To fix this problem, we propose a slight modification of the construction given by Bratley, Fox, and Schrage (1987). The idea is to attach shifted exponential distributions to the lower and upper tails of each empirical distribution. The exponential tails are chosen so that $E(X_i) = 0$ and $\mathrm{var}(X_i) = \sigma_{0i}^2(h)h$.

Our data set consists of daily exchange rates for 23 currencies against the dollar (which is taken to be currency 0), during the period from January 1989 to June 1996. Table 1 contains selected quantiles for X_i.

Table 1. Selected quantiles of daily returns for 23 currencies[2]

	0.01	0.25	0.50	0.75	0.99
AUD	−0.01564	−0.00254	0.00027	0.00295	0.01232
ATS	−0.01992	−0.00383	0.00009	0.00406	0.01954
BEF	−0.01932	−0.00377	0.00000	0.00409	0.02089
CAD	−0.00785	−0.00157	0.00000	0.00154	0.00724
DKK	−0.01813	−0.00364	0.00009	0.00413	0.01861
ECU	−0.01984	−0.00343	0.00000	0.00385	0.01793
FIM	−0.02230	−0.00365	0.00018	0.00404	0.02022
FRF	−0.01867	−0.00360	0.00000	0.00387	0.01886
DEM	−0.01926	−0.00377	0.00013	0.00415	0.01964
GRD	−0.01885	−0.00405	0.00000	0.00373	0.01771
HKD	−0.00127	−0.00013	0.00000	0.00013	0.00116
IEP	−0.01948	−0.00347	0.00000	0.00366	0.01871
ITL	−0.01905	−0.00372	0.00000	0.00373	0.01771
JPY	−0.01794	−0.00364	0.00000	0.00338	0.01944
MXN	−0.08617	−0.00292	0.00000	0.00260	0.05373
NLG	−0.01929	−0.00380	0.00012	0.00406	0.01973
NZD	−0.01447	−0.00211	0.00017	0.00236	0.01131
NOK	−0.01828	−0.00330	0.00007	0.00362	0.01732
PTE	−0.02158	−0.00358	0.00007	0.00394	0.01918
ESP	−0.02046	−0.00370	0.00000	0.00385	0.01991
SEK	−0.01985	−0.00352	0.00015	0.00384	0.01757
CHF	−0.01963	−0.00444	0.00000	0.00461	0.02035
GBP	−0.02029	−0.00326	0.00018	0.00350	0.01765

Interpolation of the value function

We will derive an approximation $\hat{V}(\mathbf{S})$ of the value function $V(\mathbf{S}) = V(h, \mathbf{S}, \sigma_0, \mathbf{r}_0)$, whose value and gradient can be calculated much faster than those of $V(\mathbf{S})$. Using the representation

$$V(\mathbf{S}) = \sum_{j=1}^{N} V_{0j}(S_j) + \sum_{1 \le i < j \le N} S_i V_{ij}(S_j S_i^{-1}) + \sum_{i=1}^{M} f_i(\mathbf{S})$$

we will approximate $V - \Sigma f_i$ by interpolating the $V_{ij}(s)$ separately.

Fix the parameter $q \in (0, 0.01]$, determining how much of each tail of the marginal distributions will be assumed to produce losses greater than VAR. The algorithm will converge faster with a larger q but at the cost of overestimating VAR. For $j = 1, \ldots, N$ define

$$\alpha_{0j} = F_j^{-1}\left(\frac{q}{2N}\right)$$

and

$$\beta_{0j} = F_j^{-1}\left(1 - \frac{q}{2N}\right).$$

Whenever $1 \le i < j \le N$ define

$$\alpha_{ij} = \frac{\alpha_{0j}}{\beta_{0i}}$$

and

$$\beta_{ij} = \frac{\beta_{0j}}{\alpha_{0i}}.$$

Now let the pair (i,j) be fixed but arbitrary. After choosing a sequence $\{a_{ijn}\}$ of revaluation points in the interval $[\alpha_{ij}, \beta_{ij}]$, $V_{ij}(a_{ijn})$ is calculated for each n by using the appropriate model for each deal in Π_{ij}. The standard cubic spline algorithm (cf. *Numerical Recipes*) is then used to interpolate $V_{ij}(s)$ on $[\alpha_{ij}, \beta_{ij}]$. Note that $V - \Sigma f_i$ is approximated locally with a quartic polynomial in S_i and $S_j S_i^{-1}$, where $1 \le i < j \le N$.

We will propose one way to pick the revaluation points $\{a_{ijn}\}$. Keeping (i,j) fixed, let $a_n = a_{ijn}$ to simplify the notation for the remainder of this section. Let K_{ij} be the set of all strike prices and barrier prices of the deals in Π_{ij}. Let $V_{ij}^*(s)$ be the net intrinsic value of all deals in Π_{ij} (as if each deal expired immediately), given that $S_{ij} = s$. Let $\delta > 0$ be a limit, in units of currency 0, on the change in V_{ij} between adjacent revaluation points. We will use the conservative approximation[3]

$$E(S_i | S_{ij} = K) = S_i(0)\sqrt{\frac{S_{ij}(0)}{K}}.$$

Starting with $a_0 = S_{ij}(0)$, we construct additional revaluation points $a_1, a_{-1}, a_2, a_{-2} \ldots$ iteratively, according to the following rules: For a_n

On $[a_0, \max K_{ij})$, set

$$a_{n+1} = \min\left\{K \in K_{ij} : K > a_n \text{ and } \left|V_{ij}^*(K) - V_{ij}^*(a_n)\right| S_i(0)\sqrt{\frac{S_{ij}(0)}{K}} > \delta\right\}.$$

On $[\max K_{ij}, \beta_{ij}]$, set

$$a_{n+1} = a_n \exp\left[\sigma_{ij}(h)\sqrt{h}\right].$$

On $(\min K_{ij}, a_0]$, set

$$a_{n-1} = \max\left\{K \in K_{ij} : K < a_n \text{ and } \left|V_{ij}^*(K) - V_{ij}^*(a_n)\right| S_i(0)\sqrt{\frac{S_{ij}(0)}{K}} > \delta\right\}.$$

On $[\alpha_{ij}, \min K_{ij}]$, set

$$a_{n-1} = a_n \exp\left[-\sigma_{ij}(h)\sqrt{h}\right].$$

If necessary, add revaluation points (and reindex) so that $F_{ij}(a_{n+1}) - F_{ij}(a_n) < 0.01$ for all n.

Maximal losses

The next step is to find a set of local maxima of the loss function $\hat{L}(\mathbf{S}) = V_0 - \hat{V}(\mathbf{S})$. We start by finding a set of points where $\hat{L}(\mathbf{S})$ is locally maximal *along one co-ordinate axis* (ie varying only one S_i). Let N_1 be the number of points we will check along each axis. A greater value of N_1 will result in more evaluations of $\hat{L}(\mathbf{S})$ and a greater likelihood of finding the globally maximal loss. Let $\pi_i : \mathbf{R}^N \to \mathbf{R}$ be the standard projection onto the ith coordinate space. For $k = 0, \ldots, N_1 - 1$ define $\mathbf{a}_{0k} \in \mathbf{R}^N$ by the conditions

$$\pi_i(\mathbf{a}_{0k}) = \alpha_{0i} + \frac{k}{N_1 - 1}(\beta_{0i} - \alpha_{0i})$$

for $i = 1, \ldots, N$. For $j = 1, \ldots, N$ and $k = 0, \ldots, N_1 - 1$ define $\mathbf{a}_{jk} \in \mathbf{R}^N$ by the conditions

$$\pi_i(\mathbf{a}_{jk}) = \begin{cases} S_i(0) & \text{if } i \ne j \\ \alpha_{0j} + \dfrac{k}{N_1 - 1}(b_{0j} - a_{0j}) & \text{if } i = j \end{cases}$$

for $i = 1, \ldots, N$. Calculate $\hat{L}(\mathbf{a}_{jk})$ for each (j,k). Choose $\mathbf{a}_1 \in \{\mathbf{a}_{jk}\}$ so that $\hat{L}(\mathbf{a}_1) \ge \hat{L}(\mathbf{a}_{jk})$ for all (j,k). Let N_2 be the number of points at which $\hat{L}(\mathbf{S})$ will be maximised. For $i = 2, \ldots, N_2$ take $\mathbf{a}_i \in \{a_{jk}\}$ to be the point at which the next largest local maximum occurs.

For $i = 1, \ldots, N_2$ start at $\mathbf{a}_i$ and perform a standard conjugate gradient maximisation of $\hat{L}(\mathbf{S})$ in the region $R = \prod_{j=1}^{N}[\alpha_{0j}, \beta_{0j}]$ to find a point $\mathbf{b}_i = (b_{i1}, \ldots, b_{iN}) \in \mathbf{R}^N$ at which $\hat{L}(\mathbf{S})$ is locally maximal (See Press, Flannery, Teukolsky and

Vetterling (1988)). If $\mathbf{b}_j \approx \mathbf{b}_i$ for some $i < j$, then discard $\mathbf{b}_j$ and reindex. Let $N_3 \le N_2$ be the number of unique local maxima found.

Adverse volatility and interest rate shocks

In this section, we will examine the effects of various shocks to the term structures of interest rates and volatilities at each $\mathbf{b}_k$.

Let (i,j,k) be fixed but arbitrary. Define

$$\Delta t = \frac{1}{365}$$

and

$$\sigma_m^2 = \frac{1}{\Delta t} \int_{m\Delta t}^{(m+1)\Delta t} \sigma_{ij}^2(h,u)du$$

for $m \ge 0$. Find $n \ge 0$ satisfying the condition that

$$\frac{\partial V_{ij}}{\partial \sigma_n}(\mathbf{b}_k) \le \frac{\partial V_{ij}}{\partial \sigma_m}(\mathbf{b}_k)$$

for all $m \ge 0$. This condition is designed to detect large time-spread positions where we are short the longer expiration. The parameter $\gamma > 0$ is an additive volatility shock, and $\eta \in (0,1)$ is a multiplicative volatility reduction factor. Both could be chosen using the historical distribution of daily changes in implied volatility. We now tentatively define[4]

$$\sigma_{kij}(u) = \begin{cases} \sigma_{ij}(0,u) & \text{if } u \notin [n\Delta t,(n+1)\Delta t] \\ \sigma_{ij}(0,u) + \gamma & \text{if } u \in [n\Delta t,(n+1)\Delta t] \end{cases}.$$

If the volatility function $\sigma_{ij}(0,u)\eta$ would result in a greater loss at $\mathbf{b}_i$, then we redefine $\sigma_{kij}(u) = \sigma_{ij}(0,u)\eta$. Define the $N \times N$ matrices $\sigma_k = (\sigma_{kij})$ for $k = 1, \ldots, N_3$.

The parameter $\lambda \in (0,1)$ is a relative change in interest rates. For $k = 1, \ldots, N_3$ and $i = 0, \ldots, N$ define

$$\rho_{ki} = \frac{\partial V}{\partial r_i}(\mathbf{b}_k)$$

and $r_{ki}(u) = r_i(0,u)\lambda^{\text{sign}(\rho_{ki})}$. For $k = 1, \ldots, N_3$ define $\mathbf{r}_k = (r_{k0}, \ldots, r_{kN})$.

Finally, calculate $L_k = L(\mathbf{b}_k,\sigma_k,\mathbf{r}_k)$ (using the appropriate model for each deal) and reindex so that $L_k > L_{k+1}$ for $k = 1, \ldots, N_3$.

The worst-case distribution and VAR

In this section, we give an algorithm to estimate an upper bound Ω on VAR, given the locally maximal losses and the marginal distributions. Let P be any probability measure on $\mathbf{R}^N$ and let P_j be the jth marginal distribution of P. For any event $E \subseteq \mathbf{R}^N$ (whose projection $\pi_j(E)$ is P_j-measurable for $j = 1, \ldots, N$), we have

$$P[E] \le \min_{1 \le j \le N} P_j[\pi_j(E)].$$

We will assume that the probability in a small neighbourhood of $\mathbf{b}_i$ is this upper bound. It is in this sense that our VAR measure is based on worst-case distributional assumptions.

Calculate the $N \times 1$ gradient vector

$$\nabla_i = [\nabla_{i1}, \ldots, \nabla_{iN}] = \left[\frac{\partial \hat{L}}{\partial S_1}(\mathbf{b}_i), \ldots, \frac{\partial \hat{L}}{\partial S_N}(\mathbf{b}_i)\right]^t$$

and the $N \times N$ Hessian matrix

$$\mathbf{H}_i = [h_{ijk}] = \left[\frac{\partial^2 \hat{L}}{\partial S_j \partial S_k}(\mathbf{b}_i)\right]$$

of $\hat{L}$ at $\mathbf{b}_i$, for $i = 1, \ldots, N_3$. Note that $\nabla_i \approx \mathbf{0}$ if $\mathbf{b}_i$ lies in the interior of the region R. For $\mathbf{x} \in \mathbf{R}^N$, define $L_i(\mathbf{x}) = L_i + \nabla_i \mathbf{x} + \frac{1}{2}\mathbf{x}^t \mathbf{H}_i \mathbf{x}$ for $i = 1, \ldots, N_3$. We assume that $L_i(\mathbf{x}) \approx L(\mathbf{b}_i + \mathbf{x}, \sigma_i, \mathbf{r}_i)$ for small $\mathbf{x}$.

We will give the details of the next step only for the case in which all of the $\mathbf{b}_i$ lie in the interior of the region R; the other cases are handled similarly. For $j = 1, \ldots, N$ find $c_{1j} > 0$ so that $[-c_{1j}, c_{1j}]$ is the projection of the hyperellipsoid defined by $L_1(\mathbf{x}) = L_2$ into the jth coordinate axis. A formula for c_{1j} is derived in the Appendix.[5]

For $\lambda \ge 0$, define the event

$$W_1(\lambda) = \prod_{j=1}^{N} [b_{1j} - c_{1j}, b_{1j} + c_{1j}] \subset \mathbf{R}^N.$$

and the probability

$$p_1 = \min_{1 \le j \le N} [F_j(b_{1j} + c_{1j}) - F_j(b_{1j} - c_{1j})].$$

We assume that λp_1 is the probability of $W_1(\lambda)$ under the worst-case distribution.

Next, define

$$m_1(\lambda) = \min_{1 \le j \le N} \{L_1(-\lambda c_{1j}\mathbf{e}_j), L_1(\lambda c_{1j}\mathbf{e}_j)\}.$$

We assume that $m_1(\lambda) \le L(\mathbf{x})$ for all $\mathbf{x} \in W_1(\lambda)$. Let $p = 0.01 - q$. If $p_1 = p$, take $\Omega = L_2$. If $p_1 > p$, take $\Omega = m_1[p/p_1]$. If $p_1 < p$, then we find rectangular neighborhoods of $\mathbf{b}_1$ and $\mathbf{b}_2$ that circumscribe the hyperellipsoids defined by $L_1(\mathbf{x}) = L_3$ and $L_2(\mathbf{x}) = L_3$, respectively.

Repeat this procedure until, at the nth iteration, we have either $n = N_3 - 1$ or $\sum_{k=1}^{n} p_k > p$. If $n = N_3 - 1$ and $\Sigma p_k < p$, we will enlarge the neighborhoods around the $\mathbf{b}_1$ as follows. Let

$$\pi = \frac{p - \sum p_k}{N_3}.$$

Whenever $F_j(b_{ij}+c_{ij}) - F_j(b_{ij}-c_{ij}) < p_i + \pi$, find $d_{ij} > c_{ij}$ satisfying $F_j(b_{ij}+d_{ij}) - F_j(b_{ij}+c_{ij}) = \pi/2$ and $f_{ij} > c_{ij}$ satisfying $F_j(b_{ij}-c_{ij}) - F_j(b_{ij}-f_{ij}) = \pi/2$. If $F_j(b_{ij}+c_{ij}) - F_j(b_{ij}-c_{ij}) > p_i + \pi$, use $d_{ij} = f_{ij} = c_{ij}$. Now take

$$\Omega = \min_{\substack{1\le i\le N_3 \\ 1\le j\le N}} \left\{ L_i(d_{ij}\mathbf{e}_j), L_i(f_{ij}\mathbf{e}_j) \right\}.$$

If $\sum p_k > p$, take

$$\Omega = \min_{1\le i\le N_3} m_i \left[\frac{p}{\sum p_k} \right].$$

We offer the following two observations. If $[c,d] = [-c_{ik}, c_{ik}] \cap [-c_{jk}, c_{jk}] \neq \varnothing$ for some $i \neq j$ and $1 \le k \le N$, then the marginal probability of our worst-case distribution on $[c,d]$ may be greater than $F_k(d) - F_k(c)$. In this case, we have overestimated the worst-case VAR. In the special case of no cross-rate or multi-pair deals, the worst-case VAR will be the sum of the local VARs of the different books.

Conclusion

The standard definition of VAR is based on strong assumptions about the joint distribution of the underlying prices, and their correlations in particular. Unfortunately, there is no reliable way to estimate this joint distribution, especially its tails, where large losses typically occur. Therefore, any VAR measure that depends heavily on assumptions about the joint distribution of the underlying prices is potentially misleading. Using the sum of the VARs in the different books as a global VAR typically implies inconsistent spot price combinations, triggering unnecessary capital charges.

In this paper we have proposed a measure of the VAR of a portfolio of currency derivatives under worst-case distributional assumptions, together with an algorithm to estimate this worst-case VAR. We begin by estimating a univariate distribution for each currency against the base currency. Next, we find the spot price combinations associated with maximal losses. Around these worst-case spot combinations, we assume the highest joint probability which is consistent with each of the marginal probabilities.

This worst-case measure eliminates the risk that VAR will be underestimated due to inaccurate assumptions about the joint distribution of spot prices. Our algorithm also avoids the pitfall of overestimating VAR by using inconsistent spot price combinations. Worst-case VAR is computationally feasible and more robust than the standard VAR measure.

Appendix

The projection of a hyperellipsoid into a coordinate axis[6]

Consider a quadratic form $Q(\mathbf{x}) = \mathbf{x}^t\mathbf{H}\mathbf{x} = \sum h_{ij}x_ix_j$ where $\mathbf{H} = [h_{ij}]$ is a symmetric, positive definite matrix. Let $d = \det \mathbf{H}$ and let d_i be the determinant of the $(N-1)\times(N-1)$ matrix obtained by deleting the ith row and column of $\mathbf{H}$ (ie the cofactor of h_{ii}). Given a constant $k \ge 0$, the equation $Q(\mathbf{x}) = k$ determines a hyperellipsoid in R^N, centred at 0. Its projection on the x_i-axis is the interval $[-c, c]$, where

$$c = \sqrt{\frac{kd_i}{d}}.$$

PROOF

Since the hyperellipsoid is a level hypersurface of Q, its extrema along the x_i-axis occur where the gradient vector ∇Q is parallel to the x_i-axis. That is, at any such extremal point we have $\nabla Q = \pm\lambda_i\mathbf{e}_i$ for some scalar λ_i, where $\mathbf{e}_i$ is the standard basis vector. Since $\nabla Q = 2\mathbf{H}\mathbf{x}$, the condition $2\mathbf{H}\mathbf{x} = \pm\lambda_i\mathbf{e}_i$ must hold at such points. So every extremal point on the hyperellipsoid is of the form

$$\pm\mathbf{H}^{-1}\mathbf{e}_i\frac{\lambda_i}{2}.$$

Since

$$k = \left[\mathbf{H}^{-1}\mathbf{e}_i\frac{\lambda_i}{2}\right]^t \mathbf{H}\left[\mathbf{H}^{-1}\mathbf{e}_i\frac{\lambda_i}{2}\right] = \frac{\lambda_i^2}{4}\mathbf{e}_i^t\mathbf{H}^{-1}\mathbf{H}\mathbf{H}^{-1}\mathbf{e}_i = \frac{\lambda_i^2}{4}\mathbf{e}_i^t\mathbf{H}^{-1}\mathbf{e}_i = \frac{\lambda_i^2 d_i}{4d}$$

we get

$$\lambda_i = \pm 2\sqrt{\frac{kd}{d_i}}.$$

It follows that the ith coordinate of any extremal point is given by

$$\pm\mathbf{e}_i^t\mathbf{H}^{-1}\mathbf{e}_i\frac{\lambda_i}{2} = \pm\frac{d_i}{d}\sqrt{\frac{kd}{d_i}} = \pm\sqrt{\frac{kd_i}{d}}.$$

(See Hungerford, (1974)).

1 *This is the definition proposed by the US Department of Treasury, the Office of the Comptroller of the Currency, the Federal Reserve System, the Federal Deposit Insurance Corporation, the Derivatives Policy Group, and the Basle Committee on Banking Supervision.*

2 *We thank Walter Stromquist and Wagner Associates for providing this table.*

3 *Assuming that* $(\ln S_i, \ln S_j)$ *is bivariate normal with mean vector* $[\ln S_i(0), \ln S_j(0)]$ *and covariance matrix*

$$\begin{bmatrix} \sigma_i^2 h & \rho\sigma_i\sigma_j h \\ \rho\sigma_i\sigma_j h & \sigma_j^2 h \end{bmatrix}$$

we have

$$E\left(S_i \middle| S_{ij} = S\right) = \frac{S^{\beta} S_i(0)^{\beta+1}}{S_j(0)^{\beta}} \exp\left[\frac{1}{2}(\beta+1)\left(\rho\sigma_i\sigma_j - \sigma_i^2\right)h\right]$$

where

$$\beta = \frac{\rho\sigma_i\sigma_j - \sigma_i^2}{\sigma_i^2 + \sigma_j^2 - 2\rho\sigma_i\sigma_j}$$

If $\sigma_i \approx \sigma_j$, *then*

$$S_i(0)\sqrt{\frac{S_{ij}(0)}{S}} \geq E\left(S_i \middle| S_{ij} = S\right)$$

for any $\rho \in [-1, 1]$.

4 *We thank Steve Zucker for suggesting this volatility function to us.*

5 *We thank Darrell Duffie for pointing out a problem with as earlier version of this step.*

6 *We thank Brian Kanaga for his collaboration on this result.*

BIBLIOGRAPHY

Basle Committee on Banking Supervision, 1996, *Overview of the Amendment to the Capital Accord to Incorporate Market Risks.*

Bratley, P., B. L. Fox, and L. E. Schrage, 1987, *A Guide to Simulation*, New York: Springer-Verlag.

Derivatives Policy Group, 1995, *Framework for Voluntary Oversight.*

Duffie, D., 1992, *Dynamic Asset Pricing Theory*, Princeton University Press.

Hungerford, T.W., 1974, *Algebra*, Springer-Verlag.

O'Brien, B., 1995, *FX Value-at-Risk Incorporating FX Options*, The Bank of New York.

Press, W.H., B.P. Flannery, S.A. Teukolsky, and W.T. Vetterling, 1988, *Numerical Recipes in C*, Cambridge University Press.

Stuart, A., and J. K. Ord, 1987, *Kendall's Advanced Theory of Statistics, 1*, New York: Oxford University Press.

CORPORATE APPLICATIONS AND FIRMWIDE RISK MANAGEMENT

Introduction

Christopher Hamilton and Bjorn Pettersen
KPMG

As well as burning the admonition "Increase shareholder value!" into our minds, business school academics have armed us with analytical models and methodologies, tools intended for our use as the new captains of industry. But theoretical problems can require practical solutions. Many of us quickly learned that, in the real corporate world, much of the input required to feed our models and methodologies was sadly lacking. The appropriate discount rate for computing the NPV of the firm's new project, generally given in business school exam questions, was suddenly an object of debate! Now, we know it must be around here somewhere...

Of course, this is something of an exaggeration. Many large firms have devoted substantial resources to modelling their businesses in recent years, in keeping with the latest innovations in corporate finance. But it is also true that some big organisations have struggled with fundamental financing decisions and risk/return analyses in the absence of a widely accepted methodology for quantifying risk.

We believe the advent of VAR has been a major development. For the first time, executives in all sorts of firms can quantify market risk. And, as a volatility-based and correlation-based methodology, using VAR means that firms must aggregate a wide variety of cash flow data in order to estimate the distributions of possible outcomes.

As corporate treasurers and finance officers started focusing on VAR as a way to measure market risk, the potential benefits to be derived from accumulating data about the frequency and magnitude of other risks did not elude them. Volatility-based risk measures such as VAR have helped managers not only to identify critical risks, but to develop strategies for mitigating them.

This has enabled firms to increase shareholder value at two levels. First, managers in individual business units can increase net present value by working on strategies to dampen cashflow volatility, and so reduce their discount rate. Second, executives can directly increase equity value by developing risk management strategies to control the volatility of the whole firm's cash flow. Capital allocations can be modified to support individual businesses, and cash flows for new projects negatively correlated to those of current business activities. After all, shareholder value - the stock price - is just the summed present values of the firm's future cash flows. And it is the discount rate based upon the volatility of those future cash flows, not just their anticipated size, that investors consider in establishing the price of a stock.

The articles in this section follow two closely related themes. It starts with pieces by risk management professionals explaining how corporations can employ VAR to control market and non-market risks. Case studies outline the way some firms use VAR in the conduct of their businesses. Most emphasise the key relationship between focused risk management and increasing the value of firm equity.

The other articles, all written by risk management practitioners and consultants, describe ways in which finance tools and models, including VAR, may be used to create a risk management framework suitable for any corporation. Each article either implicitly or explicitly relates the ultimate goal of increasing shareholder value to the establishment of a total enterprise-wide risk management framework.

Corporate applications for VAR

"What is VAR?" is the first of three excellent short

articles by David Shimko, formerly head of risk management research at JP Morgan, now of Bankers Trust. Shimko's "End-User's Guides" have appeared regularly in *Risk*, and he has a keen insight on new ways of using and interpreting VAR. He illustrates how a corporation can interpret VAR as the maximum uninsured loss from market risk that it is willing to accept. Of course, most firms "buy insurance" to protect against market risks by hedging. And by evaluating the cost of hedging relative to the reduction in VAR that the hedge "buys," corporate finance officers can make better-informed decisions on whether to accept a market risk or to pay away the "insurance" cost of hedging and invest the "saved" VAR in more productive opportunities.

Shimko stresses how VAR, properly interpreted, can add value in major strategic decision-making, well above the trading desk level to which it is frequently limited. Two more articles by Shimko, "VAR for Corporates" and "Investors' Return on VAR" appear later in this section, amplifying his point by presenting hypothetical transaction decision scenarios from the world's energy markets.

Richard Singer of KPMG extends Shimko's analysis in "VAR_{MD} = LAR". Singer believes that significant risk to corporate liquidity, the liquidity-at-risk, or LAR, persists after some or all of a commodity buyer's VAR is hedged away. Hedged market risk, he argues, will not be lost in the long run. But the firm may nonetheless be required to pay out its VAR in the form of margin calls during the term of the hedge to the extent that a commodity hedger employs marginable derivatives to reduce VAR. The size of a firm's undertakings subject to market risk are jointly constrained by its acceptable VAR limit and its liquidity resources, and Singer proposes a series of steps that may be used to quantify, monitor and control liquidity-at-risk.

In their very strong article "Handle with Sensitivity," Gregory Hayt and Shang Song of CIBC Wood Gundy propose using cash flow sensitivity modelling to estimate probability distributions for future net cash flows and the risk of not achieving revenue or earnings targets. By performing Monte Carlo simulations to estimate future distributions of financial prices, then "feeding" those distributions into a traditional budget model that includes estimated elasticities among exposure factors, managers may both estimate distributions of future cash flows and observe how they can be modified using risk management techniques such as hedging.

A similar "cash-flow-at-risk" estimation concept is provided by Chris Turner in "VAR as an Industrial Tool," which also includes an informative discussion of elasticity modelling. Turner nicely supplements the cash flow sensitivity approach discussed by Hayt and Song. Although their approaches may require quantitative skills that currently exist in few firms, Hayt, Song and Turner clearly demonstrate that important synergies can be realised by applying volatility-based risk measures in conjunction with more traditional financial models.

Turning to the real world of corporate applications, Andrew Priest of *Risk* describes how two global conglomerates use VAR. Veba and Siemens have bought risk engines from different vendors, but both use asset return and correlation data from JP Morgan's RiskMetrics database. They believe VAR has given them an improved methodology not only for measuring currency, interest rate and commodity price risks but also for managing and disclosing those risks.

Statoil, the Norwegian oil giant, takes the application of VAR and scenario testing a step further, as Martin Hiemstra reports in "VAR with Muscles." Statoil uses a form of cash-flow-at-risk modelling that has enabled managers not only to expand hedging and other derivatives activities, but also to plan mitigation strategies for risks from catastrophic operational failures, such as the total loss of offshore installations. Statoil's use of cash-flow-at-risk and scenario-based VAR includes the estimation of pre-tax earnings distributions, a link that clearly ties the Statoil risk management process to the search for increased shareholder value.

The move toward enterprise-wide risk management

Statoil's complimentary applications of VAR methodologies and traditional financial models seem very advanced. But risk management professionals everywhere are trying to meet the challenge of how to integrate the quantification of risk right across the range of a company's business activities. They are striving to develop frameworks that will permit managers at all levels of an organisation to make the most of risk management methodologies, both to minimise the risk of loss and to maximise shareholder value. The last four articles in this volume describe how firms and practitioners are striving to develop a total enterprise-wide risk management framework for the 21st century.

Sumit Paul-Choudhury's "Crossing the Divide"

sets the scene by reminding us that the aim of proactive firmwide risk management is not the establishment of a control environment sufficiently inflexible to make an auditor's heart soar. Rather, enterprise risk management aims to provide managers and boards with the tools, methodologies and technology to maximise their firm's performance. As Clifford Smout, a senior regulator from the Bank of England has pointed out, "Risk management was not invented to make banks safe but to make them money. Some banks [use it to] reduce their risk; others will increase their risk once they are confident of their measurements."

One of the main aims of enterprise-wide risk management is to ensure that managers have sufficient information to make educated risk/return decisions. Mike Baliman of Dresdner Kleinwort Benson argues that efforts to develop enterprise risk management frameworks are often incomplete, because practitioners focus exclusively on "bottom-up" tools such as VAR to aggregate market risks, and then mistake that aggregated sum of risks for the strategic risk in the firm. In "Taking it from the Top," he urges risk managers to balance bottom-up aggregations of market risk with "top-down" measures, including other volatile cash flows and their complex relationships with expenses, business or trading strategies, and human factors.

Model risk is not a trivial source of error in aggregating risks from multiple products and business activities. To meet the need for a top-down strategic model against which to interpret aggregated bottom-up risk, Kleinwort "has developed a strategic model which tracks the risk: return performance of all [its] business units over time. It also tracks the chance of a monthly loss pre-expenses, post-expenses and post-bonus." And, of course, the data to run it are derived functions of management policy and strategy, not the realised cash flows that roll from the bottom-up.

In "Together They Stand," Robert Allen, Westpac's head of global investment, argues strongly for integrating credit and market risk measures. His case is based upon the need for comparability between returns from market and credit risk, the convergence of credit and market risk measurement methodologies, and the transactional interaction between credit and market risks. This article is excellent background for readers exploring JP Morgan's recently released CreditMetrics Technical Document.

But Allen's clever exposition of an option model for pricing corporate equity and debt is, by itself, sufficient reason to class it as required reading for all enterprise risk managers. Shareholders of a limited liability firm, Allen argues, may be viewed as holding a long position of the company assets as well as a long put option on those assets, struck at the value of the firm's liabilities, which they may exercise against the firm's debtholders in the event the firm fails - when the value of its assets drop below the liability value-strike price.

Since the value and volatility of equity for a publicly traded company can be found in its share price data, and since the amounts and maturities of its liabilities are disclosed in financial statements, option pricing theory permits us to compute the volatility of the firm's assets. And from the volatility of assets and the value and term of liabilities, we may immediately infer the probability that the company will default or, going one step further, compute the fair value of the company's debt.

Allen's complete exposition of these relationships as well as a series of clear supportive examples from the derivatives product markets make a strong argument for the integration of credit and market risk management. The article is also an excellent primer on how to exploit new risk measurement methodologies in conjunction with traditional financial models to manage enterprise-wide risk.

Finally, in "Total Enterprise-wide Risk Management," Christopher Hamilton and Andrew Smith of KPMG present their vision of a top-down, integrated firmwide risk management framework that is supported by bottom-up risk measurement methodologies. They also analyse the strengths and weaknesses of alternative approaches. Hypothetical case studies show how, by applying new risk measurement methodologies such as VAR to complement the traditional strategies of corporate finance, a total enterprise-wide risk management (TERM) framework can directly increase shareholder value. By directly tying strategic risk framework elements to prospective increases in the value of firm equity, they reinforce the link to equity that distinguishes enterprise-wide risk management from narrower applications of volatility-based risk measures like VAR. It is this link that motivates continuing efforts toward integrated firmwide risk management solutions.

34

What is VAR?

David Shimko
Bankers Trust Company

Value-at-risk is much more than a statistic. Used correctly, it can help managers to run their businesses and make a positive contribution to shareholder value.

"We've calculated value-at-risk," says Joel Brown of Shell Oil. "Now that we have all the answers, would you please tell us what the question was? Specifically, now that I've got VAR, how do I use it to help me run my business?"

Risk management systems have been widely and enthusiastically adopted to calculate value-at-risk for corporate cashflows and investor portfolios. The technique has been much debated and criticised, mostly in the context of alternative risk methodologies and statistical appropriateness. But it may be that we cannot see the wood for the trees.

Forget for the moment about technical discussions of standard deviations, correlations and confidence intervals. VAR has an important meaning which is often obscured by the statistical details. VAR is the amount of capital a firm allocates to self-insurance, as a buffer against higher than expected costs or lower than expected revenues. This allocation may be explicit, as for many financial firms, or implicit, as for most manufacturing companies.

For example, an aluminium buyer with $360 per ton value-at-risk over a one-year time frame may have to come up with $360 per ton over the budgeted amount to make the requisite purchases. The $360 may come from cash reserves, the sale of liquid assets, issues of debt or equity, deferral of capital investment or cutbacks elsewhere in the firm. Companies have many ways to insure against this possible cost overrun and one of the choices is not to insure.

What is the cost of VAR?

One way or another, all companies insure. Some do so by borrowing, some use derivatives and some use the strength of their balance sheet. At first, it appears that self-insurance (hedging with the balance sheet) has no cost. Sometimes this is true. In general, however, the cost of self-insurance is the foregone premium return the dollars could earn if applied to their most productive use. For example, when a company accepts a project, its internal rate of return (IRR) exceeds its cost of capital (k) by some amount $\alpha = IRR - k$. If the premium on outside financing is greater than α, the project must be financed internally, if at all. If internal capital is dedicated as a safety cushion instead of being used for investment, it saves the company the cost of hedging (transaction and liquidity costs), but costs it the foregone investment premium. Self-insurance is free only if there is no better use for the capital.

This leads us to another implication of VAR. If underinvestment costs a firm $\alpha(VAR)$ per year in foregone expected profits, then the discounted losses are proportional to VAR. Therefore, VAR ultimately measures the opportunity loss of self-insurance. Armed with the knowledge of VAR, firms can better decide how to insure themselves. And if the cost of insuring with securities or derivatives is less than the foregone losses of self-insurance, firms should seek outside insurance.

Spend money to make money

But should big healthy firms pay profits to others in order to insure themselves? Perhaps. Take a personal finance analogy. The State of California requires all drivers to have insurance but they have the choice of using an insurance company or self-insuring by posting a $30,000 performance bond with the state. Assume a typical insurance policy requires payment of $2,500 per year, and the actuarial value of the policy is $2,000 per year; the economic cost of insurance is therefore $500 per year. Would anyone with a $30,000 bond pay $500 per year in profits to the insurance company? Presumably, the cost of self-insurance is zero, since the bond earns interest – so self-insurance is cheaper. However, many will buy insurance rather than post the bond because they can earn more than $500 per year (ie $\alpha > 1.67\% = 500/30{,}000$) by investing the $30,000 more profitably.

Companies should pay away profits to others to insure themselves if they thereby free enough internal capital to earn more than they pay away. If a company has hedgeable VAR of $2 billion, can earn a premium on investment of 3% a year and has to pay 1% a year in outside hedging costs, it can add annual value of $40 million for as long as the opportunity lasts.

Yet human nature and prudence cause us to focus on hedging costs rather than investment opportunities. Hard, tangible costs beat soft, intangible benefits every time.

Make your money work harder

The bottom line for risk management, and indeed for all corporate finance, is that companies need to struggle to maximise the contribution of every dollar of capital to shareholder value. If a dollar is used to self-insure, should it be withheld from investment? Or should it be returned to shareholders?

At the highest level, risk management is critical to running any firm, since risk management decisions affect the deployment of capital and the allocation of risk ownership. Companies should sell subsidiaries when outside valuations exceed internal ones, and they should offset risks when outsiders can bear them more efficiently than the balance sheet. Companies may sell subsidiaries at an economic loss if there are better uses for the funds and these cannot be financed cheaply by the capital markets. Transferring risks, in the end, is equivalent to selling subsidiaries. Modern financial markets create the opportunity to segregate risks and sell them off to the highest bidder.

Elevate risk management

It is unfortunate that many firms leave risk management to traders, with large trades requiring managerial approval. Risk management needs to be established at the corporate finance officer level, on a par with treasury, acquisitions and investment choice. Used correctly, risk management is not a reactive response to market risk but a proactive contributor to building shareholder value. VAR is not a standard deviation as much as it may be underutilised capital.

Handle with Sensitivity

Gregory Hayt and Shang Song
CIBC Wood Gundy Securities

The goal of a unified risk measure is proving difficult to achieve for non-financial firms. Cashflow sensitivity modelling is one possible solution.

Risk management practice in leading non-financial firms has been evolving from a focus on individual price exposures – interest rate, foreign exchange or commodity – to the management of the firm's exposure to financial prices as a portfolio of interrelated risks.

One of the early motivations for this change was that it is cheaper to hedge a portfolio or basket of foreign currency exposures than to hedge each individually. This realisation led to the development of other risk management products that hedged two or more exposures simultaneously. These products, sometimes called integrated products, link two different markets, eg oil and interest rates, to reduce the cost of hedging a firm's cashflow or earnings.

Many firms would like to take this process further and link all the firm's individual exposures to arrive at a single, consolidated measure of risk. Such a measure would relate changes in financial prices to the probability of achieving a given level of cashflow, earnings or other financial target over a defined period. The justification for the goal, beyond a reduction in hedging costs, is based on three foundations.

First, a portfolio-based measure would simplify the task of communicating exposure to senior management and the board of directors, since the consolidated measure will define exposure in terms of important financial policy variables rather than narrower market specific risk measures such as duration. Second, it is becoming increasingly necessary for senior management and the board to be active participants in setting the firm's risk tolerance, approving strategies and monitoring performance. Non-specialists cannot be expected to perform this role unless exposure is related to the same financial targets used to evaluate other aspects of the business. Third, finance theory and related empirical research imply that a firm's risk management policy should be integrated with its policies on areas such as investment, research and capital structure, all of which are typically set at a high level within the firm.

Attaining the goal of a unified risk measure has been difficult for non-financial firms. Senior management and board members are rarely well versed in the traditional, market-specific terms of exposure measurement such as duration, convexity, delta, gamma and vega. Also, these measures are not suited to consolidating price risks in different product and asset markets. Ideally, the firm would be able to sidestep the more market-specific terms and directly capture the effect of price changes on projected cashflows.

Cashflow risk

The desire of non-financial firms to find an aggregate exposure measure is similar to the problem faced by derivatives dealers when it became clear that oversight by individual market or risk parameter was an ineffective means of controlling risk. To address this problem, dealers have now largely adopted a set of aggregate exposure measures, broadly referred to as value-at-risk (VAR) measures, which ease the communication of exposure and acceptable limits between market professionals and senior management.

VAR, however, is not a suitable risk measure for most non-financial businesses. While both dealers and corporates are ultimately trying to maximise firm value, the approaches taken by each to the management of their businesses and related risk management strategies, lie at opposite ends of a spectrum. At one end of the spectrum are securities dealers that mark to market a large percentage of the firm as often as daily.

These firms focus on the market value of their assets and liabilities over short horizons. At the other end lie corporations with balance sheets containing physical assets, financial instruments and intangible assets such as capitalised research and development - growth options and brand names. Market or liquidation values are relevant for at best a small portion of the balance sheet. The focus instead is on projected cashflows over a multi-year planning horizon.

A natural definition of aggregate exposure for firms that manage cashflows over long horizons relates the size and timing of inflows to a firm's contractual commitments and investment objectives. This idea, which is becoming widely accepted, has been elegantly expressed in a *Journal of Finance* article by Kenneth Froot, David Scharfstein and Jeremy Stein. The 1995 *Wharton/CIBC Wood Gundy Survey of Derivatives End-Users* also supports this notion, finding that 91% of non-financial firms report reducing cashflow or earnings volatility as their primary risk management objective.

Cashflow sensitivity analysis

One framework for building a cashflow-based measure of exposure and setting risk management policy based on this is described by a process we will call cashflow sensitivity analysis. This defines a firm's consolidated exposure to market prices as the probability that the firm will fail to meet financial performance targets as the result of unexpected price changes. The firm's hedging strategy depends on this probabilistic measure of the firm's future performance. Given an overall strategy set by the board, tactical decisions about hedging instruments, timing and execution are delegated to professional risk managers. This definition of exposure is the easy part, however. The trick is in building a model that takes as its input uncertain financial and product prices and produces the desired probability-based exposure measure. To accomplish this linkage requires a model of the firm that is rich enough in detail to capture the effect of changes in market prices on production quantities and product mark-ups.

As illustrated in Figure 1, we believe the foundation upon which to build this sophisticated exposure model is the firm's existing budget or planning model. While not sufficient by itself to capture the firm's exposures, it serves as a firm-wide risk management "circuit diagram", capturing relationships between commodity inputs, product prices, foreign and domestic operations and contractual commitments such as debt and lease payments, to name but a few. Furthermore, the accounting framework is the logical choice for communicating exposure and setting overall risk management objectives that can be communicated both internally to managers and externally to investors, regulators and rating agencies.

To move from the budget model to an exposure management model requires addressing the two major shortcomings of the budgeting framework. First, a method of explicitly expressing the

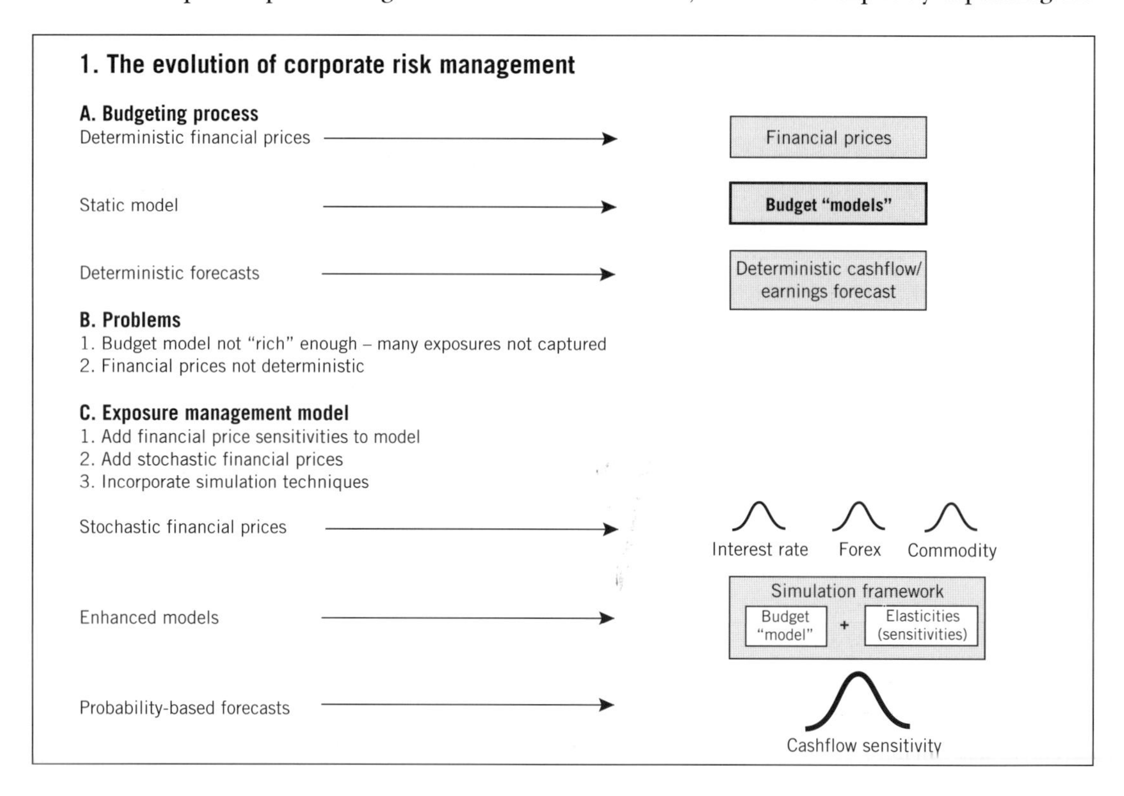

relationship between financial prices and changes in the firm's operating policies is required. For example, a change in a foreign exchange rate may affect the nominal value of an order book in the short run while changing the firm's market share in the long run as competitive advantage shifts between producers. Incorporating changes in operating variables requires managers to quantify, even if only approximately, their response to changing financial prices.

The second hurdle to overcome is the use of deterministic financial and commodity prices in the budget model. The solution is to generate stochastic prices using simulation software and models of how financial prices change over time. Use of a simulation platform and models of financial price changes adds some complexity to the process, but means management can be confident that the price scenarios fed into the model have the necessary realism.

Defining exposures

Building a model of exposure that goes beyond the base accounting model will be easier for some firms than others. Commodity-driven firms, single product firms and firms with relatively little direct or indirect foreign exchange exposure will have an easier time than multinational firms with global production and competition. However, in all cases the firm will want to identify two types of cashflow exposure.

The first type will arise from fixed contractual obligations: foreign currency accounts receivable; the amount of foreign currency debt; or an obligation to purchase a fixed amount of a commodity. The second cashflow exposure arises from changes in the firm's operating cashflows as a result of financial price changes. Contractual cashflows will be fixed in the local currency (or units of a commodity) and only their nominal value in the home or base currency will change as prices change. Operating cashflows, however, will fluctuate because the amount of product the firm sells or quantity of resources consumed will vary along with the price. In other words, operating cashflows are subject to both price and quantity uncertainty.[1]

There are many approaches one can take to linking financial prices to changes in contractual and operating cashflows. One method is to incorporate an economic pricing model into the budget framework. For example, a refiner or speciality chemical manufacturer might have a pricing model that it uses to determine the prices and quantities of its outputs given a set of input prices. Similarly, some multinational firms model the price and demand for their products given foreign exchange rates and their competitors' pricing policies. Ideally these economic models, which capture both price and quantity variations, can be incorporated into the framework of the risk management model.

However, most firms will not have such detailed models or the resources to build them. Rather than model price and quantity sold directly, these firms will find useful simplification in the idea of revenue and cost elasticities. Elasticity is simply the percentage change in one variable given a 1% change in another. If, for example, a firm's dollar revenues increase by 10% when the Deutschmark appreciates by 10% against the dollar, then the elasticity of dollar revenue with respect to the Deutschmark is one. As illustrated in the Appendix, elasticities can capture a wide variety of exposure situations whether arising from contractual or operating exposures.

Elasticity is a powerful exposure management tool. While we know that a change in foreign exchange rates might affect both the quantity of a product sold in a foreign market and its price, the elasticity concept captures the net effect of both the price and quantity change. How firms arrive at elasticity estimates will vary. Some may use economic models, but others will take a less technical approach. Asking operating managers to estimate the impact of various foreign exchange rate scenarios on their revenues and costs can lead to direct estimates of elasticities. These estimates can then be "tried on" with historical accounting results and exchange rates for fine tuning.

Elasticity also makes it easier to express the effect of a change in foreign exchange rates on revenue from domestic operations (the elasticity concept is not limited to foreign exchange – for example, one could calculate a commodity price elasticity). A purely domestic manufacturing firm facing local competition from a foreign competitor can use elasticity to express its competitive exposure. If, historically, a 10% depreciation of the foreign currency causes domestic revenues to decline by 2%, then the domestic firm's exposure elasticity will be 0.2.

The determination of exposure elasticities should recognise links between pricing in, for example, the domestic and a foreign market. Pricing cannot become completely disconnected between the two markets because of the possibility of third parties shipping a firm's goods across borders to arbitrage price differentials. In a similar vein, a firm's response to foreign exchange rate changes will not necessarily be linear. A small change in the exchange rate may cause one response, a large change may cause another.

The translation of financial price changes into changes in operating performance is by far the most difficult task of cashflow modelling. However, the challenge should not be a deterrent, since the issue, ie how the firm responds to changes in prices, exists whether the firm uses traditional characterisations of exposure or simulation-based methods. A distinct advantage of the modelling approach is that it forces managers to be explicit about the operating assumptions, and these assumptions can be examined in light of the model.

Simulating financial prices

Moving from a planning model based on fixed prices to a simulation based on a realistic model of financial prices has become significantly easier with the improvement of spreadsheet programs and the availability of software "add-ins" expressly designed for this purpose. Indeed, the knowledge of how to build a simulation model of the firm has been around for years; the renewed interest in the technique is driven by the combination of more powerful desktop computers and new insights into the uses of modelling for risk assessment and policy formulation.

Figure 2 illustrates the mechanical process of running the budget model with exposure measurement enhancements to generate a probability distribution for cashflow. One can run the model several thousand times, each time feeding the model a different series of financial prices, eg one set of prices for each quarter over a three-year period. Each turn of the model generates another revenue and expense forecast, quarter by quarter, for the next three years. The picture in Figure 2 shows different realisations of cashflow at a given point in time, eg at the end of the second year.

2. Monte Carlo simulation

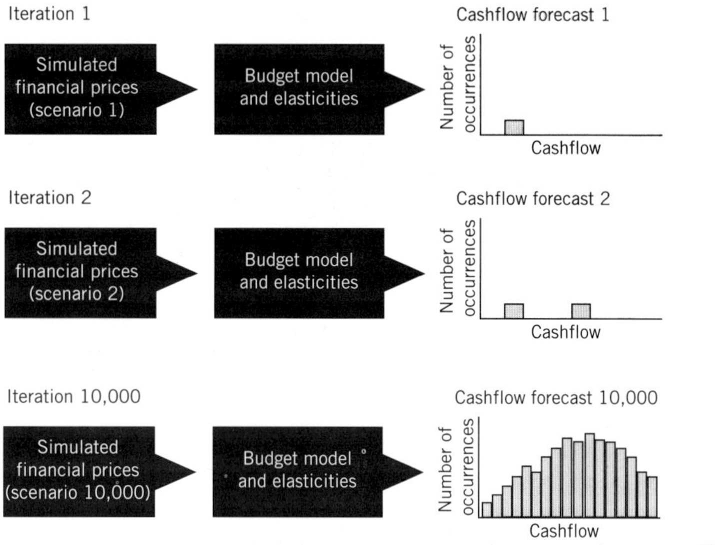

At each iteration the model needs a new input for each financial price incorporated into the model. Thus, from an initial starting value of six-month Libor or West Texas Intermediate crude oil, we need a series of quarter-by-quarter price changes. A spreadsheet will generate normally distributed random changes in prices quite easily, but a realistic simulation requires using random changes in conjunction with a model of how interest rates, foreign exchange rates and commodity prices change together.

For interest rates and foreign exchange rates it is particularly important to use an economic model such as the Longstaff-Schwartz model to generate the financial inputs for the simulation. Using an economic model ensures that interest rates and foreign exchange rates maintain a realistic relationship with each other during the planning horizon. In particular, the interest rate model will generate a yield curve for each quarter that will be realistic in the sense that there will be no arbitrage opportunities between points on the curve. Two-factor models such as Longstaff-Schwartz have the added realism of also being able to generate inverted and "humped" shaped curves.

If the simulation incorporates yield curves in two or more currencies it will be necessary to generate simulated foreign exchange rates that are consistent with the interest rates in each currency. Interest rates and foreign exchange rates are linked by an arbitrage relationship known as covered interest parity. Given the short-term interest rate in each currency and the spot foreign exchange rate, covered interest parity define the forward foreign exchange rate:

$$F_0 = S_0\left[\frac{1+r_{DM}}{1+r_{\$}}\right].$$

We can use this relationship to create a forward foreign exchange rate for each period that relates to the current state of interest rates. In a simple model, the next period's spot foreign exchange rate can be centred on the forward rate for that quarter with a normally distributed error. While not perfectly realistic, this technique ensures that interest rates and foreign exchange rates remain in economically reasonable relationships.

Implementing one of the yield curve models requires some programming, but the resulting realism in the simulated rates and prices is worth the investment. The interest rate and foreign exchange rate simulation should be done carefully, but it should also be remembered that uncertainty in the firm's basic exposure model will be likely to swamp the subtleties in the most sophisticated yield curve models. We have had success using the Longstaff-Schwartz model of the yield curve because it is well-documented, can produce inverted and humped curves and, as part of the model, provides a simulated volatility estimate as well.

Application

To illustrate the use of a cashflow sensitivity model we built a simple model around the consolidated financial statements of a hypothetical manufacturing firm. Foreign exchange and commodity exposures were added as elasticities and the firm's short-term debt was repriced each quarter at the prevailing short-term interest rate in each of two currencies. The firm is assumed to be exposed to one currency.

The distribution of the firm's total cashflow on a quarterly basis for three years was simulated using a spreadsheet and an "add-in" function. There are several ways to express the output of the model. Figure 3 shows the distribution of net cashflow for the eighth quarter, ie at the end of the second year. Combining all 12 quarterly cashflow estimates yields the three-dimensional plot in Figure 4. The quarter-by-quarter forecasts illustrate the increasing amount of uncertainty (width of the distribution) as cashflows are forecasted further into the future. Alternatively, one could plot the cumulative cashflow quarter by quarter.

Given the information about the distribution of cashflow (or some other variable of interest), the senior management of the firm must decide whether the existing degree of uncertainty is acceptable. This requires a definition of a minimum performance level by the board of directors. For example, the firm could define a minimum level of cashflow by adding contractual interest and principal repayments (net of rollovers), current dividends and planned research and development spending. If cashflow falls below this level the firm will have to increase debt, cut its dividend or forego planned investment. Figure 5 shows a bar superimposed on the histogram defining this level of critical cashflow. The probability of falling below this level is one possible measure of exposure. If this probability is too high, alternative strategies can be developed to bring in the left-hand tail of the distribution.

On a quarter-by-quarter basis the cumulative

3. Cashflow distribution of year two

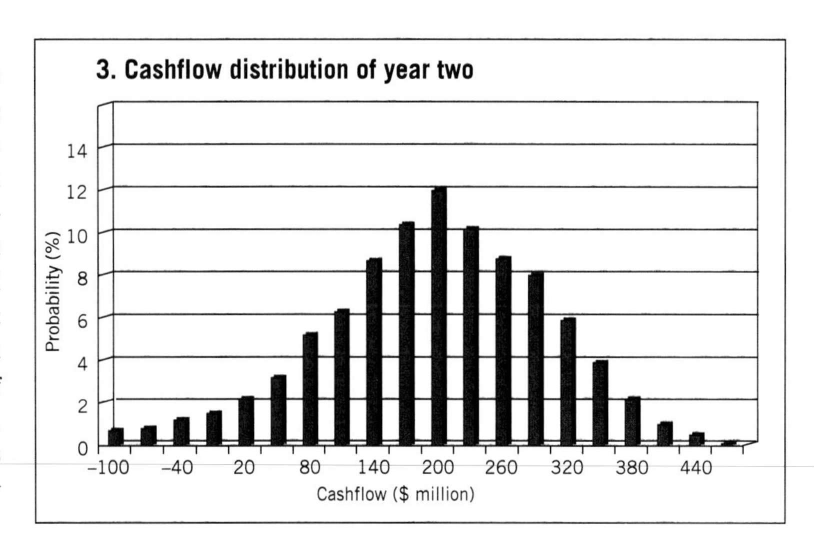

4. Probability distribution of net cashflows by quarter

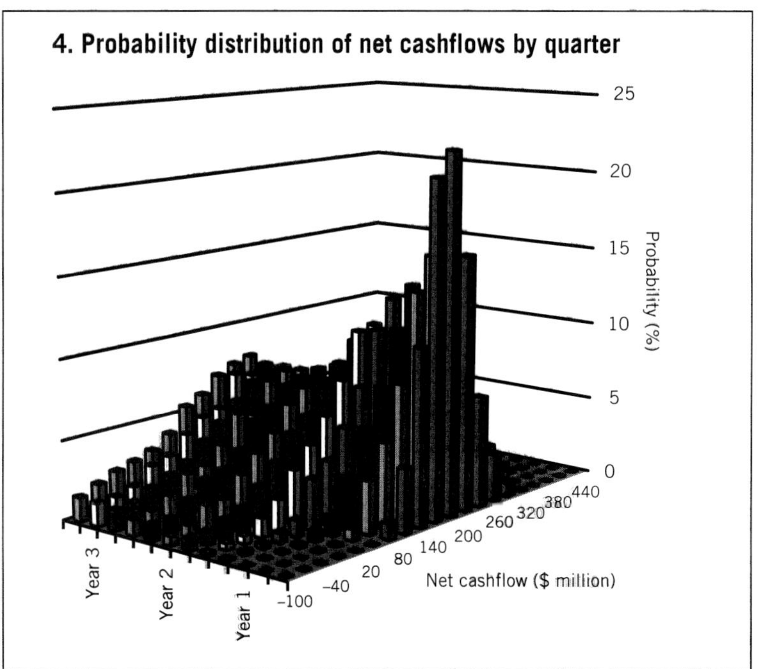

5. Risk of not achieving target

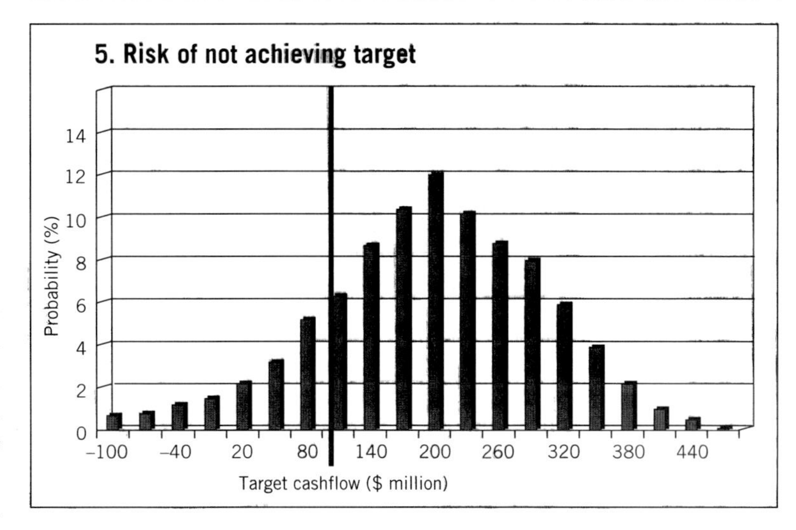

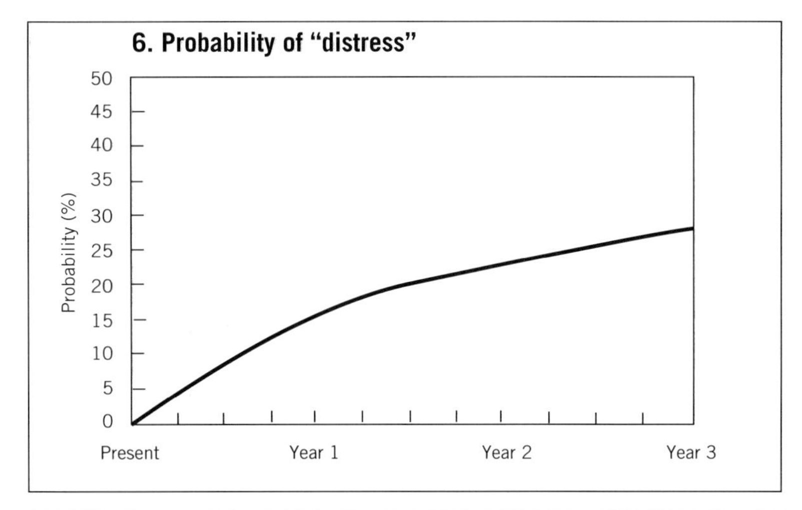

6. Probability of "distress"

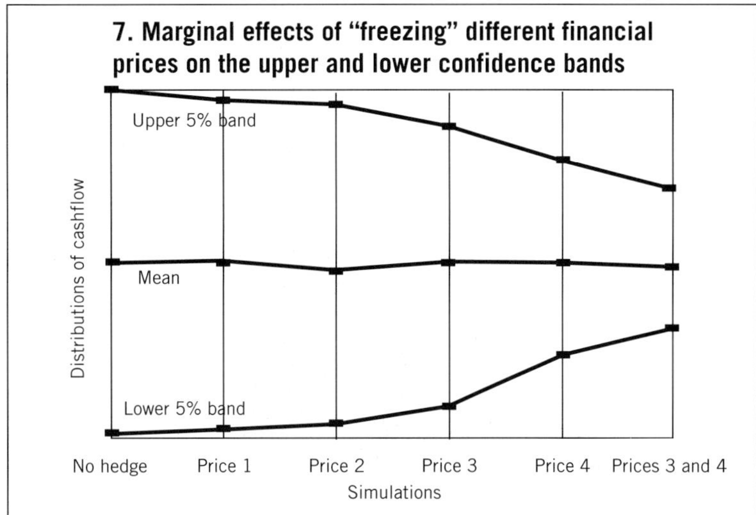

7. Marginal effects of "freezing" different financial prices on the upper and lower confidence bands

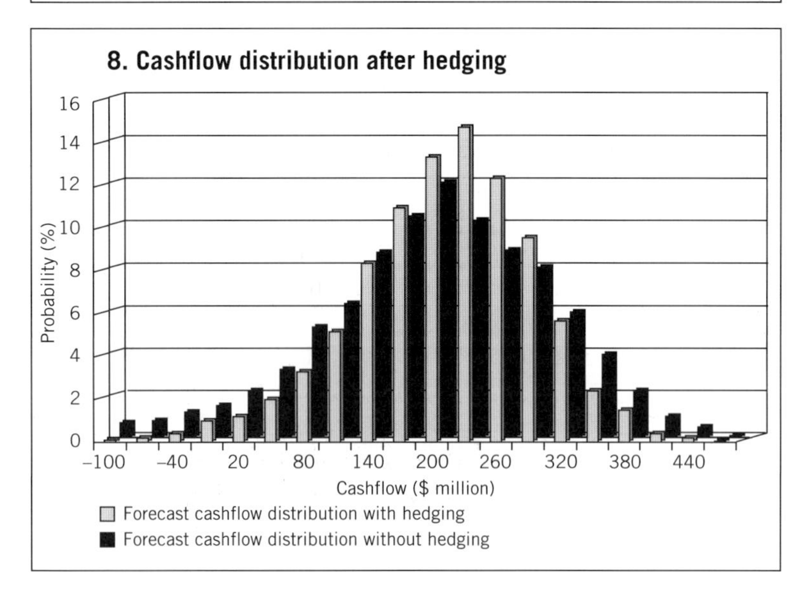

8. Cashflow distribution after hedging

cashflow necessary to meet the firm's financial plan defines a level at which the firm is in "distress". Figure 6 illustrates the probability of failing to meet cumulative cashflow targets by quarter for three years. This concise way of displaying exposure information can be extended to include multiple objectives, eg cashflow, earnings and interest coverage. By plotting multiple performance goals on the same chart, the firm can identify those areas where risk management may be most valuable.

We are aware of firms that view their exposure in terms of cumulative cashflow, earnings, self-imposed borrowing constraints, balance sheet ratios (eg interest coverage), funds available for research and development and/or investment and acquisitions, and combinations of these concepts. It is a major strength of the modelling approach that a variety of exposure definitions can be accommodated in the framework, so long as they can be expressed in terms of the balance sheet or income statement.

If the probability of failing to meet defined goals is too high, the firm can use the model to determine how this probability might be lowered. For example, the simulation software we used has features to help identify those sources of uncertainty, eg interest rates or commodity prices, that had the greatest impact on performance. Using this feature helps focus the risk management discussion on the prices and markets with the greatest impact on performance. And it may highlight the fact that the firm need only actively manage one or two critical exposures. Figure 7 illustrates the relative impact of eliminating uncertainty in one price at a time by plotting the reduction in the upper and lower 95% confidence bounds in cashflow. For this example, there is almost nothing to be gained in terms of performance by hedging the first three sources of uncertainty since the tails of the distribution are only marginally impacted. However, hedging financial prices 4 and 5 significantly reduces uncertainty – suggesting risk management strategies should primarily address those two prices.

Having isolated the critical sources of uncertainty, the model can be used to try out alternative strategies, whether on-balance-sheet or off-balance-sheet. For example, Figure 8 illustrates the change in second-year cashflow as the result of locking in one of the critical financial prices for three years via a swap. The grey bars indicate the new cashflow distribution after locking in prevailing forward prices for a part of the firm's exposures. Thus, hedges placed in specific markets can be viewed in terms of their impact on the chosen measure(s) of aggregate exposure.

Conclusion

A criticism of cashflow sensitivity modelling is that the firm must define its exposures in the model in order to use the model to define exposure! However, this criticism mis-states the process. The model-building process requires establishing the exposure to specific financial prices and markets piecemeal, in manageable stages. The model provides a realistic linkage between a potentially large number of individually defined responses inside the firm to different financial price scenarios, resulting in a single consolidated measure. The consolidated measure reflects correlations between prices and natural hedges in the firm's operations. Furthermore, by specifying exposure piecemeal using elasticities or a more elaborate model the firm can carefully examine its assumptions and operating rules.

As daunting a challenge as it may seem to specify these relationships, one must remember that the firm is either already addressing these issues as part of its existing strategy or ignoring them at great peril. In either case, the process of building a model of these exposures will force a critical assessment of exposures and risk management strategy. This assessment in turn can be expected to lead to a more integrated definition of risk that relates price uncertainty to the ability of the firm to meet its business plan.

Appendix

FRAMING EXPOSURES

Firms have to address two forms of cashflow exposure. The first arises from contractually fixed obligations such as foreign currency debt or foreign currency receivables. In the case of a US firm with a subsidiary based in Germany, a change in the dollar/Deutschmark exchange rate will not affect the local (Deutschmark) value of a receivable, but it will affect its value in terms of the home currency (dollar). The home currency value of contractual obligations in a foreign currency will change in value one-for-one with the exchange rate; therefore, contractual exposures have an elasticity of 1.

The second form of cashflow exposure is an operating exposure, often referred to as a competitive exposure. Using the above example again, the subsidiary's local currency (Deutschmark) cashflows might depend on the value of the Deutschmark relative to one or more currencies. The Deutschmark's value affects the competitive position of the subsidiary in Germany and other markets in which it operates. Since exchange rates will affect both the local currency cashflow and the conversion of the cashflow back to dollars, the total effect of an exchange rate change in terms of the home currency (dollar) could be larger or smaller than one-for-one. In other words, operating exposure elasticities could be larger or smaller than unity.

Framing operating exposures is a critical step in cashflow modelling. Inaccurate or incomplete characterisation of the firm's exposure could do more harm than good. There are several ways a firm might develop good elasticity estimates. A domestic firm selling a product in a foreign market can base an elasticity estimate on how much of an exchange rate change it can "pass through" in the local currency price of its product without changing the quantity sold. Thus a US-based firm selling into a highly competitive German market might be able to pass through only 10% of an adverse move in the dollar/Deutschmark exchange rate in its local (Deutschmark) price without affecting the quantity sold. If the firm's policy is to maintain market share, then revenue elasticity (in the short run) would be 0.9 (90% of the depreciation in the foreign currency is reflected in home currency revenue).

Another estimate of revenue (or cost) elasticity can be obtained from an analysis of the historical relationship between exchange rates and revenues (or costs). Revenue elasticity is sometimes called an exposure beta, because it is the same concept as an equity beta. Given good accounting data, one could use a regression of the percentage change in home currency revenues as a function of the percentage change in one or more foreign exchange rates. Accounting data does not always co-operate with statistical analyses, but a regression might be a starting point.

1 *For a discussion of contractual and economic exposures, see Flood and Lessard (1986).*

BIBLIOGRAPHY

Flood, E., and D. Lessard, 1986, "On the Measurement of Operating Exposure Subject to Exchange Rates: A Conceptual Approach", *Financial Management*, Spring.

Froot, K.A., D.S. Scharfstein and J.C. Stein, 1993, "Risk Management: Coordinating Corporate Investment and Financing Policies", *Journal of Finance*, 48, pp. 1,629–58.

Longstaff, F., and E. Schwartz, 1992, "Interest Rate Volatility and the Term Structure: a Two-Factor General Equilibrium Model", *Journal of Finance*, 47, pp. 1,259–82.

36

VAR as an Industrial Tool

Chris Turner
CRM Partners

Value-at-risk is a valuable technique for a wide variety of institutions. This article explains how an industrial corporate can use "cashflow-at-risk" analysis to model its operating performance.

Market value-at-risk (VAR) has become the dominant tool for risk governance by derivatives dealers. Risk managers use it to place a probabilistic limit on losses a dealer may incur on a portfolio as a result of movements in financial prices. This limit is found by examining the distribution of possible changes in the value of the firm's portfolio; the distribution itself is derived by revaluing the portfolio according to a hypothetical set of changes in financial prices.

As VAR has been popularised by dealers, some have suggested that it is not an appropriate risk measure for non-financial corporates. This is not the case. It may be thought of as a family of tools whose applications are differentiated by three factors: the composition of exposure; the definition of risk; and the cycle of measurement. By varying these factors, VAR can be applied to a wide variety of problems, for example:

❑ to measure the risk of fluctuations in interest costs, rather than changes in the asset value (by considering exposure in terms of changes in flows rather than changes in value);

❑ to measure the magnitude of foreign exchange exposure as a result of foreign-denominated cashflows (by defining risk as fluctuations in the value of the cashflows);

❑ to evaluate the foreign exchange risks resulting from the firm's equity investment in its foreign subsidiaries (by extending the length of the measurement cycle).

Some corporates are already using these techniques. PepsiCo, for example, has used VAR techniques to evaluate its exposure to credit risk. Dow Chemical Company and Mobil Corporation use the same type of approach as derivatives dealers to monitor the foreign exchange and interest rate risk exposures embedded in their debt and derivatives portfolios. For many industrial corporates, a VAR model can also be used to evaluate risk at the highest level of the firm. In this approach, which we call cashflow-at-risk (CFAR), the three factors characterising the VAR model are:

❑ The definition of exposure will encompass the firm as a whole, or at least its significant operating units.

❑ Risk is defined in terms of earnings, or some other measure of operating performance, rather than asset value.

❑ CFAR employs the same measurement cycle as the definition of risk. If the firm measures earnings quarterly, then a CFAR model applied to this definition of risk will examine quarterly changes in earnings.

This results in a measure of risk that is both simple and complete. It is simple because risk is defined in terms of cashflow or earnings. To bring it even closer to the daily discussions in the boardroom, risk is expressed as the probability of missing targets in the firm's business plan.

CFAR's measure of financial price risk is complete because it accounts fully for interactions among the firm's risks - it treats the firm as a portfolio of exposures.

This risk measure is also focused. It isolates variability in the firm's operating results linked to financial price risk. So, if the firm were an airline, CFAR might describe the impact of fuel price changes but would ignore random fluctuations in costs resulting from variations in the weather.

A CFAR model can be constructed using the firm's business model as its base. Typically, the latter includes projected values for financial prices and other uncertain variables and can pro-

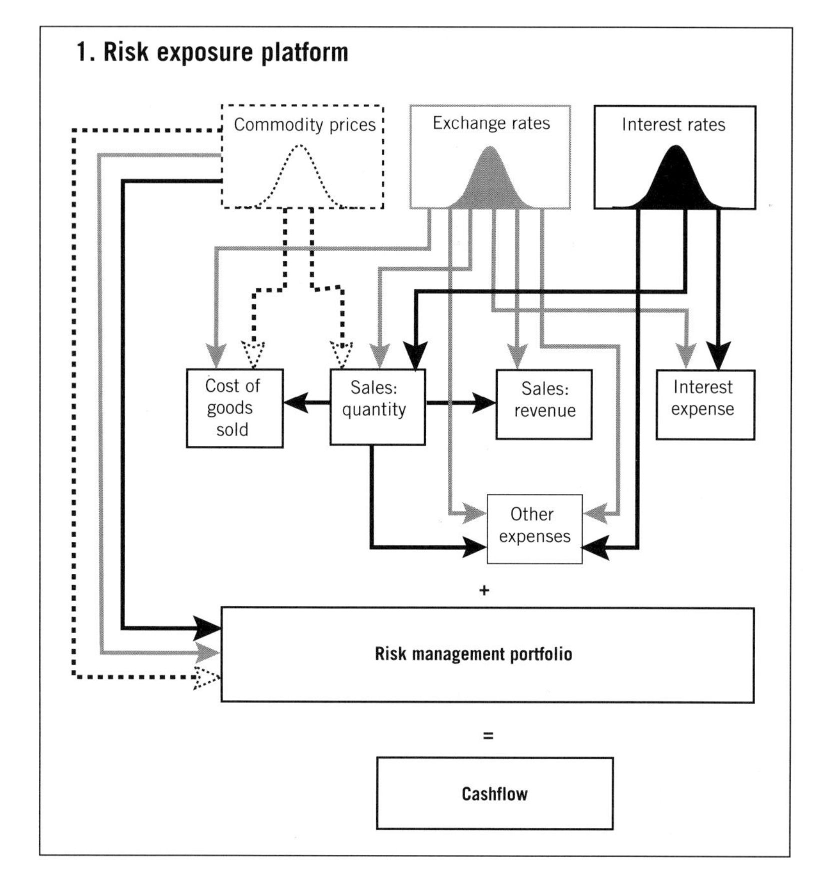

duce hypothetical financial statements. So it is able not only to summarise the firm's exposures to interest rates, currencies and commodities, but also to indicate where they are.

An ideal approach to CFAR would be to attach the firm's business model to a "simulation engine", which would replace the projected financial prices with simulated financial prices, obtained via Monte Carlo or other methods. But this is not always possible. Many firms project revenues and costs and specify exposures outside their business model. In these cases, CFAR must begin with the firm's financial statements. In this approach, key items from these statements, such as *Sales revenues*, are linked to financial price movements. These prices, and through them the relevant items in the financial statements, are simulated.

Figure 1 illustrates the critical exposures a typical firm should model in CFAR. Some firms might have additional exposures but all are likely to be exposed to financial price risk through the following items: *Sales revenues*, *Cost of goods sold* and *Interest expense*.

The relationships embedded in the income statement and the balance sheet are then used to derive the statistics, such as *Earnings per share*, employed in the CFAR model's definition of risk. In addition, changes in key financial items can be linked via "decision rules". These summarise the human element of the firm – ie discrete actions prompted by managers' decisions. Thus, managers may respond to a sustained increase in sales by initiating investment in a new plant. The decision rule to implement this action might be as follows: if sales rise above x and remain above that level for n consecutive quarters, then the firm will increase its *Plant & equipment* expenditures by z.

Exposure specification – the link between financial statement items and financial price movements – is the most critical component in the CFAR model. A well-established approach proposes that this link be modelled as an elasticity (O'Brien, 1994). That is, exposure is defined as the percentage change (%Δ) in the level of expected future values of a variable for a given percentage change in a financial price. The link between the dollar-yen exchange rate and the sales of a hypothetical corporate with exports to Japan can be described as:

$$\eta^{\text{Sales in Japan}}_{\text{\$ per ¥}} = \frac{\%\Delta(\text{Expected revenue from Japanese sales})}{\%\Delta(\text{\$ per ¥})}$$
$$\eta^{\text{Domestic sales}}_{\text{\$ per ¥}} = \frac{\%\Delta(\text{Expected revenue from domestic sales})}{\%\Delta(\text{\$ per ¥})}. \qquad (1)$$

As the figure shows, these elasticities are actually a combination of two exposures: a) transactional exposures affecting the value of sales revenue and b) economic exposures affecting the quantity of sales. The firm's transactions exposure, for example, will be reflected in the first elasticity. Since the dollar value of the firm's expected Japanese sales will move one-for-one with the value of the yen (assuming no economic exposure), this elasticity:

$$\eta^{\text{Sales in Japan}}_{\text{\$ per ¥}}$$

will equal one.

The second elasticity – that of domestic sales – will only reflect an economic exposure. If the firm faces price competition from Japanese imports, this elasticity:

$$\eta^{\text{Domestic sales}}_{\text{\$ per ¥}}$$

will be positive. The intensity of the competition will determine the magnitude of the elasticity, which will generally range between 0 and 1. The position of elasticity within this range will depend on the type of market. Firms which can pass cost increases on to the purchaser are likely to face lower elasticities than those which cannot. Specifically, firms selling commodities and other products with many substitutes are likely to face significant competition; relatively small changes in foreign exchange rates can change their competitive position. Conversely, firms selling differentiated products are more shielded from competition; larger changes in foreign exchange rates are required to change their competitive position. Other exposures can be considered in the same way. So the link between domestic sales and movements in the various financial prices to which the firm is exposed can be specified simply by adding their effects:

$$\begin{aligned}(\text{Domestic sales})_t = \Big[&\eta^{\text{Domestic sales}}_{\$\text{ per ¥}} \times \%\Delta(\$\text{ per ¥})_t \\ &+ \eta^{\text{Domestic sales}}_{\text{Interest rate}} \times \%\Delta(\text{Interest rate})_t \\ &+1\Big] \times (\text{Domestic sales})_{t-1}.\end{aligned} \quad (2)$$

In other words, the sales in any period, t, are simply the sales in the previous period, $t-1$, adjusted for the sum of the impact of changes in financial prices.

A separate set of elasticities will describe the impact of the dollar-yen exchange rate on the cost of goods sold. These formulas will be structured somewhat differently than those for sales. As the figure shows, changes in financial prices will affect this cost both directly, through changes in the cost of inputs, and indirectly, through changes in the quantity of sales. So the cost of goods sold must be modelled as a function of sales. The link between the firm's cost of goods sold and the financial prices is modelled in the same way. The cost of producing goods in any period is simply the cost that would be expected given the level of sales, adjusted for the sum of the impact of changes in financial prices.

To use this approach to link financial statements with financial items, the corporate must have estimates of the relevant elasticities. If historical internal data is readily available, this can be accomplished by using regression to estimate the historical relation between the relevant financial prices and the item in question. For example, to obtain the elasticities employed in equation (2), one need only use regression to estimate the relationship:

$$\begin{aligned}(\%\Delta\text{Domestic sales})_t = \ &\hat{\eta}^{\text{Domestic sales}}_{\$\text{ per ¥}} \times (\%\Delta\$\text{ per ¥})_t \\ &+ \hat{\eta}^{\text{Domestic sales}}_{\text{Interest rate}} \times (\%\Delta\text{Interest rate})_t.\end{aligned} \quad (3)$$

Regression analysis is, by definition, an historical measure of the firm's sensitivities to financial prices. Although it is simple to implement, its value depends on the historical relationship holding true over the time horizon of the simulation. These regression estimates are, therefore, less useful for a firm entering new markets than for a firm which is aiming to maintain its current market position.

An alternative approach to estimating exposures, described by Pringle (1991), relies more on the knowledge of managers in the corporate's operating units. In this approach, managers are interviewed and asked to rate the sensitivities of each product price to movements in the home currency relative to the local currency. The sensitivity is expressed as a rating which indicates the firm's ability to pass exchange rate changes through to the product price. This rating system can be converted fairly easily to elasticity measures of exposures.

As the figure shows, exposures to interest rates and foreign exchange rates may also enter through the Interest expense item in the income statement. By definition, this item is the sum of coupon payments on the firm's fixed-rate debt, interest on its floating-rate debt and interest costs on its short-term debt. The quantity of short-term debt, however, will vary. Increases in interest rates, for example, are likely to result in the lengthening of receivables – increasing the firm's short-term financing requirements. In addition, the firm's fixed-rate interest costs may change with interest rates if its debt is callable or if a refunding is being considered.

Standard risk management modules can be modelled through a spreadsheet that values derivatives using the simulated financial prices driving the exposures. Just a few years ago, pricing a portfolio of derivatives would have been a daunting task. Now the market for the pricing software has expanded to the point where pricing add-ins for Excel and Lotus are both readily available and easy to use.

More complicated risk management programs can also be modelled through "artificial intelligence" approaches, applied via decision rules. For example, a foreign exchange management program may include "risk avoidance" – the corporate might choose to change the location of a factory should a critical exchange rate move above a set threshold. Decision rules may be used to model context-sensitive risk management programs. For example, a firm may swap all its floating-rate debt to fixed if the yield on the long Treasury bond falls below 5%. It may swap all its fixed-rate debt to floating if the yield on the long bond rises above a trigger level, say 10%. Decision rules allow CFAR to expand beyond simple, mechanistic approaches to risk management.

A crucial portion of any CFAR model is the "simulation engine" that generates the financial prices driving the model. The financial prices must be realistic. The first critical test is consistency. Allowing interest rates and foreign exchange rates produced by the engine to violate interest rate parity may lead the model to provide misleading distributions for the firm's cashflows, leading to incorrect prices for the firm's risk management portfolio. The engine should also produce prices whose distributional properties mimic those of real financial prices. In particular, the simulated prices should exhibit, in a stochastic fashion, volatilities and correlations that vary over time.

To conclude, an industrial corporate can benefit greatly by using the measure of risk generated by a CFAR model. This measure will be readily interpretable because risk is defined in terms of cashflow or earnings and presented in terms of the firm's business plan.

As important as the output of the CFAR model is, the input can also be of great benefit to the firm - much of the effort in building a model will be in analysing the relationships between financial prices, key financial statistics and the firm's risk management plan. The end result of the CFAR approach will be both a model and a new understanding of the firm's business.

BIBLIOGRAPHY

O'Brien, T.J., 1994, "Corporate Measurement of Exposure to Foreign Exchange Risk", *Financial Markets, Institutions and Instruments*, 3, 4, New York University, pp. 1–60.

Pringle, J.J., 1991, "Managing Foreign Exchange Exposure", *Journal of Applied Corporate Finance*, Winter, pp. 73–82.

37

VAR for Corporates

David Shimko
Bankers Trust Company

Many corporates have been unhappy about using traditional value-at-risk methods for risk management. This article looks at the advantages of using a pro forma *income statement to allocate risk capital efficiently.*

Perhaps you have been overwhelmed lately with different versions of value-at-risk (VAR), a measure of how much value a portfolio might lose over a particular period with a given level of statistical confidence. VAR was first developed for investors and financial institutions to reflect the risk of financial instruments and trading portfolios that are marked to market and can be liquidated easily. Banks, consultants and software houses, each with a slightly different approach to the question, seem to have jumped on the bandwagon, approaching corporate clients with risk management solutions based on VAR.

Can VAR be applied in a corporate setting?

Many corporates have expressed unease with traditional VAR for corporate risk management, on the grounds that their future cashflows are not marked to market and, indeed, could never be traded. But they concede that VAR, as created for financial institutions, does have its place in a corporate setting, for example, when evaluating derivative positions or a foreign exchange receivables book or when considering the issuance of new equity. In these situations, VAR is really cashflow-at-risk.

For broad strategic business purposes, however, knowledge of potential short-term losses is not enough. First, risks to cashflows generally should be examined not over a short-term mark-to-market interval but over a longer period that recognises the full time elapsed before cashflows are realised. Second, corporations must be able to use VAR (or a similar concept) as a management tool to determine how the risk composition of their businesses affects return on capital at risk – this knowledge leads to efficient deployment of risk capital. The methodology must also be sufficiently robust to incorporate all of a corporation's activities, for example, project initiation, acquisitions and trading. The following example shows one way to incorporate VAR analyses into a project valuation exercise. The best corporate VAR approach is likely to contain many different facets.

A corporate VAR exercise

This exercise shows how a cashflow analysis can be used to help a natural gas producer determine whether or not it should hedge its gas price risk on a new field. The producer has both hedgeable price risk and unhedgeable volume (production) risk. To make the exercise meaningful, we assume a hedging cost of 2% of notional contract value; this could be interpreted as the sum of administrative, bid/offer and market inefficiency costs.

The goal of the exercise is to split the expected net revenue stream into two: one part which is not at risk and another which is. The analysis is similar to traditional worst-case *pro forma* (or forecast) scenario analysis. However, by explicitly splitting the expected cashflows into two separate streams, we expect to be able to draw new conclusions about the return on capital at risk and the deployment of risk capital.

In particular, by increasing the value of cashflows not at risk, the corporation can release risk capital for more efficient activities. However, it does not pay to release capital if the corporation incurs costs in excess of the redeployment benefits by increasing its value not at risk.

In the first scenario, we show a three-year standard *pro forma* for an all-equity natural gas development project.

Table 1. Risk assumptions (%)

	1997	1998	1999
95% confidence price drop	30.00	40.00	45.00
95% confidence volume drop	20.00	30.00	40.00
Correlation	0.00	0.00	0.00
95% confidence combined drop	36.06	50.00	60.21
Hedging penalty (as % of revenue)	2.00	2.00	2.00

Table 2. Scenarios

	1997	1998	1999
SCENARIO 1: EQUITY INVESTMENT			
Gas price ($/MMBtu)	2.02	1.96	1.96
Volume (MMBtu)	10,000,000	10,000,000	10,000,000
Expected revenue ($)	20,200,000	19,600,000	19,600,000
Total cost ($)	4,000,000	4,000,000	4,000,000
Net revenue ($)	16,200,000	15,600,000	15,600,000
Project discount rate (%)			13.00
Low-risk discount rate (%)			7.00
Value ($)			37,364,954
Cost ($)			35,000,000
Value-added ($)			2,364,954
Interest rate (%)			16.97
SCENARIO 2: LOW AND HIGH-RISK NET REVENUES			
Expected (from scenario 1, $)	16,200,000	15,600,000	15,600,000
"Worst-case" net revenue ($)	**8,916,786**	**5,800,000**	**3,799,237**
Net revenues at risk ($)	7,283,214	9,800,000	11,800,763
Cost of project ($)			35,000,000
Value not at risk (PV@7%, $)			**16,500,699**
Value-at-risk (cost – value not at risk, $)			18,499,301
Return on VAR (%)			23.79
SCENARIO 3: HEDGING PRICE RISK			
Expected (from scenario 1, $)	16,200,000	15,600,000	15,600,000
Hedging costs ($)	404,000	392,000	392,000
Worst case if price risk hedged ($)	11,756,000	9,328,000	7,368,000
Net revenues at risk ($)	4,444,000	6,272,000	8,232,000
Cost of project ($)			35,000,000
Hedging loss ($)			1,039,947
Value not at risk (PV@7%, $)			25,148,835
Value-at-risk ($)			9,851,165
Return on VAR (%)			36.55

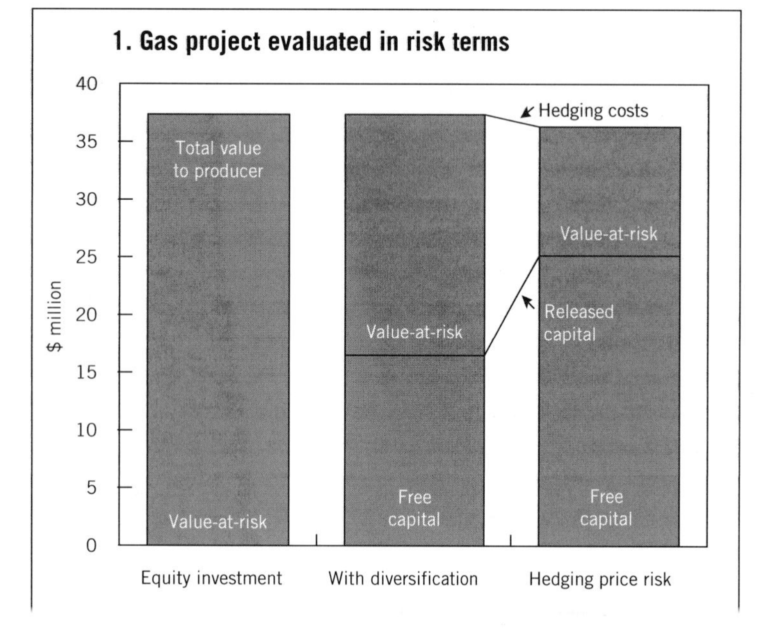

The value is calculated by discounting expected revenues at 13%. At the assumed cost, the interest rate exceeds the project discount rate, ie the project has an equity-financed "alpha" of 3.97% (16.97% – 13%).

To sensitise the *pro forma* to risk assumptions, shown in Table 1, we estimated worst-case scenarios for low gas prices and low production volumes. (A figure of 20% in Table 1 implies that the level of the variable can drop by as much as 20% over the entire period within the prescribed confidence level.) Assuming zero correlation between price and volume, the combined proportional volatility of 36.06% in 1997 reflects a worst-case drop considering the diversification benefits of bearing price and volume risk simultaneously.

When we consider the maximum drop in revenues (scenario 2), the worst-case net revenues reflect cashflows not at risk. Discounted at the low-risk rate of 7%, the value not at risk is $16.5 million. The residual value of $18.5 million is therefore at risk; its expected return (using expected net revenues at risk) is 23.79%.

We can therefore see the same project in two ways: either as an all-equity project, earning a 16.97% return, or as a project with a combination of $16.5 million in bankable value, earning 7%, and $18.5 million in VAR, earning 23.79%. This implies that the gas producer could either: (a) borrow against the value not at risk to increase shareholder value by investing in other projects; or (b) accept more profitable project risks for the same level of capital.

The analysis is particularly useful when we examine the gas producer's decision whether or not to hedge. In scenario 3, we assume price risk is 100% hedged (up to the volume of expected production) but the producer still experiences volumetric risk. However, in hedging, the producer expects to incur costs of 2% of notional contract value. Hedging therefore increases cashflows not at risk by eliminating price risk but the cost of hedging reduces these cashflows. The combined effect is that value not at risk has been elevated to $25 million (an additional $8.6 million) by hedging. The return on VAR has risen to 36.55%.

By hedging, the gas producer would lose $1 million in present value. On the other hand, hedging would free $8.6 million in risk capital. For every 1% alpha (return over required rates) the capital can earn, the present value over three years is 2.62%, implying that a one-alpha investment of the $8.6 million yields $226,954 in present value. If the alternative use of risk capital can earn more than 4.58% (=$1 million/ 226,954), the company should hedge; if the alpha falls below 4.58%, it should not.

Figure 1 summarises our results in terms of the total value of the project instead of total costs. It shows the combined impact of hedging, which can only be justified economically under these assumptions if the released capital return exceeds hedging costs. This methodology can be generalised to allow the company to determine whether trading adds value, to determine the value of diversification and to choose among competing demands for risk capital.

The decision to examine a business in terms of its risk instead of its activities is a good one – one that is especially necessary when equity capital is scarce or costly. Few firms can answer the questions: "How much equity capital are you really putting at risk?" and "What returns are you earning on risk capital?" Nevertheless, the answers could inform corporate policy, direction and, ultimately, success.

38

Investors' Return on VAR

David Shimko
Bankers Trust Company

This article outlines a new techique to help investors leverage their trading views while conserving risk capital.

Suppose you believe the price of oil will rise by \$3. How much risk capital should you budget to monetise this view, ie how much are you willing to lose on this bet? Should you establish forward positions in oil or should you buy call options? Should you write calls covered by forwards or lower strike calls? How should you choose the calls' strike prices and allocate your position between calls and forwards? How do transaction costs affect your portfolio choice? Assuming you have trading views outside of oil, how best do you diversify your information and beliefs across different investments?

Assume the Black model for options on futures applies, and current market option prices are shown in the table below. The proprietary value represents the trader's perceived value of the option at expiry, one year later.

The market prices are calculated using the market \$20 forward, and the proprietary option value is calculated using the proprietary view of a \$23 forward. The forward position has an expected profit of \$3, with value-at-risk of \$6.48, for a return on VAR of 0.46 or 46% (3/6.48). The advantage of taking a forward position is that it responds efficiently and completely to a change in market value. The disadvantage is that the forward position costs \$6.48 a barrel in risk capital.

Table 1. Option values at market and under a proprietary trading view

Strike	Market	Proprietary
17	2.98	6.00
18	2.24	5.00
19	1.62	4.00
20	1.11	3.00
21	0.74	2.00
22	0.47	1.00
23	0.28	0.00
24	0.17	0.00
25	0.09	0.00

Time = 1 year,; r = 7%; σ =15%

Ask any oil trader who has this view of the market if they should buy a call instead of buying forward. Most will say they do not want to waste unnecessary premium dollars protecting against an unlikely loss. However, although option protection appears to contradict the trader's view, it may make sense to buy call options instead of taking forward positions. This is because the liquidity costs of option purchases may be outweighed by the benefits of releasing risk capital to increase the size of the position. In other words, even though the expected profit per option is lower, the profit is earned with proportionately less capital at risk. The trader can buy one forward position or several call options for the same VAR.

In the above example, the trader expects the options to be a losing investment because of the loss of time value. Despite the built-in disadvantage, all the options outperform the forward position in terms of return on VAR. The best return on VAR is the 21 strike call at 172% ((2/0.74) - 1), but Figure 1 shows the relationship of option risk and return to the underlying forwards.

1. Portfolio efficiency: forwards versus options

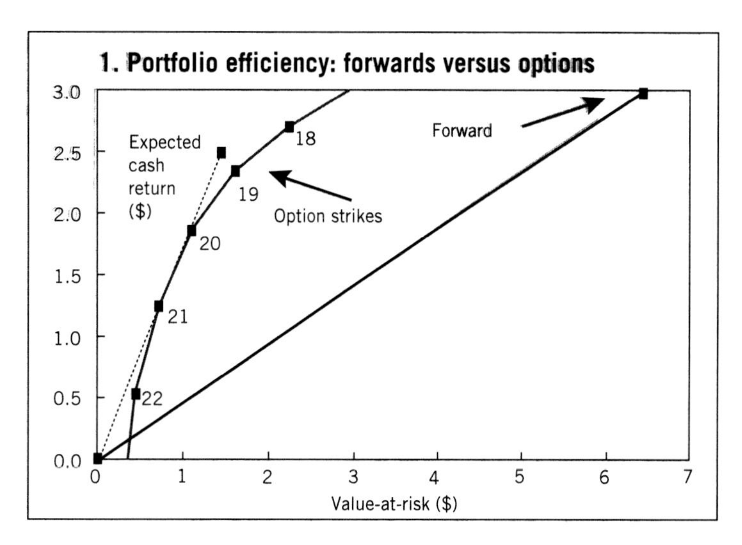

The return on risk capital can be increased by using calls instead of futures.

In this example, we did not include transaction costs or the impact large trades have on market prices. This information, though sometimes difficult to gather, can easily be incorporated. Also, the results of the analysis are parameter-dependent; this is not an exhortation to buy calls or call spreads instead of forwards in every bullish situation.

The more an investor has non-monetised views (ie alternative valuable uses of capital) and the more restricted his risk capital, the more he will value structures that preserve his risk capital. Return on VAR is an imperfect but workable way of comparing diverse and complicated positions. So investors must consider:

- ❑ How much risk capital are you willing to use?
- ❑ Are proprietary positions using appropriate levels of risk capital?
- ❑ How should positions be constructed to maximise return on VAR?
- ❑ To what use would you put more risk capital if it were available?

If portfolio realignment can give the same expected profitability for less VAR, and if released risk capital can earn a higher return by increasing positions or diversifying into new positions, maximisation of return on VAR will increase returns to a fund for the same level of capital at risk – provided the trader's views are correct! But then, that is always the hard part.

39

VAR_{MD} = LAR

Richard Singer
KPMG

Value-at-risk is all very well, but it can ignore some important risks. Risk managers should make greater use of another measure, liquidity-at-risk.

Shimko (1995) observes that a firm's VAR limit is the amount of capital it allocates to self-insurance. In other words, VAR represents the largest acceptable uninsured loss from market risk the firm is willing to suffer over a specified period of time.

Insuring against potential losses greater than the VAR limit, of course, generally involves hedging. In Shimko's example, an aluminium buyer faced with a one-year VAR of $360 per ton faces the possibility that he may have to come up with $360 per ton over the budgeted amount to make his required purchases. If his VAR limit is only $200 per ton, he must purchase insurance to cover the excess VAR of $160 per ton, typically by buying futures contracts or by entering a receive floating-pay fixed commodity swap.

But he may choose to hedge more VAR: if the cost of hedging insurance is lower than the expected return on alternative capital allocations, it makes sense to hedge away all $360 of VAR per ton. Shimko concludes that "companies should pay away profits to others to insure themselves if they thereby free enough internal capital to earn more than they pay away."

While this analysis helps the hedge/don't hedge decision from a financial point of view, it is incomplete from a risk management perspective because it ignores some of the important risks which persist following decisions to hedge. Some risky consequences of the original $360 per ton VAR cannot be mitigated – although a full hedge will ensure that none of the $360 VAR per ton will be lost, it fails to ensure against the requirement to pay out the extra $360 per ton, an obligation the firm may be unable to satisfy. The firm may be required to pay out full VAR as it meets margin calls, since the hedge instruments employed to mitigate market price risk are marginable derivatives to a greater or lesser extent. This represents a persistent risk to firm liquidity – its liquidity-at-risk (LAR).

Let us consider an extension of Shimko's example. The aluminium buyer with $360 per ton VAR needs to purchase just over 200,000 tons of aluminium. His actual VAR limit is $10,000,000, and he buys his position in three floating price tranches over several weeks. His first purchase happens to be 27,000 tons which he does not hedge, and which consumes $9,720,000 of his $10 million VAR. A second purchase of 100,000 tons is made several days later in a market that has remained quite stable. Because he is very close to his VAR limit, he hedges price risk for the entire 100,000 ton purchase by arranging a (marginable) receive floating swap. Finally, compelled to complete his programme in a market which has suddenly become more volatile, he buys the final 100,000 tons and hedges the price of that amount with futures.

First, observe that at T3 our aluminium trader has inadvertently exceeded his VAR limit. Although the quantities he price-hedged at T2 and T3 have VAR = 0, the unhedged 27,000 tons he purchased at T1 exceed his VAR limit at T3 because the market has become more volatile. Aluminium VAR rose to $420/ton from $360/ton, lifting book VAR to $11,340,000. At the end of the time horizon specified, the firm may be required to pay out an extra $11.3 million for the aluminium it needs.

Table 1. Hedge portfolio VARs and LARs

	Purchase (tons)	VAR/ton	Amount hedged ($)	Purchase VAR ($)	Portfolio VAR ($)	VAR_{MD} = LAR
T1	27,000	360	0	9,720,000	9,720,000	0
T2	100,000	360	100,000	0	9,720,000	36,000,000
T3	100,000	420	100,000	0	11,340,000	84,000,000

$VAR_{MD} = LAR$

Second, note that although book (positions plus hedges) VAR is only $11.3 million, the market value of marginable derivatives used to hedge away the remaining VAR may drop by $420/ton, resulting in required payouts totalling $84 million. However, because the 27,000 ton purchase remains floating and is self-insured, it will result in no margin call payouts. To summarise these relationships:

.99 VAR book = $11.34 million
.99 VAR marginable derivatives =
max cumulative margin calls = $84 million =
.99 LAR (liquidity-at-risk)

The liquidity-at-risk (LAR) is the maximum of cumulative margin calls requiring cash payouts in the time horizon. It is equal to the VAR of the partial portfolio of marginable derivatives for the same time horizon. If the marginable derivative hedges are perfectly efficient, then any or all of the $84 million paid out will be "recovered" as delivery is taken against a spot price $84 million lower than the hedge-fixed price.

Note the trade-off between VAR and LAR: if the firm hedges away the remaining $11.3 million at T3, so VARbook = 0, LAR grows to $95.3 million. If the firm's activities are constrained by neither VAR limits nor limited liquidity, it may switch VAR for LAR or LAR for VAR in equal amounts for only hedge transaction costs.

Of course, firms do select VAR limits to protect themselves from unacceptable losses. Moreover, since a firm must forego alternative returns from internal liquidity to meet margin calls and may also incur interest charges on borrowings used to meet them, the costs involved in converting VAR to LAR can be considerably higher than hedging transaction costs.

Naturally, firms are not blessed with unlimited liquidity, nor do they have unlimited credit. So, cost considerations aside, while VAR limits constrain the amount of uninsured market risk a firm accepts, it is clear that effective LAR limits also exist, equal to the sum of firm liquidity and borrowing power. And whether they are formally stated or not, LAR limits should constrain the amount of hedged market risk a firm accepts.

Despite the classic example of Metallgesellschaft, surprisingly few companies set formal LAR limits. One reason may be that exploring the limits of its liquidity can have awkward consequences for a firm. Let us return for a moment to the case of our aluminium buyer; suppose his firm's total liquidity and borrowing power was limited to $60 million, and that he had a $60 million LAR limit as well as a $10 million VAR limit. The awkward consequence here is that, faced with a volatile market resulting in aluminium VARs over $300/ton, the firm may not have enough liquidity resources to safely purchase and/or price-hedge the aluminum it needs.

In general, the size of a firm's exposure to market risk is constrained by specified VAR limits and by specified or effective LAR limits. Both constraints are affected not only by position size but also by market volatility. A breach of either may expose a firm to unacceptable levels of market, legal and reputation risk, as well as the simple risk of default.

Of course, it may sometimes be possible to hedge away unacceptable VAR without assuming unacceptable levels of LAR. For firms dealing in products with active options markets, long options or long swaptions strategies may provide significant insurance against excess VAR without forcing them to establish positions of marginable derivatives. But long options strategies to hedge away VAR without increasing LAR may be very costly because, in the end, option prices are influenced by the same time and volatility risk factors that drive LAR. And for firms dealing in products without options markets, opportunities to hedge LAR by buying volatility may not exist.

Risk managers interested in measuring, monitoring and controlling the LAR component of liquidity risk should consider the following steps.

❑ Determine the actual extent of liquidity resources available to support market risk for specific projects, both for individual business units and for the whole firm. Rationalise LAR limits, including benefits from rolling-up diverse business unit LARs. Make sure that senior management are happy with chosen confidence intervals.

❑ Estimate LARs daily by estimating VARs of the partial portfolios composed exclusively of marginable derivatives used to mitigate market risk. Estimate LARs both for one-day horizons (tomorrow's margin calls) and for horizons consistent with the terms of underlying transactions. Aggregate firm LAR. Consider rolling-up LAR with uncertain liquidity requirements from other corporate activities to estimate an integrated firmwide liquidity risk measure.

❑ Modify LAR limits and LAR allocations as firm liquidity resources change.

❑ Test LARs against LAR limits and report both, highlighting exceptions.

❑ Periodically estimate the costs of hedging VAR

and LAR using current market volatilities and interest rates.

❑ Explore the consequences of potential LAR "crisis events," resident in the tails of estimated LAR distributions, by scenario/stress testing the partial portfolios of marginable derivatives. Be certain to consider radical volatility shift scenarios as well as diversification benefit reductions frequently associated with market crises.

❑ Continuously review LAR estimates and actual liquidity utilisation across multiple time horizons to appropriately improve/modify LAR estimation techniques and other components of the liquidity risk management process. Inform the firm board and senior management about liquidity constraints which may impact decisions about current corporate activity levels, future plans, and financing decisions.

Active hedgers who fail to measure and monitor LAR do so at their own peril. The use of marginable derivatives to mitigate market risk, to hedge away unacceptable levels of VAR, may in turn expose the hedger to serious financial distress, potentially to the risk of default. It is imperative that senior managers of hedging firms understand that their business activities are jointly constrained by market risk as measured by LAR, and that, at least in one critical way, hedging is not like buying traditional insurance.

BIBLIOGRAPHY

Shimko, D., 1995, "What is VAR?", *Risk* 8, 12, p. 27; reprinted as Chapter 34 of the present volume.

40

Veba's Way with VAR

Andrew Priest
Risk

German industrial conglomerate Veba has set the pace with detailed disclosure of its derivatives use. This article was first published in July 1996.

Mining-to-real-estate conglomerate Veba is used to attracting superlatives. Germany's fifth-largest capitalised corporation and second-largest electricity generator was born out of one of the country's biggest privatisations. In 1995, it was the first company to acknowledge the use of JP Morgan's RiskMetrics data in its annual report. At the same time, it provided an unprecedented wealth of information about its derivatives usage, going far beyond the requirements of German accounting rules.

"Veba was aware of the concern of both the public and the press about derivatives, with regards to speculation and losses, when it was setting up its central treasury operation," says Michael Wagener, senior vice-president of the group and head of its treasury division. "We therefore decided to be very open in revealing our risk management activities."

These are bold steps for a company which used to have a reputation for outdated management structures and less than rigorous central control. "If you'd suggested four years ago Veba would be using derivatives so openly I'd have thought you were talking about a different company," says one London-based European utilities analyst.

In 1994, Veba saw a return to positive growth after an earnings slide from DM1,301 million in 1991 to DM1,203 million in 1993. Last year was particularly good, with earnings rising by 40% to DM 2,113 million. Group sales of DM72 billion were only 1.5% higher than in 1994 but this was partly due to adverse exchange rate movements.

Veba comprises five independent operating divisions (see Appendix). The holding company is responsible for strategic management while the divisions and their affiliated companies are responsible for their own operational activities.

In 1994, the group set up a central treasury group to manage financial risk – specifically group interest rate and foreign exchange exposures. RiskMetrics was introduced after that, following a presentation by JP Morgan. Since Veba went public about its use of data from the system to enhance appreciation of its financial risks, a handful of international companies have followed suit, including German electronics giant Siemens (see Chapter 42) and US household goods manufacturer Procter & Gamble. "RiskMetrics is an excellent way to measure risk," says Wagener. "This is why we decided to publish the fact that we use it in our annual report."

The partnership with JP Morgan did not end with the adoption of RiskMetrics. To use the data the system produced, Veba and the US bank jointly developed a proprietary, spreadsheet-based system to analyse risk. This had the twin benefits of exploiting JP Morgan's experience in the area and avoiding the need to buy risk management software from a third party, Wagener says.

JP Morgan was equally happy with the arrangement. "Veba had a couple of specific requirements they wished to address and we gave them some ideas and solutions," says Jacques Longerstaey, vice-president of market risk research for the bank in New York.

The customised system is similar to JP Morgan's "FourFifteen" package, an Excel-based spreadsheet program designed to calculate value-at-risk and targeted at users of RiskMetrics data. But Veba needed software which met a key requirement of its central treasury. This was to include regulatory datasets to allow the calculation of value-at-risk in line with the European Union's Capital Adequacy Directive. The FourFifteen package can handle only two sets of

1. Financial derivatives of Veba Group, Dec 31, 1995 (DM million)

Remaining maturities	Nominal volume	Market value
Forward transactions		
Buy		
Up to 1 year	339.3	(0.6)
More than 1 year	3.2	0.1
Sell		
Up to 1 year	1,057.2	(4.3)
More than 1 year	-	-
Currency options		
Buy		
Up to one year	349.6	10.7
More than 1 year	-	-
Sell		
Up to 1 year	92.2	(8.6)
More than 1 year	-	-
Subtotal portfolio	1,841.5	(2.7)
Currency swaps		
Up to one year	-	-
1–5 years	658.1	(86.7)
More than 5 years	-	-
Interest rate cross-currency swaps		
Up to 1 year	18.0	5.0
1–5 years	-	-
More than 5 years	-	-
Subtotal portfolio	676.1	(81.7)
Interest rate swaps		
Fixed-rate payer		
Up to 1 year	4.0	-
1–5 years	62.4	(1.4)
More than 5 years	224.0	(14.4)
Fixed-rate recipient		
Up to 1 year	204.0	2.2
1–5 years	48.0	4.7
More than 5 years	174.0	8.1
Subtotal portfolio	716.4	(0.8)
Total portfolio	3,234.0	(85.2)

volatility correlations – daily and monthly. But Longerstaey says a version which can handle regulatory datasets will be available by the end of the summer, targeted at corporates.

Veba uses RiskMetrics to manage interest rate and foreign exchange exposure, not commodity price risk, which is managed at divisional level.

The system also allows the current state of risk positions and associated hedges to be monitored and valued at market rates. Previously, derivative positions were assessed using sensitivity analysis, says Wagener.

Another JP Morgan development in the pipeline for Veba is the calculation and distribution of RiskMetrics data over Reuters. "This ought to be easier for us," says Wagener. "Veba already has Reuters systems installed in its treasury department and Reuters is also possibly less risky than the Internet in respect to viruses."

Other investments in technology are also evident in the Veba group's centralised management of overall risk exposure. Over the past two years, it has developed and installed a group-wide computerised financial reporting and controlling system. This allows the central corporate treasury department systematically and consistently to analyse all the group's operational and financial cashflows pertaining to financing requirements and interest rate and foreign exchange rate risks.

In 1995, 30% or DM 21.7 billion of total group sales were made abroad. The group's sensitivity to currencies is enhanced by the continuing refusal of the Deutschmark to settle into a consistent trend, particularly against the dollar. The effect of volatility in the dollar/Deutschmark rate can be grave. Veba's annual report says DM1.5 billion of losses in its Stinnes retail chain were due to "adverse currency exchange rates and the associated translation deficit".

The central treasury conducts hedges up to 12 months ahead to cover the group's foreign exchange risk. At the end of 1995, exchange hedges had been conducted for four international currencies: the dollar, sterling, yen and French franc. Shorter-term hedges are also entered into but company policy restricts their use to matching underlying transactions in terms of amount and terms.

At year-end, Veba's foreign exchange instruments covering group exposure had a total nominal value of DM1,841.5 million (see Table 1). These were all plain-vanilla instruments, says Wagener. "We are not permitted to use any second-generation or exotic structures," he adds. Veba also uses currency swaps, with a nominal value of DM 658.1 million.

The central treasury actively manages group interest rate exposure with short- and long-term swaps based on its outlook on interest rates. As with foreign exchange, no structured products are used. Hedges are typically set for up to five years. Short-term hedges, up to one year, are conducted within the same matching constraints as for currencies, says Wagener. Swaps of more than five years are also used but, as with all transactions over five years, are managed on a micro basis inspired by commercial policies. They are "harder to deal with due to the longer time frame involved", says Wagener.

Veba pays the fixed leg on interest rate swaps with a nominal value of DM290.4 million and the floating leg on swaps with a nominal value of DM426 million. Of the former, 64% of the swaps are for more than five years.

Overall, the central treasury has a derivatives portfolio worth a nominal DM3,234 million, representing 4.5% of group turnover. The minimum credit rating of counterparties the group may deal with is determined by the lifetime of the particular over-the-counter contract, says Wagener.

For commodity risk hedging, the divisional treasuries are autonomous, providing the group treasury with quarterly reports setting out the final operating risk position. Any changes in the meantime are conveyed to the central treasury by telephone or facsimile. "The system is therefore centralised and decentralised," says Wagener. "The operating divisions decide the volume they wish to hedge and when. But, if they decide to hedge any financial risk, they are obliged to deal with the central treasury as their counterparty at market rates. However, the divisions are fully responsible for their own performance and therefore make decisions independently about how to hedge."

Veba Öl, for example, hedges imbalances between daily processing and supply availability, often at short notice, with Brent crude futures at the International Petroleum Exchange in London or at the New York Mercantile Exchange.

By not only going public on its use of derivatives but also adopting a voluntary code of openness, Veba has attempted to dispel investor concern about its use of derivatives and has gained admirers in the process.

Appendix

Divisions of power

Veba was set up by the Free State of Prussia in Berlin in 1929 as a state-owned concern to tap the financial markets to develop coal mining and electricity generation in West Germany. Privatisation began in 1965 and the Bonn government finally sold its remaining shares in March 1987. The process remains one of the largest corporate sell-offs in the country's history. At the end of 1995, the conglomerate boasted a market capitalisation of around $19 billion and employed 129,000 people in some 50 units at home and abroad.

Since privatisation, Veba has been organised into five independent operating divisions within the group holding company: electricity; oil; chemicals; trading/transportation/services; and telecommunications.

Its mainstay is the electricity division. Veba is the second largest electricity generator in Germany, and the division earned DM1 billion – 48.5% of total group earnings – in 1995. Electricity distribution is organised through its wholly owned subsidiary Preussenelektra.

Veba's chemicals division, Hüls, saw its earnings rise to DM503 million in 1995, up 18% from 1994, on sales of DM10.8 billion (up 4% from the previous year). Hüls produces speciality and performance chemicals including starting products and intermediates for the pharmaceutical and crop-protection sectors, adhesive raw materials, latex and leather products.

Earnings in the company's oil production and refining division, Veba Öl, rose to DM208 million, a 45% rise over 1994, as increased production and higher crude prices offset the dollar's slide against the Deutschmark. The price of Brent, the international crude benchmark, rose from $16.38 a barrel on January 6, 1995 to $18.61 a barrel on January 5, 1996. The dollar entered 1995 at $1 = DM1.56, falling to a low of $1 = DM1.37 before rallying to $1 = DM1.45 by the year-end.

Veba's highest-selling division is trading/transportation/services. This part of the group turned over DM30.1 billion in 1995, up 1.2% on the previous year. Activities include oil transportation, a do-it-yourself retail chain, chemicals distribution, sea and land freight, building materials, retail and real estate development.

But it was Veba's telecommunications arm, Veba Telecom, which produced truly dramatic growth in 1995 following its joint venture with the UK's Cable & Wireless. Sales increased to DM339 million in 1995, up 211% on 1994.

41

VAR with Muscles

Martin Hiemstra
Energy & Power Risk Management

Statoil is one organisation that understands the importance of measuring risk. A value-at-risk system is seen as crucial to increasing the company's overall efficiency and performance. This article was first published in October 1996.

There's a 1:1,370 chance that the Norwegian oil giant Statoil will face offshore oil rig disaster next year and odds of 1:2,740 that the disaster will cost the company more than $5 billion.

Petter Kapstad, financial controller of the state-owned company, and his senior colleagues appreciate the importance of this information in their on-going respect for how risk can affect the fortunes of the company.

This knowledge stems from the company's recent introduction of a comprehensive risk management computer system. The system was introduced in August 1996, after a year in development, and has no name yet and at time of going to press no cost figures were available.

The system produces what-if reports that give the odds on potential earnings shortfalls arising from a variety of causes, be it an offshore disaster, a refinery explosion or a crude oil market crash (see Appendix A).

The system is based on the concept of value-at-risk (VAR) – a single number estimate of the price risk of the financial instruments held by a company and heavily touted by the derivatives industry because of the recommendation by the Group of Thirty report *Derivatives: Practices and Principles* in 1993 which called for the adoption of a consistent measure of market risk. VAR systems such as those offered by JP Morgan, the developer of the RiskMetrics VAR system, allow senior executives of financial institutions and companies to see daily one-page summaries of their aggregate market risk positions.

Statoil's system does much more than measure market price risk, says Kapstad. It also measures the risk to Statoil's future financial performance of most of the measurable internal and external risks faced by the company.

Statoil, founded in 1972, had revenues of Nkr87 billion (about $15 billion) in 1995 from its activities in petroleum exploration, production, transportation, refining and marketing. It's the leading exploration company on the Norwegian continental shelf and the largest exporter of North Sea oil.

The company is one of the world's largest net sellers of crude oil, producing 424,000 barrels per day (b/d) in 1995 and is a substantial supplier of natural gas to Europe, with a total production of 4.9 billion cubic metres in 1995.

Kapstad, based at Statoil's Stavanger headquarters, says the VAR system was introduced for three reasons: First, to measure overall risk. Second, senior management wanted to see Statoil's risk profile in order to make better decisions. Third, the system can aid the achievement of macro-economic targets such as those for cash-flow or return on capital employed.

The system developed from a scenario model used in individual departments, which simulated overnight risks of stock prices, interest rates and currencies and was expanded with significant help from New York-based investment bank Goldman Sachs, which helped design much of the system. The reason the system was expanded was because senior management saw the possibility of getting a complete picture of Statoil's risk profile, says Kapstad.

The lack until now of a comprehensive risk management system has meant Statoil has been a conservative user of derivative instruments to hedge price risk. The company still intends to be conservative but with the aid of the new system will look in the future towards using structured derivative products such as oil-linked bonds that

1. Shortfall risk

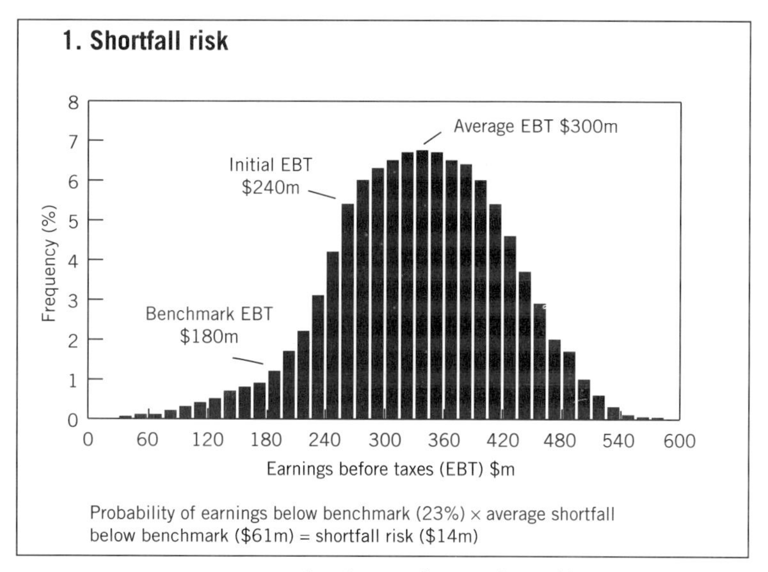

Probability of earnings below benchmark (23%) × average shortfall below benchmark ($61m) = shortfall risk ($14m)

more closely match its risk profile.

It has tended to use plain-vanilla products such as currency forwards, futures, options and swaps to manage currency, interest rate and commodity price risks.

To determine overall net risk Statoil executives first needed to establish to what degree changes in the values of assets and commodities were correlated.

They created a "correlation matrix" into which was put the currency and interest rate risks as well as the price risks associated with oil and gas, oil products, petrochemicals, chemicals and fuel oil prices in order to find the answer.

Doing the correlation work with commodities, currencies and interest rates was a "real job", says Kapstad, who gives much credit to Goldman Sachs for collecting data and analysing the correlations.

But the work with the operational risks was also tough, he says. "We did a thorough study of these operational risks, which included, for example, the risk of our reservoirs producing at less than estimated production on a portfolio level. And using a stochastic statistical model (of random events), we also added on the physical risks of all of our offshore operations.

"Our insurance coverage will replace an offshore installation at replacement cost, but the risks we were concerned with in this area were the impacts that accidents would have on production loss," says Kapstad.

There wasn't much information on this type of risk. "We had to go back to the market to determine it. What we found was that there were a total of 30 major offshore accidents worldwide between 1972 and 1993," he says. Statoil had to calculate its share, and then calculate the probability of an offshore accident and incorporate it into the VAR model.

People were brought in from the company's five major divisions to work on the VAR project covering downstream, upstream, gas, finance and economic risks.

Although still in its infancy, Kapstad says senior management are beginning to use the system to assess the impact various risks would have on the distribution of earnings and revenues.

Most companies have a good idea of their risk exposures, but no one can really know for sure without having a VAR system, he thinks.

He adds that with the system Statoil can avoid underperforming financially and unnecessary hedges now that everyone is not "sitting on their own risk and dealing with it themselves".

Appendix A

A RISK OF CATASTROPHE

How does an integrated oil company manage the risk of a catastrophe like that of Piper Alpha, an oil and gas production platform situated off Scotland's coast, which exploded in July 1988 due to a suspected natural gas leak?

The accident cost not only the rig's owners, Los Angeles-based Occidental Petroleum Corporation, but also the British government, an expected loss in export earnings and tax revenues of at least $1.2 billion and losses to insurance companies of at least $1 billion, according to reports.

Assessing the cost of such as catastrophe is something that Statoil is attempting to answer in designing its VAR system.

It's important for strategic management purposes to perform a quantitative analysis of catastrophic losses and compare it to other categories of market and non-market risk.

The loss of an offshore unit can be insured against, but the loss in oil production and refining while the unit is being replaced can be catastrophic.

Once the catastrophic risk has been calculated it can be combined with other non-market risks such as production loss risk and credit risk. Then market and non-market risks are incorporated to construct an overall risk picture of Statoil's profitability.

Appendix B

STATOIL'S DILEMMA

The dilemma facing any oil and gas company is that of finding new reserves to replace oil and gas fields that are facing production declines.

Statoil is no different and the company's three giant North Sea oil fields off Norway's continental shelf are beginning to show losses in production with crude oil output expected by analysts to decline by 1998 to one-half of their 1994 levels of 449,000 b/d.

These declines are beginning to affect the fortunes of Statoil, which saw its oil output fall for the first time in 1995, contributing to an 8% drop in the company's operating profits to Nkr13.59 million from Nkr14.74 million in 1994.

In order to avert a potential crisis in the future Statoil has spent much of the last 10 years looking for new oil and gas fields around the world. A goal the company has in mind is to raise non-Norwegian production from 2% of its total to one-third by 2005.

It has joint ventures with British Petroleum to explore in west Africa, southeast Asia and the former Soviet Union.

Statoil says it is close to an agreement with BP that will allow transmission of early oil production out of Azerbaijan. The two have also discovered a major natural gas field off the coast of Vietnam, and are looking for oil off Nigeria.

In January 1996 Statoil acquired Aran Energy, an Irish oil firm with promising offshore acreage, for $315 million.

Not so Simple for Siemens

Andrew Priest
Risk

The German engineering group Siemens is using the latest value-at-risk technology in its global risk management. This article was first published in March 1997.

The sun never sets on Siemens. With more than 400 production facilities and 370,000 employees in 45 countries around the world, from Indonesia and China to the Czech Republic and the Americas, the German engineering giant has at least one plant in operation somewhere in the world at any given hour.

Furthermore, Siemens' network of sales and marketing organisations stretches over 190 countries. Its results for the first quarter of fiscal year 1997, issued at the end of January, showed a 31% year-on-year surge in international orders to DM17.6 billion. Some 61% of sales came from outside Germany in 1996 (total turnover last year was DM94.18 billion), with much of last year's growth coming from the Asia Pacific (up 130%) and the Americas (up 37%).

This global flavour reflects Siemens' philosophy, stated in its 1996 annual report: "To grow strong local roots while reaping the benefits of its position as a global player." This policy means the company is broadly based in terms of geography as well as products – it makes power generation and transmission systems and industrial electronic semiconductors as well as telecommunications systems and domestic household appliances – but leaves it exposed to international risks, such as various economic cycles and foreign currency and interest rate fluctuations.

Last November, Siemens' share price dropped by more than 9% after it warned of stagnant profits for 1997 compared with 1996. The warning was based on price erosion in the semiconductor business, due to competition from low-cost producing countries outside Europe. Meanwhile, the company plans to cut a further 60,000 jobs in Germany – in addition to 30,000 lost in the past three years – and ratings agency Moody's Investors Service is reviewing its triple-A long-term debt rating for possible downgrade.

Such problems show the complexity Siemens' treasury faces on a daily basis – managing a company exposed to almost all the world's economic vagaries. "Siemens has to manage the financial risk arising out of foreign exchange, interest rate, equity and commodity exposure on a worldwide footing," says head of treasury Christian von Ahlefeld Weller.

The company's positive stance towards European economic and monetary union has added complexity to the treasury's management of interest rate and currency risk. On February 11, 1997, it returned to the public international fixed-income markets for the first time in 25 years, becoming the first corporate simultaneously to issue parallel bonds in three currencies – Deutschmark, French franc and Dutch guilder – all to be redenominated in the euro once the relevant currency is part of European economic and monetary union. Thereafter, the DM2 billion trio of 10-year, 5.5% bonds, will be consolidated into one euro-denominated issue.

Treasury operations are therefore structured to match the company's global reach and straddle the world's time zones – the company has a total of 45 staff at treasury centres in Munich (its head office), New York and Hong Kong. Primarily intended to reduce the possibility of intraday market risk, this strategy also allows the company to capitalise on its ability to tap the strongest economic areas around the world by having local expertise in a number of major markets. It can thus avoid cyclical local dips – a strategy more usually used by investment banks and international fund managers.

A unified approach to controlling and record-

1. Siemens' derivatives use (DM million)

	Notional amount		Fair value	
	Sept 30, 1996	Sept 30, 1995	Sept 30, 1996	Sept 30, 1995
Forward exchange contracts	29,096	23,947	(116)	357
Interest rate swaps and combined interest rate/ foreign exchange swaps	16,539	6,125	(35)	52
Options	727	3,146	9	(18)
Other forward contracts	12,480	9,737	(6)	(7)
Total	**58,842**	**42,955**	**(148)**	**384**

Source: Siemens annual report, 1996

2. Currencies included in JP Morgan's RiskMetrics

First wave: October 1994	Second wave: May 1995	Third wave: December 1996
Australian dollar	Austrian schilling	Argentine peso
Belgian franc	Finnish markka	Mexican peso
Canadian dollar	Irish pound	Indonesian rupiah
Danish krone	Norwegian krone	Korean won
French franc	Portuguese escudo	Malaysian ringgit
Deutschmark	Hong Kong dollar	Philippine peso
Italian lira	New Zealand dollar	Thai baht
Japanese yen	Singapore dollar	Taiwanese dollar
Dutch guilder	Swiss franc	South African rand
Spanish peseta		
Swedish krona		
Sterling		
US dollar		
European Currency Unit		

Methodology on modelling data for "basket-pegged" emerging currencies – including the Hungarian forint, Polish zloty, Slovakian koruna and Czech koruna, are published in JP Morgan's RiskMetrics Monitor Q3

ing off-balance sheet transactions (such as derivatives), also makes for cost savings, says Weller. Indeed, the company highlighted the centralisation of its currency hedging activities in a note to its 1996 accounts, stating: "The effect of this practice is to benefit increasingly from netting opportunities within the Siemens organisation and to reduce external hedging costs." For example, its overall currency exposure is reduced by combining cashflows from local production, supplies and investments and the firm-wide netting of exposure across the group.

However, if there is naked exposure, the company uses on-balance sheet instruments - cash investments or borrowings - and off-balance sheet derivatives - such as forwards, swaps and options - to hedge it. At the end of the last fiscal year, foreign exchange hedges were primarily denominated in US dollar, sterling and Italian lira, reflecting the balance of Siemens' core manufacturing centres outside Germany. The treasury also uses derivatives, primarily dollar and Deutschmark denominated, to manage the interest rate duration of both its cash investments and other financing activities.

In the 1996 fiscal year, Siemens used derivatives representing a notional amount of some DM58.84 billion (see Table 1), an increase of 37% on the previous year. Both listed and over-the-counter instruments were used; the majority (DM29.10 billion) were forward exchange contracts with maturities of less than a year. Further out, the company increased its use of both interest rate and combined interest rate/currency swaps in 1996, reflecting an underlying exposure of DM16.54 billion and a 170% increase on the DM6.13 billion used in the previous 12 months. Its options use, on the other hand, plunged from DM3,146 million in 1995 to DM727 million notional in 1996. Weller declines to comment on the reasons for this.

Siemens' value-at-risk systems have been developed against this background. "We realised the need for a fully integrated, centralised platform for front to back office," says Weller. The present treasury management system was installed two-and-a-half years ago. Bought from US supplier Wall Street Systems, it gives continuous assessments of current market valuations on a VAR basis, he adds. Like Veba, another German industrial conglomerate (see Chapter 40), Siemens feeds its risk management system with data provided (through Reuters) by JP Morgan's RiskMetrics system.

"The Wall Street System is fully compatible with this data," says Weller. "We simply feed it into our management system via an interface," he adds. In line with common practice among corporates, money-at-risk calculations derived from RiskMetrics data are made on the basis of 2.57 standard deviations, a 99.5% confidence level and a one day liquidation period. "We then run these results against our portfolio and hedge accordingly," he says.

"All three centres are hooked up to the same treasury system, with the full portfolio passed across according to the relevant time zone," says Weller. This allows the dual benefit of round-the-clock market risk analysis and centralised netting of exposures. But the company remains exposed to some settlement risk, admits Weller. All settlement procedures - documentation and payments - are made through the company's central treasury in Munich. "Although this facility runs from 7am to 11pm, German time, there are inevitably gaps," he says. "If something were to happen late in New York, for example, it is possible we could be left exposed for a short time. However, this small degree of risk is balanced by the advantage of having one place and type of settlement in a single process in Munich."

In general, VAR works well for Siemens, and it has been keen to take advantage of continuing enhancements to both methodology and data. "RiskMetrics started out with currency data based on the Group of Ten countries, plus a couple of others," says Weller. The widening of the system's scope to include many other currencies (Table 2) "has been a relief", he adds.

"Siemens has recently added to its operations in Indonesia and, in eastern Europe, for example, by buying Siemens Elektromotory in the Czech Republic. At roughly the same time, both the rupiah and koruna were included in RiskMetrics' correlation matrices to the Deutschmark," he says.

As Siemens continues to expand the reach of its operations, its only fear is that it will outstrip the new generation of data from JP Morgan. "Even RiskMetrics is not quite fast enough for a global player such as us," says Weller.

43

Crossing the Divide

Sumit Paul-Choudhury
Risk

Firmwide risk management has become the most fashionable phrase in risk management after value-at-risk. This article explains the reasons why.

There is a hackneyed schoolboy joke that goes something like this: - My grandfather died of deafness, you know. - How come? - He got run over by a bus. - What's that got to do with being deaf? - He didn't hear it coming.

It is not difficult to draw parallels with the predicament of risk managers and their bosses. As the débâcles of recent years have demonstrated, the lack of a system which can get the right information to the right people at the right time can make all the difference when it comes to averting losses or even collapse. The Group of Thirty's influential 1993 study *Derivatives: Practices and Principles* included among its recommendations the statement that firms - both dealers and end-users - should "establish management information systems sophisticated enough to measure, manage and report the risks of derivatives in a timely and precise manner".

The logical conclusion of such recommendations, which quickly became apparent, was that such an information system should offer risk managers and senior management a global, all-inclusive perspective - in other words, it should be a firmwide risk management system. Definitions vary, but the essence of a firmwide system could perhaps be loosely stated as follows: The systems and procedures designed to deal with the multiple types of risk (market, credit, liquidity, operational, legal and so on) that arise from dealing in different asset classes (currencies, interest rates, equities, commodities and, more recently, credit) across different time zones (eg offices in New York, London and Tokyo).

The formidable theoretical, operational and technological challenges involved in addressing this ambitious brief - and the substantial investments associated with them - might well have ensured that it remained no more than a Platonic ideal. As Clifford Smout, head of the banking supervisory policy division at the Bank of England, told a 1996 conference on regulation: "Risk management is somewhat like apple pie: we're all in favour of it so long as someone else does all the cooking and it comes free. But risk management is not a free lunch: and the more elaborate the pie, the more expensive it is."

The regulators, therefore, have chosen to adopt a "carrot and stick" approach to tightening up risk management. Richard Farrant, chief executive of the UK Securities and Futures Authority, told the same conference: "Evidence emerges constantly that firms are not only inconsistent in their risk management practices but even have difficulty maintaining their own standards and practices across their group." The stick, as exemplified in the European Union's Capital Adequacy Directive and the Bank for International Settlement's Amendment to the Basle Capital Accord, is the threat of punitive capital requirements for the market risk of trading activities, as calculated on a firmwide basis.

But if yet more motivation were needed, a bigger stick has been amply provided by the troubles of the past few years. Barings, Daiwa and Sumitomo all took massive hits because of the actions of a single "rogue trader" operating beyond the reach of the parent company's risk management process.

The scenario under which a single operation runs amok is not as pressing for non-financials, whose risk management and trading are most likely to be auxiliary to the core business. But, haunted by the ghost of Metallgesellschaft, whose New York arm implemented an apparently carefully-planned hedging policy which still went dramatically awry, many such companies have responded by centralising risk management at their global headquarters. And they have other worries too. With the federal court judgment in the case of Procter & Gamble vs Bankers Trust suggesting that swaps conducted by sophisticated parties constitute "arm's-length deals", end-users have to consider that they cannot necessarily resort to legislation when a deal turns sour. This is of particular concern given that a transaction may have been entered into without the knowledge, or understanding, of senior management.

As if these examples were not reason enough for paranoia, there remains the possibility that a dealer may deliberately structure or arrange a deal in order to conceal risks from end-user management. As one senior New York banker admits: "It is clear to me that there is – to use a very naked word – abusive stuff. The reason it's abusive is that it's always designed to fool somebody: the trader, the trader's boss, the trader's boss's boss, or the people who own the shares."

It is perhaps the shareholders who would benefit most if a firmwide system were implemented. Joseph Erickson, partner in charge of risk strategy at KPMG in New York, believes firmwide measurement will facilitate more meaningful risk disclosure in financial statements. Investors, the ultimate arbiters in matters of risk and return, will then be able to make informed decisions about a company's risk profile.

The lack of adequate risk disclosure in the past, he says, "has contributed to a number of débâcles where management has succeeded in altering the risk profile of a company without the knowledge of the investors". Understanding the risk profile of the company may be more important than the current balance sheet, he notes: investors who have bought a mining stock for exposure to metals prices may be dismayed to find this exposure has subsequently been hedged out.

But proponents of firmwide risk management have carrots, as well as sticks, at their disposal. Foremost among these is the promise that an accurate picture of the risks associated with specific businesses and product lines (including, but not limited to, derivatives) will allow their productivity to be judged more effectively, by calculating the risk-adjusted return on capital (Raroc). As Charles Taylor, executive director of the G30 at the time of its seminal report, points out: "Risk and capital are the great integrators of a large company; those are the two things which span it." Precise measurement of these two quantities opens the way for more efficient tactical and strategic allocation of resources.

Says Smout: "Risk management was not invented to make banks safe but to make them money. Some banks [use it to] reduce their risk; others will increase their risk once they are confident of their measurements." And proposals have also been made to use "earnings-at-risk" as a corporate management tool, allowing a non-financial firm to assess its performance in terms of cashflows.

But there remains much to be done before Raroc becomes a reality. For one thing, a company – usually meaning its chief executive as the ultimate risk manager – must decide where and with whom the responsibility for risk lies. KPMG risk strategy partner Christopher Hamilton identifies four different models for the firmwide risk management function. The first, and most far off, is the "virtual" model, where comprehensive information is accessible to all involved in risky activities, thus distributing responsibility across the organisation. The second is the centralised model, which is best suited to regional or small commercial banks. The remoteness of the risk function in this case is both a virtue and a weakness, in that it allows objectivity but may be too distant from the front line staff to appreciate their concerns and the risks inherent in their business.

Centralised systems do not work well for investment banks with global and disparate operations; for these the third model, a "near-firmwide" decentralised treatment, with risk management at the local level and independent oversight at the global level, is more likely to be useful. The last model, which involves the least disturbance to the corporate culture and is already used fairly widely, is to simply pass on a small amount of critical risk information (such as former JP Morgan chairman Dennis Weatherstone's now legendary "4.15" report) to senior management, typically the chief executive.

Providing this high-level information is not without its difficulties, however. In the following chapter, Mike Baliman suggests that strategic risk management is a very different beast to tactical risk management and therefore requires different measurement techniques. In particular, he believes, there are important errors associated with aggregating tactical measures of risk to generate the information used in strategic decision making. And there are more theoretical problems too; according to Till Guldimann, executive director of product management and technology at California-based Infinity Financial Technology: "There's still a big debate [over Raroc] because there's no yardstick which compares different types of risk. I think it's unlikely to become a reality until they come up with that yardstick."

While the risk management of certain activities – such as proprietary derivatives trading – is far advanced, other fields, such as managing the credit risk of a loan portfolio, are still largely fallow. Many risk managers, particularly those in banks' credit departments and in the corporate sector, think more in terms of asset and liability or duration management, which they are better equipped to handle, than value management.

The key to comparing Raroc across businesses may be the other great risk management innovation of recent years, value-at-risk (VAR). Indeed, some in the industry have argued that risk, from the perspective of senior management, is a quantity whose very definition remained uncertain until the advent of VAR. By compressing all the ramifications of risk into a single number, VAR has provided the sorely needed lowest common denominator.

One of VAR's proudest claims is that, in theory, it allows market and credit risk to be handled on an equal footing. But, as noted above, credit risk managers, particularly in the US, do not think in terms of value, meaning that the foundations for VAR-style assessment of credit risk have yet to be laid. As Guldimann says: "Today, there is no such thing as a single number for credit risk because you just can't calculate it."

Guldimann, a 21-year veteran of market risk management at JP Morgan and one of the fathers of RiskMetrics, knows more about VAR than most. He says the primary obstacle is the highly evolved credit departments created by banks to deal with the complexity of handling disparate counterparty credit ratings. For the moment, he says, active credit risk management – as opposed to simpler controls imposed by extending credit lines – has yet to find real application beyond the growing number of derivative product companies.

Many in the markets agree that a quantum leap in credit risk management is long overdue, although some argue that such a dramatic rethink is unlikely to occur without regulatory pressure. Indeed, Taylor goes so far as to suggest that "in 18 months, best practice will mean simulating market and credit risk together – and that will mean changing the 1988 Basle Capital Accord". The incentive for such integration is perhaps best summarised by Smout's observation that credit risk "is why far more banks go down than market risk, or any other risk which is mathematically quantifiable". After all, any outstanding transaction between two (or more) risky entities necessarily involves both market and credit risk. And one last factor also contributes to the importance of integrating market and credit risk: the emergence of hybrid and structured products which mix the two types of risk and therefore cannot be accurately handled without an integrated approach. Robert Allen describes these products, and the other motivating factors behind integrated market and credit risk management, in Chapter 45.

The difficulty of bringing credit risk into the fold is nothing compared to the Herculean task of managing other, less well understood risks on a firmwide or even a business-specific basis. However, just because such risks are not readily quantifiable does not mean they are unmanageable. As John Drzik, president of US consultants Oliver, Wyman & Company, points out, the conventional classifications of risk fail to acknowledge that, say, a lender's loan portfolio may have become sufficiently liquid to entail a consideration of market risk. Instead, he says, the time may have come for a reassessment: risk should be considered to fall into a "continuum". In this way, the risks associated with any given business can be located somewhere along the continuum and controlled accordingly.

But the core of any firmwide risk management effort must be the technology that supplies the management with information about the company's position. "One of the problems today in building firmwide risk management systems is that they aren't well specified," says Guldimann. "What's holding back the development of these systems is lack of experience – you can't build them from scratch." Going to a large bank and offering simply to implement an off-the-shelf firmwide risk management system is impossible, at the current stage of development, he says; instead, the bank and its information vendors must work together to evolve a specific solution for the bank.

A number of vendors have tackled this problem from various directions but for all, the largest obstacle – which Guldimann estimates takes up more than 90% of the effort in developing a firmwide system – is building a data translator which can handle the output of myriad legacy systems and assimilate them into a single coherent, computationally tractable form.

But there remains a danger that some of those caught up in the rush to build reliable and scalable "data warehouses" can't see the wood for the trees. Even assuming that a firm can manage its own information flows, many of those flows are likely to be sourced externally. Despite the best efforts of all concerned, that data is not guaranteed to be 100% reliable, consistent and useful.

With even the most basic components of a firmwide risk-management system still the subject of debate, some may doubt that such systems will be realised in the near future. This is not the belief of those already working in the arena. The common motto appears to be "each to their own", acknowledging that the single label hides a multitude of possible routes and solutions from which the prospective firmwide risk manager must draw the solutions most appropriate to his or her needs. This aim must not be to deliver a prescription for firmwide risk management, but to describe the framework within which interested parties must work.

Taking it from the Top

Mike Baliman
Dresdner Kleinwort Benson

The bottom-up, or tactical, method is currently the most common approach to managing a firm's risk. But it should be combined with top-down or strategic measures to be truly effective.

There are two perspectives on risk. The first - which may be called top-down or strategic - is driven by the requirements of senior management, whose focus is on medium term results. The frequency of publishing profit figures and the market's consequent judgement of a company's progress leads to a particular timeframe. At this strategic level, examples of important risk questions are: "what were risk levels in the last quarter compared to the previous period?"; "how has the group's risk:return performance changed?"; "what is the likely range of profits and losses (P&L) for the next period?"; and "what is the chance of making a quarterly loss?".

The second perspective - bottom-up or tactical - is driven by the needs of traders and trading management. This focus is clearly much shorter and concerns "real-time" questions of how to make a profit from principal exposures while controlling risk amid constantly changing markets.

Advances in risk management technology have predominantly been driven by the latter perspective. Against a background of a tremendous expansion in the derivatives market, the ability to price instruments competitively and to manage the risk therein safely, has depended critically on tactical measures of risk.

At the same time, the need to manage organisations as a whole has been reinforced by several high profile cases and encouraged by central banks and regulatory authorities. Given the availability of tactical risk measures, the general tendency has been to build up these bottom-up measures to produce aggregate measures which are then taken to represent the strategic risk in a firm. This article argues that this process on its own produces narrow and non-comprehensive measures of strategic risk.

Problems with using tactical risk measures as strategic measures

Operationally, strategic control of a firm's risks requires at a minimum the following elements:

- a risk budget which is an *ex ante* definition of the firm's risk appetite and risk tolerance;
- a comprehensive set of trading limits (which is compatible with the risk budget, including liquidity parameters);
- independent monitoring of the risk budget and limit compliance;
- fully documented procedures and processes.

For the rest of this article, the presence of an appropriate operational framework will be taken as read. In terms of measuring strategic risk levels, there are four main areas where using tactical measures to generate strategic risk measures will be misleading or incomplete:

- NON-COMPREHENSIVE COVERAGE The focus of value-at-risk (VAR) and stress test measures is upon the potential swings in the P&L caused by the potential impact of market moves upon principal positions held. Even if one had real-time VAR for all bond, equity and derivative instruments, one would still only be looking at principal-related risks. However, it is rare for a firm's only source of P&L uncertainty (ie the true total strategic risk) to be from principal exposures. An investment bank will generally have very significant income from "fees and commissions" which is also subject to volatility.

The income streams from principal and non-principal businesses are often inseparable and the precise (and changeable) nature of the interaction between the two is critical. For example, in a UK equity business, market-making and commission generation are inextricably linked - one cannot merely examine a market-maker's principal risks without taking into account the commission revenue which may, or may not, have been the reason for assuming the risk. The important characteristic is the risk: return performance of the business as a whole.

Furthermore, even where the fee generating process is relatively stand-alone - eg investment management or corporate finance - the volatility of the income is an important consideration and must be taken into account in the calculation of a firm's overall strategic risk. A large part of the volatility is market risk in a different guise, in that strong markets will lead to strong income (with varying lags) in these areas and vice versa.

❑ INTERACTION OF RISK WITH EXPENSES Tactical measures generally assume zero expenses (which is a reasonable assumption at the individual trade level). VAR is taken as a downside measure to operating income. However, at the firm level, expenses are highly significant. In the absence of income the consequent annual loss would jeopardise, if not bankrupt, most firms even if no principal risk were incurred. It is thus vital at the strategic level to model the chance of a post-expense loss (most financial firms rarely have negative operating income before expenses over a reporting period).

At an aggregate level, the risk to the group's profits is a function of the current average level of income, the variability around that level and the level of expenses. It is the interaction of these three factors which represents the true top-down strategic risk measure. Note that, as a further complication, variable expenses by way of bonus schemes are often themselves a function of profits. The impact of these also must be modelled to arrive at the risk to the firm's profits (see Figure 1).

1. Interaction of risk with expenses

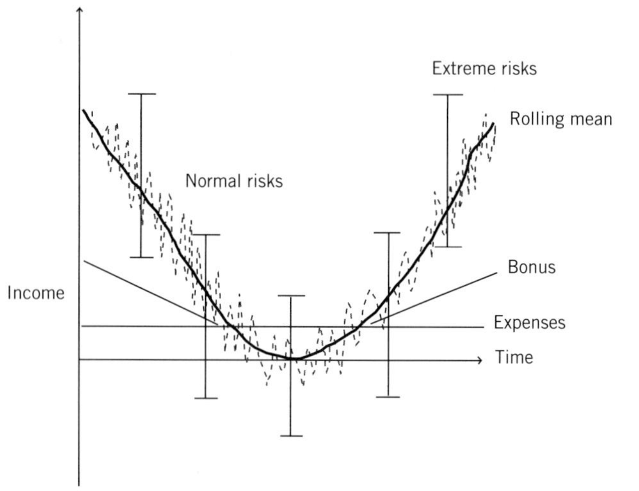

❑ AGGREGATIONAL MODEL ERROR Non-trivial financial models will always contain an error term or a degree of uncertainty as they are attempts to predict an unknowable future. As a consequence, the more models one aggregates or the more positions one applies a model to, the greater the uncertainty; the larger the number of variance/covariance assumptions, the less likely those assumptions are. This process is analogous to building a pyramid with bricks that contain a certain degree of irregularity. It would be a great surprise if the apex of the pyramid ended up in the centre.

This cumulative model risk is inherent in the bottom-up construction process. Continuing the pyramid analogy, a strategic model starts by attempting to measure the position of the apex rather than generating it.

❑ STRATEGY AND SKILLS Regulatory capital measures (or indeed deterministic calculations such as VAR) implicitly take the philosophical view that risk resides solely in the instruments held (albeit that regulators additionally examine the overall control environment). By way of analogy, the same line of argument would lead one to believe that there is an absolute level of risk in a Formula One racing car (extending the analogy, this absolute level of risk would change depending on the weather - ie market conditions). However it is certainly true that the risk is enormously greater if the car is driven by the author rather than, say, Michael Schumacher!

Even if one has the simplest trading limit - for example, a $1 million US long bond position limit - the actual level of risk will depend on the trader's strategy and skill; even the same trader will show varying risk levels depending on intangibles such as his morale (a trader who has had a "good" run will tend to trade differently from one who has had a "bad" run).

A general "black box" model of strategic risk (both for principal and non-principal risks) takes account of this factor (see Figure 2). Note that tactical risk models tend to utilise the top two inputs, but not the third. Other than for back testing of tactical models, the output is not used. If one accepts this model then, even putting statistical sampling error to one side, back testing

Figure 2: "Black box" model of strategic risk

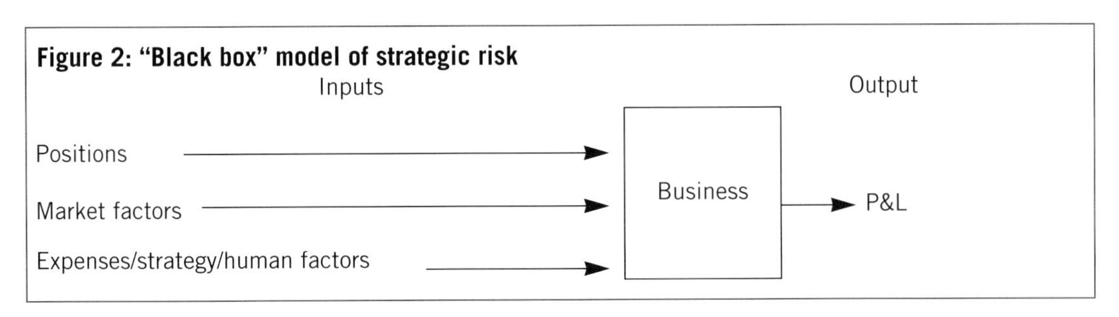

will always show a (significant) "error" term in any tactical risk measure for a business unit. This is particularly true for models based on end-of-day data (where part of the strategy will be intra-day turnover).

Measuring strategic risk

One can view the "black box" model in less prosaic terms. We can liken the positions to a thermostat and the business to a radiator. Unfortunately there is a "dodgy" connection between the thermostat and the radiator - market factors - and thus the heat output from the radiator - P&L - is variable.

The natural measure in this situation is a thermometer. In the case of the "black box" model this equates to measuring the *ex post* volatility of income. This process is fundamental to our approach to strategic risk measurement.

This approach addresses the four concerns raised previously:

❑ *Comprehensiveness* All businesses can be measured on this basis. There is no question of having to use "snapshot exposures" such as end-of-day positions as a proxy for market exposure. It is as easy to measure the *ex post* volatility of daily commission income as it is for daily trading income. Measuring the volatility of the combined P&L captures the interaction between the two.

❑ *Interaction of risk with expenses* Again, one can simply measure the volatility of operating income pre- and post-expenses. Where there is a bonus scheme which is a function of profits, naturally one observes a lower level of volatility post-bonus. As a strategic concern it is very important to measure the effect of variable compensation schemes in lowering firmwide risk.

❑ *Aggregational model error* As with all models there is model risk (see below). However, there are no aggregation induced errors as the model is top-down.

❑ *Strategy and skill* Experience shows very different *ex post* volatilities even where *ex ante* measures or limits are the same. Similarly, over time the impact of personnel changes on the risk profile of a department may be observed.

Issues with *ex post* models

The following are the main issues with models based on *ex post*, P&L volatility:

❑ *Accounting data* The thorniest practical issue tends to be the suitability of management accounts P&L. In particular, the use of accrual accounting will invariably obscure the underlying risks. Take, for example, an investment management business where income arises solely from a fee based on the annual market value of one fund. The risk is a combination of the "market value" of the benchmark on the appropriate date and the relative performance of the fund compared to the benchmark. The cashflow profile of the business is one inflow per annum. In practice, however, the management accounts would be unlikely to show 11 months of zero income but rather would attempt to accrue the revenue by spreading it over a period of time. In these cases it may be necessary to re-engineer the calculation of income to reflect better the underlying exposures.

❑ *Ex post is ex post!* A common point made is that, by definition, *ex post* models lag the risk. However:

a) an appropriate operational framework built around limits is the most important element in controlling short-term or liquidity risk - not a measurement system;

b) even *ex ante* models use *ex post* data. Any variance/covariance data will be of a historic nature and even the creation of scenarios for scenario analysis is set against a background of particular market performances. The aim of *ex ante* models is to look into the near future, with a certain inaccuracy. Thus, at best, *ex ante* models might outperform over the very short term. In practice, our experience is that for most businesses we have found that *ex post* models often have a superior predictive ability;

c) strategic measures are a complement to, not a replacement for, tactical measures.

❑ *Asymmetric P&L distributions* Clearly if one was either long or short a single option, volatility would either be a good or bad thing. However, at the aggregate business unit level, one rarely sees such extreme characteristics in the P&L and in the author's experience, this has tended to be a second-order effect. Tools to deal with this effect include skewness, kurtosis and semi-standard deviations.

Two cases are detailed below where separate (*ex ante*) modelling of extreme risks is required to supplement the *ex post* analysis as the "extreme" risks have a very different nature from "normal" risks and are highly asymmetric:

a) Credit/banking businesses Here extreme risks are always on the downside. We have implemented a system which attempts to predict possible credit losses by projecting forward recent credit experience (as captured by a transition matrix);

b) Advisory businesses One form of extreme risk is legal and reputational risks where the risks are again on the downside. These must be catered for in the overall operating procedures. The second type of advisory business risk is always on the upside in that fee sizes are non-normally distributed. They cannot be less than zero but there is (in theory) no upper bound. Similarly, many segments of advisory business show clear examples of lean years followed by boom times. The modelling approach here is to choose an appropriate statistical distribution for fee sizes and to combine this with an overall model of the fees available in the marketplace and the market shares thereof.

❑ *Statistical sampling error* Many businesses have low-frequency (eg monthly) accounting, thereby introducing a degree of measurement error. One can address this by attempting to remodel elements of the business (eg investment management fees in terms of the underlying market exposures as above). An alternative approach is to take the view that low-frequency accounting often reflects a longer business cycle and that, observed over such a timescale, the trends will be observable through the noise.

Summary

As the prime motivation for risk measurement has been the management of positions, advances in risk technology have tended to be driven by "bottom-up" *ex ante* models. This technology is very valuable and a necessary component of a sound approach to the management of risk.

In contrast, less attention has been given to the rather different motivation of wishing to measure the aggregate risk across a modern investment bank at a strategic level. Tactical measures are too limited to be fully inclusive. One class of strategic model is that based on the *ex post* volatility of income.

The approach that Dresdner Kleinwort Benson has taken is to build in parallel strategic and tactical models. We have developed a strategic model which tracks the risk:return performance of all our business units over time. It also tracks the chance of a monthly loss pre-expenses, post-expenses and post-bonus. Rather like a seismograph, this has proved a useful lead indicator of potential problems as well as a risk-based tool for allocating resources.

One advantage of *ex post* models is that, in essence, they are in some ways less of a model and more of a description of a phenomenon. In this sense, as a monitoring tool, they cannot be "incorrect" any more than historic market volatility can be "incorrect".

45

Together They Stand*

Robert Allen
Westpac Banking Corporation

Credit risk and market risk management are seldom integrated but there is a strong case for bringing them together. A look at the whys and wherefores of how this can be achieved.

Full-scale integration of credit risk and market risk management is far from common practice - arguably, it may never have been achieved anywhere. This is largely a result of tradition - credit and market risk management have long been considered totally different disciplines, and that difference has been reinforced by organisational structures. In recent years, some more progressive institutions have gone a long way towards breaking down these barriers, but there is still a long way to go.

The case for integration is strong and is based on four factors:

- the need for comparability between returns on credit and market risk;
- the convergence of credit and market risk measurement methodologies;
- the transactional interaction between credit and market risk; and
- the emergence of hybrid credit and market risk product structures.

There are two reasons why it is important that returns on capital are comparable for businesses involving either credit or market risk. First, such comparability aids the strategic allocation of capital; second, it permits bonuses to be distributed more prudently.

For the purpose of our scenario, assume it is annual plan time and capital is scarce. The lending manager says he can make another $1 million over the year if he can increase his loan book by $200 million, but the trading manager says he can also make another $1 million over the year if he can increase his position limit by $10 million.

We know there isn't enough capital to do both. Which do we choose? How can we make a meaningful comparison? Clearly, we should choose the alternative that offers the higher returns on capital, but to do that, we first need to work out how much capital is required for each alternative. How do we do that?

Capital can be viewed as the buffer that can absorb unexpected losses. However, we know we can never hold enough capital to protect us against the absolute worst-case loss scenario. We therefore have to make some choices about how bad a loss we can tolerate: we need to set a time horizon over which the possible, unexpected losses could occur and then set the required odds on survival over that period. For instance, we might say that we can tolerate only a 1% chance of losses wiping out our capital over a one-year time horizon (equivalently, that the capital requirement should provide for a 99% confidence level of survival over a one-year period).

There is no hard and fast rule on what the required survival confidence level should be, or the time horizon over which it should apply - ultimately, these are subjective judgements. But they must be applied consistently, across the lending and trading businesses - a case of comparing "apples with apples" - and allow the choice of that marginal business opportunity which maximises shareholder value. If the setting of these risk capital parameters was not integrated and, for example, the trading business used a 97.5% confidence level over a two-week time horizon, while the lending business used a 99% confidence level over a one-year time horizon, comparing the resulting returns on capital would be comparing "apples with oranges", with an overwhelming bias in favour of the trading business.

Now consider what happens when the time comes to determine annual bonuses. The lending

* *This chapter is adapted from a feature which appeared in the* Journal of Lending & Credit Risk Management, *February 1996.*

manager has generated a net profit over the year of $1 million, and so has the trading manager. The lending manager deployed $200 million in loan assets and the trading manager maintained an average open position of $10 million. Do they both deserve the same size bonus?

Clearly, this should depend on the relative returns generated on the capital required to buffer the unexpected losses that might have resulted from their respective lending and trading activities, and not just their absolute profit contributions. Again, for the returns on risk capital to be comparable, the confidence levels, time horizons and other statistical assumptions and parameters on which the capital calculations are based must be common across the businesses. This naturally requires a single, common, integrated risk measurement policy authority for the whole organisation.

An analytical framework

Traditional "gut-feel" approaches to credit portfolio management are no longer good enough. In dealing with credit risk, as with market risk, risk decisions must be evaluated within a quantitative analytical framework. Without it, there is no basis for rational decision making.

Subjective factors, however, enter into all risk decisions - a complicating factor is that tolerance of risk varies among different institutions and individuals. Few people are truly risk neutral - in evaluating risky propositions, they don't always weigh the possible gains and possible losses evenly according to their probabilities.

Not too many people, for example, would accept a bet with a 50/50 chance of a $1,000,000 loss and a $1,000,002 profit, even though the "expected" outcome is a profit of $1. But probably quite a few would buy a $1 ticket in a one-million ticket lottery offering a prize of only $100,000, even though the "expected" outcome is a loss of 90 cents.

However, it doesn't follow that as risk tolerance is a subjective issue, the entire risk assessment and decision making process might as well be subjective. Quite the opposite - there is all the more reason for adopting a quantitative analytical approach, which allows subjective risk preferences to be taken into account in a consistent fashion.

Getting back to credit portfolio management, lending decisions ultimately boil down to saying yes or no. How should decisions be made? From a purely credit perspective, portfolio theory (see Figure 1) suggests that there are only two possible reasons for saying no:

❑ the incremental impact of the deal on the portfolio is to increase the ratio of risk to return; or

❑ the incremental impact of the deal on the portfolio is to move the overall level of risk in the portfolio away from the lender's desired level.

These are quantitative questions that call for the application of similar statistical and analytical methods to those used in the measurement and management of market price risk. We need an approach to quantifying both the expected return from the portfolio, and its risk before and after the addition of the prospective deal. This measure should be a common denominator against which we can set the lender's risk appetite.

The expected return is the mean of the distribution of possible returns. However, since the revenue side of a loan, ie the spread, is generally known with certainty, what is of most concern here is the expected credit loss rate (the mean of the distribution of possible loss rates, which can be estimated from historic data based on losses experienced with comparable quality credits). Since expected returns are additive, the incremental impact of the possible new deal on the expected return of the portfolio is actually the same as that of the new deal in isolation.

In the context of market price risk, the common denominator measure of risk is volatility (the statistical standard deviation of the distribution of possible future price movements). Similarly, with credit risk, the appropriate common denominator is the standard deviation of the distribution of possible future credit loss rates.

1. Efficient portfolio theory

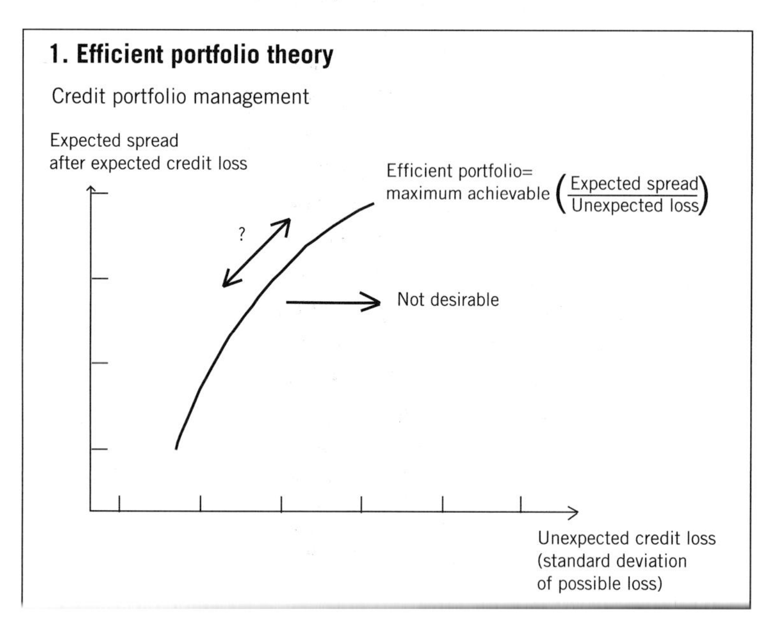

But unlike expected returns, the risk in a portfolio, expressed in standard deviation terms, is not simply the sum of the risks of all the individual deals. This is why it is the incremental impact of the possible new deal on the risk of the portfolio, and not just the risk of the transaction in isolation, that we should be concerned about.

The old adage "don't put all your eggs in one basket" has long been accepted as a fundamental principle of sound credit risk management. However, until quite recently, little was done in the credit arena to understand, quantify and exploit fully the benefits of diversification in a scientific manner.

The key to aggregating risks, and therefore the measurement of risk in portfolios, is their statistical correlation (ie the extent to which credit losses on one deal are likely to track losses in the remainder of the portfolio, and vice versa). The lower the correlation, the smaller the proportion of the risk associated with the new deal that is added to the risk of the portfolio and, since the return part of the equation is simply additive, the greater the return on risk of the resulting portfolio.

Estimating the necessary correlations of credit losses is not easy, but the potential pay-off justifies the effort. Take the management of portfolio concentrations, for example. Today, this is still pretty much a process of setting arbitrary limits by gut feelings, which may in practice actually stop the bank from writing economically valuable business.

By contrast, under a sophisticated portfolio management process, it would be unnecessary to set concentration limits at all. As portfolio concentrations increased, the correlation between similar new deals and the overall portfolio would increase. This would progressively reduce the return on risk of incremental deals with similar risk attributes. Ultimately the return on risk would decline to the point where it no longer met the required hurdle rate – at this point, subsequent similar deals would be refused purely on the basis of inadequate return on risk.

Using options theory

One of the most significant developments in the convergence of market and credit risk measurement has been the use of option pricing techniques to calculate credit default probabilities. This is possible because the market value of a limited liability company's equity is in fact the fair value of a call option on the market value of the company's assets, with the strike price and term set at the contractual amounts and maturities of the company's liabilities. This derives from the equity holder having a long outright position in the company's assets, supported by a bought put option on those assets at an exercise price equal to the value of the company's liabilities.

The net result is equivalent to a call option on the company's assets. It is the limited liability property that creates an option-style pay-off for the equity shareholders. The shareholders receive the full benefit of any potential upside in the value of the company's assets, but cannot lose more than the price paid for the equity shares – effectively the premium paid – no matter how much the value of the assets declines. In effect, if the value of the assets falls below the value of the liabilities (the strike price) at maturity, the shareholder simply exercises by handing over his stake in the company's assets and walks away. Without the limited liability feature, the downside, as well as the upside, is potentially unlimited.

Given the current market value of the equity (the option value), the volatility of the equity, the book value of the liabilities (the strike price), and the contractual maturity of the liabilities (the option term), option pricing theory can be used to infer the current market value and volatility of the company's assets (see Figure 2). For exchange-listed public companies, all the information needed to estimate the current market value of the company's assets is publicly available. The level and volatility of the market value of equity can be derived from published share price data, while the contractual amounts and maturities of liabilities are disclosed in published financial statements.

2. Applying options theory to credit default

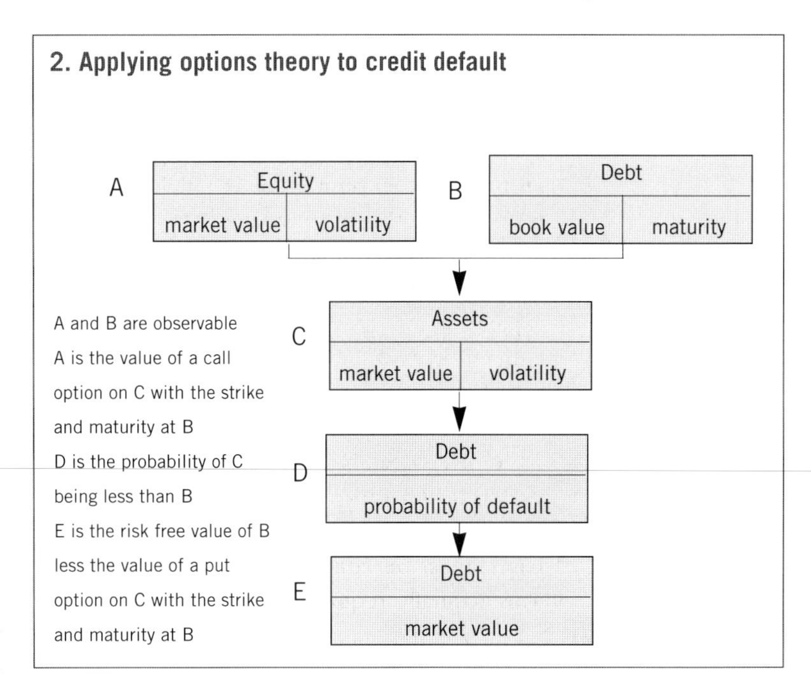

Given the market value and volatility of the assets and the value and term of the liabilities, it is then a straightforward matter to determine the probability that the company will default (ie the probability that the market value of its assets will fall below the contractual value of its liabilities).

Taking this approach to valuation based on option pricing one step further, it is possible to estimate the fair value of the company's debt - either as a check on traded-market prices, where they exist, or as a substitute for market prices where they don't.

The reasoning behind this extension of the use of options pricing techniques is that a lender's claim on a risky borrower can be broken down into two parts. The first part is a claim on which there is no possibility of default and the second, representing the risk, is a sold put option on the market value of the company's assets with the strike price and term set at the contractual amounts and maturities of the company's liabilities. The value of the debt is the sum of the values of these two components. The default-free value of the debt can be calculated by discounting the contractual cashflows at the relevant default-free market interest rates, and the (negative) value of the sold put option can be derived using the estimated market value and volatility of the company's assets originally derived from the historic market price behaviour of the company's equity.

The higher the volatility of the borrower's assets, the higher the value of the sold put option, and consequently the lower the fair value of the debt. It is interesting to note however, that the higher the volatility of the company's assets, the higher the value of the bought call option on those assets which represents the value of the company's equity. This brings to light an inherent conflict between the interests of lenders and equity investors. Lenders benefit from reducing asset volatility, whereas equity investors want asset volatility to rise.

Transactional interaction

It should always be borne in mind that credit and market risk are not additive. Imagine a foreign exchange dealer trading Australian dollars versus US dollars six months forward (see Figure 3). His overall position is square; he has some counterparty pre-settlement credit exposure but no market risk exposure. If he then does another trade, and buys another A$100 million from counterparty G, he ends up with a long position. This definitely exposes him to market risk - but has he also added to his credit exposure?

Most credit officers would most probably say he had. However, consider the possible outcomes. Since he is now long, if the Australian dollar goes up he makes money, but that is dependent on G performing in order to collect his winnings, so he has credit exposure to G.

If, on the other hand, the Australian dollar goes down, he loses money on his exposure to market risk, but as his credit exposure to G is negative, it is impossible to suffer a credit loss as well. The risk is therefore either a market risk or a credit risk. You can't lose both ways. The total assessed risk of the institution would clearly be overstated here if the risks were measured independently by separate credit and market risk functions and simply aggregated at the group level, ie if credit and market risk were not managed in an integrated fashion.

3. Credit and market risk are not additive

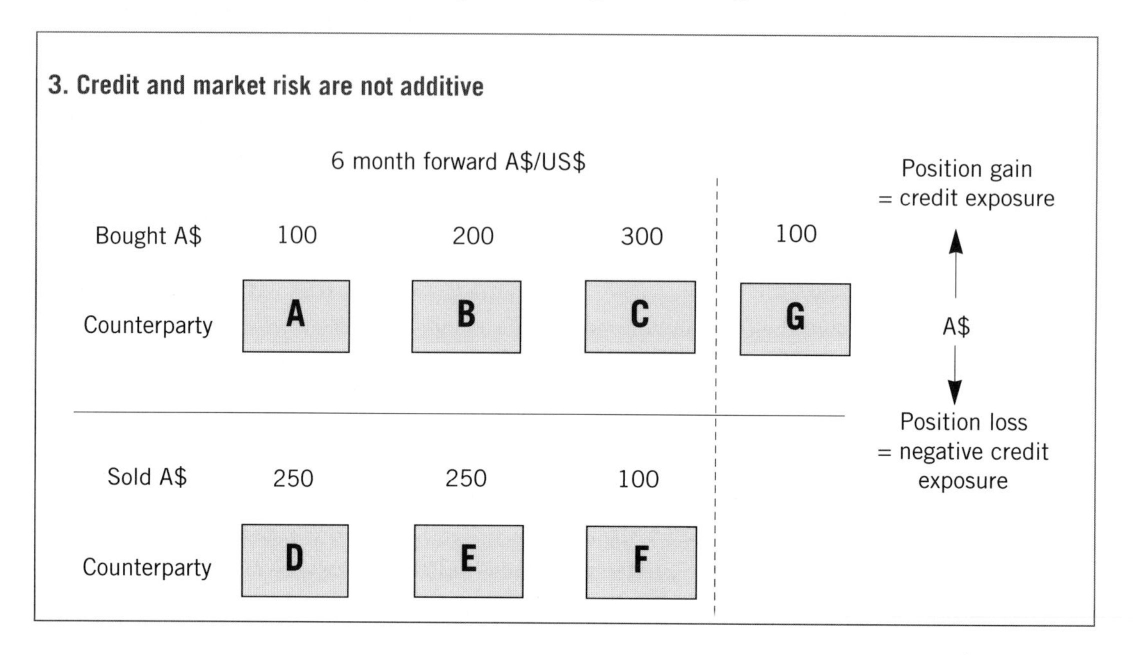

Double-counting of credit and market risk aside, a lack of appreciation of the impact of changes in market prices on potential counterparty pre-settlement credit exposures can also lead to serious overstatement of those exposures, and may even increase rather than decrease actual economic exposures.

If we look at the foreign exchange trader's portfolio (but ignoring the last trade with G), how much aggregate credit exposure is he carrying? The overly-simplistic standard approach is to add the estimated worst-case exposure for each of the six contracts. But this doesn't make sense – it assumes both the long contracts and the short contracts would simultaneously be at their maximum in-the-money values on the common six-month-forward settlement date. For this to happen, the A$/US$ spot exchange rate would have to be at its maximum and minimum possible levels at the same instant – which is clearly impossible.

Looked at in this way, it is difficult to comprehend why banks and regulators can tolerate the use of numbers derived in this obviously fallacious manner, but this is yet another real life example of the consequences of a non-integrated approach to credit and market (price) risk measurement.

A final point along this line of argument concerns the need for the trader himself to integrate credit risk considerations proactively into his market risk-driven trading decisions.

Imagine that besides G, F was also a potential counterparty for the buy-A$100-trade, but his offer was fractionally more expensive than G's. Who should our trader deal with? It is not necessarily G, even though G has the cheaper offer. Assuming there is an enforceable netting agreement in place with F, not only would there be no incremental credit exposure associated with doing the trade with F, it would also actually eliminate the exposure arising from the previous short trade with F.

By eliminating the pre-existing credit exposure, the trade with F actually reduces the amount of capital needed to support aggregate credit exposure, whereas the trade with G increases the capital required against credit risk. If F's offer was the same as G's, F would clearly be the preferred counterparty. Even if F's offer was fractionally more expensive, the lower cost of servicing the credit risk capital associated with doing the trade with F might more than offset the price disadvantage, tilting the balance in favour of the trade with F.

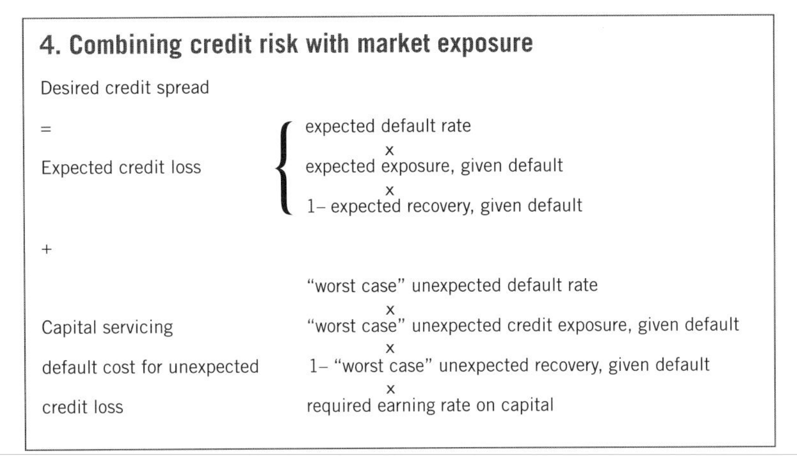
4. Combining credit risk with market exposure

Desired credit spread

=

Expected credit loss = expected default rate × expected exposure, given default × 1– expected recovery, given default

+

Capital servicing default cost for unexpected credit loss = "worst case" unexpected default rate × "worst case" unexpected credit exposure, given default × 1– "worst case" unexpected recovery, given default × required earning rate on capital

Combining credit risk with market exposure

Assume a bank wants to incorporate in its desired pricing spreads an appropriate provision for the cost of expected credit losses and an allowance for the cost of servicing the capital required to buffer potential additional unexpected credit losses (see Figure 4). Certainly the likelihood of the borrowers or counterparties defaulting on their obligations to the bank is central to the question but that is not the whole story. It is only a pure credit question if the values of the obligations and the values of any collateral held are both known with certainty.

More commonly, however, with the evolving nature of the business, the values of the obligations to the bank and the collateral it holds are not known with certainty. Consequently, the answers to questions on expected and unexpected credit losses involve the interaction of risk assessments based purely on credit default and market price exposure, using market risk measurement techniques.

With foreign exchange and derivatives transactions, for example, the size of the exposure in the event of a counterparty default depends on how the value of the contract has moved, which in turn depends on how the underlying market rates have moved since the trade was executed.

The contract value may, in fact, be negative, in which case there would be no credit loss at all, notwithstanding counterparty default. Even with conventional customer loans, the economic value of the customer's obligation is not necessarily fixed at the contracted principal amount due at the maturity of the transaction. If it happens to be a fixed-rate loan, its economic value will change as market interest rates move, in line with changes in the market values of equivalent traded fixed-rate instruments. Only loans with variable interest rates that fully reflect movements in short-term market interest rates retain a constant economic value.

The expected default rate can be generated from the bank's own loss history, from comparable external data sources or, as we have already seen, by using options pricing theory and traded equity prices.

The expected credit exposure, given default, is calculated using the same price volatility-based techniques as used in calculating market risk. Valuation of marketable collateral lends itself readily to application of the same market risk measurement techniques used to calculate expected and unexpected contract values. Estimating non-collateral recovery rates is more of a pure credit issue, but opportunities still exist to employ statistical and other quantitative analytical techniques that may have been developed for market risk management.

The same basic approach can be used to calculate the capital servicing cost. However, for the purposes of establishing a capital buffer, the possible (but unexpected) default rate for a given level of confidence is required, instead of the expected default rate, and the possible (but unexpected) maximum positive contract value for a given level of confidence, instead of the expected contract value. There is, of course, the additional step, once the required capital is calculated, of determining the income required to service the capital at the appropriate hurdle rate.

Hybrid products

CREDIT DERIVATIVES Swap structures are a simple, highly effective mechanism for the transfer of risks between counterparties: they simply agree to exchange cashflows with the required risk characteristics. The first swaps involved the exchange of fixed for floating-rate interest cashflows which allowed borrowers, lenders and intermediaries to shift their exposures between fixed and floating interest rates without the inconvenience and expense of additional borrowing and lending on-balance sheet. Initially, such transactions were single currency only.

The next stage of evolution involved the exchange of cashflows across currencies, which permitted the counterparties to convert interest rate exposures from one currency regime to another, in the same efficient off-balance sheet manner. This provided further impetus for the use of swaps to exploit arbitrage opportunities in international borrowing and lending markets, hedge existing exposures and take on risk outright. Next came commodities, and then equities.

Leading derivatives players have recently been seeking to bring credit into the derivatives arena. The same potential benefits apply as for all the other market risk types for which swaps have proved to be so effective.

Credit swaps are a much more flexible and efficient way of managing credit exposure profiles than having to originate, buy and sell on-balance sheet assets. They may even provide an answer to the fundamental conflict many banks face between the desire for a risk-efficient diversified portfolio and a cost-efficient credit-concentrated origination effort. Banks can focus their credit origination effort where they have the greatest competitive advantage, then use credit swaps to achieve the required degree of diversification.

Superficially, the basic credit swap looks little different from any other swap. The top diagram in Figure 5 illustrates how Bank A converts its risk-free cashflow from government bonds into the risky cashflows from junk bonds it desires, without having to sell the government bond and buy a junk bond in its place. And it is the converse for Bank B. The lower diagram is actually the same basic credit swap but viewed as a credit insurance transaction. In effect, Bank B is paying Bank A a credit insurance premium, in return for which Bank A guarantees full repayment of the junk bond at maturity to Bank B. The insurance is not totally bullet-proof, since it depends, like all other swaps, on the performance of Bank A, which is not risk-free.

Many more complex credit swaps (and related options structures) are being developed but the credit derivatives market is still in its infancy.

STRUCTURED DEBT INSTRUMENTS The popularity of structured debt instruments has recently suffered because of their well-publicised misuse in several financial scandals. US regulators regard even the plain vanilla floating rate note as a structured debt instrument. By implication, the natural form for a debt instrument is fixed-rate; floating-rate notes are structured by embedding a fixed-floating interest rate swap into the structure (see top diagram in Figure 6). This leads to a definition of "structure" as the introduction of some other underlying market risk (eg interest rate, exchange rate, commodity price, or equity index) or some pay-off feature (eg an option or leverage), into the valuation equation for what starts off as a pure credit instrument (see the rest of Figure 6).

Despite the recent havoc caused by the more leveraged and complex structures, there is likely

5. Credit swaps vs credit insurance

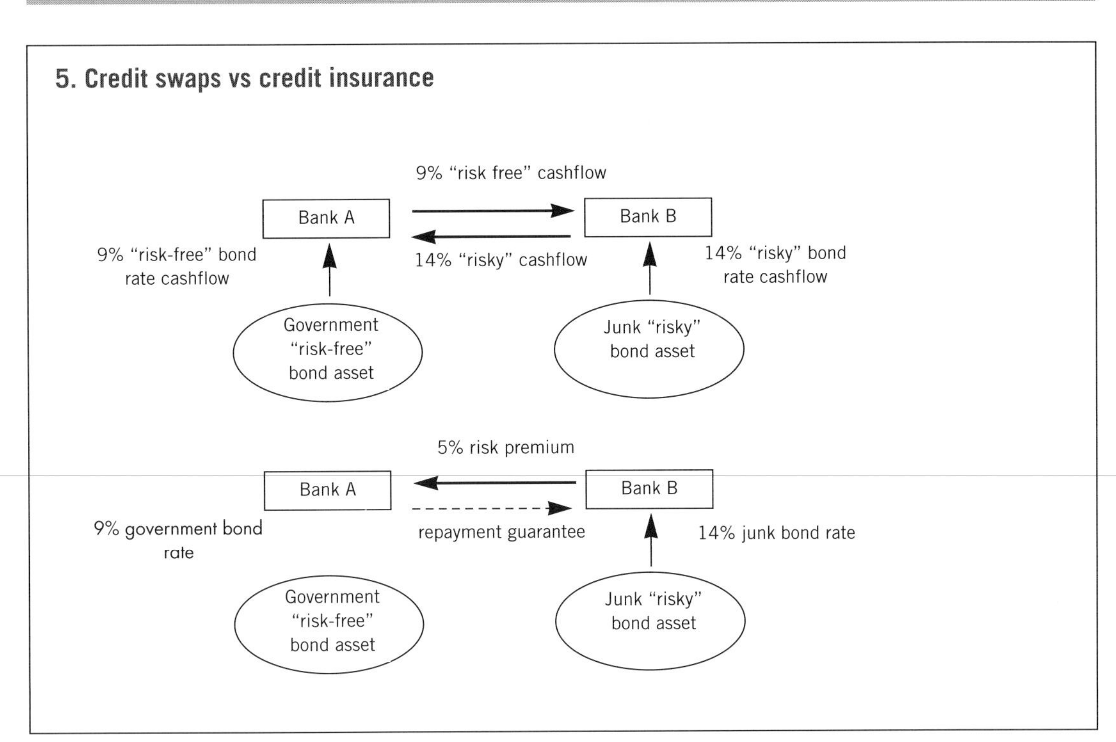

6 Structured debt instruments

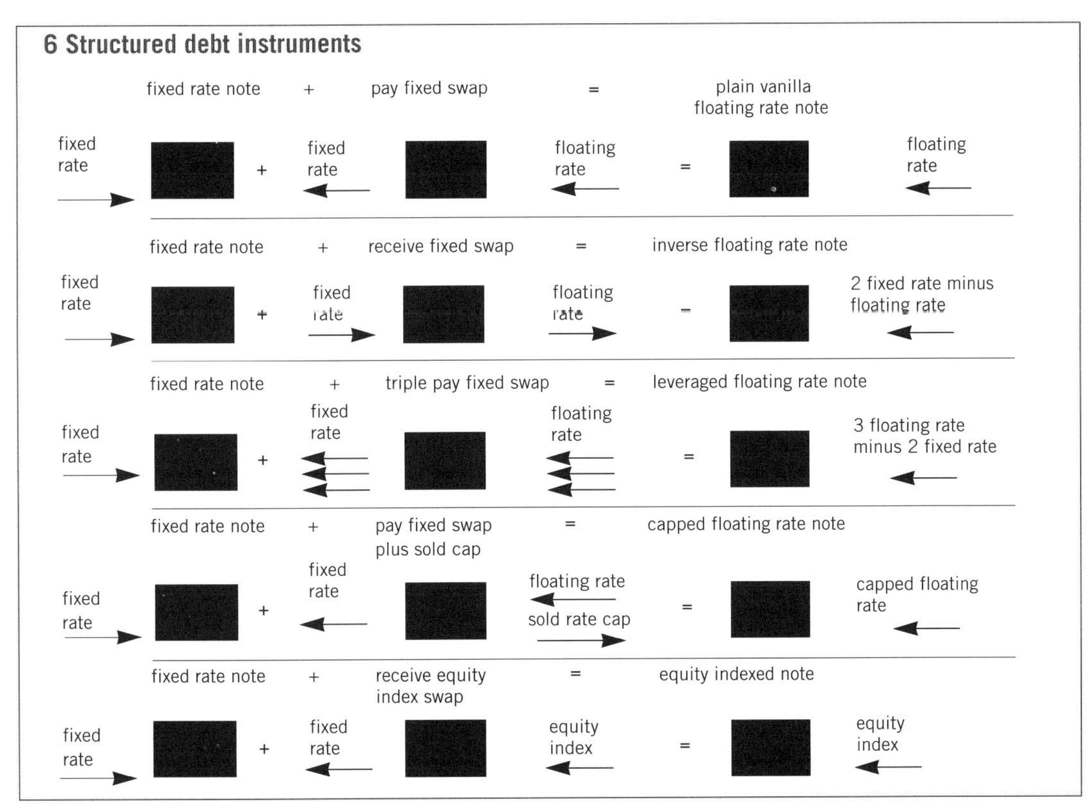

always to be a market for prudently designed debt instruments that simultaneously facilitate financing and satisfy legitimate risk management needs in a cost-effective way.

Implementation

Fully integrated credit and market risk management calls for a risk management unit with three basic powers:

❑ to operate across the entire institution;

❑ to combine responsibility for risk measurement and control policy across both credit and market risk;

❑ to combine responsibility for both credit and market risk portfolio management.

The first function would probably involve both board-level oversight and a steering committee established at the top executive level, with terms of reference specifically covering the integration of credit and market risk. There would also have to be a chief risk officer responsible for combined credit and market risk management.

The risk policy function would report to the chief risk officer and operate independently of business-line management across the entire institution. It would be responsible for developing and testing risk measurement methodologies, limit-setting and actual risk measurement and reporting. It would also approve the risk identification, measurement and control aspects of new product proposals and on the systems and models to be employed.

The portfolio management function would also report to the chief risk officer and be responsible for integrated credit and market risk portfolio analysis across the entire institution. It would combine and expand upon many of the functions commonly performed today by the units responsible for credit portfolio and asset/liability management. Its primary role would be to advise line executives on how to optimise the risk/return relationship of the institution's overall business portfolio.

From analysis of return relative to risk, risk correlations, and risk interactions (across the overall business portfolio), it would provide guidelines on optimal portfolio composition by risk class, and seek to identify opportunities at the margin to improve return on risk performance or to adjust the overall level of risk, by selectively acquiring or disposing of business with particular risk attributes.

While many of the recommendations would be executed by the line business units, the independent risk portfolio function itself would need the capability to fine-tune the portfolio (where the instruments involved, or the localised impact of the adjustments, made it inappropriate to execute at the business unit level).

This is all easier said than done, of course.

46

Total Enterprise-wide Risk Management

Christopher Hamilton and Andrew Smith
KPMG

This paper outlines a new integrated risk management framework, in which risk measurement methodologies such as value-at-risk are used to complement traditional corporate finance strategies. Hypothetical case studies demonstrate how total enterprise-wide risk management can directly increase shareholder value.

All over the world, investors consistently pay higher prices for the shares of companies that have demonstrated the ability to manage the volatility of earnings. So what approach should a firm take to achieve the ultimate goal of increasing shareholder value? We believe that the only way is to approach risk management on a corporate, or enterprise, level, rather than focusing on individual business units. And for this to happen, a sea-change is required in the traditional focus of risk management. While traditional "control" is still vital, the value of risk management and risk quantification will now be found, not in the constraints, but in the new *freedoms* they permit managers in their efforts to maximise shareholder value.

Exclusive reliance upon the traditional business models that comprise the body of modern corporate finance theory will not increase shareholder value. Rather, the integration of traditional models with powerful new quantitative tools such as value-at-risk (VAR) is required to assess the trade-offs between risk and return properly, to facilitate optimal investment, to maximise the benefits of diversification and to lower the volatility of earnings. We call this integrated approach to increasing shareholder value Total Enterprise-wide Risk Management, or TERM.[1]

TERM promises much. So it should be no surprise that a full description of the process, the technology and data management requirements, and the change management and other issues involved in migrating to a risk-oriented corporate culture will require more than this single brief article. Our goal here is more modest; we simply define our vision of TERM, provide evidence from the marketplace that leading firms are moving toward the concept, and demonstrate through case studies that the business case for TERM is valid, and that the links to increased shareholder value are real.

Recent articles in academic and practitioner journals show that enormous resources are being applied to developing the integrated approaches necessary for enterprise-level risk management. Firms are making tremendous efforts to quantify and aggregate the different risks they face from exposures to markets, credit and operations. New models for improved capital allocation are being developed around the concepts of risk adjusted return and risk-based pricing.

But while these are important steps toward the goal of enterprise-wide risk management, their power will not be fully exploited unless they find a place within a coherent framework that focuses all the tools of enterprise risk management on the ultimate goal of increasing shareholder value. The key is the link to equity, and we propose TERM as a value-based approach that focuses the application of disparate elements of risk management on equity and that also links strategic risk management directly to shareholder value.

More formally defined, TERM is a framework that permits the successful incorporation of all processes and performance measures so that risk/return decisions are optimised in both the short term and the long term, and shareholder value is accordingly maximised.

Who needs enterprise-wide risk management?

By embracing VAR methodologies as primary tools for quantifying market risk and for setting certain capital requirements, bank regulators have clearly driven the rapid development of quantitative risk measurement methodologies within financial firms. And by modifying traditional audits and examinations to focus on risk, they have also driven advances in qualitative risk management.

Other trends are driving the need for TERM as well. Businesses are becoming structured on a global basis, in which consistent risk/return decisions are required in multiple markets and management information needs to be aggregated using "apples and apples." Financial disintermediation, mergers and acquisitions and deregulation have also increased the need to re-evaluate the performance measurement of different business activities.

Banks, financial service companies, and corporates are all competing in similar markets. Given the pressures they face, it is easy to understand why financial firms have increased their focus on risk management. Several major banks, including Bankers Trust, CIBC Wood Gundy and Goldman Sachs, have invested many years in the process. More interesting is the question of whether these practices are migrating, and whether non-financial organisations perceive any value in paying more attention to risk management techniques and frameworks.

The answer is a resounding "yes!" As advocates of TERM, it is particularly gratifying to us that the reasons recently cited by four leading organisations for taking initial steps toward integrated risk management included *their* conclusions that enterprise-wide risk management was vital to increasing shareholder value.

HONEYWELL

Honeywell is the world's largest control and automation company. According to an article published in *Derivatives Week* in April 1996, Honeywell is remodelling its approach to risk management. In the past, the company followed traditional risk management methodologies, viewing and analysing risk factors independently. By viewing risk in this fashion, it is very likely that Honeywell consistently over- or under-hedged. In 1995, the company began integrating the management of external risks, which allowed it to capture economies of scale in risk measurement and eliminate any inefficiencies in hedging practices. Bottom-up tools were implemented to aggregate risks. In 1996, Honeywell was in the process of identifying its exposures and quantifying its risk appetite. It plans to subject hypothetical portfolios to stress testing and VAR analysis in the near future.

CYPRUS AMAX MINERALS

Cyprus Amax Minerals is a $6 billion mining concern with 21% of its assets outside the US. According to a *Global Finance* article published in March 1996, Cyprus was in the process of integrating currency, commodity, interest rate, and operational risks under a single executive – the director of financial risk management. Cyprus undertook this approach to save money, to give it better protection against earnings volatility, and to meet the new Securities and Exchange Commission (SEC) guidelines for derivatives disclosure. The integration has been a cross-functional, collaborative effort in which Cyprus plans to pull risks from all subsidiaries, to assess the total portfolio using VAR analysis, and to advise the board of its findings. The aim of all this is to allow the company to calculate its VAR on any given day. Cyprus is also developing risk management policies and procedures to manage its portfolio risk, and is implementing technical systems to support the integrated effort. The ultimate goal for the new risk management policy is to improve shareholder equity.

MICROSOFT

Microsoft is an $8 billion company with 56 foreign subsidiaries. It identifies risks in many broad categories: financial, reputation, technological, competitive, customer, people, operations, distribution, partners, regulatory and legislative, political and strategic. Microsoft's eventual goal is to integrate each of these risks in such a way that risk managers can quickly and easily inform upper management of current risk scenarios in order to optimise the risk/reward decisions. According to Scott Lang, Microsoft's director of risk management; "A lot of decisions made in business are based on some view of the risk-reward trade-off ... risk management should be a discipline to make sure you have an accurate picture of this trade-off."

In 1994, over a six-month period, Lang conducted a strategic analysis of Microsoft's risks, resulting in a matrix where each risk was identified and ranked according to its frequency, severity, and aggregation potential. The analysis proved that risks were larger than previously believed, and helped persuade top executives that risk management needed to be taken more seriously. Microsoft has chosen an oversight committee to integrate risk management in all business units and has developed a consulting practice within the company, Microsoft Risk Co. It has also implemented a risk management information system, and an intranet Web site that provides employees with information on corporate policy.

IMPERIAL BANK

Imperial Bank has $3.3 billion in assets, 11 regional offices in California, and loan production offices in Texas, Massachusetts, and Arizona. It recently established a Risk Management Committee to ensure continued accurate risk measurement and reporting, and to oversee a bank-wide approach to risk management. Members include Imperial's chief financial officer, chief administrative officer, chief credit officer, general counsel, and director of internal audit. The committee's "mission" is to advise the board and to assist in monitoring the effectiveness of the bank's enterprise-wide risk management process. Risk management requirements will be reviewed for new products and services prior to their implementation. The overall goal is to identify and to monitor risks so that all available resources can be employed to serve Imperial's customers and shareholders.

All these organisations have taken important steps toward integrated risk management, but their focus has been primarily on risk aggregation and on the consolidation of risk management through the introduction of centralised units. The next challenge is the development of comprehensive risk management frameworks that will permit them to exploit integrated risk management fully as a strategic tool to increase shareholder value and, at a minimum, to capture the benefits from the integration of different risk types and from the covariances of diverse lines of business, as depicted in Figure 1.

Our primary goal in the rest of this paper is to demonstrate, primarily through a series of hypothetical case studies, the direct impact TERM may have on equity.

TERM helps organisations in a number of ways, but the basic business benefits are either tactical or strategic. Tactical benefits are measured at the business unit level, while strategic benefits are realised at the enterprise level. TERM enables firms continuously to link these benefits to share price in order to quantify the potential impact of undertaking new transactions or projects or of implementing candidate financial and non-financial risk solutions. Strategic benefits flow from tactics, and they may be easy to measure quantitative results such as appropriately risk-adjusted returns or "softer," but still critical benefits such as enhanced reputation or improved market perception.

Our vision of TERM also recognises the fact that the businesses are managed using a number of metrics including earnings-per-share, efficiency ratios, credit ratings, and a myriad of others. In their efforts to increase shareholder value, corporate executives may have to serve many masters, not just their boards, but also equity analysts and rating agencies. A particular strength of the TERM approach is its capacity to "prioritise" among short-term goals and to provide tactical solutions to meet the practical needs of the moment, as well as to simultaneously address longer-term equity value strategies. For example, the TERM framework may provide immediate tactical solutions addressing the short-term goal of salvaging an endangered credit rating, while permitting the simultaneous analysis and quantification of the costs and benefits of executing "quick fixes" in the larger context of the firm's longer-term strategies.

The business case for TERM

We have now defined TERM and discussed some bold applications in the marketplace. But the critical link to equity, the ways in which the TERM helps managers directly to increase shareholder value, have not yet been demonstrated. In the five case studies below we illustrate how the integration of traditional finance models with powerful new volatility-based risk measures in the TERM framework can help managers increase earnings by optimising capital allocation,

1. Integration of risk types

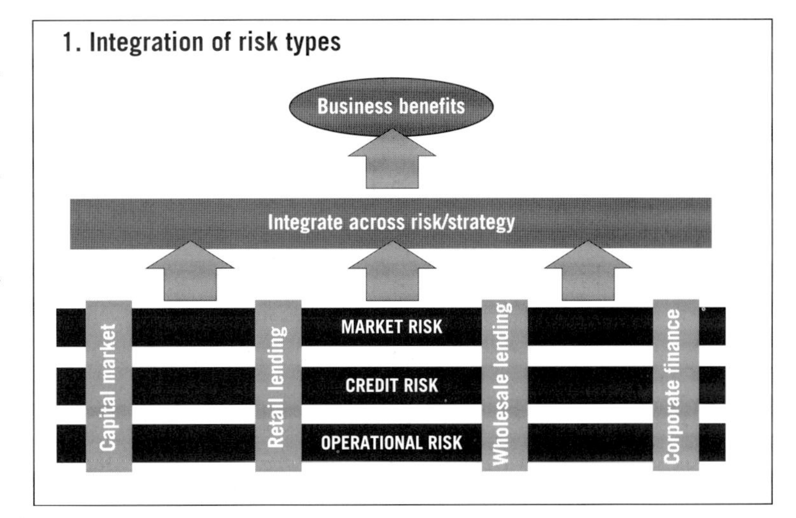

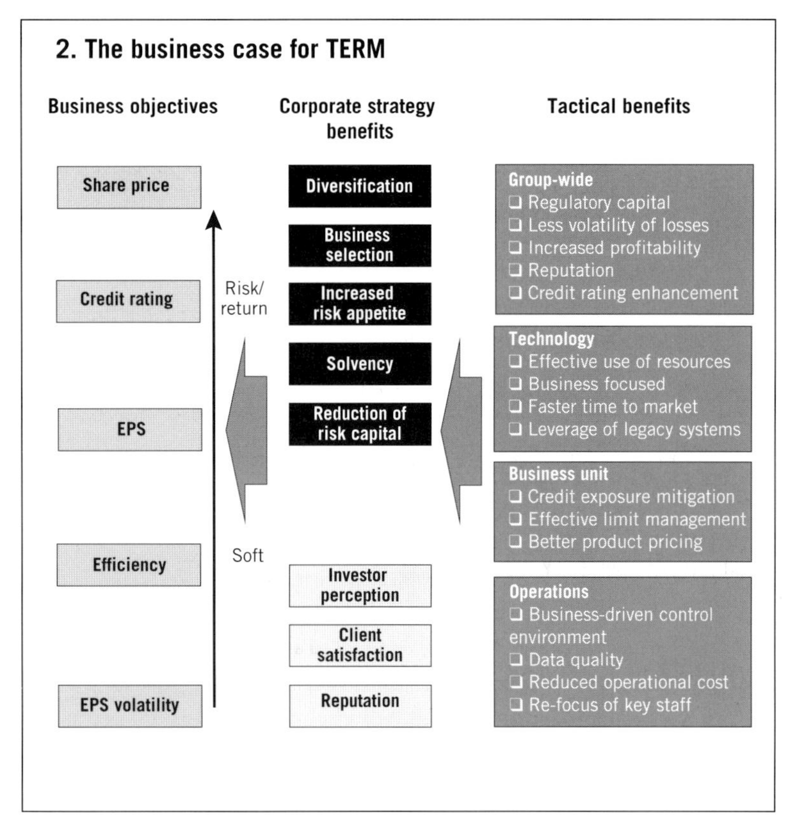

increase equity value by reducing the volatility of earnings, increase revenues through improved product pricing, and increase earnings by exploiting a proactive centralised risk management function and its immediate by-product, improved risk data. The cases we have selected illustrate only a sample (mainly drawn from the financial sector) of the many potential benefits that may follow from the implementation of the TERM framework, but they clearly illustrate its power to increase the market value of firm equity.

3. Maintaining the risk/return relationship through capital allocation

CASE 1: OPTIMISATION OF CAPITAL ALLOCATION

The optimisation of capital allocation is achievable through the use of regret models, which are used to determine optimal capital decisions based on the risk/return equation. The efficient frontier connects portfolios with the highest return for every incremental level of risk, given a particular level of capital. The optimum portfolio mix for a risk-averse investor is determined using the risk-free rate of return.[2] Depending on the risk appetite of the investors, the optimum portfolio may exhibit more or less risk and, therefore, higher or lower expected returns. Risk, in this case, is measured by VAR.

This point can be illustrated by constructing hypothetical portfolios. Assume that the portfolio may consist of any mixture of assets that are either interest rate-sensitive, equity price-sensitive, or foreign exchange rate-sensitive. The expected returns and risks for each asset type are itemised in the market data table (Figure 4). Each of these assets is correlated to some degree

4. Increase earnings by capital allocation optimisation

Initial capital allocation ($m)			
LOB	**Capital**	**Risk**	**Return**
Interest rate	46.00	5.98	3.68
Equity	9.73	2.92	1.46
FX	44.27	5.31	4.43
Total	**100.00**	**11.00**	**5.97**

Market data					
	Expected return (%)	**Volatility (%)**	**Correlation matrix**		
			Int rate	**Equity**	**FX**
Interest rate	8	13	1.00	0.30	0.50
Equity	15	30		1.00	0.20
FX	10	12			1.00

Optimal capital allocation ($m)			
LOB	**Capital**	**Risk**	**Return**
Interest rate	24.32	3.16	1.95
Equity	9.73	2.92	1.46
FX	65.95	7.91	6.60
Total	**100.00**	**11.00**	**10.00**

with others that are also listed. Our initial portfolio is comprised of assets as follows: $46 million interest rate-sensitive assets, $9.73 million equity price-sensitive assets, and $44.27 million foreign exchange rate-sensitive assets. Given the market correlation matrix, this portfolio has an expected return of $9.57 million and total risk (VAR) of $11 million.

However, given the current market data, the initial portfolio does not optimise the risk/return ratio. Through more efficient capital allocation, the expected return can be improved while keeping risk constant. By increasing the capital allocated to foreign exchange investment, which has a higher expected return and lower volatility than interest rate-sensitive assets, and by decreasing the capital allocated to interest rate investment, the expected return increases to $10 million while VAR remains constant at $11 million. The expected earnings increase from $9.57 million to $10 million, an increase of $0.43 million.

The result is an increase in Earnings Per Share (EPS) after tax of $0.28. Assuming a constant Price/Earnings (P/E) ratio of 10, risk remains constant and the increase in EPS after tax will equate to an increase in the value of the equity of 2.75. In this example, the tactical reallocation of capital results in superior asset (business) selection and achieves the broader business objective of increased earnings per share (Table 1).

By achieving a position on the efficient frontier, expected earnings have been increased while maintaining the same level of risk. Case 1 illustrates that capital optimisation is a tactical benefit of TERM that may lead the firm to increased shareholder value through increasing expected earnings without exposing it to greater volatility.

Table 1. Increasing shareholder value by increasing earnings per share

	Stock price ($)	P/E	Net EPS increase*	Stock price increase ($)	New stock price ($)
Actual position	100	10	0.28	2.75	102.75

* After-tax earnings increase = 0.43*(1 – 0.36) = 0.28. Assumption: 1 million shares issued

5. Reducing loss volatility

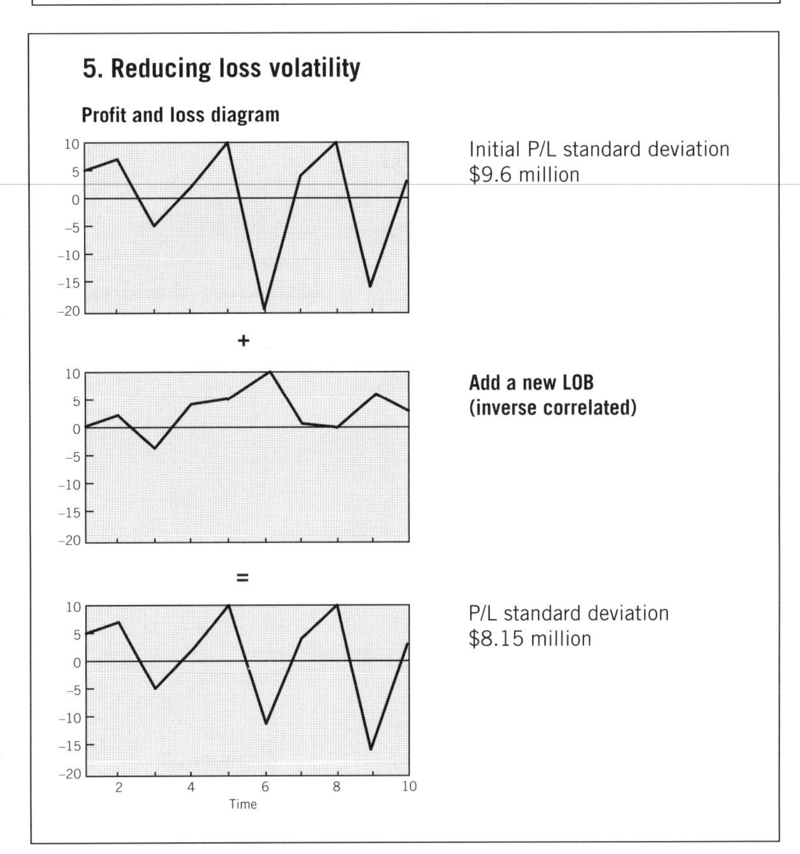

CASE II: LOSS VOLATILITY REDUCTION

The possibility of identifying and choosing investments in order to modify risk profiles is one of the major benefits that follow from the implementation of a sophisticated market risk measurement system such as VAR. In Case II, a firm considers investing in an additional business unit to add to its existing operations.

Assume that the original business operation has a P/L standard deviation of $9.6 million. Consistent with this measure, the firm has been given a credit rating of BBB+. The associated default probability of a BBB+ credit rating is 0.1%. In an effort to lower its cost of borrowing, the firm will attempt to improve its credit rating. To do so it must decrease the standard deviation of its P/L. One way this can be accomplished is by adding a new business unit that has a P/L which is not correlated with the original business operation. The inversely correlated P/L of the new business unit will have a "smoothing" effect on the aggregated P/L standard deviation. Following the integration of the new business unit, the firm's P/L standard deviation will be reduced from $9.6 million to $8.15 million (Figure 5).

The reduction in the P/L standard deviation will lead to a reduction in the probability of default. The probability of default in one year will fall from 0.1% to 0.03%, which in turn may lead to a credit rating improvement from BBB+ to A–. The reduction in default probability can be observed graphically in the left tail of the probability distributions that appear in Figure 6 overleaf. The area under the left tail of the distribution function, representing the original P/L with a standard deviation of $9.6 million, is

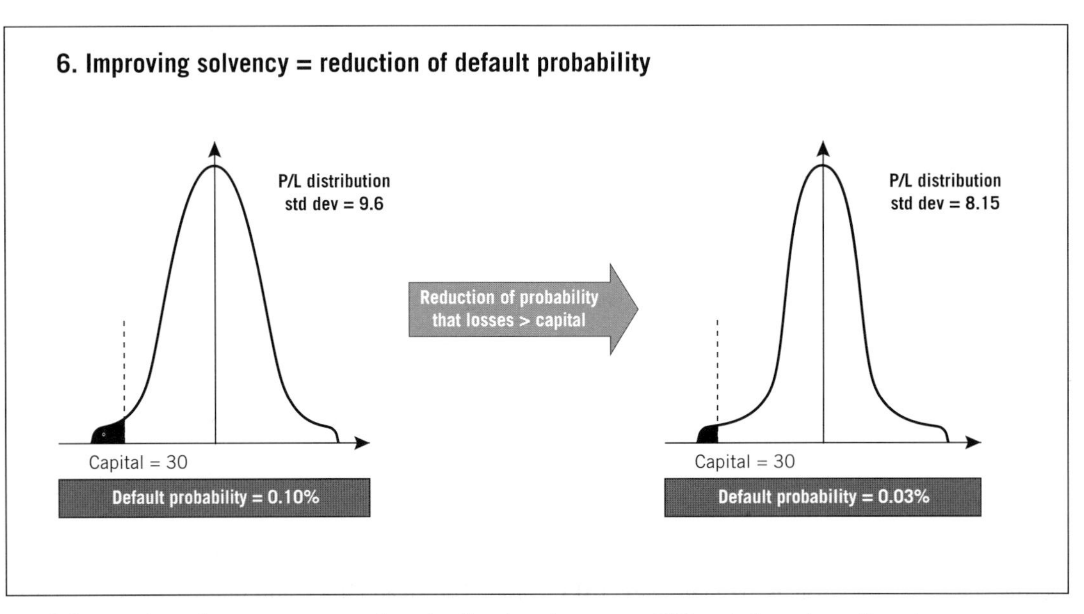

much larger than the area representing the firm's probability of default after it has completed the integration of the new business and reduced the P/L standard deviation to $8.15 million.

The potential credit rating improvement, in turn, reduces the expected cost of borrowing by 10 basis points. The 10bp decrease from the original spread of 0.27% over Libor to a revised spread of 0.17% over Libor, on a notional $60 million in long-term debt, has led to a net increase in EPS of $0.04. Assuming a constant P/E of 14, the increased earnings leads to an increased stock price of $0.55 (Table 2). Thus, in Case II, the tactical reduction in P/L volatility results in greater solvency and increases the firm's credit rating, lowers borrowing costs, and increases EPS and the value of equity.

Unlike the previous case, the loss volatility reduction created shareholder value not by increasing revenues, but by reducing the cost of borrowing.

Table 2. Shareholder value creation

Prob of default (%)	Rating	Capital ($m)	Long-term liability ($m)	Spread over Libor (%)	Net EPS increase*	P/E	Increase in stock price ($)
0.10	BBB+	30	60	0.27	0.04	14	0.55
0.03	A–	30	60	0.17			

* Assumption: 1 million shares issued. Earning increase after tax (tax rate = 36%).

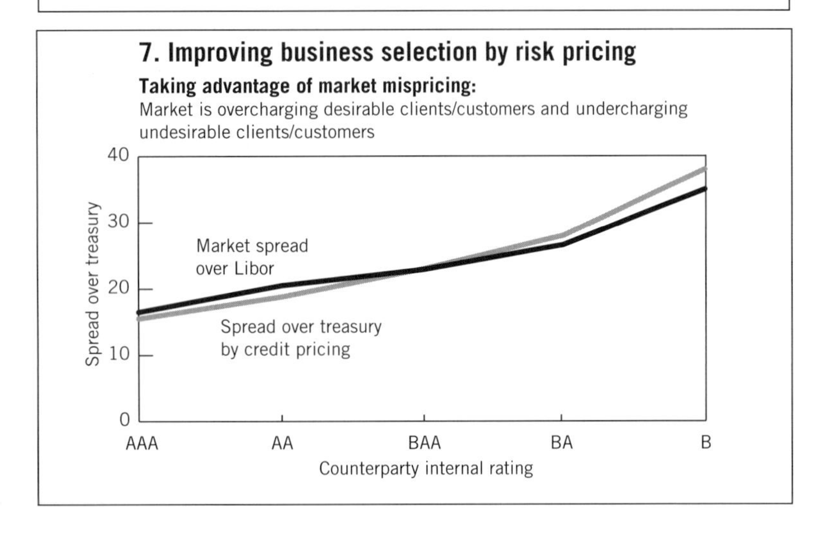

CASE III: BETTER PRODUCT PRICING

Risk-based pricing can lead to a competitive advantage by permitting the exploitation of market inefficiencies. In this example, the market consistently mis-prices loans, overpricing top tier clients while underpricing bottom tier clients. Assume in this case we are dealing in an inefficient market for bank loans. Top tier clients are expected to be low risk; in other words, relative to their low default rate, the interest rates charged are proportionally high. On the other hand, bottom-tier clients, who have higher risk, pay relatively low interest rates relative to their higher probability of default. To take advantage of this market inefficiency, the bank may implement a superior risk-based pricing method to assess the creditworthiness of its customers, pricing each individual loan accordingly. Rather than assessing loan rates based on broad categories, the bank is able to price each customer efficiently and achieve a better, more profitable customer mix.

Consider the following approach to risk-based pricing. The bank has $100 million in outstanding loans. In an attempt to price its loans more accurately, it has decided to decrease the rate of its top tier clients from 21bp over Libor to 17bp over Libor. Assuming a volume/price elasticity of 1.7, meaning that a 1% decrease in price will lead to an increase in volume of 1.7%, an interest rate reduction of 19% (4bp on 21bp) will lead to an increase in total loan volume of approximately

30%. The firm's outstanding loan balance, after the implementation of a risk-based pricing method, has increased from $100 million to $129 million. The increase in loan volume would, in turn, lead to an increase in revenue of $15,000. Given a constant P/E ratio, the stock price would increase by $0.18 (Table 3).

By taking advantage of inefficient market pricing, the firm was able to increase its market share without the use of additional investment. So risk-based pricing, a TERM concept, has led to increased shareholder value.

Table 3. Implementation of risk-based pricing methods

Current market share ($m)	Actual avg spread over Libor (%)	Actual earnings ($m)	Target avg spread over Libor (%)	Volume vs price elasticity
100	0.21	0.205	0.17	1.70

New market share ($m)	Prospective earnings ($)	Net EPS increase ($m)*	P/E	Stock price increase ($)
129	0.22	0.01	18	0.18

*Assumption: 1 million shares issued. EPS after tax (36%)>

CASE IV: THE BENEFITS OF CENTRALISED RISK MANAGEMENT

The typical role of a centralised and integrated risk management function is to aggregate risks across separate business units and to manage them across an organisation. Traditionally, each business unit focuses solely on its own operations, managing risk on a transaction-by-transaction basis. A centralised risk management function, on the other hand, focuses on capturing risk across each business unit in order to harmonise the consolidated risk position of the whole firm, permitting it to utilise and allocate its capital resources efficiently.

In the following example, assume a bank is composed of two business units, Head Office and Branch Y. The Head Office has total invested capital of $60 million, consisting of assets sensitive to equity prices and interest rates, with an associated VAR of $7.01 million. Branch Y has total invested capital of $40 million, consisting of assets sensitive to equity prices and foreign exchange, with an associated VAR of $4.73 million. The Head Office and Branch Y are maximising their individual risk/reward trade-off by selecting portfolios that meet their individual risk/reward preferences. However, instead of each business unit hedging its own portfolio, efficiencies can be captured through the creation of a single, centralised hedging function.

Aggregating the two business units, the total invested capital is $100 million with an associated VAR of $10.66 million. The diversification benefit of the aggregate of Head Office and Branch Y, measurable in terms of the spread between the consolidated VAR and the sum of the each business unit's VAR, is equal to $1.08

8. Role of centralised proactive risk management unit

	HEAD OFFICE			BRANCH Y			RISK UNIT	CONSOLIDATED		
	Invested capital	Risk	Return	Invested capital	Risk	Return		Invested capital	Risk	Return
Interest rate	50.00	5.50	5.00	0.00	0.00	0.00		50.00	5.50	5.00
Equity	10.00	3.00	1.50	5.00	1.50	0.75		15.00	4.50	2.25
FX	0.00	0.00	0.00	35.00	4.20	2.98		35.00	4.20	2.98
Total	**60.00**	**7.01**	**6.50**	**40.00**	**4.73**	**3.73**		**100.00**	**10.66**	**10.23**

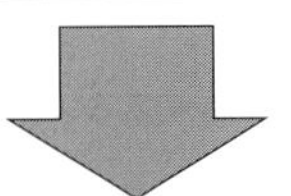

	HEAD OFFICE			BRANCH Y			RISK UNIT	CONSOLIDATED		
	Invested capital	Risk	Return	Invested capital	Risk	Return		Invested capital	Risk	Return
Interest rate	50.00	5.50	5.00	0.00	0.00	0.00	17	66.97	7.37	6.70
Equity	10.00	3.00	1.50	5.00	1.50	0.75	(4)	11.16	3.35	1.67
FX	0.00	0.00	0.00	35.00	4.20	2.98	(13)	21.87	2.62	1.86
Total	**60.00**	**7.01**	**6.50**	**40.00**	**4.73**	**3.73**	0.00	**100.00**	**10.49**	**10.23**

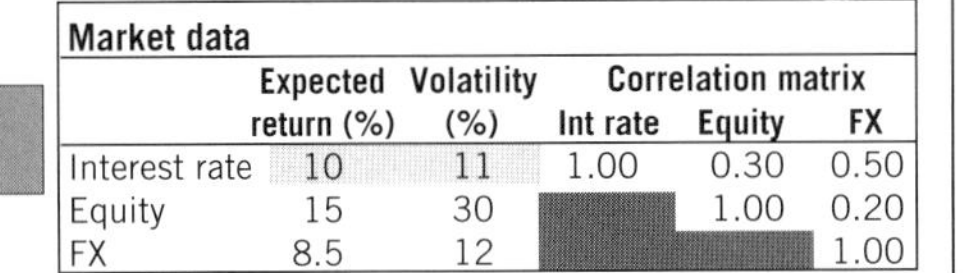

Market data	Expected return (%)	Volatility (%)	Correlation matrix Int rate	Equity	FX
Interest rate	10	11	1.00	0.30	0.50
Equity	15	30		1.00	0.20
FX	8.5	12			1.00

	HEAD OFFICE			BRANCH Y			RISK UNIT	CONSOLIDATED		
	Invested capital	Risk	Return	Invested capital	Risk	Return		Invested capital	Risk	Return
Interest rate	50.30	5.53	5.03	0.00	0.00	0.00	17	67.27	5.53	5.03
Equity	10.10	3.03	1.52	5.60	1.68	0.84	(4)	11.86	4.71	2.36
FX	0.00	0.00	0.00	35.00	4.20	2.98	(13)	21.87	4.20	2.98
Total	**60.40**	**7.06**	**6.55**	**40.60**	**4.83**	**3.82**	0.00	**101.00**	**10.65**	**10.36**

Table 4. Increasing shareholder value by increasing earnings per share

	Stock price	P/E	Net EPS increase*	Stock price increase	New stock price
Actual position	100	15	0.08	1.25	101.25

* After-tax earnings increase = 0.13*(1 – 0.36) = 0.08.

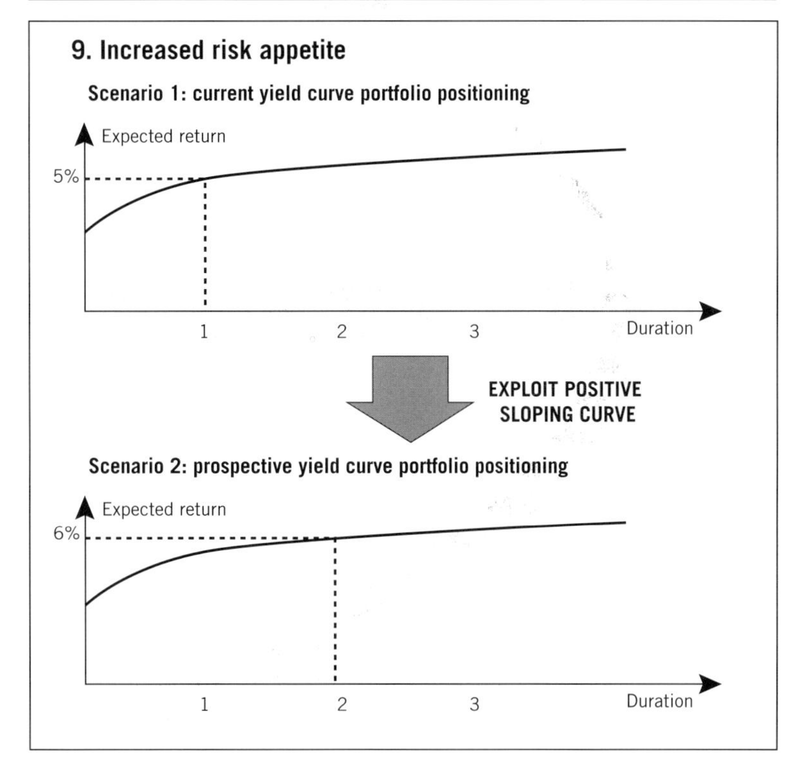

Table 5. Shareholder value creation

Actual position ($m)	Duration
100	1

Prospective position ($m)	Duration	Risk premium (%)
100	2	1

Net earnings increase ($m)*	Increased EPS**	P/E	Share price increase ($)
0.64	0.64	17	10.88

* Tax rate = 36%.
** Assumption: 1 million shares issued.

million. The centralised hedging function can rebalance the organisation's portfolio. By increasing the net capital allocated to interest rate sensitive investments, which has a higher expected return and lower volatility than foreign exchange-sensitive investments, diversification benefit has increased from $1.08 million to $1.25 million. Accordingly, the consolidated VAR has been reduced from $10.66 million to $10.49 million.

Through the creation of a centralised risk management function, the bank is able to increase its trading volume by $1 million without increasing risk above the risk-based reserve requirement of $10.66 million. The ability to increase volume generates increased profit. It is possible to translate the earnings growth into a stock price increase, assuming a constant P/E ratio. Net earnings grow by $0.08 which leads to an increase in the stock price from $100 to $101.25 in this example (Table 4).

This case has similar benefits to Case I: Optimisation of Capital Allocation. However, these benefits were created through two very different methods. In Case I, increased returns were achieved by efficiently allocating capital. By increasing investment in foreign exchange sensitive assets, the expected return of the portfolio increased while risk remained constant. In Case IV, each business unit in the first phase had allocated its capital efficiently and had achieved its optimal risk/reward given individual preferences. These portfolios began where the Case I portfolio ended. Taking the first case one step further, it is possible to gain additional efficiencies by taking an integrated approach to risk management. By aggregating the two optimally balanced portfolios and creating a centralised risk management function, it is possible to increase earnings once again by reallocating the portfolios at the enterprise level.

CASE V: BETTER DATA QUALITY

The implementation of risk control systems at various levels can effectively increase the risk appetite of an organisation. Control systems generate a consistent stream of reliable information which permits traders to utilise all available capital. In Scenario 1, assume initially that the organisation is without a risk control system (Figure 9). Arbitrarily, the organisation's portfolio has a duration of one year with an equivalent expected return of 5% (dictated by the yield curve illustrated below). The organisation has chosen this conservative portfolio risk appetite not because of its risk/return preferences, but because it lacks the information that would make it possible to assess accurately its current position and to achieve a higher expected return.

In Scenario 2, assume now that the organisation has implemented a sophisticated risk control and measurement system. With the information generated, the portfolio's return can be increased by 100bp by simply increasing the duration of the portfolio from one year to two years. Through the information provided by the control system, the shift in duration of the portfolio allowed a shift along the yield curve resulting in an increase in expected return from 5% to 6%.

Having the ability to access reliable information relating to investments, funding, and hedging allows an organisation to make calculated decisions in accordance with its preferences. In Scenario 1, the risk/return equation could not be maximised because there was insufficient information relating to firm risk. The risk control systems in Scenario 2 made it possible to assume greater risk by adjusting the portfolio duration, knowing in advance the effects on expected return.

On a position of $100 million, the 100bp increase in expected return translates to an increase of $1 million (after tax of $0.64 million) in investment income. Once again, the increase in expected earnings of $0.64 million leads to greater shareholder value. Assuming a constant P/E ratio, the increase in profitability translates to an increase in stock price of $10.88 (Table 5).

The business cases presented here have all cited tactical benefits created through the use of various analytical tools, staples of TERM. These benefits have included growth in earnings, increased competitive advantage, increased trading volumes, and reductions in expenses. In each of the cases described, TERM has led to a measurable increase in hypothetical stock price and shareholder value.

The case studies are intended to show the disciplined approach needed to link the tactical benefits of process and systems enhancement to shareholder value. Once these and the multitude of other benefits have been analysed in the appropriate manner, we advocate the use of a TERM framework and TERM measurement tools to drive implementation. The business case expectation should remain as the cornerstone of the ongoing TERM effort. However much importance we place on a well-constructed business case, the practical components of implementation are no less important. Accordingly, we will introduce the framework and a high level structure of measurement tools needed to advance the practical implementation of the preceding business case.

TERM permits a consistent and integrated view of risk and return right across the business firm, and the "pyramid" in Figure 10 attempts to capture our vision of the TERM risk management framework. The value of TERM lies in the global integration of business process, analytics and technology to achieve the goals of both preserving and optimising capital. It begins at the strategic level, incorporating elements of risk management into overall business objectives by defining the firm's risk appetite and defining the firm's mission in terms of risk elements. Processes are then developed to support the mission, to address the multiple dimensions of risk and to permit improved risk-based decision making. Finally, a risk/return-oriented corporate infrastructure is implemented to support process and mission, an infrastructure that necessarily includes elements such as risk-based organisational structure, compensation, standards, technology, analytics and policy.

10. The TERM risk management framework

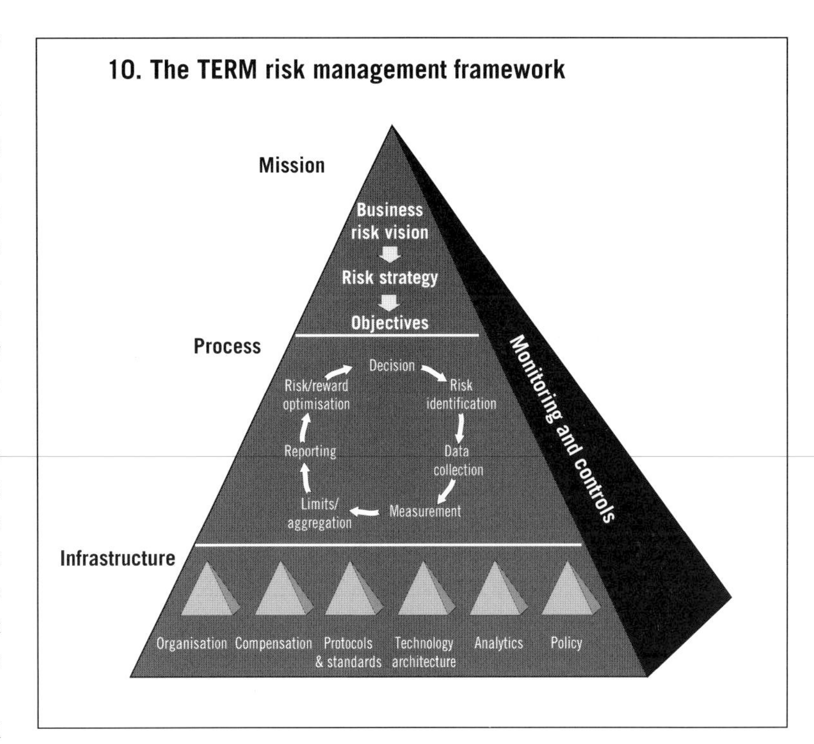

It is critical to note that that the TERM framework does not attempt to reinvent or to significantly reorganise the business firm. Rather, it attempts to refocus structures found in all firms toward risk and consequently toward the optimisation of resources and the maximisation of shareholder value. And it is important to understand that while implementing TERM may have certain technology requirements, TERM is not itself a technology solution, but a redefinition of many elements of corporate organisation and culture. It cannot be successfully implemented simply by buying machines. If anything, the greater challenge lies in ensuring management provides strong and continuing support for change management during the redefinition of many roles and responsibilities.

The TERM framework is designed to:

❑ Incorporate risk management into overall business objectives

❑ Consistently view and review risk and return across the entire organisation

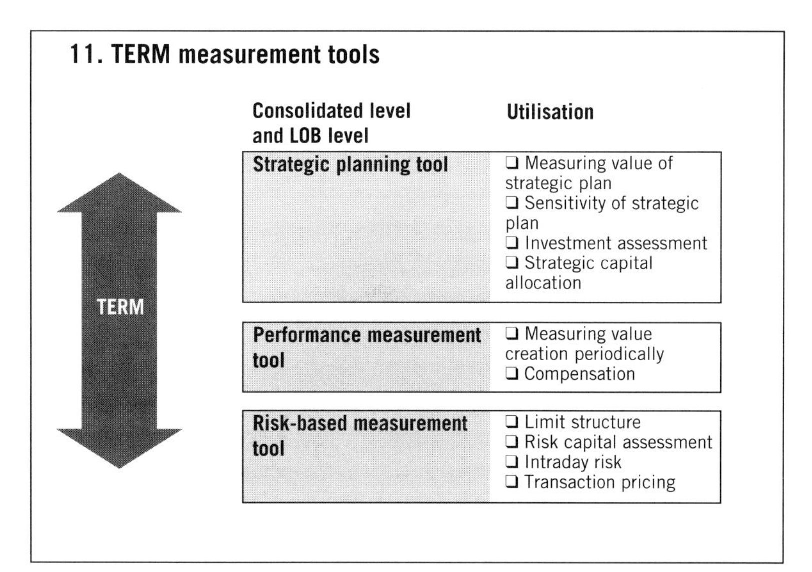

❑ Build business processes from business strategies
❑ Continuously assess and reassess all exposures
❑ Support processes with an infrastructure that addresses all dimensions of risk
❑ Be maintained through monitoring and controls appropriate to the organisation

Once an organisation's risk appetite and "mission" are defined by senior management, processes and infrastructure can be established or reoriented to support the mission, and the entire process directed through appropriate monitoring and controls. Of course, the game does not end with the creation of such a framework; it only begins there. Used properly, the framework is reflexive and dynamic, its application is circular and continuous, and its primary by-product is new knowledge - knowledge that permits management to reorder its priorities continuously, to recalibrate its risk strategy, and to modify infrastructure to meet changing needs.

While measurement tools are only one element of the comprehensive framework, their overriding importance is evident in the process of constantly linking decision making and infrastructure investment to shareholder value. TERM measurement tools include both "top-down" strategic tools such as "strategic planning" and "performance measurement" and "bottom-up" tactical risk based measurement tools (Figure 11).

Performance measurement tools are designed to measure, motivate and reward behaviour, and for this reason, they are built on current risk/ return parameters with little or no view of future intentions and changing risk profiles that may result from the application of strategic planning tools. Top-down tools are used together to identify business opportunities at the enterprise or business unit level, while bottom-up tools are used primarily to implement those opportunities. Top-down tools are used to identify opportunity. The foundations for all top-down tools are corporate earnings or cash flows. Top-down tools are used to measure the contribution of each business unit to the market value of the enterprise and to diagnose areas for improvement.

Bottom-up tools, on the other hand, are used to measure risks at the transaction level and to aggregate those risks (up) to the enterprise level. These tools are used to solve problems within the business units. It is imperative that the quantitative results that follow from applications of top-down and bottom-up tools can be reconciled - not in the sense that they literally sum to the same value - but in the sense that differences can be explained and the integrity of the model is continuously revalidated and integrated within the TERM framework and business case.

Conclusion

In this paper, we have defined our vision of Total Enterprise-Wide Risk Management or TERM, provided evidence that leading firms are moving toward a such an approach, demonstrated through hypothetical studies that the business case for TERM is valid, and shown that the links to increased shareholder value which distinguish the TERM framework are real. Our research clearly supports the business case for a risk management framework that focuses the integrated application of traditional finance models and newer risk-based methodologies on the objective of increasing the value of firm equity. This is for two main reasons:

❑ Competitive pressures in the marketplace and compressed margins are driving the application of new tools to increasing equity values.
❑ In isolation the application of strategic and tactical tools, training, technology improvements, and efforts at modifying corporate culture are each of value to a firm, but when they are integrated and focused within a TERM framework, their power to drive equity value is maximised.

The key remains the link to equity, and TERM is the value-based approach that focuses the application of disparate elements of risk management on equity and that links strategic risk management directly to shareholder value.

1 *TERM has been processed as a registered service mark of KPMG Peat Marwick LLP.*

2 *The closest approximation of a risk-free rate is the return on equivalent treasuries.*

BIBLIOGRAPHY

Business Wire, 1996, "Imperial Bank announces formation of a Risk Management Committee to improve services", November 12.

Ogden, J., 1996, "Putting all your Risks in One Basket", *Global Finance*, March, pp. 38–40.

Saleh, P., 1996, "Honeywell Remodels Risk Management Approach", *Derivatives Week*, 5, 13, p. 1.

Teach, E., 1997, "Microsoft's Universe of Risk", *CFO, The Magazine for Senior Financial Executives*, March.

INDEX

INDEX